DISPATCHES
– FROM THE –
DOGHOUSE

RVing Through North America

Dina Kalns

 FriesenPress

Suite 300 - 990 Fort St
Victoria, BC, V8V 3K2
Canada

www.friesenpress.com

ISBN
978-1-5255-7822-9 (Hardcover)
978-1-5255-7823-6 (Paperback)
978-1-5255-7824-3 (eBook)

1. TRAVEL, ESSAYS & TRAVELOGUES

Distributed to the trade by The Ingram Book Company

To Matejs
who will always be *mans mazais zakītis.*

And to John
who will always be *mans dzīves draugs.*

I will look back on this and smile because it was life, and I decided to live it.

Travelling - it leaves
you speechless, then turns
you into a story teller.
                              Ibn Battuta
Well this journey
certainly left me speechless,
and this book is merely a
feeble attempt to regain
my voice.
            Enjoy!

            Dina

CONTENTS

INTRODUCTION

THIS BOOK IS BASED ON A BLOG. A lengthy blog that documented a 3-year, full-time RV journey through North America. I did not set out to write anything quite so lengthy, never mind something that would be transposed into book form. A book that is ultimately part diary, part memoir, part travel guide and part social commentary. My original intent was to simply describe a few places, record a few exploits and throw in the odd picture so that while travelling, my Mom would know where we were and how we were doing. Then I thought that perhaps there might be a few family members and friends who would be interested in keeping up with our whereabouts. And then it occurred to me that it might be good for my husband John and I too – to help remember where we had been and what we had seen long after the adventure was over. I resolved to post at the beginning of each month, deciding that would be the simplest way to maintain a routine. It wasn't always easy to stick to the plan, but I persevered. The end result was 39 posts covering our travels from the tip of the Gaspé Peninsula in Québec to San Diego in California, from Homer in Alaska to Key West in Florida, and pretty much every place in between. Driving, hiking, biking, kayaking, boating, snorkeling and flying. Flora, fauna, geology and history. National, provincial, territorial, state, county and city parks. Cities, villages, hamlets and one-horse towns. Solitude and fellowship. Excitement and relaxation. Fulfillment and frustration. Happiness and sorrow. It was quite the ride. Would that we could do it all again!

1.

ABOUT US

THE CONVERSATION WENT SOMETHING LIKE THIS...

"Hey, John, let's get a dog!"

"Um... no... Dina, I really don't think that's a very good idea."

"Why not? It'll be great!"

"Well... dogs require a lot of work. You have to walk them and care for them, and we both work. Sometimes crazy hours. You can't leave a dog by himself at home for 10 hours."

"True. But I'll be retired soon. I'll have lots of time and he can go running with me. It'll be great!"

"Yes... but... we like to travel, and a dog would really cramp our lifestyle."

"No problem – we'll just put him in a kennel."

Five years later we were both retired after more than 30 years of policing in Toronto and had a 5-year-old Chocolate Labrador Retriever named Porter. He ruled our lives and while we continued to travel, there was never any question of putting him into a kennel. Instead, if we were off skiing or hiking or biking, Porter went to dog camp. A perfect off-leash place out in the country. This worked very well for 7, 10 or even 14-day stays. But we found we could not leave him for longer than that, no matter how wonderful the facility. It was hard on him, hard on us and hard on the pocketbook.

So, what to do? Our dream of visiting all the capitals of Europe and travelling for extended periods of time overseas was put on the back burner. But what about exploring our own back yard? What about North America? We could easily bring Porter with us! He loves the car! Well that plan also faltered. Travelling with a dog meant finding dog-friendly hotels/motels/inns and dog-friendly restaurants. There are plenty of pet-friendly accommodations to be sure, but eating establishments is another story. And there was no way Porter could pull off the role of therapy dog.

Enter the RV. Now this was a huge paradigm shift for us. When our children were young, we took them car camping to both the east and almost-west coasts, often cursing when caught behind a slow-moving behemoth on a 2-lane highway. As the kids grew older and developed their own interests (none of which seemed to include the great outdoors) we set out just the two of us – back-country camping, hiking, canoeing, kayaking. We loved the solitude, the back-to-nature, even the challenge of packing as light a pack as possible for a 10-day trek. One of our most memorable trips had us hiking the Grand Canyon from the south rim to the north, where on the first day we even had to carry our own water! So, a motor home? Oh, the horror! But it was either that or stay home.

We started our research, attended numerous RV shows, visited several RV dealers and ultimately decided on a 2016 Tiffin Phaeton 36gh. It had more bells and whistles than we really needed (or wanted) but the size and layout worked. Big enough that we would not feel cramped, yet small enough that we would be able to get into all the national, provincial and state parks on our list. And those bells and whistles? Our new abode came with a full-size residential fridge (almost nicer than the one we had at home), a 3-burner gas cooktop and a convection microwave oven (we decided to forgo the optional dishwasher), a stackable clothes washer/dryer, a reasonably-sized shower in the washroom plus a separate vanity area, and to make it completely ridiculous, 4 television sets. We didn't even have that many in our bricks-and-mortar house! One above the electric fireplace, one above the front windshield, one in the bedroom and one outside. Apparently, the outside one was for any tailgate parties we may wish to attend. Driving it required a DZ licence, so John took the requisite course. We leased out our house, put the bulk of our things into storage, donated the rest to local charities and packed up the land yacht (as we came to call it) with what we thought would be needed for a journey that we estimated would take us three years, possibly four. There were restrictions and limitations to be sure, imposed by both our health coverage and US Immigration, so certain timelines had to be followed. We divided North America into general geographic areas and hoped to follow the warm weather as much as possible. Trips home to visit family and friends were a certainty, but we hoped that family and friends would also look us up should they find themselves in whatever neck of the woods we were situated. The land yacht had a sofa that could sleep two guests and the welcome mat was always out!

PORTER. OUR *RAISON D'ÊTRE* FOR BUYING THE DOGHOUSE.

2.

IN THE BEGINNING

WE HAVE NO CLEAR MEMORY...

We took possession of the land yacht from McPhail's in Harriston, Ontario on Monday May 9th, and John drove it to our home in Port Credit, with me and Porter following in the SUV. It was like being behind a bus, and in many ways, that is exactly what it was – a 36-foot-long bus that really measured 38 feet bumper-to-bumper. We made it home without incident, parked out front and began what became the onerous task of loading up. This was certainly one aspect of "the plan" we had underestimated. Despite months of sorting, evaluating, re-sorting and purging, followed by countless trips to charities, our storage locker and the dump, we

OMG! WHAT HAVE WE DONE!

still had so much stuff! Our son Matejs was moving into his first ever condo and was thankfully able to take some of the items, but it certainly made us aware (and in not necessarily a good way) of how much stuff we had and how attached we can get to material things. In all fairness, we were moving from over 3000 square feet into about 300 so that was bound to be a challenge no matter how brutal our decision making. It was exhausting and we agreed that if we were just going to do this for 1 year, we would have left everything in situ and simply started driving. As it was, it took us 7 days before we were ready to weigh anchor. We really have no clear memory of that first week.

Our first stop was near the Rouge Valley where we spent 3 nights parked in the driveway of our dear friends Andrew and Ilze. They were a godsend, helping us acclimatize to our new digs (despite Andrew's shaky rendition of Paul Simon's *Homeless),* encouraging us to use their kitchen and shower until we had the cupboards somewhat organized and the electrical and water systems up and running. This also gave us an opportunity to reflect a bit more on the upcoming adventure. More than once we looked over at each other and said, "What have we done?" But houseguests, even if they are parked in your driveway, are like fish, and after 3 days we knew we best pull out lest we ruin a wonderful friendship.

We also knew from the start that we would not be able to actually hit the open road until early July since we had several social and other appointments during May and June. Thankfully, a place from my childhood provided the perfect locale to really settle in and work out all the bugs. Sidrabene!

St. Andrew's Latvian Lutheran Church in Toronto owns about 70 acres of land on Bronte Creek near the Niagara Escarpment and they call it Sidrabene after an ancient Semgallian castle in the home country. It functions as a summer camp for children, a spiritual retreat for adults and a social gathering place for members of the Latvian GTA (Greater Toronto Area) community, their families and friends. It was where I spent my summers between the ages of about 5 and 17. Sidrabene's council was kind enough to grant our request for a place to park, hook into some shore power and have easy access to fresh water.

The drive out to Burlington was uneventful, although the yacht did pick up some minor scratches along one side as we navigated the narrow road into the property itself. The manager Andy was very helpful in getting us situated and even engaged in some impromptu pruning to make our campsite more RV friendly. Unfortunately, the first two weeks were not spent in idyllic laziness, remembering days gone by, hiking up the escarpment, with a bike ride or two thrown into the mix. That was what I had naively envisioned. Instead, we made countless forays to Canadian Tire, the Bell Store and Costco for yet another item necessary to make things more comfortable. Unfortunately, Sidrabene is in a dead zone when it comes to cell and internet coverage, so any communication was more miss than hit. We also spent a fair bit of time reorganizing the RV and sorting through packed plastic bins for yet another purge. How many pairs of shoes was I supposed to sacrifice before this journey could take flight? The weather was unseasonably hot and humid so that took a bit of getting used to as well. We couldn't run the a/c hooked up to Sid's 15-amp service, and we were loathe to use our built-in generator and disturb the peace and quiet. Just when it looked like we were getting into a bit of a groove, my 90-year-old mother fell and broke her pelvis. Thankfully, no surgery was required, the hospital was only a 40-minute drive away and we were able to visit on a regular basis. Her recovery went well, so limited worries there. Still…

A bit about Sidrabene. The original purchase by St. Andrew's was in 1953 with the children's camp being set up the following year. Over the years, building lots were made available to congregation members enabling them to build small cabins/cottages for restful retreat. It seems that building permits were a rather novel concept at the time and subsequent generations found that the original construction techniques and materials were rather unorthodox (castoff ping-pong table roof – really?) An outdoor sanctuary was built, as was an infirmary, a large meeting hall and a house for the property manager. When swimming in Bronte Creek became more of a health hazard than summer fun, a splash pad and pool were added – all made possible through donations and countless hours by countless volunteers. During our stay, we also donated a bit of time, and John was able help Andy with some odd jobs around the outdoor church and dance floor, and had the opportunity to harness his inner cowboy by restoring the head on the old see-saw horse in the playground.

My fondest memories of Sidrabene are from the time period when the summer camp was at its peak – around the mid to late 1960's. There were so many kids it was easy for those of us who were a bit more mischievous to fly under the radar from time to time. I must admit that I was not a model camper (disliked structured activities), nor a model camp counsellor (more interested in extra-curricular pastimes). But it was the place of a lot of firsts – first best friend, first sneaked cigarette, first illegal drink, first kiss, first of many groundings by my parents. And by having the opportunity to "camp" there again it was wonderful to be able to relive some of those memories. The place has changed, of course. The old café where we would go to buy Pink Elephant Popcorn, shoe-string liquorice and Lolas, burned down a number of years ago. A new one has replaced it, and while it is in many ways superior, there is just something missing. The volleyball court that saw many epic matches (it was almost a blood sport at times) between Sidrabene and the kids from rival St. John's Camp Saulaine is barely used. The track & field area is overgrown, with the track scarcely visible in most places, the long jump pit full of weeds and the high jump dismantled years ago. But in my mind's eye, I still see the participants of many a track meet and can hear the cheers of the spectators. The one constant is the outdoor church. It is as peaceful and serene today as it was all those many years ago. The cedar-lined path leading towards it is still shaded, although the cedars are considerably larger. The trees around the sanctuary still tower overhead and the sun seems to only penetrate and shine on the altar. There truly is a sense of the spiritual being amongst nature. Yet walking along these memory lanes, I found myself wondering, "What happened to all those kids? How did their lives turn out?" I wish we could have a Sidrabene/Saulaine reunion, along the same lines of an old high school reunion. How many of the hundreds who passed through the old stone entry gates would return? How many would be able?

Yet not everything about Sidrabene is of the past. It still has a vibrant core of members, supporters and volunteers. The summer camp still operates (if only for 5 weeks), the large hall (Sidrabkalns) is rented out to both members of the Latvian community as well as the surrounding local community for public and private functions, boy scouts and girl guides are a constant presence, and social and cultural events take place most every weekend. The largest and most popular is "*Jāni*", when Latvians harken back to their pagan past and celebrate summer solstice. Traditionally this was a time when homesteads were decorated with birch and oak branches, although nettle and thistles might be attached to doorframes to keep evil spirits out. Huge bonfires were lit and jumping over them would supposedly rid one of "everything unnecessary." Staying up all night was a requisite and walking through early morning dew at dawn would bring money, and for women, washing your face in this dew ensured beauty. At Sidrabene, the community still gathers, bonfires are lit (although the jumping over seems to have waned), traditional homemade caraway cheese and home-brewed beer is consumed, and couples still supposedly sneak away to search for the flower of the fern that only blooms on this night. Now any botanist will tell you that ferns do not produce blossoms of any kind at any time, but it is a good excuse to sneak away for some private time. Garlands of field daisies for women and oak leaves for men are woven and worn with pride and singing – a Latvian cultural identifier – is engaged in with beer-fuelled enthusiasm. And while many of the participants at Sidrabene may be a bit hazy on the origins and meaning of these rituals, they look forward to and partake with gusto. This particular year, the band at the dance floor stopped playing at 1:30am, and the singing of folk, traditional and more contemporary songs ended at 4am. All in all, a great celebration and a great way to meet up with old friends and say "*uzredzīti*" until we would return again in three (?) years.

3.

THERE ARE NO PROBLEMS IN LIFE

"THERE ARE NO PROBLEMS IN LIFE, ONLY CHALLENGES AND OPPORTUNITIES," SAYS JOHN. Well July gave us more challenges and opportunities than we had anticipated. During the first part of the month we had the "opportunity" to focus on bars – although not the sort where you might have a libation or two. And given the hot, humid weather, that would have been a good idea. No, these bars were tow bars and sway bars. Quite reluctantly, I learned a fair bit about things mechanical – much more than I should have had to. First, the tow bars.

We knew from the outset that we would not be able to take our SUV, an Acura MDX, on this odyssey because it could not be flat-towed behind the RV. "Flat-towed" is the term used to describe the towing of a motor vehicle with all four wheels on the ground (as opposed to two wheels down and two up with a dolly, or sitting on and being pulled by a trailer). And in the RV world, a vehicle that is being towed behind an RV is referred to as a "toad". Get it? Very cute. In any event, John had done a fair bit of research and found that many vehicles manufactured today cannot, as a rule, be flat-towed. He started explaining the mechanics behind some of this, but I believe it was around that time that my eyes may have rolled back into my head. One promising article however, published by none other than a "towing magazine" indicated that a Subaru was equipped for this mode of travel. Excellent. We like Subarus. Off to a Subaru dealership. Unfortunately, the nice salesman, after checking with the mechanic, advised that under no circumstances could a Subaru be flat-towed. No way. No how. Strike one. Our second choice was a Jeep. In fact, in most RVing magazines with photographs of RVs towing cars, the car is always a Jeep. So off to the Jeep dealership. Same story. This salesman also advised us (after checking with a mechanic) that flat-towing was not advised. Strike two. We were starting to get concerned because we needed a car but did not want to pull one on a trailer. And besides, why did we see so many photos of Jeeps behind RVs? John downloaded the Jeep owner's manual and there on page 86 were the instructions on how to flat tow your vehicle for recreational purposes. Obviously the people at this particular Jeep dealership were not very well informed. I don't like to name names, but the dealership name rhymes with deal and peel. The second dealership, in Cooksville, was the complete opposite – knowledgeable, helpful and informed. We bought a white 2016 Jeep Trailhawk.

I'd like to say, that was that. Well that was just the beginning. Just because a vehicle can be flat-towed does not mean it comes equipped for it. We now had to have the tow bar actually purchased and installed. That meant John driving the RV back to the RV dealership, with myself and Porter following in the Jeep/soon-to-be Toad. The install was an all-day job, so we drove up the night before, parked in their lot and were ready when the garage opened at 8am. Yes, we slept in a RV dealer lot. Surprisingly, it wasn't all that bad because the dealership was out in the country surrounded by cows and cornfields. Porter, being a city dog, was quite intrigued by the cows but we were careful not to let him get too close. The installation went relatively smoothly although it was a pretty boring wait. As I said, cows and cornfields.

Then another hiccup. We had not yet left the GTA when we received a recall notice for the land yacht. Apparently, there was an issue with the sway bar. Sway bar. Hmmm. Is that important? Apparently so. In a nutshell, the sway bar is part of the steering and suspension system, and prevents the RV from tipping if you happen to drive over some bigger bumps in the road or take some curves that cause the vehicle to.... sway. This particular RV had a Cummins engine and Freightliner chassis, so no ordinary garage could tackle the problem. We had to go to a "monster" garage, where the serious trucks go. After inspecting our unit, they advised that several parts would have to be ordered before the work could begin. This set back our departure date by a few days, but I suppose we were fortunate that the issue had been identified and we were able to address it before we were half-way down the open road.

Ahhhhhh. The open road. Our original plan was to drive on as many secondary roads as possible in order to get a real sense of the countryside. In other words, no 400-series highways or interstates. But given that our departure date had been delayed by the recall, we opted for the 401 at least as far as Montreal in an effort to make up some time. Near the town of Cornwall, we noticed a rather loud and rhythmical pulsing noise coming from somewhere around the front end. We exited the highway and the pulsing increased or decreased commensurate with our speed. As luck would have it, the road we were on passed directly by a Freightliner garage. We stopped in but they were booked until the following day and recommended a garage down the road. Down the road we went, thumpity, thump, thump. Two hours later, the mechanic advised that while he heard the noise and felt the vibration, he had no idea what was causing it. He suggested getting the tires checked. By this time, it was 9pm so we spent the night in a Walmart parking lot. In the RV world this is known as "boondocking". That is, spending the night in an area that is not really meant for camping, and has no amenities such as water, electricity etc. (John maintains that "boondocking" is in fact the Latin word for "to suffer"). Generally, boondocking is accepted practice if you are in a pinch, need some-place safe to sleep, and do not abuse the locale by setting up your BBQ and staying for a week. Walmart has a reputation for being very hospitable to boondockers. There were six of us in this particular parking lot. The following morning, we presented ourselves at Cornwall Tire. As we pulled up, numerous mechanics stopped what they were doing to watch us roll in. The problem was identified in a matter of minutes.

Our land yacht had six tires. Two in front and four in the back, with each tire held in place by 10 lug nuts. Turns out that on the right rear outer tire, only 2 of the lug nuts were tight. The remainder could be unscrewed by hand. According to the mechanic, another 50 kms and that wheel would have flown off and bounced down the highway. And we have all read and seen in the news what happens when a 130-pound tire bounc-ing down the highway hits something or someone. To say we were upset would be an understatement. Not only had we narrowly avoided an accident, but we could have killed somebody. Additionally, because the outer tire was not secure and therefore vibrating, it had damaged the inside tire rim and wheel hub. Back to the Freightliner garage we went. Yep, they could fix it but nope, they needed to order the parts. And the land yacht was not driveable. We were going to be spending the next week in Cornwall. In a truck garage parking lot! After digesting this piece of news, our second order of business was trying to determine who was responsible for handing us the keys to an unsafe vehicle. The garage in Milton where the sway bar was corrected denied touching the tires. Their work was all at the front end. So that left the dealer – McPhail's of Harriston. John apprised the shop foreman of the situation and left it up to him to decide whose head should roll. We were covered by warranty.

Challenges and opportunities. We now had the opportunity to explore the area around Cornwall, with the land yacht securely situated and plugged into another 15-amp service. No cows or cornfields, but we were safe and secure none-the-less with transport trucks coming and going at all hours. According to Tripadvisor, the

#1 attraction in Cornwall is the St. Raphael Ruin. Calling something a "ruin" brings to mind the crumbling castles and abbeys one might find in Ireland or Scotland. St. Raphael was really the well-maintained shell of a church that had burned down in 1970, although its history was rather interesting. (And it wasn't in Cornwall either but rather a 30-minute drive northeast through rolling and picturesque countryside.) The church was built in 1821 and its claim to fame is that it was the first administrative centre for the Catholic Church in Upper Canada. So basically, this parish was the cradle of Catholicism in Ontario. Scottish Highlanders had originally settled the region in 1786, after leaving the Glengarry region of Scotland because of harsh economic conditions. It's difficult to imagine how harsh those conditions must have been if sailing to the wilds of Canada in 1786 was an upgrade.

We then spent a full day at Upper Canada Village near Morrisburg and to our pleasant surprise, found it quite fascinating. I am not sure if this is because as we age, we appreciate the past more, or because this was truly an interesting and educational experience. The village is really a heritage park that covers 60 acres and depicts a typical rural village in Upper Canada in the mid 1800's. It is comprised of over 40 historically accurate buildings, including a working woollen mill, gristmill and sawmill, as well as a blacksmith, cabinetmaker, baker, dressmaker, cheese maker, shoemaker and numerous other tradespeople. All the "villagers" (including children) were dressed in period costumes engaging in period activities. The flour from the mill is baked into bread that can be purchased upon departure. Delicious! We could only marvel that we had driven past this place en-route to Montreal so many times, without ever stopping in.

We also found out about The Lost Villages and the St. Lawrence Seaway & Power Project. All I remember learning in school is that the waters of the Great Lakes flow into the St. Lawrence River and then out to the Atlantic Ocean. And ships carrying all kinds of goods go up and down the waterway. Easy, peasy. Apparently, this was not always the case. As recently as 1958, any large ships on the lakes were not able to get to Montreal and vice versa because of a nasty set of rapids. The Great Lakes were in effect land locked to modern marine traffic. A collaborative effort between Canada and the United States (known as the St. Lawrence Seaway & Power Project) resulted in the expansion of the St. Lawrence River for shipping purposes while at the same time generating hydro-electric power. The project was hailed as a great benefit to both countries, was completed in four years, and came in on budget. A government project on budget. Wow. Everyone was happy. Well, not everyone. In order to accomplish this marvellous feat of engineering and progress, 6 villages and 3 hamlets, that had evolved from the early settlements of the United Empire Loyalists, were flooded, and their remains now lie submerged under the newly created Lake St. Lawrence. Over 8,000 hectares of prime farmland and mature orchards were gone. Two new towns were created and the 6,500 people whose properties had been expropriated had to pick up and relocate. While over 500 buildings were literally moved to higher ground, numerous churches, schools, homes and businesses were destroyed. Obviously, a way of life disappeared as well. The Lost Villages Historical Society set out to capture this way of life before it was forgotten altogether and volunteers maintain a small heritage village museum, comprised of original buildings depicting mid-1950's life as it was in these tiny communities. It was very charming if somewhat heavy on nostalgia. By way of contrast we also visited the "new" created town of Ingleside but calling it a town is truly a misnomer. It consists simply of a few residential streets laid out in a suburb-style grid with no central core, no main street, no churches, no shops, no heart. A small strip mall near Highway 2 that houses a Mac's Milk Variety and LCBO liquor store complete the unappealing air. I suppose from a structural and commercial engineering perspective, this project was a huge success for some, but on a social and cultural scale, it was an abysmal failure. The town of Cornwall did not come out on the winning side either.

The opening of the St. Lawrence Seaway meant that Cornwall's canal, which had been vital to marine transport since 1843, fell out of use and was in effect by-passed. Needless to say, any and all businesses associated with this waterway also fell on hard times. The main canal itself was filled in around 1971 and a large park complete with band shell and children's splash pad was constructed where ships used to dock. All that remains is the stone foundation of the swinging bridge that used to swing to one side in order to facilitate the passing ships.

Now despite our best intentions to make lemonade out of lemons, we eventually started running out of things to do. We began filling our time by touring the countryside and stopping at whatever caught our attention. We visited a creamery (Biemond – a family business run by two brothers and their wives) that produces organic yoghurt and other dairy products. The frozen yoghurt was very good. That is all I can say. John, having worked on a dairy farm in his teens, was a bit more enthusiastic and found the new milking system very informative. We stopped in at the St. Albert Cheese Coop and watched them making cheese curds, which of course we had to sample in their house special poutine. We have never been real fans of poutine, but this was something exceptional. Fresh cut French-fries topped with gravy, sautéed ground beef, fried onions & green peppers and cheese curds so fresh you could hear them squeak on your teeth. You could also hear your arteries slamming shut. Enough said.

We stopped in at a cemetery in the village of St. Andrew's West and stumbled upon the grave of Simon Fraser. Who knew that this great explorer and settler of British Columbia died in poverty in 1862 and was buried in a little town in the middle of nowhere Ontario? Actually, it wasn't exactly the middle of nowhere back then. It is at the corner of Hwy 138 and County Road 18, and at that time, County Road 18 was the main route between Montreal and Toronto. And here I always thought it was the McDonald-Cartier Freeway. But poor Simon Fraser. After all his exploring for Queen and country, and despite having both a river and a university named after him, his rather modest grave marker was only erected in 1921, and that was by the Hudson's Bay Company "over the grave where he and his wife were buried". Neither Canada nor British Columbia have seen fit to honour his final resting place. Surprisingly, Ontario's first premier, John Sandfield Macdonald (d1872) is also buried in this small out-of-the-way place, although his burial site is commemorated with a much larger and grander stone, erected by "friends from all parts of the dominion". The irony was not lost on us.

We drove along the Long Sault Parkway stopping at several parks, picnicking and admiring the St. Lawrence River along the way. We bicycled along the numerous bike paths that parallel the river and wind their way through city parks. We even tried to find signs of life in downtown Cornwall. That was a rather surreal experience as we were not able to decide if this was a town that is dead, dying or on life support. There were a few nice shops but no shoppers, one coffee shop but no patrons (other than us) and a few restaurants with no diners. Over the course of several visits we never saw more than a handful of people. I had theme music from *The Twilight Zone* in my head the whole time. But the waterfront was another story. A few blocks towards the river, Lamoureux Park (site of the previously mentioned canal) was a constant hub of activity, and the highlight of our stay was attending a 4-day ribfest featuring numerous rib cook-offs (naturally), several bands (all quite good), a midway of sorts and carnival rides. There were thousands of people – young families, older couples and more teens than I had seen in a long time, all enjoying the food and music.

"*Going places that we've never been. Seeing things that we may never see again. Just can't wait to get on the road again.*" I'm not sure which was worse. That I included in my blog a quote by Willie Nelson or that John actually knew a quote by Willie Nelson. The much anticipated and longed for tire part finally arrived on day 13 and was installed by evening. We were on the road at 10am the next day but not before the owner of the garage gifted us with wonderful T-shirts to commemorate our stay in the Cornwall Freightliner parking lot. "*Cornwall Freightliner. We'll fix your truck or we'll push it in the river and say we never saw it.*"

Heading east along highway 20, we skirted around Montreal and Quebec City, planning to stay in Montmagny. Given John's Irish heritage we hoped to take a day trip to Grosse Ile, Canada's version of Ellis Island. It is operated by Parks Canada but unfortunately, they do not allow dogs on the island. The only dog daycare in Montmagny was full, so that will have to be a trip for another time. Instead, we continued on to Saint-Jean-Port-Joli to check out the Musée des Anciens Canadiens. There was not a lot to choose from by way of campgrounds, so we pulled into Camping de La Demi-Lieue, right on the St. Lawrence River. Big mistake. Although I am almost completely French-illiterate (having skipped too many classes in high school), John has enough to be able to ask about vacancies and rates, although not enough to carry on a full conversation. The lady at check-in acknowledged she spoke English but carried on in French anyway. She advised they did not have any spots available, but we could park out by the baseball diamond/playground, without any hook-ups (so in effect, we were sort of boondocking again). Except she charged us the full fee. And when we went for a stroll through the campground, we found that there were at least 7 or 8 vacant spots. Welcome to la belle province! The Musée in town was small, but definitely worth the visit. It explained the history and cultural importance of woodcarving in Quebec and exhibited many incredible pieces by artists both old and new. Too bad most of them were out of our price range. But that is just as well. We were travelling light.

We followed route 132 along the south shores of the St. Lawrence River, and while at times a bumpy ride, it was scenic and winding with many quaint little villages to pass through. At least at first. Then, just past Ste-Anne-des-Monts things changed. It was still scenic and winding. In fact, even more so. But now there were elevation changes with 15-degree grades to contend with as well. So it was a bit like riding a roller coaster, and despite the fantastic views, by the time we reached Gaspé we were glad to get off the ride. The Gaspé region itself has an interesting history. Although its inhabitants are primarily French speaking today, prior to 1850 the population was actually 50/50 English and French. The two groups got along very well, living and working side by side, each retaining their own language and customs. It seems that things only became testy after the politicians got involved. And during WWII, there was a bit of action in the area as well. Between 1942 and 1944, German U-boats sank 23 ships during the Battle of the Gulf of St. Lawrence. Fort Ramsay naval base had been inaugurated in Gaspé in 1942 to guard the mouth of the river so I'm not sure how effective it really was. When I was busy skipping French class in high school, I must have skipped the odd history class too because I don't recall learning about Germans being on this side of the pond.

Forillon National Park, at the tip of the Gaspé Peninsula, is Quebec's only national park, having been created in 1970 through the expropriation of property belonging to

225 families. The actual negotiations were sub-contracted out to a private firm and may or may not have involved threats and bullying. No one is really saying, but in 2011 the House of Commons adopted a motion to officially apologize to these people for the "unconscionable manner in which they were treated". None-the-less, it is a beautiful place with soaring cliffs that drop abruptly into the ocean, and we were surprised that based on licence plates, there were so few visitors from out of province. The weather was perfect enabling us to go on numerous walks/hikes including one to Land's End, the actual geographic tip of the peninsula. It turns out that in Mi'kmaq (the area's original inhabitants) "land's end" is actually "gespeg" so not a great leap to "gaspé". We hung out by the ocean a fair bit (which Porter particularly enjoyed) but the absolute highlight was snorkelling with the resident harbour seal colony. There were about 200 of them spread out along a stretch of rocks that we accessed via steel hulled zodiac. Some of the more inquisitive ones swam out to take a closer look, but one little fellow must have mistaken me for a rock because while I was face down in the water, he kept climbing up onto my back, and when I turned over, he crawled up onto my belly. "Incredible" does not begin to describe it. The water temperature was only 15 degrees Celsius so 14mm wetsuits were required but it was a fantastic experience. And to top it off, we saw a lynx crouched down by the side of the road that very same day! There was some debate whether it was a lynx or a bobcat, but the longer ear tufts and less obvious spotting was the clincher. These cats are fairly elusive so what this guy was doing out in the open is anyone's guess. Wildlife sighting: 2 moose, 1 black bear cub, 4 porcupines, flocks of northern gannets, 2 whales (in the distance), numerous harbour seals and 1 lynx. July ended on a great note!

SNORKELLING WITH CURIOUS SEALS. INCREDIBLE!

4.

"PARDON, PARLEZ-VOUS ANGLAIS?"... "NO! GET LOST YOU ENGLISH DOG!"

I HAVE COME TO BELIEVE THAT THE GASPÉ REGION OF QUEBEC HAS A SPLIT PERSONALITY, SOMEWHAT ALONG THE LINES OF DR. JEKYLL AND MR. HYDE. And although Dr. Jekyll was whom we met most often, we never knew when Mr. Hyde would put in an appearance, and that was rather disconcerting. The majority of the people we ran into in the Gaspé were wonderful friendly folks and while their English was not necessarily great, it was far better than my French. So between their broken English and my fragmented French (supplemented by hand gestures and pantomimes worthy of a winning game of charades) we managed to make ourselves understood and were able to exchange both pleasantries and useful information. But from time to time we ran into people who not only spurned our feeble overtures, they made it very clear that our mere presence was not only not welcome, it was outright resented. I always started any conversation with something along the lines of, *"Excusez-moi, je ne parle pas très bien francais, juste un peu. Parlez-vous anglais?"* (Excuse me, I do not speak French very well, only a little. Do you speak English?) And then the pigeon-English and pigeon-French would begin with apologetic smiles and embarrassed laughter on both sides. But sometimes, the reply I received was an emphatic "No!" followed by a long tirade in French that of course I could not understand. Now given that more than 55% of communication is non-verbal, I didn't have to know how to conjugate a French verb in order to get the gist of the message. And it was not a mere, "Sorry I don't understand English", it was, "Get out of here you English-speaking pig-dog!"

We related these encounters to some fully bilingual Quebecers, and they all advised the same thing. Everyone in Quebec understands English, but some are so caught up in the separatist sentiment, that they practically refuse to acknowledge anyone else's right to exist. Which lead us to Percé.

We spent the first few days of August finishing up some hikes in Forillon National Park, specifically hiking to a watchtower that overlooks the tip of the actual peninsula. Incredible view! As an aside, it was interesting to note that Forillon is not actually a national park, i.e. administered by the federal government of Canada. It is a provincial park of Quebec, but in Quebec, they call their provincial parks national. As in the Quebec nation? Even the museums and interpretive centres were quite biased. If you did not know your history, anything displayed in the Gaspé would lead you to believe that only those of francophone descent contributed anything of any value to the region. Neither the Mi'kmaq nor the English-speaking immigrants get much mention. The Mi'kmaq have set up their own interpretive centre to showcase life as it was way back when, and in addition to visiting the indoor and outdoor exhibits, we sampled bannock bread and moose soup. Unique flavour, that moose soup.

In comparison to the actual town of Gaspé, the town of Percé is very touristy with the main drag lined by little shops selling touristy trinkets and all kinds of knick-knacks. I didn't check but I suspect most of the stuff is made in China. But the town of Percé has Percé Rock and that in and of itself makes it worth the visit. It's actually part of another "national" park, L'Ile Bonaventure-et-du-Rocher-Percé. The rock's weight is calculated at 5 million tonnes, of which 300 tonnes crumble off and disappear into the ocean each year. At low tide, it is possible to walk/wade out along an exposed sandbar to its base and standing at the bottom of this massive monolith looking up was rather awe-inspiring and a bit scary. In 2003 a falling piece of limestone actually struck a visiting Ontario tourist in the head. He sued and the court held the park liable because they encouraged people to walk out there but didn't advise them of the risks. Subsequently, all treks were forbidden but this was so difficult to enforce, they gave up and people (including us) were back to risking their noggins again. Estimates are that at its current rate of erosion, it will all be gone in 16,000 years. So get out there while there is still something to see! The rock is significant not just for its sheer size, but for its arch that is almost 50 feet high, making it one of the largest natural marine arches in the world. It actually had two arches when Jacques Cartier arrived in 1534 but by 1845 it looked pretty much as it does today. We walked out on a rather windy day, so the waves were quite high, making it too dicey to get out to the arch itself. Probably a good thing because the water was freezing! Not that Porter minded. He ran back and forth, pulling seaweed and whatever else he could find, out of the ocean.

The second attraction in this area is L'Ile Boneventure that lies just over 3 kms off the coast – about a 15-minute boat ride. The island is geographically quite small (about 4 square kms) and has been home to both fishermen and artists since the late 1700's. In 1971 the Quebec government expropriated the entire island (this seems to be a common practice in the region) and evicted the entire population of about 35 families. In typical government fashion, they neglected the homes and other buildings to the point where they were collapsing in on themselves and are now busy restoring everything and congratulating themselves on their commitment to heritage preservation. But the main draw is ornithology. The top half of the island is home to the largest and most accessible northern gannet colony in the world – 62,000 pairs plus their offspring. These birds spend most of their lives out at sea, mate for life, and return to the same nest every year to breed, producing just one egg that is nurtured by both partners. They are migratory and some even travel as far as Mexico before making their way back in the spring. No dogs are allowed on the island, so John and I took separate trips out to see these fascinating birds. Yes, we are now officially bird watchers. It's hard to admit, but I could have spent hours watching them. A short hike of a few kms. through a spruce forest took me right up to the colony's edge. At first, I heard them, then smelled them and finally saw a blanket of white. There were so many and so close I could have reached out and touched them (but didn't) and they seemed to have no fear of humans. The hatchlings were already a fair size, and although still covered with downy fuzz, I wouldn't exactly call them cute. At least not like baby chicks cute. And while the smell emitted by these thousands of birds was not overly offensive, it was pungent enough that my nose could only take so much. That, and the incessant squawking along with hundreds of pesky flies had me beating a hasty retreat to the pier for my return trip to the mainland. As luck would have it, a pretty severe thunderstorm blew in just as we boarded, and the boat was pitching and rolling such that a few people started getting sick. The captain was zig-zagging in order to avoid the waves hitting us broadside, the sky had turned an ominously dark blue/gray and I had the theme song from *Gilligan's Island* in my head. "*The weather started getting rough. The tiny ship was tossed...*" But we made it back to shore safely and John was waiting with the car at the dock just as the deluge started.

The town of Percé also has an additional, albeit little discussed claim to fame and we actually just stumbled across it in our reading. There is certainly no overt or public mention of this little nugget at the tourist information centre. In the late 1960's when discontented youth were rebelling against the establishment and flocking to Haight-Ashbury in San Francisco or Yorkville in Toronto, the young people of Quebec were circumnavigating the Gaspé peninsula and congregating in Percé. Amongst these were Paul & Jacques Rose, Francis Simard and Bernard Lortie of FLQ (Front de Libération du Québec) fame. In the summer of 1969, Paul Rose and company set up a drop-in centre/free hostel/coffee house in an old building in the centre of town and called it La Maison du Pêcheur (The Fisherman's House). It attracted its share of revolutionaries who were, amongst other things, upset with the poverty of the Gaspé region, and the presence of Anglophones and rich Americans in their midst. Rose et.al. of course took things to the extreme when they returned to Montreal in October of 1970, and kidnapped and murdered Quebec's Deputy Premier Pierre Laporte. But it was in La Maison du Pêcheur where Paul Rose wrote his manifesto and the Chenier cell of the FLQ was

formed. After being released from prison, Rose donated his manifesto to the archives at the Musée de la Gaspésie. Paul Rose and Francis Simard have since died, and La Maison du Pêcheur is now a trendy and popular seafood restaurant. I suspect that none of the diners had any idea of where they were sitting as they cracked open their lobster claws.

PERCÉ FROM ILE BONAVENTURE.

We left Percé on a sunny, warm day and headed south along hwy 132 towards New Brunswick. The drive was nowhere near as exciting as the north shore and we reached the border in no time. Au revoir la belle province. You can "je me souviens" all you want, but your memory is pretty selective. We spent a quick night in Miramichi and then continued along hwy 11 to Kouchibouguac National Park on the shores of the Northumberland Straight. This park had not been on our radar when we left home but after learning about it, we just had to stop and see what all the fuss was about. Because surprise, surprise, it was created through yet another expropriation! Unbelievable. But this one did not go quite that smoothly. In 1970 the federal government decided to create the park by kicking out 250 families who owned land and lived in 8 villages along the shores of Kouchibouguac Bay. These people were primarily Acadian fishermen and farmers who had been living in the area for several generations and were considered to be amongst the poorest and least educated people in New Brunswick. The practicalities were again left up to the province, and in a nutshell, they paid the people about 50% of what their own government appraiser had said the land was worth. A resistance movement sprang up with long-time resident, Jackie Vautour at the helm. Over the ensuing years, Vautour refused all offers of land and money from the government and was duly served with an eviction warrant, had his house demolished and his belongings placed in storage, was evicted from a motel by the RCMP using tear gas, and lost a court challenge opposing the eviction. The court set back resulted in 200 people rioting in the new park. Actually, there were several riots. This then resulted in a commission of inquiry that ultimately blamed the federal government. At the end of it all, new laws now prohibit Parks Canada from expropriating land for the purpose of creating new parks, and Jackie Vatour, at the esteemed age of 86, is still living on his land, in the park, albeit in a trailer without any running water, electricity or other creature comforts. The government has decided to leave him alone. The Acadian community considers him a hero.

The park itself is really nothing to write home about. It encompasses about 240 square kms, most of which is inaccessible, is crisscrossed by many gravel biking paths and has several ho-hum short hikes. Its most popular spot is Kelly's Beach, a long sand bar that can be reached via a boardwalk over salt marshes, small lagoon and some low-lying dunes. The dunes are home to the endangered Piping Plover, so dogs are not allowed anywhere near. What else is new. We didn't stay long, and we didn't meet Jackie Vatour, aka the rebel of Kouchibouguac either.

We continued on to Shediac, lobster capital of the world, although that isn't really saying much because lobster season opens up at various times in various locations throughout the eastern provinces, and more than one place lays claim to this honour. That is why you can get lobster at any time of year. Other than having a model/sculpture of the world's biggest crustacean, there isn't much going on there. But we were trying out a new method of overnighting through an association called Boondockers Welcome. It's a novel concept based on altruism, manners and a common interest in RV travel. It works like this. Through the website, you sign up as either a "host" or a "guest" (or both) and complete a brief profile. A host makes their driveway, back 40, or whatever space they have, available to travelling guests for 1 or 2 nights. They also set the parameters. Dogs or no dogs, big rigs or no big rigs, one night or two, hydro and water available or not and so on. Guests may then send a request to a particular host asking for permission to boondock on their property. The host reviews the guest's profile and if it works for them, provides their specific address. Other than a nominal fee to "join the club" there is no payment involved. Many of the host locations we saw were not along our route, but we decided to give the one in Shediac a try. I must admit it seemed a bit odd. Parking in your friend's driveway is one thing, but to pull up to a complete stranger's house is another. It went very smoothly. A recently retired couple who sail in the summer and travel south in their RV for the winter, made us feel very welcome, recommended some places to eat and helped clarify a few questions we had about being Quebecois vs Acadian (another history lesson will follow shortly). We really just wanted someplace safe to park the motorhome while we spent the day in Moncton and this location was perfect. In Moncton, we took care of some mundane housekeeping tasks, but our main objective was to visit the Acadian Museum located at Moncton University, Canada's only solely French language university. The museum was small but very interesting and between the displays and chatting with the staff, we learned a great deal about Acadian history, culture and food.

One thing we had noticed upon crossing into New Brunswick was that although many people spoke French, they would switch to English as the need arose without any of the accompanying attitude we found in Quebec. The Acadian flag (red, white and blue with a yellow star in one corner) was displayed everywhere and we got the sense that these were people very proud of their own heritage but willing to acknowledge the heritage of others as well. So how was it that we ended up with two completely separate and different French speaking communities in Canada? And they are different. Different food, different customs. Even the French language the Acadians speak is different – closer to what was spoken in France in the 1800s.

From what we were able to find out, the first group of French colonists in "New France" settled in the Bay of Fundy area around 1604 (Saint Croix Island to be exact although they moved to Port Royal a year later) under the leadership of a French nobleman named Pierre Dugua. But in 1608 Samuel de Champlain founded Quebec City with another group. Given the geographic distance between these two settlements, as well as the differing survival challenges they faced, the two groups did not interact much and over the space of about 150 years, the Acadians no longer identified with their country of origin. They were their own people and thrived through their own ingenuity. Those in Quebec City, however, continued to engage with and receive support from France, both military and economic. Unfortunately for the Acadians, France and Britain were engaged in a turf war over the new territory, and the British did not trust the Acadian position of professed neutrality, fearing they would side with the French. So starting in 1755 and for the next 8 years, the British deported over 11,000 Acadians to England, France and up and down what is now the American eastern seaboard. The Acadians refer to this as the *Grand Deragement* (the Great Upheaval) and although they were eventually allowed to return, not everyone came back – hence the Cajuns in Louisiana. It seems that the survival of this deportation and the period of homelessness that followed, forged their identity like nothing the colonists in Quebec could relate to. We visited the historical site and interpretive exhibits at Grand-Pré (one of the largest Acadian settlements before expulsion and a UNESCO World Heritage Site) and specifically Horton's Landing from where one of the first mass deportations was launched. A large commemorative cross has been placed at the exact spot where so many families were separated, and the weather was overcast and misty in keeping with the sombre tale. In 1847 Henry Wadsworth Longfellow's epic poem *Evangeline: A Tale of Acadie* was published and despite being a fictional character, Evangeline came to symbolize the history and resilience of the Acadian people. We picked up a copy and dutifully read it. However, despite our queries, we are still not clear on why France looked after their colonists in the Quebec City region, but neglected those in Acadia from the get-go, thus resulting in their sense of alienation and loss of loyalty. Perhaps some doctoral student at Moncton University has addressed this in their thesis, but it would be written in French so there ended our education on the matter. We headed south-ish.

Lunenburg. Home of the Bluenose. And more pricey restaurants and assorted galleries and shops than you can shake a stick at. Actually, that is not fair. Lunenburg is a lovely little town with multi coloured clapboard houses of interesting design, many with one or two large 5-sided dormers at the front, referred to as "Lunenburg Bumps". Not exactly arts & crafts but leaning that way. And of course, a picturesque harbour where you can admire the sailboats while sipping a glass of wine (or beverage of choice) from the patio of one of the pricey restaurants. Okay. Sorry. But being right on the ocean, there should be no need to pay downtown Toronto prices for fish and chips. And while I'm at it, why do they have to deep-fry almost everything? But it was a very charming place and had a completely different look and feel than anything else we had come across so far. We learned it had been settled primarily by German-speaking Lutheran farmers, whom the British recruited in 1753. The land was not exactly conducive to farming so the farmers turned to the sea for their livelihood, thus becoming expert fishermen. Over the space of about 10 generations, the names had changed (eg. Berhaus to Barkhouse), but sauerkraut was still readily available. The streets are quite steep in places and at times reminded me of San Francisco. Especially when you added in the houses painted in a myriad of colours – deep magenta, purple primrose, canary yellow, garish green. These rich rainbow colours are actually a rather new concept because historically, all the buildings were simply white with black trim. Most of the churches remain that way. The waterfront and first two or three streets up, cater primarily to tourists (and what else were we, but tourists) with many of the shops selling creative ceramics, paintings and clothing – but if you are not shopping for that specific something to take home, schlepping up and down the street with the rest of the window shoppers loses its appeal after a while. And there were a lot of window shoppers. The Fisheries Museum of the Atlantic had a little bit of something for everyone and while there, we learned about "bottle fishing", a time during Prohibition when fishermen could make more money at running rum than hauling in nets. In fact, one rum run to the United States could bring in more money than an entire legitimate year out at sea. So there was a lot of bottle fishing going on. And of course, all the Bluenose accoutrements you could wish for. Sweatshirts, T-shirts, sailor's caps and baseball caps, even Bluenose in a bottle. The Bluenose II herself was out at sea, but we hoped to catch up with her later on. Overall, I'd have to say that I was ambivalent about Old Town Lunenburg (although John is entitled to his differing, if somewhat more upbeat, opinion). It is another UNESCO World Heritage Site (because it is the best surviving example of a British Colonial grid-pattern street layout in North America) but despite its charm, I somehow expected more. Or maybe I expected less. Less tourists, that is. But then again, it's the tourists who significantly contribute to keeping the place alive so who am I to complain.

A confession here: We had considerable difficulty staying put in one place for very long. It was either adult onset ADD, or we were too much like crows. Oh look! There's something shiny! Quick! Turn right! Although situated in Lunenburg, we decided to take a scenic drive in the Toad along the south shore, also known as The Lighthouse Route. We got as far as Mahone Bay and Chester Basin. And it's a good thing we left the land yacht securely anchored because the road was very winding. Scenic but winding. Mahone Bay was just lovely. A few galleries, a few bistros, sailboats in the harbour and three churches side by side with their steeples reflecting in the water. Anglican, Lutheran and United. The Calvary church was a bit to one side and needed some TLC, and John lamented the fact that the Catholics had been overlooked. We went to a farmer's market in Hubbards to buy wild blueberries and fresh baked bread, and then dropped in to visit John's cousin in Chester Basin. We had not seen her since she got married eight years ago, and it just reminded us how quickly time passes. We also drove a little ways onto Oak Island, a mysterious place with a fascinating history about an unexplained "money pit", and many theories on how it came about. The most intriguing one is that Captain Kidd (of piracy fame) spent a lot of time there and buried his extensive treasure at a hidden location. There is no question that a pit exists, and it has been excavated by both companies and individuals alike (starting in the mid 1850s until this present day). They have found booby traps and channels, oak platforms and iron plates but so far, no treasure. Six people have died looking for it, and the History Channel has a reality series about it. Good thing we didn't show up with our shovels because the No Trespassing sign was pretty prominent.

And of course, a trip to Nova Scotia would not be complete without a visit to Peggy's Cove and its iconic lighthouse. We had been there years ago with the kids, but it has one of those vistas you never tire of looking at, despite all the tourists crawling and scurrying over the rocks like little ants. The day was overcast with fog rolling in and out, and that just completed the whole east coast fishing village feel. It was pretty much the way we remembered (maybe they keep it that way on purpose) and well worth the slow drive in. We were then on to Halifax which has a nice waterfront for strolling and the weather was on our side, warm and sunny. But we were anxious to get to Cape Breton. And that is when the weather turned. We left Dartmouth under an almost torrential downpour but were optimistic things would clear in an hour or two. At least that was what the weather radar showed. Well predicting weather accurately was no better in Nova Scotia than at home. The storm system just changed from downpour to drizzle, and the drizzle was accompanied by extremely heavy wind gusts. It made driving less than enjoyable. We made a small detour to Mulgrave, having read that the Bluenose II was anchored there for two days, on her way back to Lunenburg. I'm not much of a sailor (prone to sea sickness although John suggests that alcohol may be playing a role) but I'm glad we stopped despite the inclement weather. We were able to board but could not go below decks. One of the crew advised that while in Lunenburg, they typically have over 1,000 people per day come aboard. Fortunately for us, the nasty weather and out-of-the-way moorage kept the number at just over 100. Perfect. We continued on and spent the night in St Peters, just across the Canso Causeway on Cape Breton Island. A small town, a village really, it grew up around an isthmus that the Mi'kmaq used as a canoe portage route between Bras d'Or Lake and the Atlantic Ocean. In the mid-1800's an 800-meter canal was built (it took 15 years to complete) which generated a fair bit of shipping traffic up until the end of WW II. Today it is used primarily by pleasure boats, especially sailboats, that like the quick access to Bras d'Or Lake. One day per year, community members and others are invited/encouraged to swim the entire length of the canal, something that was considered a rite of passage back in the day. This particular year, 183 swimmers participated, albeit some with water-wings and others with foam tubes, while onlookers cheered from the sidelines. A very community-spirited event. The nasty weather prevented us from doing much exploring, but the locals reassured us that come morning, it was going to be lovely. "Lovely" is an adjective, and therefore, open to the vagaries of interpretation. So they weren't really lying. Come morning, the rain had tapered off to a drizzle that came straight down as opposed to sideways, so I suppose that could be considered "lovely". It didn't really clear until we neared Louisburg, so as much as I would like to say that the drive along Bras d'Or Lake was "lovely", we didn't see a whole lot of it. We checked into Mira River Provincial Park for several nights and had easy access to the Fortress of Louisburg and other points of interest in the area.

The Fortress of Louisburg was definitely worth the price of admission. Actually, it didn't cost us anything because we had purchased a Discovery Pass and that gave us admittance to all Canada's National Parks and Historic Sites for the next two years (in honour of Canada's 150 years in 2017). But this is one place worth visiting regardless of cost. A few interesting facts: The Fortress of Louisburg is actually a reconstruction (1/5th of it really). The original was destroyed in 1758 and some of the stone from its walls was used in the construction of buildings in Halifax and Boston. And a "fortress" encloses an entire town, as opposed to a "fort" which does not. This particular fortress was built by the French over the span of 28 years to help them prevent the British from gaining access to the St. Lawrence River (and thus Quebec City and Montreal), to protect France's hold on the Grand Banks fishing grounds, and to provide a base for France's profitable fishing industry (more profitable than the fur trade). All well and good, except the British had other ideas and successfully laid siege to the place on two separate occasions. It became in effect a bargaining chip in the on-going war between the two countries and having achieved the upper hand at the end, the British destroyed and then abandoned it. But during its original construction, the French kept meticulous records that had been archived, so when Parks Canada commenced their reconstruction, they had the exact plans to work from. Everything is true to the original, down to the 4-sided nail heads in the floor planks. Staff in period dress (from governor to soldier), go about their daily tasks and are happy to answer any questions. The only exception to authenticity was that some of the "soldiers" today were female, complete with make-up and earrings. It was, after all, 2016. For a fee, visitors can fire a cannon, fire a musket and children can be marched around in military drill, complete with their own wooden muskets that they load, aim and fire. It was all very informative, and in a way entertaining, but I must admit I have never thought of war as a game (hence my dislike of military video games) and couldn't help but think about the real soldiers who drilled, fought and died there. It's easy to romanticize and marvel at their way of life when the sun is shining, the café is open and there is no imminent threat of attack, but in reality, their lives were full of hardship and trepidation. On both sides. For example, following the first 7-week siege, 100 attacking New Englanders died in battle but a further 900 died afterwards of disease and harsh winter conditions. And they were the victors! Interestingly, the vast majority of the geographic area has not undergone any extensive archaeological digging because there is just too much buried there. Perhaps in the future the exhibits will be expanded, but as it currently stands, it is impossible to see everything in one day. We considered staying longer but the Highlands were calling.

Ceud Mile Failte! (*Cead* if you are Irish.) A Hundred Thousand Welcomes! Nova Scotia and The Cape Breton Highlands have close ties to Scotland and in the past little while there has been great interest in the revival of the Gaelic language and culture. In fact, most of the village names are posted in both English and Gaelic, and a Gaelic College (teaching language, history, music and weaving) is situated pretty much in the geographic centre of the province. We started our journey by visiting Baile nan Gaidheal (Highland Village) near Iona, another outdoor museum displaying the lives of the Gaelic Scots as they progressed from leaving Scotland (most after the Battle of Culloden), settled in Nova Scotia, prospered, moved away and are now returning. The "village" was high on a hill overlooking Bras d'Or Lake (really an inland sea) and the view was beautiful. No rain this time. Through character actors explaining their specific roles, we learned a great deal about how the Scots came to settle here (some arriving on decommissioned slave ships) and how they are now reclaiming their culture through language (eg. *Tha i breagha an diugh* – It's lovely today.)

We then had to decide whether to drive the Cabot Trail through Cape Breton Highlands National Park with the RV towing the Toad, or park the RV somewhere and continue on by car alone. The advice we received from fellow RV travellers was 50/50. Some said it would be no problem as long as we drove carefully and took our time. Others, with sincere consternation, said no way no how. Too steep, too winding and too many switchbacks on a poorly maintained two-lane road with no shoulders. We had already reserved a campsite for 10 days at Broad Cove, just north of Ingonish, so decided to do the RV/Toad combo and take it slow. After all, the RV was our home. The weather was perfect as we set out, feeling if not exactly apprehensive, somewhat on guard. The road surface for the first 10 kilometers was very poor, rattling both the dishes in the cupboards and the teeth in our heads. And once the pavement smoothed, the curves started. They were not as bad as we expected and there were only two places where a Hail Mary may have passed John's lips. The first involved a very narrow hairpin turn that forced us to enter the lane of an oncoming motor home. Thankfully, timing was on our side and no screeching brakes were involved. The second was a bit more frightening. We were making our way around Cape Smokey (an elevation gain of 725 feet in 2.1 kms) with the road hugging a cliff on one side and the ocean a long way down on the other, when we came around a blind corner and found an old battered pick-up truck, loaded with firewood, at a dead stop in the middle of the road. No flares or hazard triangles set out, no four-ways flashing, just one brake light. Are you kidding me?!?!? We quickly stopped, as thankfully did the cars behind us, and waited for traffic in the oncoming lane to clear. The tricky part was that the oncoming lane also had a blind corner so we couldn't tell whether more cars were on the way. I think I heard a Jesus, Mary and Joseph after that one. The rest of the drive went, if not smoothly, without further incident and we arrived at the campground with plenty of time to set up, unhook the Toad, relax and plan our hikes for the next couple of weeks.

The Cape Breton Highlands are truly beautiful with untouched forest-covered mountains, panoramic ocean views, rugged coastlines and even sandy beaches. It was just a matter of deciding what to do which day. Driving the Cabot Trail itself was exhilarating with oohs and aahs around every curve in the road. I took way too many pictures at each lookout, convinced this was the money shot, only to find a more stunning view around the next bend. It's not surprising that this drive is rated as one of the top 10 most scenic highways in the world. We hiked, picked wild blueberries, hiked, picked wild raspberries, hiked, and from time to time, checked out various beaches where Porter was in his element. Nothing in the water was safe from his retriever instinct. He was fearless. In a few places we left the Cabot Trail highway and drove along some local roads through small fishing villages and isolated coves. The most northern point we reached (along a pothole filled gravel road) was Meat Cove. Historically, this part of the Atlantic witnessed many hundreds of shipwrecks, and given local tides and currents, countless carcasses (both animal and human) washed up on the beautiful beach, hence its name. Today, it is dotted with sunbathers from the small campground on the bluff that overlooks it.

But being in this park only exacerbated to our A.D.D. We had not sat still since we left Sidrabene and we kept saying, "Okay, tomorrow let's just stay by the campsite, lay in the hammock, read a book." Then tomorrow would come, the sun would be shining, and we'd say, "Okay, let's go do [insert hike name here] and tomorrow, we'll stay put." We were exhausting ourselves. And then we pulled out the bikes! We had seen quite a few people biking along the highway, complete with bulging panniers, so they weren't just out for an easy pedal. If they could do it, so could we. What were we thinking?!?!? The Cabot Trail has some incredibly steep sections – 15% grades that continue for literally 5 winding kms. I don't know what kind of shape you have to be in to tackle that type of topography, but those days, if they ever existed, are long behind us. We decided to drive the entire loupe and scout out those sections that would be within our more modest capabilities. And while we found plenty of hills to coast down, there were just as many to climb up and several of those were brutal. I thought I might heave a lung on some of those never-ending ascents and I'm not ashamed to say that on more than one occasion, I wanted to just get off and push my bike to the top. I was certain I was going to fall off into the traffic out of sheer exhaustion. Because we did not want to leave Porter in the RV by himself, we took turns biking (while the other hiked), so I cannot attest to how many times John did or did not get off his bike. He says he never got off. Hmmmm. Thankfully, the motorists were very courteous in sharing the road and we never felt unsafe, despite having no shoulder most of the way. When passing cyclists, drivers pulled either completely or halfway into the opposite lane. If there was oncoming traffic, they simply waited for clearance. I never once had anyone try to squeeze by me. Maybe they felt my pain and figured it just wasn't sporting to add to it. Of course all this heart pumping, chest heaving, leg burning biking was definitely going to make any cycling in Prince Edward Island a breeze. And it was time to move on. However, leaving was difficult. Words can never describe, and pictures can never capture how magnificent and breathtaking it truly was, and we would highly recommend at least a full week here. Now you may recall that we received conflicting advice on driving the motor home through the park along the Cabot Trail. No problem vs. no way. Well, we had entered the park along the east side, via North Sydney and this counter-clockwise approach was definitely the easier way. Because while scouting out bike routes in the Jeep, we came to see exactly what the nay-sayers meant when they said too windy, too steep, don't do it etc. etc. The north and west sides of the park are where some of the more panoramic views are, but they are also where some of the more gut wrenching, heart-in-your-throat,

knuckle whitening switchbacks are. And to add just a bit more challenge, gravel, due to road construction and re-surfacing. Agreeing that discretion is the better part of valour, we left the park the same way we came in, knowing that there was only one really steep and winding section awaiting us, instead of four. On to Prince Edward Island!

I DIDN'T GET OFF MY BIKE EITHER!

5.

POTATOES, POTTERS
& PAINTERS

HOW TO DESCRIBE PRINCE EDWARD ISLAND... POTATOES, POTTERS
AND PAINTERS, WITH A FEW COWS THROWN INTO THE MIX. While
we often associate PEI with potatoes, that may be a bit too one-dimensional, because as
soon as we crossed the Confederation Bridge, we were greeted with views that can best
be described as pastoral. Gently rolling hills with fields of green-purple clover, bright
yellow canola and buff coloured wheat ready for harvest. Wheat? Really? Well, being
city folks, we couldn't tell a wheat field from an oat field, but they were definitely grains
of some kind. And peacefully grazing cows. Black and white ones that after some discussion we agreed were Holsteins. Although there were plenty of brown ones too. So where
were the potatoes? It seems that either PEI has diversified, or we don't know anything
about this province.

Getting to PEI today is very easy compared to 25 years ago, when you had to reserve
a spot on the ferry (the MV Abegweit), which only made a limited number of crossings
per day between Cape Tormentine in New Brunswick and Port Borden in PEI. "Abby",
as the locals called her, was an icebreaking ship that carried both people and vehicles.
But she didn't sail if the seas were too stormy, thus making any and all plans contingent
upon the weather. I recall one rough crossing while on holiday with Matejs when he
was about 8 years old. The water was so choppy that while making our way down the
vessel's passageway, we literally staggered along like over-acting drunks in a movie. It
is still possible to take a ferry to the island but that is the crossing from Caribou, Nova
Scotia to Wood Islands, PEI. Most people prefer to take the "new" bridge between Cape
Jourimain, New Brunswick and Borden-Carlton, PEI. The Confederation Bridge (or

Fixed Link as the islanders originally called it) was built between 1993 and 1997 at a cost of one billion dollars and is the longest bridge in the world that goes over ice-covered waters. Ten minutes to cross 13 kilometers at a height of between 40 and 60 meters above sea level, leaving ample clearance for marine traffic. There is a toll, but you only pay it when leaving the island. And you have to drive. No pedestrian or bicycle traffic. If you don't have your own motor wheels, you have to take a shuttle. Some island residents are a bit miffed that they have to keep paying a toll to drive to the closest Costco (which is in Moncton), but the griping is kept to a minimum because it is still considerably easier and cheaper than booking the previously mentioned ferry (although it does add an additional $46.00 to that Costco bill). Proposals for some form of crossing to the mainland (other than marine) were floated as far back as the 1870's and they included both a railway tunnel, as well as a rock filled causeway augmented by a bridge or tunnel to accommodate shipping. The causeway proposal was rejected because the tidal currents through any gap would be in excess of 18 knots (33km/h for us landlubbers) making it virtually impassable for commercial ships, and the railway tunnel was a non-starter. In true federal government fashion, nothing was seriously done about any proposals until it became too costly to maintain the aging ferry service. And they had to do something because PEI joining Confederation was contingent upon the federal government always ensuring the islanders would have some means of accessing the mainland. However, when talk of a bridge started edging closer to reality, the inhabitants of PEI were split on whether it was a good thing or not. Two groups were formed: Friends of the Island, made up mostly of fishermen, environmentalists and academics vs. For A Better Tomorrow, made up of business, tourism and labour groups. Arguments devolved into the ridiculous with some on the nay side maintaining that a bridge would give everything from killer bees to prostitutes easy access to the island. The matter was decided by plebiscite with 60% of the residents voting "aye", but quite a few friendships never regained their footing. And the killer bees and prostitutes never arrived.

Our first stop was Charlottetown, that vaunted "Birthplace of Confederation." The romanticized version would have us believe that our great forefathers had the astuteness to organize a conference specific to uniting the provinces for the benefit of us all. The reality? In 1864, delegates from PEI, Nova Scotia and New Brunswick had gathered in Charlottetown to discuss the union of the Maritime provinces. Only the Maritime provinces. They weren't exactly looking to include the west. Representatives from the province of Canada (which then consisted of Ontario and Quebec) arrived to pitch their notion of a nation stretching "from sea to shining sea." Keeping in mind transportation methods of the day, they sailed into Charlottetown harbour by ship and then rowed ashore. But when they landed, no one was around to greet them. A circus happened to be in town and most of the Islanders had gone to see the show. Government and circuses hand in hand right from the get-go. It's perfect. Once the actual circus left town (the one with the clowns, that is), the officials got around to talking about the concept of a new "Canada." Hence, PEI's place in our history as the "cradle of confederation". The specific discussions took place at Province House but during our visit, this edifice was closed for renovation, so I was spared feigning any enthusiasm over that. Charlottetown's waterfront, at Peake's Wharf has pretty much what you would expect from a tourist destination and cruise ship port. Crafts, clothing, souvenirs and a few places to eat. Thankfully, no ships were anchored when we arrived, so we were able stroll about relatively un-trampled. Two blocks up from the water were more shops and restaurants, a bit more upscale and interspersed here and there with statues of the various fathers of confederation, seemingly engaged in discussion or deep in thought. I took the time to share a park bench with Sir John A. Charlottetown also has a great little farmer's market just outside the core, closer to the university. Wonderful artisan breads, wild mushrooms, and cinnamon rolls that were amongst the best we have sampled. And we had sampled quite a few in the preceding weeks.

Other than getting in some cycling, our plans for the island were very fluid. We were on the "No Plan" plan. We spent the first week at a wonderful campground in Cabot Beach Provincial Park overlooking Malpeque Bay and the Gulf of St. Lawrence. We were situated right on the water facing south/west and thus able to take in some spectacular sunsets. And because the closest town was Malpeque – as in Malpeque oysters – we had to try some of these pricey bi-valves. I still maintain eating the raw ones is like swallowing snot, no matter what kind of fancy sauce you cover them with. We even tried raw quahogs (which I had never heard of – hard shelled clams) and they were as bad as the oysters, only "chewier". John would like to point out that my critique does not necessarily reflect his opinion. He quite enjoyed them. I stuck to seafood chowder and lobster after that, and there was plenty available. Although surprisingly, quite costly. While the seafood was obviously very fresh, just because you are 500 yards from the source does not mean you are going the get a deal on the price. And some places didn't always put in the culinary effort either. I know that Oysters Rockefeller are not just baked oysters with some spinach and cheddar cheese on top! We even ate at one place where they served frozen fries! In PEI! Imagine! I think there is a tendency hit up the tourists while they are around, and many dining establishments close after September, some even at the end of August. But eating was not all lunch bag letdown. The best fish and chips I have ever had, ever, ever, ever were at Rick's Fish& Chips in St. Peter's, and the caramel bread pudding with blueberry sauce at 21 Breakwater in Souris was to kill for. We ate more lobster rolls than we can remember, and occasionally switched them up for just lobster, skipping the bread altogether. However, given all the gastronomic indulging, it was time to get in a bit of exercise so out came the bikes. We started with The Confederation Trail.

The trail itself runs from Tignish in the west to Elmira in the east, a distance of 274 kms, (370 if you include the spurs) and is built entirely on an old single gauge railway line. Interestingly, PEI joined confederation in 1873, in large part because of the huge debt it had incurred in building this railway in the first place. But as improved roads and cars gained in popularity, rail travel declined and by 1989 the railway had been abandoned. The islanders saw an opportunity and it is now Prince Edward Island's portion of the Trans Canada Trail. Mostly crushed cinder stone, its steepest elevation changes up or down were never more than 2 degrees. Considerably easier than the Cabot Trail in Nova Scotia. We biked sections of it in 30 to 40 km stretches and while pleasant, I am sorry to state I found it a little boring. Too many segments were just long, narrow and straight trajectories hedged in on either side by trees that blocked your view of anything else. But then it does follow the old rail line, so that makes sense. This is not to say that there were not interesting and scenic parts, and you could always stop at villages along the way to visit an art gallery or pottery studio (more on that later). Along one particular stretch, I kept seeing random, lone apple trees and not the sort that are found in abandoned orchards. These were very old, had obviously never been pruned, had no logical connection to the surrounding landscape and were even to my inexperienced eye of different varieties. They were along old railroad tracks for heaven's sake! I then came across an information panel that explained the whole mystery. Back in the day, rural people taking the train to any given destination would also bring along their lunch, often containing an apple or two from the homestead's tree. After eating the apples, they would pitch the cores out the train window and from some of these cores, over a hundred years later, we have trees producing heritage apples the likes of which cannot be found in grocery stores. Their aroma filled the air as I cycled along, so I got off my bike at various places and picked some (those I could reach), brought them back to the RV and made apple loaf cake (after cutting out the many wormy bits). It was so flavourful! Thank-you to those long-ago litter bugs! The prettiest and most scenic section of the trail is a 15-km stretch between Morell and St. Peters where it actually follows the shoreline for a bit and crosses a longish bridge over the Morell River. Considering the rest of the trail is, as stated, a rather monotonous "tunnel", anytime it came into a clearing, never mind provided a water view, was cause to sit up and take notice.

We then took to cycling along the roadways and looking at a road map of Prince Edward Island, you will see that there are very few straight or logical routes to be found. Proof positive that neither the Romans nor the British army were here to help lay things out in an orderly manner. But it was definitely more enjoyable – scenic and rolling so that both our eyes and our legs got a bit of a workout. I even came across a signpost for the town of Baltic. Well that warranted a detour. But after peddling several kilometers (and crossing the Baltic River), I came to an intersection where although another sign welcomed me to Baltic, all I could see was a house on one corner and a huge (smelly) poultry farm on the other. Certainly no Latvians or Lithuanians to greet me. I then did a bit of research. It turns out that the name "Baltic" is really a corruption of the Gaelic word "*bailtech*" meaning "belonging to a village". And considering the area was settled in 1775, it is highly improbable that any Baltic people were amongst the earliest immigrants. So much for finding any long-lost relatives. The roads themselves were not in the best of shape and it was obvious asphalt maintenance was not high on any government's agenda. And many of these roads, while clearly indicated on the map with solid lines (eg. route 303), are really just red dirt tracks. As in, have never been paved. On more than one occasion we wondered if we had perhaps taken a wrong turn and were simply driving through some farmer's potato field, about to come face to face with a tractor! But no, eventually we reached pavement again. It's a good thing we had purchased a Jeep instead of the Smart car we had briefly considered.

But what about those PEI potatoes? Well everything you ever wanted to know about potatoes can be found at the Canadian Potato Museum (& Antique Farm Machinery Museum). And we went. I kid you not. It wasn't large but it certainly contained a lot of information about a food staple that we take so much for granted. It turns out China is the biggest potato grower in the world, followed by Russia, to a tune of almost 110 million tonnes. I'm not sure what the Chinese do with theirs, but the Russians make a lot of vodka. Canada harvests around 5 million tonnes, with PEI accounting for about one third of the amount. That doesn't seem like much except when you break it down into a population to production ratio, PEI accounts for 10,000 kgs per person. In other words, the potato capital of the world. And they are quite proud of that honour. As a food stuff, potatoes are not indigenous to Canada, but estimates are that they were introduced by European settlers to New France around 1700. In Europe itself, they hadn't shown up until the late 1500's and even then, were used mainly as animal food. It took periods of famine before they were seen as suitable for human consumption and even then, only by the poor and often only after royal decree, be it in England, Germany or Russia. People just didn't want to eat these things. But they really are a very healthy food, undeserving of the bad rap we give them. Cholesterol-free, high in fibre, containing vitamins B and C as well as iron, calcium, magnesium and other minerals, and actually quite low in calories. The average potato contains only 80 to 100 calories. It's all that butter, sour cream and bacon bits we add that seem to cause all the problems. And what about those French fries? How did they come about? Well for them we may have to thank the third President of the United States, Thomas Jefferson. When he wasn't busy founding the Republic and authoring the Declaration of Independence, he was serving "potatoes cooked in the French manner" at official dinners. It turns out that while Ambassador to France in the 1780's he developed quite a liking for deep fried ones and brought the recipe with him when he returned to America. So there you go. A president is partially responsible for the obesity epidemic in America. And there are so many varieties of potato – so many more than the Russet and Yukon Gold we are limited to at our local grocery stores. And they all have different uses. How do you tell whether a potato is better for mashing vs. for stew? Here is the trick. If you place potatoes in a salt-water solution, some will sink and others will float. Those that sink are higher in starch and therefore, become fluffy when cooked. So they are better for baking, mashing or frying. Those that float have lower starch so are better in soups and stews. Now you know. Don't make that mistake again! Following our tour of the museum we indulged in some baked potatoes at the local cafe, mine loaded with the usual sour cream, bacon bits etc., and John opting for the more gourmet offering with lobster and hollandaise sauce. Either way, they were more than 80 to 100 calories!

We then decided to check out some lighthouses. PEI is about 140 miles long, has 2,184 square land surface miles and 1,100 miles of coastline. So prior to today's modern methods of navigation, lighthouses were crucial for marine traffic and safety in the waters around the island. Today there are 63 lighthouses and range-light buildings, of which 37 are still active. That means one lighthouse for every 34 square miles – the highest concentration of lighthouses in any province or state in North America. Yes, somebody actually took the time to calculate all that. We first drove to West Point Lighthouse in Cedar Dunes Provincial Park. We had been there years ago with the children and I am really glad we returned because it is just lovely. Constructed in 1875, it counts as a "second generation" lighthouse. Lighthouses built prior to 1873 are considered "colonial" in that their shape is octagonal and they were built when timber was abundant in the province. Those built after 1873 are square tapered and the large timber required for construction had to be imported from New Brunswick because by then, PEI was all out of big trees. In addition to distinctive light flash patterns, each lighthouse has its own unique markings (eg. white with one large horizontal black stripe vs. white with four average sized horizontal black stripes), and it is these differences that helped sailors identify or confirm their nautical positions. Obviously with today's technology, this manner of navigation is obsolete, and lighthouses are really more nostalgic and decorative than functional. The one at West Point also operates as an inn, restaurant and museum, so diversity is the name of the game to ensure maintenance and continued survival. Having been to West Point, we decided we should check out East Point Lighthouse as well. It is nowhere near as attractive as West Point, but it does have a more interesting history. Built in 1867, it was unfortunately situated about half a mile from its designated position on marine navigational maps. So in 1882, the British warship HMS Phoenix was wrecked off the coat of PEI, in large part because the lighthouse was not where the maps said it was. In 1885 they moved it to within 200 feet of its assigned location. Since then, it has been moved back to its current placement due to erosion. There have not been any further serious incidents, despite the fact that the waters are quite turbulent, with three major bodies of water, the Atlantic Ocean, Northumberland Straight and Gulf of St. Lawrence all meeting there. When we visited, the wind was almost enough to sweep you off your feet. But it had been very windy since we left Cabot Beach and relocated to Red Point Provincial Park. Gusts up to 70 km/h.

Red Point was another beautiful park, almost deserted given that tourist season was pretty much over, and we were blessed with another sweeping view out over the water, where we could just faintly make out the outline of Nova Scotia on the horizon. We deliberately stayed away from PEI National Park and Cavendish for two reasons. First, the national park prohibits all dogs on their 40 kms of beach until October. This is because the piping plover nests in the dunes and they don't want the four-legged creatures disturbing the two-legged ones. And Porter is a retriever after all. It would be bad form if he came back with one of these endangered little shorebirds clutched in his jaws. Interestingly, the provincial parks do not have this restriction despite having similar flora and fauna. And thankfully, Porter was more interested in pulling out seaweed and rolling in the sand than chasing birds. And we stayed away from Cavendish and the whole Anne of Green Gables shtick too. I have never been an Anne of Green Gables fan (obviously neither has John) and we had heard that the whole area is very contrived and touristy with nothing but shops selling Anne paraphernalia – Anne wigs, Anne hats, Anne music, Anne apple pie. The list goes on and on. Whatever they can think of to get you to buy, it's there. Perhaps people are waxing nostalgic about life during a simpler time in a simpler place, and that is all well and good, but it won't be accomplished by fighting with tour buses for a parking spot. And speaking of vehicles...

While driving to Red Point, we passed a couple of Amish horse-drawn buggies.

Now what was up with that? PEI has an Amish population? Well as of 2016 they do. About 80 people from two southern Ontario communities (one near Woodstock and one near St. Jacobs) had taken up residence on the island and were setting up two separate hamlets. Given that they do not use electricity the move cannot be prompted by Ontario Hydro antics, so what gives? Apparently, farming in PEI is more in keeping with their simpler lifestyle, and they are getting out of Ontario where modern life and modern farming methods predominate. I can't say I blame them. Life here is less pretentious, less cluttered and quieter – the people more sincere. What more could we ask for?

Well, there could be a few improvements in communication and the accuracy of disseminated information. As is often the case, the Tourist Information Centre was a treasure trove of what to see and do in the province. We picked up several maps of scenic drives, interesting locations and sites of historic or cultural importance. If only they had been up to date. We drove along a rutted road looking for PEI's largest tree (an elm with a circumference so big it takes four people to encircle it) but to no avail, only to be told later at the information centre that it blew down in a storm 2 years ago. We drove out to an apple orchard that markets itself as having over 40 varieties of apples, only to see a sign stating that it would not open to the public until the following weekend. We drove to a pick-your-own blueberry farm (after checking on their website and confirming they were open) only to pull up to a closed sign. We drove to a fresh vegetable farm only to find a weather-beaten homestead where the "open" sign had fallen away from the overturned bucket it had been propped up against, and the garden looked overgrown and neglected. The best description I can give would be "creepy". I think I saw Norman Bates' mother in the upstairs window. We didn't stop. We drove to an historic church to look at an old bell with an interesting history. Forged in France in 1723, it had been used by the Acadians residing in St. Peter's Harbour, but with deportation looming, they buried the bell for safekeeping and forgot about it. And so it remained until 1870 when some farmer discovered it by accidentally hitting it with his plough. From then on it was used by the present-day Acadian community. But when we got to the church, the doors were locked. We found out (again later), the church had been deconsecrated and no-one knew what the present-day Acadians had done with the bell. All these outings would have been a colossal waste of time except the drives themselves were so scenic, we didn't really mind. It was the journey, not the destination.

And driving along on these numerous "journeys" we passed sign after sign after sign for pottery studios, art galleries and craft shops. Every hamlet, no matter how small, seemed to have their own resident artist (or artists). This island must have the highest concentration of craftsmen/women per capita than anywhere else in the world. If someone had the time to calculate how many lighthouses there are per square kilometre, surely they can figure out how many painters and potters there are. And saying "a lot" wasn't the answer we were looking for! And further, how do these places survive? Are there really that many tourists buying artwork? And while many of the pieces clearly are "art", others would fall into the knick-knack category. It's a tough call. Sea-glass pendant vs. refurbished lobster trap chair? T-shirt rubbed with red PEI soil vs. lighthouse model? Stoneware teapot vs. savoury snacks. We did visit one gallery however, that is deserving of special mention. Disclaimer here: the owner (and potter extraordinaire) Peter Jansons is a fellow of Latvian decent who was also, and here is the connection, one of the kids at Sidrabene when I was there as a child. His establishment, The Dunes Gallery and Cafe, is in the north/central part of the island at Brackley Beach and while he started out with pottery, he has expanded to such an extent (18,000 square feet), it is impossible to describe all the treasures to be found both inside and out. Pottery, of course, but also jewellery, blown glass works, clothing, paintings, woodcarvings and furniture (even dining tables and chairs made from the salvaged wood of boats wrecked in the Indonesian tsunami) as well as works imported from Bali. Add to that an upscale café and beautiful outdoor gardens on 20 acres, and you can easily spend a day just wandering and admiring art for art's sake. It was great to say hello, catch up a bit and pass on greetings from friends back home. We wish we could have spent more time.

Another visit I particularly enjoyed was to The Inn at Bay Fortune. Not another art gallery but rather, a culinary one – the "home" of Chef Michael Smith. A number of years ago, his show *The Inn Chef* was popular on the Food Network and I was always impressed by his emphasis on using fresh, local ingredients to create the best flavour in different dishes. Although we were neither staying at the inn nor staying for dinner, the staff invited us to wander through the gardens and look around. The guys in in the kitchen invited me in as they prepped chanterelles and chatted about their work. It was all very friendly and informal – just like being in somebody's kitchen (albeit it on a slightly larger scale). Michael Smith himself was leading a small group of people around on a little tour of the grounds, and he greeted us with a casual "howdy folks" somewhere between the dill and the arugula. Dinner at the inn is a 4-hour affair that starts with different tasting stations and ends with all the guests (a regulated number) sitting around a large table and dining together. Unfortunately for us, we had Porter to contend with and we were not yet at the point where we were comfortable leaving him alone for that length of time in the yacht. And this was certainly one time we could have used a doggie daycare. It just so happened it was our 20th wedding anniversary and a nice dinner prepared by one of my favourite chefs would have been great. But not if I would be worrying about Porter every 20 minutes. We opted for a romantic dinner at an excellent restaurant (21 Breakwater) in Souris, where the timing was a bit more manageable and we could leave the brown menace in the car.

As our days started counting down, we talked more and more about how much the island had grown on us. At first, we simply appreciated its beauty, which was more tranquil than dramatic. But after spending time on the byways and coastlines, we came to appreciate more than just the view – although the beaches did contribute in no small way to the overall appeal. Some of these were laid-back while others were on the busier side. Some could only be accessed by walking through huge dunes and grasses before reaching a fine light-coloured sand. In places, walking in this sand produced an audible squeak with each step – something akin to wet running shoes on a gym floor. They refer to this as "singing sand" and it has something to do with the type and size of each sand grain, the presence of silica and a specific level of humidity. It was a very peculiar experience. In other places, the sand was of a coarser variety, tinged red in keeping with the sandstone cliffs from which it was crumbling. At Red Point, we actually took the time to sit on the beach, watch the waves and fishing boats, and wait for the ferry en route to Ile de la Madeleine to pass by. Did I mention we love the ocean?

However, one thing PEI does not have is wilderness. Every square acre has been hunted, logged, farmed, ploughed, cultivated or altered in some way. There are no large animals, predatory or otherwise, and the last bear was killed sometime around 1927. The odd red fox may put in an appearance, but there is nothing else left that might cause the unexpected disappearance of little Fido or Fifi. Except bald eagles. We saw them on five separate occasions, and it is estimated they number between 500 and 600. As an aside, during this particular month I had been reading a book by Annie Proulx entitled *Barkskins*. Set in the east coast between 1693 and 2013, its overarching theme is logging, and it was disturbing to read how rapacious and destructive the approach to logging was several hundred years ago. A feeding frenzy if you will. Proulx did her research well, and it is obvious Prince Edward Island was not spared, as evidenced by the need to import lumber for lighthouses within a few generations. North America truly was another world prior to contact. Off on a tangent here... Driving through northern Ontario, be it heading to the cottage in summer or admiring the autumn colours in fall, we forget that the forests of today consist of mere saplings compared to the giants they once held. Because although the feeding frenzy started on the east coast, it did not stop there. Algonquin Provincial Park in Ontario has a small logging museum (albeit a sanitized version of what life in a logging camp was really like) where visitors can see the odd massive stump, log or slice of white pine that was once so abundant in our province.

All of it now gone. At least we still have bears. For the time being. Okay. I'm getting off my soapbox now. I'd highly recommend *Barkskins* as a read though.

We left PEI on a rather miserable day, with high winds and rain. In a way, we had to leave, because all the provincial parks were closing for the season. They didn't exactly kick us out, but they were turning off the power that night, so it was a pretty strong hint. We headed towards New Brunswick. The drive as far as St. John was fairly easy and would most likely have been quite scenic if it had not been for the drizzle, mist and fog. But one thing was obvious right away. Fall was just around the corner. Many of the aspen trees had yellowed leaves, and tinges of red were evident on the maples. How had the summer passed by so quickly? We hit a little speed bump just before St. John, when the motor coach's engine light went on. Oh oh. Now what? We took it to a Cummins dealer in town right away and they advised all that was required was a quick update with the Cummins computer. Almost like the update you do periodically on your personal computer or tablet. Unfortunately, the Cummins computer was down for most of the day, so we were at a bit of a loose end – homeless, with a dog, in the fog and rain. We quickly found out that St. John is not a very dog-friendly city. Other than an off-leash dog park, and short of checking into a hotel, there was literally no place to go. So we took turns. One of us stayed in the car with Porter while the other shopped. In this manner, we covered Costco, Winners, Pet Value, Best Buy and the downtown Farmer's Market. The market was quite a nice venue. Not huge, but very pleasant, with the rafters built to resemble the inverted hull of a ship. It is actually Canada's oldest continuous farmer's market, having been established in 1876, and one of the vendors has been in operation for over a hundred years. But you can only wander aimlessly for so long and we eventually ended up back at the garage waiting room. At least they had huge comfy chairs. The update was completed by evening, so we thankfully retrieved our home, boondocked for the night and hoped for sunnier skies the next day because we were off to Campobello Island.

Why Campobello Island? Well, it is our son's fault. One of the conditions of employment with his agency is a willingness to accept a posting anywhere in Canada regardless of from where you hail. Yukon/Alaska, Manitoba/North Dakota, New Brunswick/Maine. Following training, any remote border crossing is a distinct possibility. Fortunately for him, his luck held out and he received the posting of his choice. But a close colleague was not so fortunate and ended up at Campobello/Lubec. Although Campobello Island is legally and literally Canadian soil, the only way to get there by car is through Maine, hence the border check. It is busy in the summer with tourists from both Canada and the United States crossing back and forth, but come winter, border services officers complain of feeling like the Maytag repair man. We read up on Campobello and found out that it is home to the Roosevelt Campobello International Park, a park administered, staffed and funded jointly by both Canada and the United States. Given that we were sort of in the neighbourhood, we thought we'd check out where Matejs could have ended up. The park itself was created in 1964 as a symbol of the close relationship between Canada and the US, and as a memorial to President Franklin D. Roosevelt. His parents had purchased a house on the island in 1883 and as a child, young man, and even as president, FDR spent many summers there with his family. His visits only decreased after he contracted polio at the age of 39, although his wife Eleanor, their children and grandchildren continued to visit until Eleanor's death in 1962. The cottage (really a rather large summer home – 34 rooms, with 18 bedrooms and 6 bathrooms) has been preserved and contains all the original furnishings used by the family. It was interesting to see that despite its size, they lived a relatively normal and simple life. Definitely not ostentatious. But then they only occupied it for 2 months a year during the summer! The visitor's centre showcases the story of the Roosevelt family's life on the island as well as the legacy of friendship between Canada and the US. There were several hiking trails throughout the 2,800-acre park itself, as well as picturesque coastal drives along the rest of the island. The weather on our first day was rather foggy, but it did make for some interesting photographs and we quite enjoyed listening to the foghorn in the distance at night. On our second day we attended a one-hour presentation called "Tea with Eleanor". A limited number of guests are treated to bottomless cups of tea (in lovely china cups) while staff give an overview of Eleanor Roosevelt's life and achievements. What an amazing woman! The projects she tackled and the changes she was able to effect make the accomplishments of subsequent first ladies (and even subsequent presidents) pale in comparison. I'm not too sure about the success of her children though. She raised 5 to adulthood, and between them, they have registered 19 divorces! Ouch! But short of immersing ourselves further into the lives of the Roosevelts, two days on the island was about enough. We were starting to run out of time (we hoped to be back in Ontario by early October) and still wanted to see the Fundy Tides.

It is only a one-hour drive through Maine, to get from Campobello to St. Stephen, New Brunswick. St. Stephen is known as Canada's chocolate town, and the land yacht seemed to have a will of its own as it pulled up outside the Ganong Bros factory. Ganong Bros. is supposedly Canada's oldest candy company, and they claim to have introduced the concept of heart-shaped boxes of chocolate on Valentine's Day to North America, as well as sold the first "wrapped" chocolate bar. We may have dropped a dollar or two there but the quality, while good, doesn't beat Godiva. On to St. Andrews-by-the-Sea. Another charming resort town with a quaint main street, we were able to secure a camping site right on Passamaquoddy Bay. And although the tides here do not ebb and flow as dramatically as elsewhere, it was great just being on the water. We only stayed one night and then continued on to St. Martins. But en route, we were passing just a hair's breadth away from Wolfhead Smokers Ltd., an artisanal smoked salmon smoke-house and once again, the land yacht veered off the highway. It was just a short detour, but I would have gladly driven triple the distance for the cold smoked salmon they produce. Thank goodness they also ship anywhere in Canada and we left with their busi-ness card securely tucked into John's now considerably lighter wallet. We made it to St. Martins in no time and were fortunate to be camped right on the Bay of Fundy facing the sea caves, a local attraction. That was certainly one benefit of travelling in the shoul-der season. The great summer rush was over and choice sites were fairly easy to find. We settled in although high tide prevented us from walking out to the caves themselves, as they are only accessible when the tide is low. That had to wait until the next day. We set out around 11am and even before we got there, could see evidence of how high (and low) the tides get. Boats that were floating beside the dock yesterday were now lying on the ocean floor 15 feet down. Walking out to the sandstone caves was relatively easy for

us, but hard on Porter's paws because at this location, the ocean floor is made up more of smoothly rounded river rocks than sand. A huge bald eagle was sitting a little distance out on some clumps of seaweed and kelp, keeping a wary eye on us as we approached. And I had left my zoom lens in the car! It was a nice outing, but we had pretty much seen everything there was to see within an hour.

ST. MARTINS HARBOUR AT LOW TIDE.

We then drove along the Fundy Trail Parkway (not to be confused with the Fundy Trail Highway) – touted as the last "undeveloped" stretch of wilderness coastline between Labrador and Florida. It starts about 10 kms east of St. Martins and runs for about 20 kms following the shore. By 2018 they hoped to connect it with Alma and the Hopewell Rocks (our last east coast destination). The drive itself was very scenic with the road winding in and out, offering stunning views of the Fundy coast from numerous look out points. I had not imagined there would be cliffs along this stretch! And when we dropped down to sea level, with the ebbed tide we easily walked 500 meters out before reaching the water. The area is part of the Trans Canada Trail, as well as the Fundy Biosphere Reserve and a UNESCO Global Geopark. Fancy authorities meaning they will try to keep it as natural and undisturbed as possible. Lots of picnic tables but no organized camping. Worked for us!

LUNCH ON THE OCEAN FLOOR, WITH COLLAPSED ELEPHANT IN THE BACKGROUND.

The most impressive place to witness the magnificence of the Fundy Tides is at the Hopewell Rocks at Hopewell Cape. Technically, at this point it is really Shepody Bay, but the water is coming from the Bay of Fundy. And the amount of water that flows in and out of Fundy within one day equals all the water, running into all the oceans, from all the rivers on earth, over a 24-hour period. It is mind boggling. The phenomenon has been named one of the Seven Natural Wonders of North America and depending on the phase of the moon the tides can vary by 50 feet in height. And they change at a rate of 6 to 8 vertical feet per hour. The rocks themselves are sandstone sea stacks (or flowerpot rocks as they are called there) that have been eroded by the tide over thousands of years. There are 17 of them in various shapes and sizes with many given specific names depending on their outlines. Elephant rock, one of the more photographed formations (it actually appears on the New Brunswick health card) lost half its mass on March 14th of this year when about 200 tons fell off during the night. Now you see it, now you don't. They are unstable to say the least, and warning signs and roped off areas are a constant reminder that this area is nature in motion. Despite the risks (albeit minimal), visitors are encouraged to walk out on the ocean floor at low tide, but once the water starts to rise, park staff do a "beach sweep" to make sure everyone has returned safely. Otherwise it is a long cold and wet wait until the coves are clear again. There is no scrambling up those cliff faces if you are caught out! The ocean floor itself alternates between coarse sand and rock, and boot-sucking mud. It is one of those places you have to experience to really appreciate. And judging by the huge parking lot, a lot of people come for the experience. Thankfully, towards the end of September most of the crowds were gone, but we did notice a bus carrying tourists pull up just as we arrived, so we picked up the pace to get ahead of them. It wasn't really necessary because the area covers so much terrain, a hundred people could easily get lost there.

While driving in New Brunswick, one thing we were careful to avoid were roads that had covered bridges. Yes, they are charming and romantic, but they are not something the land yacht was designed to cross. And New Brunswick has a lot of covered bridges. Sixty of them. Mostly in the southern part of the province. And why cover them? Early bridges were more often than not, built of wood, and bridges built of wood have a life span between 10 and 15 years. But if they are covered and protected from the elements, they can last 100 years. So it made economic sense. From a human-interest perspective, covered bridges also offered a private moment for couples to steal a kiss or two, so were sometimes referred to as "kissing bridges". The longest covered bridge in the world is in Hartland, New Brunswick with a span of 1,282 feet over the St. John River. Amusingly, when it was being built, a petition went around with the signatories trying to prevent the bridge from being covered. This because a local minister said that is would corrupt the region's youth. One government official said, "If the morals of the young people are so badly bent that it only requires a covered bridge to break them completely, there is little we, as a government, can do about the matter." So Canada has the world's longest covered bridge. Of course today, bridges are no longer made of wood, so any new covered ones are simply built in order to attract tourists.

By the time we left New Brunswick, in fact even by about the third week of September, autumn was no longer hinting at arriving. It had arrived. The tinges on the leaves had turned to a more definite colour, the underside of clouds had that dark grey look and the temperature was at times 10 degrees C during the day, dropping to 2 at night. We were thankful the motor home had both electric and propane heat, and the little electric fireplace gave off enough warmth to makes things cozy. But in retrospect, I wish we had not been so quick to dismiss the heated floor option when making our purchase. Those floor tiles got really cold. Time to bring out the thick socks and fleece, and head for Ontario. The drive north through eastern New Brunswick along the Trans Canada (Hwy 2) was one of the prettiest we had undertaken to date. The highway follows the St. John River valley and the terrain there was quite steeply rolling – very Appalachian as opposed to Laurentian. Abundant green forests with accents of yellow and red – a perfect picture postcard...

... Although not quite as picture perfect as Algonquin Provincial Park in Ontario. We stopped in for a few days to check out the fall colours and due to the unseasonably hot and dry summer, they peaked a bit later than usual. Perfect timing for us. They were magnificent! We had not been to Algonquin for at least 20 years and it was nice to be back, although there was some added drama to our return. When checking in at our campground, the park ranger advised that our reserved site was not available because of an earlier fire at the adjoining site. What? This is a forest. How bad can it be? It's not like a hotel where our room would have smoke damage or anything. It turned out that the "fire" was somebody's luxury motor coach going up in flames. Nothing left but a charred metal skeleton. Thankfully nobody was hurt, and the fire did not spread to the rest of the campground or park, but while it was burning, campers had to evacuate leaving their various modes of abode behind. Rumours were rampant about how it started, and the people directly across from it knew enough to say that the owners had actually not been around for over a week, so who knows what kind of malfunction occurred. Needless to say, that was a solid reason for not leaving Porter alone in the RV by himself for any length of time. And while late September is technically the shoulder season for camping, it is high season in Algonquin due to the leaves. The place was packed, and we had never seen the hiking trails so full of outdoor enthusiasts, some lugging expensive camera equipment while others tottered along on high-heeled wedge sneakers. There were several buses full of Chinese tourists who would dutifully disembark, take the requisite photo or selfie by some colourful foliage and then set out along the directed trail. Some were more intrigued by Porter than their surroundings, but they all seemed to be having a good time. Cars were stopped along the shoulder of Hwy. 60 where-ever there was a brighter flash of red or orange and the Ontario Provincial Police were out in full force making sure some of these nature lovers did not wander out into the traffic. However, I was starting to think that when it came to wildlife, someone was pulling a fast one on us. All along Hwy. 60 from the east gate to the west, there were numerous signs warning of moose crossing, the entrance to the campground warned of bears in the area and a whiteboard inside the kiosk listed all the recent animal sightings, including a wolf just the other day. Other than a chipmunk, we didn't see a darn thing. I think they just post that stuff to add a little excitement to people's lives and make them believe they are really getting back to nature.

Some final observations about this inaugural leg of our journey. We packed way too much stuff. Things that we thought would be essential to our existence weren't even looked at. There would be some more purging before we headed south. Driving a motor coach on secondary roads was not fun, since many of them were in pretty bad shape. It was better to park the coach at a campsite and then take side or day trips in the Toad. Easier on us, on Porter and on the vehicles. It is far better and considerably cheaper to camp in national or provincial parks than private ones (except Algonquin where the prices are just stupid). Sites are bigger, have more privacy and are generally in prettier locations with numerous back-to-nature things to do. We ate out way too much. But that could be because we were on the east coast and who can resist all that seafood chowder and all those lobsters. Technically, we didn't exactly "eat out" since we usually got the "take out" because of Porter, but I suppose that is splitting hairs. Gluttony is still one of the seven sins, so we hoped to show a bit more restraint in the future. We didn't get in as much biking and hiking as anticipated. Originally, I thought at least one ride or hike a day, but we were nowhere near that. Not sure why. Possibly because we were so busy learning about new things and new places. On the positive side, we established an almost daily yoga routine, so all was not lost. We missed our family and friends. Travelling was fun, we enjoyed each other's company and we relished sharing new places, sights and experiences with each other. But sometimes it would have been nice to see a familiar face or two at the dinner table. Not to mention catch up on gossip.

6.

DOES THIS MEAN WE ARE ALMOST SNOWBIRDS????

OCTOBER STARTED OUT PRETTY MUCH AS PLANNED. We were "home" by the 3rd, dropped the RV at McPhail's for service and spent several days in the guest suite of our son's condo. Although he offered the pull-out couch in his living room, his place was really too small for three adults (one of whom was working shiftwork) and a spoiled, high maintenance dog. Being "homeless" was certainly a bit more hassle than expected. Our original idea to simply check into a hotel if ever we found ourselves without the big wheels got to be very expensive. And it wasn't like going away for a vacation or romantic weekend getaway, where you really don't mind the cost. This was more like dropping the bucks just so you had someplace to sleep. So we were very happy to stay at Matejs' building for considerably less cash and once the RV work was complete, returned to Sidrabene for the remainder of our hiatus. It was quite a contrast from our initial stay in June. The nights were cool, bordering on cold, we had frost a few mornings, and many leaves had already fallen. Matejs came over for Thanksgiving and preparing dinner without the use of a large oven required a bit of creativity. It turns out that extra stuffing can be cooked in a portable bbq/grill without too much difficulty. Who would have thought? Two weeks flew by in a flurry of appointments and meetings, both social and professional. We visited with friends, but didn't get to see as many as we wanted, spent time with family, but not as long as we had hoped, and ran around like chickens with our heads cut off, trying to take care of all those things we had put off while on the road. A favourite phrase, "We'll take care of that when we get home" came back to haunt us.

We left Toronto on the 16th heading east along highway 401 towards Gananoque and the Thousand Islands. It was a lovely drive with the leaves in full colour. The border crossing into New York state was uneventful (the only question asked was how much cash we were carrying – none) and we were officially on our way south. Did that make us snowbirds? Not sure I liked that moniker. It sounded like we were old and should be wearing white shoes and pastel coloured sweatpants. I refuse! The first part of the drive was fairly easy although the road (Interstate 81) was not in the best of shape – very bumpy. We reached Watertown by 4:30 so decided to put a few more miles behind us, and boondock in Syracuse. Unfortunately, the Syracuse Walmart did not permit overnight parking and by then it was 6pm, getting dark and starting to rain. But we were forced to press on and that's when things got nasty. Horrific is the only way to describe it. Although still on the Interstate, the asphalt became rutted and rough, as if it was being resurfaced. In many places, construction and concrete barriers narrowed the already narrow lanes. It was winding. It was windy. It was dark. It was raining hard. Downed leaves blew across our path. I had my eyes closed much of the way. John says he kept his open. We blundered our way into Binghampton and said a prayer of thanks that other than damage to our nerves, we had made it. We vowed to never again drive under those kinds of conditions. The following morning dawned with high cloud cover and a few foggy patches, but overall, the view was spectacular. Mountains covered in vibrant shades of red, yellow and gold. The Appalachians on one side and the Catskills on the other.

We set out in a much more positive frame of mind, heading for the guitar mecca of Nazareth, Pennsylvania – C.F. Martin & Co. guitar factory – where we spent the bulk of the day. Now when I say we, I mean John. Porter and I hung around (no dogs allowed inside) while John went on a tour of the factory itself, wandered through the museum checking out rare and vintage instruments played by the likes of Elvis Presley, Bob Dylan, Johnny Cash, and Crosby, Stills & Nash, and strummed various higher end guitars, one priced at a mere $10,000.00. It just so happened that it was John's birthday, but that was one present he was not going to get. Christian Frederick Martin founded the company in 1833 in New York, moving to Nazareth in 1838. The company is known for its innovations in acoustic guitar design, including the Dreadnought, which is now standard for most of today's acoustic guitars. They employ 600 people and churn out 165 guitars per day, although the custom ones can take up to 2 years to make. In 2004 they made their millionth guitar and inlaid it with 40 rubies and diamonds. It has an estimated value of 1 million dollars. We made the requisite stop in their souvenir shop but all we could afford was a T-shirt and some guitar picks.

The next stop was another boondocking location in Reading. As in the Reading

Railroad of Monopoly fame. And it was fitting that we fell asleep listening to train whistles in the distance. The following day was spent trying to activate communication devices through Verizon. Despite considerable research beforehand, we found ourselves without internet and high roaming fees on our cell phones. It's amazing how isolated that can make you feel. Not to mention frustrated at not being able to research the next destination. We got things semi-resolved and headed off to French Creek State Park in Lancaster County, Pennsylvania. It is a huge park as state parks go (almost 8,000 acres) and it was odd to be camping where the scenery was all autumn hues and falling leaves, yet the temperature was in the low 80's F (27C plus for you Canadians). The area used to be covered with old growth American chestnut trees, but they were all chopped and burned to create charcoal, required for the local iron producing forges in the 1700s. By 1883 the area was completely denuded of all trees. Once the furnaces closed, about 100 years ago, beech, hickory, maple and oak trees moved in. And there were a lot of oak trees. If we hadn't been able to tell by the leaves, we would certainly have figured it out by the countless acorns that kept raining down on the roof of the RV. Literally raining down. And quite noisy too. Being in Lancaster County, we were in close proximity to the Amish and Mennonite communities, so we set up the land yacht and unhooked the Toad.

Our initial foray into the world of the Amish was very disappointing and discouraging. We had read that being a farming community, the Amish were spread out over a considerable geographic area. But two particular towns, Bird-In-Hand and Intercourse, were at the heart of this society making it very easy learn about the Amish and their lifestyle. Yes, yes, we snickered too. Intercourse. As a town name? Really? But the word "intercourse" has no sexual connotation here; it refers to the fellowship and camaraderie shared within these faith-based groups. So get your mind out of the gutter. We arrived at Intercourse, and saw all kinds of horse-drawn buggies, men with long beards and straw hats, and women wearing plain clothing, caps and aprons. But they were all busy going about their daily lives and were certainly not about to pull over and talk to a couple of tourists. And wouldn't that just be the height of ignorant? "Excuse me, I know you are busy, but would you mind telling me why you don't drive a car and wear that funny cap on your head?" We went into some shops that were advertising Amish merchandise (quilts, knickknacks, small wood items) but it all seemed so gimmicky. We then had the misfortune of stumbling into an area known as Kettle Kitchen. Oh my! It was as if a cruise ship had disgorged a group of elderly, overweight, garishly dressed Americans into a location that combined Santa's Village with a tacky Niagara-on-the-Lake and mixed in a bit of food court for good measure, all concentrated on about 2 acres. Except in this case, it wasn't a cruise ship to blame, but tour buses. Many tour buses. And many incredibly out of shape people waddling along (or sitting on benches to catch their breath), eating ice cream cones and shopping for trinkets. Signs everywhere saying Amish this and Amish that for sale, but not an Amish person to be seen. It was depressing. Bird-In-Hand was not much better, although the stores were a bit more spread out. We beat a confused and hasty retreat, and decided to just drive around the country roads. We needed a breath of fresh air, if you will.

The countryside here is indescribably lovely and being fall and harvest time made it lovelier still. It is all rolling pastureland dotted with countless family owned farms – each with white-washed barns, several grain silos, rambling farmhouses and tidy vegetables plots. The homesteads are not laid out in a grid-pattern, but rather patchwork, and the narrow roads wind around curving fields. Very few fences. We turned left and right, not following any real plan. We saw numerous horse-drawn buggies, some black, some gray, some open, some covered. We saw women pushing their way down the road on scooters. We saw men baling corn husks and loading the bales onto wagons, all the while being pulled by teams of draught horses or mules. We drove past one-room school-houses and across covered bridges. We saw herds of Holsteins and goats and the occasional chicken. It was like being on an anthropological field trip. The only problem was that we did not really know the significance of what we were observing, and our limited knowledge of this community came from the media and Hollywood. We couldn't even tell who was Mennonite and who was Amish. What to do? We had passed a Mennonite Information Centre in our travels and decided that might be a place to start. Lucky for us! The centre was full of books, DVDs, and pamphlets, but best of all, we were able to "hire" a local fellow (David) who came with us in the car for a 2+ hour ride through the county, all the while answering our questions and taking us to various farms for a walk about. David was 76 years of age, of the Old Order River Brethren (a more liberal group) and was a wealth of information. We learned a great deal, including how the Amish came about in the first place.

It all started with the Protestant Reformation in the early 1500s. Martin Luther did not like how the Catholics were doing things, so he split from the church, implementing some changes. The Anabaptists did not think Luther went far enough with his changes, so they broke off forming another group. A fellow by the name of Menno Simons had originally joined the Anabaptists (around 1536), but somewhere along the way, decided to branch off and take his followers with him. These were then referred to as Mennonites. All was good until the late 1600s when another fellow, Jakob Amman, didn't think the Mennonite were strict enough so he and his followers started to worship on their own, and eventually came to be called Amish. Both Mennonites and Amish were persecuted in Europe, so they moved to Pennsylvania in the late 1720s where they were allowed to worship as they pleased and live in peace. And this is where things get confusing. It seems that every time a segment of a particular order disagreed with how things were being done, they simply broke off and formed another order. Almost like being on a baseball team where if you and a few fellow players don't like what the coach is doing, you just go off and form a new team with a few different rules. Whenever we saw something that seemed inconsistent with what we had read or heard, David just said, "Oh, that's a different affiliation." Picture a tall tree. Looking up the trunk is like looking at the progression from Catholic to Lutheran to Anabaptist to Mennonite to Amish. But when you get to all the many branches and twigs at the top, that seems to be the Amish today. It is most confusing. There are about 40 Amish affiliations throughout North America all with different names, different types of dress and different rules on interacting with society at large (us "English"). They have no central authority, such as a pope or synod, so each can decide what works best for them.

However, the largest and best-known affiliation is the Old Order Amish – those whom we associate with austere living and old-fashioned dress. But as stated, they are all variations on the theme. They drive gray horse-drawn carriages (the Mennonites drive black ones), they use horses or mules to pull farm equipment in the fields, use diesel or gasoline for power instead of electricity, may have a phone but it will be out by the road in a phone shanty – never in the house – and have their own one-room schoolhouses where formal education only goes to grade 8. Men wear dark suits with no lapels and black or straw broad-brimmed hats, while women wear modest dresses of solid-coloured fabric, and aprons and head coverings. Most of these rules serve to reinforce their "separateness" from the surrounding community, but this is in keeping with their basic tenet that they are in this world but not of this world. They emphasize humility, community and family. Much of it seems rather quirky and can be circumvented if the need arises. Amish do not own cars, but they will ride in one being driven by a non-Amish driver. They do not use electricity unless they make it themselves using a gas or diesel-powered generator, and will retrofit equipment to use oil, air or battery power. They cannot market their own products, so will contract an outsider to do it for them, thus giving them access to global markets. They do not dance as that is considered immodest and worldly. They do not like to have their picture taken as it goes against Exodus 20:4 re: graven images. So why do we see photographs of Amish people? They probably belong to an affiliation that has no such prohibitions. In fact, most of the postcards in the Mennonite Information Centre were of David and his family members – riding in buggies, working the farm etc. – his being a more liberal group. All for the benefit of us tourists.

Tourism is a touchy subject, and opinions range from positive to negative. The Amish of Lancaster County seem to have started the tourist business as a means of generating some extra income during lean farming years. Sewing colourful quilts (that are much too ornate for their own homes) and producing furniture for tourists has helped make Lancaster one of the more prosperous Amish counties. But others resent this incursion into their lives and blame the media and Hollywood (the Harrison Ford movie *Witness* was filmed in and around the town of Intercourse) for this unwelcome attention and exploitation. But regardless of how it started, tourism is here to stay and has brought with it its share of problems. The tourists need places to stay, so chain hotels have moved in. The hotels need staff, so non-Amish have arrived for jobs. The staff need places to live, so suburbia is encroaching on farmland causing land prices to go up. These staff also need schools and other infrastructure, so taxes are going up. Even the Outlet stores have arrived. All the while, "outsiders" in Amish costumes are offering "Amish" buggy rides and selling "Amish" products made in China. Which brings us full circle to our first day at Kettle Kitchen. The original quaint Amish/Mennonite towns of Bird-In-Hand and Intercourse have pretty much succumbed to faux-Amish tourist tackiness. The real Amish go about their daily lives, in this world but not of it, all the while navigating their buggies around circling tour buses. Thankfully, once you leave Lancaster county, you can still find Amish communities without the sightseer onslaught.

The paradox is striking, but our next destination moved us from the peaceful pacifism and non-resistance of the Amish, to the terrible war that pitted brother against brother. We were off to Gettysburg. Neither of us are Civil War buffs, and while *Gone With the Wind* is my favourite movie of all time, I will grudgingly admit that there are more accurate sources of information covering this period in American history. We had been advised that prior to visiting the site, we should watch *Gods and Generals* as well as *Gettysburg* with Robert Duvall, Martin Sheen and Jeff Daniels. Although they are Hollywood productions, they do lay out for the uninitiated how the battle unfolded and do provide a bit of context. Still, we were not prepared for all that we saw and learned. It was sad. It was sobering. It was so vast it was difficult to take in.

We started our visit at the Gettysburg National Military Park Visitor Centre, which is huge. It houses a museum, a cyclorama depicting Pickett's charge, extensive bookstore/gift shop, and a detailed film *New Birth of Freedom*. It would take a full day to really do that any justice. And then there is "the battlefield". In reality, there are several battlefields spread over 6,000 acres and in order to cover all that territory, a 24-mile long car tour takes you to 16 salient spots where you can get out, read about the specific skirmish and walk around. We had purchased an audio guide for this car tour, but it did not work properly so we read up on things as best we could as we drove along. We had decided against going out with a ranger who would have provided the narrative and in retrospect, I am glad we did. At one location I eavesdropped on one ranger's presentation to an enrapt group and the detail was excruciating. "Now the 1st Minnesota cavalry was about 100 yards from Hancock's 2nd and at 1:30 pm they charged at Wilcox's brigade across the Emmitsburg Road just west of Codori farm advancing 20 yards before they met..." For some people, the Civil War is a hobby – their only hobby. We preferred to read a bit about the significance of a specific area to the overall battle and then quietly walk out on the field. As I said, it was hard to take it all in. Over 3 days, over 11,000 dead, over 40,000 wounded, captured or missing, and the war would still go on for another 2 years. I wondered about how you can go "missing" when all the action is taking place in a huge farmer's field. Not-withstanding desertion, if you take a direct hit from a 12-pound cannonball, there is nothing but pieces left, and they didn't have DNA technology back then. So for too many soldier's families, their boys were "missing". When the war finally ended with General Lee's surrender, 620,000 soldiers and sailors had died – just under 2% of the country's population. A loss like that on today's scale would be about 6 million people. Try to wrap your head around that!

And driving along on this sunny, peaceful Saturday we saw hundreds and hundreds (there are about 1,400 actually) of statues, monuments, markers and tablets, each dedicated to a specific brigade, corps or regiment, at the location where they had mustered and fought. Some of them were magnificent, others humble. Initially, veterans from the specific units had them erected, but eventually the War Department pitched in and today, the Gettysburg Foundation together with the US National Park Service maintain them, in large part through monies generated by the fees at the visitor's centre. How can you mind paying? There is, however, a level of disingenuousness to some of the information presented. A great deal of emphasis is placed on the fact that the Civil War ended slavery, and much importance placed on President Abraham Lincoln's Gettysburg address, "Fourscore and seven years ago... a new nation... conceived in liberty... all men are created equal." It plays well and who today would disagree with these noble words? But any learned historian will tell you that not only did Lincoln himself own slaves, he married into a very prominent slaveholding family from Kentucky, and only jumped onto the abolitionist movement when it became politically expedient to do so. His main reason for engaging in the war was to preserve the state of the Union, since the Confederate States had elected themselves their own President (Jefferson Davis) and adopted their own constitution. The main goal was to bring the seceded states back into the Union fold. Slavery was really a secondary issue. So if you are going to go to all the trouble of compiling and preserving history, then present it in its complete accuracy, warts and all.

Our Civil War tour also took us to Harpers Landing, a quaint little town, at the picturesque confluence of the Shenandoah and Potomac Rivers. George Washington had chosen this site for a US Armoury back in the early 1800s and the town housed many factories and industries related to munitions. In 1859, abolitionist John Brown decided to spark a rebellion by arming enslaved people, so he and 18 followers seized the armoury as their opening assault. Ironically, during the raid the first person to be shot was a free black man who was loyal to his Union employers. Things just did not go according to plan and the rebels were forced to take refuge in the fire engine house (subsequently called John Brown's Fort) where some were subsequently killed, and others captured. John Brown himself was tried for treason and murder, convicted and hanged by none other than General Robert E. Lee. But this uprising did help move the issue of slavery a bit more to the forefront on the political agenda. There are so many Civil War battlefields and sites in this part of the country that we had to "just say no" and move on, lest we miss out on much of the other surrounding beauty.

ALONG THE SKYLINE DRIVE

And beauty there was plenty – in the Shenandoah Valley, Shenandoah National Park and the park's Skyline Drive. We situated ourselves in Shenandoah State Park (because they had hook-ups, as opposed to the National Park which had none) and took day trips in the Toad. Skyline Drive runs along the crest of the Blue Ridge Mountains for a distance of 105 miles, and at its southern tip, joins up with the Blue Ridge Parkway that runs for another 470 miles into Great Smokey Mountains National Park. In effect, a scenic drive bearing south-west all the way from Virginia to Tennessee. We started on the Skyline where the speed limit is a strictly enforced 35 miles per hour and stopped at many of the 75 scenic overlooks that provided beautiful panoramas of the valley below. The highest point is 3,680 feet, so you really get a bird's eye view. There were also numerous hiking trails, some of which intersect with the Appalachian Trail, so we took the time to walk along that a little way too. A bit of an explanation on its significance to us. We have both done some extensive hiking over the years and from time to time, wished we were young and crazy enough to tackle the full length of the Appalachian Trail (at least I have, anyway). The Appalachian runs 2,015 miles (over 3,200 kilometers) from Georgia to Maine and takes several months to complete. And having read Bill Bryson's *A Walk in the Woods*, I even started to seriously think about it. But then reality checked back in and I knew it would probably never happen (probably – never say never). Neither would the Pacific Crest Trail for that matter (which runs from Mexico to British Columbia). Still, it's nice to dream, so when we had the opportunity to walk a short distance along the venerated Appalachian, we took it. No 35-pound pack mind you, but it was great just the same. The weather was sunny, albeit on the breezy, cool side and the leaves were still green in many places, brown in others. The trees were predominantly oak as opposed to maple, so the colours lacked the vibrancy of Ontario or Vermont. But it was still spectacular. We wondered about the presence or absence of wild animals because even though it is a wilderness area, it does get a lot of heavy tourist and vehicular traffic. I had just finished saying to John that I seriously doubted any bears were in these woods, when a mama black bear ran across the road not 20 feet in front of us, followed by two little cubs! I couldn't get the camera up in time. And driving back to our camp site, a deer jumped out in front of the car, causing John to stand on the brakes. A day later, the camp host at this location bemoaned the fact that she had just struck a deer in the morning and now her radiator was punctured. So there is wild life a plenty in them thar hills!

And there was plenty to see below ground as well. Virginia has at least seven known underground caverns, so we went to visit Luray, one of the larger ones, spread out under 64 acres. A one-hour walking tour along one mile of artistically lit pathways took us past some incredible stalactites (coming from the ceiling) and stalagmites (coming from the ground). They "grow" at a rate of about 1 cubic inch in 120 years. Where they grow into each other, columns are formed. And they are massive columns! Luray is a family owned establishment and during the summer, they average about 5,000 people per day, 3,000 in the spring and fall. At $26 a ticket (for the short tour), that is one successful family. The caverns were actually discovered in 1878 when a small quarter-sized sinkhole was emitting very cool air on a hot August day. A few hours of digging gave access to an entrance and the rest is history. Within a few years it was a tourist attraction, and up until 1920, visitors were encouraged to bring their own hammers and chisels so they could bang off a stalactite or two as a souvenir! The cavern is 164 feet deep at its lowest point and contains a small lake that is only 18 inches deep. The water is so still that the formations reflect as if off a mirror. But the pièce de résistance, is the stalactite organ. Between 1954 and 1957, an engineer (Leland Sprinkle) located 37 stalactites with perfect musical pitch, and set it up so that electric charges would cause rubber hammers to strike the requisite stalactites. The organ can actually play recognizable tunes, one of the favourites being Mendelssohn's wedding march. Approximately 500 couples have been married deep within this cavern to the sounds of what is touted as the world's largest musical instrument. Only in America. Surprisingly, dogs are allowed but only if you carried them. Porter weighed almost 80 pounds, so had to forgo the experience.

Not everything was going smoothly, however. We were still struggling with the communication issue and getting contradictory information from Verizon, Sprint and AT&T. It seems that having home internet, as opposed to roaming, is much easier and cheaper to set up. And all the advice we received at the Apple Store back home was speculative at best. "Sure, all you need to do is buy an unlocked phone and switch up the sim card when you get to the States." I wish! The main stumbling block seemed to be that in order to access the cheaper and more extensive US data packages, we needed not just a US address, but a US social security number too. We could get travel packages, but those cost pretty much double. Ten gigs for $100.00 for us, but 24 gigs with monthly carry over for residents. It took John quite some time to unravel it all.

And our planned excursion to Arlington National Cemetery was foiled as well. At least 6 months prior I had done some research and was pleased to find that dogs were permitted throughout the grounds, except at JFK's tomb. Excellent. It was a two-hour drive from our campsite and when we were almost there, I brought up the website for the specific directions to the main gate. That is when I saw the change in their pet policy, effective that very same day. Dogs, except service animals, were no longer permitted. Had we gone the day before, all would have been fine. So that was another location added to our ever-growing bucket list of "have to go back to". The day was not a total failure, however. While grocery shopping that evening, John found our favourite ice cream that has been missing from Canada's shelves for many years. Ben & Jerrys – Coffee Coffee Buzz Buzz Buzz. Coffee ice cream containing chocolate slivers that have been coated in espresso grounds. Eat that after 8pm and you won't be sleepy until 3am! We purchased a few extra tubs to make up for the many years of drought.

And speaking of time, two hours south found us at Monticello, the home of Thomas Jefferson, 3rd president of the United States and drafter of the Declaration of Independence. During his presidency he negotiated the Louisiana Purchase and backed the Lewis & Clark Expedition. Over a period of 40 years, he designed and oversaw the building of his home on a hill outside of Charlottesville, Virginia that is now a designated

World Heritage Site. The home's image is found on the back of the US five-cent coin. So I had great expectations. I can't say I was disappointed because the grounds are nicely maintained, the view is expansive, and efforts are being made to recreate the gardens and slave quarters as they would have been in Jefferson's time (he lived 1743 – 1826). It had been a working plantation after all. But the actual house itself was considerably smaller than I expected. Not at all what is depicted in photographs. It is supposedly 11,000 square feet, but I'm not sure what is factored into that calculation. Timed tours are given of the first floor and it was during the tour that I came away with the opinion that while Jefferson may have been a creative over-achiever, he was also eccentric, compulsive, introverted and lived consistently beyond his means. Upon his death, his entire estate – land, buildings, furnishings, equipment and slaves were sold to settle his debts. The rooms in the house itself were not very large and all beds were placed in alcoves so as to utilize space more effectively. The dining room was painted a rather garish yellow, a colour that can still be purchased today if you so wish – Ralph Lauren Monticello Yellow. Better paint a test swatch first. But the man himself was either a hypocrite or a victim of his time. Although he considered slavery "an abominable crime" he owned 600 slaves, of whom he freed only 6. And while he did not personally purchase slaves, he had no qualms about giving them away to family and friends. And DNA has confirmed that he fathered six children with one of his female slaves, although he denied any such relationship and did not acknowledge any of the children as his own. Okay. Not a saint. But he was definitely on to something when it came to the notion of democracy. He wrote, "What would be the value of a democratic republic if it existed in an intellectual stupor caused by inattention." Wow. Given what is going in in today's political arena, he must be rolling in his grave.

We then started the drive south along the Blue Ridge Parkway, and there is a reason it is considered one of the most beautiful drives in America. It differs from the Skyline Drive in that the Skyline is entirely within Shenandoah National Park, so a fee is charged for the drive. The Blue Ridge was designed as a motor corridor linking the Shenandoah and Great Smokey Mountains National Parks, crossing through Jefferson and Pisgah National Forests, but also at times through private farmland. So no fee is charged. The drive is basically along the crest of a long mountain ridge and there are countless white-knuckle turns. The views are even more spectacular than on the Skyline, with elevation changes from 650 feet to 6,050 feet and at times it was almost like looking out an airplane window. Mount Mitchell at 6,684 feet is the highest point east of the Mississippi River, although we opted not to take that detour. But it was also very slow going. We rarely went faster than 30 miles per hour, and that's not because someone was in front of us – traffic was very light. The road was too winding and too narrow to go any faster. Steep changes in elevation, several cliff faces, no shoulders, and tree limbs growing out over the road forming natural tunnels that while pretty, kept hitting the RV's antenna. John said three days driving the Blue Ridge made the Cabot Trail seem like child's play. You had to stay focused and could not take your eyes off the road for a second. The colours were again, more russet than crimson given the preponderance of oak over maple, but still beautiful and in many places along the drive, the leaves slowly floated down like large snowflakes. Similar to back home, they had a dry summer, the colours were about two weeks behind and in some places the leaves had fallen without changing colour at all. But it all depended on the altitude and longitude. Around the 140-mile marker, huge rhododendron bushes lined the road and we could only imagine what the drive must be like in the spring when they are in full bloom.

Around the 215-mile marker we officially crossed into North Carolina. There are 26 tunnels along the drive, and towards the south end we had to divert to the interstate (just before the Smokies) because the tunnels were too low for our rig. One had a clearance of only 10 feet 6 inches, and we were 12 feet 7. So we resolved to return to those in the Toad. There was no difficulty securing camping spots within the park because it was end of season and all campgrounds were closing at the end of the month. But they are rather "rustic" campsites, built around the 1950s so not designed for the big rig RVs of today. Had there been more large coaches vying for spots, we may have run into trouble. They actually get snow in early November, but we were lucky in that the weather was sunny and unseasonably warm (80 degrees most days). And of course, more hiking trails than you can imagine, some intersecting with our beloved Appalachian (insert wistful sigh here). We took the time to stop at an outdoor interpretive centre that depicted life in rural southern Appalachia around the 1920s, complete with a gristmill and a whisky still in the forest. It too had been re-constructed in the 1950s so could use a bit of restorative work, but it was interesting none-the-less. And we stopped at the Blue Ridge Music Centre where locals just randomly show up for jam sessions, playing "mountain music" on instruments ranging from fiddles to mandolins to banjos to zithers. And an obviously custom-made Martin guitar that John kept eyeing. The music is a combination of bluegrass and folk. Think George Clooney in *Oh Brother Where Art Thou* and you'll get the idea. It was really very enjoyable. And a very interesting museum displaying stringed instruments used throughout the years for playing this genre of music. Another great stop was the Folk Art Centre, close to Asheville, where the Southern Highland Craft Guild displays the work of its various members.

The Guild was formed in 1930 for the purpose of creating a market and network for mountain craftspeople. Corn-brooms, loom-woven runners, pottery, jewellery and woodcrafts. It was fascinating. Depending on the timing, it is possible to watch these masters at work. We were lucky to see both the weaving and corn-broom construction. Given it was Halloween I seriously considered buying a broom, but they were too beautiful to fly around on.

SOUTHERN APPALACHIAN GRISTMILL FROM THE 1920S

And Halloween? It was so strange not to be carving a pumpkin and getting ready for all the little ghosts and goblins. Not to mention eating the left-over candies and chocolates. Maybe next year we would be in a more populated area and could get back into the spirit of things. And we wished a very happy birthday to the brown menace, born on Halloween 6 years ago. Without him we would never have started this journey.

7.

THE HAVES AND THE HAVE-NOTS

EVERY COUNTRY HAS ITS SHARE OF DISPARITY – BE IT IN WEALTH, HEALTH OR EVEN BEAUTY. But nowhere does this seem more pronounced than in the good ol' U.S. of A. Perhaps being on the North Carolina/Tennessee border exacerbated that sentiment, but the magnitude of it was truly astounding. A nation that produces some of the finest athletes imaginable also has some of the most physically unhealthy people I have ever seen. Same goes for looks – breathtaking beauty and drug-addled meth-heads all within one city block. And real estate? Don't get me started. Haves and have-nots. A country of contrasts.

November 1st saw us settling into a nice little RV park near Cosby, Tennessee on the northern boundary of Great Smokey Mountains National Park (GSMNP). We opted to stay outside of the park because the RV sites inside did not have hook-ups and the whole dry-camping/boondocking thing, while cost effective, was getting a bit tiresome. I didn't like to have to think about how much water was in the gray tank, never mind the black. Just plug me in somewhere and let's get on with it. The downside was that staying outside the park meant driving several miles to get into it, and for the GSMNP that meant driving through Gatlinburg. And Gatlinburg is as if the old tacky part of Niagara Falls met Toronto CNE's Midway, and they both overdosed on steroids. The economy depends primarily on tourists who visit the park, yet the permeating tasteless and cheap vibe of the town is a complete antithesis to the natural and quiet beauty of the park itself. Wax museums, pin-ball arcades, t-shirt shops, tattoo parlours and even quickie wedding chapels next to "rent a bridal gown" shops. Flashing lights enough to bring on an epileptic seizure. Mind you, they also had a Ben & Jerry's ice cream shop, so it isn't a complete write off. And then, as if someone had drawn the proverbial line in the sand, scenic winding roads, steep tree covered embankments, and mountain ridges as far as the eye can see. At one point, the road actually cork-screws. It's hard to describe. We went in on a sharp curve, under a curved viaduct, kept curving, now over that curved viaduct and curved out the other side. All on a 10-degree grade. It was enough to make me nauseous. But thankfully, not a neon sign in sight.

GSMNP is geographically situated with the north half in Tennessee and the south half in North Carolina (and the Appalachian Trail, naturally, running smack dab through the middle). It was created in 1934 in an effort to preserve the last of the southern Appalachian forest that once covered more than 4 million acres. The forest had been virtually eliminated by logging and fire. So yes, more people getting bought out or kicked off their land. But I suppose it was worth it. The park has such a huge variety of animal and plant life (more tree species than in all of northern Europe) that it is now a UNESCO World Heritage Site and Biosphere Reserve. It has a relatively high concentration of black bears (they estimate around 1600, so about 2 per square mile) but we didn't see any. And it also has European wild boars that found their way in around the 1950s, but we didn't see any of them either. Just half a dozen elk in a roadside stream causing a traffic jam and photo ops for some pretty excited tourists. Elk were re-introduced to the park in 2001 after being extirpated by the mid 1800s through overhunting and habitat loss. They now number about 130 and are monitored very closely – for their safety as well as for the safety of over-zealous tourist photographers. The park is huge, so much of our time was spent in the car. On one outing we drove as far as the road would take us, up to Clingman's Dome, the highest point in the park at 6,643 feet (2,024 metres). To reach the actual top meant walking about half a mile along a steep footpath and once at the summit, up a viewing platform. It was quite enjoyable, but I was a bit concerned for some of my fellow "hikers". Given that the path was paved, many were under the illusion that it was literally a walk in the park, and as they waddled, wheezed, puffed and gasped their way to the top, I mentally reviewed my CPR training. I am not kidding. Those were heart attacks in the making. The ranger advised me that they have a de-fibrillator on hand, and yes, they have had to use it. An ambulance would take 40 minutes to get there, coming all the way from Gatlinburg.

The view from the top was lovely although hazier than I had expected. The original inhabitants, the Cherokee, described these mountains as *"shaconage"*, meaning "blue, like smoke", but this smoke was a bit more literal. It turned out that the previous week, a 400-acre forest fire had broken out on the North Carolina side and without any breeze, the smoke was still lingering in the air, veiling a lot of the panoramic vista. By the time we were out on the coast – 6 days later – numerous other fires had ignited and spread, with mandatory evacuations taking place. They suspected arson. And if that wasn't enough, at the end of November a fast-moving fire ignited by high winds carrying sparks from a fire at Chimney Top Trail, swept through Gatlinburg, killing 14 people, injuring 134 and destroying or damaging 2,000 homes, businesses and resorts. It moved so unexpectedly quickly that at one golf course, golfers were not able to make it back to their cars and simply fled in their golf carts. Over 17,000 acres burned, 11,000 of those within the park. Very sobering to think we had been there just a few weeks prior.

We also drove to the town of Cherokee located on the Cherokee Indian Reservation just outside the park's southern boundary. The main drag is lined with faux trading posts selling Indian trinkets, dream-catchers, moccasins and the like, but we were headed for the Museum of the Cherokee Indian. It is an excellent museum that traces the origins of these people back to the Paleo period and carries through to present day. As is typical of most aboriginal/white contact, the Cherokee did not fare well in the land claims department. Despite their efforts to live peacefully, President Andrew Jackson signed the Indian Removal Act in 1830, forcibly exiling the Cherokee to Oklahoma in a 2,200-mile winter trek that became known as the Trail of Tears. Thousands died. Interestingly, those Cherokee living within the boundaries of what is now GSMNP were not subject to removal because they were legally living on a white man's private land (as opposed to communal Indian land) and together with about 200 souls from the Nantahala region, became known as the Eastern Band of the Cherokee Nation. And a twist on their history – it is believed that the original Cherokee were a breakaway group of Iroquois from the north. The museum's gift shop contained many "textbook" type books on Cherokee history and my only complaint was that everything closed up at 5pm and we had to leave.

Another day, we decided to take a drive along a gravel road to what was supposed to be a beautiful valley once populated and farmed by early settlers (before the park bought them out). A scenic drive to a scenic place is what we imagined. Big mistake. We have never, and I mean never, driven on such a steeply winding, twisting and unforgiving road. We only had to cover a distance of 30 miles, but turned back after about an hour, found the interstate, and took the road more travelled. And once we eventually arrived at this wonderful valley, there really wasn't all that much to see. A field, a stream, a forest. And that took us all day. I must admit that this was the first time in our entire journey up to that point when I was really ready to move on (other than our Cornwall wheel mishap). I was tired of the winding roads and to a certain extent, the falling leaves. I was ready for concrete, asphalt, civilization and some common sense. Common sense? Let me explain. The little town of Cosby does not have a grocery store and the closest place to get milk was at the Walmart in Newport about 15 miles away. I went grocery shopping at Walmart. Yes, I did. And while there, I passed the alcohol section and grabbed a bottle of wine. No big deal, right? Well, they carded me at the check-out! Now I like to think that I take reasonably good care of myself and am in reasonable shape, but there is no way on God's green earth I could be mistaken for someone under the legal drinking age. Are you serious? Look at me! Do you really think I am a minor? "Well Ma'am, y'all have to realize that this here is the law here in Tennessee." I did not have my i.d. with me and the check-out clerk would not budge. "Y'all have to realize that this here is the law here in Tennessee." That was all she would say. "Y'all have to realize that this here is the law here in Tennessee." It was like talking to a parrot. I left without the wine.

Next stop, Asheville, North Carolina. Asheville is a charming little town with a compact downtown core full of quirky little shops and inviting restaurants. It is also home to several universities and colleges so there were a lot of energetic young people out and about on a warm Saturday afternoon. And it is also very dog-friendly, so Porter received more than his share of attention. We had a great dinner on an outdoor patio where Porter was able to lay under the table with his own special bowl of water. Now that is civilization. But our main reason for stopping there was the Biltmore Estate. Talk about the "haves". Biltmore House itself is pegged as the largest private house in all of North America, and was completed in 1895 by George Vanderbilt, the great-great-great-great-grand uncle of Anderson Cooper of CNN fame (Anderson's mom being Gloria Vanderbilt of quasi-designer fame). The family tree is a pretty tangled mess. But the house, while offending my sense of balance and symmetry, was quite something to behold and well worth the price of admission. It was designed along the lines of a French Chateaux and took 1,000 men 6 years to build. In fact, George V. wanted to replicate a European working estate and he certainly had the money to do it. It has 250 rooms, 33 guest bedrooms, 43 bathrooms and 65 fireplaces. In other words, 4 acres of floor space. The main banquet hall is 70 feet by 40 feet with a 7-story ceiling, 500-year-old Flemish tapestries on the walls, a table that seats 38, and a huge pipe organ. There are Renoirs, Napoleon's chess set, 10,000 books, Ming vases, the list goes on and on. It is very much a museum that depicts the lives of the uber-rich and those who served them during the height of the Gilded Age at the turn of the century. The estate itself covers 8,000 acres (they sold 87,000 acres to the government in 1914) with acres of walled gardens, Italian gardens, rose gardens, azalea gardens, shrubbery gardens and a bass fishing pond. The landscape architect was Frederick Olmsted of New York City's Central Park fame. We did our best to take in what we could over one day, but to visit the entire estate would take a week. My only criticism is that being a tourist attraction, they switch up seasonal décor themes and during our visit were all set for "Christmas at Biltmore". And the Christmas decorations were so over the top, over-elaborate and cluttered, they obscured many of the home's finer features and true artworks. I suspect springtime would be the best time to visit because the gardens must be fantastic! If ever travelling through North Carolina, this is worth a visit if for no other reason than to gawk.

BILTMORE "HOUSE."

We then stopped for few days in Atlanta to spend some time with my dear friend and old college roommate Evia and her husband. We left the land yacht parked in front of their house (much to the curiosity and delight of the neighbourhood children) and savoured their gracious hospitality. Our timing was very fortuitous because we were able to take shelter and watch the U.S. election results in the comfort of their lovely home, all the while adding our own commentary to the pointless drivel of both CNN and FOX. It was a very entertaining evening although none of us were able to stay awake for the final tally. That had to wait until morning, and given we were in a traditionally Republican state, there were no demonstrators or malcontents out disturbing the peace. Porter was in his water dog element, taking advantage of their pool and we were able to take care of a number of housekeeping issues before saying good-bye and heading towards Florida. Our original plan had been to go to the Outer Banks of North Carolina, but Hurricane Matthew had inflicted considerable damage on his swing through and many of the roads were still impassable. I was particularly disappointed not to be able to learn more about the Roanoke Colony, so we added yet another destination to the "return" list. Instead, we made our way south-east to explore the Golden Isles of Georgia, specifically Jekyll Island and St. Simons Island.

Jekyll Island is the smallest of the islands – only 7 miles long and 1.5 miles wide. The eastern, ocean side shore, sports low rise budget hotels and a sprinkling of vacation condos while the western, marsh side houses the remains of the exclusive Jekyll Island Club, once the domain of America's turn of the century elite – Rockefeller, JP Morgan, Vanderbilt et al. I cannot for the life of me understand why these men, whose wealth is difficult to comprehend, would choose to vacation here. Except perhaps that they owned the whole island, but then they owned half of the country so that is a rather weak argument. In terms of view, there is nothing to draw your eye upwards, as in magnificent mountains, nor anything to gaze down onto, as in picturesque valleys. There is only the monotony of a swamp, or as John corrected me, a marsh. To-may-to/to-mah-to. You can dress it up and call it the Intracoastal if you want, but that doesn't change the view. It's still monotonous. Their exclusive little domain fell upon hard times after the Depression and was eventually purchased by the state of Georgia who were no better at turning a profit than the big boys – no real surprise there. It was then acquired by a conglomerate who restored the buildings to their former glory and now operate the entire compound as supposedly one of the top resorts in Georgia. I still don't get the appeal. The buildings are lovely, but that's about it. And everything sits at only 12 feet above sea level. One big tsunami and you know where it is going to end up. Yep. The swamp. There is, however, a very interesting beach at the north end of the island – Driftwood Beach. Given the prevailing winds and ocean currents, any large debris (read ripped up by their roots, trees) from storms, hurricanes and the like wash up on the beach, to lie bleaching in the sun. And there they remain, just waiting for beachgoers to lean up and use them as back-rests. Unfortunately for us, we had chosen an overcast, windy and cold day as our beach/ biking day, so there was neither strolling nor cycling, but they sure would have made for some fantastic pictures in the right light. Maybe next time. Instead, we paid a visit to the Georgia Sea Turtle Centre, a research, education and rehabilitation facility that works to increase awareness of sea turtle endangerment to the general public. It is also a working sea turtle hospital where they provide emergency veterinary care to injured and ailing sea turtles. Once again, we learned a lot. I now know that sea turtles have flippers, while aquatic, marsh and pond turtles have webbed feet and claws, and tortoises are not really turtles at all. They are "land terrapins". They never enter the water and if they did, would sink. Go figure. These oddly cute creatures have been around since the time of the dinosaurs and yet today, all are on either the endangered or threatened list. Only 1 in 4,000 will make it to breeding maturity (which for turtles is 30 years of age) to continue the reproduction cycle. Amazing.

St. Simons appealed to me much more than Jekyll. It is a peaceful little island, about 12 miles by 3 miles of mixed vacation and full-time residents, as well as some places of historic importance. Nice little stores and restaurants complete the draw. We took time to stroll along the beach, fronted by high-end vacation homes that were well out of our price range. It's nice to window-shop. The sand is of a very fine, almost powdery consis-tency and Porter was once again overjoyed at the opportunity to get into some saltwater. The only downside was that all this fine sand got into his coat and came back to the RV with him, creating some cleaning challenges later on. Thank goodness the land yacht had central vac! We also visited Fort Frederica National Monument. So for this month's history lesson... Fort Frederica played a very important role in the ongoing battle between British and Spanish forces in the 1700s. Both empires claimed the territory between St. Augustine, Florida and Charleston, South Carolina, so in 1735 Britain established a colony on St. Simons to serve as a kind of southern frontier buffer. A village and fort were in place by 1740 and it soon had a population of 1,000. This, of course, aggravated Spain who saw any British settlements as a threat to their claim to Florida. And so the fighting began. British forces prevailed and people here still say that if not for Fort Frederica, the southern US would be speaking Spanish today. (Although we did hear a lot of Spanish regardless.) The fort and village itself fell into ruin by 1758 because once peace was settled, the soldiers departed and with them so did the demand for goods produced and supplied by shopkeepers and tradespeople. The National Park Service acts as a sort of caretaker for the few ruins that remain (they were archeologically excavated in the 1960s) and it was interesting to stroll around and look at the various artefacts on display. The buildings themselves had been made of a construction material called "tabby", a type of coastal concrete consisting in large part of oyster shells. The shells were mined from thousand-year old Indian middens (shell mounds), burned into a type of lime powder and then mixed with sand, water and whole shells to form a crude sludge. This was then poured, in several courses, into wooden frames and voilà – a wall was up. An interesting and efficient use of local resources. But what captivated me most of all were the old Spanish Moss-covered trees. The trees themselves are Live Oaks, so named because they are never without leaves. They just perpetually renew themselves, the same as a fir or pine tree might, and the only thing they have in common with our more northern oak trees are the (smallish) acorns. The leaves do not look at all like oak leaves (more like euonymus) and their branches are huge! And Spanish Moss (also

known as Tree Hair) is not really moss at all, but a non-parasitic plant that derives its moisture and nutrients from the air with no need for a root system. Once divested of its creepy-crawly inhabitants (ticks, spiders, millipedes, even snakes), the moss was used as stuffing for pillows, mattresses, furniture and even spun into

SPANISH MOSS AT FORT FREDERICA

rope. It could be woven into horse blankets or primitive clothing and Henry Ford used it to fill the seats of his Model T Fords. Talk about a thousand and one uses. I just think it looks hauntingly beautiful.

And on the topic of trees, we took a little detour into the town of Brunswick to see a Live Oak that arborists have determined to be 900 years old. Spectacular! Talk about "old growth". It was located at an intersection in Historic Brunswick ("Historic" really being code for "neighbourhood of lovely old mansions that are falling into disrepair because the city has gone for a shit") and we jumped out to grab a quick picture before hightailing it back to the highway. We actually had one unsavoury character yell after us, "Hey, whatch y'all lookin' fer?" John said the guy probably thought we were lost and wanted to offer us directions, and suggested I was overreacting when I told him to just step on the gas and not look back! In all fairness, we did look a little out of place as we circled the block a few times in disbelief. How could a community that was once so obviously grand be allowed to decay like this? We are not city planners, but still... Next stop, Florida.

The Sunshine State wasn't really living up to its sunshine claim as we crossed the state line and headed for St Augustine. The first few days were overcast and quite cool, bordering on cold. But our campsite at Anastasia State Park was great. We were sur-rounded by Live Oaks, various palm trees, Magnolia trees and all kinds of vegetation that gave the illusion of being in a jungle. All that was missing were the alligators. At least we hoped they were missing and not just hiding. The park has a wide 4-mile long beach that we biked along at low tide, but since pets were forbidden, we didn't spend much time there. Instead, we drove to a dog-friendly one (Vilano) where Porter could run around and enjoy the surf. Hurricane Matthew had packed a pretty good wallop as it moved up the Florida coast in October and evidence of its destructive power was everywhere. Many of the beach houses had their lower levels simply washed away and all that remained were the concrete footings. I suspect they are now condemned, though I suppose that is the risk you take to have an unobstructed ocean view.

The town of St. Augustine itself is the longest continuously European inhabited city in all of North America, having been settled by the Spanish in 1565. Actually, Ponce de Leon (of mythical Fountain of Youth fame) landed in and around the area in 1513 and claimed all of North America for Spain, calling it La Florida. (He thought he was on an island.) As we all know, he was being rather overly ambitious and optimistic on that call. It all just became one never-ending, 300-year battle for supremacy between Spain, France, Britain, the newly formed United States and of course the original Seminole inhabitants. With some marauding pirates thrown in to keep everyone on their toes.

And trying to keep track of who was aligned with whom at any given point in history was a challenge. When they started talking about the second Spanish period, I gave up. I am not a history major. But we did learn some interesting stuff. The old fort, La Castillo de San Marcos was erected by the Spanish in 1672 to guard the old city, taking 23 years to complete. It was actually built 10 times, because the first 9 versions were constructed of wood and therefore easily rotted or burned to the ground by an assortment of invading forces, both natural and human. But the last version, along with many buildings in the old town, was built of a material called "coquina." Coquina consists of millions of tiny seashells that, over many years, bonded together through some geological forces beyond my comprehension, and now form a type of soft shell-rock. The rock was quarried and became the perfect building block because it did not crumble, but rather, absorbed the many cannon balls that were lobbed at the fort. It some places you can still see the indentations of those that struck their mark. In the end, the Americans prevailed and have been the caretakers of the Castillo since 1821. Between 1875 and 1887 they used it as a prison for captured Great Plains and Southwest Indians, including Geronimo's wife and family. No shortage of sad history.

There is also much to see of a more recent history in the town of St Augustine itself. We followed a friend's advice and took a driving tour of the city on a 6-seater electric golf cart with a somewhat eccentric guide. Even Porter came along for the ride as we zigged and zagged along the narrow streets and listened to some interesting commentary. It's surprising the town has not been re-named Flaglerville. Henry Flagler (who together with John D. Rockefeller established Standard Oil) was another beyond comprehension wealthy American. Upon visiting St. Augustine, he found it so much to his liking that he changed the town's entire architectural and economic picture. He built the Hotel Ponce de Leon (which is now Flagler College), the Hotel Alcazar (which is now the Lightner Museum) as well as the Memorial Presbyterian Church (which is still a serving church and the Flagler Mausoleum), all for the benefit of the affluent so they could come south for the winter. He even built a railroad to make the journey from New York a little easier. (He eventually extended this railroad all the way down to the Florida Keys and was instrumental in making Miami and Palm Beach the desirable destinations they are today). The buildings are magnificent. The lobby of Flagler College (née Ponce de Leon Hotel) has a 24-karat painted domed ceiling and its dining room houses the largest collection of Tiffany windows in the world (protected from the outside by bullet proof glass). Beautiful. But once again, we ran out of time and were not able to do all the buildings justice. There was just too much to take in! Definitely another return-to place.

Our next Florida stop was Jonathan Dickinson State Park, near the town of Jupiter (home of Burt Reynolds, while he was still alive). And as much as Anastasia was big on vegetation, Dickinson was wide open with lots of low-lying scrub, lots of cycling paths and lots of warning signs about alligators. We actually biked past one guy, about 12 feet long, just sunning himself in the ditch beside the road. We stopped to take a few pictures and I may or may not have disregarded John's admonishment that I was getting too close (is 10 feet too close?), when the alligator suddenly lunged sideways, scaring the life out of us (me?). It is hard to retreat quickly and gracefully when you are straddling a bicycle with both feet firmly planted on the ground, but thankfully the gator was mainly interested in getting into a culvert that had been built under the road. If he had decided to come up onto the road, things may have been a bit dicey. Yes, yes, John was right. We then rented a canoe and spent the better part of a day paddling the Loxahatchee River. Given our many years of canoe tripping, it felt wonderful to be back on the water, gliding in and around mangrove and centuries-old cypress swamps, watching ospreys soaring in the sky and wading birds and box turtles closer to eye level. We even saw a manatee blowing his spout in the distance. But we had been warned ahead of time not to get into the water, nor even land the canoe anywhere. There were lots of alligators around. That was a bit unnerving considering how low to the water we were sitting, but fortunately (or not), the gators were off somewhere else. Or maybe we just didn't spot them. I had this image of their dead, reptilian eyes following us as we blithely drifted by.

The park itself is named after Jonathan Dickinson who was shipwrecked off the Florida coast in 1696, and along with fellow survivors, came ashore where the park currently sits. He kept a journal of the group's trials and tribulations while they made their way north towards St. Augustine, describing in great detail the shipwreck, their capture by local Indians, as well as the suffering they endured over their 6-month journey. The journal was first published in 1699 and can still be purchased today. So this month's literary classic – *Jonathan Dickinson's Journal or God's Protecting Providence*. It's a bit of a slog since it is written in old English, but it does provide a fascinating first-hand account of how harsh life was back in the day. A far cry from the Florida of today. And I must say, Florida grew on me. I had only been there twice before, once making the requisite pilgrimage to Disneyworld when our son was 9, and once to visit friends in Panama City Beach for a few days. Both times I was left with the impression that Florida is mostly strip malls, condos, gated communities and manicured golf courses connected by long stretches of highway. Well there is a lot of that. But the Intracoastal is beautiful here, wide open and boarded on both sides by seriously high-end real estate. What do these people do for a living?! And there is also the more natural side. You just have to get off the beaten track a bit to find it and when you do, it's terrific. Even if it does require exercising a bit of caution around the wildlife.

Despite the first few days, the weather was generally great so it's easy to see why people flock here in the winter. Warm bordering on hot, mostly sunny, a bit of a breeze, limited humidity. Only thing that takes a bit of getting used to is that the sun rises and sets very quickly. Dawn and dusk are so short-lived you have to move quickly to capture those sunsets on camera. We bounced around a few parks along the eastern side and it was interesting to compare both the facilities as well as the clientele. Sebastian Inlet was our least favourite. Poorly maintained, with racoons running rampant in the garbage bins, and boats with their accompanying anglers at every turn. It was more like a blue-collar fishing camp. Add to that, our first experience with No See-ums – almost invisible biting gnats so small they can get through window screens. You don't see them, you don't hear them, you just feel their bite that is like a burning pinprick! Which gets very itchy two days later. We kept the windows closed and were grateful for air conditioning. The smallest place we stayed was one managed by the Army Corps of Engineers beside the locks on the St. Lucie River. Only 9 RV spots and 3 tent sites, all with a great views of the water and the occasional boats that went by. Very relaxing.

However, water management has been a huge issue in south/central Florida for the past while. Almost shades of the Walkerton, Ontario tragedy we had a few years back. As I understand it, farmers in the centre of the state use copious amounts of nitrates and chemical fertilizers which make their way into Lake Okeechobee and subsequently the water drainage system. The contaminated water, if it were allowed to follow its natural course, would slowly flow south, through the Everglades and eventually end up in the ocean. But there are a lot of people with money in the southern part of the state, and they do not want polluted water flowing past their front doors and through their aquatic play areas. So the water is diverted to flow east to the Atlantic and west to the Gulf. This past year, excess amounts of nitrate laden water produced over the top toxic algae blooms, making any waterways east towards Stuart and west towards Ft. Myers literally poisonous. Dead fish floating to the surface like corks, and rendering the water too dangerous for human use, recreational or otherwise. Of course by the time anyone caught on to what was happening, numerous people had become ill, lost limbs or died. A water-avoidance ban was in place for about a year and just recently lifted, but few people were venturing back into the water with any confidence. Wow. As if the alligators weren't enough to keep you out! Thankfully, the algae dissipate when they hit salt-water so the impact on the oceans is limited.

On another environmental note, all is not well with Florida's citrus industry either. While grocery shopping, we noticed that oranges and grapefruits were quite expensive.

In places, even more costly than at home. And while driving, we passed acres and acres of seemingly abandoned orange groves, trees with branches barren of most leaves and just some occasional fruit on the odd straggler. What was going on? Blame the Asian Citrus Psyllid. It's a tiny bug that showed up in 2005, and it carries a bacteria that attacks the tree's vascular system, eventually killing it. Production is down by more than 60% from a decade ago, and there doesn't seem to be a cure. Some farmers are using more insecticides and spraying more often (and we all know where the excess goes). Others are switching to blueberries and strawberries, while along the coast, groves are being ripped up and replaced with hotels and vacation homes. Some are suggesting the entire citrus industry in Florida could be gone within a few years and that seems unthinkable. It would be like Quebec without maple syrup or Georgia without peaches. No-one knows where it will end so enjoy that glass of oj while you still can.

And then there is the Kennedy Space Center. Like most places we visited, it really requires two full days, but we had given ourselves only one. And to quote Charles Dickens, "It was the best of times, it was the worst of times." Our expectations were minimal – see a few rockets, learn a bit about the space programme. But what caught us off guard from the get-go was the Disneyesque approach to the whole thing. Long line ups contained by metal railings, whining children, non-stop music over loud-speakers, gift shops and food cafes. I half expected to see Mickey Mouse come around the corner singing, *It's a Small World After All*. Although I suppose they have to make it relatively child-friendly so as to maintain the interest of any future Buzz Lightyears. We started with a 2-hour bus tour that transported us from the Visitor Center out to the actual launch pads that had supported both the Apollo and subsequent space shuttle programmes. We saw the Vehicle Assembly Building where the spaceships are put together as well as the huge crawlers that transport the rocket ships to their launch pads. And we saw work under way for the new launch pad that will support the new Orion Programme. As much as that may sound interesting, it really wasn't, because these were all just drive-bys. We didn't stop (not even for photo ops), didn't get off the bus, didn't even really have too much of an explanation provided. Maybe we just had a bad driver. But on the positive side, we were dropped off at the Apollo/ Saturn V exhibit hall, which has been built around the actual Apollo launch control center (which we were able to go into). The hall itself is huge and we wandered around looking and learning about the various Apollo Missions. NASA really promotes being able to "touch a moon rock", but in reality, the "rock" is a small black object (about 1-inch square and ¼ inch thick) that has been completely smoothed over from so many fingers reaching into its glass enclosed case. John said he remembered going down to City Hall in Toronto and watching the moon landing on a huge screen set up at Nathan Phillip Square, but I have no such memory. Since it occurred on July 20th 1969, I was probably at Sidrabene where electronics of any kind were forbidden. The bus then took us back to the Visitor Center where we could opt to see several IMAX movies, wander around the Rocket Garden (displaying various rocket ships from years past), visit the Heroes and Legends Hall (the US astronaut hall of fame), or queue up with the ten thousand other folks who wanted to have "lunch with an astronaut". We chose to visit Atlantis. That was our best call of the day because they have done an excellent job there. A short movie introduces the space shuttle programme, the floor-to-ceiling screen rises and there she is – the massive space shuttle Atlantis, atmosphere re-entry scuff marks and all. Of course the accompanying music rising to a crescendo helps dramatize the whole thing, but it was very moving. And I'm not even a patriotic American. Some people had tears in their eyes. Atlantis was 1 of 5 space shuttles but she flew 32 missions primarily resupplying the space station prior to being retired in 2011, along with the entire space shuttle programme. There is also a sobering retrospective commemorating the Challenger and Columbia disasters with touching memorials to the lives of their 14 lost astronauts. It was very well done. NASA's new programme, Orion, has been in the works for a few years and there is considerable chatter about landing on both Mars and asteroids. Just thinking about it makes my brain hurt.

It was hard to believe, but at this juncture we had been living in the land yacht for just over 6 months. Does time pass more quickly when you are on the road? Our daily routine was pretty well set although we continued to make minor adjustments, as circumstances required. Were there any creature comforts I missed? A few. I missed having double sinks in the bathroom, a washing machine that could handle large loads, a big kitchen table that I could spread stuff all over, and fine china. Corelle is very practical but it's just not the same. And most of all, I missed my cleaning lady. Living with a dog in less than 300 square feet meant vacuuming every single day. Other than that, no complaints. Porter, on the other hand, turned out to be a somewhat insecure traveller. I suppose that is natural. Although he knew the land yacht was "home", his "home" kept changing locations and that was rather unsettling for him. One time we left him inside on his own for 30 minutes and returned to find him sitting at the front window with his muzzle resting on the dash, looking forlornly out in the direction he last saw us. Talk about rip your heart out. It became day care or bust for the brown menace. We appreciated all the blog comments and "contact us" e-mails received, and while we did not initially reply to each and every one, it was heartening to know there was interest in our journey. We missed seeing our friends and while the RV lifestyle did have a certain social aspect to it, it was not the same. We hoped our friends continued to stay in touch.

8.

AND SO THIS IS CHRISTMAS???

HISTORICALLY, WE HAD NEVER TRAVELLED ANYWHERE IN DECEMBER. January or February? Yes. Those were the months to either avoid the cold by heading south or embrace it by going skiing. But December? December is the Christmas month. Come the first Advent Sunday, our house would be sparkling clean from top to bottom, the decorations would be up, and the first Advent candle would be lit. Then we'd start thinking about Christmas cards, gifts, social schedules and food. Yet this year, on the first Advent Sunday, we were in Florida getting ready to drive to Key Largo. There was something seriously wrong with the picture. "Freshly" cut Christmas trees were being sold under the shade of palm trees, inflatable Santas could be purchased alongside paddle boards, and twinkling lights adorned both cabin cruisers and motor homes. It was surreal. And very difficult to think about Jack Frost nipping at your nose. But given that some of our campground neighbours were getting into the decorative spirit of things, we also went out and purchased a small artsy representation of a tree for inside the yacht and some coloured lights for outside. For the first time in my life we wouldn't be undertaking the family trek to the great white north to chop down our own tree. It was kind of sad. However, Christmas Eve was traditionally spent at my parent's house and since we would be heading "home" late December, we knew we would get our fill of the real deal there. In the meantime, the Key Largo tree would have to do.

Our arrival in Key Largo was a bit worrying at first. Driving south along US1, we were almost across the causeway when we noticed a large portable electric road sign on the right shoulder. "Screwworm Alert! Call 1-800 for information." Oh. Oh. We quickly did a google search. Not good. The New World Screwworm (*Cochliomyia hominivorax*) is a fly larvae (in other words, a maggot) that infests warm-blooded animals including livestock, pets and even humans. Thankfully the human infestations are rare, but pets are a bit more at risk. The larvae enter the animal through any open wound and feed on its living flesh. If not treated within a week or two, it can be fatal. The frightening thing about all this, was that while Screwworms are found throughout most of South America and in five Caribbean countries, they had not been seen in the United States for over 50 years! The US Department of Agriculture confirmed Screwworm presence in Big Pine Key in October and immediately started an eradication programme. Their primary goal – contain the infestation so it does not spread beyond the Keys. Their secondary goal – save the Key deer, a subspecies of the white-tailed deer, living solely in the lower Florida Keys. These tiny deer only numbered somewhere between 25 and 50 in the 1950s, so were placed under the protection of the Endangered Species Act. The population rebounded to around 1,000, but they are very susceptible to Screwworm. Authorities were taking all this very seriously and had established a mandatory animal health inspection zone covering the Keys, and all animals were to be given a health check at Mile Marker 106. In other words, any creature headed for the mainland had to be inspected. Of course Porter, once realizing he'd be rewarded with a jumbo Milkbone for being so co-operative each and every time, was quite happy to submit to these examinations, which were really quite cursory at best.

And the weather? The prior month I thought Florida weather was "warm bordering on hot with limited humidity". I took it all back. At least as far as Key Largo was concerned. Here it was hot and humid, humid, humid. Average temps around 86F (30 C) with 85% humidity. What must it be like in the summer?!?! We were staying in John Pennekamp Coral Reef State Park and experienced fairly heavy showers most every night. Not for long, but long enough to ensure continued humidity the following day. Of course that makes sense. Key Largo is surrounded by water and sits at about the same latitude as Nassau, Bahamas. So what do you expect? It was also quite breezy so unfortunately, many of the snorkelling trips out to the reef were cancelled, but even more unfortunately, not breezy enough to keep those nasty No See-ums at bay. They were merciless. We were covered in bites in no time and I resorted to taking Benadryl every night just to ease the itch and get some sleep. The locals advised it was a waste of money to use insect repellent because it is ineffective against these miniscule gnats. The only thing they suggested was slathering on oil – coconut oil, baby oil, any kind of oil. The wings of these tiny pests are so small they stick to the oil, foiling any opportunity to bite. Get out the Mazola! An Avon product, Skin So Soft, is also a supposed help but unfortunately there weren't any Avon Ladies around making RV house calls.

We weren't overly troubled by the weather-curtailed snorkelling because although staying in Key Largo, our primary focus at this point was Everglades National Park and creatures found therein. This is not to say that there weren't interesting creatures within the state park – there were plenty. One afternoon, an iguana wandered through a neighbouring campsite, cautious, but with a rather self-assured air. He was over 3 feet long and orange in colour. I'd never seen one so big nor so close. Technically, he was a Green Iguana but the males are orange during mating season. It turns out that iguanas are not indigenous to the Keys, but some people imported them from South and Central America to keep as pets. Naturally, a few escaped and others were deliberately released. Because they have no native predators, they multiplied at a rapid rate and are causing no end of controversy. Some people want them eradicated because they are pretty vociferous eating machines, munching on plants of all kinds, especially flowering ones. Others don't consider them a threat because they are herbivores, so how bad can they be? Herbivores or not, they didn't look very friendly to me.

We stayed at Pennekamp for 12 nights, using it as a base to explore the area, and resisted the urge to continue south. Key West was going to have to wait until our return in January. But there was much to see and do at the north end too. We first drove to Homestead, not too far from Miami, and checked out the Coral Castle. This was a "must do" on our list, only because of the Latvian connection. Much of the genesis behind the story of the Coral Castle is of questionable veracity and has in all likelihood been embellished over time, but the "castle" is real, and its construction is nothing short of miraculous. It all began with Edward Leedskalnin, born in Latvia in 1887. At the age of 26, he was engaged to a young girl, 10 years his junior. On the eve of their wedding, she changed her mind. Heartbroken, Ed left Latvia, wandered for several years working in lumber camps throughout Canada and California, and eventually ended up in Florida where he constructed a castle of sorts, made entirely of local coral, that he quarried himself. Actually, it is not really coral but rather oolite limestone. And it is not really a castle but more of a compound. That in and of itself is not necessarily miraculous. But what is, is the fact that the quarried stones weigh literally tons. 18 tons, 23 tons, 9 tons and so on. And he moved them all by himself, using simple hand-made tools that he formed himself, often from old car parts. No-one helped him and no-one ever saw him working (he had built a high coral wall around his property and worked only by oil light late at night). He carved tables, rocking chairs, a very precise polaris telescope, a sun dial, reclining couches, the list goes on and on. And everything he fashioned weighed thousands of pounds. Ed himself stood 5 feet tall and weighed in at 100 pounds. He constructed the complex between 1920 and 1940, dedicating it to the love of his life, but sadly for Ed, she never bothered to show up. When his project was complete, he invited visitors in to see his work, charging them 10 cents for a tour. When asked how he was able to construct all this without the use of heavy machinery or assistance of any kind, he stated that he understood the laws of weight and leverage, and that he knew the secrets of the pyramids. Now Ed was not a formally educated man, having ended his schooling after grade 4. But to this day, many of his building secrets are unknown, and no one has been able to replicate his work. For example, the compound can only be entered through one of two gates. The first gate is triangular in shape, weighs 3 tons, and is balanced on the axle of a Model T Ford. There are no gears or bearings in the rotating mechanism. I was able to easily move it with just a simple push. The other gate is about 15 feet by 7 feet and almost 2 feet thick. It weighs 9 tons. It could be moved by the push of one finger. Engineers and scientists had measured, probed and x-rayed it, but couldn't figure out how Ed was able to balance this uneven shape so perfectly. Of course this lead to all kinds of rumours, ranging from supernatural to space alien assistance, and the gift shop has more paranormal junk than any real explanations about the man and his work. And the whole unrequited love story appeals to romantics and helps fuel the tourist traffic. Billy Idol wrote his song *Sweet Sixteen* about Ed and the castle in 1986. Not being a Billy Idol fan and therefore unfamiliar with his music, I checked it out on Youtube. Still not a Billy Idol fan.

Fortunately for us, there were a few days with calm seas, so we were able to get in the snorkelling that Pennekamp is famous for. And it was amazing! The first day was out at Grecian Reef, a fairly shallow area where we spotted all kinds of colourful coral and fish, including barracudas. The next day we were out at Molasses Reef, which although deeper, had better visibility. A nurse shark, several types of parrotfish, angelfish, butterflyfish, blue tangs, scrawled filefish, hogfish, grunts and many other fish with equally curious names. And I have since learned that octocorals, such as sea fans, are flexible and

therefore sway in the ocean current while stony corals, such as brain coral, have a limestone skeleton around their bodies so they appear solid. We ended up purchasing a field guide to the fish and marine invertebrates just so we could check off all that we had seen. Pennekamp Park itself was actually created to protect a portion

ALMOST SCUBA?

of the only living coral barrier reef in the continental United States, extends 3 miles out into the Atlantic Ocean and is about 21 miles long. There are countless reefs spreading down towards Key West so we hoped the weather would cooperate when we returned in January and February. I was almost tempted to take up scuba diving but that may be a bit too technical. John assured me it's no big deal but I suspect that if something really big swam by I'd panic and forget the rules. After all, it was only about a year or two ago where if the water wasn't 90 degrees and chlorinated, I wouldn't go in. Some progress has been made.

And let's not forget the alligators and crocodiles. Florida is the only place in the world where both coexist in the wild, so we became quite conversant with both their similarities and their differences. Alligators are more common, live in either fresh or brackish water, are born with all their 80 teeth, are dark green/gray in colour, have a broad head, and despite being predators, do not generally consider humans as food. Unless they have been fed by humans, which changes the whole ball game. It appears that was the situation for the poor little boy who was killed by one in Disneyworld earlier in the year. In an effort to entertain themselves, tourists had been routinely tossing the alligators all kinds of picnic lunch leftovers, excitedly congratulating themselves when the reptiles voraciously lunged at the food. It was a tragedy just waiting to happen. When their jaws reflexively snap shut, they exert 3,000 pounds of pressure per square inch. No way you are going to pry those choppers open. Most alligators under 4 feet are not really dangerous unless they are being handled, but any bite, even if not fatal, is serious. The wound cannot be sutured, but rather, must be left open to continuously drain. Alligator mouths contain a toxic mix of bacteria that will cause serious infection if not allowed to ooze freely. Charming. And you are guaranteed a pretty nice scar at the end of it all. Florida reports about 50 unprovoked bites per year.

Crocodiles, on the other hand, live more in salt, or brackish water (but have been found in fresh), have a narrower, elongated head with a more tapered and upturned snout, and are green/brown in colour with a "spikier" tail. They are actually quite shy so are not seen as often. We were lucky to see both, although the gators definitely outnumbered the crocs, thirty to two. Both are members of the Crocodylia family, and while alligators have been removed from the federal endangered species list, crocs are still considered threatened. So that meant no crocodile handbag for me. Kidding. We visited an alligator farm where we were able to see some hatchlings of various ages, observed a scheduled feeding, and watched a "show" that was really closer to a pathetic circus act than anything else. The attendant sat on the gator's back and bravely (I use that term loosely) rested his chin on the snout of the gator's upturned open mouth. I half hoped he'd try sticking his head inside the gator's mouth too. Now that would have been a show. While not really being into reptiles, and despite their dangerous reputation, I found myself feeling a bit sorry for these creatures. They should be out in the wild doing their thing (which is mostly nothing) instead of being dragged around by the tail inside a concrete and sand enclosure by some guy who thinks it is sporting entertainment. As luck would have it, we did get the opportunity to see them in their natural habitat.

On our next outing we drove into the centre of Everglades National Park to go on a 15-mile (24-km) bike ride through the vast Everglades wilderness. The bike path itself is flat, paved and slightly raised with nothing but freshwater marshes on both sides as far as the eye can see. And freshwater marshes contain, you guessed it, lots and lots of alligators (along with all kinds of beautiful wading birds). The gators come up out of the water to warm themselves along the path, and we easily counted thirty as we pedalled along. I couldn't resist stopping to take some pictures. They were just lying there! We e-mailed one picture to our son, but he was less than impressed, cautioning me that I could well become a recipient of the posthumously awarded Darwin Award. The Everglades themselves do not have a "take your breath away" kind beauty, but they are interesting, often referred to as a 100-mile long "river of grass". Elevation above sea level is measured in inches instead of feet, and small dense island forests called tropical hardwood hammocks can be found on those slightly higher areas that rarely flood. Supposedly they are home to panthers, but we didn't see any. Only pictorial road signs warning of their presence. Like most national parks, Everglades was created in an effort to preserve a unique ecosystem, but today's park encompasses only one fifth of the original Everglades area. Development keeps encroaching. We also drove down to Flamingo on the shores of Florida Bay, a destination as far south as the road would go. There used to be a small settlement nearby, but it was wiped out by Hurricane Katrina in 2005 and wasn't rebuilt. It's easy to understand why. Even though this was the "dry" season when bugs supposedly ease up a bit, John had no sooner stepped out of the car at the visitor centre when he was swarmed by mosquitos. Five seconds, tops, and he was back in the car. We've done a fair bit of back country hiking and canoeing in northern Ontario but have never experienced anything like it. How can anyone possibly survive here in the summer? But having driven all this way, we felt compelled to do something, so we rented a kayak and paddled out into Florida Bay. No bugs what-so-ever. It was great. And as a reward for our tenacity, we saw two crocodiles (one rather close to the kayak) and John saw a manatee surface for a brief moment. Parts of the bay itself are quite shallow (it's really just a shallow estuary), in some places only about six or eight inches, and we almost grounded ourselves on several occasions. Now who do you suppose would have had to get out of the kayak and push us off if we got stuck? Good thing we extricated ourselves because neither of us wanted to risk stepping into those waters! Further inland, we also stopped to hike along the Anhinga Trail, the Anhinga being a cormorant type bird found only in the southern parts of the United States. The hike wasn't anything to write home about, but the preparation for it was interesting. Blue tarps and bungee cords are provided free of charge at the trailhead, so that motorists can cover up their

cars prior to setting out. Apparently, the local buzzards have taken to ripping off windshield wipers and any rubber moulding they can get at. We dutifully wrapped up the Toad, completed the hike (which turned out to be a short one-mile walk along a boardwalk) and returned without incident. Not a buzzard in sight.

IS THIS TOO CLOSE?

Having spent so much time out communing with nature, we decided that a visit to Miami Beach was in order. Talk about contrast. And we were both surprised at how much we enjoyed it (despite Porter being banned from the beach). This is what happens when city people like us spend too much time away from concrete. South Beach itself was quite nice with high-rises fronting soft white sand and not crowded by any stretch of the imagination. But the best part was Ocean Avenue with all its Art Deco buildings lit up by neon lights and littered with outdoor cafes and restaurants. It's the sort of place where you just want to sit down, sip a libation or two, and people watch. Regrettably, the Miami Beach of today may not be the Miami Beach of tomorrow. Blame can be placed equally on the shoulders of Mother Nature as well the arrogance of man. The city of Miami Beach was really built on nothing but mangrove swamps and what has been referred to as a glorified sand bar. In the early 1900s, the mangroves were cleared, channels were dredged, and actual soil was brought in to build up the land mass. Real estate agents and warm weather vacationers followed, together with gangsters, corruption, wealth and beautiful people. And very little has changed, except the Chicago gangsters of yesterday have been replaced with the Eastern European organized crime gangs of today (read Russian mob). And when Castro emptied his prisons back in the 1980's, guess where many of the newly emancipated ended up? Yep, living side by side with elderly Jewish retirees. It's an eclectic mix to say the least.

But they all may be living on borrowed time because Mother Nature is no longer playing ball. Not that she ever really was. The city of Miami Beach has, for most of its history, pumped sand up from the ocean floor in order to keep the beaches nice and pristine and pure. Pumped up at a cost of millions and millions of dollars because the ocean, day and night, works at washing that same sand away. Things have now reached the point where the original ocean bed source no longer has any sand left to pump and Miami Beach officials are scouting around looking for other appropriate sand sources. And not just any sand will do. Sahara Desert sand is considered too smooth and river sand too rough. They are currently eyeing the Bahamas. But that is just the beach. The real problem is flooding. Ocean levels are rising, and Miami Beach is built not only at a very low elevation (two feet above sea level), but on top of porous limestone. Storm sewers that were designed to carry rainwater away, now act as conduits to bring sea water in, and with a porous limestone foundation, instead of fresh surface water seeping down and away, salt-water is seeping in and up. It is most noticeable whenever there is a King Tide. That is, high tide during a full moon. Then, entire neighbourhoods are knee deep in water. Apparently this type of flooding is becoming increasingly frequent but many clueless residents believe they are dealing with something no more challenging than a broken water main. City officials are investing millions into pumps and other drainage systems that are beyond my comprehension while at the same time, scientists are warning that these efforts are no more effective than spitting into the wind. Who knows how it will be resolved but it certainly seems like the whole "buying swamp land in Florida" joke is cycling around again. Either way, if we win the powerball lottery, we won't be investing in any Miami Beach real estate any time soon. Except perhaps to help re-locate Joe's Stone Crab.

Joe's is one of Miami Beach's local landmarks and people come from all over for the famous stone crab claws and key lime pie (which was the best we had ever tasted). The restaurant was established in the early 1900s by a Hungarian immigrant (Joe Weiss) who moved from New York to Florida for his health, at a time when Miami Beach was not yet a "destination". If marketing is to be believed, Joe introduced stone crab claws as a culinary menu item at a time when they were merely southern Atlantic Ocean crustaceans. Before 1920, no one even knew they were edible! The place was, and still is, a family run business five generations later, and over the years has catered to average folks as well as some pretty big names – Joseph Kennedy, J. Edgar Hoover, Amelia Earhart, Frank Sinatra, even Al Capone (although he used the name Al Brown when making reservations). You can dine in to be served by tuxedo-clad waiters and rub elbows with the who's who, or you can order take out. The food is the same although the dining room menu does provide a few more options. Porter was with us, so we opted for take-out and had a tailgate picnic in the parking lot. Excellent seafood bisque, excellent stone crab claws, excellent key lime pie. The conch fritters, not so much. After doing a bit of post-dining research, it turned out Joe's wouldn't need any of my hoped-for lottery winnings to re-locate. In 2013 it was ranked as the second highest revenue-generating restaurant in the entire United States, with over 35 million in earnings. We sure can pick 'em.

And then around mid-month came the painful readjustment to "climate change". We had arranged to leave the land yacht in Florida for some maintenance while we drove home for Christmas in the Toad. On the first day, around Macon Georgia, the temperature dropped by about 20 degrees F from the mid-90s to the mid-70s. In Canadian parlance, mid-30s to the mid-20s. Okay. We could handle that. On the second day, around Lexington Kentucky, it dropped by more than 25 "Canadian" degrees to minus 8C. OMG! I know I had said to John at the beginning of the month (while complaining about Florida's humidity) that I longed for a nice breath of clear, cool, fresh air, but I didn't mean it quite that literally. John quickly switched up for some sub-zero windshield wiper fluid (that froze anyway) while I scrambled to find my hat and gloves. The weather forecast was for some pretty serious winter weather through Ohio and Michigan (we were coming up I-75) but we really were not sure what to expect since there is such a tendency for the media to exaggerate things. They have even taken to naming their winter storms, the same way they name hurricanes. Seriously! They were talking about Winter Storm Decima one morning. Really?! Thankfully it was smooth sailing until London when we finally started getting a bit of snow.

I wish I could say that finding pet-friendly accommodations went as smoothly as the driving, but such was not the case. While many hotels advertise themselves as pet-friendly, that amenity comes at a cost. One place we contacted (Marriott) wanted an additional $75.00 on the top of the posted room rate, ostensibly for cleaning purposes. Other places charged $10, some $50 and others nothing at all. This posed a dilemma. On the one hand, we didn't want to stay in a place where dogs are allowed in rooms that are not followed up by some extra cleaning. Not everyone's dog is as well behaved and well-mannered as our precious Porter. But on the other hand, if we fork over the extra $75, are they really steam cleaning every room a pet stays in? Our cynicism prevented us from truly believing that. Still, we'd rather err on the side of naïve faith in humanity and pay the surcharge than stay in a room where Fifi or Fido slept on the bed and did their business on the carpet with nothing being said or done. Once we got over the shock of below zero temperatures, it was nice to settle in and enjoy a somewhat white

Christmas with family and friends. We rented a condo at Queens Quay in downtown Toronto through airbnb and it was great looking out over Lake Ontario, watching the flights at Billy Bishop Airport come and go. But as anticipated, the two weeks flew by in a flurry of appointments, forays to the mall and socializing. We spent Christmas Eve the same way as I have done my entire life. Evening church service followed by a traditional Latvian feast and gift exchange at my parent's home. But Christmas Day found us at a loose end. John and I had always hosted dinner on Christmas Day, complete with turkey and trifle but given that we were "homeless", that was one tradition we could not pull off. Matejs had to work so we pretty much just hung out and didn't do much of anything. It was very strange, but at the same time, probably a good thing because the rest of the week consisted of visit, eat, drink: repeat. I wasn't sure I wanted to step on the bathroom scales when we got back to Florida. John took the time to check in with his barber and chopped off the long locks he had been growing since retirement. He donated his tresses to a company that makes wigs for people undergoing chemotherapy, and then started the process all over again. And in the blink of an eye, two weeks were gone, and we were ringing in 2017 hoping for health, happiness and peace in the New Year!

9.

WASTING AWAY IN MARGARITAVILLE

"THE CLIMATE HERE IS TOO RELAXING TO BE CONDUCIVE TO WORK."
So said American philosopher and educational reformer John Dewey, referring to his time spent in Key West. Truer words have never been spoken. The place simply has a negative impact on one's ability to think. I found it extremely difficult to sit down and gather my thoughts, much less string together some sentences in any semblance of a coherent manner for my January blog post. Or more accurately, to think about something other than where to laze around next. Lounge chair or hammock? Inside or out? But perhaps that was exactly what we needed.

There is no way to say this without sounding entitled or unappreciative, and truthfully, we are not that. We are in fact, exceedingly grateful for the opportunity to have been on this journey and to have traveled to all these incredible places. But... after 7 months on the road, we were in dire need of a vacation! I realize that from one perspective we were on vacation. However, that isn't an entirely apt description. Yes, we were travelling. Yes, we were seeing new and wonderful things. Yes, we had escaped the winter cold. And best of all, no, we were not punching a clock. But that did not mean we had been relieved of the mundane responsibilities that make up everyday life. We still had to grocery shop, make meals and do dishes, budget, track and pay bills, wash laundry and clean house. All the while in new environments where I didn't necessarily know how to get to the closest wine store. And constantly researching the next destination, next route and next RV site. So it was at times, demanding. Thankfully, our plan to stay in Key West for the month of January, and part of February, was just what the doctor (or therapist) ordered.

The drive home for Christmas, the social activities enjoyed while there and then the drive back to Florida was very tiring. And not everything went according to plan. We had left the motor coach at an RV centre in Palm Bay Florida for some minor service and repairs (eg. a window latch had broken, the door locking mechanism was reversed, some scratches needed to be buffed out) with the agreement we would pick it up on January 3rd. We had to be at our reserved place just outside Key West by the 4th. But when we checked in with the RV people on the 2nd, they did not appear to know who we were nor what we were talking about. John spoke with 4 different employees in the service department over 2 separate days (while driving down I-75), all of whom said they would call right back (the manager even definitively said "in 15 minutes") and then – nothing but crickets. That is never a good thing. We started imagining all kinds of scenarios. They didn't do the work and were now scrambling. They did the work, but it was so long ago they forgot. They couldn't find the RV on their huge lot. They had crashed it. They sold it. Someone stole it. Oh no! When we finally showed up, it turned out they had completed only four of the eight jobs requested (blaming the manufacturer Tiffin for not providing them with updated information, parts and advice) and suggested we slide on over to Red Bay, Alabama to get the work done at the source. Even though Red Bay was almost 800 miles away, it was probably the most reasonable thing they ever said, and by that point we would have driven to California if only to get out of there. And our departure would have been immediate if only they had been able to locate the keys! Unbelievable! We were forced to contact management at Bluewater Key RV Resort in Saddlebunch Key to advise we would be arriving a day late. And through all this, we were dealing with a Kafkaesque situation involving the Royal Bank of Canada.

Although discussing finances is in some ways considered ill-mannered, this is one tale that must be told. If Kafka were still alive, he would be using it as a plot line. In a nutshell: the exchange on the Canadian dollar was quite unfavourable (what else is new?) and when using Canadian credit cards with their added-on fluctuating foreign currency exchange rates, we were at times paying an additional 39% on the dollar. Ouch is right! So while home for two weeks in October, we had applied for a RBC American dollar Visa card so that we could make our purchases in US dollars and pay the balance from our US dollar account. There is a $95 US fee for the privilege of possessing said card, but such is the price of doing business. So far, so good. We explained to our branch manager that we were travelling and would not be able to pick the cards up until late December, but he assured us this would not be a problem. That should have been our first clue. The cards were issued in late October and immediately assessed the $95 fee – even though we did not have them in our possession, had not yet activated them, were obviously not using them and thus were not aware any charge had been levied. We were driving through Pennsylvania for heaven's sake! We became aware of the situation when we returned home for Christmas, but by that point we were "in arrears" and had been red flagged. Our US funds were in the Toronto Police Credit Union, so we immediately transferred them over to RBC and tried to electronically pay the outstanding amount. But RBC had placed a 14-day hold on the transfer (actually 24 days because weekends and holidays don't count, and they added an extra 3 days for some inexplicable reason). This because the funds were coming from another financial institution and RBC needed to be sure it was a legitimate transfer. Yes, you can't be too careful when dealing with the Police Credit Union. Who knows what kind of nefarious Nigerian fraud scams are emanating from there. We were still in limbo by the time January rolled around and started the drive back south. Over the course of several days, and being transferred from one RBC department to the next, placed on hold for innumerable hours, and being told it was "the system", "the computer" and "not possible", we finally came upon one enterprising soul who understood the absurdity of the situation and was willing to move the measly $95.00 over so the balance owing could be paid. Problem solved? Not so fast. In checking our statement the following day, we found not only had the payment been reversed, we had been assessed an additional $45.00 for making a payment from a frozen account. How is this even possible? And all the while, we had to keep using Canadian credit cards because the US RBC card was supposedly blocked. Although only intermittently. Sometimes it worked at grocery stores and gas stations, sometimes not. Nobody could explain it. We danced this ludicrous dance for three weeks before things levelled off. So yes, we needed a vacation. And what better place than Key West, where the notion of reality is just as elusive and rare.

I should point out that Key West is an entity of its own, differing in many ways from the rest of the Florida Keys, which start just before Key Largo at Mile Marker 110. (Everything here is measured in mile markers with Highway 1 starting at mile marker 0 in Key West and ending 2,369 miles north in Fort Kent Maine, making it the longest north-south route in the United States.) The drive down is for the most part beautiful, with turquoise, azure and brilliant blue-green water on either side of the two-lane highway. There is not a lot of land mass and many of the Keys are joined by bridges (42 in total), the longest one being the creatively named 7-mile bridge. Yes, its span is seven miles. Key lime pie shops, snorkelling concessions, storage facilities, boat repair places, tiki hut bars and restaurants line the highway wherever geography allows. The only thing to mar the view is the occasional abandoned or dilapidated roadside restaurant or business that didn't survive the latest storm. From time to time, side roads lead off into gated communities where elegant homes face the water (Atlantic or Gulf of Mexico), all with the requisite boat moored out front. In other areas, the communities are not gated, and the homes reflect a more humble (to put it mildly), live-and-let-live air. If we were buying real estate we'd definitely go for the gated community.

Our favourite Key turned out to be Bahia Honda, home to Bahia Honda State Park at mile marker 37. We had tried to reserve a RV spot there but even though we started the booking process 11 months earlier, luck was not on our side. The sites are so few and the hopeful travellers so many, those who are fortunate enough to secure a place truly have won the lottery. We actually struck out at all the state parks in the Keys but it's funny how life really does give you what you need. There are several private RV parks in the southern Keys, where visitors are packed in cheek to jowl and in retrospect, we were very fortunate they didn't have room for us either. I would never have survived that level of intimacy with complete strangers. But the crown jewel, Bluewater Key RV Resort at mile marker 14.5, supposedly the no. 2 ranked luxury RV resort in the country, had room. For a price of course. All the sites are privately owned, and the owners can rent them out, or not, as they wish. All are beautifully landscaped and artistically lit up at night, come with private docks and tiki huts (some so elaborately furnished with high end amenities you don't even need your RV) and the facility caters only to high end motor coaches. Although we were quite proud of our lovely land yacht, we were definitely more towards the entry level here. We had never seen so many Prevosts and King Aires with custom paint jobs and matching Toads. But the people were friendly, it was relatively quiet and if we got tired of staring at the ocean, we could always go hang out by the pool. Porter was in heaven, being able to wade along the shore or jump off the dock depending on his mood. The only challenge was when we tried to go kayaking. He just about lost his mind, first swimming after John's kayak and then trying to climb into mine. We resorted to leaving him in the yacht with the night shade down so that he couldn't see what we were doing. Yes, we were way over budget, but what is the price of a six-week vacation in what many call paradise? As the saying goes, "Life is short. Take the trip. Buy the shoes. Eat the cake."

Bahia Honda State Park has one of the few really nice beaches in the entire Florida Keys and the water is that fantastic clear Caribbean blue. The fee was $9.00 per day for the joy of digging your toes into the soft white sand but it is worth every penny. The only drawback is that no dogs are allowed on the beach proper, despite its 3-mile length. We found a secluded spot at one end where John and Porter were able to swim while I was out on the snorkelling boat but unfortunately, a rather overly officious volunteer descended upon them and demanded their immediate withdrawal, so they were forced to hang out by the marina, where Porter further endeared himself by growling at the monstrously-sized manatees that call those waters home. The snorkelling out at Looe Key Reef, a 30-minute boat ride from shore was fantastic! The water was incredibly clear, and the fish were considerably larger than those we had seen off Key Largo. Lots of sergeant majors and yellowtails, but also several species of butterfly fish, a midnight parrotfish and even a huge black grouper. Some people in my group said they saw sharks but thankfully I was spared the excitement. Did I say I love snorkelling? It isn't <u>like</u> entering another world – it <u>is</u> entering another world. Sadly, that underwater world, much like our terrestrial one, is threatened and dying. As the oceans continue to absorb more and more carbon dioxide, they are becoming more and more acidic, causing the coral reefs to disintegrate at an increasingly rapid rate. And of course the reefs are crucial fish habitat. I was very new to this "sport" but even my novice eye could see the die off. Nevertheless, as with many environmental issues, it's out of sight, out of mind. Where were the activists when you needed them? Oh, yes. They were busy arranging the boycott of designers who had the temerity to "dress" the new first lady. There are priorities, you know. Sorry, I digress. On another day, we left Porter in the RV and took the kayaks to Bahia Honda to explore the shoreline. The water on the Atlantic side was a bit choppy but we managed to paddle out to a little island off-shore with a great view back to Hwy

1, and what remains of Henry Flagler's East Coast Railway (which was washed out by the great category 5 hurricane of 1935). Small Portuguese man o' war jellyfish were easily visible in the crystal-clear waters closer to shore, so we gave them plenty of room. Staying at the park would have made these activities so much more accessible. Maybe another time it will be our turn to win the lottery.

AT BAHIA STATE PARK WITH FLAGLER'S HURRICANE DESTROYED BRIDGE IN THE BACKGROUND.

We also took time to check out the National Key Deer Refuge at Big Pine Key (mile marker 30), home of the endangered Key deer. This is the only place in the world where they are found and at present, only number around 800. They are a subspecies of the Virginia white tailed deer, but over thousands of years, evolved and adapted to an environment that is both short on food and water. In fact, Big Pine Key is the only one of the Keys to have naturally occurring fresh water reservoirs, enabling these "toy deer" to survive. They really are very tiny, with fawns being about the size of small cats and the adults weighing around 75 pounds. A few short walking trails lead into their wild habitat, but we only saw one little guy out there, and he was too busy eating to pay us much notice. The locals say if you park in a residential area you'll see plenty of them, making themselves at home in the gardens where plants are more plentiful and easier to access. So much for wildlife. At least of the four-legged variety. On to Key West.

It was difficult to get a real feel for the town of Key West itself simply because it is so eclectic. Cruise ship tourists and seasonal snowbirds rub shoulders with washed-out bohemians, street performers and local bar-flys. Sun worshippers and gawkers mix in with wanna-be-Hemingways, sport fishermen and average working folks. Talented (and some not so talented) musicians, gays, newlyweds, nearly-deads. They were all there. But it's not surprising. The history of the place is equally eclectic, involving pirates, wreckers, spongers, cigar makers, bankruptcy, tourists, literary types, entrepreneurs, hippies and more tourists. The founding fathers were basically pirate fighters. Back in the late 1400s when the "new world" was being discovered and all its riches were being hauled back to Europe, shipping reigned supreme when it came to transportation. By the 1600s, around these parts anyway, Spain held the upper hand. Galleons loaded with gold, silver and precious stones were tempting quarry for the pirates of yesteryear. And these were not your Johnny Depp *Pirates of the Caribbean* type pirates. These were nasty men (and some women) who committed unspeakable acts of pure torture just for the fun of it. If caught, the offence of piracy was punishable by death, but it wasn't that simple. Blame the privateers. Given Spain's unprecedented wealth, other European countries began attacking the Spanish ships for a share of the booty. The attacks were conducted by private ships but sanctioned by European governments who received a specific share of the plunder. However, it was such a lucrative business, it soon became difficult to tell the pirates from the privateers as everybody in the region seemed to be in on the action, sometimes authorized, sometimes not. In theory, privateers did not attack ships from their own country but given the profits to be made, there was considerable playing fast and loose with the rules. And the shallow waters and bays around southern Florida's Keys were the perfect place to hide out, pounce and disappear again. By 1822, the United Stated government had had enough of its ships being attacked and sent the US Navy to the Florida Keys to protect its shipping interests. The southern-most point of the United States was chosen and soon, 1,500 people were living at the naval base, all for the sole purpose of eradicating piracy. The move was a success and within 2 years, most of the pirates were gone and maritime trade throughout the Caribbean was once again safe for all countries. Safe from pirates, at least. Unfortunately, the waters around the Keys contain many shoals, reefs and other navigational hazards, and marine charts at this time in history were either non-existent or very poorly marked. This resulted in numerous shipwrecks, sometimes averaging two per week. Enter the wrecking industry. Or in today's parlance, a form of salvage.

As soon as a shipwreck was spotted, anyone with a boat scrambled to get there first, ostensibly to save lives but really, to claim the cargo. Whoever got there first, kept 50%. The rest would be divvied up on shore through a quasi-legal process involving auction-eers, agents, lawyers, insurance companies and a ragtag assortment of interested parties. There was big money to be made and not all of it legal. Accusations of impropriety (many legitimate) were common; ship captains deliberately colluding with wreckers in order to defraud insurance companies; auctioneers, purchasers and judges often one and the same person. Nice work if you can get it. The wrecking business was so profitable, that between 1828 and 1850 Key West was considered, per capita, the richest city in all of North America. Of course, in between wrecks, there was not much to do so gam-bling, discussing politics, smoking Cuban cigars, and drinking to excess were common pastimes. A bad combination because this often led to a fifth activity: duelling. Pistols, at dawn, at the beach. It seems that today, only the duelling has been removed from the list of acceptable practices. Alas, all good things must come to an end and with the advent of rail and road, shipping rapidly declined. The people of Key West had to find another source of income. Sponging! No, not what teenage children do to their parents. Sponging, as in the collection of sponges from the sea floor.

Most of today's bathing sponges are synthetic, but back in the day, sea sponges were used as packing material, furniture stuffing, even woven with wool or cotton to produce broadcloth. Those good times didn't last either because a deadly fungus destroyed most of the sponge beds. So next up... cigar making. In 1831 there was only one cigar making factory in Key West, but during the Cuban Revolution, thousands of Cubans emigrated to Key West, bringing their cigar making skills (amongst other things) with them. By 1890, there were 129 very profitable cigar factories employing large numbers of Cubans and providing the perfect venue for political activism against Spain. But as with any business, there are problems, and strikes, tax-free land offers and cheap labour saw many entrepreneurs enticed away to the Tampa area. Key West lost its status as America's leading producer of hand-rolled Cuban cigars. During prohibition, rum running was a considerable source of income creating many wealthy KW inhabitants, but the Great Depression hit hard and at one point almost 90% of the city's population was receiving some form of government assistance. The other 10% were doing quite well, thank-you very much. Ernest Hemingway and his monied wife Pauline Pfeiffer had rolled into town and between house renovations, fishing charters and his bar tab, they managed to not only employ quite a few locals, they gave everyone something to talk about. More on Hemingway later. Other artists and bohemians followed, as did tourists looking for an authentic getaway to what really was just a poor fishing village. The only problem being, whenever tourist hordes descend, nothing stays authentic for long and many of the original inhabitants took flight. By 1912 Flagler had managed to extend his railway all the way to Key West and that just made it too easy. People left in droves only to be replaced by other people arriving in droves. (Even though the railroad was wiped out by the 1935 hurricane, the government simply used Flagler's bridges to build Hwy 1, all the way down to Mile Marker 0.)

While many of the changes and developments were simply a reflection of what was going on in the rest of the country, some events are too unique not to mention. For example, the inhabitants of Key West seem to have an odd penchant for threatening secession from the Union when things do not go their way. Case in point. In 1985, the U.S Border Patrol set up check points along Hwy 1, stopping each and every car, looking for narcotics and, given the proximity to Cuba, illegal immigrants. This caused considerable traffic delays and inconvenienced many locals and tourists alike. Complaints to the federal government were ignored so Key West City Council took the position that since these checkpoints were in effect border stations, and anyone leaving KW was being treated like a foreign national, they might as well become a foreign nation. Since local citizens are referred to as Conchs, they called their new country the Conch Republic. The Mayor was declared Prime Minister and he immediately declared war on the United States by symbolically breaking a loaf of stale Cuban bread over the head of a man dressed in US military uniform. One minute later, he surrendered to this "military man", and demanded 1 billion dollars in war reparations and foreign aid from the United States. The roadblocks were taken down shortly thereafter, and tourism increased yet again. And here I thought federal politicians were crazy.

But what is it that draws the tourists? Yes, the weather is great. For the most part. It was quite windy the first few weeks we were there, and snorkelling and kayaking days were few and far between. The locals said they had never experienced a winter as windy as this. Just our luck. There are no real beaches to speak of. What little sandy stretch there is, is covered with baking bodies from one end to the next, and Bahia Honda is 35 miles to the north. The geographic area is small. Old Town is about 1 mile wide and 2 miles long, making it possible to hike from the Atlantic Ocean to the Gulf of Mexico. We did it several times. Sounds impressive, doesn't it? The rest of the "island" was built up by landfill, and that is where the airport, chain hotels and shopping malls are located. Yet people come in huge numbers. Tourism and the Naval Base/Air Station at Boca Chica Key (mile marker 10) are what keep the economy afloat. As an aside, the naval air station made its presence felt in a very audible way. Almost every morning, the roar of fighter jets streaking overhead drowned out any other sound, manmade or otherwise. Sometimes one, sometimes three. And again, in the afternoon, same ritual. It was like having our own daily private air show. Our full-time neighbour at the resort suggested we go to Boca Chica "beach" that runs perpendicular to the naval runway. You can go out there and have the jets literally scream over your head as they take off and land. It was pretty impressive, albeit deafening. The beach is generally used only by locals and he did warn us it is clothing optional. Why is it that those people who should leave their clothes <u>on</u> are the ones who feel they need to take them <u>off</u>? Enough said.

Old Town Key West was rather enjoyable except perhaps for Duval Street, the main drag. Yet Duval Street is where most of the tourists flock (save Mallory Square at sunset). To me, it seems Duval Street consists primarily of beer-soaked bars of questionable ambiance interspersed with a plethora of cheap t-shirt shops, sandal shops, hat shops and faux Cuban cigar shops, with the odd over-priced restaurant thrown in. And the people in the drinking establishments are the exact ones you would find parked by the swim up bar at some big-name Caribbean resort. Drinking too much, laughing too loud and not noticing the passage of time. And there is no mistaking it. Alcohol plays a very important role here – over and above what might be found at any other vacation destination. If you live there, the prevailing sentiment is that if you show up to work sober, you are management material. If you show up drunk, that's ok, you still have a job. For tourists, most on the other side of 50, it brings out a sophomoric delight at being able to legally exit an establishment with cocktail in hand, and stroll down the street to the next venue. At Jimmy Buffet's Margaritaville bar, you can even leave with your booze in your own mini blender. For serious drinkers, it is paradise. Sloppy Joe's (at the corner of Greene and Duval streets) vies with Captain Tony's (on Greene south of Duval) as the "real" Sloppy Joe's, where Ernest Hemingway spent many a soused afternoon and evening. It is a badge of honour to be able to say you drank where the great H. drank. I can think of quite a few more worthy pursuits. In reality, both bars can legitimately claim the Hemingway connection. He did drink at the Captain Tony's locale (although it was called Sloppy Joe's at the time), but when the landlord raised the rent, Joe moved his bar to the current location and Hemingway followed. Old Town even has a nude bar, the Garden of Eden, where locals will take unsuspecting visitors just to watch their reactions. We were too chicken to go in. And as sunset approaches, the bars empty, leaving only the truly committed drinkers to continue honing their craft. Everyone else goes in what one author referred to as a "lemming like march" to congregate at Mallory Square and partake in the setting sun ritual. Buskers and musicians of various talents and abilities entertain the throng; cameras, i-phones and selfie-sticks are wielded with varying degrees of proficiency, and as the last sliver of light from the bright orb drops into the ocean, the crowd breaks into appreciative applause. And then they all head back to their bar stools. The show is over for another 24 hours. Such a curious tradition. And yet we too attended on numerous evenings, albeit minus the alcohol generated glow emanating from many of the spectators.

Another curious tradition, this one not involving booze, is the line-up for a photo beside an oversized buoy demarcating the southern-most point in the continental United States. Thirty or more people, waiting patiently (and politely) in the hot sun in order to immortalize their arrival at this holiest of holies. You'd think they had summited Everest. I wondered how many of them were aware that despite its markings, the buoy really isn't the southern-most point. In fact, that lies at the Truman Annex about 900 feet further south, but since it is on naval property, tourists are not allowed access. Fort Zachery Taylor State Park, which is accessible to the masses is another 500 feet further south, but there is no "X" to mark the specific spot, so what kind of a picture would that make? Even the "90 miles to Cuba" sign is a rounded off figure, in that Cuba actually lies 94 statute (81 nautical) miles south. I didn't have the heart to say anything. They looked like they were having such a good time.

Walking around Old Town was not difficult, and there were quite a few historic buildings, museums and galleries to visit. But one rather quirky feature that took some getting used to was the freely roaming roosters, hens and little chickens. They were everywhere. Roadways, sidewalks, parking lots, laneways, gardens, porches, patios, marinas and parks. And they were not timid. They would strut out into the middle of the road, obstructing traffic, almost daring you to shoo them along. There are two versions on how they came to be there, both involving Cubans. The first, when Cubans originally came to Key West to work in the growing cigar industry during the mid/late-1800's, they brought their domestic life with them. And that included barnyard fowl. When the industry moved north to Tampa and Miami, the Cubans followed, leaving their chickens and roosters behind. They have been running free ever since. I'm not sure why, if you took the trouble to take them with you from Cuba, you wouldn't take them along to Tampa as well, but maybe there wasn't any room. Who knows. The second version is similar except that it contends the Cubans brought the roosters not to contribute to the family food supply, but rather for cock fighting. This barbaric form of entertainment was outlawed in the 1970s so the Cubans released all their roosters in protest. The second explanation gets my vote. Some people want them culled because they are such a nuisance, but others maintain they should be protected because they are great at keeping the insect population down. No grasshoppers or cockroaches in KW. Either way, they are there and don't seem to be leaving any time soon. And as usual, Mother Nature has a way of keeping things balanced. One reason these birdies have not completely taken over the city is the hawks. On two separate occasions I saw a hen scratching in the dirt with her little hatchlings alongside, when a hawk swooped down out of nowhere, grabbed one little unsuspecting chick, and was gone. There was much clucking and clacking by the adults but that's life in the big city. And this was, literally, in the city. Porter, of course, was torn between his bird dog instinct and his city dog excitability, with some not so pleasant results. On one occasion he made the tactical error of getting too interested in a mother hen with her little chicks and didn't heed her warning clucks. One sniff too many and she came at him with her feathers puffed out, hopping up and down, wings flapping, all the while pecking at him. Our poor brown menace didn't know what to do other than beat a confused retreat. Another time, we were walking down the sidewalk with me holding Porter's leash firmly in my hand. Passing a narrow laneway, I failed to see the rooster, but Porter didn't. He lunged, slamming me backwards into a post and I went down like a ton of bricks. It happened so fast! My favourite camera lens was busted ($400 US – thank-you very much) and I either cracked my ribs, badly bruised them, or both. Three weeks later, I still couldn't sleep on my one side and did my best to avoid sneezing or coughing. And just so you know, roosters don't only crow at dawn. They crow whenever they feel like it, day or night, and they feel like it a lot! I'm thinking a cull might not be such a bad idea after all. This whole free-range poultry thing has gone a little bit too far.

And then there is Hemingway. Even though he only spent eight years of his life there (between 1931 and 1939) his presence still lingers. Actually, it doesn't just linger. It is cultivated, nurtured and promoted. A bit like Elvis at Graceland or Lenin in his tomb. Every July, Key West holds a Hemingway Days celebration with Hemingway look alike contests, a three-day marlin fishing tournament, even a "running of the bulls" event. And for those who are not there in July, Hemingway t-shirts can be found at every shop, Sloppy Joe's bar is a "must do" on the drinking circuit, his books are everywhere, and a tour of his house draws visitors like moths to a flame. It turns out, I am more of a moth than I like to admit. I'm not an English lit major and have rarely enjoyed in depth analyses of literary works. Sometimes a tree on the hill is just a tree on the hill. But I had to go. If not for him, at least for the descendants of his polydactyl cat Snow White. The sixth toe is caused by a recessive gene and is considered to bring good luck in the nautical world. She was a gift from a sea captain, and being both nautically inclined and quite superstitious, Hemingway took great care of his beloved feline. Today, there are over 50 cats wandering the grounds, cared for by their own veterinarian and a host of volunteers. Most are spayed or neutered but several are specifically targeted for breeding so that this legacy too, can continue. The house and grounds sit on one full acre in Old Town, where real estate is priced by the square inch, not the square foot. On today's market, if you don't factor in its literary significance, the place is estimated to be worth over 30 million dollars. I took the 30-minute guided tour and while quite informative, it was also possible to wander around on your own. Hemingway lived there with the second of his four wives. She was the one with all the money and all the connections and introduced him to a lot of the right people. Maybe that is what got him noticed. Hemingway himself was what is described as a "man's man". Handsome in a rugged sort of way, adventurous, hard drinking and hard playing. Though quite disciplined. He rose every day at 5am, working in his little studio above the coach house until 2pm. Then he went out to indulge in his two favourite pastimes: deep sea sport fishing and drinking. But he did manage to churn out some of his better-known books while living there, including *The Old Man and the Sea*, which earned him the Pulitzer in 1953 and contributed to his being awarded the Nobel Prize for Literature in 1954. But for me, the tree on the hill is still the tree on the hill.

And speaking of trees, Key West has some interesting vegetation, in particular the Kapok tree and the Banyon tree. The Kapok has a trunk that grows out in a fan shape at its base, while the Banyon's roots grow from the branches down into the ground. Both can be found gracing the lawns of public buildings and some of the more stately older homes, although it is the smaller cottages that are a true depiction of what Key West was really like before it was "discovered". One curious feature, however, was that each and every house, be it humble abode or gracious manor, had a metal roof. This is required by law. In April of 1866, a fire broke out in a coffee shop and burned for 12 hours, destroying much of the city centre, including 16 cigar factories, 200 houses and numerous warehouses. Since then, the city requires that all houses have metal roofs so that any potential fire cannot spread as rapidly as that one did.

Another place that was definitely worth visiting was the Mel Fisher Maritime Museum. It is the only fully accredited museum in the Florida Keys and houses much of the treasure recovered from the 1622 Spanish shipwreck, Nuesta Senora de Atocha. The Atocha, along with her sister ship Santa Margarita, was en route to Spain loaded down with a small fortune (legal and smuggled) when both galleons sank in a hurricane, 35 miles off the coast of Key West. Atocha was carrying 450 million in gold and silver bars (about 40 tons worth), unset emeralds (70 pounds worth), intricate jewellery and about 100,000 gold and silver coins, amongst the first minted in the New World. And there she lay on the ocean floor for over 350 years. In 1980, along came Mel Fisher. He was not new to treasure hunting, having had success with an earlier 1715 wreck but this would be the mother lode if he found it. Together with his family, he searched for over 16 years before finally realizing the dream. To date, they have recovered about 500 million's worth but according to the ship's manifest, there is still another 120 million to be found (plus 166 million from the Santa Margarita). And then there are the smuggled emeralds and gold that could be worth over half a billion. The entire undertaking is explained and displayed throughout the museum, including the government's attempt at seizing the find. Maritime law on "finders keepers" can be a bit vague depending on the origin and location of the treasure, but in this case it appears Fisher was in the right. Despite being aware of his efforts, the government did not make a move until the find was announced. In effect, letting Fisher do all the heavy lifting. Then they sailed in and said it belonged to the nation. Fisher said no, but I'll give you 35%. The government said, no we want the whole thing. Fisher took it all the way to the Supreme Court which ultimately ruled the entire find belongs to him. For once, the little guy won. The museum is not large but the artefacts it displays are spectacular. Many of the coins and lesser pieces can be purchased, but sadly, most were way out of our price range. We settled for a musket ball. It somehow seemed fitting.

Towards the end of the month, Matejs flew down for a short visit. He quite enjoyed trading the grey monotony of an Ontario winter for the sunny skies and balmy breezes of KW, and we were very happy to see his smiling face. Porter was in heaven, having his buddy to wrestle, swim and play water coconut football with. We managed to get in a few touristy activities, explore a bit more of Old Town, and got him hooked on kayaking as well as snorkelling under John's expert tutelage. The kayaking came quite naturally to him, but snorkelling... as much as he enjoyed it, he managed to snort and drink a fair bit of ocean during his initial foray so perhaps his idea of getting his own gear is not a bad one. Out at Looe Key Reef, water visibility was 40 feet and he was quite fortunate to see a nurse shark, a baby goliath grouper (they can weigh up to 800 pounds) and a barracuda, in addition to all the other colourful fish. Lucky guy! His corrupting influence had us checking out the cigar shops on Duval, which I must say were just as unappealing to me afterwards as they were prior to going in. Despite Key West's Cuban cigar history, it is still illegal to sell Cuban products in the U.S. so the guys had to settle for some inferior product that they declared was just awful. I could have told them that before they bothered to light up. But the days flew by in a flurry and before long we were driving him back to KW's one runway airport. We'd see him again when we returned home over Easter. 'Till then, we had until mid-February to search for that lost shaker of salt.

GOOD TIMES IN KEY WEST. BAD CIGARS.

10.

OH YOU GOT TO HAVE FRIENDS

THEY CALL IT THE KEYS DISEASE AND THE LIKELIHOOD OF CONTRACTING IT INCREASES EXPONENTIALLY WITH THE PASSAGE OF TIME. We almost succumbed, and the entire North America tour was in jeopardy. Perhaps that is a bit of an exaggeration, but there is something about the Florida Keys that makes you want to stay put. For the entire 6 weeks we were there (plus 2 weeks before Christmas) the weather was practically perfect (save for a few sporadic days of rainy and cool) and there was much to see and do – more than we had anticipated. And the people were a very curious mixed bag, albeit more aging rocker than Birkenstock vegan, but all fairly close to our age. Perhaps it was just that time of year and summer brings out a different crowd, but the baby boomers were definitely in the majority during the winter months.

February did not exactly start off on a high note, thanks to an unanticipated and ultimately costly kayaking capsize. And what is most irksome is that we should have known better. We do know better. We have done enough kayaking over the years to know the rules. And we have always followed those rules. Rule number one. Anything that needs to be safe and dry goes into a dry bag and into the hatch. Period. No debate. But the seas were calm. The water was aquamarine blue. The sun was shining. And we decided to paddle out to Indian Key State Park, a distance of about ½ mile offshore, near Islamorada at mile marker 78. We had found a doggie daycare close by and although it was a bit on the sketchy side (they leave the dogs unattended and unsupervised between 4pm and 6pm during "shift" change – what could go wrong?) we estimated we would be back before 4, so Porter would be okay. Indian Key is an interesting place and one of Florida's smaller state parks at only 10 acres. It was the site of a small settlement of about 50 people at the height of the "wrecking years" and included a profitable store, hotel and numerous wharfs and warehouses. Unfortunately, it was also vulnerable to hostile Indian activity and in 1840, during the Second Seminole War, a band of 100 Indians attacked. Most of the inhabitants were able to escape but several were killed, and the buildings looted and burned. Although the little island was used on and off in the ensuing years, it never regained any sense of community and had been totally abandoned by 1880. The Florida government purchased it in 1971, designating it an historic site. Many building foundations are still visible, and it was a bit like walking around an archaeological ruin with groomed pathways following the original street layout. Given its water only access (and no facilities or fresh water once there), only 10 other people were wandering about, so we had the place pretty much to ourselves. We had brought along a picnic lunch and spent a great day feeling a little bit like explorers ourselves. We also brought along our snorkelling gear as per prior research, but the water was too choppy and murky to go in. Towards late afternoon we started the 30-minute paddle back to the mainland and were almost across when I wanted to take just one more picture. But the camera was in John's kayak. He reached out to hand it to me and leaned just one millimeter too far. There was no chance to recover. He was in the brine, along with his snorkelling bag, camera and i-phone. The snorkelling bag was easy to grab, and the camera was our underwater one with an attached float, but the i-phone – it is now sleeping with the fishes. It just goes to show you can never be too old to make stupid mistakes. Thankfully, there was an AT&T dealer in Islamorada so we put a new U.S. sim card in my phone until UPS delivered a new phone for John a few days later. Ka-ching. Live and learn. Unfortunately, things ended on a considerably more tragic note that day for award-winning Canadian underwater documentary filmmaker and marine biologist Rob Stewart. We didn't know it at the time, but he had been scuba diving and working on his next film *Sharkwater: Extinction* not far from Indian Key the day before. Upon resurfacing from his dive, it appears both he and his diving buddy lost consciousness. While the boat crew were attending to his friend, Stewart slipped under the water and disappeared. We saw low flying helicopters while we were out paddling but did not know that they were searching for him. Sadly, his body was recovered a few days later.

Which leads to another macabre sort of topic. Key West is quite proud of its 20-acre cemetery and a readily obtained pamphlet encourages visitors to take the self-guided tour. So we did. We found out that the residents are just as eclectic in death as they were in life. The cemetery was established in 1847 following a disastrous hurricane in 1846 that pretty much washed the first cemetery (and its inhabitants) away. According to the local port inspector of the day, "the dead were scattered throughout the forest, many of them lodged in trees". It seems hurricanes down here can take out more than just bridges. The "burial" ground was re-located to the highest point on the island at a time in history when there was a movement to establish park-like landscaped cemeteries, where people could spend a peaceful afternoon while simultaneously paying their respects to the dead (this mainly because the private and churchyard ones were overcrowded and running out of room). Think of the arboretum approach found at Bonaventure in Savannah (*Midnight in the Garden of Good and Evil*, anyone?) or Mount Pleasant in Toronto. Unfortunately, the historic Key West cemetery is anything but landscaped and park-like. I don't know who they are trying to kid. Since it is situated on limestone, traditional ground internment is limited. Instead, most of the dead are stacked above ground in square concrete sarcophaguses, sometimes three high with many of the stacks listing precariously to one side. Filing cabinets of human lives once lived. Another good hurricane and there might be a repeat of the original calamity. Like many old cemeteries, it is divided into sections based on faith – Jewish, Catholic, Protestant and the rest – Cuban martyrs, city founders, prominent residents and ordinary folks. One area contains the remains of 260 sailors who were killed when the US battleship Maine blew up in Havana harbour in February 1898, and helped kick off the Spanish-American war. There are even graves for veterans of the Civil War. But overall, the place has a very neglected air, despite some of the more quirky and amusing epitaphs that are promoted as drawing features by city tour guides. "I told you I was sick" for the hypochondriac, "Devoted fan of singer Julio Iglesias" for the fervent follower and "I know where you are sleeping tonight" for the philandering husband. We only found one of the three and I suspect the tour guides may be taking a bit of artistic licence recounting the inscriptions. Supposedly Hemingway's buddy "Sloppy" Joe Russell is buried there too but we couldn't find him either.

In the early part of the month our friends Andrew and Ilze, who were on a road trip of their own, came to visit for a few days. It was wonderful for us to have the pleasure of their company and Porter was more than delighted to once again be in the embrace of the two people who spoil him the most. We had a relaxing, laid back time just hanging out, strolling around town, eating too much and fantasizing about real estate purchases. And we can never thank them enough for the opportunity they afforded us. They took care of Porter for a day so that we were able to get out to Dry Tortugas National Park. It is not easily accessible (the only way to get there is by float plane or 2 ½ hour ferry ride) so any trip required a bit of planning. We opted for the ferry – Yankee Freedom III. It was a very pleasant crossing despite the fact we had to be at the ferry terminal by 7am. Thankfully they provided a fairly decent breakfast and lunch, although I must confess to a bit of queasiness part way across. The seas were fairly calm with just a mild swell but after about an hour I started to feel it. Breakfast no longer held any appeal, however stepping outside into the fresh air and staring at the horizon helped immeasurably. Not so for one of our fellow passengers who succumbed fairly early on and spent the majority of the trip with his face buried in his barf bag. If only he had stepped outside as well, instead of subjecting those inside to the sounds of his retching.

Dry Tortugas consists of seven keys (there used to be eleven but four were washed away by hurricanes over the years) and lie all by themselves 70 miles west of Key West. They were discovered in 1513 by none other than Ponce de Leon and called Las Tortugas (Spanish for turtle) after the numerous turtles to be found there. "Dry" was added to nautical charts later on to indicate they had no fresh water source. Most of the turtles have long since disappeared and to say there are seven keys is also a bit of a misnomer. As we were approaching Garden Key (the site of Fort Jefferson and our designated dock) the captain announced we were passing the first three keys. All we saw were 3 sand bars, maybe 100 yards long. And I mean sand bars. No trees, no scrub, no nothing. Apparently they are prime nesting habitat for sea turtles and are off limits to visitors. And did I say small? Garden Key, the second largest landmass, is only 22 acres and Fort Jefferson itself takes up most of the terra-firma. Construction of the fort began in 1846 when Americans realized they needed a garrison at the Tortugas in order to control navigation in the Gulf of Mexico. They worked on it for 30 years, but it was never finished and never saw any military action. It did, however, serve as a prison during the Civil War and its most famous inmate was Dr. Samuel Mudd who was convicted of complicity in the assassination of Abraham Lincoln. We wandered around the fort for a bit (they are constantly working on restoration), went snorkelling (visibility was quite poor that day) and then walked around Bush Key, finding huge conch shells and coral pieces that I was most tempted to slip into our backpack. John, acting in his capacity as Jiminy Cricket, reminded me that we were in a National Park and it is against the law to remove anything. If only he had looked the other way. There were reports that a crocodile was occasionally spotted in the moat surrounding the fort but wasn't it just our luck that on this particular day, said crocodile had decided to leave the moat and hang out on the beach – right where we were walking. We just couldn't get away from those guys! But they are quite shy creatures and as I crouched down to take a picture of this one, some approaching fishermen startled him and he scurried back into the ocean. That would be the same ocean where we had just been snorkelling! Yikes! Nobody knows how he got out as far as the Tortugas (remember they are 70 miles from the closest land mass) and they call him Cletus, the loneliest crocodile on the planet. Despite this atoll's tiny size, this is one place that we have definitely added to the "return to" list. There is a limited first come first served primitive campground in one corner and campers rely on the daily ferry for fresh water and a hot meal. The ferry arrives around 10:30 am, disgorges the day-trippers and then rounds them back up and departs by 3:00 pm. The rest of the time the place is deserted. Imagine! Being on this tiny speck in the middle of the ocean. No noise. No light pollution. A handful of likeminded people. A few frigate birds soaring overhead. And of course, Cletus. It would be fantastic!

SEARCHING FOR JESUS.

Back in the Keys we also managed to get in another snorkelling day out at the reef although this required driving back up to Key Largo so that we could put Porter into the only legitimate off leash day care facility around. That is one thing that is sorely lacking around there. Lots of kennels, but nothing off leash, and we just can't bring ourselves to lock him up in a puppy prison. We opted for the extended snorkelling trip that had us in the water at three different reefs for a combined time of over 3 hours. The water was 75 degrees and even wearing a shortie, after that period of time, we were both really cold. Lucky for us though, the captain took us out to Dry Rocks so that we could snorkel with Christ of the Abyss, or as he put it, "go find Jesus". Christ of the Abyss is a 4000-pound, 8½-foot bronze statue of Jesus Christ that stands at a depth of about 25 feet. Italian scuba manufacturer Egidi Cressi donated it to the Underwater Society of America in 1966 and they subsequently had it placed just off John Pennekamp Coral Reef State Park. There are actually three such statues all cast by sculptor Guido Galletti, one submerged in The Mediterranean off the coast of Genoa, Italy and one in St. George's Harbour in Grenada. The original was created at the request of Duilio Marcante in memory of Scuba pioneer Dario Gonzatti who died in a scuba accident in 1947. Every few years, the Society would go down and scrub off the marine life that was attaching itself to Jesus' hands and body, but a number of years ago Florida Parks decided to just leave it be and let the ocean do its thing. Visibility wasn't the best, but it was better than not seeing it at all.

There were also a few days when the water in the bay off our dock was like glass, and we took advantage of that to get out in the kayaks and explore. An interesting thing about the bay. The Keys contain hundreds of little bays and inlets with small fingers of land, barely above sea level, jutting out into the water. It is on these fingers of land that small neighbourhoods and RV resorts spring up. But the water itself is very shallow, in places only two feet deep. Except for about 20 feet right at the shoreline. There, its depth is between ten and fifteen feet, courtesy of the United States Army Corps of Engineers. Back during World War II, they dredged out channels all along these shorelines in order to store the army's considerable supply of torpedoes. Today, that depth is perfect for the passage of motorboats and other small watercraft. With our kayaks we were able to get into the shallow water as well, and this made for some really easy marine life viewing. Lots of sponges, orange tube coral, upside down jelly fish, crabs & lobsters, even baby nurse sharks. We did have one little mishap though, where after one paddle, John was attempting a new disembarking procedure and smacked his head on the side of the dock as he flipped over. A nasty gash to his ear with lots of blood but thankfully he was out of the water before the barracudas showed up.

One day we drove into town to check out Fort Zachary Taylor State Park. We didn't actually get around to visiting the remains of the fort itself and despite talking about going back, time slipped away on us. The park is a popular place with both locals and those visitors staying in town, and it was easy to see why. The beach is beautiful with numerous picnic tables amongst the palm trees that provide the perfect amount of dappled shade to guard against direct sun, as well as space to string up a hammock. No dogs allowed on the beach, naturally, but we let Porter get into the water at the park boundary anyway. Nobody complained. And the sunset from there was even better than from Mallory Square. Trees to frame the shots and considerably fewer people. Another day, we drove to Sombrero Beach in Marathon. This is a public beach so no problem with dogs in the water. It was actually a planned social day for both us as well as for the brown menace. While travelling Canada's east coast the previous summer, we bumped into some fellow Tiffin RV'ers several times at several locations. First in the Gaspé, then Lunenburg, then Baddeck. They were travelling with their dog Carson, and he and Porter hit it off famously. We had exchanged contact information and it just so happened they were in the Keys too. So the canines had a blast in the water for an hour or so and then the humans had a lovely lunch while catching up a bit. It was a wonderful day although Porter (and us by extension) paid for it later. The waves were pretty high at the beach and in his excitement, Porter swallowed a lot of sea water swimming after his ball. At lunch, he tanked up on lots of fresh water and by evening he was in distress. We've seen stuff come out both ends before, but this time he was also sluggish, his breathing was laboured and he had no interest in dinner. When a lab is not interested in food, you know there is something wrong. A visit to the vet was in order. By this time, the vets around Key West were closed so we had to drive back to Marathon, a distance of about 35 miles. It was the right thing to do. The vet moved the air that had built up in Porter's belly, gave him a shot, plus some pills to coat his stomach. By noon the next day he was his old self. We decided that in the future we'd have to keep him out of big waves no matter how much fun he thinks he is having. Someone here had to be the responsible party.

READY TO LAUNCH AT FORT ZACHARY TAYLOR STATE PARK

A rather understated place we visited (and never got around to touring inside) was President Truman's Little White House in old town Key West. Originally constructed in 1890 by the U.S. Navy, Thomas Edison lived there in 1918 while developing weapons for the army during WWI. During Truman's presidency, from 1946 to 1952, it was used as both a retreat and functioning official White House. Other presidential couples have stayed there (eg. Carters, Clintons) but the most intriguing visit was by John F. Kennedy in 1961, ostensibly for a summit with the British PM to discuss the situation in Laos. Yet the Bay of Pigs invasion took place 23 days later, so there is considerable speculation that there was more being discussed than just a civil war in a far-off little country. And when it comes to politics, and by extension immigration, Cuba is never far off the radar. Given the situation at home and its proximity to Key West, many Cubans have attempted to sneak into the United States by making a rather perilous journey by water. They are called *balseros* – people who try to leave Cuba illegally in small boats or home-made watercraft. Not only is the sea unpredictable, but this journey can take up to four days in contraptions that are barely seaworthy. One enterprising group used empty 55-gallon drums to keep their vessel afloat, together with a pick-up truck engine to propel it along. Still, if they can land on American soil, they can make their claim to stay. In 2015, 10,000 Cuban rafters were granted asylum while another 3,000 were returned home because the Coast Guard intercepted them at sea. This is the "wet foot, dry foot" policy, where-in those migrants who make it to land can stay, while those who are caught at sea, are immediately sent back. Some are so desperate, they will seriously wound each other en route, knowing that the Coast Guard must take them to a U.S. hospital for treatment where they can then claim to be "on land." It is a constant game of cat and mouse.

Sadly, our vaycay in the Keys was over too soon and it was time to pack up and head north west. I'm not sure why it was so difficult to leave. Perhaps we had just stayed too long in one place and got attached to it. Or maybe we were coming down with Keys Disease. It's a good thing we had a travel plan of sorts to keep us on track.

Our next stop was the complete antithesis of a civilized luxury RV resort. A mere five- hour drive and we were set up in Big Cypress National Preserve bordering Everglades National Park, with no hook-ups and more mosquitoes than anyone should have to endure. And this was the dry season! And if that wasn't enough, a neighbouring camper advised John (and showed him a picture) that water moccasins were quite prevalent in and around the campground. As of course, were alligators. I was starting to doubt the wisdom of our decision to check out the whole "swamp" experience. There were lots of ATVs and swamp buggies around and I half expected to find the guys from *Duck Dynasty* at the next bend. Early in the planning days, I had half-heartedly hoped to go on a 3-hour guided swamp walk with park staff (where you have to wade in thigh deep swamp water), but the spots had all been booked up weeks in advance, so I set off on a short little walk along a marked route by myself. I didn't last 30 minutes. The dried-up sections weren't too bad, but in those places where the cypress trees stood in water, pausing to take pictures was an open invitation to any blood sucking flying insect within a 50-foot radius. And I had even doused myself with bug spray in preparation, but John said mosquitoes just view that as a condiment. So much for getting back to nature. Although the epiphytic bromeliads were intriguing. These lovely plants grow on trees and are sometimes referred to as "air plants" because their roots are not anchored into the ground to absorb nutrients, but rather anchored onto trees (or rocks) for support. They obtain their nutrients from moisture in the air so are not parasitic to the tree they grow on. Fascinating. We drove over to Everglades City just out of curiosity and even though we did not have any expectations, we were unsurprisingly underwhelmed and couldn't fathom why anyone would want to live there. A whole lot of nothin' going on. But one very nice place we visited in the Cypress Reserve was Big Cypress Gallery that houses the work of Clyde Butcher. Confessing my ignorance, we learned that Butcher is an internationally renowned photographer whose black and white photos of natural wilderness landscapes are displayed in museums and galleries around the world. Almost Ansel Adamish. Butcher must really find swamps inspiring because what else would motivate him to stay there! Thankfully our "swamp stop" was only for a couple of nights and we were soon on our way to an RV resort along the gulf coast. I should point out that our accommodations of choice really were state and national parks, and our preference truly was to be close to nature, but during the winter months, Florida's public parks are reserved months in advance. And given that we wanted to keep our route fairly flexible, we sometimes had to compromise on where we stayed. And so we ended up at privately owned Riverside RV Park, about an hour's drive north of Fort Myers, where the only real "nature" were the sand cranes wandering around like they owned the place.

The reason for our stop there was my 90-year-old mom. As a young girl growing up in Latvia, she was dear friends with another young girl, Maria. But the war came, their families fled in different directions and the two lost touch with each other. Mom ended up in Canada and Maria in the United States. When mom got married, Maria saw the wedding photo in the Latvian newspaper (it has a North American circulation) and the two reconnected. Maria became godmother to my eldest sister. But as often happens in life, their contact became less and less frequent and other than exchange occasional letters, they had not seen each other for over 30 years. Since our RV route was going directly past Maria's home of Punta Gorda, we convinced mom to fly down for a few days so that she could see her old friend. Our son Matejs got her on the plane in Toronto, and we picked her up in Fort Myers. The following day, we drove her over to Maria's house and left the two "girls" to catch up. John and I then did a whole lot of "nothing exciting." We engaged in some needed shopping, maintenance on the RV, housekeeping responsibilities and basically hung out at the RV park, marvelling at how many northern U.S. and Ontario licence plates we saw. It was a large park with over 500 sites, and it was obvious that the residents had settled in for the long haul. We were squarely amongst the dedicated snowbirds now. Many had planted flower gardens, some had huge semi-permanent gazebos set up, others even edged their very spacious sites with white picket fences. And the scheduled activities were endless: computers for beginners, mah-jongg tournaments, aqua fit, square-dancing, horseshoes, bible study, book club and the ever- popular shuffleboard. It was like a summer camp for adults, except nothing was compulsory. Everyone was incredibly friendly and God bless them for that, but we were way too young to be there. Maybe in 20 years it will be something to consider.

We finished off February with even more socializing. Our friends (and neighbours) from Port Credit had just purchased a vacation home on Sanibel Island and as luck would have it, invited us to spend some time with them. We were in the area. How fortuitous was that? Their yellow lab Maggie is Porter's blonde girlfriend back home and it was incredible to watch the two of them carry on. For three days they were running, playing tug-of-war, pawing each other and competing for belly rubs. It was heart-warming. And we ourselves fell in love with Sanibel. It is not a large island, and has the perfect mix of shell covered beaches, preserved wilderness, elegant homes and interesting shops.

No huge developments, no traffic lights and a three-story height restriction on any building. And while vehicular traffic may be a bit heavy, it doesn't really matter because everybody bicycles everywhere along well-maintained bike paths. We had a wonderful time kayaking through a wildlife preserve, checking out the best local farmer's market I had ever been to (the only thing that saved us from buying out the place was that we had just come from a delightful breakfast spot), dropping in on a bookstore that was equal parts charming and extensive, and hanging out at the beach. And collecting seashells, naturally. I found one rather large conch about 10 inches long but when I picked it up, realized that not only was it alive, it was "eating" another two shells. Yuck. Gross. I took a quick picture and tossed it back out to sea. And we saw the green flash! Twice! This is a rare atmospheric event that occurs at sunset (although physicists say it can occur at sunrise as well) and is caused by light refracting in the atmosphere. But to call it a "flash" isn't a very accurate description. More like a one to two second glow that comes and goes very quickly. Just as the setting sun sinks into the ocean and the last sliver of orange light is visible on the horizon, it momentarily changes to a bright lime green. And then it is gone, and all that is left is a coral coloured sky. A perfect way to end the month.

11.

TRADING BEACHES FOR BEADS AND BAYOUS

WHAT IS THE DIFFERENCE BETWEEN SNOWBIRDS AND PEOPLE WHO RANDOMLY TRAVEL SOUTH IN THE WINTER? I may not be able to provide a succinct answer, but I can say without hesitation, "We are not snowbirds!" There is a definite difference between those folks who cover ground in their motor coaches, and those who just move from point A in the north to point B in the south and back again. Both may be in the warmer climes during winter, but there is a world of difference in attitude, enthusiasm, energy level and interests. While travelling in Canada during our first summer and driving down through the States in the fall, we met many people like ourselves. On the move, exploring, curious about who the neighbours were, where they had been and where they were going. We traded travel tips, RV maintenance tips, cooking tips, even border-crossing tips. It was all very social, fun and informative. Not so with the stay-put crowd. They have formed little communities in their RV park of choice, brought all their homey accoutrement with them and have no interest is going anywhere outside a 5-mile radius. Other than wanting to know how long we were staying, there was little to talk about. It was almost as if they did not want to invest any emotional energy because they knew we would be gone within a day or two. Additionally, true snowbirds seemed to flock to private RV parks, while travellers more like ourselves migrated amongst the state and national parks. So it was with considerable reluctance that we checked into yet another private RV park in Crystal River, but only because there were no state parks around.

The sole reason we went to Crystal River was to swim/snorkel with manatees. Disappointingly, it was not everything it was cracked up to be, although that can be partially attributed to timing. As in a little too late in the season. And that was our own fault. We should have dragged our butts out of Key West a little sooner. But to be honest, the entire manatee encounter took place in a setting that was not at all what we had envisioned, so that only adds to this less than enthusiastic review. A bit of background on manatees. These huge gentle mammals, also called sea cows, are related to elephants and as adults, have no predators. They weigh around 1,200 pounds (although can reach 3,000), grow to more than 12 feet in length, and were once hunted for their meat and hides. They were placed under the protection of the Endangered Species Act in 1973 and their current population in Florida is estimated to be around 5,000. The best place to see them, supposedly, is at Three Sisters Springs, Crystal River, geographically just south of where the Florida panhandle begins. Why there? Because Crystal River contains several springs that release fresh water at a constant temperature of 73 degrees. And manatees need that warm water during the winter months in order to survive. Despite their huge size, they do not have any deep layers of blubber (like whales) and are very susceptible to changes in temperature. When the water drops into the low 60s, they experience cold stress and can die. So as the waters of the Gulf of Mexico start cooling off, the manatees head for where things are warmer and Three Sisters Springs Wildlife Refuge in Kings Bay is one of their preferred hangouts. It is also one of the few places in the world where it is possible and permissible to swim with these funny looking creatures. But therein lies the problem. Everybody and his brother want to either a) partake in the experience or b) make money from those wishing to partake in the experience. So things can get pretty crowded. And it doesn't help matters that the location has been written up in *National Geographic Traveller*, and *1000 Places to See Before You Die*. Furthermore, although Three Sisters Springs is in a "wildlife preserve", the preserve itself is in the middle of a residential area, complete with man-made canals, houses, docks and motorboats, typical of Florida water-access communities. It is a bizarre set up to say the least. Not knowing the lay of the land, we reserved a spot with a tour operator (Fun With Manatees) who was highly rated on Tripadvisor, and showed up at the appointed time. After a short briefing on what to expect, what to do and what not to do, we were issued our wetsuits and headed off in a small "houseboat" type boat with four other people. For two hours, our "captain" guided his craft up and down the river, in and out of the canals, all the while searching for those elusive manatees. Considering there are supposed to be several hundred of them gathered around this watering hole, their apparent absence should have been our first clue. Captain Fantastic finally spotted one loner, ordered everybody into the water (quickly and quietly so as not to spook it away) and we all got to get up close and personal for no more than 2 minutes before the lumbering giant swam off. We were a considerable distance away from the clear waters of the spring by this time, so the water was a bit on the murky side. Back into the boat. Then another siting. Back into the water. This time the visibility was worse than murky. It was hardly even worth getting wet. But the captain was quite enthusiastic, saying we had "nailed" the experience. What B.S.! We could have been gathered around a huge floating log and not known the difference. We obviously understood that when dealing with wildlife nothing is guaranteed, but there was no need to play us for fools. We knew very well that once the water starts warming up, the manatees head back out to the Gulf and that is why there were so few around. Their "season" was coming to an end. The following day, in an effort to make this stop worthwhile, we drove back to the same general area, launched our own kayaks from a public park and paddled across the bay and up into the preserve. We saw several manatees in the clearer water by the actual spring itself and I

was sorely ticked our snorkelling gear was back at the RV. We could have done our own swimming with manatees at no cost! Still, I am glad we took the time to give it a shot. If we were to do it again, I'd say let's go in January when there are sure to be more of them around. Then we will be certain to "nail" it.

I HOPE THEY ARE AS GENTLE AS THEY SAY!

Leaving Crystal River, our next stop was Grayton Beach State Park on the Gulf of Mexico, about 25 miles west of Panama City. But somewhere along the way, it was as if we had crossed that proverbial line in the sand. The warm/hot tropical weather we were used to became more like early spring in Ontario. The trees had small bright green leaves just starting to emerge, colourful shrubs were blooming and there was a definite crispness to the air. In the Keys, we experienced maybe a two or three-degree change in air temperature after sunset, but now, there was a huge drop. In fact, on our first night at Grayton Beach, we had the heater on because the temperature dipped to 45F (8C). WTF! Manatees be damned! We should have stayed further south! But Grayton is a lovely park, albeit small and the weather soon warmed up. The sand on the beach was an incredible powdery white and in places it squeaked when walked on, the same as the "singing sands" of Prince Edward Island. But that is about all the beach had going for it. White. Powdery. Singing. A parks employee said that this part of the

Gulf contains the cleanest beaches he has ever seen. But by "clean" he was not referring to garbage and other human detritus that may wash up (of which, thankfully, there was very little). What he meant was, devoid of any natural wash up. No shells, no coral, no seaweed, not even a piece of driftwood. And nothing offshore to break the monotony of the horizon either. So other than lying on the beach and tanning, there is really very little to do. Yet people come to this stretch of the Gulf. In fact, they come in droves. At one end is Panama City Beach with its high-rise condos, high-rise hotels, discount beach shops, water parks and mini putt courses. One travel article describes it as "an area synonymous with frolicking, fun-loving spring breaks and affordable family vacations". That about sums it up. In fact, just prior to our departure, it was obvious the area was preparing for the annual influx of college and university students on their March break, ready to "frolic". Signs were posted all around that no-one under 18 was allowed on the beach after 8pm without adult accompaniment. Let the debauchery begin. Fifty miles to the west along highway 98 is Destin, which is even more extreme. Strip malls, big box stores, fast food joints, garish arcades and even more high-rises. Precisely the type of Florida we had been trying to avoid. Both places truly are deserving of their moniker "The Redneck Riviera" no matter how much the tourist board promotes them as part of "The Emerald Coast."

Yet interspersed between these two examples of humanity's penchant for tasteless overdevelopment are a handful of small state parks, all trying to preserve some vestige of a more natural shoreline, with large sand dunes, dune lakes, oat grass and migrating birds. However, at Grayton Beach State Park they have taken their preservation efforts to such an extreme and are so keen on enforcing their petty rules, it got rather annoying. Although the beach itself is very wide with large 25-foot dunes inland, signs (joined by either ropes or slat fences) are posted every 20 feet: "keep off the dunes". So are signs for no dogs on the beach (naturally), no bikes on the beach, don't leave any personal items on the beach, don't launch your canoe here etc. etc. As the Five Man Electrical Band sang, "*Sign, sign, everywhere a sign.*" One morning, we were taking Porter for a walk past the park's administrative office and were strolling along the entry lane. Not a vehicle was in sight, but the volunteer inside opened her little window and insisted we turn back and go around the kiosk so as to walk along the exit lane. Unreal. We should have made up a sign to remind her of the rule about walking against traffic when there are no sidewalks. And our campsite neighbour was chastised for letting her English Sheepdog sit on the beach boardwalk while she took a picture of him with the ocean in the background. As I said, annoying. But if you can get over the staffing and regulation issues, it is a lovely park and one of the highlights was kayaking around in the dune lake.

Dune lakes are actually very rare and South Walton County in north Florida has 15 of them – the largest concentration in the world. Others are found in New Zealand, Australia, Africa and the Pacific Northwest. These are bodies of water found inside the dune ecosystem and within 2 miles of an ocean shore. When the water in these lakes reaches a higher than normal level (due to heavy rain, groundwater seepage, tributaries etc.), the lake water breaks through the dune creating an outlet or outfall into the ocean. Subsequently, saltwater washes in and the ensuing mix of fresh into salt and salt in to fresh is vital to the fragile dune ecosystem. Each dune lake is unique depending on its salinity, so some are primarily fresh, some are brackish and some quite salty. Judging by the numerous water lilies on Western Lake where we were paddling, it was more on the fresh side.

Along highways 98 and 30A, where state parks have not been established, small vacation communities have sprung up, obviously designed to off-set the madness that is Destin and Panama City Beach. Yet they may have taken things to the other extreme. Beach towns with names like Water Color and Seaside, laid out with such engineered cuteness they come across as Stepford dollhouses, trying too hard to be chic. No buildings higher than four stories, palm tree lined boulevards and white picket fences. The tacky beach shops replaced by upscale boutiques charging upscale prices just because they can. No centre. No soul. At least that was our initial impression. But once we got to walking around these designer communities, we found they were not really all that bad. Just bland. While many of the mixed-use areas had a European feel with tree shaded courtyards, park benches, and a relaxingly peaceful air, they still came across as contrived. So those were the choices along this Emerald Coast. Overdeveloped tackiness, uber-regulated "wilderness" or upscale sophistication. We abhorred the high rises, were tired of the park rules and couldn't afford the upmarket exclusivity. So we headed for New Orleans, trading beaches for beads and bayous.

Pronounced by locals as "Naw-Lins", we had deliberately scheduled our visit post Mardi Gras, figuring that if we arrived two weeks later, the worst of the hangovers would be over, and the city should have returned to some semblance of normalcy. That is, if "normal" is a term that can be applied here. It is a city that has a depth of character that only history and time can impart. Architecture that is simultaneously uniform yet unique, conforming yet creative. Then there is the music. And the food. And the museums. We had originally planned on staying five days, but quickly extended that to ten and could have easily stayed for twenty. Historically, New Orleans was founded in 1718 by two French Canadians, who had been sent to the region by the government of New France in order to secure a foothold at the mouth of the Mississippi River.

They secured a foothold all right, establishing the settlement on the highest ground they could find, but still surrounded by hundreds of miles of cypress swamps. This is the part of the city now referred to as The French Quarter. Not to bore with too many dates, but in 1762, the area was peacefully transferred to Spain resulting in a huge influx of Spanish laws, language and culture. In 1803 it was transferred back to France and then sold a few months later by Napoleon to the United States as part of the Louisiana Purchase. In fact, that document was signed in New Orleans itself! At this point in time, the city was already what we today might call "multicultural". Primarily French and Spanish but also Haitian, African, German, Irish and Italian. Plus Creole. This is where it gets confusing. Prior to 1803, if you came from another country (eg. France or Spain) you were considered French or Spanish. But if you were born in New Orleans, you were considered Creole. French Creole, Spanish Creole, Haitian Creole. Even "free person of colour" Creole. Although not if you were a slave. You couldn't be black slave Creole. They drew the line at that. And many free people of colour owned their own slaves. It gets even more confusing, considering that today, the term "Creole" refers to people of mixed racial, as opposed to ethnic, heritage. So back in the day, everyone lived in and around the French Quarter. Then the Americans showed up. To say they did not think much of the existing Creoles in the French Quarter would be an understatement. And the Creoles with their established European customs and traditions did not think too highly of the "uncouth" Americans either. So the Americans moved "up river" and established what is now The Garden District complete with Antebellum mansions on huge tracts of land. With all this history and diversity, we were at a bit of a loss on how to make the best use of our time, so we started with a few guided walking tours.

The first one was through the Faubourg Marigny and along Frenchmen Street. Music is a driving force here, as well as a considerable source of pride, and given that this is where jazz was born, that is to be expected. Ironically, when outsiders talk of New Orleans, Bourbon Street is often mentioned as the place to go for jazz music and nightlife. Nothing could be further from the truth. At least as far as real jazz goes. We took a walk along Bourbon Street and found it to be dingy and sleazy, with strip clubs of Larry Flint Hustler variety, and the permeating stench of stale urine and vomit that no amount of sidewalk pressure washing can erase. The true jazz musicians have long since moved to Frenchmen Street in the heart of Faubourg Marigny, playing at clubs like The Spotted Cat, D.B.A. and Blue Nile. Interestingly, the only club on Frenchmen Street to have a bad rep (and have protestors outside from time to time) is Bamboula's, whose owner/operator has several clubs on Bourbon. The locals just don't want that debauchery to follow them here. But you don't necessarily have to go to a club to hear good jazz. Many of the street musicians are incredibly gifted (although there were some whose enthusiasm far exceeded their talent) and our favourite was Doreen Ketchens. We just happened to be walking around in the French Quarter and came upon a crowd gathered at the corner of Royal and St. Louis. And it was easy to see why. She was fantastic – clarinet and vocals, accompanied by her daughter on drums, husband on sousaphone and friend on guitar. Turns out she has been referred to as the female Louis Armstrong, Lady Louis and Queen Clarinet, and has played at venues as far north as Chicago. But it seems that the gender wars can permeate everywhere. Doreen took her show to the street, having found that the jazz industry does not make room for female band leaders. Breaking into vocals or piano is hard enough but leading a band? Forget it. Over the course of our stay, we returned several times to hear her sing and play, bought a CD and regretted we didn't buy more.

We also went on a Voodoo walking tour and although there wasn't really much walking involved, it was quite informative. Our guide Robi, advised that both his mother and grandmother were practitioners of Voodoo and he himself was an actual Louisian', and Haitian Voodoo priest. I was (and still am) a bit sceptical as to his actual role, having found him a bit on the theatrical side but he seemed passably knowledge-able about true Voodoo as opposed to the fictional American Horror Story kind. He facilitated the lecture/tour by assigning roles to several of us in the group, and John and I were appointed the Voodoo Father and Voodoo Mother. I'm still not exactly sure what we were supposed to be doing but it was fun none-the-less. New Orleans is full of palm and Tarot card readers, fortune tellers, Voodoo shops, ghost tours and cemetery tours all catering to the naïve, superstitious or gullible tourists who hope to either find out or understand why their lives are such a mess. They buy all manner of lotions, potions and candles, and walk away from the palm readers exclaiming, "She knew exactly what I have been through!" The walking tours of the various cemeteries (or "cities of the dead" as they call them) are complete with bogeymen and haunted history stories. In reality, Voodoo is a rather peaceful religion, originating in Haiti but really being a compilation of African practices involving one god and the intercession of ancestors in accessing that god. It was brought to New Orleans by Haitians fleeing the 1791 slave rebellion in Santo Domingue (as Haiti was then called) and was easily adopted by New Orleans slaves since its structure was so similar to the Catholicism that was being imposed upon them by their owners. It has nothing to do with hexes, blood worship, sacrifices, chicken bones, chicken feathers or zombies but does involve copious amounts of alcohol and prolonged drumming. The most famous voodoo priestess in New Orleans was Marie Laveau whom the mid-1800s establishment feared because of her uncanny ability to know what was going on in their personal lives. In reality, she just had an extensive spy network and used the information she gleaned from her spies as leverage to bargain for what she wanted – mostly improved living conditions for the slave community. And on the subject of slavery, being a slave in Louisiana at this time was in some respects "easier" than in the rest of the country, largely because of French civil law, the strong influence of Catholicism, and intermittent Spanish law that was even more liberal than the French. Under the "Code Noir" slaves were not required to work on Sundays, and this gave them the opportunity to gather, socialize, practice their own culture, and create their own music, all in present-day Congo Square just outside of the French Quarter. It was also possible for them to purchase their own freedom – hence the large number of "free people of colour" in the area at the time of the Civil War. In fact in New Orleans, the distinction between different groups was often along the lines of economic class rather than skin colour. This was very confusing to the Americans from the north who saw things literally in terms of black and white, being more familiar with conditions on the cotton plantations of Georgia and Virginia.

We took a day trip to visit one of the Louisiana plantations, Oak Alley, located about 45 minutes north of New Orleans and considered to be one of the most beautiful plantations in the state. Well maybe it is, but that is only because of the 300-year-old live oaks lining the walkway from the Mississippi River up to the Big House. The house itself is of modest size although it is surrounded on all side by huge verandas and columns, which give it the illusion of being much bigger than it really is. Reconstructed slave quarters at the rear depict life on a sugar cane plantation in the mid 1800s. There are several plantations in the area that are open to visitors but that is not surprising considering there used to be 500 of these vast estates along the Mississippi River prior to the Civil War. But following the war, most families lost their holdings and the great houses fell into disrepair. Oak Alley was in such a state that cows roamed freely through the dining room and the circular staircase had long since crumbled, when the Stewart family purchased it in 1925 and began extensive restorations. I pensively wondered what ever happened to the original family of this once grand home. The guide advised me not to be too concerned. The great-great-grandson, Jay Roman, is President of New Orleans famous Café du Monde, so he is definitely not hurting fiscally. And although the term "plantation" may conjure up romanticized images of genteel southern life prior to the Civil War, it really is just another word for homestead, ranch, hacienda or farm, some large and prosperous, some small and struggling. It just depends which part of the country you are in.

Back in New Orleans we did the one touristy thing that I do somewhat regret. It wasn't really all that bad, but it just wasn't worth the time and money. We took a short 3-hour cruise on the Mississippi River aboard the Steamboat Natchez, touted as the last authentic steamboat on the river, complete with live jazz music and southern lunch. Talk about being sucked in by a romantic image. The days of slowly gliding past the antebellum homes that lined the river have been gone for over a century, and Tom Sawyer and Huck Finn are just fictional characters. What were we thinking?!? New Orleans is a working port, one of the ten busiest in the world, 100 miles inland from the Gulf of Mexico, with over 20 miles of wharfs to facilitate the shipping of steel in and grain out. The river itself is lined on both sides by pollution spewing industries of all kinds, and there were more barges, tugs and cargo ships about than I could count. Lunch was okay for cafeteria style, the live jazz was a two-bit-trio (John thought that was a rather harsh description), the weather was cold and drizzly, and there really wasn't anything to see. But I suppose we can claim we have been on a steamboat on the Mississippi! Been there. Done that. Won't do it again. But what I would do again is return to Mr. Roman's Café du Monde and indulge in some more beignets and café au lait. The café itself has been in operation since 1862, and is open 24 hours a day, 7 days a week, only closing on Christmas Day. The beignets are covered in mounds of icing sugar and although I'm not normally a coffee drinker, their coffee is mixed with chicory, so I gave it a try. Delicious! It is quite the tourist trap and people dutifully line up for hours to get in. One of our earlier tour guides had given us a tip. Don't stand in line. Just walk in the side door (as the locals do), sit down at the first table you see, and you will be served in no time. She was right. We were in, seated and served within 10 minutes. It is possible to buy the beignet mix to bring home, but it just wouldn't be the same.

And on the topic of food, New Orleans prides itself on its cuisine and rightfully so. It's all good and sadly, our fitness/yoga regiment, which was already ailing, gave up the ghost. The beignets started it. Then we discovered red beans and rice. Nothing fancy, but so full of flavour. And wouldn't you know it, it was crawfish season. Or mudbugs as they are affectionately called. Okay, those I can do without. They were alright, but way too much work for the return. Give me some fresh Gulf shrimp instead. Gumbo? Love it! Muffaletta sandwiches? The best! Real French pastries? Save me from myself! It's a good thing we did a lot of walking. And walk we did. Admiring the architecture of the French Quarter – which is more Spanish than French (because two huge city fires burned down almost all of the French buildings, which had been made of wood) and then taking the trolley up to the Garden District. The trolley itself was kind of fun, a rickety antiquated affair with wood seats and leather hand straps but at $1.25 per ride, we weren't complaining. The St. Charles Avenue line, the one we were on, is the oldest continuously operating street railway system in the world, although it did suspend operations for a brief period of time after hurricane Katrina. We spent a full day on a self-guided tour of where the Americans settled, wandering around and admiring the spectacular homes with their incredible architecture. Many were built around the mid-1800s and range in style from Gothic to Greek Revival, Germanic Chalet to Queen Anne. And quite a few celebrities did or do own homes there as well. John Goodman, Sandra Bullock, Anne Rice, even the Mannings of football dynasty fame. Nicholas Cage lived there for a while as well, until the bank foreclosed on him. But as much as the houses are charming and even jaw dropping, the streets and walkways themselves could use a lot of work. The roadways are uneven with more buckling than smooth sections, and the sidewalks are for the most part brick pathways that have not been levelled since they were first laid down 150 years ago. Large exposed tree roots only serve to augment the tripping factor. But the Garden District is by far one of the nicest places to stroll around.

UPTOWN MARDI GRAS INDIAN

By way of contrast, we had occasion to go "uptown" near A. L. David Park. We hailed a taxi in the French Quarter and when we told the driver where we wanted to go he said, "What you want to go there for? Nobody want to go there." Oh dear. Were we making a mistake? Our sole reason for going was to see the Mardi Gras Indians (although these were not really Indians but rather local black people). They hold a parade on the third Sunday of March, celebrating the end of Carnival season, and their costumes were said to be spectacular. A bit of history here. During the 1700s in Louisiana, runaway slaves were often taken in and protected by the local aboriginal population and over the years there was some blending of cultures with masking, beads and feathers being common to both. Today, the black community honours this history by hand stitching elaborate bead and feather costumes and headdresses – costumes that take a full year to make, can weigh more than 100 pounds and are worn only once. There are about 40 Mardi Gras Indian "tribes" throughout New Orleans and they can roughly be divided into Uptown and Downtown, with the Uptown costumes being somewhat abstract in design and the Downtown more pictorial. The two sides come together on "Super Sunday" as it is called, forming a parade of sorts, engaging in mock wars and vying to be deemed as having the "prettiest" costume. In the not too distant past, violence was used to settle scores that had built up over the preceding year. We knew we had been dropped off in the right location, given the number of people milling about, but this was definitely not the Garden District, nor would it ever be promoted in tourist brochures. The majority of houses were neglected, boarded up or simply abandoned with no windows or doors. Beat up cars. Lots of weeds. A fair bit of garbage. Yet everyone was getting ready for the parade. The route was lined with impromptu food stands and barbeques made from oil barrels cut in half. Propane tanks left and right. Smoke filled the air. One entrepreneur even had a makeshift bar (not too badly stocked) set up in the back of his pick-up truck. And no rock concert even comes close to the amount of weed that was in the air. The parade itself was disorganized chaos with tribes coming along at no discernable intervals. Sometimes three bunched up, then nothing for 15 minutes, then a straggler or two, then another group. And the crowd itself seemed more interested in eating and socializing. It was really just a day-long street party with the police taking a complete hands-off approach. Yet the tribes themselves take the matter very seriously. We happened to be on a side street when one of the chiefs was exiting his house, getting ready to join the parade. There was much fanfare, shout outs and chanting. He stood on the steps and addressed his tribe in rhyming verse, most of which we could not understand. And then they were off. I felt like a cultural anthropologist engaging in non-participant observation and was acutely aware that I would never be able to accurately explain what I had seen. It is just one of those things you have to experience.

But all the parades and parties can't cover up the fact that New Orleans is hurting. I don't know if that is because they have not fully recovered from Hurricane Katrina or if that is just the way it has always been. There were many vacant and boarded up buildings both in residential neighbourhoods, and in the business part of town. Empty commercial real estate means a limited tax base, and that translates into waning infrastructure everywhere. We saw a lot of transient street youth with their signature fatigue clothing, numerous piercings and requisite pet dogs, all begging for change. Although one engaging young man unabashedly said if we gave him some money, he would gladly go buy some more pot to smoke. As for Hurricane Katrina, we went to one exposition that provided a before, during and after of the tragedy (and offered up a "why" as well). And the saddest thing is that the "why" was to a large extent man-made. Given its proximity to the Mississippi, New Orleans always worried about being flooded by the river. So they built spillways and levees to avoid that. But these spillways helped destroy coastal wetlands, wetlands that had traditionally guarded against flooding from storm surges coming from the Gulf of Mexico. So in effect, they traded river flooding for ocean flooding. And as the population grew, the city expanded, draining swamps to create low-lying subdivisions. The end result? A city that was once situated on a narrow crescent along the river, less than 20 square miles, has now expanded to over 200 square miles, half of which sits below sea level. In 1965, the area was struck by Hurricane Betsy with tragic consequences. Congress authorized the U.S. Army Corps of Engineers to construct a hurricane protection system. It was supposed to be completed by the mid 1970s. Funding issues, internal squabbling, environmental issues, lack of cooperation between local and state flood control agencies stalled things and the project was still incomplete in 2005 when Hurricane Katrina came ashore. As I understand it, not much has changed, fingers are still being pointed and the people of New Orleans continue to party. Music and Mardi Gras. Beads in the trees.

PADDLING THE BAYOU.

Having learned a fair bit about the role water plays in this area, we took the kayaks and headed out of the city itself to explore a bit of the bayous. The difference between a swamp and a bayou? A swamp is a piece of land, often wet and spongy, while a bayou is a body of water, often slow moving or stagnant. We launched not far from the town of Slidell on the Pearl River, where some of the "swamp tour" operators are based. We were not impressed with them at all. In an effort to amaze their paying customers, they have taken to feeding the alligators that live in these bayous. Hot dogs, no less. It is dangerous. It is irresponsible. It is stupid. I got to chatting with one of the local fishermen while John was setting up the boats, and he advised they tried to get the U.S. Wildlife Management people to ban the practice, but it is so difficult to enforce it is almost useless. Terrific. And here we were, heading out to sit 5 inches above the water line, in a bayou with alligators that associate humans with food. Not to worry my new friend said. "If you see one coming at you, just splash your paddle. He'll go away". Well that was very reassuring. Off we went. It was some of the best paddling we have ever done. Because a bayou has very little current, it took very little effort to move along. The air was still, Spanish moss hung loosely from the Cypress trees, we could hear birds and frogs of all kinds, saw great blue herons, white herons and pileated woodpeckers, numerous turtles sunbathing on partially exposed logs and then suddenly a loud splash with an accompanying large wave. Yikes. Apparently, while focused on drifting closer and closer to those sunbathing turtles, I didn't see that sunbathing alligator. Yes, they are shy, and no, we were not in any danger. It was a great day and we left the New Orleans area on a positive note. Next up, the Natchez Trace.

As any traveller knows, there are places you read about in brochures that seem so idyllic you can't wait to get there, but when you do, the reality doesn't live up to the hype. Then there are the places you didn't really know much about, hadn't planned on staying long but upon arrival, wish you had budgeted more time. Such was the case with the Natchez Trace Parkway. At least from a bicycling perspective. The Parkway runs a distance of 444 miles following an earlier foot path between Natchez, Mississippi in the south and Nashville, Tennessee in the north. Originally an Indian trail, it was used extensively by trappers and "Kaintuck" boatmen from Ohio who floated their goods down the Mississippi River, sold everything (including their boats) in New Orleans, and then walked 500 miles back north along the path. It has seen so much traffic that in places where the ground is soft, it has been worn down into gullies. There are all kinds of interesting sites to see along the way. Ancient Indian mounds, ruins of antebellum mansions, even a marker to commemorate where Meriwether Lewis (of Lewis & Clarke fame) died. And it is the perfect cycling route with only gradual changes in elevation along the way. If only we had known! But we were due back in Canada by mid-April so had to be content with driving, starting in the town of Natchez.

Natchez is rather sad. It prides itself on its large collection of antebellum homes that are open for tours during the spring, complete with southern belles in hooped skirts sipping mint juleps. And you can't argue with that. Some of the mansions are quite spectacular. In its hey-day Natchez boasted that half of America's millionaires (back when being a millionaire meant something) had homes there. But get off the beaten track and you clearly see how the down and out live. Wooden shacks resting precariously on concrete blocks with the requisite junkyard scattered about in front. Even Main Street had numerous boarded up storefronts and was devoid of life, save for the odd straggling tourist. Vestiges of a time gone by. Driving along the Trace, we stopped off to view Emerald Mound, an aboriginal religious and ceremonial earthen mound that covers 8 acres (the second largest in the country). It was used between 1200 and 1700 by the Mississippians, ancestors of the Natchez Indians, but there really isn't anything to see there anymore other than the knolls themselves. A few miles west of the Trace are the Ruins of Windsor, once one of the largest antebellum mansions along the Mississippi. It emerged from the Civil War unscathed, and then burned to the ground in an accidental fire in 1890. All that remains are the iron topped Corinthian columns, but even so, it was pretty impressive. It would have been great to bike along at least a portion of this route, but the days were ticking by and we still had the Blues Highway explore.

Our first stop was Clarksdale to visit the Delta Blues Museum, located in an old railroad depot. As museums go, it was neither large nor sophisticated, but that seems fitting given the history of the blues. Lots of memorabilia, guitars and clothing worn by the early bluesmen, as well as informative panels explaining the poor and humble roots of these early artists. We both love this genre of music, but I must confess to getting an extra kick out of the bluesmen names: Muddy Waters, Blind Lemon Jefferson, Pinetop Perkins, Howlin' Wolf and Hound Dog Taylor. But unless you're really into blues history, it may not hold your interest for any length of time. We then had lunch on the porch of Ground Zero Blues Club (no dogs inside) that has deliberately been left to look like an old rundown juke joint. The food was okay, but we really only gave it a try because Morgan Freeman co-owns it. We walked around town a bit, stopping in at the Hambone Gallery, a combination art studio/blues drop-in club and got to talking with the owner, Stan Street. It turned out he creates all the artwork for the annual Port Credit South Side Shuffle, our own local blues and jazz festival which we attend whenever we are home. What a small world! And we stopped for a quick picture at the Crossroads, the intersection of highways 49 and 61, where legend has it that bluesman Robert Johnson sold his soul to the devil in exchange for the ability to play the blues.

Names aside, B.B. King is my all-time favourite bluesman, so we headed off to his hometown of Indianola to check out the museum dedicated entirely to "The King of the Blues." It was excellent. A professionally laid out exhibit of his life, his music and the changes he experienced over the years personally, professionally and societally. Born on a cotton plantation in Mississippi in 1925 and rising to musical heights unimaginable to anyone at that time. Pictorial displays, video interviews, concert clips, Lucille, and everywhere the sound of his music. We had seen him in concert in Toronto twice, with the last time being in 2013, and at that performance it was obvious he was not well. He passed away two years later at age 89 so it was nice to tour this tribute to his talent. We played B.B. King CDs in the yacht for several days afterwards.

But driving around Mississippi, in and around the small towns, and along the Blues Highway, it was obvious that this is an area of considerable poverty. So many decrepit trailer homes, bare unpainted plank houses and dirt driveways. And since this is primarily a rural area, miles and miles of empty cotton fields just waiting to be planted. The towns themselves were like something out of a *Twilight Zone* episode. Picture a

1950's era smallish Main Street with a handful of storefronts, diners and businesses, and angled parking. Then picture that street without any people, without any cars (parked or moving), boarded up or papered over storefront windows, and "closed" signs in those windows that still have some semblance of products on display (mostly second hand or consignment). All that was missing were old newspaper pages blowing down the street. In Indianola, we were hoping to get a bite to eat, but there were only two diners in town and only one of them was open. And it was operating out of what was clearly an old gasoline service station. Betty's Place. Having said that, we had some of the best ribs we have ever had, the owner was incredibly friendly and much to his wife's dismay, insisted on coming outside to throw the ball around for Porter. Another lunch place, located in an old general store along the highway near Lorman (The Old Country Store Restaurant), served up the best fried chicken we have ever had. It was so good we bought extra to take with us for the following day. But it too would never have received any ambiance/décor award. We also popped into a "typical southern" grocery store in Grenada to pick up some milk and a few staples. Very few brand names on the shelves, nothing along the lines of mineral water, and don't even think about Evian or Häagen Dazs. And at the meat counter? Very little beef. A few scrawny chickens. Some ham. And lots of chicken gizzards "for frying", chicken necks, smoked turkey necks, pork stomachs (folded up accordion style), fresh pig ears and something called "fresh pork fries". A Google search revealed those were pork testicles. I couldn't bring myself to ask if they had fresh beef marrow bones that I usually buy for Porter. Yet the people were ever so polite and friendly, even if the boy who carried out our groceries said, "You're not from around here are you?" Was it that obvious? Time to head north!

12.

LONG LIVE THE KING!

I DO NOT KNOW WHY I AM AN ELVIS FAN. He was 23 years old when I was born, already the star who would change music history. I certainly had no exposure to his music from my parents, since they were more about Prokofiev than Presley. I never made it to any of his concerts and only had one of his albums, but I can clearly remember the day he died. August 16, 1977. My older sister told me in a casual off-hand, kind of way, "Hey did you hear Elvis died?" and when my eyes teared up, she teased me mercilessly, "Dina is crying. Dina is crying." For the record, I was not crying. I teared up. There is a difference. And I'm not the rabid, cult-of-Elvis, never missed a commemorative vigil type fan. I'm more tongue-in-cheek, but still, a fan. I have always loved his voice and his music and would now have the opportunity to visit The King himself, albeit posthumously. We were going to Graceland!

However, before we got there we had to make a quick stop in Red Bay, Alabama. Where? Why? Red Bay is ground zero for the Tiffin Motor Coach Company. The place where all Tiffins are made and the place where Tiffin owners can go to get major or minor repairs done by the home team. Or to just tour the factory and watch new Tiffin coaches being made. Someone told me they make about 15 per day. (Insert big yawn here.) Our route was taking us so close to Red Bay, it would have been foolish not to stop in and take care of the few small issues that had cropped up. Fix broken window latch, check water pressure valve, retrieve tv remote that had fallen behind the fireplace (don't even ask how that happened). Tiffin has an interesting set up. They don't make service appointments but operate on a first come, first served basis. And depending on how busy they are (and the level of repairs required) people can find themselves there for a few days or a few weeks. But it all runs very smoothly. They have a large "campground" (really just a huge parking lot with full hook-ups) and upon check in at reception, customers are assigned a site number and provided with paperwork where they list all their repair issues. The following morning, Norris (who had such a southern drawl I could scarcely understand what he was saying) comes by to go over the list and advises how long the wait will be. We were told two or three days. Okay. Now what? We wandered around chatting with some of the other Tiffin owners and started thanking our lucky stars that our problems were so trivial. No structural cracks in the body, no need to replace engine compartment doors, no seized slide-outs, no leaking roof. Granted some of these people had older models but still, the possible future calamities were too depressing to contemplate so we looked for something more positive to do. Mother Nature had plans of her own.

It was very warm and large thunderclouds were forming. At 4pm a siren went off. It was at this exact time that most of the Tiffin employees were heading for their vehicles to go home so we naively thought it was just an end-of-shift whistle. Sort of like in the Flintstones when Fred finishes his workday at the Bedrock quarry. But then at 4:30, that same siren went again only this time accompanied by a broadcast message advising everyone to head to the closest tornado shelter. What?!?! Where is it? Are they serious? Should we go? Our neighbours to one side came out and asked the same questions. We looked up and down the rows of neatly parked coaches and didn't see anyone heading for higher ground, so we stayed put as well. Torrential downpour, hail, strong winds and it was over. On the news they announced that a tornado had passed just east of us by 8 miles. Okay then. That was enough excitement in Red Bay. We decided that the next day we would go further afield to keep ourselves occupied, even though the further afield options were only marginally more interesting than hanging out in a trailer park with tornados on the horizon. No matter how much we want to dress things up by calling them luxury land yachts, when it comes to acts of nature, there is no difference between us and the dentally-deficient guy living in the doublewide.

Bright and early next morning, we started with a short drive to Tupelo, Mississippi, birthplace of The King. Might as well get this pilgrimage started at the source. As expected, there wasn't much left other than the restored home he had been born in. A tiny two room wood frame that Elvis' father Vernon built when his mother Gladys was expecting, typical of poor rural southern homes of the time. Of course the house is not in its original location and a small museum and gift shop are located close by, but it was interesting to see the humble beginnings of this great entertainer and certainly provided some insight into his future lifestyle choices and behaviour. We also drove past the hardware store where Gladys bought Elvis his first guitar on his 11th birthday. Apparently he wanted either a rifle or a bicycle but she deemed those to be too dangerous. Thank-you

Gladys. The family moved to Memphis when Elvis was 13 so his history in Tupelo is quite brief.

Next stop, Ivy Green in the town of Tuscumbia, birthplace of Helen Keller. For those who have forgotten (or never knew), Helen Keller was born a healthy little girl in 1880 but at the age of 19 months was struck by an illness (probably scarlet fever or rubella) that left her completely blind and deaf, and with limited speech. In effect, incapable of communicating with any one in any way. At the age of 7 she was introduced to Ann Sullivan, who as a teacher and companion, taught her sign language and braille amongst other forms of communication. Keller became the first blind-deaf person to attain a baccalaureate degree and went on to become an author, lecturer and strong political activist (especially for women's suffrage, civil liberties and the rights of blind and disabled persons). An excellent movie starring Patty Duke and Anne Bancroft, *The Miracle Worker,* depicts her struggle. So we drove over to her homestead and walked around a bit reading up on her life and accomplishments. The exhibits themselves were of a dated and somewhat amateurish quality, and the entire outing took no more than 30 minutes. I had somehow expected more. I'm not exactly sure more of what, but just more. More details? More accolades? More recognition? Perhaps given the rights so many of us take for granted today, we forget the work and struggles of these early pioneers.

NO POODLES OR LAPDOGS ALLOWED.

And then the highlight of our stay in Alabama – a visit to the Coon Dog Cemetery. It is the only one of its kind in the world. I kid you not. Not only does it exist, but at the Alabama Visitor's Centre, you can pick up a pamphlet that describes its inception and the requirements for burial. Located out in the country not too far from the town of Cherokee, it was founded in 1937 by a man (Key Underwood) whose love for his faithful coon dog Troop was so great, he buried him out in the wilderness by a popular camp where they had hunted together for 15 years. Other hunters soon started doing the same, and today more than 300 coon hounds are interred in this quiet forest clearing. Underwood was once asked why other dogs could not be buried there and he replied, "You must not know much about coon hunters and their dogs, if you think we would contaminate this burial place with poodles and lap dogs." Ouch. In order to have the privilege of such eternal rest, three criteria must be met. 1) the owner must claim that their dog was an authentic coon dog. 2) a witness must declare that the deceased was a coon dog, and 3) a member of the Key Underwood Coon Dog Memorial Graveyard Inc. must be allowed to view the coon dog and declare it as such. What can I say? Let sleeping dogs lie? We didn't really know much about coon dogs prior to going but we sure know about them now. Coon Dogs are hounds, trained specifically to hunt racoons (at night) and this American "sport" is a holdover from Colonial times. There are various breeds of these dogs but all can trace their lineage back to English foxhounds (except the Plott Coonhound that goes back to boar hunting Germany). The last big funeral was in 2011 when a world-champion black and tan from Illinois was buried. Over 400 mourners with a processional stretching over half a mile. They take "man's best friend" to a whole new level here.

After all these stimulating sojourns, we thought we'd better sleep in the next day and rest up for another round, but the phone rang at 8am. Our coach was due in service-bay #10. What time? Right now? Big scramble! They have 47 bays at this Tiffin hub, each staffed by 3 technicians. The guys were very friendly, and Tiffin encourages all owners to stick around during the service, watch the work being done and ask as many questions as desired. I couldn't stand so much excitement, so John stayed while I went to the owner's lounge, a spacious area complete with huge comfy couches, television, kitchenette and a pet friendly and pet free side. Very civilized. The work was completed in less than 3 hours without any problems and we were on our way. Memphis here we come!

Now although Memphis is to a large extent associated with Graceland, there is considerably more to it than that, so we divided our time between the Elvis Pilgrimage, the continued Blues Trail and the history of Rock and Roll at Sun Studios. John even managed to get in a tour of the Gibson guitar factory but thankfully walked away without any major purchases. We started at Graceland and I am at a bit of a loss in trying to describe what we saw and experienced. Graceland itself is the home/mansion that Elvis lived in, along with (at various times) his parents, grandmother, wife, daughter and entourage. Built in 1939, it originally belonged to a University of Tennessee doctor/professor and his high society wife. They were the ones who originally called it Graceland, but Elvis liked the name so much it stuck. By today's standards the house is not all that grand and is literally frozen in time, with nothing having changed from the day Elvis died. Formica counter tops in the kitchen and shag carpeting throughout, including on the ceiling (although they say that was for acoustic purposes since they did do some recording there.) It is the second most visited home in the nation, surpassed only by the White House. Elvis had wanted to live out in the country where he could have some measure of privacy, far from the frantic and fanatical fans, but being busy with his filming schedule, he had his parents do the leg work and they were the ones who actually found the place. At that time, it was literally out in the country, with cows grazing in the fields all around. They bought it in 1957 – on 13.8 acres for $103,500.00. But Memphis expanded and today the compound is situated in a less than toney suburban part of town on the east side of Elvis Presley Boulevard. And Elvis Presley Boulevard itself is really a busy 6-lane major traffic artery. The property is surrounded by a huge stone wall that acts as a barrier between the manicured gardens on the inside, and the fast food joints and muffler shops on the outside. Tours of the mansion's main floor, outbuildings and grounds are available for a considerable fee. The second floor is off limits as that was not only Elvis' private living space but also the place where he died. Following his death, he was buried beside his mother in the local cemetery but two years later, his father had both bodies moved to the meditation garden at Graceland in order to preserve some level of privacy and dignity. Visiting Graceland left me feeling rather sad. Especially considering the type of person it seems Elvis was. Naïve (and at the same time quirky), shy, polite, trusting, generous to a fault, and by all accounts a nice person. All he cared about was music, performing and taking care of his family and friends. Coming from incredible poverty, neither he nor his parents were savvy, sophisticated business types and this made them vulnerable to those in the music industry who knew a cash cow when they saw one, especially his manager Colonel Parker. This is not to say that "The Pelvis" was an angel. He was not. He was quite a hound dog himself, enjoying the excesses that fame brought. But he was also surrounded by sycophants and hangers-on who simply lived off his success and generosity. Including his own personal physician who in the last 8 months of Elvis' life, prescribed over 8,300 pills, all in order to ensure that Elvis would make it through one more performance. Most reports state that Elvis died of a heart attack although at post-mortem it was found he had more than ten times the acceptable level of codeine in his body. Thank-you Dr. Tragic. Sad. An unparalleled loss to the world of music.

And forty years after Elvis' death, it seems family/associates are still desperately trying to get the goose to lay just one more golden egg. Across from the actual Graceland estate, on the other side of Elvis Presley Boulevard, an extensive complex dedicated to his achievements just opened up, with ex-wife Priscilla cutting the ceremonial ribbon. It is comprised of huge pavilions, each housing mementos and treasures from The King's life. One for all his cars, one for all his motorcycles and other motor toys, one for all his gold records and awards, one for all his over-the-top costumes, one for his army years and one for all the accolades from current and past musicians. (Keith Richards said that with Elvis' arrival the world changed from black and white to vivid colour, while John Lennon said that before Elvis there was nothing.) And each and every pavilion with its own accompanying gift shop full of Elvis souvenirs. Mugs, t-shirts, scarves, socks, jackets, sunglasses, stuffed toys, calendars, pencils, jewellery, decorative plates. Whatever you could put his name, face or signature on, it's there. And of course, all his recordings and DVDs. I bought a two-part biography by Peter Guralnick that details his rise (*Last Train to Memphis*) and demise (*Careless Love*). It makes for some interesting reading. A combination of the times, the advances in technology and his incredible talent made it all possible. But as Elvis himself said, "The image is one thing and the human being is another. It's very hard to live up to an image." I still find him fascinating, still love his music, yet at the same time, find it depressing to see how this incredible talent was manipulated both in life and in death. It is unlikely anyone such as him will come along again.

THE MUSICAL GATES AT GRACELAND. I EVEN WORE MY BLUE SUEDE SHOES.

Yet despite the overarching presence of Elvis, there is a lot of other history in Memphis. It is where Memphis Blues were born. It is where Rock 'n Roll was born. And sadly, where Martin Luther King Jr. was killed. Memphis Blues differ from Delta Blues in that they incorporate more instruments in their sound (eg. harmonica), although not as many as heard in Chicago Blues. And Beale Street is where many of the original Delta bluesmen migrated in order to make a living. From around the 1920's and into the 1950's, big names like Louis Armstrong, Muddy Waters, and Memphis Minnie could be heard throughout the clubs that lined both sides of street. It was here that Riley B. King earned his moniker as the Beale Street Blues Boy, eventually shortening it to B.B. King and going on to international acclaim. Located in a predominantly black neighbourhood, with black businesses and black clubs, frequented by members of the black community who were forbidden by segregation to hang out elsewhere, Beale Street was the place to go for great music, great nightlife and more than the occasional murder. Unfortunately, by the 1960s the area was in serious decline with many of the clubs having closed and many businesses boarded up. And the race riots that broke out prior to and following the assassination of Dr. King lead to a further economic spiral from which there was no recovery until the mid 1980s. Today, it is a major tourist attraction with lots of neon lights, blues clubs and restaurants, and at less than 2 miles long, very walkable. But at the same time, somehow missing that spark one would expect from such a music mecca. Perhaps we were just there at the wrong time or perhaps today's musicians just can't replace those giants have long since moved on.

However, one place where the presence of those early musicians still lingers is Sun Studios on Union Street. The main floor is a café cum t-shirt shop, but upstairs is a small museum with memorabilia depicting the work of Sam Phillips as he introduced the world to rock and roll, blending blues with country music. Long before Elvis walked through the door, Phillips was cutting records for B.B. King, Howlin' Wolf and Ike Turner. And after Elvis, he continued recording with Johnny Cash, Carl Perkins, Jerry Lee Lewis and Roy Orbison. In the café hangs a huge framed black and white photograph, referred to as the "million dollar photo" of a young Elvis sitting at the piano, surrounded by young Cash, young Perkins and young Lewis, taken during an early recording session well before any of them hit the big time. It's hard to take your eyes off it. And the basement houses the actual recording studio where it is possible to stand exactly where these greats stood as they recorded those tunes that changed our musical world. It is even possible to hold the microphone that Elvis used, although our tour guide did caution us to please not kiss it or use it to engage in any other sort of sexualized activity. He said we wouldn't believe what some of the more fervent fans are capable of, even these many years later. The studio is still used by numerous artists today, with U-2 having recently left a drum set behind in case they need it when they return. It's enough to give you goose bumps.

We also spent a fair bit of time in the Blues Hall of Fame that although not huge, provided an excellent overview of the early artists, not just from an historical and pictorial perspective, but from a hands-on acoustic one as well. It's the sort of place you could easily spend an entire day. And to give it an even more positive review, when we walked in with Porter, the staff said, "Oh, he looks like a Service Dog. Come on in." Perhaps those weren't the exact words, but it was a very dog-friendly place. And just across the street is the Lorraine Hotel/Civil Rights Museum. I have to confess that I know very little about the civil rights movement in the United States and even less about the assassination of Dr. Martin Luther King Jr. I attribute that to two things. One, I was only 10 years old when he was killed and world events such as this were beyond my interest, scope and understanding. I was more concerned with perceived injustices in my own home between my older sister and myself. Why did she get to stay up later than me?

And two, negative race relations were just not within my life experience. I grew up quite sheltered in a middle-class, suburban, predominantly white neighbourhood. I had a black girlfriend in grade school, ran track & field with a black friend in middle school, and was casual friends with a black guy in high school, but was blissfully ignorant of what was transpiring south of the border. Of course I was aware of the differences in our skin colour, but it just did not occur to me that skin colour was a basis for discrimination. Things like that had happened long ago and far away. Talk about naïve. On April 4th 1968, Dr. King was shot as he stood on the balcony just outside his room at the Lorraine Hotel. He had gone to Memphis to support striking black sanitation workers and was preparing to go out for dinner that evening when James Earl Ray, crouched in the washroom of a rooming house across the street, shot him in the back of the neck. King was 39 years old and his strategy of peaceful civil disobedience to effect change seems to have faded. The hotel is now part of the Civil Rights Museum and although we did not go into the museum itself, it was poignant to be standing at the spot where this tragedy played out.

Lingering in Memphis was great, but we were very much aware of how quickly the days were flying by and we didn't want to exceed our allotted 183 days on the U.S. side of the border. Consequently, we chose to skip Nashville on the road home. We did see the Grand Ole' Opry from the interstate that runs right past it and perhaps if we had been attending a performance of some kind it would have been worth the stop, but to just go look at the building... no. Our destination was Cleveland where we stayed with one of my childhood friends from Sidrabene days, Andi, and his lovely wife Cindy. I felt old acknowledging that Andi and I have known each other for almost 50 years. How can that be? They showed us around Cleveland, and we were really impressed with both the downtown food market (similar to St. Lawrence Market in Toronto only in a much nicer building) and with the incredible restored theatre district. Five huge theatres all brought back to their 1920s glory days complete with gold leaf decorative trim and huge marble columned lobbies. We toured Hofbrauhaus where Andi has a business interest and we'd be most happy to see that enterprise brought to Toronto. Prost! And then we were off to the Rock and Roll Hall of Fame. What better way to end this music themed month than with a visit to a venue dedicated to all the great rock and rollers. All I can say is that I can't believe we have lived so close for so many years (it's really only a 6-hour drive by car from Toronto) and never checked it out. Everything from the early roots of rock including gospel, r&b, bluegrass and folk, to fifties, soul and heavy metal. And the legends: Elvis, the Beatles, Rolling Stones, Janis Joplin, Jimi Hendrix. And the guys behind the music: Les Paul, Alan Freed, Sam Phillips. It's interesting that both Memphis and Cleveland claim to be the birthplace of rock 'n roll, although as best as I can figure it out, Memphis is where Sam Phillips first started recording this new sound, while Cleveland is where disc jockey Alan Freed first used the term to describe the music he was sending out over the airwaves. And it was music that was not necessarily well received. The Hall has many quotes by people during the early fifties who were beside themselves with the wickedness of this new genre. It seems comical now, but these folks really believed what they were saying. "Rock and roll is the means of pulling the white man down… It is a plot to undermine the morals of the youth of our nation." Wow. Consider me immoral. And another interesting tidbit – the actual phrase "rock and roll" was code for sexual intercourse in early blues music, first heard in Trixie Smith's 1922 recording of *My Daddy Rocks Me (With One Steady Roll)*. Definitely immoral. I can't begin to list everything there is to see, learn and experience. Another one of those places where an entire day can easily disappear. We vowed to return.

And now, another confession. Or more accurately, an embarrassing admission and heartfelt apology. We have all heard stories about people who, blithely following the instructions of their GPS, turn off perfectly good roads and drive into rivers, fields or in Europe, end up in wrong countries. And we laugh at their stupidity. Well, it turns out that we are amongst those stupid people – although we weren't following GPS but rather, Google Maps. And we didn't end up in the wrong country but rather, the wrong state. I suppose it was mostly my fault, but I am blaming John for not double checking my coordinates. Leaving Cleveland, we had arranged to drop in for the evening to visit with friends who live in Troy, Ohio. Yes, we reassured them, we are leaving now and will be at your place around 4pm. Get the BBQ ready! I put their address into Google Maps and off we went. Just after 4pm, we had navigated the incredibly badly potholed roads around Detroit and were closing in on their address northwest of the city, congratulating ourselves that we were going to be on time. But then, when we were within a mile of their house, the address on Google Maps changed. It went from being Seneca Street to Serena Street. No, no, no. That can't be right. Type it in again. Nope. No more Seneca. Those with a more in-depth knowledge of U.S. geography will have probably caught on that Detroit is in Michigan. And Michigan is considerably north of Ohio. To make a painfully mortifying story short, upon entering their address into Google Maps, I had just clicked on the first Troy that popped up. The one in Michigan. Troy, Ohio was a little further down the list, and about a 4-hour drive south of where we found ourselves. OMG! It's bad enough when you mess up, get lost and inconvenience yourself, but something totally different when you inconvenience someone else. And have to own up to it. So, to our dear friends in Troy, Ohio, once again, we are so, so sorry. However, there is some truth to the saying that every cloud has a silver lining. Troy, Michigan is actually not that far from where John's aunt lives. We had planned to visit with her en route home, but a quick call had us parked in her driveway that very evening. Thank goodness for Aunt Katherine. We had a lovely visit and she e-mailed us later to advise that having the coach parked in her drive had generated a fair bit of chatter amongst the neighbours, including speculation about an upcoming vacation, as well as some wishes from a little boy who longed to live and travel like us so that he wouldn't have to go to school!

The following evening, we pulled into Sidrabene, and set up in our "usual" spot. Things certainly looked bare compared to when we left the previous summer, and spring was definitely several weeks behind what we had experienced further south. From Mississippi to Alabama, through Tennessee and Kentucky, we were constantly just on the cusp of warmer weather. The trees were in a perpetual phase of emerging leaves and the Redbuds and Mountain Dogwoods were in full bloom. But somewhere around northern Kentucky it started to look rather bleak and by the time we reached Ohio and Michigan, it was pretty much like Ontario. Gray, drizzly, cool days and cold nights. The land yacht was equipped with both electric and propane heaters, so the ambient temperature was warm and cozy. But the ceramic floor? Not so much. It was freezing since there was no insulation underneath. Some coaches do come equipped with heated floor tiles but that was one option we didn't go for. Hindsight is twenty-twenty. We jokingly proposed that when we got to Alaska, we would pick up some fur pelts and strew them about. But it was great to be back, catching up with friends and family and taking a bit of a break from the road. Easter was spent at my parent's house and it was odd, being the first year John and I did not host Easter Sunday dinner. Even though it's a fair-sized coach at 38 feet, that would have been a little bit too tight a squeeze. And then we started making "the list". There was so much to take care of. Coach for service, car for service, computer for service, repair cracked car windshield, clean carpets, doctor appointments, dentist appointments, hair appointments, submit income tax, bikes in for a tune up, need a new bike hitch, need kayak covers, re-pack and purge (again). And most importantly, spend time with family and friends. May was going to be a busy month.

13.

HAPPY ANNIVERSARY!

IT WAS HARD TO BELIEVE, BUT COME JUNE WE HAD BEEN LIVING IN THE LAND YACHT FOR AN ENTIRE YEAR! It seemed like just yesterday that we were, with no small degree of trepidation, pulling away from our bricks and mortar home and embarking on our temporarily nomadic lifestyle. Two sayings come to mind. "Time flies when you are having fun" and "As you get older, time goes by faster." A fantastic three hundred and sixty-five revolutions of our little blue planet passed in the blink of an eye. Another saying also fits. "Never go on trips with anyone you do not love." We learned a great deal during the first twelve months. About ourselves, about travelling, about RV life, about family, about friendships both old and new. And given that the entire month of May was spent parked at Sidrabene, we had time to reflect a bit and review both the highs and the lows of the year gone by. The best places we visited as well as the not-worth-it-places, what we'd do differently, what we missed, what we didn't.

Being able to situate ourselves at Sidrabene again was a blessing. We were able to take care of the many housekeeping and maintenance issues on our "to do" list, (both vehicular and personal) and spent as much time with family and friends as we possibly could. It was an odd state of affairs. Although we met and made friends with many wonderful people during our travels (some of whom we have stayed in touch with), there is something about seeing familiar faces that adds an additional layer of comfort to get-togethers. Whether attending our condo board's annual general meeting and chatting with the neighbours, or taking part in the spring clean-up day at Sidrabene (in Latvian known as the "*talka*") there is a sense of belonging, a sense of grounding that is missing when you are constantly on the move. Lunches, dinner parties, barbeques, breakfast meets, book club meets, coffee dates and Christenings. We treasured them all, trying to pack a year's worth of socializing into six weeks. Having said that, we were also itching to get going on the next leg of the journey, this time across Canada to British Columbia where the plan was to regroup prior to heading towards southern California when the weather turned cold. Our route had not been planned out in as much detail as the first year but that was simply because we knew that heading into Florida required advanced accommodation bookings. Canada would afford us much more flexibility and we hoped to be dipping our toes in the Pacific Ocean by September.

Spring in Sidrabene was beautiful despite starting off on a rather soggy note. The rain was torrential and unrelenting, the air was quite cool and at times we questioned the wisdom of returning to the great white north so early. "April showers bring May flowers?" I think not. More like deluges and torrents with the odd soggy daffodil thrown in. I can't claim to have ever spent much time at Sid during the spring, but I have never seen the waterways so swollen. Dead Man's Creek, which I always thought was just a dry gully, had turned into a river. The water level in Indian Creek was such that it over-flowed the road that leads to the cottages, making motor vehicle access impossible. The culvert underneath the dance floor became clogged with debris so water gushed all over the surface and down the embankment. And a huge puddle, bordering on a pond, started forming beside our yacht. Perhaps the yacht's water referenced moniker was about to become literal. At one point, the creek was flowing so fast and the water level rising so quickly, we packed up and put the coach into travel ready mode just in case we needed to move to higher ground in a hurry. It was certainly a far cry from the unseasonably hot and dry spring we experienced there the year before. Thankfully things eased up a bit and the promised May flowers arrived. Trilliums, Lily-of-the-Valley, Forge-Me-Nots, Lilacs of purple and white variety, apple and crabapple blossoms, tulips, daffodils and narcissus. And all the trees a beautiful bright shade of green that only lasts through spring. It was wonderful. And the birds! Baltimore Orioles, Red Breasted Grosbeaks, Goldfinches, Housefinches, Cedar Waxwings, Robins and Blue Jays. Even a Pileated Woodpecker. All singing their hearts out, some with considerably more melodious voices than others.

But we didn't just walk around admiring nature's beauty. There was work to be done as well. The rocking horse head at the children's playground, that we had so lovingly restored the year before, didn't make it through the fall much less the winter but that wasn't a complete surprise. We knew while repairing it that being made from particleboard, it was vulnerable to the elements and despite using as much sealant as possible, moisture got into the wood and the poor horse literally lost his head. So John formed another one out of more solid plywood and I set to painting again, hoping this one would be a bit more durable. John also helped the groundskeeper here and there with a few odd jobs, and during the *talka* he repaired baseboards in the great hall while I helped paint the new storage shed by the church. If work can be considered "fun", it was just that. "Fun" to be part of a community again. It was something we sorely missed while on the road.

And then we went to school. Cooking school that is. We had an opportunity to attend a workshop, where one of the Latvian community's most experienced and respected cooks taught about 30 of us how to bake traditional Latvian "*klingeris.*" This is a type of yeast based sweet bread, flavoured with saffron, cardamom, citrus and raisins, served at special occasions be they birthdays, weddings or other commemorative gatherings. There is a real art to making *klingeris* correctly and the uninitiated churn out all manner of substandard product that guests quietly criticize under their breath. Too dry, too yeasty, too many raisins, not enough raisins, on and on it goes. John and I had tried to make it in the past ourselves, with less than stellar results (actually a complete disaster) so a chance to learn from the master was one we were not about to pass up. Bright and early one Saturday morning, we were all gathered at the café, pencils in hand, ready to take copious notes on exactly how much of this and how much of that was necessary to make the perfect *klingeris.* Chef Ausma explained how the morning was going to unfold and then started with the ingredients. First, three egg yolks. You can use whole eggs if you like, but her preference is just the yolks. We dutifully wrote that down. Then you will need some salt. She poured a quantity into her hand and sprinkled it into the bowl. Near bedlam ensued. "What?" "How much was that?" "Did she measure it?" "Was that a teaspoon?" "It looked like more!" "Calm down. Calm down. That was about a teaspoon." Well I saw exactly what was in her hand and there was no way that was a teaspoon. More like a tablespoon. Okay, we got through that and moved on. Now the flour. Start with about one cup. More bedlam. "What?" "That's not a cup measure! That's a coffee cup!" "It was mounded!" "How much flour was that?" And so it went.

Such is the way of the masters. They have done it so often for so long, it is all a matter of touch and as Ausma said, we novices will learn by trial and error to get the right feel for the dough. It was a wonderful community learning experience, the finished product

THE FINISHED PRODUCT.

turned out great and I'm sure I speak for the group when I say that we all left with a sense of confidence and optimism that one day, we too will be able to bake if not the perfect *klingeris,* at least a reasonable facsimile thereof. *Paldies* Ausma!

And as we started our second year, what else had we learned? We learned that John is a saint with infinite patience while I am a mere mortal given to bouts of occasional Tourette's. That may be a slight exaggeration. In reality, we supported each other although he may have done a bit more of the heavy lifting. I have no tolerance for uncooperative computers and rely on John to rescue me from whatever hole I have over- clicked my way into. It has happened more than once. On the road, our roles and responsibilities evolved along fairly stereotypical lines. He took care of most of the mechanical and vehicular things, as well as all of the driving. There was no way I was going to get behind the wheel of the beast. I took care of most of the domestic and social things, as well as destination ideas. We both took care of Porter. Some friends wondered if it was difficult to live in such close proximity 24/7. In two words, "Not really." That requires an explanation. Perhaps it is just the nature of our relationship, but we never felt the need to "get away" from the other. This is not to say we didn't do things apart. We did, but not as an escape. More just an interest thing. I might go for a walk to take photographs while John stayed by the campsite reading or playing guitar. Or John took Porter for a walk while I stayed "home" blogging. The difficulty of close quarters only came into play when we were physically inside the coach. The living/kitchen area was fine but in retrospect, if we were to buy this thing all over again, I would consider conceding to John's suggestion that we get the 40-footer with a bigger bathroom. Or at least one with double sinks. And a bigger bedroom. Or at least one with a king bed. And a bit more closet space. Other than that, no complaints. When it came to the actual travelling, we learned that choosing destinations and the best way to reach them was best done together. That way there was less chance of heading off in the wrong direction or under-estimating driving times. And no-one to point fingers at. If we messed up, we messed up together (except when differentiating between Ohio and Michigan – that was my fault). And en route, if we got to a destination ahead of schedule, we stayed put instead of "pushing on". Weather and road conditions can change quickly and driving the yacht at night along winding roads through pouring rain while pulling a car with kayaks on the roof and bikes on the back is not fun.

In terms of our favourite places to visit, and ones that we hope to return to: Key West, Dry Tortugas National Park and New Orleans. Key West for its laid back, casual approach to life (and close proximity to excellent snorkelling), Dry Tortugas for its beautiful solitude and New Orleans for music, food and culture. Places we could have done without? It's hard to say. While we could have spent less time in Cornwall and didn't appreciate some of the "Frattitude" in the Gaspé, we were still glad we went and had the chance to see and experience those parts of the country. That is partly what this journey was all about. Seeing the everyday, not just what is promoted in travel brochures. One thing we did not miss was the insanity that continues to accompany and reinforce political correctness. Living in travel mode, we didn't follow the news with too much attention and people we bumped into were more interested in talking about great hikes and sights as opposed to perceived slights and historical wrongs. Obviously we were aware of current world events but more on a macro level. If the Russians attacked, we'd know about it. That said, staying put during May saw us reading the paper on a daily basis and watching the nightly news. I could only shake my head in amazement at how many new and novel ways there are for people to join the cult of the perpetually offended, and how eager the media are to inflate the importance of contrived angst. Arguments over "cultural appropriation" and whether or not uniformed police officers should be allowed to march in the Toronto gay pride parade. Even why the first lady doesn't hold the U.S. President's hand. Really?!? As John said, turning nonsense into news. We were more than ready to take another break from that!

And a note about keeping a monthly blog. My blog started out with three objectives. First as a journal for ourselves so that at the end of the trip, we would have a record of not just what we saw, but what we felt and experienced along the way. Second, as a way to keep family and friends apprised of where we were and what we were doing. And third, as a way to keep in touch with family and friends so that we would know where they were and what they were doing. Somewhere along the way, the blog also morphed into a motivational entity. There were times when I didn't feel like writing and laziness set in. But knowing I had a deadline (self-imposed as it was) and knowing that there were people who enjoyed reading about our exploits, gave me the incentive to sit down, gather my thoughts, do a bit of typing, and then organize and edit the photographs. Without this process, we would have just ended up with a huge jumbled mess of images and random memories. The effort was well worth it.

14.

OF MICE AND MEN AND BUTTERFLIES

SCOTTISH POET ROBERT BURNS WROTE THAT THE BEST LAID PLANS OF MICE AND MEN OFTEN GO AWRY. To be more precise, he actually wrote, "The best-laid schemes o' mice an' men/ Gang aft a-gley" and that was in his poem, "*To a Mouse, on Turning Her Up in Her Nest by a Plough, November 1785*," but really, that is neither here nor there. It's just a side note, if you will. All I know is that Burns' sentiment described our situation to a tee. Our June plans definitely went "a-gley." We had anticipated pulling out of Sidrabene on the 8th to start our westward journey via northern Ontario with a few stops along the north shore of Lake Superior. We didn't even come close. First, one of John's aunts passed away and the service was scheduled for the 10th. Naturally we wanted to go and pay our respects, and at that point time was not really an issue. A couple of days in a three-year-plan was not going to make all that much difference. It was nice to see all the cousins but as is often the case with large families, regrettable that it took a sad occasion to bring everyone together again. Then, our tenants called and advised there was a problem in the second-floor laundry room as it related to the clothes dryer. Apparently, the plastic vent cover on the outside wall had broken off and some enterprising birds capitalized on this new access point to make themselves at home, complete with a cozy nest inside the ductwork. That would be the ductwork that leads from the wall outside to the dryer inside. To compound the matter, the plastic cover was supposedly connected to the duct itself by way of an extension somewhere inside the wall. That connection had become detached. Did I mention "somewhere inside the wall?" The duct cleaning contractor was not sure of the specific location. Rectifying the situation would require cutting through drywall inside the laundry room, reattaching the ductwork, and then patching and repainting the drywall. We decided we best hang around a bit to at least make sure we were happy with the work. And then I had a medical issue pop up where my doctor decided to send me to a specialist, and our medical system is far from speedy. So by the 8th, we knew that we would not be leaving until at least the 21st, possibly later. No way we were going to make the Calgary Stampede. What to do now?

First, get in some regular biking. While Appleby Line in Burlington is a bit dicey traffic-wise, with narrow pot-holed shoulders, and motorists and gravel trucks seemingly oblivious to the 70 km/h speed limit, Walkers Line and Bell School Line up around Rattlesnake Point are less travelled. Both incorporate some pretty good ups and downs that definitely gave our legs and our lungs a work-out. And it was very scenic to boot with all manner of wildflowers lining the roadway. We even stumbled upon an old pioneer cemetery with burials from the early 1800s. Unfortunately, the weather was not that cooperative, and the regular biking became somewhat sporadic. Then we did some hiking up the Niagara Escarpment and along the Bruce Trail to Mount Nemo, starting off near the intersection of Walkers Line and No.2 Sideroad. There is a small yet convenient parking lot directly opposite the country cemetery where as teens, we used to sneak away from camp to go and scare the bejesus out of each other. I had not been up that way for years and it brought back some great memories of camp expeditions, complete with hot dog cookouts and lemonade that tasted faintly of Clorox bleach. (I think the lemonade was made of Realemon, sugar and water, with the bleach used to kill off any bacteria!) When our son was a camper, they actually practiced rock climbing and rappelling down the cliff faces of the escarpment but those were not activities on anyone's radar back in "my day." The view from the top was still quite scenic and although the city has grown considerably closer, by-laws and zoning should prevent it from encroaching much further. In most places the trail was fairly level but there were a few sections where Porter needed some assistance getting up and down the ladders. We were careful to keep him away from the numerous fissures and crevasses, as well as the cliff edge because the drop is easily 100 feet. The odd inattentive hiker has died from the drop after straying too close to the lip, but Porter is quite an obedient dog, so we had no issues there. The Bruce Trail itself actually runs from Niagara Falls all the way up to Tobermory on Georgian Bay, but I think it is at its best through the Burlington/Milton areas. And being quite close to many urban centres, it was surprising we saw so few people. Maybe it needs to be promoted it a bit more.

Another day we decided to tackle a longer hike from Rattlesnake Point to Crawford Lake, a distance of about 15 kms return. Although the Bruce Trail runs along the escarpment's edge there as well, offering up some pretty expansive views, the Halton Conservation Authority maintains a parallel trail (the Nassagaweya) that has less roots and rocks than the Bruce and is easier on the knees. So we took the path more travelled but were still pretty tired at the end of it all. Hiking aside, Crawford Lake is an interesting destination in its own right and can be easily reached via Guelph Line, if walking through the woods isn't your idea of a fun afternoon. It's a small, tree and cliff-lined lake, encircled by a boardwalk with several bench/rest areas to sit and enjoy the quiet solitude (although faint traffic noise from Guelph Line does intrude from time to time). The lake itself is pegged as a very rare meromictic lake. That is, its layers of water do not intermix (as opposed to a holomictic lake where at least once a year, surface water mixes with deep water at the bottom). Because of this, Crawford Lake has very little oxygenated water below 50 feet, in effect making it impossible for anything to live in the bottom 30 feet, and leaving all accumulated sediment virtually unchanged. That makes it the perfect time capsule for archaeologists wanting to know who and what was around the area in years gone by. By studying core samples, they found high levels of corn pollen deposited between the 12th and 15th centuries, and speculated that Iroquois Indians must have lived in close proximity. Sure enough, digs revealed the remains of an ancient Indian village about 1 kilometer from the shoreline. This village has now been re-constructed, complete with several longhouses, and made into a bit of a hands-on educational experience for life prior to contact. It is not an overly sophisticated exhibition but there were several school groups on a class trip, and it was obvious that both young and old alike enjoyed the experience. Or maybe the kids were just happy to be out a classroom. Probably the latter. Perhaps it was the location or perhaps it was the time of year, but we saw numerous butterflies flitting about, including Eastern Tiger Swallowtails and the largest butterflies in North America, Giant Swallowtails. Their wingspan was easily four inches across, and they were just beautiful.

And then it was *Jāni*. Although all our appointments had been taken care of by the 21st, we decided that since it was so close to the summer solstice celebration, we might as well stay the weekend and head out on the 26th. We'd be able to get in one more social event and save ourselves the trouble of trying to find a camping spot on the weekend. We helped out at the *talka* in preparation for the festivities and John managed to place himself on the receiving end of some poison ivy while trimming back the vegetation on the road in. Hands and legs! The weather was on the cool side but sunny overall, so everyone was happy. Many of the usual suspects were in attendance, daisy and oak leaf garlands were worn with various degrees of panache, traditional "*Jānu siers*" (homemade caraway seed cheese) and beer were enjoyed, and as per custom, the requisite singing and dancing went on into the early morning hours. Those early Latvian pagans knew a thing or two about having a good time. But if I am honest, the appeal of the whole thing was starting to wane. A considerable number of our friends and acquaintances no longer put in an appearance, and I didn't recognize many of the younger crowd who did. Perhaps it is just a passing of the torch and I am nostalgic for how things used to be. Or perhaps I should get out onto the dance floor a bit more.

ALL HITCHED UP AND READY TO START YEAR TWO!

We pulled out of Sid on the 26th. There is no question that we looked forward to leaving, but not with the same level of unbridled enthusiasm as the year before. The novelty of our new living arrangements and playing house in our cozy home on wheels had worn off, and despite our love of travel, we now had a greater appreciation for what we left behind. It is a totally different feeling being away for months as opposed to weeks. We had a last breakfast with Matejs in Oakville and then headed for the family cottage near Bracebridge so I could say bye to my mom. One night there, and we were off, well aware it would take us at least three days to get out of Ontario. We stopped for a break at the new visitor's centre where Hwy 69 crosses the French River and decided to go for a short 3-km hike. Why not? We weren't in a hurry and have crossed that bridge too many times in the past without checking out the surrounding terrain. Most of Canada's explorers, missionaries and fur traders (Brulé, Champlain, Jesuit martyrs, Coureurs de Bois) used the French River as a vital canoe route to get from the east to the west and in our past canoeing years, we had made a half-hearted effort to plan a few days on the water along these shores as well. That never came to fruition, but I haven't totally abandoned the idea. Maybe one day. The hike was okay although the path itself was very rocky with many exposed slippery roots and puddles from an earlier rain. We could hear thunder approaching and saw dark clouds gathering but made it down to the river and back before the real deluge began. Porter, of course, just wanted to stop and play in the water but the mosquitoes and blackflies were enough to keep us from lingering. A quick overnight in Sault Ste. Marie and we pressed on. We had opted to take highway 17 that hugs the shoreline of Lake Superior and is considerably more scenic than highway 11, which curves to the north and runs through North

Bay and Kapuskasing. And scenic it was. Fairly steep up and down grades along winding roads with panoramic views out over *Gitche Gumee*. Gordon Lightfoot is one of my all-time favourite troubadours and his epic *Wreck of the Edmund Fitzgerald* kept playing in my head – "*The legend lives on from the Chippewa on down, Of the big lake they call Gitche Gumee. Superior they said never gives up her dead when the gales of November come early.*" And didn't we just happen across the point where the famous laker went down. We had stopped at a scenic pull off at Alona Bay to admire the view and upon reading the information placards, learned that in 1975 the iron ore tanker Edmund Fitzgerald had sank 15 miles off shore of the point just to our south, with all 29 hands on board lost. And Canada's first uranium discovery in 1837 was on Theano Point just to our north. Lauren Harris of the Group of Seven spent much of his time painting along the north shore of Lake Superior and given its rugged beauty, we could see why. The only thing we couldn't see is why, given its relatively close proximity to the golden horseshoe, we had not spent more time up there. Well, we would find out soon enough, but first we had to get past Wawa and its iconic Canada Goose.

There is some dispute over the origins of the name "Wawa". Some say it is a corruption of the Ojibway (Anishnabe) word "*wawank*" meaning "clear water springs" while others say it is a corruption of the word "*wewe*" meaning "snow goose." In any event, the first Wawa goose statue was erected in 1960 as a means to lure people, travelling along the newly completed Trans-Canada highway, into town to spend a bit of money. Sadly, this first attempt was made of chicken wire and paper-maché, and given the winters in near northern Ontario, barely lasted two years. A second one was constructed of more durable material, but it too was starting to show its age. So this year, the third goose was going to be unveiled on Canada Day. And it certainly has achieved its purpose, being one of the most widely recognized city symbols. While we were there, they were just putting the final touches onto Wawa the Third, in preparation for its official launch. The original sits outside the general store in town while the second was cut up into sections with individual pieces going to wealthy benefactors who donated funds for the upgrade. Would that be the same as fabricating a chicken? We continued on just past the small community of Schreiber stopping for the night at Rainbow Falls Provincial Park, with our camping site right on the shore of the big lake. Which brings us back to why we may not have spent a lot of time up here. The location was beautiful enough and the fact that it was still relatively light out at 10pm only added to the allure. But we weren't the only ones enjoying the great outdoors. The blackflies were quite enjoying it as well. We have never experienced anything like it and can clearly see why these swarms of flies can drive forest animals mad. They were insidious. I had been wearing a loose t-shirt and the following morning, had a ring of red bite marks all around my neck. Almost like a ruby necklace, but then those at the front swelled up so that it looked like the beginnings of a goiter. Charming. Poor Porter's belly and groin were covered in angry red raised areas, and John even managed to get a bite on top of the poison ivy he was dealing with. This was the glamorous side of the adventure we were on. One thing is for certain, as much as I would like to return there and do some paddling, it isn't going to happen in the spring or summer. I'd rather have cold and no bugs than be warm and eaten alive.

We continued on towards Thunder Bay, passing all kinds of beautiful wildflowers growing along the side of the highway: Orange Hawkweed, Daisies, Buttercups and Lupines of purple, pink and white. But the weather was not on our side. We had hoped to spend some time checking out Thunder Bay and the surrounding area including Sleeping Giant Provincial Park as well as Kakabeka Falls (of which I have a vague child-hood memory) but the weather was just abysmal. The grey morning sky and light drizzle that we woke up to in Rainbow Falls had turned to a steady rain and the closer we got to town, the heavier it came down. By the time we entered the city limit, it had become a torrential downpour and we decided to push on. That is just as well. I had a lump in my throat through this whole stretch. I can't think of Thunder Bay without thinking of my older sister Benita who very tragically died there while studying nursing at Lakehead University. She was 23 years old and I was 21. Perception is such a strange thing. Even though that was oh so many years ago, in my mind, she is still older than me and can still kick my butt. I miss her..... Leaving Thunder Bay behind, the highway leads away from the shores of Lake Superior and the terrain became less dramatic and more rolling with shorter coniferous trees, numerous marshy areas and small shallow lakes. Very sparsely inhabited but with many moose crossing signs. We switched from the Eastern to the Central Time Zone and shortly afterwards, saw a sign indicating that we were now at a latitude where all water flows towards the Arctic Ocean. We were definitely no longer in Kansas. The weather eased and we stopped for the night in Dryden before pushing on towards Manitoba, "the friendly province." But not without pausing at Kenora's famous chip truck for lunch. I really needed those extra calories. Not!

15.

IT'S A CULTURAL THING

HAPPY CANADA DAY? A lot of ground was covered during the month of July. A lot. We commemorated Canada's sesquicentennial in Winnipeg and although we are not usually given to participating in huge group festivities, we decided to give this one a shot. It was, after all, 150 years. I'm not sure about how things went in the rest of the nation, but Winnipeg's effort was decidedly lacklustre. First, we went to a residential neighbourhood street party on Osborne Avenue (a fairly major artery) which had been shut down to vehicular traffic for the supposed celebration. The roadway was packed, with almost everyone in attendance sporting some variation on the red and white theme. But that was about it. Numerous vendors were set up along the centre line selling cheap body soaps, bargain basement clothing, dog treats and that sort of thing, two mediocre bands played at either end of the street and people just shuffled back and forth waiting for something to happen. It was like being at an outdoor flea market. In a word, boring. So we drove over to The Forks, at the confluence of the Red and Assiniboine Rivers (which have very silty/muddy water), in what is more downtown. The area has historical importance in that it has been a gathering place of sorts for over 6,000 years, starting with aboriginal peoples and moving on through European fur traders, Métis buffalo hunters, settlers and immigrants. Today, it is promoted as a major Winnipeg tourist destination but if you take away the historical significance, it is really just a nice 9-acre park on the river with a band shell and some sculptures. There were lots of people around, a Francophone band was on stage, a few food vendors were flogging mediocre foodstuffs and people just seemed to be hanging out, enjoying the day. But there certainly wasn't any energy. At least none that we could feel. Given that at this latitude it was still quite light out at 10pm (in fact even at 10:30, there was still a bright orange/fuschia glow to the west) the fireworks were set for 11, but we were party poopers and by 5pm had had enough. We returned to the land yacht that was set up at a campground in the countryside, less than 30 minutes south of town. As privately-owned RV places go, it was clean and quiet enough, although the sites themselves were so close together privacy was virtually non-existent. But we wanted to spend a week to really get a feel for Winnipeg, so it served its purpose.

From a cultural perspective, two things are very obvious in Winnipeg. There is a considerable Aboriginal presence there, and a strong French-speaking community. But the whole Aboriginal, French and Métis issue is very convoluted. I wish I had paid more attention in school although given how we are busy re-writing history these days I probably would have learned the wrong perspective anyway. This is how I currently understand it. In 1670, not too long after first contact, King Charles II gave the Hudson's Bay Company a charter, in effect control over all land and waters flowing into Hudson's Bay. Rupert's Land, as it was called. Obviously, the many indigenous peoples living in and around the area were not consulted. Most of the trappers and hunters that worked for the HBC were Scottish and French with a few Irishmen thrown into the mix. A great many married Aboriginal women, and their offspring and descendants became the Métis, belonging to neither the white nor the Indian communities. Over time, the Métis developed their own language and culture, adding an additional wrinkle to this already elaborate mosaic. And if it wasn't confusing enough, the Métis of the lower Red River area were of Scots descent with different customs, language and religion than those of the upper Red River who had French roots. Winnipeg, at the time called Fort Garry, was an important HBC trading post in the Red River Colony. Destroyed by a flood in 1823, it was rebuilt 30 kms to the north and re-named Lower Fort Garry. (More on Lower Fort Garry later.) Around the time of Confederation, the American Civil War had just ended, and the Americans were caught up in the frenzy of Manifest Destiny – i.e. that they should spread out across North America and pretty much grab anything in sight. This was of great concern to our first Prime Minister, Sir. John A. who, in order to prevent the Americans from thinking that north of the 49th parallel was easy pickings, became obsessed with building a railroad "from sea to shining sea", and thus ensuring fairly effortless access for European immigrants and settlers loyal to Canada. At this point Manitoba had not yet joined Confederation, HBC was negotiating to sell Rupert's Land to the new Dominion and the Métis were very upset that McDonald and his railroad surveyors were completely disregarding their several generation presence on the land. Enter Louis Riel.

Considered today to be the founder of Manitoba, Riel lead the Red River Rebellion (which was pretty mild by rebellion standards – more like a prolonged sit-in), ensuring that Métis concerns pertaining to rights and culture were addressed by the federal government. Shortly thereafter, Manitoba joined Confederation. Of course Riél couldn't leave well enough alone and fifteen years later lead another rebellion in present day Saskatchewan, for which he was convicted of high treason and hanged, partially because this uprising went beyond simple occupation and resulted in the killing of twelve North West Mounted Police officers. (Riél also had mental health issues and a serious messianic complex but his followers loved him anyway.) The sad thing is that many of those who took up arms were not rejecting Canada – they just wanted the same full and equal participation that was being given to others. In 1982, the Métis were legally recognized as one of Canada's three Aboriginal peoples, along with First Nations and Inuit. Back to Lower Fort Garry. Although it was the only fort ever built of stone in western Canada, it was really just an administrative centre for the HBC and the stone was used simply to make it look impressive. But despite its early-settler chic construction, everybody else stayed at the original Red/Assiniboine River location and continued trading, building and expanding. What gives Lower Fort Garry its dubious honour is that it was at this location, in 1871, that the first numbered treaty between six representatives of the Ojibway and Swampy Cree, and Canadian officials, was signed. Treaty No.1 (of more than 70) – the spirit and intent of which is still being disagreed upon today. No big surprise there. Of the six aboriginal signatories, two were supported by only half of their own people. The other half backed someone else, sought different terms and refused to comply. And somewhere in there were the Métis. It is no wonder that we are where we are today.

And on the theme of "why can't we all just get along," Porter spent a day at daycare while John and I checked out the National Museum for Human Rights. Opened in 2014, it is the only national museum located outside of the Ottawa area, and the only one of its kind in the world. Media mogul Israel Asper was the driving force behind its inception and to a large extent posthumously, its construction. Architecturally, it is interesting although very cavernous. We climbed the stairs up into the Tower of Hope to get a panoramic view out over Winnipeg and admired the Spanish alabaster ramp walls, lit from within, that gave them a warm glow. There are no right angles in the entire place, ostensibly to symbolize the fact that human rights cannot be put in a box. But other than the exhibits on the Jewish Holocaust under Hitler, and the Ukrainian Holodomor under Stalin, the content was often superficial, some politically correct and some downright ridiculous (although the curators maintain that the purpose of the museum is to generate discussion and dialogue so from that perspective, I suppose it works). Upon entering, a voice-over promoting the virtues of international human rights announces, "You shouldn't feel scared to say what is on your mind." Yeah right, I thought. Tell that to all the right-leaning intellectuals who are being pilloried for expressing views that go against the left-leaning social media mob. One exhibit has Alan Borovoy (of the Canadian Civil Liberties Union) expressing his dismay that then-Prime Minister Pierre Elliot Trudeau invoked the War Measures Act in order to contain the FLQ Crisis of 1970, and another addresses the 2012 angst of Quebec university students when it looked like the province was going to increase their ridiculously low tuition fees. Suggesting these are human rights issues somehow related to the horrors of true genocide and genuine human bondage is just intellectually dishonest. All in all, I'm glad we went and if you are on a road trip through Manitoba and find yourself in Winnipeg, it might be worth a stop. But I wouldn't say worth a specific detour.

One detour that we did take, however, was to locate some long-lost Latvians. My exposure to the Latvian experience has been from the perspective of those who fled Soviet occupation following the Second World War. But there had been an earlier exodus back in the late 1800s /early 1900s, with many Lettish (as they were then called) migrating to Canada, others to Brazil, all seeking a better life and a place to call their own. The Canadian contingent settled around the Winnipeg area where land purchase fell within their meagre means, clearing forests and setting up humble homesteads. Most of these early pioneers have long since melted into the larger community, and the farmland overtaken again by trees, but it was neat driving around the region and finding names that were clearly of Latvian origin: on street signs, cottage communities, even cemeteries: Lagsdin, Karklin, Kalnin, Grausdin. In the Lettonia cemetery, it was interesting to note however, that save for one, the inscriptions on the headstones did not have any Latvian dedications. All were in English and the one with the Latvian inscription was in old orthography and with a Polish surname! (It occurs to me that quite a few of our excursions included visits to cemeteries. I am not morbid. It's just that there is such a sense of history in these places.) I found a book written by one of these early settlers, describing life at the turn of the century in the Lac du Bonnet region, *The House Beside the Rock Hill* by Aina (Gulbis) Turton and could only smile at how closely their customs were the same as those we still follow today.

And then it was time for a self-guided walking tour of Winnipeg itself, although we ended up driving most of the route. The weather was unseasonably hot and the distance between points of interest so far, we chose the lazy vehicular air-conditioned way. And thank goodness for that. Of all the places suggested, only the Manitoba legislative building, the St. Boniface Cathedral and an area known as The Exchange were really worth exploring. The rest was just big city blocks with big city construction and big city noise (although dropping into the home of the Royal Winnipeg Ballet was nice even if the season was over, and we didn't get around to visiting the Winnipeg Art Gallery either, which houses the world's largest collection of Inuit art). The legislative building is impressive and incorporates a great many hidden symbols that lead some scholars to believe its architect designed it as a temple to Freemasonry with religion, numerology and astrology all playing a role. I'm no expert, but there were some odd pieces – including sphinxes at the roofline and the "Golden Boy" on the roof itself. He is supposed to be Hermes, son of Zeus, and has been twice gilded with 24 karat gold leaf. Inside, two life-size bison statues weighing 5,000 pounds each flank the grand entry staircase. In order not to scratch the marble floor during installation, they were placed on two huge slabs of ice and then slowly slid into the building. Very innovative. It is possible to take the Hermetic Code Tour and get the inside scoop on all the mysterious symbols, but we decided to leave that to the DaVinci Code enthusiasts. Further on, an area known as The Exchange is a thirty-block district containing numerous buildings constructed between 1880 and 1920, many restored to their original beauty. I think it is the most charming part of Winnipeg with bistros, galleries, shops and places to just sit in the shade of a leafy tree and enjoy a cup of coffee. We didn't take the time to savour that. Our bad. We were off to the French side of the river to check out St. Boniface Cathedral-Basilica. The original cathedral was built in 1908 but completely destroyed by fire in 1968. Those walls that were left standing, were incorporated into a new church, that now sits in an almost courtyard type setting. Definitely making use of the original structure in a very practical yet aesthetic way. Louis Riel is buried, with a modest marker, in the old cemetery just outside.

A few more observations about Manitoba, in no particular order. The soil there is very dark, almost black, when compared to Ontario's brown or PEI's red. It looks very fertile and perhaps that is why canola grows so well. We loved the canola fields. As far as the eye could see, gently undulating waves of brilliant, warm, almost neon yellow that could brighten up even a dull day. Like sunshine solidified. Interspersed with still green fields of hemp, flax and wheat. The sight never got old. It would have been perfect to just bicycle along and enjoy the scenery, but we realized too late that we had had a little mishap with the bikes back in Ontario. When we made our final stop at the cottage prior to heading out, the bikes were already loaded on the rack at the back of the Jeep. This partially obstructed the view through the back-up camera. You know where this is going. John inadvertently backed up into a tree. It was just a small bump, not even enough to get out of the car and look. Just an "oops" and we were off. It turned out that small oops bent the rear wheels of both bikes, enough to make them inoperable. Now what? Should we fix them or hold off until we get to Alberta where we had planned on buying new ones anyway (remember, no provincial sales tax in Wild Rose Country). We decided to hold off and gave up some of the easiest cycling we would have ever done. Sometimes sacrifices had to be made.

But a bit more physical exercise would have been beneficial from a health standpoint. People in Manitoba love their cinnamon buns. They even have a cinnamon bun trail that criss-crosses the province highlighting the better-rated establishments. Sadly, they do not keep it up to date because we took the time to stop in at the listed café in a two-street town (Austin), but the new owner was not aware she was on the registry. She only made butter tarts. It was such a sacrifice eating those instead. However, Austin did have a still utilized old-fashioned grain elevator situated beside the railroad tracks that run through town. These were once found in every small community throughout Manitoba and Saskatchewan, but most of the old wooden ones have fallen into disrepair. Austin's had been covered with aluminum to protect the wood from the elements but in many other villages, they have been replaced with large concrete towers. Supposedly more durable, hygienic, and safe but they just don't have the same charm. We stopped by the little town of Inglis where five of these old prairie sentinels are being renovated in an effort to preserve a bit of western Canada's agricultural history, but they are now for show as opposed to function. We learned that many of the older constructs list to one side because over the years, they have been consistently unevenly loaded on the trackside. Another oops in the making.

While fuel, both gas and diesel, was considerably cheaper than in Ontario (86 cents for a litre of regular), the roads were by far the worst we had driven on to date. By far! Vertical cracks, horizontal cracks, patched sections, potholes. And although the coach does have a good suspension system, the ride is much harder than in an SUV, so we felt every jolt. At one point, we had stopped for a break and Porter refused to get back in when it was time to head out again. Noooooo! I can't take anymore! We knew exactly how he felt. I'd like to say things improved in Saskatchewan, but such was not the case. Equally bad. We covered considerably less miles in a day than we had in either Ontario or in our swing through the eastern provinces.

Out first Saskatchewan stop was in Verigin to check out the National Doukhobour Heritage Village. The Doukhobours were (and still are to some extent) a religious sect (for lack of a better word) who left Tsarist Russia after running afoul of both the Tsarist Regime as well as the Orthodox Church during the 17th and 18th centuries. They are total pacifists and in 1895 took a decisive stance against militarism and all forms of violence by burning all of the firearms they possessed. After which they also became vegetarians.

Go figure. They obviously didn't see that one coming. Their guiding principle is that in struggling for a better life they will only use the spiritual power of love rather than any form of violence. They were persecuted for their beliefs by both the Orthodox Church and Tsarist authorities so in 1899 about 7500 of them (almost a third of the entire population) migrated to Canada settling primarily in Saskatchewan, living an agricultural communal lifestyle. Their first hamlet was established in Verigin and it became their administrative and spiritual centre. The Canadian government had reassured them that they would be free to practice their faith but after five years, changed the rules with respect to swearing an Oath of Allegiance. So the majority packed up and moved to the Kootenay region of British Columbia where said oath was not required. Like many immigrant groups they prospered, but over the years have been slowly absorbed into the larger community and their customs and traditions watered down. The Heritage Village had a small museum and a compilation of buildings that illustrated life on the prairie in the early 1900s, but it was not high tech or sophisticated by any stretch of the imagination. The Chairman of the village happened to be at a loose end, so he gave us a personal tour of the place which greatly enhanced our learning experience, but considering we were the only visitors, that isn't saying much, and it certainly does not bode well for their future.

We bumped our way down the highway to our next stop, the not so scenic Little Manitou Lake. It promotes itself as North America's "Dead Sea" but in reality, although its mineral density is three times that of the ocean, the salinity is only half that of Israel's Dead Sea. Still, it allows for effortless floating and supposedly, the lake has therapeutic properties curing all manner of ailments from smallpox to eczema to gangrene. We went for a short swim and while it didn't magically alleviate the bursitis in my hip, I do think my skin was softer. The downside was that the lake itself is not very picturesque (not even close), the beach (trucked in coarse sand) is maybe 100 feet long and the immediate village and buildings have a rather passé, neglected look to them. Calling it a resort is more than a misnomer. When a commemorative plaque extolling the virtues of the place lists such recreational activities as checker games, swings and a merry-go-round, you know they are reaching. Apparently in the 1930s, Americans and Europeans found it as popular as Banff and while I suspect that is a bit of a stretch too, there is a certain fascination with water that heals. The lake is fed by underground springs, has no outlet and its mineral content has been measured to be 180 grams per litre. That's incredibly high considering many spas market mineral water soaks at 1 gram per litre. If the place were more accessible, had better infrastructure and looked more upscale chic than abandoned fifties sanatorium, I would have been tempted to return and soak a little bit longer. Who knows what improvements might have resulted?

Perhaps we would have learned how to tell time while travelling through time zones because we ran into a bit of confusion over that. The cell phones and i-pad showed one time, but the lap-top and microwave clock an hour later. Now how could that be? We had reset everything when we crossed from Eastern to Central time just past Thunder Bay. Where did we gain an extra hour? Is there another time zone we don't know about? How many zones are there? It was a puzzle. Research revealed that Saskatchewan does not practice daylight savings time. No spring forward or fall back for them. Except for the town of Lloydminster on the Alberta border, which does. There is always somebody who has to be different. And on the topic of being different, it seems that Ma Bell is *in*different to its subscribers in the prairies. We drove through most of Manitoba and central Saskatchewan without any phone or internet service, save for when we were in bigger cities like Winnipeg and Saskatoon. Which makes it all the more important that map-reading skills be taught in school. Sooner or later, Google Maps will not be there to bail you out.

We spent a few days in the Saskatoon area with our campsite in a RV park right in the city. It was very green, quite private, and you'd never know that downtown was a few short minutes away. Our first evening was a bit unsettling because severe thunderstorms were forecast and while we had skated on some of those warnings before, we weren't so lucky this time. The hail was incredible! About the size of Werther's candies and when it pinged off the roof of the RV, the sound was deafening. Media reported there were 5,366 lightening strikes within the city itself. I'm not sure whose job it was to count them. Thankfully, we were spared, there was no ensuing damage and we were able to continue exploring the area. We started with a short drive to Batoche National Historic Site, where Riel's last battle took place. It wasn't knock-your-socks-off impressive, but it was nice to put a visual on what we had been reading about. Truthfully, our main reason for heading to Saskatoon (or running back to... lol... thank-you Burton) was to visit the Wanuskewin Heritage Park on the outskirts of town. We had read an article about it in *Canadian Geographic's Travel* magazine and it seemed very interesting with several kilometers of hiking trails, archaeological digs, interpretive programs and the like – "working to connect non-Indigenous and Indigenous people." Very commendable. Unless those people happen to be travelling with a chocolate lab. Then the entire area becomes "sacred ground" and a dog's presence somehow desecrates it. I'm not sure about the relationship between Aboriginal people and dogs but apparently at Wanuskewin, children's day camps and playgrounds are okay, as are film crews filming segments of *The Amazing Race*, but a leashed dog walking along a 6-km trail will contaminate the entire hallowed 600 acres. John was more accepting of their policy, but I left in a huff. Just wait until I get on Tripadvisor! We went to the Taste of Saskatoon food festival instead, held downtown in Kiwanis Memorial Park. The turn-out was amazing considering that the event runs 11 hours a day for 6 days straight. Thirty local restaurants dish out food samples for a nominal price and not surprisingly, we ate too much.

Our next course found us heading in a southerly direction and near Moose Jaw we stopped in at a Burrowing Owl Interpretive Centre. Actually, it was just time for a lunch break and the centre had a huge parking lot so perfect timing. I'd never even heard of burrowing owls, much less knew that they were endangered so it was a pretty opportunistic learning experience. They are tiny little things, about the size of large robins, and their endangerment comes from habitat loss since they build their homes in the prairie grassland that is rapidly being depleted. They are the only owls in the world that nest underground. And just in case you were wondering, the only way to tell the males from the females is through a blood test. So now you know. Save the owls!

Our ultimate destination at this point, however, was Grasslands National Park in the southern part of the province, a few kilometers from the U.S. border. The drive south from Saskatoon was horrendous. I can only reiterate that the roads here were really, really bad. And if the paved ones weren't bumpy enough, access to and driving within the park itself was all wash-boarded gravel. Kilometer after kilometer after kilome-

TALK ABOUT YOUR WIDE-OPEN SPACES!

ter of wash-boarded gravel. We were both clenching our teeth by the time we reached the campground. But once set up and hooked in, it was all worth it. Spectacular! Not in a grand majestic kind of way, but in a wow-this-is-vast kind of way. This is by and large cattle country although the park itself is mixed-grass prairie and has a herd of about 500 bison (they were reintroduced in 2005) that roam around its 900-square kilometers. And the air! At the risk of sounding like a pretentious sommelier describing a fine wine, the air was literally perfumed with the scent of dried wild grasses and freshly cut clover with hints of camomile and a soupcon of sage. Not cloying, not overwhelming, just heavenly. Now I know what people mean when they talk about air smelling sweet. John said it was the type of gentle scent you wish you could bottle up and take with you. The air temperature, however, was another thing. During the day it was extremely hot (about 34C/94F) – it was a dry heat – but as soon as the sun went down it plummeted to about 14C/57F. The mornings were decidedly chilly. We drove (in the Toad) an 80-km scenic loop through the backcountry to see if we could spot some bison and to check out the declining Black-tailed Prairie Dog colonies. This park is the only place in Canada where these little rodents still live in their natural habitat – although you wouldn't think they were an at-risk species given how widespread their little clusters of raised burrows were. Some had even dug holes in the middle of the road and would sit on the edge of their mound, watching our car approach. At the last minute, they would dive back into the ground. A prairie dog version of the game of chicken, if you will. We passed numerous stone tepee rings (there are over 12,000 in the park), reminders of a bygone Plains Indian era and took a rest in some red Adirondack chairs that Parks Canada places at many of its more scenic viewpoints. This pair happened to be situated about 3 kilometers from the Montana border, but we didn't see any illegals trying to sneak across. Given the terrain, it would be very foolhardy to try. Miles and miles of grassland with nary a tree nor water source in sight. And the bison? Well, that encounter was a little closer than planned.

I had walked about 150 yards out into a prairie dog colony, along a designated path I should point out, hoping to take some pictures because the little critters really are very cute. (John stayed in the car, parked along the roadside with Porter.) About five or six bison were off in the distance but I figured that if they got too close, I'd snap a few pics and then hurry back to the car. While I was busy taking pictures of the prairie dogs, unbeknownst to me, two other bison came up out of a coulee behind me, near the trailhead. In effect, cutting off my planned escape route. They were literally between me and the safety of the car. Why there? The parks people had installed wooden posts to prevent anyone from driving out onto the walking path itself and the bison like to use these as scratching posts. The small "herd" on my right was getting closer and closer, apparently planning to join up with the two already having a good rub. To the left of the path was the deep coulee and I didn't know if any other stragglers were down there. Things were not looking good. Thankfully, John motioned for me to walk out into the prairie dog colony and parallel the road for a stretch, angling towards the roadway where he picked me up with the car. Now that I think about it, prairie dog burrows are also home to rattlesnakes and black widow spiders. Was that really the best getaway route he could think of? Hmmm. We then looped back to the trailhead where we watched these massive beasts from the safety of the car at a distance of about 40 feet. Awesome! We would have loved to stay longer at Grasslands, but the campground was very small, perhaps 20 sites that have power, and with the weekend coming, they had already been reserved. So we were forced to move on to Cypress Hills Interprovincial Park at the extreme southwest corner of the province where it straddles the Alberta border.

The park itself was okay but a far cry from the expansive solitude of Grasslands. This was more your poorman's resort type park, complete with swimming pool,

OH.OH. BETWEEN A ROCK AND TWO *TATANKAS*. THAT'S MY CAR!

tennis courts, riding stables and ice cream huts. The weather had been extremely hot and dry (fire bans everywhere), but a thunderstorm did develop and provided some wonderful photo opportunities. I had just happened to drive to a lookout point near Bald Butte, supposedly the highest elevation between the Rockies and the Torngat Mountains in Labrador (I know, I know, this was Saskatchewan!) and it provided a panorama over a vast valley. When the storm came through, it was unbelievable just watching it move across the valley floor! And the sunset afterwards was fantastic. I think I am running out of superlatives. We didn't spend much time in the park though. Instead, we drove over to Fort Walsh, site of the first North West Mounted Police (later to become RCMP) post/ headquarters in the west, established in response to the Cypress Hills Massacre. Back in the early 1870s there were already concerns about a wild-west mentality forming in the new frontier with lawlessness and illegal whiskey trade on the rise. A bill was before McDonald's parliament that a police force should be created in order to maintain law and order, but same as today, the decision making in Ottawa was moving at a snail's pace. While they were debating, the massacre of numerous Plains Nakota took place. In a nutshell, wolf hunters in the area accused local Indians of stealing their horses. In their minds, justice was not forthcoming quickly enough, so they took matters into their own hands, attacking a Nakota camp and slaughtering twenty warriors, elders, women and children. This accelerated the usual foot dragging that governments are known for, and the North West Mounted Police started marching west in 1874, establishing Fort Walsh in 1875, just two kilometers from the sight of the massacre. By all accounts, the Superintendent of the fort (James Walsh) got along very well with Sitting Bull of the Lakota Sioux (who had fled the U.S. following his trouncing of Custer at Little Bighorn) and the area was quite peaceful and prosperous. After the railroad went through, the RCMP headquarters was moved to Regina and the fort was abandoned until the 1940s when it served as a breeding and training centre for the Mountie's familiar musical ride horses. Given our policing background, it was relatively interesting although obviously there is very little similarity between the duties of a police officer then versus today. And not just with respect to salary. A staff sergeant at Fort Walsh earned between $1.00 and $1.50 per day. Even by today's standards, that may be a bit high.

Overall, we were very pleasantly surprised by the beauty of Saskatchewan. It was not the endless monotonous flats we had anticipated, although perhaps that is because for the most part, we stayed off the Trans-Canada highway. The locals say that as long as you go twenty-five kilometers north or south of that route, it is quite rolling and picturesque. We couldn't agree more. However, there is quite a difference between the north where it is more agricultural with canola and wheat fields galore and the south with more grazing herds and grassland. But the area is so vast, 360 degrees of vast, that the grazing cattle were often just tiny black specks on the horizon. Unless of course they had decided to come right out and block the roadway, which they were quite prone to do. In terms of camping, it seemed everyone had either a straight-out trailer or a fifth wheel (those trailers that have the front sitting in the bed of a pick-up truck). And most everybody had a pickup truck. We saw very few class A motor coaches such as ours although perhaps that was because those owners knew how bad the roads were and stuck to the Trans Canada. There was, however, one annoying camping feature. When staying at provincial parks, the overnight rate was advertised at "X" number of dollars, usually around $40 for electric and water. Not a bad deal. But if you wanted to reserve ahead of time, there was a $10 to $12 reservation fee. (And given the size of our rig, we found we needed to do that during peak season.) That is an additional 25%, even if it is just for one night. And when you actually pulled into the campground, they charged around another $10 per day per vehicle and that additional charge was not mentioned anywhere. What do they think people are going to do? Walk in 5 miles from the park boundary carrying their tents and gear? So really, they get an additional 50% on top of their advertised rate. Sneaky. You can't trust the government about anything.

Leaving Cypress Hills, we had just crossed into Alberta when we were forced to pull over for a mandatory watercraft inspection. The authorities there are so concerned about zebra mussels and other invasive water creatures that boats of any kind must be cleared before launching in any Alberta waters. In fact, in Waterton National Park, motorized boats have been banned from all bodies of water in an effort to curtail the spread. Thank goodness we had kayaks! We passed inspection and continued on with our clearance certificates firmly in hand. But the further west we went, the worse the air quality became. This because of the forest fires burning out of control in British Columbia with even a few in the Banff area. Back country camping in the Kootenays and certain parts of Banff had been temporarily prohibited. It was hard to imagine that the devastation so far to the north was affecting us so far to the south, but driving along wide open spaces where you should theoretically be able to see forever, was more like driving through a light fog. Everything was hazy. It would be as if a forest fire in Quebec City were to obstruct a view of the CN Tower in Toronto. We had one quick overnight in Lethbridge before pulling into our previously arranged site through Boondockers Welcome, near Pincher Creek just north of Waterton National Park. On an average day, you can clearly see the Rockies in all their glory from our host's sizeable homestead (2,000 acres!!!) but these were not average days. By the time we were set up, the haze was so thick it completely obscured the mountains and things only improved after a few days. Very disappointing from that perspective. But we loved the surrounding area regardless. Perhaps I was a prairie farmer or rancher in a previous life, but I felt so at home and comfortable in those wide-open spaces. We stayed with our generous hosts for three nights, exploring the area and getting the lay of the land over at the national park, an hour's drive away. We had not realized that 90% of the sites in the park were on a reservation basis and of course by the time of our arrival, all of them had been booked. So using the ranch as a base, we visited Head-Smashed-In Buffalo Jump as well as Frank Slide. Both interesting for different reasons.

Head-Smashed-In, a UNESCO World Heritage Site, is deemed to be one of the oldest, largest and best-preserved buffalo jump sites in the Western Plains. Native peoples used it from about 6,000 years ago until about 150 years ago – although there is a 1,500-year gap when it was not used at all and archaeologists don't know why. It is really very ingenious. The Plains Indians relied on buffalo for their very existence and prior to contact, had neither horses nor guns to take these massive beasts down. Going one-on-one armed only with an arrowhead was dangerous to say the least. So utilizing their understanding of the region's topography as well as bison behaviour, they would stampede the herd over a 50-foot precipice. This was accomplished by forming drive lanes as far as 8 kilometers away from a cliff edge, herding the buffalo in the right direction and then causing them to stampede. Those that were not killed by the fall were dispatched by bow and arrow as they lay injured at the bottom. The hunts were communal affairs, and everyone pitched in to butcher and process the meat and hides. We often read that native peoples lived in complete harmony with nature, never wasting but rather utilizing every part of a hunted animal. Not so at Head-Smashed-In. A good hunt could result in 100 dead bison so only the choicest labā omā. parts were used with much being left for the coyotes, crows and other carnivores. Another myth shattered. But the site was well worth the visit. An excellent interpretive centre examines the lifestyle of the plains people (in this case the Blackfoot), the buffalo hunt itself, how things changed with contact and how archaeologists have been able to unearth so much information. Definitely worth the short drive off the highway.

Frank Slide in Crowsnest Pass was next. Set in an incredibly beautiful part of the Rockies (although the forest fire smoggy air still impacted the view for us), it is hard to fathom the tragedy that befell the small coal mining town of Frank with its 600 inhabitants at the base of Turtle Mountain in the early morning hours of April 1903. Around 90 million tons of rock broke off the mountain and in 90 seconds slid down like a huge avalanche burying 3 square kilometers of the valley, including half of the town and its sleeping population. It is estimated the slide travelled at 120 km/hour and left a debris field that is up to 45 meters (150 feet) deep in places. Over 1&1/2 kilometers of Canadian Pacific Railway was wiped out, as was the road. Despite some miraculous survival stories, ninety people died, and most remain buried under the massive pile of jumbled rock. It is still North America's deadliest rockslide. Explanations for the disaster are threefold: the mountain's overall unstable geological structure, the coal mining at the base of the mountain and the large amount of water in the cracks of the rock near the summit that froze when spring temperatures suddenly dropped to an unseasonal -17 C. The mountain is still unstable today, and geologists predict that another slide is imminent although this next one will only be about one sixth the size of the original. How imminent? They can't say. Tomorrow, next week, next year, next century. We walked along a short trail that winds in and around the massive boulders and I could only hope that the money for the next slide was on next year. Interestingly, the wiped-out railroad was repaired, up and running again after 17 days. They brought in over 1,000 men to expedite the restoration. In contrast, at the time of our visit, the people of Churchill Manitoba had been without a railway for over two months (and it's the only overland way to get in and out of town) and private industry and various levels of government were still bickering over who should foot the cost for repairs. Because of this, a 4-litre jug of milk cost over $12.00! It is shameful.

Not wishing to outstay our welcome with our boondocking hosts (who had even invited us for dinner one evening), we managed to secure a site in a RV campground just outside the Waterton National Park boundary. It was nowhere near as peaceful and scenic as our boondocking location (in fact it was rather crowded and shabby), but it was two minutes from the park gate and that was what we needed in order to undertake all the hiking and kayaking we had planned. Most of the smog had dissipated by then so the views were spectacular. We went on three hikes, each progressively more challenging: Blackiston Falls near Red Canyon (more of a stroll really), Bear Hump overlooking Wateron Lakes and the town-site (steep vertical – lungs could have used a bit more oxygen), and Wall Lake that technically took us across the border into British Columbia (legs felt that one simply because it was quite long.) I had also hoped to attempt Crypt Lake which required an early morning rise and a boat ride to the trailhead but that was not to be. The trail is rated as one of the twenty most thrilling hikes in all of North America by *National Geographic Traveller* and would have been a challenge with ladders, tunnels and narrow ledges but unfortunately by this time, Porter, who had been a real trooper so far, started limping. (He has arthritis in his front paws.) Despite a few days rest we did not think it prudent to set out on an 8-plus hours long trek when he was not in top form, and we couldn't leave him alone in the coach for that long. No doggie day care around. It is interesting to note that in Canada's national parks, dogs are not just permitted but are actually encouraged to go out on the trails. Perhaps that is because there are so many cougars and bears around (black and grizzly) that even aggressive dogs seem tame by comparison. In any event, we were very thankful for this enlightened and welcoming policy since it allowed us to experience the beauty of the park together instead of taking turns (as we were forced to do in U.S. national parks).

So instead of Crypt Lake we opted for a 2-hour boat ride (where Porter was also welcome) to the southern end of Waterton Lake, into Glacier National Park, Montana. The two parks are actually called the Waterton-Glacier International Peace Park and much of the administration is shared between our two countries. Passports were not required when we stepped ashore unless we wanted to go on an extended hike into the U.S. interior. The passport policy seems a bit over-the-top. There is literally nowhere to go! This is the wilderness. Yes, there are hiking trails up into the mountains, but the closest road is 35 miles (that is 56 kilometers) away! You'd really have to be a desperado to brave that kind of terrain, never mind the bears and cougars, to get into the U.S. without proper documentation. Yet there is actually an American border station (read: "hut") complete with Homeland Security checking passports for those wishing to spend the day at the south end of the lake. American tax dollars at work.

Back in Canada, we went for "afternoon tea" in the iconic Prince of Wales Hotel. I just needed a bit of a civilization fix and a glimpse of what my life used to be like. As afternoon teas go, it wasn't really all that great, but what it lacked in proper cucumber sandwiches it made up for in setting. The scenery was sublime with huge picture windows in the lounge providing a commanding view out over the water to the mountains. The hotel itself was built in 1927 and is absolutely charming. With a charming price tag to boot, but then what is the price of beauty? We had a choice. One night in the hotel or six in the crummy campground. Same price. Okay, we cheaped out, stayed in the crummy campground and squeezed in some more wilderness experiences. We spent one day taking turns kayaking on the southern-most portion of Cameron Lake, which is also strictly speaking, in the United States, so yes, we both snuck back into the U.S. without our passports and returned with no-one being the wiser. The fact that the lake is glacier fed and surrounded by mountain peaks with no road access what-so-ever on the U.S. side is irrelevant. For a short time, we were illegal aliens! The park is known for its wildlife and we did see a few black-tailed deer on the hiking trails. I spent a fair bit of time trying to get the perfect picture to no avail. The next day, one was nonchalantly strolling down main street in town and another resting in the shade on someone's lawn. Of course, I didn't have my camera with me! We saw several bears in the distance, and one quite close in our campground, up on a hill where we had gone for an evening stroll the night before. Yet another was at the edge of the roadway, contentedly dining on berries and completely ignoring the car and still another meandering along the beach where we had set up to just hang out for half a day. I happened to be out in the kayak and got a few pictures from the water of that guy. It turns out that bears don't just shit in the woods. They quite like leaving huge piles on the beaches too! Getting closer would have made for some great photographs but since *National Geographic* wasn't paying me and I still had memories of bison in my head, I stayed at a safe distance. A local guide advised us how to tell the difference between black bears and grizzlies. If you climb up a tree and the bear follows you, it's a black bear. If you climb up a tree and the bear pushes it over, it's a grizzly. Very helpful, these guides. A few times small herds of Bighorn Sheep crossed the road in front of us (they were the exact colour of the surrounding rocky peaks), and we heard that a cougar had been roaming around town the evening before. Only us tourists got excited about that sort of thing. We finished off our stay in Waterton with a two-hour trail ride. While it was great to be in the saddle again, the outing was a bit underwhelming. It's not really fair to compare this kind of ride to the multi-day Rocky Mountain excursions we have undertaken in the past, but a bit more effort could have been put into trail and destination selection by the folks at Alpine Stables. Basically, we rode single file along a dusty trail out to a meadow (where we could then spread out), crossed two streams and then rode back along the same dusty trail. Yeehaw. John's horse (Norman) was less than enthusiastic about heading out in the first place so there was no danger of him riding off into the sunset. An adventure shop in town had as its slogan, "Live Inside the Postcard." That precisely summed up how we felt about July. It was picture postcard perfect. Busy. But picture postcard perfect.

16.

DIGGING FOR DINOSAURS; WALKING WITH WOLVES

THERE ARE OCCASIONS IN LIFE WHEN THE ANTICIPATION OF AN EVENT TURNS OUT TO BE BETTER THAN THE ACTUAL EVENT ITSELF, AND WHEN IT CAME TO GOING ON A DIG FOR DINOSAUR BONES, THAT IS EXACTLY WHAT HAPPENED. Many years ago, when Matejs was at the tender age of nine, the two of us went on a certified dinosaur dig managed through the auspices of the Royal Tyrell Museum in Drumheller, Alberta with what was then call the Day Digs Programme. And it was fantastic as much as Matejs might say otherwise. He was the only child amongst a group of adults, was afforded extra attention and got to do a great many extra things, including casting a partially excavated bone. A few of the adult wanna-be-palaeontologists were a bit miffed by all this additional consideration and I suppose their chill is what tainted Matejs' opinion. The RTM no longer offers this programme, but it is still possible to partake in a similar experience through Dinosaur Provincial Park, about a two-hour drive from Drumheller. I couldn't wait. A full day in a bone fide bone bed with a bone fide palaeontologist working at a bone fide on-going dig. The price was a bit steep, considering anything found goes to the Museum (it is against the law to remove any dinosaur bones from dig sites or even backyard gardens) but what the heck. If I had not gone into policing, I would have studied archaeology, so money was not going to hold me back. And besides, I would be contributing to ongoing research at the RTM. John stayed behind with Porter, saying that he had no interest in brushing away grains of sand with a paintbrush. His loss.

The day was very hot (around 40C/105F) without a cloud in the sky and I met my four fellow stone and bone enthusiasts bright and early – a young couple from Calgary, and a father and son from Saskatoon. Things looked promising until we met our guide and tutor. He had obviously spent way too much time playing in the dirt because he had the personality of a soil sample. I'm still not sure if he was simply having a bad day or if he thought taking us amateurs out into the field was beneath him, but he offered very little information, answered questions in a perfunctory manner but rarely expanded on them, and had no sense of ha-ha. We paying volunteers exchanged looks and quiet comments throughout the day that this was not quite what we had envisioned. But despite his attitude, I enjoyed it. First, we drove several kilometers out into the Red Deer River valley where, if you knew where to look, petrified wood and dinosaur bones tens of millions of years old were essentially sticking out of the ground. We stepped over and onto so many, I really began to question why one of the smaller pieces couldn't quietly slip into my backpack. Only the thought of a possible $50,000.00 fine deterred me. Once at the site, the morning was spent literally chipping away at a limestone layer in order to clear the way to the bone layer below. Not too exciting, but not everything can be *Indiana Jones*. I kept singing that song, *"Breakin' rocks in the hot sun... I fought the law and the law won...."* Our guide didn't even crack a smile. After the included lunch (the saddest ham and cheese sandwich ever!) we crawled and inched our way through various micro-beds looking for minuscule pieces of teeth, vertebrae and shells, all indicators of the area's earlier tropical environment. And then back to the salt mine. We didn't get to work at unearthing any bones (although one beautiful rib was right at my feet) nor did we form any plaster casts. Breaks were spent wandering around the parched earth examining the bones that littered the terrain, and it breaks my heart to know that I just left them there. And then we were done, back in the van bouncing our way back to the visitor's centre. Was I disappointed? Yes. Would I do it again? In a heartbeat. Montana was supposed to have a similar programme somewhere so I hoped when we made it to that part of the country, I could try it again although given my review, I suspected John would once again decline. We made a quick stop at the Royal Tyrell Museum and again, despite the potential, it too, was a disappointment. Not the museum itself. It is ranked as one of the world's top palaeontology museums and was just as interesting now as 22 years ago, but the children! OMG! I have rarely been in the presence of such an unruly horde of whirling dervishes. Obviously the parents thought that their little darlings would enjoy seeing numerous full dinosaur skeletons as well as true-to-life mock-ups, including T-Rex and Stegosaurus. Not so. The unappreciative little wretches ran about the museum as if it were a playground, chasing each other, shrieking and generally behaving as children with unbridled energy are wont to do. And the parents all seemed okay with it! Unbelievable! Now that's where a $50,000.00 fine would have come in handy! We left without truly enjoying our visit. Had there been a suggestion box, I would have recommended having certain days or hours where anyone under 10 years of age is not permitted. Okay, I'm just kidding... Sort of.

SEARCHING A MICRO-BED FOR BONE FRAGMENTS. IS THIS FUN OR WHAT?

A short drive from Drumheller, we spent the night boondocking at a supposedly genuine ghost town – Rowley. It isn't really a ghost town because there are 6 inhabitants still in residence, but all the shops along the unpaved main street have long since closed and its rather abandoned air has made it a destination of sorts for Hollywood. Parts of Clint Eastwood's *Unforgiven*, and *Legends of the Fall* (Brad Pitt, Anthony Hopkins), as well as Canada's production of *Bye Bye Blues* were filmed there. It used to have a population of 500 but that was in the 1920s and it has since been dying a slow death. The final blow came in 1997 when vital train service was cancelled, and the tracks were torn up – rails sold to China and ties to Japan (or vice versa). It was nice having a quiet place all to ourselves, albeit a bit creepy. Just us and the empty grain elevators. All that was missing were tumbleweeds. Next stop was in Red Deer at a RV dealer because the steps on the yacht were giving us problems. They were supposed to extend and retract commensurate with opening and closing the door, but the motor was making a loud grinding noise and they were not fully extending. The dealer advised he needed to order a part that would take two weeks to arrive. Okay, call us when it's in and we'll return.

On to Edmonton where we checked out the West Edmonton Mall – that monument to excessive consumerism. It is the largest mall in North America at 5.3 million square feet (or about the size of 90 football fields) and employs about 24,000 people. So bigger than most of the towns in the area. It had all the usual shops and then some (although no Saks or Nordstrom), plus a huge skating rink, a massive wave pool/water slide complex that visitors can zip line across, several roller coasters, a performing seal aquarium, two hotels, countless movie theatres and over 100 dining establishments. So to call it a mall is not really accurate. More like an amusement park with optional shopping, eating and sleeping facilities. However, once you get past the "wow" factor, it's not really that appealing. The skating rink (close to the size of a football field itself) was undergoing a 3-million-dollar refurbishment so was closed. There were several hundred people in and around the wave pool, many of them little children and we all know what little children do in pools. I overheard two ladies discussing how disgustingly dirty the change rooms were with soiled diapers and toilet paper strewn about. The poor performing seals, surrounded by faux pirate ships and swinging rope bridges were a pretty sorry looking lot and the roller coasters would be considered pretty tame by today's newer death-defying rides. Prices in the stores were the same as anywhere else, although considering there is no provincial sales tax in Alberta, I may or may not have purchased one or two pairs of shoes. We spent the entire day in the mall but didn't get around to seeing everything. It was exhausting. And while on the topic of shopping, I should confess that we also took advantage of the tax situation by purchasing our new bikes while passing through Calgary. Carbon frames and so much lighter than what we were used to. There would be no stopping me on those up-hills now! We left our old bikes with the shop staff who advised that they will donate them to a community charity where, once the wheels were fixed, they would be put to good use. I was a bit sad saying good-bye to my old bike. It had safely taken me on so many great rides including to and from work when I was in a fitness frame of mind. So long old friend.

And then we were off to Jasper, the first of the so-called Rocky Mountain Parks (Jasper, Banff/Lake Louise, Yoho, Glacier and Revelstoke) having made a change to our anticipated route. We had originally planned to drive up to Slave Lake, Peace River, loop around through Grand Prairie and then south again but the more we researched, the more we realized it would be a long road for little reward. And if we were honest, we really just wanted to kayak and hike in the mountains. Heading towards the Jasper/Lake Louise/Banff area during summer was going to mean tourist hordes but it couldn't be helped. We didn't have any reservations but much of the area is first come first served so we crossed our fingers and headed west. We also kept a close eye on the wildfire situation in British Columbia lest it spill over into Alberta, having heard it was the worst forest fire season since 1958 (by month's end that had changed to the worst in B.C. history) and that an area the size of Prince Edward Island was aflame (by month's end an area twice the size of PEI had burned.) Hard to get your head around that. Smoke was certainly going to impact the view, but you can't have everything. Were we ever clueless. Upon arrival in Jasper we found out that the big rig friendly (read: have electricity) campgrounds were totally on a reservation basis with the booking process starting in January. So we were out of luck there. And the first come, first served campgrounds were all full. A quick drive through in the Toad showed that even had there been vacancies, most of the sites were too small for the yacht anyway. We were directed to Snaring Campground overflow. I thought we had won the lottery. It was excellent. While the approach was a bit haphazard (no numbered sites, just set up where you find a spot) it was wide open, affording unobstructed views of the surrounding mountains. Tent sites were tucked into the trees and coaches, fifth wheels and trailers could situate themselves in the big clearing or hide alongside some copses for shade. We opted for a shaded spot since the weather was predicted to be sunny and quite hot. The price was the same as the regular campground (dirt cheap at $15.70/night) and the only thing lacking at some of the sites were picnic tables. At times it was a bit breezy and dusty but overall, it was by far one of the loveliest spots we had camped. Having said that, overflow means limited "amenities". Certainly no water, sewer or electric hook-ups and that meant being very conservative with water use and regularly running the generator to ensure our batteries stayed fully charged. Parks Canada has very specific rules about when you can run your generator (8 – 9:30 in the morning and 5-7 in the evening) and the parks staff did check. We were busted on two occasions, once for running 15 minutes beyond the allotted time. Sheesh! And we also learned that Porter, who isn't even fazed by thunderstorms, hates the sound of train whistles. The sound that I find so hauntingly beautiful causes him to jump up, head for the door and start growling. Now in all fairness, there were a lot of trains that passed through the Jasper region (day and night / freight and passenger) and the tracks were quite close to the campground, but we could have used a bit less drama from the brown menace. Still, we weren't complaining since we were in fairly close proximity to all the lakes and trails we planned to explore. "Planned" being the operative word. If we had listened more closely, we would have heard God laughing.

Jasper itself is a quiet town and despite being surrounded by the same beauty as Banff and being located within the boundaries of a national park, there the similarity ends. It has a permanent population of about 4,500 people who live in about 1,600 houses. You cannot buy a vacation home there, nor can you move there to retire. You can own property, but you cannot live in it unless you are an "eligible resident" and can demonstrate to Parks Canada a "need to reside". These rules are in place so as to avoid the over development that seems to infect all places of natural and pristine beauty, and to keep real estate prices within a range that is affordable to those people who actually work and contribute to the local economy. While there are a few "outdoor" stores and souvenir shops along two of the busier streets, there is no Lulu Lemon or Roots pushing out the autonomous entrepreneurs. A few nice independent restaurants but no Keg or Old Spaghetti Factory. Definitely a more unassuming and home-grown feel to the place than Banff, although they have capitulated and approved a Tim Horton's franchise.

The first several days were almost perfect. "Almost" because there was a slight haze in the air from the wildfires, with one quite close in the Verdant Creek area of Kootenay National Park and at Assiniboine Provincial Park, about 200 kilometers to our south. We drove along the Icefields Parkway (considered to be one of the most beautiful and scenic drives in the world – and we thoroughly agree with that assessment!) to the Athabasca Glacier where you can either walk up to the toe or pay a tourist fee to have a bus drive you out onto the ice itself. We opted for the walk (thanks to Porter) and it was amazing how rapidly the temperature dropped from 35C in the parking lot to 5C at the glacier's edge, with chilly air sweeping down from the ice. Access to the glacier from the trail itself is prohibited, although the occasional tourist has disregarded the posted signs, walked out, tumbled into a crevasse and died from either the fall or hypothermia. The last fatality was in 2001, although in 2014 the glacier gave up the body of a man who had disappeared in 1995. I recall being there as a child in the 1960s, with Matejs in 1994 and with John in 2005. With each visit, the glacier has noticeably retreated and at today's accelerated rate, climatologists predict it may completely disappear within 100 years (it has lost 60% of its volume since 1885). However, it has advanced and receded several times since it originally formed during the Late Wisconsin Ice Age about 10,000 years ago, so who's to say. And the difference between a glacier and an icefield? A glacier is "a constant body of dense ice that moves under its own weight" while an icefield is a large accumulation of snow that over time and through compression turns to ice, usually covering a very large area. Many glaciers form in icefields and are, in effect, the movement of ice out of the icefield. So there you go.

We hiked and walked around various waterfalls (Sunwapta, Athabasca and Tangle Creek) and were relieved to find that most of the throngs of sightseers who disgorge from tour buses rarely venture more than 100 yards from the parking lot. We never achieved anything even remotely close to solitude, but there were quite a few locations where we did find some peace and quiet. The Sunwapta and Athabasca Rivers are actually very fast flowing. Deceptively so because they are quite wide and shallow in places. And yes, the odd tourist has waded in upstream only to be caught by the current and then swept over the falls downstream, usually with fatal results. Given how many people visit these places, it is a miracle there have been so few tragedies because there really is a tendency for some people to want to treat the area as a giant water park. The rivers themselves are glacial and in places run a milky gray colour and in others a lovely turquoise blue. This due to what is referred to as "rock flour". That is, finely grained particles of rock that have been ground down into a silt-like texture by the glaciers themselves and are now suspended in the water.

With the warm, sunny weather we also spent a day taking turns kayaking on Maligne

Lake, considered by many to be one of prettiest lakes in the Jasper area. Bright blue water surrounded by mountains, yes, although not as dramatically pretty as say, Lake Louise. It is the largest natural lake in the Canadian Rockies at 22 kms long but unfortunately for us, the real beauty was at the water access only end. About ¾ of the way down its length is Spirit Island (which isn't really an island, more like a point), one of the most photographed places in the country. And did I get a picture? No! It was at least a 2-hour paddle one way, and since we were taking turns on the water (someone always had to babysit Porter), we just couldn't pull it off. There is a $70.00 boat cruise that we considered but unlike at Waterton Lakes, dogs were not allowed. Why? Because Spirit Island, all 25 feet of it, is Aboriginal land and therefore, you guessed it, sacred. The argument that Porter and I would just stay on the boat and not disembark didn't hold any water. I think that this whole "sacred" designation is being applied rather loosely. The waters of Maligne Lake flow out along the Maligne River into the misnamed Medicine Lake, because Medicine Lake isn't really a lake at all. It is just a place where the water pools before it disappears into an underground river and eventually emerges and empties into the Maligne Canyon several miles downstream. The analogy? A slow draining bathtub that fills with water (creating a lake) and eventually empties (creating a river) depending on the time of year. Early aboriginal peoples thought the lake had medicinal and magical properties because of its fluctuating water levels. Given the volume of water that moves through various channels, some geologists believe this may be the largest underground river in the world. To see where the water emerges requires a trip to Maligne Canyon and a hike up the ravine itself, and there are several access points allowing for either a shorter or longer trek. We found this to be a very picturesque walk, if somewhat congested. The top end was super touristy with countless selfie-stick wielding day-trippers in flip flops disembarking from their travel buses and setting out to take as many selfies as possible. It made for a curious study of human nature. They were more interested in taking pictures of themselves, than they were in taking pictures of the beauty that surrounded them, and while they busily posed, mugged and smiled for the camera they seemed totally oblivious to their natural surroundings. After which they rushed off into the gift shop/restaurant.

That said, I am neither above appreciating nor succumbing to the lure of tourist traps in the guise of art galleries myself, and the gallery at the top of the canyon did carry some authentic, if somewhat overpriced pieces. And the minute I walked through the door I saw one particular piece that I had coveted yet not seen for almost 25 years. It was a limited edition, multi-media sculpture of a timber wolf head entitled *"Nokona – The Wanderer."* Life size. Majestic. I had thought I would never see it again. I had to have it. Negotiations ensued both with the proprietor (no way I was going to pay his asking price) and John

(Honey, I know it weighs almost 80 pounds and takes up a lot of space in the coach, but we can take it home at Christmas) and after a few days, I was a happy camper. John even promised to build a suitable base to display it on once we returned to our bricks and mortar life. We also made a brief stop at the Miette Hot Springs, touted as the hottest springs in the Canadian Rockies, but they are not the natural ones that can be found in Gwaii Haanas or even the Tofino area, but rather, large swimming pools the same as at Banff and Radium, where all manner of humanity soak away their aches and pains. We had no desire to get into what is really just a huge hot tub with a hundred other people, but the surrounding scenery was worth the several-kilometer drive up Miette Road. A couple of the peaks actually reminded me a bit of Half Dome in Yosemite. Very Ansel Adamish.

We had given ourselves two weeks to explore the Jasper area and were then going to spend two weeks around Banff and Lake Louise. But the wind started to change direction and smoke from the forest fires drifted our way. A definite haze was in the air when we hiked up the Overview Trail above the town of Jasper to look out onto Patricia Lake and Pyramid Lake, with Pyramid Mountain in the background. It was still hot and sunny, but the smog was such that one of the most recognizable peaks, Mount Edith Cavell, was almost entirely obscured, as was the Athabasca River and the townsite itself. On a clear day the view must be spectacular. One thing that was still very noticeable, however, was the damage being done by the western mountain pine beetle. There were huge swathes of green that had been turned to a rusty-red as this little pest, which is actually indigenous to the area, took out acre after acre of pine forest. The beetles usually target older, over mature trees as well as those that are diseased, so this could all be an indication that these forests are at the far end of their life cycle. However, it is a huge concern in the area because the dead trees heighten the risk of forest fires. There is no easy solution. As the air quality deteriorated, we decided to drive down to Lake Louise to see if things were a bit better there. Even worse. We could literally smell the smoke. And it wasn't just a, "Hey, does that smell like smoke to you?" There was no mistaking it. It was almost like standing downwind of a smoky campfire and after a few days my throat started feeling like I had smoked one too many cigarettes the night before. And the views? Almost non-existent. When we thought we had haze in the Crowsnest Pass area, we had no idea what we were talking about. That was nothing compared to this! I found myself feeling very sorry for all those people who had come long distances from places like Germany and Japan (and there were many of them!) and all they saw was smog. So thick that at times it was down at ground level, visibility was less than a kilometer and not a glacier nor mountain in site. Not even a mountain ridge! The temperature changed overnight as well, with the car thermometer indicating that on one drive, the outside temp was 4 degrees! In August! Time to fall back and regroup. Although we had not quite kicked the habit of real vacationers who desperately try to fit everything into their one or two-week time limit, we did have the luxury of readjusting our plans as necessary. And after four days of waiting for visibility to clear, we gave up. The RV dealer in Red Deer called to advise the ordered step part was in, so we decided to declare the entire Jasper/Banff experience a "do-over."

Our route back to Red Deer had us heading south on the Icefields Parkway again to pick up highway 11 east, but a good 90-kilometer section of the Parkway (on either side of the Athabasca Glacier) made the roads of Manitoba and Saskatchewan seem smooth as glass. Heaving pavement, lateral cracks and crumbling shoulders challenged us. And this was not wear and tear that just occurred last winter. It had been years in the making. Considering all the money the feds had poured into advertising Parks Canada's 150th anniversary they could have taken a quarter of that investment and used it for road improvement. With all the international visitors to the park, it was a national disgrace. We were never so glad as to leave the park boundary and drive where the provincial government's responsibility for road maintenance kicked in. Thank goodness. The step repairs were completed within a few hours and we found ourselves in a "now what?" situation. We had already committed to postponing the thorough Jasper/ Banff exploration to another time, but still had to drive through the area to pick up Highway 1 towards Golden, after which we hoped to drop south and west of the fires, thereby avoiding the smoke. We decided to spend two nights in Banff, two in Lake Louise and move on. How bad could the smoke be? Well God was sure getting a chuckle at our expense.

We arrived in Banff and found clear, sunny skies. This after we had already cancelled our Lake Louise sites and made reservations in Golden. Are you kidding me?! They didn't last of course, and the shifting wind alternately blew in and blew out the smoke over the next few days. We spent the time lightly checking out the area but not starting any great paddles, bikes or hikes (save one.) We walked around Banff townsite one day and could only marvel at how much it had changed from when we had been out there skiing 20 years earlier. The surrounding beauty was still breathtaking, and it is easy to see why people flock to the area, although judging by the pedestrian traffic, these were not folks who were going to venture far off the beaten track. They may have been wearing the requisite hiking boots, but those puppies were never going to step in a creek or be covered with trail dust. And I was good with that. The longer they stayed in town, the longer they stayed out of my wilderness. Very selfish, I know. Then again, there is nothing wrong with sitting on an outdoor patio with your libation of choice, admiring the fantastic views in every direction either. That works for me too. We then spent two nights in the Lake Louise area where campers were directed to one of two campgrounds. Those with tents or soft-sided trailers (i.e.

popups with canvas sides) had to stay in a zone that was surrounded by an electrically charged (7,000-volt) fence. About a dozen grizzlies and several black bears live in the Lake Louise area and while they do by nature try to avoid human contact, expanding development increasingly encroaches on their territory. Every effort is made to keep us away from them and them away from us, but there are always those who don't play by the rules. On both sides. Since we were in a hard-sided unit, we were deemed to be safe and could stay outside the enclosure, although the regulations were very strict as to what could be left outside the rig. Other than camp chairs? Nothing. No need to invite trouble.

One beautiful clear morning we set out on a day to hike through the Valley of Ten Peaks from Moraine Lake to Eiffel Lake, a distance of about 12 kilometers return. Moraine Lake is an unnatural turquoise blue colour and used to be featured on the old twenty-dollar bill. It was a lovely starting point but ridiculously crowded. We pulled into the parking lot at

VALLEY OF TEN PEAKS OVERLOOKING EIFFEL LAKE

7:10am and found only a few spaces left. Those arriving after 7:30 ended up parking several kilometers back along the edge of the road. Thankfully, the "late" arrivals also tended to mill about the near end of the lake with the more "adventurous" strolling along its edge to the far end and back, a walk of about 45 minutes. Only a handful set out on the longer hikes, so we were able to enjoy a fair bit of solitude. The trail we had chosen started with a steady and winding incline, was followed by ten switchbacks that were quite steep and rather lengthy, levelled out through alpine forest and then crossed a lengthy stretch of scree. And the song in my head this day? Again. "*The ole' gray mare just ain't what she used to be, ain't what she used to be...*" My legs were shaking, my lungs were heaving, and my heart was beating double time. But the views were those that hikers say are "earned". Indescribable! Soaring peaks, retreating glaciers, alpine meadows, wide open blue sky. And the occasional marmot whistle piercing the silence. We lunched and rested for almost two hours overlooking Eiffel Lake (which was really the size of a big pond), discussed hiking further to reach the Continental Divide, lamented we were not prepared to add two more hours to the outgoing route, rested some more and started heading back. One or two of us may have had a nap prior to setting off again. It was the perfect day. Tiring, but perfect. However, we seriously reconsidered dragging Porter along on these extended forays. Like most dogs, he is loyal to a fault, but it was obvious on the return trip, he had had enough. He only perked up when we got back to the lake where he was able to splash around a bit and cool off.

Leaving the Lake Louise area, we headed west along the TransCanada towards Golden for one specific purpose. The opportunity to walk with wolves! My wild animal soul mates. We had read about the Northern Lights Wolf Centre, a conservation and information organization of sorts, where it is possible to walk in the wild with these magnificent animals – freely, with no boundaries (although not for free, of course.) They promise no more than six participants accompanied by the two owners and three wolves, and they only go out once a day first thing in the morning. We showed up at the appointed time and found out they had "made a booking error" and there were actually nine participants. Hmmm. Not sure I buy that one. They had ten wolves at the centre, all of which were born in captivity so from that perspective, they are not truly "wild". They live in a several acre enclosure and only a few are trusted enough to be taken "outside." We headed off with three of them in the back of a covered pick-up truck and within ten minutes were actually out walking alongside these misunderstood and mistreated carnivores. At times they ran around doing their thing and would only return when the owners rattled a food container. It was fantastic. Two hours went by in a flash. I wish we could have spent the entire day. The owners themselves were not really that personable and left the impression of being almost militant environmentalists with "Mr." constantly spewing vitriolic comments and dropping "f" bombs about governments, loggers and the fish industry. I would have appreciated a bit more information about the wolves themselves, but that was available back at the centre. It is sad to say, but almost every province allows for their hunting, trapping and poisoning, and some even have bounties, mostly for the sake of livestock protection. Unbelievable! As if habitat loss wasn't enough of a challenge for them. Wolves, like honeybees, are considered a "keystone" species in that their presence maintains a balance in the natural environment, impacting both fauna and flora.

WALKING WITH WILEY, THE 15-YEAR-OLD ALPHA. MY FAVOURITE.

Do away with bees, and crops don't get pollinated. Do away with wolves and everything from deer populations to grasslands to waterways get thrown out of whack. Yet you don't hear too many cries to "save the wolves" and they are still on the endangered species list. The only really positive story has been the re-introduction of wolves into Yellowstone National Park, back in 1994, when 66 of them were released into the wild. Today, they number close to 100 and since their return, the entire ecosystem has rebounded. Save the Wolves!!!!

We ended up staying in Golden for longer than expected because the weather was quite good (read: limited smoke) and it gave us fairly easy access to Yoho National Park. And the drive between Yoho and Golden was beautiful. In many places the roadway is literally carved into the side of the mountain with just concrete barriers between the asphalt and a long dramatic drop into the abyss. Along one curve, a herd of Bighorn sheep liked to hang out, sometimes walking along the edge of the road, sometimes in the middle of the road, and on one occasion a little guy was skipping along the narrow top of the barrier like a gymnast on a balance beam. This is the TransCanada for heaven's sake! We had checked into a small RV park that is part of the Golden Golf Club and seeing the golf carts go by the perfectly manicured greens and hearing the "ping" of a perfectly struck ball made me wish we were still golfers. I mused that perhaps when the journey was over, we could pick it up again. But until the then, the mountains were calling. Lake Louise is literally just on the other side of the mountain from Yoho, in effect, closer than Golden, but the two towns are worlds apart. While Lake Louise suffers from the Banff effect of tourist crowds, Golden is just an ordinary place that seems to cater to the more serious adrenalin junkies (although it had a wonderful little bookshop/cafe should the weather have prevented outdoor activities). White water rafting down the Kicking Horse River and paragliding in summer, steep skiing and ice climbing in winter. We stuck to hiking and kayaking.

With Porter at daycare, we set out on a 17-km loop to Twin Falls, a hike that brought back quite a few childhood memories. I couldn't believe my parents actually took us on this walk given the terrain, but I clearly recalled the Teahouse at the top where mom bought me a sugar cookie, and I ruined my favourite shorts by sitting down in some pine sap along the route. Unfortunately, the Teahouse was closed on this occasion as the owners had hiked back down for supplies. I wondered what the price of a cookie was today. Returning, John and I took a less popular route along Marpole Lake that turned out to be considerably more challenging than the Yoho Valley route up, in part because some much needed sign-posts were missing. If there is one thing that Parks Canada needs to improve, it is their trail markers. This was not the first time we took a wrong turn and added additional unnecessary wear and tear to our knees. The hike back was also a bit rushed because we had lingered at the top a bit too long and Porter's daycare closed at 6pm. We returned the following day to explore Takakkaw

Falls, supposedly Canada's second highest waterfall at 380 meters with a 254-meter free fall. We scrambled up part way near the base and the cool mist quickly covered our sunglasses, making picture taking a challenge. Loved it! The only place in Yoho that reminded us of the Lake Louise crowds was Emerald Lake, another one of those Rocky Mountain unnaturally blue/green lakes. We completed the 5.5 km walk around it one afternoon with Porter, and then returned without him to launch the kayaks the following morning. It was heavenly. Not too many sightseers in the early morn', the mountains reflecting in water that was smooth as glass, and a pair of loons swimming alongside. Life was good. And the people were a constant source of amusement. We decided to have our picnic lunch at the far end of the lake and disembarked, leaving our boats sitting on a stretch of sand bar while we situated ourselves on a log about 25 meters/80 feet away. Presently, four obviously foreign tourists came meandering along the hiking/walking path, which is about 60 meters/200 feet from the water's edge and espied the boats. Ahhh. Kayaks. True Canadiana. They walked around them admiringly and took a few pictures. Just the boats. Then the boats with mountains in the background. Then standing beside the boats. And the pièce de résistance, picking up the paddles and posing with them in a majestic manner, gazing off into the mountains. I was half afraid that the next picture would have them sitting in the boats. We would have been forced to say something at that point! Because the entire time, they acted as if we were not there. I don't know if they were oblivious, overly self-absorbed or just rude, but they could have asked! It was hysterical.

The next park along the route was Glacier N.P. and although we had hoped to spend a few nights there, the smoke from the fires was thick, the sky had that yellow/brown tint to it, and we could smell the smoke from inside the coach. We even saw several active spots less than a kilometer from the highway where the smoke and flames were billowing up from the forest floor, so we continued as far as Revelstoke N.P. And despite Revelstoke being just the next mountain ridge over, the air was almost perfectly clear. But that only lasted a day. Long enough for us to know what we were missing because 12 hours later things got hazy again. We lingered for a while hoping for yet another shift in wind direction, but no such luck. If anything, it got worse. Our goal still remains to return another time and explore all those places we had to forgo. Overall, we liked Yoho and Revelstoke better than Jasper and Banff simply because they are more rugged and less crowded but that is being picky. All these Rocky Mountain parks are spectacular. To date, this month was the most difficult to recap. We saw and did so much it was almost overwhelming trying to compile the information, sort it through in my mind and put it down in some semblance of a coherent manner for the blog. And our constantly changing plans only made things more complicated, with the entire month being like a game of hide and seek. Us trying to hide from the smoke and the smoke seeking us out. We hoped the next month would not require so many references to the road atlas!

17.

HEINZ 57

SEPTEMBER TURNED OUT TO BE A RICH KALEIDOSCOPE OF EXPERI-
ENCES AND EVENTS, FEW SEEMINGLY CONNECTED TO EACH OTHER.
Put another way, a real Heinz 57. We started the month in Merritt B.C., located along
the Coquihalla Highway (aka Hwy. 5) – a small town that prides itself on being the
Country Music Capital of Canada. At least that is what they have painted on the
numerous murals that cover the cinder block walls of their squat one-storey downtown
core buildings. Colourful likenesses of various country music stars, none of whom I
recognized. But then, I'm not a country music fan so no surprise there (though John
did try to enlighten me). How Merritt achieved this dubious honour was never fully
established although it probably had something to do with the country music stars who
once attended the annual Merritt Mountain Music Festival. The festival was cancelled
in 2005 due to poor ticket sales, but the town keeps hoping for a revival. We were simply
using it as a rest stop, having vowed to pull off at the first place that had sunshine and no
forest fire smoke. Merritt fit the bill. It afforded us the opportunity to weigh our future
travel options and ended up being a good base for a quick day trip to Kelowna. The surrounding area looks a bit like high mountain desert and was primarily ranching country
back in the day. Given the dry summer, I can't say if the landscape always looked like that
but rolling hills of dried yellow grass interspersed with groves of dark green evergreens
provided a very pretty visual. The drive to Kelowna was quick because the posted speed
limit was 120 km/h. Very considerate but it took a little getting used to since I normally
drive a touch over the speed limit anyway. Our purpose was to buy some local fruit
(fantastic peaches and tomatoes) and see if the area was worth adding to our "return to"
list. Probably yes. Forest fire smoke was still a factor to contend with, so we hit the road
with a quick stop in Chilliwack – supposedly home of the best corn-on-the-cob in B.C.

Yes it was excellent, but I'd still have to tip my hat in favour of Ontario's.

An interesting side trip was to the Othello Tunnels (not far from the town of Hope) once part of the Kettle Valley Railroad, considered in its day to be the most difficult railway in the country to operate. It provided freight and passenger service between the Kootenays and the Coast for 48 years, with a stretch over the 300-foot deep Coquihalla Canyon, passing through such hazardous terrain that many believed the trains were scheduled to cross only at night so passengers would not become unduly alarmed when seeing their surroundings. Conductors had to contend with rock, mud and snow slides (during the first 7 years the line was out of service more than it was in service) and when heavy rains washed out an entire section in 1959, the Coquihalla Line was shut down. The engineer who had designed the route in the early 1900s (Andrew McCulloch) was a real Shakespeare fan so many of the tunnels and stations were named after his favourite characters – Othello, Romeo, Lear, Portia and so on. Apparently, he used to read Shakespeare to his work crews in the evenings after dinner. No information on whether they appreciated his efforts. We spent a lovely afternoon walking along abandoned rail routes, through dark tunnels and across old bridges, and given the narrow span and precipitous drop, I can fully understand why people did not want to see where they were going. The area is not well marketed and the turn-off from the highway is not well marked, yet there were a lot of people out and about enjoying the day. Judging by the licence plates on the cars that lined the access road (the parking lot is extremely small), this is a local/B.C. secret so I'm glad we made the effort to find it.

The following two weeks found us set up at a RV "resort" in Abbottsford. Why is it that just because there is a swimming pool, no matter how small, people feel compelled to use the term "resort"? Talk about taking artistic licence. Actually, it was not bad except for the location itself. Right beside Hwy 1, so the noise took some getting used to. The surrounding vicinity consisted mostly of blueberry farms and fortunately for us, it was harvest time. Since these are cultivated blueberries, they were nowhere near as flavourful as the wild ones in New Brunswick or PEI, but I took what I could get. However, despite being in the Fraser Valley, this particular area was not all that picturesque. Huge garishly modern multi-generational homes were simply plunked down amidst rows upon rows of blueberry bushes, with an assortment of farming equipment scattered about nearby, and there did not appear to be any effort made to separate living space from working space. So while these farmers may be making a pretty good income off their berries, it is obvious the entire concept of landscaping and curb appeal has eluded them. The only positive was that on a clear day, we would catch glimpses of Mount Baker over in Washington State, standing out from the other surrounding peaks like a sore thumb – in a good way.

Being situated so close to the U.S. border we managed to get in a few bike rides along the rural roads and in particular, along Avenue 0. This made for an interesting visual. Two parallel country roads separated by a one-foot deep grassy ditch. Canada on one side. The United States on the other. And every five kilometers, a silver or white delineating marker. We were literally pedalling along the 49th parallel. I wonder if The Donald was aware how porous his border really was. One morning we came across a small camper truck that was in said ditch, with three US border patrol cars parked around it. We saw two people sitting on the ground in the shade of some blueberry bushes and a couple of US border patrol officers standing over them. Hmmmm. Did this guy really try to jump the border (literally) or was he just mindlessly following his

erroneous GPS? There is no way he overlooked the actual border crossing because it was about 2 kms west of the location and you can't miss it with the usual signs, flags, line-ups and duty-free store. We didn't have the nerve to stop and ask what was going on. Even the pictures I snapped were taken in pedal-by fashion given that immigration is such a hot

OOPS! I'M AN ILLEGAL ALIEN!

button topic these days.

We then spent ten days apart. John and Porter stayed with the coach (and completed a thorough and much needed interior and exterior cleaning of both vehicles) while I flew home for some medical appointments. This also gave me the opportunity to see my parents, catch up with a few friends and hang out with Matejs. Talk about your role reversal. I stayed with him at his condo where I did my best to respect his space, but he still managed to admonish me with "my house, my rules". He later admitted he had been waiting for many years to level that phrase at me. We took in Port Credit's annual *South Side Shuffle* – a Blues and Jazz Festival, binged on *Frasier* re-runs and generally just enjoyed spending time together. At least that is what I am telling everyone. Visiting with my parents, however, was bitter-sweet. Following the natural order of things, their advancing years were accompanied by advancing infirmities and seeing them every three months (as opposed to every three days when we lived at home) only seemed to make their aging more pronounced. And as much as it remained unspoken, we were all very much aware that each time we say good-bye, we could be saying it for the last time. And even though I talked this all over with my mom before we set out on this journey, and even though we were both on the same page with respect to staying versus going, and even though I was just a short plane ride away should emergencies arise, it didn't make leaving any easier. Perhaps the angst was just exacerbated because we had always lived in fairly close physical proximity to each other. So many families live hundreds if not thousands of miles apart so who were we to complain. But I have to admit that when I returned to the yacht, it took me a few days to get back into the groove of things. I missed my bricks and mortar home, I missed my favourite coffee shop, I missed my predictable routine. But most of all I missed knowing that Matejs, my parents and our friends were just around the corner. It's all very psychological. So the first order of business was to book an apartment through air-bnb so that we could be home for three weeks over Christmas. We didn't know where we would be coming from, but we would be home on December 19 and staying until January 9, so hoped that would give us the socializing time we needed.

Once that was settled, we got in touch with the west coast family contingent, my "favourite" uncle and aunt – Ojārs and Ilga, who immediately invited us over for dinner. That sounds rather formal. It was really more of an expectation (on both our sides) that of course we would get together and catch up. It was just a matter of arranging the date and time. And as luck would have it, two of my three cousins along with their better halves were able to make it as well. It was so wonderful seeing everyone again and catching up on family events, and I could only marvel at my aunt and uncle's zest for living. In keeping with propriety, I cannot divulge Ilga's age, but she still plays golf twice a week! I want to be like her when I grow up. We also went over to my one cousin's place in Harrison Springs, a small acreage and hobby farm of sorts, where he showed me how to milk goats and explained how goat cheese is made. I can't say I was much help in collecting the milk (okay, I only managed to get in a few squirts, he did all the rest) but Porter sure scored. The full bucket was momentarily placed on the kitchen floor and guess who got his opportunistic brown nose in it! Lots of goat milk for him but no goat cheese for us! Actually that is not true. We were gifted with fresh eggs and fresh goat cheese! Fantastic. Who needs a farmer's market when you can go straight to the source. We spent a wonderful afternoon and even drove to the top of a mountain where my cousin used to go hang-gliding. All the power to him because as much as I like to think I would enjoy it, I'm not sure I'd have the guts to jump off a cliff no matter what was strapped to my back!

And then we were off to the Sunshine Coast. We have been out west numerous times (Vancouver proper, Vancouver Island, Whistler) but had never travelled north along the coast itself. Very remiss of us. The ferry crossing from Horseshoe Bay to Langdale on the Sechelt Peninsula is only 40 minutes, is very picturesque with soaring peaks all around, and is pet-friendly in a manner of speaking. Dogs are not allowed on the passenger decks of the vessel, but we had the option of leaving Porter in the coach or taking him to the pet area. This was a small room on the car deck that had a few kennels along with several chairs and benches (and clean up supplies for accidents.) It was noisy but quite light and airy. We were not sure how Porter would react to being "at sea" in the coach, so alternated between babysitting him in the pet room and enjoying the view from the passenger deck. He didn't seem phased at all so next crossing we left him in the RV with no problematic results save for his usual "you didn't take me with you" look when we returned. We spent one week at Gibsons RV Resort, where they have taken the term "resort" to a whole new level of misnomer. It was more like a run-down trailer park. Of the 67 sites, more than 60 were occupied by long term (read: permanent) residents whose fifth wheels and trailers had seen better days. Far better days. And that is being kind. One sad shack even had the bench seat of a car placed under its sagging awning to be used as a couch. OMG! I kept expecting to hear banjos. During our entire stay we only spoke to two people. One a young aboriginal man who advised he had moved away from his family "because of all their nonsense" and another young man whose family was in Kelowna but since there was no work, he'd come to the coast to try his luck in the logging industry. Accommodations are hard to find and too expensive for most of these folks, so they buy old trailers and set them up in these little communities where an entire month's rent runs just over $500. In all fairness, the place was quiet and we didn't spend much time there so we shouldn't judge. And, it was the only game in town. Plus, we were off exploring!

Gibsons (originally known as Gibsons Landing) is the name of the actual town and its claim to fame is that it was here that the long running CBC series *The Beachcombers* was filmed during the 70s, 80s and 90s. I can't say I ever watched it but reading up on the history was quite interesting. The show ran for over 380 episodes, considerably longer than better-known sitcoms such as *MASH*. Much of the action took place around Molly's Reach on the waterfront, which has now been turned into a restaurant, and diehard fans (yep, they do exist) still continue to make the odd pilgrimage. Gibsons itself has a cute little harbour with a few interesting little shops and cafés and the overall vibe is pretty casual and unpretentious. While there were some uber homes here and there, most fit into the more "modest" category despite their upper end price tags. My only complaint would be that they roll up the sidewalks at 4 o'clock. Even the two coffee shops close at 4! Now that is not civilized. Driving along Hwy 101 towards Sechelt (which is more sprawling with a strip-mallish feel) was nice for all the green but lacked the wow factor of other west coast drives. And beaches? Nada. They have a few places where it is possible to access the water but there is almost no sand to speak of. Lots of large round barnacle covered rocks and huge washed up logs, but they aren't going to be holding any sandcastle building competitions here. That was okay with me. Just sitting on a huge sun-bleached log watching the Oyster Catchers picking their way through the kelp was my idea of a perfect day at the "beach". The only down-side was that the rocks aggravated the arthritis Porter has in his front paws, so walking was a bit difficult for him. We managed to find one area that had a small stretch of sand and he was busy rolling in it in no time. Again, I was so grateful the land yacht had central vac! We had hoped to do some kayaking but there weren't any areas that really seemed worth it. That sounds spoiled. But this is the Pacific Ocean where one has to contend with currents and tides in addition to the usual wind and chop. So we were looking for sheltered bays and coves to explore. We found one area that had potential but by then, the weather was not cooperating. Overall, the temperature was around 16C (while back in Ontario we read about heat alerts) and clouds often hid the sun. You can't have everything. Near Earls Cove (the jump off point for the next ferry crossing to Powell River) we took the time to go on an easy 4-km hike to the Skookumchuck Narrows (Chinook for "strong water"), a place where the tide ebbs and flows between the Georgia Straight and Sechelt Inlet with such speed (up to 30 km/h) that the roar can be heard from the hiking trail. It was a beautiful walk through the forest although evidence of prior logging was everywhere, and clear cuts could be seen on almost every distant peak. We watched two sea lions feeding on salmon in the rushing water and although our timing was off for the big show, the highlight was really the walk in the woods. We enjoyed it so much, we went back a second day, had a picnic lunch on the rocks and watched Porter pull bull kelp out onto the shore.

The crossing to Powell River was on another perfectly sunny day and once again, cruising through the various channels was lovely. We even saw a humpback whale near the shoreline. And staying in Powell River was very convenient. We had stumbled across a municipal campground right on the water and it actually had a bit of a sandy beach. Local Tla'amin artisans were carving a canoe out of a large cedar log as part of the wide-ranging reconciliation process, and any interested persons, aboriginal or not, were welcome to participate. Once completed, it will be ceremoniously presented to the Tla'amin Nation to honour the teachings of the Tla'amin people. No word on what exactly their teachings are. The cynic in me thinks that these projects, while well-meaning, are really just an exercise in preaching to the choir. Those who believe in the reconciliation concept, both aboriginal and non, will joyfully participate and truly believe they are effecting change. And those who do not believe in reconciliation, again on both sides, couldn't give a rat's ass. I am still uncertain as to which camp I am in. The Tla'amin were in the news last year because as of April 2016 they became a self-governing nation, free of the Indian Act. All 1,100 of them, 60% of whom live in a small settlement just north of town. And you know it when you get there. It has the same run-down reservation look as many other aboriginal communities throughout the country. Their new autonomy grants them self-governance, law-making authority and even tax authority over people living on about 8,000 hectares of former Crown and Reservation land. But the federal government will still be providing tens of millions of dollars to prop them up. So what they now have is a Constitutionally protected modern treaty. Troublingly, there were many within the Tla'amin community who were not in favour of this new arrangement (the vote barely passed by majority) and considerable resentment and hostility still exists. I don't profess to have a deep understanding of the Indian Act nor the Constitution for that matter, but it seems to me that the aboriginal signatories of the first numbered treaty signed back in 1871 at Lower Fort Garry like-wise did not have the full support of their people, and that one didn't work out too well either. And so it goes. *Plus ça change...*

The town of Powell River itself had its heyday in the early 1900s with a pulp and paper facility, the largest one in the world at that time, employing almost 3,000 people. Starting in 1930, old WW I and II transport ships, collectively now known as The Hulks, were brought in and strategically placed to act as a breakwater for the log pond. Many of these ships were actually built of reinforced concrete, at a time when there was a shortage of plate steel for ship construction. Once the wars were over, the concrete ships were found to be too heavy in relation to their cargo carrying capacity and were not able to compete with the steel cargo vessels that replaced them. What to do? Reuse and recycle! They looked very out of place from the roadway that overlooks the factory, especially considering the natural beauty that surrounds them, but paddling up close was an entirely different matter. Almost creepy. They looked like they belonged in some post-Soviet naval facility. Or something out of a post-apocalyptic movie set. Change that to definitely creepy. The mill has downsized over the years (they now have 400 employees) but the town still chugs along despite its shaky economy. While it tries hard to promote itself as a tourist destination, and the surroundings are lovely, it just didn't quite have that upbeat tourist vibe. Perhaps some vacationers are turned off by the neighbours they inherit when overnighting in the campgrounds. At Willingdon Beach, where we were set up, policy limits stays to 14 nights in any calendar year. Yet it was obvious that quite a few sites had been occupied considerably longer than the allotted two weeks – mostly by single men in run down campers who were less than fastidious in keeping things tidy. I don't know if they were working at the pulp & paper plant, logging, fishing, or just down on their luck. But this lifestyle seemed to be a pattern in this part of the country. It was a bit off putting.

PADDLING PAST ONE OF THE TEN HULKS – LIKE SOMETHING OUT OF A POST-APOCALYPTIC MOVIE

The highway ends in the town of Lund. Literally ends. Or starts. Mile 0 of Highway 101 – which then stretches 24,000 kilometres south to Quellón, Chile. Now that would be a drive! The little hamlet isn't made up of much more than a small harbour, a few eating establishments (fantastic cinnamon buns at Nancy's Bakery) and the historic Lund Hotel that dates back to 1889 when the town was founded by two Swedish brothers. (Under the new "treaty" it is now Tla'amin property.) A few high-end vacation homes are perched on the rocky shores on either side of the inlet, but the main draw is its proximity to Desolation Sound and the Copeland Islands Marine Park, a kayaker's delight with numerous coves and bays to explore. The water is very clear, and all manner of colourful starfish can be seen clinging to the rocky shores. We were only able to secure daycare for Porter on two days but took full advantage to be out paddling as much as possible. Although the weather had turned and it was definitely west coast cool (and rainy one day), very little beats being on calm water in a kayak where you can hear the sound of seals breathing as they come up for air. They are ever curious and would often pop up behind the kayaks just to get a better look at us. The Copeland Islands are a short paddle out of Lund harbour and we quite enjoyed ourselves despite the weather. Another day we paddled up Okeover Arm and came across numerous oyster farms. I've never been a fan of oysters on the half shell (I prefer Rockefeller) but we did discover some interesting oyster facts from talking to one of the owners. Oysters take two years to grow to market size (sometimes three) and the best tasting ones are those that are harvested during April. Supposedly they have the sweetest taste. Those collected in the summer months have absorbed too many algae and plankton flavours making them taste too fishy. So next time you belly up to the oyster bar, ask when they were gathered.

If not April (winter is ok too) feel free to turn up your nose.

Savary Island was another little gem that we stumbled across. Accessing it required a 15-minute water taxi ride from Lund and once there, many of the trappings of modern life slipped away. There are no paved roads. No hydro. Electricity to cottages is through generators and solar panels. No garbage receptacles. Pack it in, pack it out. Only a few cafes and galleries (that were closed for the season.) But the wonderful wide sandy beaches and relatively warm shallow water make it a popular summer destination. The island is less than 8 kms long and 1 km across yet is the most sub-divided of any island in the Salish Sea (1,750 small lots) with local residents determined to maintain its pristine beauty and prevent further development. Typical selective hypocrisy. Development is fine while you are looking to buy, but once you have joined the club, "Oh no, we can't have any further expansion. It's bad for the environment!" We spent a beautiful sunny day enjoying a deserted beach where only two other people (with a chocolate lab, no less) set up at the other end. Porter was in his element. Water, sand, seagulls. What more does a dog need? And for us? Peace, rest and rejuvenation. Our departure from the Sunshine Coast coincided with a stretch of beautiful sunny fall weather so we considered staying longer but since the next phase of our journey was towards Utah, we wanted to be through the Cascade Mountains before winter weather moved in. As it was, I had already taken to wearing long underwear beneath my hiking pants. Plus, we were hearing about snow in the B.C. interior. Therein lies the drawback to this mode of travel.

Sometimes you find the great places a bit late in the game, and having discovered Savary Island, I wished we had gone there sooner rather than spent an entire week in Gibsons. And as much as I liked to think we would return, that list was starting to get a bit long. Sacrifices will have to be made.

A DAY AT THE BEACH — SAVARY ISLAND.

18.

IS THIS WHERE WE SHOOT OUT THE TIRES?

INTO EVERY LIFE A LITTLE RAIN MUST FALL AND ALTHOUGH WE STARTED OCTOBER ON THE SUNSHINE COAST, IT WAS APPARENTLY OUR TURN. It didn't rain literally, just figuratively. We had decided to spend one more night on the Sechelt Peninsula instead of rushing to the ferry, so we scouted around for a suitable camping spot in Porpoise Bay Provincial Park. So far so good. But while guiding John into said suitable camping spot we had a small boo-boo with the yacht. Actually, we were not sure how small it would be once the insurance company took a look, but I didn't think it was all that bad. (Based on my non-extensive experience with insurance appraisals.) In a nutshell, the manoeuvre required a three-point turn on a tight narrow curve and while nosing forward, the rear wheels of the yacht went into and out of a deepish gully/ditch. This would not have been a problem except the overhang at the back of the bus is a good 6+ feet and it was this section that caught onto the ground. John had to reverse out and that exacerbated the problem, causing damage to the right rear bottom corner and twisting one of the basement doors. In an effort to assuage our dismay, we listed all the things that had not happened. No one was dead. No one was injured. The yacht was still driveable. The damage was hardly noticeable. And the Tiffin Motor Coach Company could do the repairs. All that was required was another trip to Red Bay Alabama. We formulated a plan to drop it there so the work could be done while we were home over Christmas. Insert a big sigh here.

We left the Sunshine Coast on an appropriately sunny day and caught the 10:50am ferry from Gibsons Landing to Horseshoe Bay, planning to drive as far as Yakima in Washington State. Didn't even come close. While the ferry crossing was as smooth as they come and a fitting way to say good-bye to this lovely part of the country, there was no safe place to hook the Toad back up to the coach once we disembarked (it is cheaper to cross unhitched while on board the vessel) so we essentially drove separately until the border. En route, there was a pretty serious traffic accident just before Vancouver's Port Mann Bridge. I got through in the Jeep with only about a 10-minute delay, but John was a few kilometers back and those few kilometers translated into a good 30 – 45 minutes off schedule. And then at the border crossing, U.S. Customs sent us into Secondary! What?!?! In all our travels this has never happened to us! First, the drug/bomb dog sniffed around both vehicles – twice. We thought that was kind of funny. But at the booth, the officer asked all kinds of questions about the food we had with us. He obviously didn't like the answers because we were given an orange slip and directed to another lane. Porter was locked up in a kennel outside (!!!) and we had to go inside to answer more questions about everything from food to weapons to medication. This while the coach was being searched. At the end of the day, they seized Porter's dog food (because it was in a plastic Rubbermaid type bin, not the usual dog food bag, and they could not be sure of its country of origin) and some smoked pork sausages I had in the freezer (also because they were not in their original packaging and therefore suspect). Plus, one apple and one avocado. I had several freezer bags of homemade stew that they did not take, nor were they concerned with a bag of Porter's frozen beef marrow bones, none of which were labelled. Talk about arbitrary seizure guidelines! At least they didn't find the... never mind. Just kidding. And then we were off! Considerably behind schedule, but once again, south of the border.

The drive down I-5 towards Seattle was very picturesque (especially on a clear day) and seeing glimpses of Mount Baker, and eventually Mount Rainier in the distance only made it lovelier. We planned on exploring the area more thoroughly on our return journey, but at this point with the weather turning cooler, we were focused on getting to Utah with a quick stop at Craters of the Moon National Monument in Idaho first. We headed east along I-90 through Snoqualmie Pass. Rugged mountains, blue sky, winding roads, what's not to like? Once through the pass, however, the landscape changed rather abruptly. Suddenly we were in high foothills and ranch country again. All the green disappeared. It was very windy and ploughed fields had their thin topsoil layer lifted into the air causing considerable haze and poor visibility. It was how I imagined things getting started when reading Timothy Egan's book, *The Worst Hard Time* (about the big dustbowl of the 30s) although we weren't exactly in America's high plains. Dark clouds blew in, the temperature dropped, and it began to rain. Terrific. But by the time we reached Twin Falls, Idaho things had cleared up again. We had not planned on stopping in Twin Falls, but I had underestimated our driving time and Craters of the Moon was still another 2 plus hours off. Just as well. John remembered it was at Twin Falls in 1974, when with much media coverage, Evel Kneivel made his unsuccessful attempt at jumping over the mile-wide Snake River Canyon on his rocket propelled motorcycle. Apparently, his parachute opened at take-off and he harmlessly floated back down to the launch pad. Had he landed in the river he would have drowned under the weight of his safety equipment. In 2016 the reckless feat was finally accomplished by another daredevil, on a motorcycle built by the son of the man who had built Kneivel's bike. Such symmetry. It's still possible to see Kneivel's launch area and diehard fans have erected a monument of sorts to commemorate the effort. Looking down into the beautiful deep gorge, I could only marvel at their stupidity. But then, they were not the only ones risking life and limb. All kinds of adrenalin pumping activities still go on today. We came across a group of young people BASE-jumping off the I. Perrine Bridge that spans the Snake River gorge at a height of 485 feet. BASE-jumping is an extreme sport where participants jump off a Bridge, Antennae, Structure or Earth, usually at a height that does not permit emergency manoeuvres should something go wrong. In most places it is against the law given the high mortality/injury rate but apparently not in Twin Falls. We were walking across the bridge to get a better vantage point for a picture of the gorge when we saw what looked like someone hanging a garbage bag over the railing. The next thing we knew, he had jumped. Instant horror followed by instant disbelief. Seconds later, we realized the "garbage bag" was really his parachute as he floated down to the bottom. We hung around and watched three other people do the same thing except their chutes were strapped to their backs. My hands still sweat just thinking about it.

Craters of the Moon National Monument was definitely worth the drive even though Mother Nature was having a good laugh at our expense. It was snowing when we arrived just past noon and we were the only people in the campground. By evening 6 other foolish travellers had arrived. Why foolish you might ask? Because the campground has no hook-ups and the temperature was predicted to drop to 23 Fahrenheit that night (that is -8 C!!!). And it did! Our propane heater ran all night yet in the morning, the thermometer registered a chilly 57F inside. John had wrapped a disposable heating pad (the kind you'd use for a sore back) around the water pump in the wet bay just in case and brought all the Perrier and Coke bottles that were stored in the "basement", inside. Which was probably the right thing to do. We had left a large plastic tumbler full of water outside just to see what would happen and come morning, it was frozen solid! On the plus side, there was not a cloud in the sky so the sun warmed things up quite nicely by noon. If you can consider 8C "nice". They say in the summer, air temperature can hit 100F (38C) with the ground reaching 150F (65C)! We could have used a bit of that heat during our stay. Since it was Canadian Thanksgiving weekend, I prepared a "cheater" Thanksgiving dinner using stuffing from a box and gravy from a mix, but the turkey was real, as was the pumpkin pie. Not quite the same as at home but you work with the tools you've got. Happy Thanksgiving! And then we began exploring.

I can't say that volcanoes have ever held much fascination for me but as we started walking along the various trails, it really was very informative. The landscape was vast and barren with all kinds of craters and lava flows, and we learned it was not just one volcano that blew its lid and could be credited for the creation around us but rather, lava coming from numerous deep fissures in the earth. Collectively known as the Great Rift, it started about 15,000 years ago with the most recent eruption being only 2,000 ago. Shoshone Indian lore passed down through generations indicates that their ancestors may very well have witnessed this last eruption, and scientists believe more will come in the future. Two predominant features here are cinder cones and splatter cones. A lesson in volcanology: cinder cones form when gas-rich volcanic froth shoots up into the air from a ground vent and the resulting cooling cinders fall to the ground in a conical shape. The more cinders the higher the cone. The surface of a cinder cone is quite granular and easy to walk on yet almost completely inhospitable to plant life. It took almost 2,000 years for the tiny dwarf buckwheat flowers we saw to take root. In contrast, splatter cones are like mini volcanoes that spew blobs of lava into the air that harden and produce an uneven, jagged surface upon landing. Walking on this stuff can ruin even the best hiking boots. It is called "A'a" (pronounced Ah-Ah), a Hawaiian term meaning "hard on the feet." There were miles and miles of A'a. And fluid molten rock squeezing up through fissures like toothpaste coming out of a tube, hardens into various smooth, rough, striated or rope-like shapes. To me, some of them looked like huge cow patties. And the third feature we explored were lava tubes and caves. As lava flows, its surface cools and hardens although underneath the molten rock keeps moving. Almost like an underground river. Eventually the source of the "river" runs dry, leaving an empty space beneath the hard exterior. Sometimes these surfaces deflate, like a soufflé and other times they shatter like peanut brittle, filling in the space below. But in still other places they just remain huge hollow cavities to be explored thousands of years later. We walked, crawled and clambered our way through some of these tunnels, finding new lava formations at almost every turn. I never would have thought to find this fascinating, but it was. I guess there are just some things you have to experience to appreciate. Were we now volcanologists?

Leaving Idaho, we headed to the Salt Lake City area to check out not just the geological features to be found, but the cultural/religious ones as well. Great Salt Lake itself is quite beautiful from the shore, with salt encrusted shallows and dull brown mountains in the backdrop, although it is so huge (the largest natural lake west of the Mississippi), you'd really have to see it from the air to appreciate its size. It is all that remains of ancient Lake Bonneville that once covered more than 20,000 square miles during the last ice age. The salinity is too high to support any fish life, so sailing is the only recreational activity around. And the high salinity comes from the fact that although four rivers carrying over 2 million tons of minerals flow into it each year, the lake itself has no drainage. Only evaporation. Leaving all those minerals and all that salt behind – along with numerous salt/mineral processing plants that while creating a bit of an eyesore, are really only visible on the drive west along I-80 to the Bonneville Salt Flats and the Bonneville Speedway. Naturally, we had to go. The drive is rather flat and straight with only a few distant brown mountain peaks breaking the monotony. The salt flats are so vast it was like driving along huge fields of bright white snow. And the salt actually glistened just like snow. Near a rest stop, we were able to walk out onto them and the further out we went, the warmer it got. I could only imagine how easy it would be to become disoriented in such an expanse, because shimmering mirages were all around. These salt flats were actually a huge impediment to the early pioneers trying to make their way west. The tragedy that befell the Donner-Reed party (of stuck in the deep Nevada-Sierra snow and resorting to cannibalism to survive fame) is partially attributed to the problems they encountered trying to get across this area. An eerie yet dangerous beauty would best describe it. Closer to the Nevada border, is the famous Bonneville Speedway where starting in 1896, men have been trying, failing and at time succeeding at setting world land speed records, with the first event being a carriage vs. bike race. No indication on how fast they went or who won. The first official record was noted in 1935 when Sir Malcolm Campbell achieved a speed of 301.13 miles per hour. The record to date was set in 1997 by Andy Green at 763 miles per hour in a car powered by two Rolls Royce speys jet engines. But that didn't happen at Bonneville. That was at Black Rock Desert in Nevada. It appears this obsession with speed knows no geographical boundaries. The Bonneville speedway itself is 80 feet wide and 10 miles long, and is prepared annually for the races, although some years they are cancelled due to heavy rains that cover the salt, as happened in 2014 and 2015. There is some concern that the salt surface itself is becoming a problem. When these competitions started, the salt layer was three feet thick. But over the years, as machines have pushed it around in an effort to smooth the surface, it is now at a depth of less than one foot. *Quelle surprise.*

And then there were the Mormons. Or as they are more properly known, members of The Church of Jesus Christ of Latter-Day Saints (LDS). They make up over 63% of the population of Utah and over 35% of the population of Salt Lake City. And rightfully so. They did, after all, settle the place. Founded as a new restorationist church by Joseph Smith in 1830, the Mormons were persecuted for their faith and practices (including polygamy) in New York State, so they picked up and moved to Illinois. Their presence wasn't appreciated there either, with Smith himself killed by a mob. Brigham Young stepped up to the plate as second president and led the adherents to the unsettled west where they hoped to practice their faith in peace. They got as far as Great Salt Lake and decided this was the place to build the new Zion. And industrious they were, following one of their guiding principles that everyone should work together in a productive, cooperative fashion in order to build something bigger than themselves. Like honeybees. Hence the honeycomb symbol on all Utah State highway signs. The best place to learn about the Mormons was at Temple Square, 35 well-landscaped acres of religious devotion in downtown Salt Lake City, housing large, impressive buildings such as the Tabernacle and the Temple, not to mention two libraries, a conference centre (seats 21,000 people), office buildings, two visitor centres and a host of other buildings. And everywhere, clean cut people of all ages and races welcoming visitors and unobtrusively engaging them in conversations of faith. In a way it was nice, but at the same time, a bit discomforting. The visitor centre was more of an indoctrination centre and the interior reminded me of a huge funeral home with high ceilings where everyone spoke in hushed tones. Actually, the entire complex is like an indoctrination centre, but then you can't fault them for looking for converts. And we were, after all, there of our own volition. The Temple, built over the span of 40 years and completed in 1893 was quite beautiful, but very few people are allowed to see the interior. In fact, not even LDS members are allowed inside without passing an interview first. Said interview to determine if they are worthy to step inside this space that is considered to be the most sacred place on earth. Suffice to say, we were only able to view a cut-away model in the visitor centre.

But one place where all are welcome, and that I found remarkable, was the Tabernacle. Originally built as a meeting and conference centre in 1867, it is now home to the Tabernacle Choir of Temple Square (formerly known as the Mormon Tabernacle Choir) and Orchestra. It also houses one of the largest pipe organs in the world with 11,623 pipes. And the acoustics! Unbelievable! We attended a short noon-time 30-minute organ recital, and prior to commencing the performance, the organist demonstrated the acoustics of the building by dropping a straight pin onto the pulpit. Sitting at the back, about 175 feet away, we clearly heard the pin drop. This, without a microphone in a room that seats 7,000. The concert was, as expected, outstanding, with the organist playing everything from *Bach* to *Danny Boy* to *Phantom of the Opera*. And the world-famous choir? We were in luck. They practice every Thursday evening and anyone from the public is welcome to attend. So back we went. Choir and orchestra together. I can't say which I enjoyed more – the organ or the choir. Both really were celestial. And all free of charge.

But despite these enjoyable musical interludes, I'm not about to convert. And not just because I would have to donate 10% of my pre-tax income to the church, and give up alcohol and caffeine. I'm simply too sceptical. Smith got his religious revelations in 1823 from the Angel Moroni who told him that two gold tablets with Egyptian hiero-glyphics were buried in a New York State hillside and once he found and deciphered them, voilà, the new true church of Christ was formed. The angel then took back the tablets. I'm also too cynical. Those LDS members who have to pass an interview and are judged to see if they are worthy to enter the temple? Who is interviewing the judges? It seems to me they have quite the exclusive little club going on in there. And I'm far too suspicious. 10% of all pre-tax income from almost 15 million people worldwide is a lot of money. Where does it all go? Really. Yet I do admire one position the LDS seem to hold. Both Joseph Smith and Brigham Young, the founding fathers of this church, were practicing polygamists. A custom that most people, including LDS members today, consider abhorrent. Yet there is no debate about removing their statues nor striking their names from schools and boulevards because of it. Maybe there is hope for Sir John A. Macdonald after all. As an aside, the LDS officially abandoned the practice of polygamy in 1890 (mostly due to threats of property confiscation from the government), but there are off-shoots – fundamentalists (FLDS) – that still think it's a good idea for some 65-year-old guy to have 14-year-olds amongst his numerous wives. Warren Jeffs and Winston Blackmore come to mind. Suggested readings: *Under the Banner of Heaven* by Jon Krakauer, and *The 19th Wife* by David Ebershoff. Both completely different yet excellent books on the topic.

Heading south to Zion National Park, we made a short detour to check out a genuine U.S. ghost town – Frisco, at the base of the San Francisco Mountains, suppos-edly one of the most extensive ghost towns in America. It was a mining town that sprang up almost overnight when the Horn silver mine opened just after 1875 but was then pretty much abandoned 10 years later when the mine literally collapsed. In its heyday the Horn Mine was considered the richest silver mine in the world and provided the U.S. with almost half of its silver supply, along with other ores such as gold, copper, lead and zinc (worth 60 million in 1885 money – about 1.3 billion in 2016 money). It had

16 levels of tunnels and shafts with one shaft over 1600 feet deep and although some areas were cleared following the disaster, and the mine reopened years later, it never achieved its former production level. But it is the town that had the rowdy reputation. Frisco was considered to be the wildest town in the wild west, with multiple murders happening every night and a corresponding extensive cemetery to receive the hapless victims. The 23 saloons and numerous brothels may have had something to do with that. (For Louis L'Amour fans, the name Sackett supposedly appears on many of the cemetery headstones.) In reading the history, I envisioned something like the town in the HBO series *Deadwood*, only worse. But this was LDS Utah, so a Marshal was brought in and given free reign to administer law and order. He believed neither in jails nor judges and summarily shot lawbreakers on sight. The town became quite law-abiding very quickly. I used to teach my criminology students that Deterrence Theory proposes that in order for crime control to be effective, justice must be severe, swift, and certain. It certainly worked in Frisco. And although the town once had a population of over 6,000, by 1930 the place had been totally abandoned and over the years, the buildings have all but disappeared. A few shells remain (mostly from those structures that were built of stone) as well as some of the headframes at the mine entrances. We had read not to go near the mines since many still emit noxious gases, so we stayed clear. But it was interesting walking around the vast desolate area seeing all kinds of rusted-out detritus, from food cans to boilers to what looked like an old oven, and imagining the lives once lived. We also came across 6 huge beehive shaped kilns (in relatively good condition given their age) and sticking our heads inside, could still smell the smoke from all those years of charcoal production. But try as we might, we couldn't find the cemetery. Judging by pictures posted online, it should have been easy but no such luck. We left that for some other explorers and continued south.

We spent one night at Sand Hollow State Park beside a manmade reservoir simply because we could not get into Zion N.P. yet – and found that racing OHV – off highway vehicles – over sand dunes is a favourite pastime in this part of the country. Not my cup of tea at all and Mother Nature was on our side. It was incredibly windy. So much so that no-one was out racing around disturbing the peace but rather, seeking shelter in their trailer of choice. The wind blew all night creating a veritable sandstorm. The following morning all was calm, and the racers were off to a slow start, so we were able to get out and walk around a bit in the newly created sand dunes. The sand was a beautiful deep orange/red colour and with a consistency as fine as flour. Porter loved running around in it and when mixed with his saliva, it created a sort of paste that stuck to his mouth and nose. Not that he minded. Upon leaving, we found that the wind had created sand drifts across the highway and a parks guy was using a bobcat to plough it off to the side. Now that was a windy night!

And then we hit Zion. I love this park! We visited briefly nine years ago while on a Utah/Grand Canyon circuit but our time in Zion was limited to 2 days then. Now we had scheduled six and I loved every minute. Its beauty is difficult to describe. Majestic. Grand. Awe-inspiring. Imposing. Glorious. I could go on and on. Red, orange, pink, beige and grey sandstone and limestone cliffs tower up to 7,000 feet overhead as quiet shuttles whisk sightseers up and down a 10-mile long valley/canyon floor. The national park service instituted a free shuttle service in 1999 simply because the visiting masses were clogging the road and turning it into a virtual parking lot (5,000 cars showing up for 450 parking spaces). The shuttles work great, making 10 stops up and down the canyon where hikers and nature lovers can simply hop on and off at their leisure. And because other motor vehicles are prohibited from using the road (at least between March and November), it was the perfect cycling route. A bit of a challenge going up canyon where it is mostly up hill (steep enough for a workout but not so steep as to humiliate) and a breeze coming back down canyon. My trip meter said at one point we were going 45km/h. What a ride! And the hiking? Superb! Treks of every length and for every ability. We chose to tackle the most difficult one first, since it had been closed for repairs during our earlier trip.

Angel's Landing. It is rated as difficult and not for people who are afraid of heights (it ends 1,500 feet above the canyon floor) but those who make it to the top are rewarded with breathtaking views up and across the canyon. Actually, "breathtaking" can be applied to more than just the views. It was breathtaking just climbing the numerous steep and close switchbacks, and it was breathtaking hanging onto the chains that have been attached to the cliff faces along the narrow ledges with unprotected drop offs that we cautiously crept along. And while in motion, it was best not to look down! Even near the top where we paused for some pictures, it was dizzying simply because we were so close to the edge of a sheer 1,000-foot drop. And by sheer, I mean straight down. We had reached a point just past Scout Lookout and saw the actual peak of Angel's was about another 1/3 mile ahead along a steep narrow spine. In effect, the most difficult part of the hike. We had to make a decision. The clock was ticking, and the odds of us getting up and back down again in a timely manner were slim (Porter's daycare closed at 6). It wasn't so much the distance, as the number of people that concerned us. We were very much caught off guard by the countless hikers trying to scale this beauty. And the narrow ledges and chains had to accommodate those people both making their way up and those making their way down. In quite a few sections, sweaty strangers and I literally embraced as we tried to pass each other without one of us taking a dive down to the valley floor. My hands still sweat at the memory. So this slowed the process to an excru-ciating crawl. We decided that discretion was the better part of valour, enjoyed the view from Scout Lookout and gave up the bragging rights for Angel's. We then trekked a short distance in another direction and found complete solitude. Not as heart-stop-pingly dramatic a climb, but still with breathtaking views. There is always a trade-off.

THE VALLEY FLOOR OF ZION N.P. – ALMOST MADE IT TO THE TOP OF ANGEL'S LANDING.

One last comment on crowding. There is a certain etiquette to hiking. Specifically, when on a trail you don't crowd the person in front of you, going up or down (the down is obvious – if you slip, you will take out the person in front of you). But on an uphill, if you catch up to someone, you pass them. If you can't pass them, you hang back giving them lots of space. On the first 2+ miles of this particular trek, a woman who had obvi-ously not read the hiker's handbook, kept catching up to me, would keep pace at my heels for a while and then fall back. Over and over again. I knick-named her George, after a *Seinfeld* episode where George Costanza wishes to buy an expensive suit but has to wait for it to come on sale. The entire segment has him going through various she-nanigans in an effort to beat other interested shoppers to the purchase. In the end, he is successful but upon wearing his new duds to an important dinner, finds the pants make an audible whistling noise because his thighs rub together as he walks. This particular hiker had the same problem with her pants, and I could always hear her coming. A "whistle while you walk" if you will. It was annoying but funny at the same time. I don't know if she ever made it to the top.

Another day we tackled The Narrows, Zion's signature hike. Calling it a hike isn't entirely accurate since most of it is wading up current through the waters of the Virgin River as they flow down a canyon that gets progressively more and more narrow. The water level is mid-calf most of the time although there are places where it is thigh-high and if you are not careful, waist high. And in several stretches, the walking is downright easy along embankments of sand and stones. Having said that, the water is cold. 47F (8C) cold. At least that is what the sign said as we waited to board the shuttle. (The sign also said that it was tarantula mating season so if we see these huge spiders we should just leave them alone. As if there were any time I would consider not leaving them alone!) When we got on the shuttle that took us to the trailhead, we saw several people kitted out with neoprene lined booties, hip waders and even full body suits. And we smugly muttered to each other, "Well isn't that a bit of over kill?" Apparently not. I was wearing ankle high neoprene socks inside my closed toed Tevas (quite the fashion statement I might add) so didn't find the water temperature all that bad, but John was barefoot in his Tevas and the first hour or so, he was not a happy hiker. He maintains he became acclimatized to the cold, but I suspect he just lost feeling in his feet. The surroundings were fantastic. The canyon walls soared easily a thousand feet overhead in myriad shades of red and orange, in places streaked gray and black where waterfalls appear and disappear depending on rainfall. The river has carved all kinds of curves, hollows and holes over its tens of thousands of flowing years and huge boulders lie scattered about where they have cleaved from the cliffs above. So many colours, hues, shapes and textures. It was fantastic! The only downside? We never reached the actual narrowest part of the canyon where the walls almost form a roof overhead. Blame Porter. We love him dearly but once again, we had to turn back in order to make it to the daycare centre before it closed. Arghhhhh! Foiled again. And then again!

On one of our bike-rides up canyon, John got a flat tire, so that necessitated a drive into the town of Springdale for a new inner tube and pump. Springdale is a cute little place with many nice cafes, bistros and restaurants along with several art galleries and adventure shops and of course, hotels, inns and b&bs. I only wished we were there for a month so we could thoroughly explore the place. As it was, we only managed one nice dinner at The Switchback Grille in order to celebrate John's birthday. Excellent food! And speaking of switchbacks, one bike ride saw us huffing and puffing up the switchbacks that lead to the Zion-Mount Carmel tunnel. The 1.1-mile long tunnel was completed in 1930 and provides easy access from Zion to Bryce National Park and beyond. We wanted to check it out ourselves because when it was built, no-one envisioned the large rigs of today passing through. In fact, its height is 13 feet 2 inches at the centre and 11 feet 4 inches at the sides. So large coaches or buses must travel along the centre line in order to have the necessary clearance (our coach was 12-7). National Parks have set up a system where for a fee of $15, the tunnel is closed to oncoming traffic when larger vehicles pass through. This causes a bit of a delay for traffic in both directions, but no one has come up with a better plan. We were advised we would also have to unhook the Jeep because the tight curves in the tunnel will not accommodate the extra length either. I didn't look forward to the drive. That aside, I wished we did not have to leave Zion, but our reservation had run out and there was not a hope's chance at getting an extension. This is such a popular park that people book campsites up to 6 months in advance (a full year if they want to stay at the lodge). We had just had a spot of pure dumb luck when someone cancelled at the same time we were looking to book. Everything else was reserved solid well into mid-November. So off we went – heading for the tunnel with John driving the yacht and myself following in the toad. The suspense was agonizing. I

thought the roof of the yacht would scrape the roof of the tunnel at every curve and John said that his hands were cold as ice throughout the entire passage. Thankfully we emerged unscathed on the other side and after a short drive of continued spectacular scenery, were able to re-hook at the park's east gate and continued on to Bryce Canyon National Park.

OMG! OMG! IS HE GOING TO MAKE IT?

I should mention at this point that we were also transporting a hitchhiker, one who was uninvited and who would not leave of his own accord. A few nights earlier we were watching television and I thought I saw something move out of the corner of my eye. A scurrying of sorts along the floor. No. Couldn't be. It must have been the light from the tv. Nope. There it was again. And this time John saw it too. A mouse! How it got into the coach we have no idea, but he (she?) had made himself at home in one of the upper cupboards where we stored the junk food. John mentioned that when he went to get the Doritos earlier in the day, he thought it unusual the bag was ripped so badly but didn't give it much more thought. And ate the Doritos! Yuck! So we set out two traps and it took us three days, two nights and several bags of ruined popcorn before we caught the little rascal. Apparently he was partial to Brie cheese and thus ended his free ride. Although John did set the traps for a few more nights just in case there was more than one.

Bryce Canyon is another one of those fantastic national parks that although not huge, contains such a vast array of rock formations that rounding every corner of every hike brings a new feast for the eyes. Due to erosion, huge walls of limestone, sandstone and mudstone have been shaped into thousands of spires, fins, pinnacles, holes, bridges and mazes, collectively referred to as "hoodoos", in wonderful hues of red, orange, purple, white and gray. Limestone is generally a pale beige/cream/gray colour, but the red tones are caused by high iron content and the purple/blue shades from magnesium oxide. Mixed together they make for a lovely artist's pallet. This small area experiences extreme and rapid temperature swings (high heat during the day and below freezing at night) for about half of the year, allowing water to seep into cracks when it is warm and freeze during the night (a process called frost-wedging). We had −8C at night and +20C during the day. And the constant temperature fluctuation accelerates the breakdown of the limestone into its whimsical shapes. Technically, the place is not really a canyon either, but more a series of huge amphitheatres that you can look down into. Walking along the rim trail that overlooks this huge horseshoe shaped "canyon" provided a vast panorama that was especially beautiful at sunrise and sunset. But hiking over a vertical mile down into the canyon itself was what made it magical. The hoodoos were in such fanciful shapes that it didn't take much to imagine a stegosaurus head, a sinking ship, an owl or castle ruins. And several phallic formations just to liven things up. We saw so many fascinating shapes that I wanted to photograph them all. But of course you can never capture on film what you see with your eyes. There were many hiking trails to choose from (we chose the 8+ km Peek-a-Boo Loop) but what differentiates them from other hikes we have undertaken is that we had to go down into the abyss first and then make our way back up again when we were good and tired. This was certainly a challenge because at an elevation between 8,000 and 9,000 feet above sea level, the air is quite thin and our lungs were taking in only 70% of the oxygen they were used to. And as much as it might be a physical mystery, I swear the uphill was steeper than the downhill. Much huffing and puffing, wheezing and gasping accompanied our wobbly legs as we slowly made our way back to the top. An analogy comes to mind. After a long day of hard skiing, when the sun has gone behind a peak and the light is flat, there is still that last ski-out to negotiate. Your quads are burning, your skis are chattering, and you are one millimeter away from catching an edge and hosting a yard sale. But once safely down (or in this case, up) the feeling of satisfaction is wonderful. Worth every lung-busting step. However, if we ever do this again, I am going to suggest we take advantage of the horses that can be hired for said trek. It will be so much easier. Another plus for this park is that it is considered a dark sky preserve, being one of the darkest places in North America that can be accessed by paved road. And with the high elevation and thin air, the stars and the Milky Way were spectacular. I even attempted some night-sky photography and although the results were not a complete write-off, there is still a long way to go.

I could have stayed at Bryce longer, but there are so many wonderful parks in southern Utah, we had to push on. As much as we liked to say we were following the "no plan plan", certain timelines had to be heeded. We started heading east along highway 12 towards Capital Reef National Park, an area so remote and desolate it was one of the last places in America to be discovered by white settlers (not until 1866). The drive alternated between heart-stopping scenic vistas and overlooks, to moments of sheer terror. Okay, that second descriptor may be a bit of an exaggeration but motoring along the winding section of roadway referred to as Hog's Back was a white-knuckler. And I wasn't even holding the steering wheel. Completed in 1935 at a cost of over $1 million, it joins the towns of Escalante and Boulder (which was such an isolated place it has the dubious honour of being the last town in America to have its mail and supplies delivered by mule train), and the road engineers decided that the crest of a narrow fin of rock with the canyons of Escalante a straight drop on either side, was the best location. A vehicular tightrope might give you a visual. What were they thinking?! One guidebook described this stretch as a "swallow-your-gum" type drive. A spot-on description.

We made it to Capital Reef in one piece, settled in and compared the three parks. Zion has soaring cliffs with cottonwood and juniper trees, where you hike up to enhance the experience. Bryce has wide canyon amphitheatres filled with multi-coloured hoodoos and pinyon pines where you hike down to explore. And Capital Reef has narrow canyons with deep red cliffs, slickrock and mesas that you hike up, down and all around. Or go on scenic drives many of which require high clearance vehicles since they follow dry washes. Signs are posted all over cautioning drivers not to head out if a storm is forecast since the back country turns to mud and the washes can become raging torrents. And to bring lots of water and extra gas because there is no-one out there to help you if things go wrong. Game on! We first went for a full day drive into the interior of the park following a bumpy dirt road for about 30 miles that paralleled Waterpocket Fold, North America's longest monocline at 100 miles long (a monocline being a high step-like fold in horizontal layers of rock) that formed 65 million years ago when the earth's crust buckled upward. We then turned onto the Burr Trail Road which required navigating a series of steep switchbacks (800-foot elevation gain in ½ a mile) where once at the top, we stopped for lunch. The view was never ending without a sign of civilization in sight. The Burr Trail was actually used back in the late 1800s by ranchers moving their herds to the other side of the Fold. Part of this entailed driving through the aptly named Long Canyon, a narrow 6-mile stretch of imposing dark red canyon walls that were easily 300+ feet high. Indescribable! We passed several places where people were boondocking and enjoying the remote solitude. I envied them but this was terrain that the yacht could never handle. Too steep, too rutted, too rugged, too narrow, too winding. We started toying with the idea of returning in a "B" Class, and really staying off the grid for a time. Who knows what the future holds? The road eventually wound its way into Grand Staircase-Escalante National Monument that showcased even more of the same. Slickrock, canyons, desert, stone arches, mesas, buttes, weird rock formations and arid plateaus. Legend has it that Butch Cassidy and his gang hid out in this area for a time in the late 1890s and I can see why. There are so many places to lose yourself.

We were staying at Fruita Campground, the only organized camping spot in Capital Reef (the rest is back country) which has a rather interesting history itself. It is an oasis of fruit orchards in an otherwise totally inhospitable landscape. In the late 1800s Mormon pioneers settled the area and planted all manner of fruit trees, irrigating them using water from the Fremont River. The pioneers are long gone, but the orchards remain (almost 3,000 trees) and are tended to by the parks department. When in season, campers are encouraged to

PICTOGRAPHS FROM THE ARCHAIC PERIOD: 5,000 – 8,000 YEARS OLD.

pick whatever fruit they desire (for a small fee.) We just caught the tail end of apple season with only a few ripe apples left on the trees. The lone surviving settler home has been turned into a café/gift shop where the fruit is baked into the most delicious pies I have ever tasted. Since there are no predators out here (except for perhaps the odd mountain lion), wild turkeys and deer roam freely throughout the orchards and the campsites, totally ignoring us interlopers. Porter just about lost his mind. But the Mormons were not the original inhabitants of this seemingly desolate environment. That honour goes to the ancestors of the Hopi and Paiute Tribes. Archaeologists call those people who lived here between 300 and 1300 AD the Fremont Culture, but the Indians refer to them as "*Hisatsinom*" – People of Long Ago. There is no evidence of their presence here after 1300 and archaeologists speculate that they were assimilated into other cultures. The Hopi reject that theory and believe that their ancestors left the region in order to complete their journey to "*Tuuwanasavi*" – the centre of the universe. I certainly have limited knowledge of these ancient peoples but in looking at the petroglyphs that they had chiselled into a nearby rock face, it didn't take much imagination to wonder if those little figures didn't look a little bit like space aliens. And we really weren't that far away from Roswell, New Mexico. More on rock art later.

We managed to get in a few hikes, and one in particular stands out. Capital Gorge is an easy walk through a deep dry canyon that for over 80 years was the route of the main state highway for south-central Utah. Every time a flash flood rolled new boulders down onto the road, Mormons would labour to clear a path so their wagons could pass through. It was only with the completion of highway 12 in 1962!!! that the road was abandoned. Having read about this before we set out, I wasn't sure what to expect but once we started walking along the narrow gulch, I could not believe that people actually drove their cars down there. Cattle and carts okay, but motor vehicles?! There were a few petroglyphs along the way as well, although not in the best condition and evidently graffiti is a rather human tradition. One wall contained the chiselled-in names of several early Mormon pioneers, some dating back to 1888. Part way along the trail, there is an area where a bit of scrambling took us up to what are referred to as water tanks or waterpockets. These were large potholes in the slickrock where water collects after a rain or snowmelt and they are crucial for the few animals and birds that call this inhospitable place home. They seemed so out of place in this arid environment.

We finished off the month in the town of Moab which despite its relatively small size was the perfect jumping off point for exploring Arches, Dead Horse Point and Goblin Valley parks, as well as the perfect place to get caught up on laundry and other housekeeping tasks that we had neglected far too long. Moab is situated by the Colorado River and was originally settled by the Mormons in 1855 when they established the Elk Mountain Mission, one of their shorter lived endeavours that only lasted a few months. Relations with the resident Ute Indians soured quickly, fighting ensued (with both missionaries and Utes killed), and the Mormons packed up, hightailed it back to Salt Lake City, and did not return for two decades. Not a very auspicious start. In 1952 a down and out prospector discovered one of several major uranium deposits and almost overnight, Moab became one of the richest communities in the U.S. (although judging by the real estate, you'd never know it – lots and lots of double-wides). The boom lasted until 1970 when demand for uranium dropped off, but then the outdoor enthusiasts moved in. Moab is a mecca for hikers, rock climbers, river trippers but most of all, mountain bikers who coast along the slickrock at adrenalin pumping speeds. We chose to forgo the more hazardous pursuits and continued exploring by foot, starting with Dead Horse Point State Park. And yes, the reason behind the name is as you would expect. We hiked a 4-mile loop with numerous overlooks, in many cases gazing 2,000 feet down to the Colorado River. It was almost like a mini Grand Canyon. In fact, parts of *Thelma &*

Louise were filmed there, as were segments of *Mission Impossible II*, *City Slickers II* and *Indiana Jones and the Last Crusade*. Being a state park, Porter was able to come with us on the hike, but sad to say that at 7 years old, our Hallowe'en baby was starting to show his age. Perhaps it was because we were not by the ocean, but he was really lagging after the first 2 miles despite all the water and treats we brought along for him. Day care was going to be required if we planned to be out for more than a few hours. We also checked out some fascinating pictographs (painted figures) and petroglyphs on the walls of Sego Canyon, about 40 miles north of Moab. There is a lot of rock art along the Colorado River and up its tributary rivers and side canyons, and archaeologists have classified it into three distinct periods. Archaic, from 6000 – 1000 BC, Fremont from 450 -1300 AD and Ute from 1300 on. The Ute style is easy to identity because their figures include horses, which were introduced by the Spanish in the 1600s. But it's the 6,000-year-old Archaic style figures that have the bug eyes and antennae, and look the most like aliens. Makes you wonder doesn't it? Hmmmmm.

And then there was Arches National Park. It contains the largest concentration of natural arches anywhere in the world (over 2,000 catalogued) and is a hiker's paradise. The trails are not difficult (for the most part) but if hiking is not your thing, amazing rock formations can be seen just by driving along the newly-paved 20 miles of roadway. We started with a 45-minute hoof out to Delicate Arch, often seen on promotional photos of Utah, and it was lovely. Especially in the evening sun. It sits at the edge of a natural amphitheatre and we were lucky to get there when we did, because within 20 minutes a large group of foreign tourists showed up. They were either unaware or didn't care that their voices were being amplified for everyone to hear. Not that we could understand what they were saying but it was quite annoying. And the difference between a natural arch and a natural bridge? Natural bridges are caused by rushing streams or other fast flowing waters as they erode the rock above them. Arches begin as recesses in limestone fins that slowly enlarge as water seeps in, freezes and thaws, ultimately cracking the stone. Gravity does the rest. We hiked out to several of these – Landscape, Double O, Partition, Turret and couldn't decide which one we liked the best. Maybe Partition. Some places along the routes required a bit of balancing as we had to walk along high fins but there was never any real danger of falling as long as you watched where you put your feet. The arches themselves are constantly changing. In 1991 a large section of Landscape arch came tumbling down (caught on camera by one lucky soul) and sightseers are now no longer permitted to walk underneath it given its unstable nature. The park also asks people not to scramble up onto the tops of the arches but there are always those who believe the rules do not apply to them. We saw two such idiots. I was half hoping for a mishap. Does that make me a bad person? And then there were the slot canyons. We only tried one, Little Wild Horse near Goblin Valley State Park. It is a very popular hike given its proximity to the park and is one of the few slot canyons in the area that can be explored without any canyoneering equipment or experience, so off we went. Gaining access required a bit of a scramble up and around some slickrock crags, but once in, it was fantastic. The entire loop is 5 miles long, but we turned back after about an hour simply because we didn't want to wade through a pool of water that was blocking our path. No biggy. The most scenic part was near the mouth anyway. It was a great "walk" and the smooth, curved sandstone walls were amazing. In places the passage became so narrow we had to turn sideways to move forward. Thankfully, given the time of year, we only met six other people along the way. I managed to smack my head quite hard on a large boulder we had to crawl underneath, by straightening up too soon, but that was the only ouchie. Slot canyons can be very dangerous at the wrong time of year, mostly when thunderstorms bring on flash floods. But that is how the stone gets sculpted, so forewarned is forearmed. You never go in without getting a weather report first.

As had become customary, I hated to leave. Too many canyons and arches were left unexplored. Plus, I really wanted to try slickrock biking and rock climbing before it was too late. What if the outfitters advised me there is an age limit? Perhaps I've already passed that limit, but I'd still like to try. How old is too old? John and I always joked that while on this journey, if we found a place that we really, really loved, we'd just shoot out the coach's tires and stay put. I was pretty close to shooting out the tires. Not necessarily to live in Moab but somewhere in southern Utah. It is glorious.

DELICATE ARCH, UTAH. I'M READY TO SHOOT OUT THE TIRES.

19.

SHHHHHH! I THINK I HEAR SOMETHING!

NOVEMBER WAS PART NEW MEXICO, PART TEXAS MONTH, ALTHOUGH WE DID TAKE A SHORT DIP INTO NORTH-EASTERN ARIZONA TO SEE MONUMENT VALLEY NAVAJO TRIBAL PARK ALONG THE WAY TOO. It was so close to our route, how could we not? The road in is along highway 163, passing through what is referred to as Navajo Nation Tribal Lands, the current parlance for Navajo Indian Reservation. Sadly, the shoulder of the highway was blanketed, literally blanketed, with beer cans, and green and brown beer bottles, some broken, some not, that glistened in the rays of the afternoon sun. I have never seen so much deliberate despoilment of what otherwise would be a picturesque drive. Perhaps it's a right-of-passage to toss empties from passing cars, or perhaps they just don't care, but either way there is no excuse. The "sacred" designation that is applied to so many native places out here was obviously overlooked along this stretch. There were also numerous lean-to type shelters advertising the sale of "authentic" and "handmade" Navajo jewellery, dream catchers and the like, but many of them looked abandoned, listing precariously to one side or another. Yet the park itself was clean and efficiently run with a museum and a modern hotel that architecturally blended so seamlessly into the surrounding landscape you could almost overlook it. The $20 entrance fee allowed us to drive a 17-mile loop along a very rutted dirt road to get closer views of the iconic buttes and mesas. To clarify these terms, a butte is an isolated high cliff-like tower with steep sides and a flat top, taller than it is wide, while a mesa is similar but has a much larger surface area. Buttes generally start out as mesas. We chose not to drive the entire loop. The posted speed limit was 15 miles per hour, but the road was in such bad shape, we barely went faster than 5. Back in 1939, Hollywood director John Ford filmed his first motion picture here (*Stagecoach*, which launched John Wayne into stardom) and almost singlehandedly brought the genre of Westerns back into movie vogue. More "recently", movies like *Easy Rider, Forrest Gump* and *Back to the Future III* used the locale. Driving up and around the area it all seemed so familiar, but that is probably because well over 60 movies, tv shows and commercials have used this beautiful terrain as a backdrop for one scene or another. Whether I consciously realized it or not, I had seen these vistas many times before.

We deliberately bypassed The Four Corners, the only quadripoint in the U.S. where the four states of Utah, Arizona, New Mexico and Colorado intersect. Two reasons for our decision. First, we didn't want to pay for the privilege of placing our four extremities in four different states at the exact same time. Signs lead to an area that claims to be the exact locale, but it is fenced off (another Navajo Tribal Park) and payment is extracted prior to entry. But more importantly, it may not really be the correct place anyway. There is considerable controversy that this location is not where Congress intended to put it in 1863, following the Civil War. The problem stems from the imprecise surveying technology of the time, and GPS today points to a spot 1,807 feet west. But the Navajo have a pretty profitable business going there with over 250,000 visitors each year and they are not about to give in to the correction. It's a little bit like all those people in Key West lining up to have their photo taken at the "southern-most point" marker, which really isn't. And truthfully, there was a third reason. We were tired, the road was bumpy, and we had a long way to go. So on we went.

We entered New Mexico in the north west corner of the state, and I can't say I liked it much, if at all. It was desolate, but in a very forlorn, unwelcoming sort of way and appeared quite impoverished. Trailer homes, double-wides and aluminum-clads outnumbered houses at easily 25 to 1. This is natural gas and ranching country although the ranches were not affluent by any stretch of the imagination and Lord only knows where the cattle (the few heads that we saw) actually found anything nutritious to eat amongst all the sage scrub. And the people living in these trailers were what we referred to as "external hoarders". It seemed that every type of once motorized vehicle that they, their father, their grandfather and all their aunts and uncles ever owned, was randomly abandoned hither and yon, scattered throughout the property. Along with half-finished sheds, listing outhouses, children's toys, weathered wooden skids and rusting barrels. I shudder to think what they had inside. John said whatever wasn't abandoned was covered in rust and dust. Well put. And if impressions of places can be described in colours, while Utah was a lovely rich deep red/orange, New Mexico an unappealing pale

Dijon mustard yellow. My opinion became more positive as we made our way south east, but that was my first reaction. So why were we there? We wanted to get to Chaco Culture National Historic Park, a UNESCO World Heritage Site. It was easier said than done.

The park is located about 60 miles from the closest town (Bloomfield) and although it has a campground, RVs over 35 feet are not permitted. So we left the coach in an RV park in town and set out in the Jeep. The first several miles were easy highway driving. Then we turned onto a bumpy "country" road, which soon turned to gravel, which soon turned to wash-boarded and deeply rutted hard packed dry mud. It was horrendous. Seven miles of horrendous. But once we reached the park boundary, relatively smooth pavement again. We asked at the visitor's centre why portions of the road were in such bad condition and the ranger at the desk just rolled her eyes saying that the really bad stretch was on Navajo land and they just refused to fix it, ignoring all written and verbal entreaties. Rather ironic given that in the literature the park makes available, the relationship between the Parks Service and the local Indians is described as amicable and cooperative. Obviously just on paper. And as usual, this was a sacred area, so we were to enter with respect. I did so as much as I was able because this whole living in harmony with nature and each other was getting a bit rich. Chaco Culture Park, located in Chaco Canyon is an important archaeological site that reveals much about the Ancestral Puebloan civilization that once thrived there. Conventional misconceptions have us believing that the Navajo and Apache have lived in this area since time immemorial, but it turns out that is not true. From what we were able to learn (compiling information from various sources), the Chaco Canyon area has had some form of human habitation for well over 10,000 years. The Chaco people (or Ancestral Puebloan as they are more commonly called) were one of the first groups to be identified, where starting in the mid-800s and over the span of 400 years, they established a far-reaching commercial and social community. They built three and four story stone buildings using masonry techniques that archaeologists have determined were very unique for the time, quarrying stone from the huge cliffs around them, and by the early 1100s, Chaco Canyon was a ceremonial, administrative and economic centre with roads linking over 200 large, many-roomed houses throughout the region. Pueblo Bonito alone had over 600 rooms and 40 kivas (circular subterranean ceremonial chambers). The Hopi and New Mexico Pueblo people consider the Chaco to be their ancestors but why they left the Canyon is unknown. How the Navajo and Apache came to dominate the region is glossed over, other than to say, "the Navajo are not a Puebloan people, but they came to occupy much of the former Puebloan homelands." Gee, I wonder how they accomplished that? Probably through peaceful dialogue and scared ceremonies. The Navajo and Apache peoples originated in the Athabaskan culture of Canada and Alaska, with the Navajo only showing up in the southwest between 1200 and 1400 and the Apache in the late 15th century. That's about the same time as the Spanish, give or take 50 years. And also around the time the Puebloan peoples starting abandoning Chaco Canyon and moving to cliff dwelling abodes. Coincidence? Hmmm. Somebody should write an objective thesis on this timeline. Interestingly, the Ancestral Puebloans are also historically referred to as Anasazi, yet they object to this label. Why? Because "Anasazi" is the Navajo word for "ancient enemy" or "enemy ancestor." Yep, the native people were all just one big happy family until the Spanish showed up in 1539. But I digress. More on that later. One very interesting perspective the park did present was a comparison of Chaco buildings to other structures that were being erected throughout the world at the same time. Angkor in Cambodia, Durham Cathedral in England, L'anse aux Meadows in Canada. It really helped put things into perspective. But the park is huge, covering 53 square miles with too many pueblos/great houses to explore in detail, so we focused on Chetro Ketl (3 square acres alone) and Pueblo Bonito which is even bigger, marvelling at the intricate brick work and labyrinth layout. We scrambled up the high cliffs to get a bird's eye view of the canyon, keeping a close watch on Porter so he would not get too close to the edge and just sat for a while contemplating what life must have been like in such a seemingly inhospitable land so many hundreds of years ago. All in all, I am glad we went but as became very apparent throughout the month, it was very difficult to get the real history of Indian, Spanish and Anglo relations without political correctness getting in the way. Very tiresome.

We left the northwest part of the state and started making our way east towards Taos, still puzzling over the word "pueblo". I had always thought that a pueblo was a type of dwelling house, found predominantly in the southwest, historically constructed of a building material called adobe (which I learned is made of mud or clay mixed with sand and bound together with straw or grass) and inhabited by southwest native Indians. And that is true. A pueblo is a house. But a pueblo is also a village made up of pueblo buildings forming a community, of which there are 19 in New Mexico. As in Acoma Pueblo, Taos Pueblo, Santa Clara Pueblo. And a pueblo is also a people or tribe, including Hopi and Zuni who believe their ancestors are the Ancestral Puebloans. And when the word "pueblo" is used in the village sense, it also denotes a particular cultural affiliation. Each pueblo village has its own diversity and style of eg. pottery, with the Acoma being very different than the Taos. (White clay adorned with black stripes vs. brown clay with no pattern.) Similar, I suppose, to how different regions in Latvia have different patterns for their mittens, sashes and national costumes. Except its more confusing in the southwest.

As we continued east, the sage and scrub gradually turned to grass and the ranches, if not of a JR Ewing calibre, were at least marginally better kept. But that didn't last long. We drove across the Rocky Mountains (yes, they do extend this far south!) and were soon down in scrub again. And it was flat, flat, flat with the Sangre de Cristo Mountains in the far distance. We were quite close to Taos when we noticed some very bizarre buildings, houses of a fashion, scattered throughout the wide open plain. Many were half submerged in earthen mounds and all had their windows facing south-west. They looked like they had been designed and constructed by artsy hippies, on acid, influenced by aliens. Then John had the Ah! Ha! moment. This was an Earthship Community, formally known as The Greater World Earthship Community, brainchild of architect Michael Reynolds. He had an epiphany in 1988 that houses do not have to be built from raw materials such as lumber but can be self-sustaining and built from discarded garbage. He constructed his first home shortly thereafter using cast-off tires packed with dirt for the exterior walls and recycled old bottles and cans for the inside. Other environmentally conscious people jumped on the bandwagon and these communities have since sprung up in 50 other states and 20 other countries. In the Taos area, the neighbourhood sits on over 600 acres and has no power, water, gas or sewage lines going in or out. Everything is self-generated or recycled, including water, which is collected, treated, filtered and reused. Each home even has its own greenhouse. The only "outside" help at some homes is a propane tank that can be used to aid with cooking or heating water. The "Earthship Biotecture" has been referred to as "a supermodel of sustainable living" and if you are so inclined, it is even possible to rent some of the homes and studios through Airbnb. The jury is still out on this one. I'm all for helping save the planet but aesthetically, they have a long way to go.

Just past these eco-conscious pioneers, we came to the Rio Grande Gorge. It just suddenly appeared as a huge gash in an otherwise totally flat plain. The Rio Grande itself is the fifth-longest river in the United States, starting in Colorado, flowing 3,000 kilometers to the Gulf of Mexico and for 2,000 kilometers being the actual border between the U.S. and Mexico. Near Taos, the Rio Grande Gorge Bridge, built in 1965, spans the river at a dizzying height of 650 feet and is the second highest suspension bridge in the country. Only the Royal Gorge Bridge across the Arkansas River in Colorado is higher (at 955 feet.) We took the time to walk out so that we were directly above the water, which was only about 60 feet wide at this point, and saw three kayaks making their way down the slight rapids, but from this height they were so small we could only make out the boats, not the paddlers. We were curious to see what the river would look like in Texas because we planned to stay in Big Bend National Park once we made our way further south. But for the time being, we were in Taos.

We stumbled across a RVing blog where the author recommended camping at BLM campsites down in the gorge and that worked out very well. BLM stands for Bureau of Land Management and is in effect, the U.S. version of Crown Land. Except in the southwest, they do a much better job of making it accessible for recreational use. This particular area, Orilla Verde, had three campgrounds strung out along a county road that followed the course of the river just south of town. They were small with no more that 15 sites each and not fancy (are campgrounds ever fancy?) but did provide electric hook-ups and water. It was just what we needed. The river is not really that impressive at this point and made me wonder where the term "Grande" came from. It was neither deep nor fast flowing. More of a meander. It actually reminded me a bit of Bronte Creek near Sidrabene except with the rocky cliffs on either side. Perhaps Grande refers more to length than width. Our first morning we decided to drive into Taos but had gone no further than 100 yards when we were confronted by a herd of Bighorn sheep. Photos were in order. Some of the rams were quite large and although a bit skittish, were not about to make way for us. One was actually lying down in the middle of the road. They eventually moved off to graze elsewhere although not before three of the larger ones waded across the river and nimbly leapt up the uneven rocks that soared several hundred feet above us. Pretty impressive.

TAOS PUEBLO

Our first stop was the Taos Pueblo, which promotes itself as being the oldest continuously inhabited community in the United States, with a 1,000-year history. We learned later that quite a few other pueblos in the southwest make the same claim, although this one does have a UNESCO designation. I'm not sure how their past was verified because the Taos Puebloans say they have a "detailed oral history which is not divulged due to religious privacy." What?!? Most of them are Catholic! About 150 people live in the Pueblo full time, in the same manner their ancestors did 1,000 years ago, carrying water by pails from the nearby creek into the homes for cooking and washing. Others live in conventional houses close by, where they can avail themselves the luxurious conveniences of electricity and running water but come to the Pueblo to operate small craft and food shops. We thought we'd sample some traditional "fry bread" at one of these shops. This is a bread that is fried in a deep iron skillet (as opposed to baked in an oven) and is made from both regular corn flour or blue corn flour, sprinkled with icing sugar and then drizzled with honey. Though tasty, it was also very heavy and sat uncomfortably like a brick in my stomach the rest of the day. Good thing I didn't try the chiles. The Taos Pueblo complex has two churches, although one is really just a ruin. It was first built in 1619 but destroyed during the Pueblo Revolt of 1680 when the various southwest Pueblos joined forces, rose up against their Spanish colonizers and drove them south as far as Mexico. Taos Pueblo was headquarters for the revolt with a San Juan Indian named Popé as their leader. But following this tenuous victory, it seems that many Puebloans didn't necessarily want to return to their pre-Spanish existence, and since each Pueblo is self-governing, Popé's edicts of following the old ways were pretty much ignored. So much for a united front. The Spanish came back 12 years later albeit this time with less enthusiasm to eradicate the Puebloan culture and religion. We were off to a slow start in learning about the Spanish influence in the southwest, so we headed off to check out one of the oldest remaining haciendas in the area, la Hacienda de los Martinez. It was a bit of a bust not the least of which because we had jumped forward by a few hundred years into the early 1800s. The hacienda was built in 1804 and stayed in the Martinez family until the mid 1930s when it changed hands several times, fell into disrepair and was eventually bought and turned into a museum. Its claim to fame is that it is one of the few remaining northern New Mexico late Spanish Colonial period "great houses" more or less still in its original form. At least on the outside. It was built fortress-like because New Mexico was suffering from continuous Comanche raids during the 1700s, so the walls are 2 feet thick. That is about the only interesting thing I can say about the place. If ever in the Taos area, feel free to skip this side trip.

Next up was the old San Francisco de Asis Church (aka St. Francis of Assisi if you are Italian) located in Rancho de Taos a few miles from the centre of town. It is a plain but beautiful adobe church, considered to be one of the best examples of mission architecture in the southwest. The only problem is three different sources provided three different time frames for when it was constructed. Between 1710 & 1755, between 1772 & 1815, or between 1813 & 1816. Take your pick. I'm going with 1710 - 1755 because it was built in the centre of a fortified plaza – fortified because of Comanche attacks, and the Comanche were most active in New Mexico around the mid-1700s.

While the church itself has obviously been lovingly maintained, that cannot be said for the rest of the plaza that surrounds it. I'm sure back in the 1700s it was an active square that played a central role in the life of the community but today it is just a dirt parking lot surrounded by abandoned, derelict buildings, many with caved in roofs and boarded up windows, some still bearing their former business signs – eg. Andy's La Fiesta Saloon and Discount Liquors. I wouldn't want to be going to midnight Mass in that neighbourhood.

But there was one church and its surrounding environs that I find difficult to describe, partly because of the effect it had on both of us, though mostly John. It was my decision to go there although I can't say I knew much about it, and John had no prior knowledge of its history, nor its significance. He was simply indulging one of my, "Hey, let's go here" suggestions and agreeably chauffeured us out to the country. When we stepped from the car in the parking lot, John said he immediately felt the hair on his arms stand up and could sense an indescribable spiritual energy. Something he felt deep in his core. I should point out here that neither one of us are overly active in our religious lives. Me, a few times a year church going Lutheran who wishes for stronger faith and he a spiritual yet fallen Catholic who questions the merits of organized religion. And here we were at El Santuario de Chimayo. This is what we learned. The Chimayo area was settled by Spanish colonists in the 1700s although an Indian pueblo, famous for having a natural healing spring, had originally existed there. Legend says that around 1810, the local friar saw a light emanating from a hillside. He started digging and found a crucifix. Three times he brought the crucifix to Santa Fe and three times it mysteriously vanished only to be found in its original hole in the Chimayo hillside. Another legend claims that it was a local farmer who while ploughing his fields, had a vision telling him to dig beneath his plough, and there he found the crucifix. Either way, the dirt within which this crucifix was found, was considered to be holy and possessing healing powers. A tiny chapel was built over the site of the find but so many miraculous healings occurred they had to build a larger chapel (constructed between 1813 and 1816), the one that we were able to visit. The said crucifix itself still hangs in this chapel, and a tiny room to one side has a small 1-foot diameter dirt well or pit (*el pocito*), purportedly the exact location of where the crucifix was originally found. Visitors are able to take some of this holy soil from the well away with them if they so desire. Another small anteroom contains a collection of crutches, canes and other mobility aids that pilgrims have left behind after they were healed. The walls in the room, as well as throughout other niches on the grounds are plastered with thousands of pictures of people for whom prayers of healing have been said, or from whom prayers of thanks for healing have been offered. All manner of crucifixes and rosaries hang from trees, fences, statues and posts. The Santuario is in effect a spiritual place of healing, often referred to as the "Lourdes of America". About 30,000 people go there each year, most making their visit a pilgrimage, although there are people like me who were more motivated by curiosity. Yet once there, one is enveloped with such a sense of serenity, of calm, of spirit, it is difficult to explain. As if all the hundreds of thousands of heartfelt prayers were somehow concentrated into a spiritual energy that permeated the air. I can't describe it without sounding like a fruitcake.

EL SANTUARIO DE CHIMAYO – A PLACE OF INDESCRIBABLE SPIRITUAL ENERGY.

We left the church and headed off to the village (really just a crossroads) where we wanted to stop in at Ortega's Weaving Shop, a small family business that has been making rugs, blankets and the like for over 300 years. Nine generations of Ortegas have laboured there and while they do contract out some of the work, we were able to watch Robert, the current owner, operate a huge loom as he created yet another masterpiece. He appeared to be about our age and said that while he enjoyed the work, he was getting a bit old for the physical part of the business. We were sorely tempted to buy either a rug or mat as a memento of our southwest sojourn, but there were so many to choose from and truth be told, my head was still back at the Chimayo church. I just wasn't in the mood for shopping and that is really saying something!

Not too far a drive from Chimayo, are the Puye Cliff Dwellings, ancestral home of the Santa Clara Pueblo people who had left Chaco Canyon around 900 AD and migrated south. Located on a huge plateau, the site consists of small cavities in the cliff face as well as ruins on top of the mesa. All really very interesting and we could have easily spent more time there if not for the whole day is drawing to a close problem. Obviously we were still trying to cram too much into too short a timeframe. Having said that, the Puye Cliffs are not on public land, (i.e. National Park or Monument) but rather, Native land, so prices were a bit silly for what was offered. The visitor's centre contained very basic information and in order to walk up to the base of the cliffs, we had to pay $10 each. And with that, we were only permitted to explore about 50 yards along the wall. If we wanted to go further, or go up to the top, it was $20 per, and even then, it would be with a guide and only for one hour. That is a rip if ever there was one. There is no way to cover all that area in an hour! Just for spite, I climbed part way up one of the ladders to see what they would do. No one even noticed. There are quite a few cliff dweller locations throughout New Mexico so we decided to forgo further privately-owned offerings in favour of public ones where with our Annual Parks Pass, we could head on in and spend as much time as we like. The perfect place for that was Bandelier National Monument in the Frijoles Canyon. It has 70 miles of trails but suffice to say we covered considerably less. About 68 miles less. We opted for the 2-mile Main Loop Trail that took us along a cliff face where the remnants of cave dwellings and old pueblos still stand, past numerous petroglyphs and up to Alcove House, a niche that was only accessible by climbing up 4 rather long wooden ladders. Not for the faint of heart nor the short of breath. The interesting thing about these dwellings is that many were actually 3 to 4 stories high, made possible by anchoring what were in effect floor trusses into the cliff wall and thus ensuring stability. Sadly, most of the cliffs are easily eroded sandstone that over time, take the man-made structures down with them.

Next stop, Santa Fe – capital of New Mexico. This is a lovely city that although set at an elevation of 7,000 feet (we found ourselves a bit out of breath a few times), boasts 325 days of sunshine a year (although it was cloudy and rained when we first arrived) and can be quite cold (daytime temps were around 65F, nights were around 32F), and the locals said this was a warm November. Founded in 1610 by Spanish colonists, it is the oldest state capital in North America, refers to itself as The City Different (supposedly because of the mix of Native, Hispanic and Anglo cultures) and has the Palace of Governors, a low-rise adobe building that is the oldest continuously occupied government building in the U.S. Beneath its portals, Native American artisans from many of the regional pueblos sell their handcrafted jewellery and other trinkets as they have done for generations. It is all state sanctioned and to an extent, regulated, so that shoppers can meet the actual artists and know they are actually purchasing locally hand made goods as opposed to imitation knock-offs. The knock-offs do exist, and some Santa Fe shops have been raided by police for selling imitation goods that they purport to be the real deal. The city also has the oldest church in the United States (San Miguel Mission) built just after 1610, and as much as I would have liked to have gone inside, I think there is something just wrong about having to pay money to enter a place of worship, no matter how historic. So we walked around the outside. This after we had already paid to go into the Loretta Chapel in order to view its supposedly mysterious spiral staircase. The chapel was built for the Sisters of Loretto in the 1870s, and legend has it that when it was completed, the Sisters realized they did not have stairs leading up to the choir loft. Not knowing what else to do, they prayed. A mysterious carpenter arrived and constructed a circular, helix shaped staircase that has 33 rungs, makes two complete 360-degree spirals and has no central support, nails or screws. The carpenter disappeared without payment and no one knows who he was or where he obtained his supplies. The devout believe he was St. Joseph himself. It was only after we paid and were inside that we found out that although it is a very beautiful chapel, the nuns had long since sold it to a private firm and it is really run as a museum (although it can be rented for weddings too). The sign outside saying "as seen on *Amazing Mysteries*" should have been our first clue but we weren't really paying attention. Literature in the gift shop continues to promote the mysterious carpenter angle, but without getting into details, simple physics and engineering explain the construction perfectly. And the "mysterious stranger" has been identified by an historian as Francois Rochas, a skilled craftsman from the area. So much for miracles. But it does make for a good story and brings in the cash. Ours included.

Santa Fe is also known for its incredible galleries and shops that are more like small, privately owned museums. It is, in fact, the third largest art market in the country. Going in and out of so many was almost overwhelming. We admired the work of gifted painters, potters, sculptors, woodworkers, weavers and jewellers both at the Plaza (the central core) and along Canyon Road a bit to the east. It's a good thing we were living in a motor coach and space was limited because I could easily have taken out another mortgage and gone on a spending spree. Canyon Road in particular had some pretty high-end galleries, many with wonderful sculptures and contemporary paintings, although there were also those pieces where you wonder whose kid had access to the paints. As it was, we limited ourselves to a few humbler purchases to simply commemorate our swing through the southwest. That said, some of the jewellery deserves special mention. A great many of the pieces featured turquoise and while some were quite intricate, many were god-awful clunky ugly. I can't imagine where or even why anyone would wear them. They made some of the old heavy Latvian brooches look delicate by comparison. And since turquoise is in many ways a symbol of the southwest, and figures so predominantly in both jewellery, furniture and art, we thought we'd educate ourselves on that a bit too by driving along The Turquoise Trail, a highway that runs between Santa Fe and Albuquerque. We got as far as Madrid, an eclectic collection of shops in a little village that was once an abandoned ghost town.

Called the Sky Stone, turquoise comes primarily from mines in Nevada, Arizona and Colorado with the New Mexico mines being mostly small, privately owned ones. More by-hand-rock-chipping quarries than deep mines. To the early Native Americans, the stone was considered to have spiritual and life-giving qualities, but it really caught the attention of jewellers when Tiffany & Co. (yes of blue box Tiffany) became interested in a mine at Cerillos, just south of Santa Fe. A semi-precious stone, turquoise is geologically the hydrated phosphate of copper and aluminum, and the higher the presence of copper, the bluer the colour – a deep robin's egg blue. The higher the presence of iron the greener the colour – like a dusty olive. There is a lot of fake turquoise being generated (China has apparently become a major producer of the synthetic stuff) and it is difficult to differentiate between the natural and the non, not to be confused with the natural and the stabilized. Crash course: Natural turquoise comes in various hues and has a matrix – brown to black veins and markings throughout. Stabilized turquoise is turquoise that has been hardened under heat and pressure to keep small or crumbly pieces together and is often uniform in colour. This is all okay. Fake turquoise is either plastic and will melt if a hot pin is stuck into it or is simply a dyed stone. This is not okay. We saw some very creative uses of stabilized turquoise where artists have taken crushed or pulverized pieces, mixed them with a type of epoxy and then somehow injected the substance into the cracks of wood they are using for a given project, be it a bowl, a vase, a knife, a cheese tray, even a chair and coffee table. They were beautiful. I wanted to re-decorate my house.

And on the subject of art, as much as we planned on visiting numerous museums, the only one we got around to was the Georgia O'Keeffe. While I was passingly familiar with some of her work, my knowledge of her as a person was non-existent. Born in 1887, she is one of America's most influential artists well known for her large-scale flower paintings, with abstracts being a favourite genre. She painted New York skyscrapers in her early years, but by 1949 had permanently moved to New Mexico, loving the dramatic landscape and wide-open skies. She once said, "It's so beautiful there it's ridiculous." She continued to paint until 1977 when macular degeneration forced her to relinquish her independence. Never a quitter, she took up pottery although it never replaced her love of painting. She died in 1986, at the age of 99. The museum is not large, and while some of her work doesn't do anything for me, they did exhibit the one piece I was most familiar with, "Ram's head, blue morning glory." Loved it. I left the museum very motivated and most tempted to purchase a steer skull to bring it home (they were available in the Plaza) but couldn't imagine where I would put it once we were back. Somehow, I didn't think it would look right above the fireplace in Mississauga, Ontario. That is the problem with buying things when travelling. Everything starts looking good in the shop (including that clunky turquoise jewellery) but once you get it home... different story. Another appealing quality of Santa Fe was its size. It is not huge and therefore pleasantly walkable. And because it does not have a limitless supply of water (green lawns are discouraged and washing your car on the street will generate a fine), there is no industry, and with no industry, there is limited pollution. The economic engine is government, followed by art and tourism. And most of the architecture is pueblo/adobe style. Did I say it is lovely? And gas is cheap, cheap, cheap; even with the exchange rate. The lowest price we saw was $2.28 per gallon for regular, which roughly worked out to about 57 cents/litre. Diesel was slightly higher at $2.79 or 70 cents/litre. (Later on, in Texas, it was 2.09 and 2.39 respectively.) If only that were so in Canada.

And then there was the food. I love Mexican but it has to be the real deal. Guacamole from scratch, not Taco Bell. We had read about a good place along the aforementioned Turquoise Trail – the San Marco Feed and Café – and decided to stop in for lunch. What we hadn't done was read the fine print, so we were a bit confused after pulling off the highway, out in the country, miles from town. The first thing we saw was the red and white checked Purina symbol, along with large feed bags, hay bales being moved by cowboy-looking types from one flatbed truck to another, farm implements scattered about, and wandering chickens. This couldn't possibly be the place. But around the corner was a small neon sign that said "café". Okay then. We'll give it a shot. It was wonderful. A small cozy alcove with southwest décor, and the most genuine Mexican dishes served by sincerely friendly staff. We both had burritos, and I learned that if you want both red and green chile sauce on your meal, you order "Christmas". And extra sour cream to help with burn. The green was deadly. And keep in mind there is a different between chilli and chile. They also had the best cinnamon buns I have ever had, although for some inexplicable reason, they are to be eaten prior to the main course. Worked for me.

Continuing south, we passed through Albuquerque and the only reason I wanted to drive through there was because of Bugs Bunny. I can't see or hear the name "Albuquerque" without thinking of the episode where Bugs is tunnelling along to where-ever, pops up in the wrong location, and says, "I must have taken a wrong turn at Albuquerque." I can't explain it. I find it hysterical. We considered stopping at Petroglyphs National Monument, which is quite close (practically an Albuquerque suburb) but were pretty much petroglyphed out. Same with cliff dwellings. Gila Cliff Dwelling National Monument was also within a reasonable distance but by this point, we had seen so many is was not likely that we were going to learn or see much new. Instead, we headed off to the National Radio Astronomy Observatory, also known as VLA (Very Large Array). I should point out that this was totally John's idea. The whole space/"final frontier" thing just freaks me out, so I try not to think about it. The site is literally miles from nowhere, the location selected to be as far away from the interference of man-made radio pollution as possible. We even had to put our cell phones on airplane mode or turn them off when we got there because their radio frequency interferes with the work being done. I will attempt to explain what this complex is all about, but it will not be easy. Most of what I heard and read was wa-wa-wa, quasar, wa-wa-wa, gamma ray bursts, wa-wa-wa, microquasar, wa-wa-wa, superdense neutron star, wa-wa-wa, quadrillion calculations, wa-wa-wa, cosmic radio waves, wa-wa-wa. My pea brain can only comprehend this information in a very simplistic way.

HEY! IS ANYBODY LISTENING?

The VLA consists of 27 huge disc shaped antennas that are 82 feet across, each weighing 230 tons. They are purposefully placed in a "Y" shape over an area of about 22 miles. Each dish collects radio waves from galaxies and stars billions of light years away. The data collected is then grouped together so that basically all these discs function as one giant radio telescope. What?!? Objects in the solar system emit radio waves. Planets, the sun, chemicals within comets, the Milky Way, other galaxies, all have radio waves that travel through space just the same as light. These waves can be intercepted by the radio telescopes and through the magic of computers, can be converted into pictures for us to see. Still with me? Put another way, the VLA is a huge radio telescope that, by compiling and processing radio waves, makes detailed digital images of objects in space. So, when astronomers examine these radio images, they can see things that optical telescopes cannot. The computers they use for this process perform 16 quadrillion calculations per second. I don't know how many zeros that is. An information panel at the visitor's centre explained that if every person on earth performed one mathematical calculation on a computer every second, it would take all 6 billion of us an entire month to collect what the VLA computer processes in 1 second. My brain hurts. So far, VLA has shown that the planet Mercury has water ice (okay, I get that), detected radio waves from mysterious Gamma Ray Bursts (huh?), discovered the first "microquasar" (oh sure), and found a billion-light-year-across empty "hole" in the Universe (WTF??). And other stuff too. The only thing that really registered with me was that Jodie Foster filmed parts of her 1997 film *Contact* out here. And I have yet to watch it.

So there. As much as I have difficulty wrapping my head around this stuff, it was pretty neat being able to walk up to one of these huge dishes. And while we were standing there, it and all the others started to rotate in unison, making about a 180-degree turn. Like a perfectly choreographed ballet. We were there in the late afternoon and since the place is so remote, decided to boondock in a large gravel parking area a fair distance from the visitor centre, albeit still on VLA property. Being so far from light pollution it would be the perfect place to practice taking pictures of the night sky before turning in. All went according to plan until 12:30 am, when we were awakened by a knocking at the RV door. It was Security telling us we were not permitted to stay overnight. Why? Because our presence interferes with the collection of the radio signals. Really? Are the radio signals that come in at night different than the ones that come in during the day? We didn't give him a hard time. He was actually very nice and acknowledged that they really should put up some no over-night parking signs so people like us don't get caught out. He also directed us to another gravel lot about 100 yards away that was off VLA property where we could stay. When we awoke the following morning, we found we were actually situated considerably closer to the huge discs than when we had been on their property. So much for radio interference.

Our next destination was White Sands National Monument but en route, we just had to stop and have lunch in a town called Truth or Consequences. With a name like that, who could resist? It actually used to be called Hot Springs but in 1950 the residents voted to change the name to commemorate the 10th anniversary of the tv game show by the same name. It went off the air in 1988. Supposedly the town is quite popular because the hot springs still exist, but we found it rather tired looking. Not pretty. Not posh. And certainly not what you picture when you hear, "spa town". The restaurant we had planned to eat at (after checking Tripadvisor) was closed (this being a Sunday), but another casual place near-by looked if not enticing, at least respectable. When we walked in, we found that it was definitely a local favourite and while the needle didn't exactly screech off the record, it was obvious we were strangers in town. The food was again very tasty authentic Mexican, but I found that having consumed chile sauce at almost every meal several days in a row, my stomach was starting to protest. I should have stuck to oatmeal.

White Sands National Monument is one of those places you have to see to believe. It is an anomaly at the northern end of the vast Chihuahuan Desert in the Tularosa Basin. After miles and miles of pale brown scrub and distant pale brown San Andres Mountains, a seemingly never-ending panorama of white sand dunes appears. Except the dunes are not sand per se but rather gypsum – 275 square miles of gypsum – the largest gypsum dune-field in the world. By its nature, gypsum is a water-soluble mineral so is rarely found in a sand like form. But at White Sands, there is no water drainage. Anything washed into the basin by rain becomes trapped. The water evaporates, dry lakes are formed and strong winds blow the remaining gypsum into beautiful grey-white dunes as far as the eye can see. It's like being in a huge white desert. When we arrived, we noticed a sign at the visitor centre that sleds could be rented. What?! Driving further into the park, we saw why. Children and adults of all ages were having a great time sliding down the huge dunes on plastic discs. Image! Sledding without snowsuits and mitts or freezing your nose and your toes! We went on a short ranger led walk (where even Porter was allowed to come along) and the sunset afterwards was magnificent in beautiful shades of deep fuchsia/coral. The only tricky part? This Monument sits smack dab in the middle of the 4,000-square mile White Sands Missile Range and getting to it requires driving along highway 70. About twice a week both the highway and the park are closed for about 2 hours while the defence department tests a few range missiles. Do they ever go astray? Thankfully, we were spared any such excitement. And another minor point of contention? The park sits less than 100 miles south of the Trinity Site – location of the world's first atom bomb detonation in 1945. Should we have invested in a Geiger counter? Were we glowing? If so, we were going to fit right in at our next destination, Roswell.

Neither one of us is the type to believe in conspiracy theories, especially ones involving government agencies. We have both worked for the government and know first-hand that there is no way things can be kept secret for long. Someone always talks. But once we finished touring The International UFO Museum and Research Centre, we both came away convinced that an attempted government cover-up of some kind had definitely occurred in the case of "The Roswell Incident". Now whether it involved little green men I am not sure, but it certainly makes you wonder. Short summary. In July of 1947 an unidentified airborne object crashed in the Capitan Mountains during a storm, about 75 miles northwest of town. Numerous farmers and townsfolk, including the local sheriff, were involved in the initial response until such time as the air force showed up and took over the crash site. The air force originally issued a statement saying that a flying saucer had been recovered, but 5 days later, recanted and said it was just a weather balloon. Considerable pressure was put on the everyday folks who had seen or heard things, to remain silent. And most of them did. But the museum is in possession of (and displays) numerous affidavits from these people, their families, as well as from air force personnel, detailing their specific roles in the recovery effort. Many of the affidavits were sworn to in the 1990s, while some were letters that had only been opened posthumously. Individually and collectively, they all point to the same thing. Something alien (using the word specifically and generally) had occurred. And interestingly, the testimonials are all from people who were boots on the ground, so to speak. Nothing from anyone high up the food chain. Having worked in policing and seeing how issues are dealt with once politics come into play, I can certainly see a cover-up of sorts taking place. The Museum also displays photographs of unidentified flying objects from around the world (which may or may not be doctored – I couldn't tell), as well as letters from people purporting to have witnessed or experienced strange phenomenon. Some are definitely of the "one-too-many beers" variety but others come from seemingly rational, sober military/law enforcement-type personnel during the course of their duties. One thing that keeps me from being 100% convinced, is that there is very little by way of "new" evidence – i.e. nothing from the past 10 or 15 years. Couldn't they at least get in touch with the people at the Very Large Array? I'm sure someone would have heard something by now.

After Roswell, we continued making our way towards Texas, stopping briefly at Carlsbad Caverns National Park, one of the largest cave systems in the world. I'm not much of a spelunker but this was pretty impressive. It is massive! And much more natural than the privately-owned Luray Caverns in Virginia. At least we had no fear of having to listen to *America the Beautiful* being played by a stalactite pipe organ! Carlsbad has over 30 miles of explored passages, with the deepest chamber being over 1000 feet below surface, but only about 3.5 miles of them are lit and accessible to tourists such as ourselves. We walked down about 750 feet following a winding, paved pathway and were thankful for the paving because some areas were rather dark. But the lit areas were really something to behold. We saw the usual stalactites and stalagmites, but also learned some new terms. "Soda straws" refer to stalactites that are thin and hollow, and collectively all the decorations are referred to as "speleothems". I hope to remember that for the next time I play Trivial Pursuit. One extraordinary occurrence that takes place there every evening between June and October is the massive bat exodus. Tens of thousands of bats (mostly the Brazilian free-tailed variety) live deep within a section of this cave system (in the creatively named Bat Cave), and every evening at dusk they leave the cave in a gigantic swarm. Their departure can last as long as 2-1/2 hours. That is a lot of bats! So many, that when the caverns were first being explored in the early 1900s, bat guano inside was over 40 feet deep! Apparently it is an excellent fertilizer so guano mining was quite profitable until the caves were declared a national monument in 1923 (and achieved "park" designation in 1930 – which really just means they get more government money). I can't say bats have ever held much fascination for me, but I'd be willing to return in the summer just to see the flight display. By late October they have all left for warmer climes in Mexico. Smart bats.

And then we were in Texas, spending the first few nights in Guadalupe Mountains National Park. It was okay, but nothing to knock your socks off. The only thing that piqued my interest was that prior to starting out on a hike, for the first time I noticed warnings and instructions about what to do should a mountain lion be encountered. Running away is not recommended. I sincerely hoped to see one but no such luck. We continued on to Big Bend National Park located at the northern end of the Chihuahuan Desert on the banks of the Rio Grande, with Mexico on the other side of the river. I had high hopes for Big Bend. And as much as I'm glad we went, it isn't a place that we will in all likelihood return to. It fits into the "been there, done that" category and while the park is substantial at over 1,250 square miles, the drive in seemed never ending. It can be divided into three distinct regions. First is the Rio Grande Village area (where we were staying) – all desert. Dirt and cactus as far as the eye can see, and between 10 and 15 degrees hotter than the Chisos Basin area. That said, the campground itself is by the river in a grove of cottonwoods. Many are dying due to an on-going drought but thankfully they do still provide a bit of shade. I'm not sure why they call it a "village" because other than the campground there is only a small general store stocking very basic staples and a few souvenir items. The second area, Chisos Basin, is referred to as an island of green mountains in a brown desert sea. Or something like that. We drove about 40 miles just to check it out, following a steep winding road that is not recommended for RVs or trailers longer than 20 feet. There were still cacti around, but this section had all kinds of trees, and soaring rocky peaks in every direction. I suspect this is where the mountain lions and bears live. There were warning signs for them posted all around too, but once again, we didn't see any. This was by far the most crowded part of the park, with a dated lodge and a restaurant for those who are not into roughing it. The views out over the desert were okay but limited due to a haze caused by dust being kicked up by the blowing wind. And then there is the river. Not overly deep, not overly wide, not overly picturesque, and quite silty with a moderate current. In places, it was easy to access and walk along the sandy banks while in others, it was steep canyon that required a bit of exertion. The prettiest area was by the Santa Elena Gorge where we flaunted the rules by ignoring the "no dogs" sign and took Porter along for the walk. People along the path were very friendly and reassured us that park rangers rarely venture out onto the trails, preferring to spend their time in their air-conditioned vehicles.

We explored as much of the park as we were able, but everything required driving, driving and more driving. And very little was provided by way of information. The park map/brochure indicated where, for example, the ruins of Sam Nail's ranch were, but nothing by way of who Sam Nail was, why he came here or why or when he left. Another area near some hot springs (of which we also learned nothing) had the remains of what we assumed was a small guesthouse/inn (given the peeling and faded Mexican-themed frescos painted on the walls) but again, we were left wondering who, when, why? Same with flora and fauna. What information was readily available pertained mostly to safety although we learned on our own that almost everything in the desert is prickly. The cacti, of which there are a huge variety, have spikes and thorns ranging from miniscule to 3 inches in length. Even the most innocent looking shrub is just waiting to get you. We had scrambled up one overlook when I noticed a brown smudge on my pants. Not thinking, I brushed it off. Big mistake. Barbs, almost microscopic in size were now imbedded in my palm. So small that they were scarcely visible with the magnifying glass once we were back at the coach. And they really hurt!

Then there were the tarantulas. The first one we noticed was crawling across the road, directly in the centre of our lane. We actually drove over it before simultaneously saying, "I think that was a tarantula!" We backed up to examine it more closely. It isn't every day that something looking like a huge black golf ball with legs crosses your path. He (she?) didn't seem too concerned with our attention and just kept booking along. I considered trying to get him to crawl up onto my shoe, but not knowing too much about their venom, decided against such folly. We learned later that their bite, while very painful, is not deadly to humans. We saw six of these creepy-crawlers in total, each time on or along the roadway so who knows how many more were lurking in the underbrush. We also saw quite a few roadrunners. While they are capable of short flight, roadrunners spend most of their time dashing along on the ground, often near roadways, and can reach speeds over 20 miles per hour. I was able to get quite close to one along a trail and found they have a beautiful spot of blue right on the back of their head. We saw a coyote too, but he was just crossing the road in front of us, and not chasing any roadrunners. Go Wiley E.! And then there were the Javellinas (not that we saw any of them either). They are often mistaken for pigs or wild boars, although the two species are not related in any way. Parks personnel were concerned about them because they travel in small packs of a dozen or so, and since they will eat just about anything, have been known to destroy the campsites of campers who have carelessly left food lying about. Hence the metal food storage bins and signs posted at all sites. The park has numerous back-country campsites too, for those wishing to find complete solitude (and perhaps a Javellina or two) but these can only be accessed with high clearance vehicles. We drove along some "unpaved" roads in the Jeep and they were pretty rough so I can't imagine what the "high clearance" ones were like. But at least you would be assured freedom from the park rangers. We had occasion to interact with one officious officer who really was in dire need of a "lighten-up" pill.

One morning I was sitting outside the yacht, brushing Porter. Said officer was about 100 feet away across a grassy common area, called out "Is that your dog?" and started walking over. "No," I thought to myself, "I just happened to grab this stray because I felt like brushing something." But her voice had piqued Porter's attention. "Oh goody! Someone wants to play with me!" He started racing around the Jeep, running in circles (as he does when overly excited) and then running towards her. She brought up a leg as if to kick him, but he whistled right around her and raced back towards me. Twice. Well didn't I get a lecture. Everything from how coyotes hunt in packs and will kill domestic pets, to how dogs must be on a leash at all times – even when moving 7 feet from the coach door to the car door, never on any trails ever, and if this happens again we will receive a citation. Sheesh. If those hungry pack-hunting coyotes were going to attack anything, it would be the 20-pound kid who was playing with a stick by himself at the edge of the clearing far from the protection of his parents, or the 5-pound shaggy rat pretending to be a dog that was on a 20-foot leash, also a good distance from any cover. So many things I wish I could have said, but by this time, John had shown up and his presence prevented me from letting my inside voice come out. I suppose I should be grateful she didn't shoot on sight.

We also had an incident with our American Visa cards. For some reason, RBC had blocked them so when we went to pay for our stay, the staff in the visitor's centre advised they had been declined. We had used them a few days earlier without incident at Guadaloupe Mountains so what gives? Were we too close to the Mexican border? The park has no cell service and the pay phone at the little camp store was not working, but the store owner let us use her's to straighten everything out. Not that we really received any explanation from RBC for the inconvenience other than some mumbo jumbo about algorithms and patterns. And then there was the windstorm. It was only after the fact, that I recalled reading an article posted by more seasoned RV travellers warning that if wind comes up in the desert, close all windows and vents right away. We foolishly did the opposite. Noticing a slight breeze in the morning, we thought, "How wonderful – it will be nice and cool, and the yacht's interior won't heat up too much while we are away exploring. Let's open all the windows." (This campground had no electric hook-ups, so a/c was not an option unless the generator was running.) That slight breeze became a strong wind in our absence and by the time we returned several hours later the interior was nice and cool, as anticipated. But what we had not anticipated was the layer of dust and grit that came in along with said breeze and now covered everything from floors and counters to pillows and books. And this wasn't the kind of dust that you sometimes see gently floating in a beam of sunlight as it shines through your window. This was ugly stuff. I'm calling it air born silt. Start up the generator and plug in the central-vac. Live and learn. But at least we were not in as dire a position as some of the tenting folks. Several tents had collapsed (I think one had bent poles because upon returning, the owners packed up and left) and one tent had its pegs pulled up and was 30 feet from the site resting against a fire hydrant. There was a lot of regrouping going on.

All said and done, we found this park to be a bit run down and "tired", certainly in comparison to other national parks and even some state ones. I don't know why. Perhaps it doesn't get the number of visitors to warrant a much-needed cash infusion, or perhaps they rely too much on volunteers (all 250 of them) but either way, it could use a bit of updating. I don't think it is asking too much to have access to potable drinking water when in the desert. Well, technically you could drink the water but a sign in the visitor's centre window indicated that the quality did not meet required health standards and contained excess amounts of certain sulfates. Uh-huh. And that means???? We spoke with a husband and wife volunteer team and he said he would never drink the stuff, while she said she does, but had initially gone through a bout of cramping and gastro-intestinal distress. We had filled our water tanks before arriving so were thankfully all set but did buy a few extra gallons of spring water at the store in case we started running dry. It is amazing how cognizant you become of wasting water when you think it could run out.

WAITING AT THE RIO GRANDE TO CROSS INTO MEXICO.

And on the subject of water, we actually got out onto the Rio Grande. Not in our kayaks and not on a raft trip. We took what was really no more than a rowboat across, into the small village of Boquillas, Mexico. What a hoot. The U.S. side of the border is actually manned by National Parks staff in a small adobe building situated just up from the north bank. The ranger went through a little lecture on what could/could not be brought back and *ándale* we were off, walking down a dirt path to our watercraft, operated by an entrepreneur named Juan (I think – maybe it was José). $5.00 for a round trip. Porter was free. It took 3 minutes to cross. Once on the Mexican side we had the choice of walking half a mile into town, riding on a horse, riding on a burro or riding in a pick-up truck. Since we had Porter, the horse/burro option was a non-starter, so we opted to walk. Twenty minutes along a dusty, dirt road and we were checking in with the Mexican Federales in a small trailer. Nope. Nothing to declare. Actually, the officer didn't ask anything – just wanted to see our passports. John had stayed outside because of Porter, but the customs agent said I could sign on John's behalf. They take this border crossing stuff very seriously there. And then we were free to wander about and explore. There really wasn't much to see. One shop, two restaurants and several dilapidated houses built of cinder block and mud. It was really quite sad seeing what simply being born on the other side of the river can mean for your opportunities in life. All the squat one-storeyed/one-roomed buildings were incredibly derelict, not quite yet ruins but heading in that direction. The roadway was stones, dirt and dust. Burros appeared to be the main sources of transportation, but I suspected they were mostly for the benefit of the tourists since we didn't see any locals riding them. Lots of Chihuahuas and mongrels roaming freely, all yapping excitedly as Porter went by. They weren't vicious, just curious, and easily cowered when I shooed them away. The tidiest buildings were a small church, hospital and school. And that was it. We had seen everything there was to see. Some of the resident women were displaying what looked like embroidered tea towels for sale and sent their 3 and 4-year-old children towards us tourists in the hopes of making a sale. Start 'em young. How do you say "no" to a little street urchin with huge brown eyes? Easy. "*No, gracias.*" I said that a lot. We had lunch (a pretty humble burrito with bland guacamole for me and a so-so poblano chile rellenos for John) and we were done. Other than the novelty of such an unconventional crossing, I'm not sure why people feel compelled to go there. It is small. It is impoverished. It is dusty. The closest neighbouring town is 175 miles away and that is a long way to go without a car. The locals go once a week for supplies. Prior to 9/11, there wasn't even an official border crossing between the two countries. Young people from the U.S. side would just wade across the river, drink warm beer all day and then wade back, but following the attack, the entire border was shut down. It only opened up again in 2014 with the small parks building now acting as the clearing point. Returning, we were directed to a remote audio/visual kiosk and connected to an American Border Services officer in El Paso. A few cursory questions, a passport scan and we were back. Shortest trip to Mexico I ever made. Not to be outdone, the Mexicans make their own quick trips to the U.S. side of the river, illegally wading or rowing across and, along the hiking paths, unobtrusively setting up little unattended displays of the same homemade souvenir trinkets as found in Boquilla. Based on the honour system, a small jug is left close-by for payment. Parks personnel warn that officials can seize these items if we purchase them, since this type of transaction is illegal. Given the few dollars that might conceivably change hands, you would think Customs would have bigger smuggling issues to concern themselves with. And they do.

Driving through southern Texas, on three separate occasions we were forced to stop at roadside Border Patrol checkpoints and produce our passports when we said we were not U.S. citizens. They didn't come on board to search mind you, so I suppose we didn't look too suspicious. But human smuggling and illegal immigration is a serious problem there. Upon leaving Big Bend, we noticed that flags at the roadside checkpoint were flying half-mast. Why? Two nights earlier, an officer was following some suspicious tracks and subsequently ambushed. His head was smashed in with a rock. When his partner came to investigate, he too suffered serious head injuries and, in all likelihood, would not recover. There are some extremely vicious people sneaking into the United States. There is no excuse. A "wall" may not be the answer, but I certainly would not want that rock-wielding migrant moving into my neighbourhood.

On a more personal note, we were getting pretty tired from never sitting still for any length of time. That was mostly my fault, although we did cover a lot of geography over the month. And in my defence, there was so much to see. I wanted to explore and experience everything – fully realizing that was not possible, but still trying. By this point, our fitness regimen had fallen by the wayside, the yoga mats sat unused in a corner, the bikes were getting dusty and I swear I could feel my muscles atrophying. A strict personal trainer was the only solution but that was not possible. Christmas would only make things worse. So after the holidays, we planned to re-prioritize with something simple like 30 minutes of cardio before any sightseeing. Until then, *"otra margarita y más guacamole por favour."*

20.

DO I HAVE TO "REMEMBER THE ALAMO?"

WHEN WE STARTED OUR ADVENTURE IN MAY OF 2016, I MADE A COMMITMENT TO POST A BLOG ENTRY AT THE BEGINNING OF EACH MONTH DESCRIBING OUR EXPERIENCES IN THE PRECEDING +/- 30 DAYS. I kept that commitment. But as time passed, it was obvious each post was getting progressively longer as the journey unfolded. November's dispatch continued the pattern. In fact, it was so long I had to include the last week of November in December's entry in an effort to alleviate reader fatigue. So to continue...

We left Big Bend National Park November 23rd heading for San Antonio along highway 90. The drive was non-too exciting, the landscape not quite desert but not quite pastureland, the road mostly flat and straight with the occasional curve thrown in to prevent highway hypnosis. We pulled off around 4 pm, deciding to boondock overnight at a picnic area by the Pecos River Bridge, a secluded spot about a mile in off the roadway – so not your typical roadside rest area. This was, after all, southern Texas and we had covered miles and miles of emptiness between non-descript towns. The view over the river was lovely and we had the place to ourselves until two other vehicles with Texas plates pulled in. One a van and the other a car. Although they were not travelling together, they made me a touch uncomfortable. Other motor homes, trailers, fifth wheels, okay, but people sleeping in roadside rest stops in their cars screams... I don't know what it screams but whatever it is, I didn't like the sound of it. And besides, this was the evening of American Thanksgiving so why weren't these people at home eating turkey with their families? The evening passed uneventfully, and we went to bed around 11pm, but I slept with one ear open. Around 4am I heard an odd "ping" type sound but couldn't place where it came from. It wasn't the fridge or anything else I had heard before, but it didn't repeat and Porter was still snoring (we had no illusions of him being a guard dog) so I went back to sleep. Around 5:30am the car pulled away and when we got up around 8, the van was gone too. All without incident. Okay. So maybe I was being paranoid. Not so fast. We had left the Jeep still hooked to the coach, and the bikes were locked onto a rack at the back of the Jeep, covered with a tarp that was tightly secured with bungee cords. John found one of the bungee cords lying on the pavement under the car. No way that thing just flew off by itself overnight. That must have been the "ping" I heard. Someone was snooping around. I mention this because this was the first (and what we hoped would be the only) time people violated the traveller's code. You simply don't touch other people's stuff, be it lifejackets and paddles along a kayak route, chairs and mats on a beach, or bikes on the back of a car in a rest stop. Which brings me back to my still tingling Spidey senses. You just can't trust people sleeping in cars. Except perhaps in Walmart parking lots, which is another story.

We continued on to San Antonio without further issues and checked in at a RV park with full hook-ups. That was a necessity because the laundry had really piled up. It was an okay place, if somewhat noisy at night – the noise coming from freight trains passing nearby. We had never, not even in Jasper, heard train whistles that went on for so long. Three blasts with the third one easily lasting 8 seconds. Count it out. That is a long whistle. And there were at least 5 trains a night. Porter was not a happy camper. Train whistles are the only thing that set him off. We don't know why. Once the mundane housekeeping chores were taken care of, we played tourist and headed over to the Riverwalk. I had been to San Antonio twice before (John once), both times for work so we knew what to expect. The shores of the not-too-wide San Antonio River, where it winds through the downtown core, have been landscaped and paved with pedestrian friendly walking paths, and bridges every few hundred feet make it easy to cross back and forth. Restaurants, cafes and shops line the walkway and seating areas under the canopies of large trees provide a nice, cool shade from the city heat. Riverboats (rafts, really) cruise up and down the waterway with the operators giving an overview of San Antonio's history. It is all quite charming, but the Riverwalk is a serious tourist draw (second only to The Alamo which is half a mile away) so the tourists are served tourist food at tourist prices. And crowded! OMG! It was the shuffle of the living dead trying to manoeuvre from one side of the river to the other. Throw in a few baby strollers and the odd wheelchair and it makes you want to push people into the river. In all fairness, it was the Thanksgiving long weekend, but still... After a quick unsatisfying touristy lunch (Margarita from a mix!) we wandered over to the Alamo, dodging more strollers, and eventually made our way to the information panels where we could finally brush up on our Texas history. Brush up? I was starting from scratch.

The growth of America as a nation is often presented from the perspective of the British colonists, with the Spanish contribution taking a back seat. Well in southern Texas, it is the other way around. It is all Spanish, all the time. *Reader's Digest* version: Starting in the 1500s, Spain made inroads into the new continent from the south, and laid claim to vast tracts of land. So Texas was technically part of the Spanish colony of New Spain. But it's one thing to say something is yours and another thing to actually control it. Sort of a talk the talk versus walk the walk kind of thing. They literally did not have enough settlers to populate the geography and their competition in Britain knew it. And if worrying about the British wasn't bad enough, those pesky French were showing a bit too much interest in the Texas frontier as well, so in an effort to strengthen their claim, Spain had Franciscan monks build six Missions along the San Antonio River during the 1700s. These Missions were used to transform the local Coahuiltecan population into Spanish subjects, by converting them to Catholicism and teaching them a more Spanish-based lifestyle. This went rather smoothly, each Mission being pretty much self-sufficient with its own church, fields, granary, living quarters etc. The only flies in the ointment were those churlish Comanches and Apaches who didn't appreciate the civilizing efforts, and periodically raided the stores. Hence the construction of protective walls. Of all the Missions built, The Alamo is the most famous (originally called San Antonio de Valero), although its legendary status came much later. As far as Missions go, its only claim to fame at the time was that it was the first one built. Mission San José was considered to be the strongest and most beautiful and today, Mission Conceptión in the best preserved/least altered. Of the six originals built, five are still standing and four actually still function as active parishes. We took the time to visit four of the five and they were interesting to a point. Information got to be a bit repetitive after a while. Build a church, teach religion, farming, language to Coahuiltecans. Shelter from marauding Apaches. Repeat. However, one advantage to exploring the missions in the San Antonio area was that they were in fairly close proximity to each other, (as opposed to California where you'd have to drive hundreds of miles to compare a few) and there were very few visitors, so we managed to get them all done within one afternoon.

Except "The Alamo". That one was so jam packed it was unreal. At the risk of sounding sacrilegious, you really have to wonder why it is such a big deal. I didn't voice that out loud of course. Since its construction, The Alamo has been a mission, a fortress, a battlefield, a warehouse and today, a shrine. It is *The* Texas shrine – the most visited site in the entire state. And once I learned a bit more about the region's history, I didn't just wonder, I became convinced, that myth and hype are obscuring many of the facts. And if behaviour is any indicator, I suspect most of the coon-skin hat, Bowie knife gift-shop-purchasing Alamo visitors really didn't have a clue about any of it. To understand The Alamo's place in history means having to understand the four main conflicts that took place in this part of the world within about a fifty-year period. Mexico wanted independence from Spain. Texas wanted independence from Mexico. The United States wanted everything. Following which they couldn't agree on how to govern what they had.

A brief overview. After three centuries of rule, the sun was setting on the Spanish Empire and Mexico wanted out. Hence, the Mexican War of Independence fought between 1810 and 1821. At this point, the geographic area we now know as Texas was part of Mexico but that didn't last long. Fourteen years after that first conflict, Texas wanted out of Mexico. (The United States, having won its independence from Britain in 1783, was continuously expanding west, and many settlers had migrated to the Texas area.) Hence, the Texas Revolution fought between 1835 and 1836. There were numerous battles during this war, but the one at The Alamo gets all the press and I'm still not sure why. Perhaps because of who died there, specifically Davey Crockett (of bar-killin', coon-skin cap fame) and James Bowie (of Bowie knife fame – more on him later). Texas became its own independent state following the Mexican defeat. If only that were the end of it. Nine years later, in 1845, Texas was annexed by the United States. Not only was it annexed, but its western border expanded as far as the Rio Grande. Mexico, never having recognized Texas' independence in the first place, could not accept so much loss of territory, hence the US-Mexico War, lasting from 1846 until 1848. Mexico should have quit while it was still ahead because by the end of that war, it had lost almost half of its territory including what is now California. We visited the Palo Alto Battlefield (near Brownsville), site of the first battle in this war and it really was very informative in helping understand how the US came to be geographically so big and Mexico so small. And then the American Civil War started (1861-1865) with Texas fighting for the Confederacy. When talking about the Civil War, Texas doesn't exactly come to mind, but it played a huge role in helping keep the Confederate war machine humming. In fact, the last battle of the Civil War was fought in Texas at Palmito Ranch (also near Brownsville) in May of 1865. This, despite the fact that almost four weeks earlier, the other major Confederate armies had already surrendered at Appomattox Courthouse in Virginia. The news just hadn't reached Texas. Talk about poor communication. (The Confederates won, by the way.)

So with all these battles, losses, victories and shifting borders, what's with The Alamo? It can't all be because of Bowie. Or can it? There was a special exhibit in one of the Alamo buildings, dedicated entirely to Bowie and his trademark knife. And while there was a bit of information on the man himself (which did not necessarily paint him in the best light, so again, why the hero tag?), most of the exhibit centred around the knife – how he killed someone with it in a brawl in Mississippi (which naturally made it very popular), how it is forged, how to tell a legitimate one from a knock-off, and the effect the knife has had on pop culture (from David Jones changing his name to David Bowie, to its use in Sylvester Stallone's *Rambo* movies). James Bowie himself was born in Kentucky, lived in Mississippi and "relocated" to Texas in 1830. Why? Because he was a swindler – selling real estate he did not own to unsuspecting settlers. When his crimes came to light, he "relocated" to Texas, which at that time was still part of Mexico. Lucky for him there was no US/Mexico extradition agreement at the time. He was also an active participant in the illegal slave trade, seriously abused alcohol to the point of irreversible physical illness and had a violent temper. But he was also one of the leaders of the Texas Revolution so maybe that ameliorates things for some people. Yes, he did die "defending" The Alamo but even that is not an entirely accurate use of the word. He was actually sick in bed with an unidentified illness (possibly alcohol induced) during the Alamo's entire 13-day siege so he didn't exactly go out with guns blazing. Still, the masses flock to read all about him and his famous knife. And buy replicas at the gift shop.

Leaving San Antonio, we stopped in Kingsville thinking we would visit King Ranch, the largest ranch in Texas at 825,000 acres (almost 1,290 square miles). Or about the size of Rhode Island. We quickly realized that we didn't have time to take in one of the tours they offered, so put that off for the return leg, and just checked out the King Ranch Saddle Shop where they supposedly still make their saddles by hand. It was rather disappointing. A lot of lovely high-end leather goods, furniture, clothing and the like but nobody working on any saddles. And much of the stuff manufactured in India and China anyway. So much for making America great again. We had left the RV parked on the street with Porter inside (the generator and a/c running) while we went browsing, but upon our return, saw two police cars with lights flashing parked behind it and an officer knocking at the door. Oh. Oh. It turned out street parking was prohibited in Kingsville. The younger officer was a bit chippy, ("Do you always park in the middle of the road where you come from?") but John worked his magic and the older officer was soon shaking his hand and wishing us well. Lesson learned. I missed most of their exchange because I just had to stop and photograph a sign in front of what obviously used to be a movie theatre but was now a gun shop. "Guns. Don't be scared, be prepared." Only in Texas.

Our next stop was South Padre Island, about as far southwest as you can get in this huge state, pretty much where the Rio Grande enters the Gulf of Mexico. The "island" is really just a huge sand bar, 34 miles long and only half a mile wide at its widest point, accessed via a long causeway from the mainland. Only the southernmost 5 miles are developed so four-wheel drive vehicles are recommended for driving along the beach. We were blessed with great weather – hot and sunny – and spent our days exploring the area, walking along the miles and miles of beach, and collecting seashells. I found lots of them, but apparently shell collecting is not what it used to be due to a serious decline in mollusc populations. The reason? Commercial ocean trawling, over-harvesting and oxygen-deprived dead zones. And if that wasn't bad enough, one thing that struck us was the amount of flotsam washed up. "Marine debris" as it is politely called. Garbage, to the rest of us. Lots of plastic pieces – large, small and miniscule – old ropes, aluminum cans and the odd shoe but mostly bottles – plastic and glass alike. And this was not new stuff. Judging by the crustaceans that were attached to some of the pieces, they had been floating around in the sea for quite some time. When vacationing at a Caribbean beach resort where the sand gets raked clean every night, it's easy to forget just how much garbage is out there drifting around in our oceans. South Padre Island has a lot of beach and no-one is going out there to tidy it up on a regular basis while we are asleep in our beds. We are all collectively responsible for this mess. Enough said. Yet despite this reminder of mankind's penchant for despoilment, we had a great time and Porter was in heaven, quickly forgiving us for dragging him all around the desert in the preceding weeks. When he wasn't splashing in the water, he was rolling in the sand and then shaking it off on us. Although sadly, much of it still came back with him to the yacht so the vacuum cleaner worked overtime. And it's a good thing there was so much beach for him to run around on because the grass was definitely a place to stay away from. Seemingly innocuous lawns contained tiny little burs called "stickers", about the size of an eraser on the end of a pencil, and hard as rock. The barbs on these stickers were very sharp and very painful. When stepped on, they would imbed themselves in Porter's paws completely crippling him. They were difficult to remove without tweezers because they would just transfer themselves from paw to hand. And the prick they inflicted burned. Almost like a bee sting. I don't know what the scientific name for them is, but apparently they are quite common in coastal dune areas. Porter got to the point where if his ball rolled onto the grass, he would just sit down and wait for me to retrieve it. Another reason for staying away from the grassy areas was the mosquitoes. They were abundant and aggressive, despite the park area supposedly being sprayed a week earlier. Needless to say, we spent our time either at the beach or in the yacht.

A DAY AT THE BEACH. PADRE ISLAND NATIONAL SEASHORE

The small town, Port Isabel, was really nothing more than a strip of roadway lined with numerous cheap beach shops selling discounted towels, wake boards, kites and the like, with a few eating establishments thrown in. But they did have small town community spirit. We were driving to a restaurant for dinner one evening and part way along found the main road was closed. Why? It was December 1ˢᵗ – time for the annual Santa Claus Parade. I've never seen one held at night, but I guess it was cooler that way for spectators and participants alike. Even Santa (a rather thin, young-looking fellow) riding on top of the local fire engine was wearing shorts. John maintains he was also showing off his Christmas "bells", but I didn't see anything. The floats (using the term loosely) were mostly cars pulling small trailers decorated in red, white and green lights, carrying school-aged children who looked a bit uncertain about the whole thing. A few local clubs (Boy Scouts, Gymnastics, Karate) were marching bravely along, throwing in the odd cartwheel or kick, and older kids were tossing candy to the onlookers who were sparsely stretched out along the route. There was one middle school marching band playing Jingle Bells rather off key, and quite a few enthusiastic cheerleaders. The whole thing was pretty amateurish but so community-spirited we couldn't help but smile, wave back at the floats and return the calls of "Merry Christmas". We didn't hear any "Happy Holidays". It was great. But at the same time, difficult to think about Christmas given the warm temperature. And completely incongruous to be standing in line at the grocery store, looking at the palm trees outside, and listening to *Walking in a Winter Wonderland* playing inside. We were staying in a state park that was quickly filling up with "Winter Texans" (as they were called there), everyone settling in for their few months in the sun, arranging patio furniture and stringing up clotheslines along with Christmas lights. Our neighbour even had a small vegetable garden going, complete with tomato plants. We kayaked on the lagoon side one day and saw a few interesting birds (and one small alligator) near the bird watching centre, and considered snorkelling but were told that visibility isn't really all that great. Supposedly there was a golf course somewhere. So other than collecting shells and surf fishing, there is really very little to do. Great if you need to boost your Vitamin D and de-stress for a week or so, but three or four months? I could not for the life of me imagine being there for three or four weeks never mind months. This part of the United States (i.e. the Rio Grande Valley) has the highest concentration of RV and mobile home parks in the country so obviously lots of budget-minded people love it but it just wasn't my cup of tea. Certainly the weather is warm, there is very little humidity and the sun shines a lot, but how many seashells can you collect before you start losing your mind?

And then there was the little incident of the ants in my pants. Except they were not ants, but sand fleas. There is no delicate way to explain this. Nor any way to avoid embarrassment. I suppose I could omit this part of the narrative entirely, but then that would not be a true account of all the ups and downs of our journey. So please, laugh with sympathy, not derision. The day we went kayaking, we were on the lagoon side of the strip where there aren't any dry sand dunes but rather just a vast expanse of flat wet hard packed sand and mangrove trees. At low tide, it's about a 300-yard walk before you reach the water. Our boats were all set to go at the water's edge, when I decided I needed to "go" too. And it was a good twenty-minute drive back to the yacht. So I popped behind some reeds, quickly did my business and was all set. Easy, "peesy", so to speak. Unfortunately, not. You know where this is going. The following day, I had nasty red bites and welts all over my belly, torso, back, backside, even "other" parts. OMG! I counted at least 100 of them. They were sand flea bites. And itchy? Ten times worse than mosquito bites. I could have ripped my skin off. Thank goodness for Benadryl which is doubly effective when washed down with wine. It took three weeks before the agony subsided and even at month's end I was still covered in red dots. It was a good thing there were no bathing suit beach vacations in the immediate future. Moral of the story: Be careful where you drop your drawers.

On that cheerful note, we returned to Kingsville, took in a tour of the King Ranch, and learned a fair bit about Texas ranching history. And it wasn't easy since our guide threw around terms like "soft breaking", "cutting horses" and "bump gates" as if we knew what he was talking about, but we did manage to retain some of the information. King Ranch is actually considered to be the birthplace of American ranching, because back in 1853 Richard King purchased a number of Spanish/Mexican land grants and brought cattle that we know as Texas Longhorns up from Mexico. These were the only cattle that could survive in this inhospitable land (classified as wild horse desert) because they could eat anything, including prickly-pear cactus, and thus thrive during drought conditions as well as on the long cattle drives to market. Over the years, as other means of transportation became available (trains, barges, trucks) and demands of the market changed to "fattier" beef, the ranch diversified and today raises primarily Santa Gertrudis (a hybrid breed of Brahman and Shorthorns, in case it matters). The Longhorn herds are kept for historical purposes, a nod to their bygone contribution to this billion-dollar industry, and as a symbol of the Old West. As beef cattle go, their meat came to be considered too tough for the human palate. Lucky for them. But their luck may be running out. The trend is again changing towards leaner meat and Longhorns certainly fit that bill, with cholesterol levels even lower than skinless chicken breasts. The only hiccup to switching over is one of supply and demand. In the United States, well over 100,000 head of cattle are required each day to meet beef demand. Texas Longhorns only number 100,000 in total. So there is going to be a long wait before we routinely see Longhorn beef on dinner menus.

The King Ranch is a family business (you have to be a direct descendant of King to sit on the 120-member board) and their success can largely be attributed to diversification. Half of their acreage is leased out for game hunting (deer, javelina, turkeys, even an imported herd of nilgai from India), they are big into cotton, oil and gas, and raising quarter horses. And that's just in Texas. They have citrus groves in Florida, horses in Kentucky, and more cattle in Canada, Australia and Morocco. This is one very wealthy family. The "big house", built in the early 1900s is 32,000 square feet, has 17 bedrooms, 19 washrooms and stained-glass Tiffany windows. No one really lives in it now. They just use it once a year when the entire clan gets together to re-connect. But it all started with cattle ranching in the middle of nowhere. Two facts I thought were quite interesting: cattle will not go more than about 1 mile from a water source when grazing, so wells are crucial; and in times of severe drought, the spines of prickly cactus can be burned off so the cattle will eat it as food. Who knew? I did have one question, however, that did not really get answered to my satisfaction. That is partly my fault. Our guide was at least 85 years old, and a very amiable, kind fellow so I didn't want to argue with him. He advised us that when the grazing cattle are about 700 pounds, they are transported to feedlots where they are fed a scientific diet of mixed grain pellets, including corn (engineered and processed so that the cattle can digest it) and after they put on another 500 pounds, off to market they go. In their promotional literature, King Ranch even says, "our cattle were derived from the need for performance in feedyards." This is where I have a problem. A few years ago, my book club (okay, okay, it was really a wine club with a reading problem) discussed *The Omnivore's Dilemma* by Michael Pollan, where in one section he traced the path your average steak takes from pasture to table. It completely turned me off supermarket beef. Read it at your own peril. Sometimes ignorance is bliss. And five years ago, we were driving through Texas and saw some of these feedlots.

They were horrific. Animal cruelty is an appropriate term. Hundreds and hundreds of cattle, tightly bunched together near troughs, nowhere to go, milling around in their own excrement, without a blade of grass in sight. We often smelled them before we saw them. Today, when I buy beef, I try to get it from a reputable butcher who sells organic, grass-fed, hormone free, yayda, yada, you get the idea. Maybe I'm naïve, but I just can't get those feedlot images out of my head and am now engaged in my own little feedlot boycott. I wonder what a Tofu burger tastes like?

We wanted to explore one more seaside park before turning the yacht towards Red Bay for service/repairs, so we headed off to Padre Island National Seashore, not far from Corpus Christie. As much as it is technically the northern extension of South Padre Island, the two places could not be more dissimilar. This was what coastal wilderness looked like before condos and cottages. Miles and miles of uninterrupted beaches, dunes, grasslands and tidal flats. I loved it. And there were no mosquitoes. The Seashore actually protects the longest undeveloped stretch of barrier island in the world, at 70 miles long, with 60 miles of it being beach driving (although you need 4-wheel drive after mile marker 5). The campground was small and basic, in that there were no hook-ups, but sites had picnic tables and shelters, and best of all, they faced directly onto the Gulf about 100 feet back from the water's edge. We had a beautiful unobstructed view of the ocean through our front window, where we could watch as the waves rolled in. If only the weather had cooperated. The first few days can only be described as dismal. It alternated between downpour and drizzle for 72 hours straight, the wind driving the rain sideways, with gusts strong enough to rock the yacht, a daytime high of 40F/5C and one night it dropped to 30/-1. On our third rainy day we drove into Corpus Christi, dropped Porter at a daycare (they are a godsend) and spent the day being mall rats. It was okay since we managed to get a start on our Christmas shopping, but I would have preferred sun and sand. The fourth day we awoke to a snow-covered landscape. It turned out that this was the first snowfall Texas had received in 13 years. Not the beach vacation I signed up for! It was hard to accept that only four short days earlier, we had been sweltering in 80-degree heat.

SOUTH TEXAS HAD NOT HAD SNOW IN 13 YEARS! JUST OUR LUCK.

Another unexpected and unpleasant surprise was our one campground neighbour, someone who we officially labelled a "Poo Head". Upon arrival, we had barely finished setting up when the camp host was knocking at our door. Apparently, Mr. Congeniality had gone and complained that with our coach nose-in and facing the beach (as opposed to his smaller C class that he had backed in), our door now opened up towards his picnic table (which he wasn't even using). He did not think this was right. Are you kidding me? We reassured the host that we would be careful not to encroach on the space, and noted that there were several other coaches set up the same as ours. End of story. But that was the first and only time we met someone so inimical and petty. People living this lifestyle tend to be very good-natured and friendly. If anything, sometimes too much so, talking your ear off while they relate where they have been and what they have seen. This guy was just miserable, never said one word to us (not even "hello") and never made eye contact. Thankfully we didn't see too much of him. I hoped he got sand fleas in his pants. But after the shaky start, the weather improved and although it was still a cool 19 degrees, the sun was warm and we spent several days just hanging out at the beach, collecting shells, avoiding Portuguese Man-of-War, reading, and engaging in some community service work by picking up garbage washed up on the beach. The Parks Service invites people to help where they can with signs posted to "pack out more than you came in with." I don't think things are this bad along every shoreline and suspect the ocean currents are patterned to deposit more along this stretch than elsewhere, but it was depressing. Whatever you can think of that is made from plastic or aluminum was washed up. Combs, pens, lighters, toothbrushes, bags, bottles, caps, cans, flip-flops, cutlery. Where does it all come from? Our little contribution was less than a drop in the bucket and we knew that come the next high tide, there would be more. I can't imagine what must lie on the ocean floor. I decided that once the trip was over, ocean clean up would be added to my list of favourite charities.

Leaving Padre Island, we drove straight through to Waco where we needed to pick up some Texas-themed Christmas gifts. It was almost dark by the time we completed our purchases so decided to spend the night boondocking in the Walmart parking lot. Which brings me to my second observation about people sleeping in cars. We had set up the yacht off to one side of the Walmart lot and I took Porter for a walk while John went into the store to doublecheck that it was okay to overnight there. This was a 24-hour store so quite a few cars were still parked near the entrance but tucked off to one side was a very dated Ford pick-up truck with a small generator running in the bed. The generator was surrounded by a few buckets and tarps, the kind of stuff someone engaged in painting or plastering might have. While a foil sunshade covered the front windshield, through the driver's side window I could see a small television playing on the dash. Someone was definitely living in their car. Later that evening, I noticed that both the driver and passenger windows had little blinds pulled down – the cheap, plastic kind you attach with suction cups. It was pretty cold (39F/4C) and the generator ran all night, so I was glad that at least this person was warm. The next morning, around 7:45, I looked out and saw a tall, slender man, late forties/early fifties, dressed in a t-shirt and blue jeans, standing barefoot beside the truck bed. He was pouring hot coffee from a little 4-cup coffee pot into a mug. He then covered the pot up with a tarp and got back into the cab with his cup. The soles of his feet were black with dirt, so who knows when he last had a shower. By 8:15 he was gone, I suspect off to work. I'm not sure how I felt. Certainly, it was one of the few times in my life where I wanted to go up to someone and just hand them some money. Homelessness is a huge problem in the United States and while I have little sympathy for the fatigue-dressed, multi-pierced, pot-smoking youth who panhandle along the crowded sidewalks of many southern cities, this guy represented that entire class of people who are still trying to maintain some shred of independent dignity. It was so sad and the image of him in the cold morning air with his bare feet and coffee cup stayed with me. Perhaps I'm conferring onto him some romanticized nobler character and in reality he is just a fugitive from the law, but I don't think so. I'm not a bleeding heart by any stretch of the imagination, but the disparity between rich and poor in this country is truly obscene.

The rest of the journey home was pretty uneventful, and after covering so many miles of desert and scrub, it was lovely to see trees and grass again – even if the trees were bare of leaves and the grass was brown. We left the yacht with Tiffin in Red Bay and were once again impressed with the efficiency of their entire set up. Our every concern was documented and inspected in preparation for the maintenance work, the insurance appraiser arrived the next day for the body work and we left feeling completely confident that things would go smoothly. John had located a small storage company where he stowed the kayaks and bikes, we loaded up the Jeep (Porter a bit confused that his lounging space was now considerably reduced) and we were off, looking forward to seeing family and friends. We had been home less than 48 hours before I was exhausted. I had anticipated a relaxing few days with a little bit of last-minute shopping before Christmas but such was not the case. It started with our Air BnB condo.

December prior, we had rented someone's actual home and although it was great, the location was not the best. We were right downtown on the waterfront yet most of our social activities were in the west end, so there was a lot of back and forth. This time around, we rented a place through a company (Elite) near Mississauga's largest shopping mall – Square One – making it easier to split our time between our son in Oakville and my folks in Mississauga. The location was the only thing good about it. Our contract had us checking in at 3pm, but when we called to arrange the key pick-up, were advised the unit would not be available until 4:30 because they weren't finished cleaning it yet. Hmmm. Okay, a few more trips around the block. When we finally got in, this "fully furnished" 2-bedroom suite was anything but. While spacious, the kitchen had next to nothing by way of cookware or utensils. Nothing along the lines of cutting board, mixing bowls, bake ware, wine glasses, not even a can opener or tea towel. In terms of furniture, there was a couch, a rickety table with four flimsy plastic chairs, tv (no batteries in the remote and no cable), and just a bed in either bedroom. Certainly not what the advertised pictures had shown. The company would have been hard pressed to have a cheaper set up. We contacted them right away and they were fairly prompt in bringing over a few of the necessities (like a corkscrew) but that was about it. They declined to provide a cup measure or place mats saying those were "extras". Needless to say, we quickly gave up on the idea of entertaining. The building itself was only a year old, one of those glass tower creations, yet the construction was so poor that I suspect within a few years they will be levying huge assessments to repair failed widows and inoperable elevators (of which there were only 4 for 50 floors so loooong wait times). During the first two weeks, the fire alarm went off on three separate occasions during the night, once at 2am, another time at 5am and on a third at 7am. Each time, the ear-piercing signal sounded non-stop, on average for 30 minutes. Porter was crawling under the bed. We made the best of it. I tackled gift shopping on behalf of my parents whose aging had limited their mobility and scrambled to put together some semblance of a Christmas day dinner. Thank goodness for Whole Foods. Sadly, John and I didn't make it to either of the two Christmas Eve church services. My family opted to attend the ridiculously early 3pm service and going to the 5pm would have meant throwing off my sister's hosting plans, so for only the second time in my life, I didn't go to church on Christmas Eve. But the evening passed in the usual manner at my parents' home with too much food and too many sweets. Our son finally had his condo feathered the way he wanted and invited us over for a lovely Boxing Day dinner. He is quite the cook, and it was wonderful evening with he and his fiancé, albeit a touch surreal. At what point did our roles get reversed? No-one warned me about that transition. And the over-indulging pattern continued into the new year as we tried to meet up with as many friends as possible. Despite being home for two weeks there was not enough time to accomplish everything on our list. I was not complaining. We are truly blessed to have so many wonderful people in our lives and only wished we could have spent more time with those who we did see and had had more time to see those who we did not. It was great having a legitimate white Christmas although I could have done without the bone-chilling temperatures, and John came down with a very bad cold that naturally, he felt compelled to share with me. It was, after all, the season of giving.

SEARCHING FOR CLETUS — FORT JEFFERSON, DRY TORTUGAS NATIONAL PARK

CANOLA FIELD — OUTSIDE WINNIPEG, MANITOBA

OVERLOOKING WATERTON LAKE FROM BEAR'S HUMP, ALBERTA

PADDLING WATERTON LAKE, ALBERTA

PADDLING EMERALD LAKE, YOHO NATIONAL PARK, ALBERTA

HIKING THE VALLEY OF TEN PEAKS, LAKE LOUISE, ALBERTA

BONNEVILLE SALT FLATS, UTAH

WALKING UP THE VIRGIN RIVER, ZION NATIONAL PARK, UTAH

LITTLE WILD HORSE SLOT CANYON, GOBLIN VALLEY STATE PARK, UTAH

HITCHIN' A RIDE — MONTEREY BAY, CALIFORNIA

YOSEMITE NATIONAL PARK, CALIFORNIA

YOSEMITE N.P. FROM OLMSTED POINT

GETTING READY TO PADDLE — MUNCHO LAKE, NORTHERN BRITISH COLUMBIA

THE SPIT, HOMER, ALASKA

PURE GLACIAL ICE — MENDENHALL GLACIER, ALASKA

INSIDE AN ICE CAVE, UNDERNEATH THE MENDENHALL GLACIER, ALASKA

SUNSET IN PARADISE, TOFINO, BRITISH COLUMBIA

THE BROWN MENACE.

21.

YACHTLESS

JANUARY GOT OFF TO A DECIDEDLY SLOW START AND THE PACE NEVER REALLY PICKED UP. First, we received word from Tiffin in Red Bay that service on the yacht was about two weeks behind. Apparently they take their Christmas breaks seriously down in Alabama. So what to do? Our Air B&B rental agreement expired January 9, and to be honest, we were quite thankful to get out of the place. The entire Square One area of Mississauga is turning into a huge cesspool, no matter that Holt Refrew was just a short walk across the parking lot. Mega-storey, high density, cheaply constructed buildings with no green space does not bode well for the future. Thankfully, the guest suite in our son's condo building was available for six days so we packed up our belongings and skedaddled over. There is a lovely park across the street (complete with frozen pond) so Porter was a happy camper once again. The days flew by with time spent visiting my parents and taking care of some minor issues at our house. And when it finally came time to hit the road, it wasn't easy. There had been a marked decline in my parent's health so once again, difficult good-byes all around. Lugubrious. The weather continued to be bone chillingly cold – the kind of cold that makes your forehead hurt – and as per Ontario winters, the skies were gray, gray, gray. We took our time driving south along I-75 and stopped in to visit our friends in Troy, now that we (I) knew the difference between Troy, Ohio and Troy, Michigan. It was great to be able to catch up, although the temperature was not much warmer than in Toronto and there was a fair bit of snow on the ground, considerably more than what they were used to. And then we imposed on our Atlanta, Georgia friends – and they had freezing temps and snow too! In Atlanta! Go figure. Porter spent a fair bit of time gazing longingly at the pool through their sunroom window, but we were not about to indulge his request at that time of year. It was a relaxing few days just hanging out, talking about family and discussing current events although we naturally failed to reach a consensus on how to solve the world's problems. Red Bay still wasn't giving us any encouraging news, and despite my friend's urging to stay as long as necessary, it was time to move on and let them return to their usual routine. We truly felt rudderless and I, for one, was getting very tired of living out of a suitcase. No matter how small the square footage of the RV, it was still our "home" and we wanted to get our journey back on track. There was still so much to see and do, and we were very cognizant that our time south of the border was limited to six-month increments. But being "yachtless" also made us realize how important it really is to have a home base, regardless of whether it is bricks and mortar, or motorized. Everyone needs a place to call their own. We had several more days to kill before picking up the coach so we moseyed on down to New Orleans. It was only a 7-hour drive – why not? We love it there.

We found a dog-friendly hotel in the Garden District, quite close to the doggie daycare we had used before, and the St. Charles Street trolley to the French Quarter passed right by the front door. Perfect. We had the opportunity to re-visit some of the previously explored places and checked out a few new ones as well, including the Jazz Museum, formally known as the New Orleans Jazz National Historic Park of Louisiana, and curiously, run by the National Parks Service. I still can't figure out that connection. Unfortunately, the foray was rather disappointing. It is located in the old Mint building on the border of the French Quarter and the Marigny, so while the local street youth were numerous outside, the same cannot be said for the exhibits inside. One small room with limited information and a few audio displays on the contribution women have made to Jazz, a wall size information panel on Louis Armstrong (that was really just one type written paragraph made large), Fats Domino's piano (that had been recovered from his home in the 9th ward after Hurricane Katrina) and that was about it. It was a real shame because New Orleans played such a huge role in the birth and growth of this music genre, and most of us don't know too much about it. We picked up a Parks Service pamphlet which provided some basic information, but that hardly made up for the lack of artefacts and articles in the "museum". On the plus side, however, we did catch a short 45-minute concert by jazz pianist David Torkanowsky, which was very enjoyable, and somehow stumbled upon a room displaying eight Mardi Gras Indian costumes from carnivals of years gone by. They were fantastic, with intricate beadwork, sequins, crystal stones and feathers, and accompanying explanation panels alongside. Although we had been to the parade last year, being able to stand and admire these works of art up close was a bonus.

And on the topic of Mardi Gras, with Easter falling on April 1st this particular year, New Orleans was already gearing up for the festivities. We were due to depart Friday the 26th and the first parade was set for the 27th. Decorations in purple, green and gold (representing justice, faith and power) were being strung up along parade routes, main streets and side streets, and it was interesting to watch the whole city become more alive and cheerful with each passing day. When we originally arrived, they were still reeling from the previous week's weather inflicted damage. The thermometer had dipped well below freezing for several days and that caused the aging water mains and pipes to burst, resulting in low water pressure in some places and no water at all in others. For three days, restaurants were closed, hotels were forced to turn away potential guests, and boil water advisories were issued all around. Timing is everything. We wandered around the French Quarter, enjoyed beignets at Café du Monde (again), filled up on excellent red beans and rice at Joey K's, and sampled King Cake, which is only baked for Mardi Gras. The cake is supposed to commemorate the Epiphany, and each one contains a tiny baby figurine symbolizing the Christ child. As cakes go, it's so-so. Really just a cinnamon type coffee cake with purple, green and gold icing, but it was available for sale in every store. We read up a little more on the Mardi Gras tradition itself and decided that one day, we will return for the full Carnival experience and take in the Cajun celebrations as well. As one author put it, "Mardi Gras is not a parade. Mardi Gras is not girls flashing on French Quarter balconies. Mardi Gras is not an alcoholic binge. Mardi Gras is the love of life. It is the harmonic convergence of our food, our music, our creativity, our eccentricity, our neighbourhoods and our joy of living. All at once." I think it bears checking out. But being there so early in the year, things were considerably quieter, and it seemed to me that the street musicians were not quite as talented (we couldn't find Doreen Ketchens anywhere), the panhandlers were more prevalent and prior to the decorations going up, things looked generally more run down. But we still loved it. We stocked up on packages of gumbo, red beans and rice, and jambalaya (cheater versions, I know) that were considerably cheaper in the grocery store than in the tourist shops ($1.50 vs. $5.99) and vowed to learn how to make them from scratch.

The weather was a sunny and balmy 15 degrees one day, so we decided to treat Porter to a day at the beach, driving 2 hours out to Grand Isle State Park on the shores of the Gulf of Mexico. Grand Isle itself is a constantly shifting barrier island, formed as a result of the Mississippi River's flow into the Gulf. In the late 1800s, it was a holiday destination with vacationers staying in elegant hotels that had once been plantation homes, but a deadly 1893 hurricane pretty much wiped everything off the map. From about 1940 on, the petroleum industry has been the major presence there. The drive out was uneventful through miles and miles of wetlands, but they were not as "pretty" as the wetlands of Florida. Partly because in every direction there are signposts of industry – cranes, shipyards, oil rigs. The houses (full time and vacation alike) were built on incredibly high stilts so that the first floor is literally one and a half stories up from ground level. They have their fair share of high-water surges. And the beach? Well, Louisiana does not really have the prettiest beaches. The sand was an unappealing black/brown in many places and I'm not sure if that was still a vestige of the huge BP oil-rig disaster of 2010 (that over 3 months spilled more than 200 million gallons of crude into the Gulf) or if that was just how Nature made it. Coincidentally, the movie *Deepwater Horizon* (about that very disaster) was on television the following night and is apparently a rather troublingly accurate depiction of what happened. And while we are unlikely to return, I am glad we checked the area out so we have a visual of what the terrain looks like when viewing a map of the Mississippi delta.

And then we received some sad news. My much-loved Godfather had passed away. John drove me to the airport so I could fly home for the funeral, while he continued on to Red Bay to pick up the coach. I certainly had not expected to return to Toronto quite so soon. Life is funny. I have a genuine fear of flying, yet my Godfather had been a Captain with Air Canada, piloting for over 33 years. Despite many conversations, he was never able to ease my anxiety over this mode of travel. Descending into Pearson airport late at night with all the city lights spread out in every direction, it was really quite beautiful. The plane was early so we had to circle a few times, and I could only smile at how many times my Godfather must have enjoyed this very same sight. Perhaps he was trying just one more time to alleviate my fear. *Vieglas smilits, Krustēv.*

We ended the month crossing back into Texas, although bouncing around from condos to friends to hotels had knocked us somewhat off our stride. Coupled with the health concerns back home, this January hiatus served to dampen our carefree wanderlust somewhat and we really needed to give ourselves a bit of a pep talk. The closest international airport to Red Bay is Memphis so John parked the coach in Southaven and met me at the airport upon my return. We spent two nights in a small RV park, re-orienting ourselves and planning our Texas trek. Who am I trying to kid? It was not a RV park. It was a run-down trailer park, pure and simple. Of the 40-odd sites, ours was the only one available for travellers. Everybody else was a down and out permanent resident. All we needed was a tornado and we too would be wandering around in a confused state searching for our lost dog. Things could only get better in February.

22.

JFK, COWBOYS & CACTI

WHAT CAN I SAY ABOUT TEXAS? Obviously, we did not get to tour the entire state – it is simply too big, and since we were in the southern Gulf half before Christmas, we headed back west through the middle/north end (although not the panhandle). It was a dicey decision because the temperature was for the most part, quite cold. Our first lengthier stop was in Dallas/Fort Worth, cities that could not be more dissimilar. Dallas prides itself on its arts and sports while Fort Worth is all about cowboy culture. I never thought I'd say it, but I like cowboys! And I can't think of any other group of people in North America who are more culturally identifiable simply by the manner of their everyday dress (except for maybe the Amish). The first thing we did was go to the Fort Worth Stock Show & Rodeo, held in a huge area reminiscent of Toronto's CNE grounds, only bigger. The show runs for three weeks and we managed to catch the second last day. It reminded me a bit of Toronto's Royal Winter Fair, only on a much more massive scale. This was serious! With serious cowboys. Stetsons, boots and spurs in every direction. I must have been the only person wearing Converse running shoes, and was sorely tempted to buy some boots just to fit in. But where would I wear them afterwards? Downtown Toronto? We wandered in and out of numerous livestock buildings, along the boulevards, and into an exhibit hall where vendors sold every cowboy-themed item imaginable. Everything from cowhides to bull whips to toy ponies. The cowboys themselves were all unfailingly polite and being addressed as "ma'am" with a tip of the hat was ever so charming. One curious observation though: most of the men had pleats pressed into their jeans. Perhaps so they can tell their dress jeans from their work jeans? Even though we had missed the horse exhibits, we were able to see some of the cattle/calf competitions (ho-hum) but the highlight was the rodeo. Neither of us had ever been to one, so in the future, I will be able to say with complete truthfulness, "This is not my first rodeo." I have to admit to being a bit conflicted about enjoying the event so much simply because there is an obvious element of animal cruelty involved. Especially with the bull riding. But I am getting ahead of myself.

Held in a huge arena, with red white and blue banners hanging from the rafters, it started in a very solemn and patriotic manner. First the mounted flag bearers (USA and Texas flags) slowly walked their horses around the perimeter of the ring and as they passed, everyone stood up, with the men removing their cowboy hats. (There were very few ball caps.) Then a prayer led by the police Chaplain, then everyone recited the pledge of allegiance and then a small chorus sang the national anthem. There was no hootin' or hollerin' or whistlin'. Just quiet respect. And then the fun began. Bareback broncos, saddled broncos, barrel races, calf roping, chuck wagon races and bull riding. Two hours of excitement with me quietly cheering for the beasties. Because despite being awed by the skill of the riders, and the power of both horses and bulls alike, it must be traumatic for these animals. With the bronco competition, scores are assigned based on the both the ability of the rider to stay in the saddle and the intensity of bucking by the horse. And how do you ensure the horse bucks for all its worth? Why kick him with your spurs of course. And for bull riding? Again, points are allotted for staying on his back for the required period of time (8 seconds) but the anger of the bull is also taken into consideration. And how do you ensure he is angry? Tie a flank strap around his midriff to squeeze his abdomen, causing considerable discomfort and pain. As soon as the cinched rope is released, the bull tends to calm down. Of course some of the bulls are so ticked off by this point, they run around the ring a few more times, looking to gore anyone in their path, hence the very skilled "clown" cowboys who divert attention from the rider, who having been bucked off, is usually lying in the dirt or scrambling to get out of the way. So exciting? Yes. Conflicted? That too. But I'd still go to another one. Cowboy culture is alive and well in Fort Worth.

We then spent a day at the old Fort Worth Stockyards that have been "repurposed" into a tourist destination of sorts. Not in a tacky wax museum sort of way but rather in a more realistic tribute to the history of "Cowtown" and its role in the cattle drives of the past. The working stockyards of today have moved 300 miles north to Amarillo so this is a rather sanitized approach, but it was fun and interesting none-the-less. There were many genuine cowboy apparel shops (albeit with higher prices than what we saw at the Stock Show), a museum (with old stockyard photos showing that the treatment of cattle was no better in the past than it is in the feedlots of today), numerous restaurants and even an old renovated hotel (where Bonnie & Clyde hid out for a while). But the highlight was the twice-daily cattle drive where cowhands in historic garb lead a small herd of Texas Longhorns (16 of them) along East Exchange Avenue. They aren't really going anywhere.

Just moving at 11:30am from one pen, down the street to another, and then back again at 4:00pm. The tourists, including us, loved it. I'm not sure why, but we did. The only really disingenuous part in the whole area was Billy Bob's Texas bar – supposedly the biggest bar in the world, accommodating up to 6,000 people. I went to check it out, paid my $2.00 to go inside and quickly realized it was all just hype. Yes, it has some unique aspects. A live bull-riding ring (no mechanical bulls here), an opportunity for patrons to sit on a stuffed bull as if they were actually riding, and a Texas sized dance floor. But the reality is that at 27,000 square feet, it is just a huge arena that has been divided into various rooms with 26 different bar stations and several stages for live acts. Celebrities like Garth Brooks, Willie Nelson and Waylon Jennings have performed there and the place has been featured in numerous TV shows and movies, but at the end of the day, it is just a dingy drinking joint that smells of stale beer, and is so huge that customers wander from one room to the next, never to find their friends again. They could just as well be walking around a cheap cowboy themed casino. Claiming it's the biggest bar in the world is ridiculous.

Our next foray into understanding a bit of Texan mentality was at a Gun Show. We had never been to one and were curious with respect to the type of people it attracts. Actually, we already had a pretty good idea but just wanted our suspicions confirmed. We were not disappointed. A rather paranoid lot, many with what John called "crazy eyes" and several young people (teens) who were in my estimation, way too interested in all the firepower on display. By gun show standards, this was a rather small one – only 400 vendors. The big one with 1,200 vendors was the following weekend but we would be gone by then so had to settle for a more modest venue. It was just as well. We lasted less than two hours because after a while everything started to look and sound the same. In addition to the numerous offerings of handguns and assault rifles, there were lots of scopes, holsters, knives, ammunition and what would be prohibited weapons in Canada – brass knuckles, butterfly knives, even the odd grenade. One female merchant tried to convince me I needed a stun gun just in case the nefarious fellow who was following me around in Walmart decided to follow me out to my car. "Imagine how much more confident you would be if you had this in your hand! It has 20 million volts plus a flashlight and an audible alarm. I got one for my daughter when she went away to college!" And all the while she kept activating the device, as if its crackling noise and arcing blue lights would convince me to dish out twenty bucks. It would have been a waste of breath to tell her that if I felt someone was following me around in Walmart, I would go find security, not head for the parking lot. But she typified the people there: a siege mentality focusing on the fear of an unknown attacker. I eavesdropped on the discussion a youngish female handgun purchaser was having with another supplier, and that was disturbing as well. Her primary interest was the colour of the grip. Should she get pink or green? Glossy or matte? OMG! This is a weapon!!! John tried to engage some of the dealers in conversation about the assault rifles but as soon as they found out we were from Canada (so would obviously not be purchasing anything), they were not interested. When asked about the purpose of assault rifles, they all said, "for hunting." But anyone who knows anything about firearms will tell you that a bolt-action rifle has more accuracy for hitting any intended target. They were not about to engage in that dialogue. They just wanted to sell something. Texas is the largest civilian gun market in the country. We left feeling quite unsettled.

And on the topic of firearms, we also went to Dallas to learn more about the assassination of John F. Kennedy and get a visual on the significant locations involved. Since it all took place in 1963, we were obviously too young to have any independent recollection of the events, but it is impossible not to be aware of the tragedy and the ensuing conspiracy theories that still persist all these many years later. And ironically, it is not JFK's death, but rather these very theories that keep the story alive (and have subsequently generated quite a few tourist dollars for the city of Dallas). The grassy knoll, JFK's liberal policies, the Mob, Castro, the Russians, even the Vice President as suspect all have their believers. I'm certain that if I suggested it was Bobby Kennedy who was jealous over his brother's relationship with Marilyn Munro, someone would buy into it. But as reporter Hugh Ayensworth said, "We can't accept very comfortably that two nobodies, two nothings – Lee Harvey Oswald and Jack Ruby – were able to change the course of world history."

There are several ways to approach this visit and by far, the best is going to Dealy Plaza and touring the sixth floor of the Texas Book Repository, which has been turned into a museum of sorts. Following along a pictorial and audio guide (with some video clips), visitors are informed about the Kennedy family's history (although there is no mention of Kennedy Sr.'s bootlegging past), the political climate of the 1960s, JFK's policies, Lee Harvey Oswald himself, the assassination, the aftermath and funeral, the investigation, and even the numerous conspiracy theories. There is also a scale model of the plaza setting, roadway and motorcade, showing the trajectory of the bullets fired by Oswald from the sixth-floor window. And from that window, we were able to look down onto the roadway (Elm Street) where two large "X"s have been painted on the asphalt, indicating the exact location of the motorcade when two of the bullets hit the President. It was interesting but rather macabre. Unfortunately, we ran out of time in the museum because we had also arranged for a guided tour to other related areas – Oswald's rooming house, the location where Dallas police officer J. D. Tippit was shot, the theatre where Oswald was captured, even the garage where he was later shot by Jack Ruby. Other than seeing places we had only read about (which was great), the tour itself was a bust. We could have just as easily (and for way less money) hopped in a cab and directed the driver to take us around to the various addresses. Our tour guide through Viator – and I use the term "guide" loosely – was an ill-informed conspiracy theorist who attempted to make the drive more titillating by making vague allusions to circumstances that were clearly just that. Circumstances. We should have stayed in the museum. I purchased and read *Four Days in November* by Vincent Bugliosi – a shorter version of his book *Reclaiming History: The Assassination of John F.* Kennedy (a bit lengthy at over 1600 pages but I'm intrigued enough to maybe buy it) and it concisely lays out along a chronological timeline who was doing what the day the president was shot, and what happened immediately afterwards. I would highly recommend it for anyone who is interested in the topic but doesn't want to get bogged down in textbook gobbledygook or out-there conspiracy theories.

Leaving the Dallas area, we headed west on I-20 towards El Paso and this was definitely not a route that will be listed amongst the top scenic drives in America. The stretch of highway, especially through Midland and Odessa was a wasteland of industrial petroleum pollution. Oil drills, oil refineries, oil tankers, abandoned scrubby parking lots with abandoned manufacturing machines, rusting disjointed lengths of pipeline, collapsed sheds, collapsed houses and more garbage strewn along the highway than I have ever seen. We had originally considered a small detour to Wink, childhood hometown of Roy Orbison, but quickly abandoned the idea. Why subject ourselves to more of the same *Mad Max* landscape. Even Orbison himself said later in life that he was glad to get away from the place because it was nothing but oil, grease and sand. We did, however, stumble across a small oasis of a park that other than having the faint smell of petroleum product in the air, was fairly decent. Monahans Sands State Park. It was in a hollow of sand dunes, so we were spared any reminders of what was around us (although there was an oil drill by the picnic area). But it was just a one-night stop and we continued on. Cutting across the lower southwest part of New Mexico didn't change things much, other than the oil rigs were gone, only to be replaced by decrepit trailers and junkyards. It looked more like a destitute slice of Mexico as opposed to the affluent United States. Numerous signs along the highway warned of dust storms, advising drivers to pull over, park and stay buckled up when they hit. Wow. Thank goodness we were spared that additional excitement. The impoverished air of El Paso also caught me off guard (although in all fairness we were just driving through along the interstate), and it seemed to seamlessly flow into Ciudad Juarez on the Mexican side of the border. The entire area reminded me of pictures I have seen of the poorer sections of Mexico City. A seemingly never-ending sprawl of densely packed squat homes with dirt and rubbish-filled yards, and crumbling pavement on roadways. All that was missing were the burros. And then we got to Tombstone – the "Town Too Tough to Die." Or so the saying goes.

Location of the infamous shoot-out at the OK Corral, where the Earp brothers along with Doc Holliday successfully took on the reprehensible Clanton/McLaury gang, Tombstone started out as a mining town in 1877, when silver was discovered in the mountains, and quickly became one of the more violent and immoral places in the southwest. Shootings in the streets were quite common as was evidenced by our stroll through the Boothill Graveyard. From 1878 to 1884, it had been used as the burial site for about 250 of Tombstone's residents, young and old, good and bad alike. But when a newer cemetery was opened, the Boothill Graveyard was left neglected until the 1920s when some interested Tombstone residents restored it as best they could to its original state, and through extensive research, compiled as thorough a list as possible of those interred there. It provided a fascinating snapshot of the time. Some of the markers were obviously sad (eg. babies who died of illness) but by and large most people met violent deaths, either by shooting, stabbing or hanging. It was interesting to note that the headstones recorded the deceased's name, year of death and cause of death, but rarely age at death – eg. "Harry Curry 1882 Killed by Indians" or "Miles Sweeney 1880 Murdered." Some were downright humorous. "Here lies Lester Moore, Four slugs from a 44, No les, No more" or "Here lies George Johnson, Hanged by mistake, 1882, He was right, We was wrong, But we strung him up, And now hes [sic] gone." Tombstone itself was okay to visit but is really just a tourist attraction depicting life during those turbulent years. People in period dress offering ghost tours, shops selling historical western garb for men and bordello type clothing for women, a "shoot-out" two times a day and carriage rides up and down main street. It was a bit like stepping onto a movie set. Neither of us was really into the whole western outlaw theme so we poked around a while and were soon on our way to Tucson.

Our main reason for going was to explore Saguaro National Park and the high concentration of Saguaro Cactus located there. But we found that Tucson had a lot more going for it than just the park. One day, we drove 28 miles up Mt. Lemmon to the southern-most ski hill in the U.S. Okay, it was small with only two chair lifts, but they

BIKING THROUGH SAGUARO NATIONAL PARK.

did have snow on the ground in a few places (although not enough to ski on). The drive was very winding and scenic, and it was interesting how the vegetation changed along with the air temperature. We started in the desert with Saguaro cactus and 82F/28C degrees, and as we climbed, the Saguaro were replaced by Yucca, which were then replaced by small pines, which were then replaced by large pines. By the time we got out of the car in the small community of Summerhaven, it was 45F/7C degrees, and we could have been somewhere in Canada's ski country. We stayed long enough to grab a hot chocolate and then headed back down to warmer climes. To get a real sense of the national park, we left Porter in the yacht for a few hours while we set out to bike the winding 9-mile loop road through the park's interior. I don't know what I was thinking. It was brutal. I had somehow imagined a leisurely pedal in and around the huge Saguaros, with some gentle slopes to get my heart rate up a bit. Gentle slopes? I just about heaved a lung. A steep downhill at the beginning should have been my first clue but it was too late. There was more than one uphill where I had to get off and walk because my legs were just done. Wobbly jelly done. John said he never got off his bike, but I was so far behind him how would I know? However, the Saguaro were fascinating. Some tall and straight like telephone poles, others with one or two upwardly bent arms, and still others with numerous arms pointing in numerous directions. We found one with 15 arms, but I believe the record is 75. They actually don't grow any of these arms (or branches) until they are about 70 years old and will only reach their full height of 40 to 50 feet at the ripe old age of 150! Some of the taller ones can reach 75 feet. Amazing.

There were other things to do in Tucson as well, but our timing was a bit off. There is a huge outdoor aircraft museum (Pima Air & Space Museum) with 800 aircraft spread over 8 acres (yawn), but through Pima and by special arrangement you can also visit Davis-Monthan Airforce Base where over 2,000 (!) army, navy, airforce and NASA airplanes are stored, regenerated or recycled. They call it the boneyard. Just driving by on the road, we could see hundreds of these planes, neatly lined up in equidistant rows, waiting to be called up. The arid climate is perfect to protect them from rusting out, but since this is Department of Defence territory, the tours can only be had by booking 10 days ahead of time so that a thorough security background check can be done. We weren't going to be around that long. And we missed The Gem Show, a huge event where gemstones for the wealthy, and rocks and minerals for the frugal, can be admired, compared and purchased. The event is so big and so popular, and brings in so many tourists, we had difficulty finding a place to stay.

Which brings me to my next observation about RVing through North America. Accommodations. This month saw us check into the most eclectic of places, from the trailer parks of the almost-destitute, to the RV parks of the winter snowbirds, even to God's waiting room. Let me expand on this a bit. Large cities tend not to have RV parks located within their downtown cores, so while visiting Dallas/Fort Worth, we made reservations at an RV park about 30 minutes from town. One that also advertised corrals and stalls for horses too. The internet pictures looked lovely and we envisioned a bucolic country setting. It was not. It was a long-term trailer park for the down-and-out with more rules than you can shake a stick at. The overarching air was one of neglect, and although there were cars parked in front of every shabby site, we rarely saw any people. But they must have seen us, because during our three-day stay, we received two texts from management, first advising that someone had complained about Porter doing his business in a "non-designated" area along the road (even though we always stoop and scoop) and second, that our kayaks, despite being placed under the coach's slide-out, were resting on the grass. If you can call brown weeds and burrs "grass", then yes, they were. I had an image of beady eyes watching our every move from behind broken blinds. But I suppose if I were one pay cheque away from living in my car, I'd be in a bad frame of mind too. We were glad to leave.

While visiting Tombstone, we found ourselves in a place located about 10 miles from town, full of snowbirds, quite a few of them Canadian. Well maintained large sites that were nicely landscaped with many varieties of cacti. Most of the residents were obviously there to escape the winter cold and were engaged in all manner of activities to keep themselves occupied. Everything from movie night to Tai Chi classes. The owner/ manager proudly showed me the swimming pool, weight room, pool room and so on, saying several times that he hoped we enjoyed our stay. Well, our stay was only for one night and we probably wouldn't have played pool anyway, but it was a refreshing change from the aforementioned trailer park.

And in Tucson, we found ourselves in God's Waiting Room. All because of the previously mentioned Gem Show. There were no national/state parks with camping facilities near-by and every RV park we contacted was booked up. Then I came across a website for a lovely gated RV resort exclusively for people over 55. Well, I guess that's us. How bad could it be? RV stands for recreational vehicle. Apparently these folks have a different definition of vehicle, because when we checked in, we found that of the almost 500 sites, a good 95% were occupied by park model homes – those small cottagey looking places that were perhaps manoeuvred into position by a vehicle, but were not themselves capable of any motorized operation. And so closely crammed together, one neighbour could literally pass a cup of sugar to another through the window. We had been assigned a narrow space with one of these park model homes on one side and a large palm tree on the other. It was the tightest spot John had ever had to back into and it took all his skill to make sure he did not hit either the tree, the neighbour's carport or the "home" across the way. Inch by inch he reversed into the site, with me running back and forth outside as a second set of eyes. And while we were doing this, a small group of seniors had gathered to watch the entertainment. When we were finally in position, they broke into spontaneous applause and came over to congratulate John on a job well done. It must have been a slow day at the resort. Yet these were the friendliest people we had ever met. Our "neighbours" on either side of us, as well as from across the "street", all came over to introduce themselves and welcome us to the complex. Literally everyone who walked or biked past, smiled, waved or said hello. It was unnerving. And many were, again, northerners seeking warmth and sun while others were clearly well beyond their golden years but still staying relatively active. God bless them. I can't for the life of me ever imagine living like that for months at a time (three days was enough), but it is not fair to judge. Not everyone can afford high-end villas in exotic locales or go on extended back-to-back-to-back cruises. They were happy. Good for them.

And then we were finally able to check into my kind of place. Organ Pipe Cactus National Monument, way out in the Sonoran Desert, sharing a border with Mexico. Nothing but wilderness for 516 square miles. And while we were still the youngest people there, our neighbouring RVers were at least engaged in similar activities. Hiking, exploring and enjoying the peaceful beauty of the natural environment. The Monument was designated an International Biosphere Reserve by the United Nations in 1976 since it contains so many unique species of plants and animals, including the Organ Pipe Cactus which although common in Mexico, is rare in the United States. And we saw way more Saguaros than around Tucson. Curiously, it rained the first two days, a gentle steady drizzle, but that served to bring out flowers on the Ocotillo bushes, so it was just lovely. We extended our stay by several days (ultimately staying a week) and spent our time hiking and driving the several trails and routes. The only downside to being so far from civilization was that internet could only be accessed by sitting inside the visitor centre (about 1.5 miles from the campground) and there was obviously no television (so we could no longer follow the Olympics). There were no hook-ups and generator hours were limited (8-10am and 4-6pm), but we managed just fine. We were glamping once again. And being so close to Mexico, it seemed that every other vehicle we saw was Border Patrol. Pick-up trucks, all-terrain vehicles, motorcycles. We even saw sections of a wall, literally running up a hill that separated Lukeville USA from Sonoyta, Mexico. Can't blame The Donald for that one though

– it was built 15 years ago. And for the first time ever, park literature contained a safety blurb advising to hike in pairs, avoid contact with anyone carrying bundles, backpacks or black water bottles, and if seen, report their location to authorities as soon as possible. Not exactly reassuring, especially considering that we had to hike separately since Porter was not allowed on the trails, and we didn't want to leave him in the coach without a/c. Fortunately, we never had any run-ins with anything more menacing than a Gila Woodpecker and some Gambel's Quails.

That said, along each trail, signs were posted that illegal activity does take place in the area and to exercise caution. I asked a park ranger what kind of illegal activity they were concerned with and he said mostly drug smuggling (as opposed to illegal migration or human trafficking). By the park's Kris Eggle Visitor's Centre, a commemorative marker indicated that the centre was named after Park Ranger Eggle, who was killed in the line of duty in 2002. I inquired about that a bit further and was advised that Eggle was responding to a request for assistance from Mexican authorities who were pursuing two members of a drug cartel. The pair had committed a series of murders south of the border and had crossed over into the park. Ranger Eggle and Border Patrol officers responded. Eggle was shot with an AK-47 and died of his injuries before he could be evacuated. He was only 27 years old. One of the bandits was subsequently captured on the US side of the border while the other attempted to flee back towards Mexico. The Mexican authorities were waiting for him and opened fire, saving taxpayers a lot of money. During that year, US border authorities intercepted 200,000 migrants and 700,000 pounds of drugs in Organ Pipe alone. Very sobering, and really put things into perspective. That was just along one stretch of the border.

Interestingly, while out hiking (miles and miles from nowhere) on three separate occasions we came across locations where blue flags on high flimsy poles fluttered in the light breeze. Checking them out, we found that at the base of each flag was a large barrel of water and some canned food. Emergency supplies for the smugglers lest they get lost in

JUST A LITTLE SOMETHING TO HELP THE DRUG SMUGGLERS.

the wilderness. The system is maintained by a volunteer organization called Humane Borders and although it in a way supports illegal activity, the park allows it since they would rather not have desiccated bodies, no matter whose they are, turning up within their boundaries. There is something wrong with this picture.

But we really did enjoy our time there. The Sonoran is only one of four deserts in North America (the others being Chihuahuan, Mojave and Great Basin), and geographically covers ground in the southern parts of Arizona and California, down the Baja Peninsula and into north-west Mexico. It is called the green desert because it has two rainfall periods, so much of its vegetation has a green tint to it - Saguaros, Organ Pipe, Prickly Pear and the nasty Chain-fruit Cholla, sometimes referred to as the "Jumping Cholla." Porter and I have first-hand knowledge as to why the cholla has such a descriptive name. The lightest brush up against it results in the transfer of nasty spines that have tiny barbs on the end. Porter made the mistake of sniffing one and got a muzzle full, while I ended up with several imbedded in my leg – through denim jeans no less! The spines are very fine, almost like the tips of acupuncture needles, and I did not notice them until evening. By then a couple had worked their way about ¼ inch into my leg and required tweezers to get them out, leaving a small drop of blood at each extraction point. Ouch! I had encountered them while biking in Tucson as well, but not to this extent. However, one of the more beautiful plants in these parts was the Creosote bush. It isn't really much to look at, but it gives off a wonderful aroma. John said it smelled like rain. I opined that it smelled like sweet caramel. He said I was having an olfactory hallucination brought on by my self-imposed severe sugar deprivation. Ha! I will admit I was trying to cut back on sweets but only because I was trying to get back into shape after the disastrous consequences of overindulging during December and January. I will not be discussing weight gain at this juncture but suffice to say that this was one detail that had to be nipped in the bud. We put yoga on the back burner and focused on cardio and a bit of strength training. My knees were complaining in no time.

Yet despite my love of wilderness, I am still a city girl at heart, so it wasn't long before we headed to "town" in search of a coffee shop. "Town" was a place called Ajo – about 40 miles away. It is trying very hard to reinvent itself as a retirement community (their motto – "Where Summer Spends the Winter") but in reality, is just an abandoned old mining town struggling to survive. Digging in the area first started around the 1850's and 100 years later, their New Cornelia mine was the largest producer of copper in Arizona (and the third largest open-pit mine in the USA). The pit itself is 1,100 feet deep and 1&1/2 miles across. At its peak, it employed 3,000 people and produced 40,000 tons of copper a year. And then the wheels came off the bus. Demand for copper dropped, prices followed,

and in 1985 the company gave everyone two weeks notice that they were closing operations. The town has been on a downward slide ever since. There were a few dubious RV
parks around the vicinity (enough to sustain the grocery/hardware store), a town square
(with one struggling coffee shop), small homes that had seen better days, two closed baker-
ies and a Pizza Hut. They have a long way to go. We didn't stay long.

And continuing on the theme of "a long way to go," it seemed our yacht problems
were not over. The people at Tiffin had completed all the maintenance and bodywork
asked of them over the holidays but had neglected one small detail. They failed to
reattach the hanging bracket that secures the tailpipe to the RV frame. Without that
bracket, the protruding tailpipe bounced around the outlet of the RV's fibreglass body.
So guess who now had cracked and chipped fiberglass at the back of the coach? We
didn't notice it until setting up at Organ Pipe and John was forced to contact the insurance company yet again. As vehicle damage goes, it was neither an insurmountable nor
time-consuming repair, but when that vehicle happens to be your home, things get
complicated. John secured the tailpipe with a screw and duct-taped the damage until we
could get it to a body shop. OMG! I was driving/living in a vehicle that was being held
together by duct-tape! That said, we didn't look too out of place pulling into the little
town of Quartzsite, 20 miles east of the California state line.

I had never heard of Quartzsite when we started this journey, but we kept bumping
into people who said we have to go there just to see the place. It is the boondocking
mecca of America. RVers can show up and for virtually nothing, camp pretty much anywhere they wish in the seemingly never-ending surrounding desert. In order to protect
the desert ecosystem and prevent its overuse, the Bureau of Land Management set aside
over 11,000 acres and called it a Long Term Visitor Area (LTVA). For a measly $180.00,
snowbirds and others can purchase a permit that allows them to stay up to 7 months,
between September and April. If staying for two weeks, it costs $40.00. And if just
passing through and only staying a few nights (like us) it is free. But it is only available
to self-contained RV units. No tenting, because there are no facilities of any kind. Even
garbage has to be packed out. I'm not sure how they enforce all this because the area is
so big, there are no real roads to follow and everyone is incredibly spread out. So on my
momentous 60th birthday (more on that later), I found myself parked in a vast, sparsely
vegetated (mostly mesquite and creosote bush) BLM desert with our closest boondocking neighbour more than a hundred yards away. The fulltime population of this little
town is only 3,000 souls, but in January and February, can swell to an unbelievable 1
million. The main draw during those two months is geology. There are some major
mineral and gem shows here (more mineral than gem), where serious rock-hounds and

collectors can admire, trade and buy to their heart's content in what is in essence, a huge outdoor mall. Some of the vendors come from as far away as Australia and China, and of course there were spin-offs. Fossils, one-of-a-kind jewellery, clothing, even pottery. And although I still don't know the difference between azurite and bornite, it was an interesting experience and it's amazing to think that some pretty incredible beauty lies in the dusty ground beneath our feet. On the other hand, the rock-hounds themselves are an odd bunch. When they are not driving around the country to various rock shows, they are out hammering away at the ground hoping to find just one more pretty stone.

On a somewhat related theme, Quartzsite is also associated with America's first and only attempt to introduce camels to this continent. In the 1850s, the U.S. army decided to import 77 camels from the Middle East in the misguided belief that given their desert origins, they would be perfect for transporting army supplies through the arid southwest into California. They even hired a lead camel driver from Syria in the vain hope that camels would respond better to the Arabic language – Phillip Tedro, a Muslim convert who went by the name Hadji Ali. Not too concerned with proper pronunciation, Hadji Ali became Hi Jolly to the Americans. There are several explanations for why the camel experiment failed: army officials found the animals to be smelly and mean-tempered, the other pack animals (burros, horses etc.) were afraid of them and the sharp rocks in America's deserts (as opposed to Sahara sand) cut the camel's feet. Within 10 years, the camels were sold, sent to zoos and circuses, or released into the desert to fend for themselves. Hi Jolly spent the rest of his life in and around Quartzsite (he died in 1902) and is buried beneath a small, camel topped rock pyramid in the town's cemetery. Several businesses, campgrounds and streets bear his name, and the 1954 movie *Southwest Passage* is based on these exploits. So that was where I spent my 60th birthday. Not exactly the most elegant or sophisticated place to celebrate the big day, but it was certainly memorable. And upon reaching that sexagenarian milestone, I was not certain if I should tell people I was 55 and have them think I looked old for my age, or tell them that I was 65 and have them think I looked great!

And then the shitty side of life showed itself again. We had just set up in the Sedona area when I received word from home that my mom's health had taken a sudden, severe and rapid turn for the worse. She was being admitted to hospital and the prognosis was not good. I caught the first flight home from Phoenix while John stayed behind making arrangements to put the coach into storage, following which he and Porter drove back in the Jeep. Mom was not going to make it. We took turns, together and separately, sitting with her so that she was not alone. And we grieved. What else was there to do? For the most part, life is still beautiful, but sometimes it really, really hurts.

23.

THE PAUSE BUTTON

THERE WAS NO "RVING THROUGH NORTH AMERICA" DURING MARCH. Mom quietly slipped away from us on March 2ⁿᵈ and while my plans and God's were way out of sync this time, I was grateful for the opportunity to have been with her to say good-bye. Many have walked this path before and know how difficult it is. The caring support and expressions of sympathy received by our entire family were sincerely appreciated. So the first few weeks of the month were spent dealing with loss, taking care of practical arrangements and adjusting to our new reality. John and I were calculating when we could return to the road, when we discovered that two elderly and very dear friends of John's were grappling with health issues of their own. He battling leukemia, albeit the slow moving kind, while at the same time, trying to care for his wife who was undergoing a battery of tests for dementia and Alzheimer's. They were already well beyond capable of living safely in their condo and it was up to John to make sure they were settled before we headed off again. If only it were that easy. We became quasi-experts on long-term care homes, retirement homes, independent living, assisted living, memory care floors, and what services are and are not readily available in the community. In Ontario at least, it is one unwieldy, uncoordinated and more often than not, ineffective system. After searching long and hard we found a great place where she could be on a secure Memory Care floor and he could be two levels up in Independent Living, enabling them to still spend their days together. But, when all was said and done, they decided that they did not want to leave their condo and would rather take their chances on community services, hedging their bets that nothing drastic would occur. In our estimation, a big mistake, but everyone is entitled to make wrong decisions, regardless of age. And how does this relate to RVing?

Well, prior to setting out on our journey, we discussed what we would do should a situation such as we found ourselves in this month, arise. Our plan was simple but naïve: whoever had to get home in a rush would fly, while the other remained behind to put the coach into storage and then start driving with Porter. Given the horror stories we heard then (and continue to hear now) about how dogs are treated by airlines, there was never any question of Porter flying cargo. He would certainly never fit under the seat in a cabin, and his impersonation of therapy dog is shaky at best. So when we received word that Mom was ill, I was on a flight home within 12 hours and John stayed to "put the coach in storage" before heading out on the cross-country driving marathon. That was much easier said than done. Although there are numerous RV storage facilities, and twice as many advertisements for them (especially in the southern states), the good ones (i.e. covered/sheltered and with shore power) were full up. There was absolutely nothing available within a good 100-mile radius of Phoenix. He finally found a place that offered secure outdoor storage but no power. So that meant getting rid of all the food we had in the fridge and sadly, throwing out all my previously prepared and portioned out stews and chilis and other comfort foods that were in the freezer. We left the dried foodstuffs (cookies, crackers, cereal etc.) as is in the cupboards, and hoped no mice would be tempted to move in during our absence. I had no idea what the coach's internal temperature would get to with the windows closed, no a/c and the sunny outside temp hovering around 91F/33C degrees.

But what difference would a few more days make? We decided to stay put over Easter and while no-one was really looking forward to Easter Sunday morning brunch without Mom, life marches on and we must march with it. We prepared the usual Latvian fare complete with *pīrāgi, galerts* and *rasols*, we coloured eggs using traditional natural dyes from onion skins and red cabbage (with which we had Easter egg "fights") and we did our best not to weep over one less place setting at the table. We were fortunate, and I'm sure Mom's spirit was with us. Happy Easter!

24.

GETTIN' OUR KICKS ON ROUTE 66

WE RESUMED OUR JOURNEY APRIL 8TH, LEAVING MISSISSAUGA ON A CHILLY ALBEIT SUNNY DAY, ALTHOUGH THE SUNSHINE DIDN'T LAST LONG. It was cloudy and snowing by the time we reached Fort Wayne, Indiana with single digit temperatures to complete the entire "spring" experience. Temperatures in Phoenix were projected to hit 100 degrees so we were a bit concerned as to what we would find in the coach upon our return but there was nothing we could do about it at that point. Our planned route was along I-44 and I-40, basically travelling down Old Route 66 aka America's Main Street or The Mother Road. Sadly, Mother abandoned her Children a long time ago. Or perhaps her children abandoned her. If anything, Old Route 66 should be called Abandoned America Road. A short background. Originally commissioned in November of 1926, Route 66 was the first national highway to cross the mid-western part of the United States, running east-west about 2,448 miles from Grant Park, Chicago Illinois to the Santa Monica Pier in Santa Monica, California. It traversed eight states and crossed three time zones. Although the route itself actually existed well before 1916, it was really just a collection of muddy, rutted, and often impassable rural roads, and its unification and paving made it possible for truckers and travellers to reach their destinations with considerably more ease. (And subsequently replaced trains as the preferred mode of transportation.)

In the early years, thousands of migrants escaping the dust bowl of the 1930s followed it to a "better" life in California. Think Steinbeck's *Grapes of Wrath*. In the 1940s, it was a major supply line for the armed forces, and following the war, many returning servicemen settled in the small towns along its way. In 1946 musician Bobby

GETTIN' OUR KICKS ON ROUTE 66 – OR WHAT'S LEFT OF IT.

Troop coined the infamous phrase, "get your kicks on Route 66." During the 1950s Americans fell in love with automobile tourism, and it was at this time that the small towns through which the new highway ran, reached their zenith, meeting the needs of travellers with gas stations, diners and countless drive-up motels, many with kitschy themes and bizarre architecture. But during the 1960s the interstate highway system kicked into high gear with I-44 and I-40 replacing 66 as the main transportation corridor. In some straight, open stretches the interstate was paved literally over the old road. In other places, the interstate runs parallel, with 66 becoming almost a service road. And in many places where 66 once ran straight through town, the interstate now diverts traffic away and acts as a ring road. As each new interstate segment was completed, the thousands of cars that once passed through these towns on a daily basis disappeared. And shortly thereafter, so did the businesses that relied on them. Motels, gas stations and diners closed down or were abandoned as people moved away searching for another livelihood. Very few towns survived this exodus, and despite a 1980s resurgence of Route 66 nostalgia and concerted efforts to rejuvenate tourism along the old road, it is all too little too late for most of them. While state tourism brochures tout the attractions of their respective small communities, driving through them was quite depressing. Countless shuttered motels with weed-overgrown parking lots, derelict old gas stations and boarded up diners, all with a dated 60s motif. Rusting remnants of a time long gone. It was rather creepy. We only passed through three towns that we considered viable: Gallup, New Mexico (kept afloat by its over 100 Native artists, traders and galleries), Winslow, Arizona (thank The Eagles – more on that later) and Williams, Arizona (its claim to fame being it was here that the last segment of Route 66 was officially by-passed in 1984, plus it is only 1 hour from the Grand Canyon).

I'm not sure what I expected travelling this road, but after a while I could only generate so much enthusiasm for yet another black and white Route 66 road sign, and yet another claim of "original" Route 66 memorabilia for sale. And an endless supply of Route 66 T-shirts, ball caps, coffee mugs and other soon–to-be discarded trinkets. And it seemed every other little town had a Route 66 Museum, where the "collections" were basically just old 50s and 60s junk. I really didn't need to "take home a piece of Route 66." We stuck to the interstate most of the way and only detoured onto 66 when it appeared there might be something worth seeing but most of the time it was not worth the effort. While we occasionally found one kitschy shop or diner still in operation, the surrounding buildings were generally vacant. Near Gallup, we drove into a dust storm where the visibility was so limited it was almost like driving through a heavy fog. Only the odd tumbleweed that blew across our path reminded us we were still in the desert. Crossing the Texas Panhandle was not too exciting either. Despite the sunshine, the landscape was rather bleak with hundreds and hundreds of wind turbines as far as the eye could see. And near Amarillo, cattle feedlots that stretched for over a mile. I cannot even begin to guesstimate how many steers were just lying there, crowded together, sweltering in the unseasonably warm weather. It's enough to turn a person vegetarian. That, and the smell emanating from the abattoirs.

But things did improve. We had really enjoyed Santa Fe when we stopped there in November, and were passing so close, we decided a one-night stop was in order. It was a much-needed break from the interminable monotony of I-40 and we were able to find a dog-friendly B&B (Las Palomas), which was really a charming cluster of renovated adobe dwellings grouped together like an old pueblo, all furnished with period pieces. (And owned by a retired MET opera singer. Go figure.) Such a nice change from the nondescript interstate hotels. We revisited some of the galleries and shops, and I finally purchased a bleached buffalo skull that I intend to decorate, à la Indian style. The ones I saw in the galleries, adorned with colourful beads, dream-catchers, turquoise inserts, eagle feathers and furs, were considerably out of my price range but I was able to plagiarise some pretty good ideas. How hard can it be? I'm going to cover mine with some of the seashells collected along the way and call it, as John suggested, "Surf and Turf."

And then we reached Winslow, Arizona. Tourists come from far and wide (about 100,000 each year) just to stand on its one famous corner. And we did too. All because of a song. *Take It Easy*. The first hit single for The Eagles, it was actually written by Jackson Browne (Glenn Frey's former roommate) but he never completed it, much less recorded it. Credits say Browne and Frey co-wrote it, but in reality, Frey just finished off the second verse with, "*It's a girl, my Lord, in a flat-bed Ford, slowin' down to take a look at me.*" Browne had already included the line about "*standing on a corner in Winslow Arizona*," reflecting on a day when car trouble left him stranded in Winslow back when Old Highway 66 was still a major thoroughfare. The Eagles ended up recording the tune and the rest is, as they say, history. It was a cool and very windy day when we showed up, but undaunted we dutifully waited our turn to stand on the celebrated corner to take a picture beside the flat bed Ford. There isn't much else to do in Winslow.

There is, however, a wonderful old hotel just one block away from "the corner" with a fascinating history. La Posada (the Resting Place) was designed in 1927 as a Spanish hacienda by one of the Southwest's greatest architects, Mary Colter (whose name pops up again at the Grand Canyon). It was the last and some say the most elegant of the illustrious Fred Harvey Hotels built by the Santa Fe Railroad, at a time when rail travel was everything. (Fred Harvey is known for having "civilized" the west by introducing fine china and impeccable service to railroad travel and his well-mannered waitresses came to be known as The Harvey Girls. Hollywood even made a movie about them, starring none other than Judy Garland.) But why build in Winslow Arizona? Winslow was the headquarters of the Santa Fe Railroad and everything there was to see and do in northeast Arizona was within a day's drive. Every passenger train running from Los Angeles to Chicago stopped there, and anybody who was anybody stayed there: Howard Hughes, John Wayne, even Albert Einstein. I suspect choice of accommodation might be the only thing those three men had in common. At the time, Winslow was bigger than Flagstaff and even Sedona. But by the 1950s, passenger rail and automobile travel declined, with most people opting to fly to their destinations and like everything else along Old Route 66, the hotel fell upon hard times and closed its doors in 1957. It was only restored to some of its former glory in 1997. Perhaps we had just been staying in too many cookie-cutter hotels, but we really enjoyed the elegance of this old building with its numerous galleries, lounges and gardens, despite the fact that it is literally right beside the still operational railroad tracks. About 100 trains per day pass by, with the Amtrak run between Chicago and L.A. still stopping twice a day. In fact, our room came with complimentary earplugs but surprisingly we didn't need them. The walls were pretty thick. Porter was allowed everywhere except the dining room, but those of us travelling with pets were able to order a tray and dine in "the ballroom", surrounded by artwork, Navajo rugs and southwest furniture. I tried not to think about the bill but rationalized by telling myself this was our last luxury before moving back into the yacht.

The next morning, in the interests of time, we skipped Petrified Forest National Park (I was a little fossilled out) but did stop in at Meteor Crater, marketed as the "best preserved and first proven meteorite impact site on Planet Earth." Being privately owned and with a tag like that, I fully expected it to be a very hyped and hokey little hole in the ground. It was anything but. There isn't much about "space stuff" that piques my interest, but this exhibit had a very well-presented interactive discovery centre with all manner of artefacts and displays describing how this crater came to be. About 50,000 years ago, a meteor approximately 150 feet in diameter, weighing several hundred thousand pounds, travelling at 64,000 kilometers per hour slammed into the Earth with a force greater than 20 million tons of TNT. Put in more understandable terms, if you saw it flashing through the sky in Paris, it would have crossed over New York 8 minutes later, and then crashed into the Arizona plateau 5 minutes after that. It left a hole 700 feet deep and about 1 mile across. Today, that hole is only 550 feet deep because over the thousands of years, erosion has levelled it a bit. The only piece of the original meteor actually found is the Holsinger Meteorite that weighs in at a measly 1,410 pounds and was on open display. We took turns walking through the museum and around part of the rim and learned that between 1963 and 1970 even the Apollo astronauts trained there. I had to admit that not all "space stuff" is yada yada yada.

Six days after leaving Mississauga we moved back into the yacht. No damage, no mice, no unpleasant surprises. Still, it was difficult. When I had last been there, Mom had been alive and I was looking forward to talking her into visiting us on the west coast. It really hit me that I wouldn't be sending her any more postcards nor chatting with her about what we had seen and done. No more, "Hey Mom! Look at this! Look Mom! No hands!" It's a huge hole in the heart. We spent our first night in a lovely state park by Scottsdale and then set out for Sedona, returning to the same RV park we had checked into a month prior. Despite having paid for 7 days but leaving after 3 (without any compassionate refund, I might add), they were not willing to credit us for the previously unused nights. Bad form – especially considering this was their high season and they re-rented our spot in a nanosecond. But all the other parks were full, so we were forced to suck it up.

Sedona is lovely. Deep orange/red rocks against a deep blue sky, accented with deep green vegetation, surround a picturesque community that is very artsy if somewhat chi-chi. Even the boulevards are meticulously groomed and manicured, and there is neither a trailer park nor vacant lot in sight. Plus, it has all the hiking and trail biking anyone could wish for, even within the city limits. We drove part way (and walked the rest) up to a fascinating sanctuary that almost seemed to have been hewn directly

CHAPEL OF THE HOLY CROSS – MORE TOURIST ATTRACTION THAN PLACE OF WORSHIP, BUT IMPRESSIVE NONE-THE-LESS.

from the surrounding rock. The Chapel of the Holy Cross. First conceived in 1932, influenced by Franklin Lloyd Wright, originally slated for Budapest and ultimately built in Sedona in 1956, as a memorial to the visionary's parents. Up close it is huge but when viewed from a distance, illustrates just how vast this area is. It offers a commanding view of the surrounding countryside both when standing outside, as well as from within looking out. My only gripe would be that there were so many people milling about (doing pretty much exactly the same thing as us), it seemed more tourist attraction than sanctuary. But it was Sunday, after all. Another day we got in a couple of hikes, the morning spent scrambling up Bell Rock and the afternoon, strolling along Boynton Canyon, two completely different experiences. Bell Rock is a stand-alone exposed rock formation with lots of smoothed areas and no delineated path. We walked, crawled, clambered and occasionally backslid (not on purpose) until we reached a ledge where we enjoyed our picnic lunch and the view out towards town. It was marvellous. Boynton Canyon was great too, but almost the opposite with respect to terrain. A demarcated path along a box canyon floor, through trees and brush, with soaring red cliffs all around. We did not reach the end however because we had to pick Porter up from daycare. And not a minute too soon.

We had left him at Hillside Canine, not too far from our RV place, where everything seemed on the up and up. Appearances can be deceiving. When we walked into the office at 6pm, the attendant said, "Oh I just checked on him and he was fine. Just lying there panting." It was a hot day so ok with the panting. But why was she "checking" on him? He was supposed to be out with supervised care, playing with other dogs. When we got back to the RV, I have never seen him drink so much water. Two full bowls went down immediately and then part of a third. It was obvious that he had been kennelled and without water for who knows how long. I am still working on a scathing critique. On a lighter note, it was also after we returned to the yacht that I learned our two hiking locations had taken us through two of the largest and most powerful psychic vortexes in the Sedona area. What?!? A vortex is supposedly an area of enhanced vitality where "in-tune" individuals can feel a concentration of metaphysical energy. Guides will even take you out and teach you how to harness this energy. For a fee of course. Sedona has more than its fair share of psychic healers, palm readers, aura analysts and who knows what else, all because around 1980, a psychic by the name of Page Bryant (who was temporarily living there) announced that she had psychically channelled an "entity" that described these specific energy locations. Bryant then generously plotted them on a map and New Agers have been flocking to Sedona ever since. I'm all for exploring the spiritual/psychic side of things but I question the veracity of Ms. Page's claims. One of the vortexes she mapped, with specific co-ordinates I might add, was near a runway by the airport and when pilots started complaining about too many people wandering around out on the tarmac seeking their inner selves, she conveniently moved the co-ordinates a few hundred yards away. I wonder what the "entity" had to say about that.

But the Sedona area has more to it than healing, hiking and biking. A short drive south in the Verde Valley is Montezuma's Castle, a 5-story, 20-room cliff dwelling that was constructed sometime between 1100 and 1300. Although built by the Sinagua people, the early settlers assumed it was Aztec (at a time when early reports were emerging from middle America), hence the name Montezuma. It was pretty impressive although I had to admit I'd about had my fill of cliff dwellings. At least for the time being. Then we took the time to drive to another one of the ubiquitous ghost towns, this time Jerome. It has to be said that ghost towns in the south-west are pretty much a dime a dozen. Every place where a mine of any viability once operated (and there are many such places), little towns sprang up, filling with all manner of people, from labourers to opportunists and from bartenders to brothel owners. And when the mines invariably played out, everything was abandoned. Those places that are still standing often claim to be the badest, wildest, wickedest, meanest – you get the picture – all in the hopes of attracting a few tourist dollars. Some stage shoot-outs at high noon, all sell faux western apparel and after a while they all start looking the same. There is such a fascination with the wild west out there. Jerome falls into the ghost town category too, but what differentiates it from the others is that it is set 5,000 feet up a steep hillside (Cleopatra Hill) and overlooks the Verde Valley. In its heyday, Jerome was the fourth largest town in Arizona, complete with the requisite brothels and bars. Its copper mine was prolific but after the crash of 1929, the price of copper dropped, and the boom times were over. The mine and town hung in there until 1953, but things went from bad to worse. The hill upon which the town was built, was one and the same they had been dynamiting for years to get at the copper. And when the town started sliding downhill at a rate of 4 inches a year, it only hastened the exodus. Today, however, it has become a day-tripping tourist destination of sorts simply because of the numerous galleries and art shops that have opened, and its fairly close proximity to Sedona (about a one-hour drive). We walked around a bit and while it certainly had character, all the little shops and all the merchandise was starting to look the same. That is the problem with RV travel. I was limited in what I could buy because there was limited space in where to put it. No curio cabinets it the yacht! So I was not really a motivated shopper at this point. We ultimately left Sedona without doing justice to the many art galleries in town, without buying anything for ourselves and without experiencing any metaphysical awakening.

Next stop – The Grand Canyon. Full disclosure: we had been there before. About 10 years ago we went out on one of our best vacations ever. We hiked from the south rim, down into the canyon, across the Colorado River, and then back up to the north rim. It took us three full days and two nights, carrying packs that were as light as possible, but still too heavy. It was tough, but the exhausted feeling of exhilaration upon reaching the top of the north rim is inexpressible. We then hooked up with a rafting company and spent two weeks running the river where it flows through the national park, experiencing the thrill of seemingly un-survivable rapids as well as the serenity of gentle flat-water floating during the day, and slept out in the open under the stars at night. They say, "you can never go back" and so it was with this visit, although we knew from the outset that we were just going to reminisce a bit. On this 3-day stop, we walked along segments of the south rim (the paved trail runs for about 13 miles) and experienced all the canyon's weather. Sunny and warm one day, cloudy, windy and cool the next, and snowy, rainy, foggy and cold on the third! Not like the freezing rain that was coming down in Ontario, but cold none-the-less. We admired Mary Colter's Desert View Watchtower, Hopi House and Kolb Studio (that she deliberately designed to blend in with the surrounding rocks and reflect Ancestral Puebloan buildings) and wistfully wished we were staying at the historic El Tovar Hotel. Reservations are required at least a year in advance so perhaps another time. Given the park's age (it became a National Monument in 1908 and National Park in 1919), the camping facilities were not able to accommodate a rig our size so we set up in a private "park" (pretty much a parking lot) just a few kilometers from the boundary. That was ok because we only returned there to sleep and were grateful for hook-ups when the temperature dipped to freezing at night. But during the day, looking down and catching the few glimpses of the Colorado River that are visible from the south rim, we vowed to return and complete another rim-to-rim hike before our knees give out. That better happen sooner rather than later. The canyon itself is indescribable because the mind has difficulty grasping the enormity of it all. (On average, 1-mile deep and 10 miles wide.) And because it is so magnificent, I took picture after picture, trying to capture its grandeur (which is impossible – I should know better), and ended up with countless photos that then had to be sorted, edited and discarded. A daunting and unenviable task, because I wanted to hang on to each and every one. We would have enjoyed spending more time there, but being a National Park, our recreational options were restricted because of Porter. I've said it before (I think) and I'll say it again. The National Park Service in the United States is decidedly pet un-friendly. I think they go out of their way to be so. Dogs are only allowed in specific campsites, in parking lots and on some paved walkways. That's it. But only in the National Parks. National Monuments, National Forests, Bureau of Land Management, State and County recreation areas are all very accepting, with a few reasonable rules. I just don't get it.

We were en route to Death Valley when we opted to visit just one more ghost town. Oatman. Not for the gunfights (although they have one there too – daily at 1:30), but for the wild burros. Around 50 camps and mines (primarily gold) operated in the area between 1904 and 1934, and Blue Ridge Camp was renamed Oatman in 1909. At its peak it had over 10,000 residents. Geographically situated on the road through the Black Mountains, it eventually became part of, you guessed it, Route 66, although the bypass of I-40 was in this case, a blessing. It was one steep and winding road to get there, even with the Jeep. At the turn of the century, burros had been brought to the region by early prospectors and were used to haul both rocks and ore from the mines, as well as water and supplies for the miners. And as the mines shut down, the burros were released into the surrounding desert to fend for themselves. They survived quite well, and their descendants now roam wild. But not so wild that they don't come into town during the day looking for handouts. That is the only reason anyone goes to Oatman today. To feed these "wild" burros. For $1.00 tourists are given a small paper bag of grass pucks. The burros are smart and will follow those people with the goodies and can become quite obstinate if they think you are holding out. One pesky fellow refused to leave the side of a car where he obviously thought more treats should be forthcoming. And they don't like dogs, often mistaking them for coyotes, so we were careful to keep Porter on a short leash. One kick from those beasties and our brown menace could suffer serious injury or worse. One other claim to fame for Oatman – it was here that according to the Oatman Hotel, Clark Gable and Carole Lombard enjoyed a short honeymoon after their quick 1939 wedding in Kingman. I suppose it's possible, but hard to imagine Hollywood's glamour couple staying in a town like this. Even in its prime. However, several sources confirm that Gable did indeed return to Oatman numerous times to play poker with the miners. I guess everyone needs to get away from their real lives once in a while.

And finally, we made it to Death Valley. I had originally wanted to spend at least a week there, but given the time we spent back in Ontario, we had to adjust our schedule and only stayed four days. Which was probably for the best. It was hot!!! At the Visitor's Centre, the digital thermometer showed 109 F (almost 43 C), but that is not surprising since this place holds the record for hottest air temperature ever recorded on earth. That being 134 F (57 C) at Furnace Creek (apt name) on July 10, 1913. And ground temperature can be 80F (26 C) hotter than the air! I wondered how many people have been tempted to try the ole' fry-an-egg-on-the-sidewalk experiment? And if I were to say that the breeze was as hot as sitting in front of a blow dryer, I would be accused of exaggeration. But that is exactly how it felt. We had set up our chairs in the shade of the coach at 5pm one evening, thinking it would be lovely to just sit and marvel at the landscape, and while the landscape was indeed marvellous, it was also exactly like sitting in front of a blow dryer. I am not joking. We didn't last long. Only nighttime was sit-outside time. Death Valley is a place of extremes – extremely hot, extremely arid, extremely rugged and extremely unforgiving to the ill prepared. And while I wouldn't say it was extremely beautiful, it was well worth the visit. Most of our exploring was done from the comfort of our air-conditioned vehicle, but that was a necessity as well. Death Valley National Park is huge – the largest park below Alaska – at 3.4 million acres. You definitely need wheels to get around.

Being such a seemingly lifeless place, you would think that there was nothing there but rocks and more rocks. And while there were plenty of those, there were interesting things to explore too. We saw pupfish, a small 1-inch-long species of fish that is endemic only to Death Valley. It has survived for more than 20,000 years in a shallow trickle of water that rises up from an aquifer, and given the mineral content of the area, is four times as salty as the ocean. And there is other life amongst all this desolation. Beautiful cactus flowers. Mostly fishhook and beavertail, in such vivid shades of fuschia that they were impossible to miss. We walked out into The Devil's Golf Course, an area where evaporation has caused salt spires to rise up into gnarled shapes, reaching heights of two feet and looking like uninviting reef coral (and just as sharp too). And we checked out the remains of Harmony Borax Works, where between 1883 and 1888, labourers mined and processed three tons of borax per day, which was then transported in 30-ton loads by 20-mule teams a distance of 165 miles to the railroad town of Mojave. The mule teams averaged 2 miles per hour, and it took them 30 days to complete one round trip. Backbreaking work for both man and beast, yet borax is considered Death Valley's most profitable mineral.

But the two areas I found particularly impressive were the Badwater Basin and the Racetrack Playa. Badwater is the lowest point in all of North America at 282 feet (86m) below sea level. As recently as 2,000 to 4,000 years ago, it was still a 30-foot-deep lake, but it's evaporation left behind a 5-foot deep layer of salt. We took turns walking a mile or two out onto the surface (no way Porter could have tolerated that heat even had he been permitted) and it truly was remarkable. In places, the salt had formed into lopsided pentagonal shapes that constantly changed as wind and rain (less than 2 inches per year), affected the salt crystals. Supposedly on a really hot day you can hear a metallic cracking sound as the salt pinnacles expand and contract, but I didn't hear anything.

I guess it wasn't hot enough at 109F! There were quite a few people at this location (including some from two tour buses), but few ventured more than a hundred feet out. Given the heat, I can't say I blame them. And there were of course, the usual Darwin Award contestants who set off without hats, sunglasses or water. This despite warnings everywhere that if going outside in Death Valley, the body needs about 1-2 gallons (4-8 litres) of water a day. Even the washrooms had urine "colour charts" posted on the walls indicating stages of dehydration. What were these people thinking?!?

The second place, Racetrack Playa, took considerably more effort to get to. Located in a remote region of the park, it is home to the Moving Rocks, a phenomenon that puzzled scientists for countless years. The Playa (dried lakebed) is about 3 miles long and 2 miles wide. Around 10,000 years ago it was still an aquatic lake, but the changing climate completely dried it out, leaving behind a mud layer that is 1,000 feet (over 300 meters) thick. That in and of itself is nothing unique. But at the south end of the playa are about two dozen large rocks, some in the 35-inch circumference range, that have very obviously moved along the dried mud, some as far as 1,500 feet, leaving indented grooves or furrows and at times, even changed direction. Yet no-one has ever seen the rocks slide and the playa bed is perfectly flat. The area is too remote and inaccessible for this to be hoax. So we had to go and see for ourselves. A 35-mile drive along the highway led to a bulldozed, rutted and rock-strewn spur road, recommended to be traversed only by high clearance 4x4 vehicles. We had a Jeep. How hard could it be? We started driving but as much as our Jeep was trail-rated, it was not trail-rated for this type of rugged back-country nonsense and we were forced to turn back. But we were determined to see those mysterious Moving Rocks. Conveniently, the park has a small concession near the Visitor's Centre where heavy-duty Jeeps with heavy-duty tires can be rented for the heavy-duty rate of $250/day (plus gas and insurance). We went for it. The drive was challenging, through a saddle and into another valley where at one point, Joshua trees covered the sloping landscape. It was quite beautiful and marginally cooler (only 86F/30C) But it was slow going. It took just under 2-1/2 hours to cover 28 miles. We were bouncing merrily along with the air conditioning going full blast when we heard a loud roar coming up from behind us. This was a one-lane track and my first thought was that some idiot was racing up behind us. Wrong! One split second later a huge fighter jet buzzed over our heads, flying at maybe 100 feet off the ground. We looked at each other and in unison said, "Hoooooly shiiiiiit!" And as it flew off down the valley, the pilot waggled the wings in greeting. Possibly as consolation for almost giving us heart attacks!

We made it to the playa without further excitement and strolled out onto the cracked dried mud. Since it was so remote and there were only two other people around (who left shortly after our arrival), we broke the rules and let Porter come out with us. At first, he raced around with great enthusiasm but quickly succumbed to the heat and took to walking at a more sedate pace. That became a problem too because the mud surface was incredibly hot and obviously burned his paws, so we quickly got him back to the car. The moving rocks with their trailing tracks were very intriguing. Just as we had read. Over the years, numerous theories had been proposed in an effort to explain this anomaly, some suggesting that a rare combination of ½ inch rain together with 50mph winds would make the mud slippery enough for movement. But no theory was unanimously accepted. The great mystery was finally solved in 2014 by yet another group of scientists. They found that with enough rain, the south end of the playa becomes a shallow lake. In winter, if it gets cold enough at night, the water freezes into thin sheets of ice, embedding those rocks that from the forces of erosion and gravity, had tumbled onto the surface from the surrounding mountains. With heat from the morning sun, the ice breaks into sheets and the strong breezes blow the sheets with their implanted rocks

in the prevailing wind direction (usually north). This explains why many of the rocks have left parallel paths. Over time, the ice melts, the water evaporates, and the rocks are deposited in their new position, having left a gouge in the wet mud. And there they sit until the phenomenon repeats itself again, sometimes many years later. Mystery solved.

THE MYSTERIOUS MOVING ROCKS OF RACETRACK PLAYA.

Our last stop was in Las Vegas, plans that had also been impacted my mom's passing. We had originally reserved two weeks in March at a lovely resort (Las Vegas Motorcoach Resort) with arrangements made for our son to come down one week, and then our friends Andrew and Ilze for a few days. As things turned out, those plans were completely cancelled, and we hoped to do our best to make them up at a later date. It was such a shame because the resort was great. Other than our spot not being on the ocean and having a private dock, I would say it was nicer than Bluewater Key in Florida, with elegantly landscaped sites, a huge clubhouse, five swimming pools (one central and four satellites in each corner) and more 45-foot Prevosts, Newmars and Entegras than I had ever seen in one place. There was a lot of money tied up there. As it was, we did manage to get in some family time. John's sister from Oregon was celebrating a milestone birthday and had come down with her husband and daughter, also joined by John's brother and other sister from Toronto. The last time all the siblings had been together was five years ago, so it was a nice reunion. But Las Vegas had not changed. To some it is Disneyland for adults. To others it is sin city. And the countless hotels and restaurants run the gamut from classy to mediocre to sleazy, attracting corresponding clientele accordingly. To really enjoy Vegas, I think you have to be in the right frame of mind and I just wasn't "feeling it" this time around. We went to the "downtown" area of old Vegas along Freemont Street and it had a carnival/midway vibe, 'though I'd be hard pressed to say in any appealing way. Much of the "entertainment" was of a shock-factor nature. A woman dressed in a nun's habit exposing her well-past-their-prime breasts, muscular shirtless "cowboys" simulating sex acts on the sidewalk with older less-than-fit female tourists, the pervasive smell of weed in the air. And as much as an effort has been made in the last few years to improve this particular area, the overall air was one of tired seediness. Along the "newer" Strip, Donnie and Marie, as well as Wayne Newton (!), were still on the billboards and many of the people wandering outside along the street, and inside along the cavernous hallways of Caesar's Palace, seemed a little too desperate to have a good time. There were numerous "Team Bride" and bachelor group merrymakers who had obviously seen the *Hangover/Bridesmaids* movies and hoped to capture some of that magic for themselves. There were quite a few ladies seemingly testing the tensile strength of spandex, and others tottering along in unaccustomedly high heels, trying to look elegant but not quite pulling it off with their tattooed sleeves. But a lot depended on where you went. The Bellagio is still my favourite hotel with its glass flower lobby ceiling and fantastically designed topiary conservatory. The 1,200+ jet fountain out front in the 8+ acre lake still shoots water 460 feet into the air every 30-minutes (set to music of course – we listened to Frank Sinatra's *Fly Me to the Moon*) and the clientele inside seemed a bit less frantic. I am not a gambler but did allow myself to throw away a few dollars at the slot machines. I watched some people playing Blackjack but it was all too fast for me. What I would really like to do when we return (either with Matejs or our friends) is play Blackjack at a table with just us. That way, I can count on my fingers without too much embarrassment and hopefully the dealer will be patient. I wonder if I can use a cheat-sheet? Viva Las Vegas! We'll be back!

25.

CALIFORNIA DREAMIN'

MAY ROLLED AROUND FOR THE SECOND TIME, MARKING TWO YEARS SINCE WE MOVED INTO THE YACHT. It was hard to believe. We had covered a lot of ground and seen many wonderful things. Some people, friends and strangers alike, said they envied us. Said that we were "living the dream." And in many ways that was true. Yet it seems we human beings are never content with our lot. Or maybe it's just me. When I was working full time, all I wanted to do was travel and would spend countless hours researching and planning the next holiday. But once we were travelling full time, all I wanted to do was stop and sit in one place for a while. There is no denying that visiting all these fantastic places was great, yet even though we were supposedly footloose and fancy free, it still required a considerable degree of planning and scheduling. Constant scheduling. And that could get tedious and at times very stressful. Nowhere was this more apparent and necessary than in California. Why? It's a combination of things. Obviously, a popular destination. Agreeable climate (for the most part), ocean, mountains, desert. What's not to like? But while state parks are abundant, their accommodations are limited in number and some are day use only. Many would argue the country's best national parks are in California (and I may agree) but they were crowded and certainly never designed for rigs the size of ours. The terrain is in many places rugged, making access to some locations difficult and to others, impossible. The user fees are ridiculously high, both public and private alike. Add a dog that is in many locations, not welcome, and it made for a lot of scrambling.

Our first hiccup was at Joshua Tree National Park. We had left Las Vegas at a reasonable time, making a quick stop at Colbaugh in Kingman. All the turquoise that comes out of the Kingman Mine (one of the largest turquoise mines in the United States that is still producing) gets processed at Colbaugh and we were able to pick up some stabilized chips for future artistic endeavours without breaking the bank. We congratulated our-selves on being ahead of schedule so decided to press on to Joshua Tree NP to spend the night. I still don't know what happened. We didn't get there until well past 7pm, and each campground we came to was either full, or could not accommodate our rig size. It was early May! What were all those people doing there? We flagged down a park ranger who advised that the park does not have any sites that fit anything over 35 feet. Terrific. He suggested some BLM land outside the park's boundary, about a 30-minute drive away. By this time, it was dusk. We couldn't find the BLM and given some of the dilapidated shacks we saw along the road, weren't about to set up just anywhere. Thank goodness for casinos. The town of 29 Palms doesn't have much by way of high-end real estate, but it does have a lovely new casino and they were willing to let us boondock for the night. This was a blessing because in California, there is very limited boondocking. Especially along the coast. No rest areas, no Walmarts, no roadsides. This is understand-able because given the mild climate, the homeless and transient population is quite high, and neither businesses nor residents want makeshift encampments taking over the local parks and parking lots. Lesson learned. While in California, reservations are a must. Let the scrambling begin.

Our first destination was San Diego where a fellow traveller at the Las Vegas Motorcoach Resort had recommended Chula Vista RV and Marina. We checked in for several nights (the state parks with their relatively few sites were already full) and found it to be quite nice. I have to admit that my first impression of San Diego was not good, but that's simply because of the weather. It was overcast, cool and breezy when we arrived, and cold and rainy the following day. But as soon as the sun came out, every-thing changed. It was lovely. Flowers and flowering trees the likes of which I had never seen, in a kaleidoscope of rich and vibrant colours. Some enhancing the landscaping of luxurious homes that overlooked the ocean and others seemingly just growing in ditches along the roadway. We dropped Porter at daycare and decided to explore Balboa Park on our bikes. Well, we may have been on bikes, but there wasn't much cycling done. There was too much to stop and look at. Balboa Park was founded in 1868 and is set on 1,200 acres of land, pretty much in the centre of the city. In 1915, it hosted the Panama-California Exposition to celebrate the opening of the Panama Canal and at that time, many Spanish-Colonial style buildings were constructed along El Prado, the park's main street. (John maintains that my enthusiasm for going was because I misread it as El Prada and thought shopping might be in order.) In 1935, even more exhibition halls were added, and today these halls have been repurposed into museums. Lots of museums. San Diego Museum of Man, SD Museum of Art, SD Natural History Museum, SD Air and

Space Museum, the list goes on and on. I think I counted 9 museums, plus the Botanical Building and my favourite, the Spreckels Organ Pavilion. We didn't even try to tour the museums (we'd need a full week for that) but as luck would have it, a grade 5 school group had arranged for a demonstration of the organ so who were we to walk away? The Spreckels Organ is the largest outdoor organ in the world with 5,017 pipes (the smallest about the size of a pencil and the largest at 35 feet) and was first played on December 31, 1914 at the launch of the Exposition. Funded by two wealthy brothers (John and Adolph Spreckels, naturally) they donated it as a gift to the people of the world. The brothers' only stipulation was that performances were to be free of charge. This at a time before commercial radio. So in continuing that tradition, free organ concerts are held every Sunday at 2pm. The sound carries for three miles! The city residents sure are lucky. We also managed to explore the Spanish Village art centre, home to 27 resident artists, as well as the Rose and Desert Gardens. But we didn't bother to give the world-famous zoo a shot. It was all too much. If I lived in San Diego, I'd be there every other day. What a fantastic park!

We then took the time to actually put the bikes to some use and cycled along the oceanfront from Belmont Park by Mission Beach as far as Children's Pool in La Jolla, a distance of about 6 miles/10 kms, one way. Our original plan had been to kayak but the water was too choppy and the rocks along part of the shoreline too jagged. Still, it was a nice pedal and gave us a taste of San Diego's seaside scene. Belmont Park wasn't really my thing, especially the old wooden roller coaster; Mission Beach frontage was lined with side-by-side-by-side tri-story vacation rental houses that were literally on the beach, which was full of sun-seekers despite the cool breeze; and the La Jolla neighbourhood can definitely be described as upscale, with beautiful views out over the ocean. Children's Pool was enjoyable too. It is really a small cove, sheltered from the ocean's waves by a curved jetty and was originally intended as a place for small children to swim in safety. Unfortunately for them, seals and sea lions decided that they quite liked the locale too and have pretty much taken over. Now there are competing interests debating as to who should get priority – the seals or the kids. When we were there, the seals had prevailed and we walked out onto the jetty to watch them as they lolled around, basking in the sun. Biking back, we made sure to stop in at Cinnaholic, where John may or may not have purchased some gourmet cinnamon rolls which may very well be the best he (we?) have ever had. San Diego has been added to our "return to" list.

About one hour north of San Diego, we made a quick stop at Mission San Juan Capistrano. John stayed with Porter in the coach to make phone calls with respect to some RV maintenance concerns (he had discovered a hydraulic fluid leak while filling up the propane back in San Diego) while I went and toured the Mission. The Mission itself dates from 1775 and historically functioned as one of 21 missions along the California coast. But it's more recent renown (and why it is a tourist attraction today) comes from the swallows that nest under the church eaves. As the story goes, a certain Father O'Sullivan (pastor of the Capistrano Mission between 1910 and 1933) was walking through town one day when he noticed a shopkeeper using a broomstick to destroy the mud swallow nests that had been built beneath his shop eaves. The birds were flying around in great distress. When the good Father questioned the shopkeeper what he was doing, he was informed that the birds were a nuisance and needed to be gotten rid of. Father O'Sullivan told the swallows to come to the Mission where he would give them shelter. The very next morning, he discovered the birds building their nests just outside the church. These particular swallows are migratory birds, travelling 6,000 miles to and from Argentina, but each spring they have returned to nest under the eaves of the old church, specifically on March 19th, St. Joseph's Day. Father O'Sullivan related this story in his book *Capistrano Nights* which was subsequently popularized in the song *When the Swallows Come Back to Capistrano* in 1939 and again in 1949. People from all around the world started coming to Capistrano to marvel at this miracle. A very romantic tale. Except for the ending. In 1990, the powers that be decided to stabilize the ruins of the old church and in the process, removed all the mud nests that had been constructed over the past 60 years. Guess who didn't show up March 19th? Lots of disappointed tourists milling about, but no swallows. Without their nests, the birds diverted to other parts of town and Capistrano lost its star tourist attraction. What to do? What to do? In consultation with a cliff swallow expert (yes, they do exist), town council decided to lure the birds back, first through broadcasting tape-recorded swallow mating calls and then by constructing a replica wall with man-made nests. As of 2013, a few pairs had been spotted building new nests, but it's a far cry from the hundreds that once showed up. Just goes to show – no good deed ever goes unpunished.

And while I was busy learning about bird migration patterns, John was busy learning about the paucity of service locations when it comes to RV maintenance. We had run into this issue on the east coast, but not to such an extent. All John wanted was for someone to take a look at the affected hydraulics but every RV service place he contacted advised they were booking appointments into June and July. We certainly couldn't sit around that long! He finally made contact with a place near Sacramento that could take a look in 10 days, but that meant putting Yosemite NP on the back burner. Very disappointing but there was nothing we could do. The hydraulics were necessary to keep the levelling jacks functioning properly and we were not about to mess with that. One of the roof ac/heater units was also making an incredible rattling racket when turned on (which was apparently a cracked blower wheel), and the flush valve on the black water tank had dried and clogged while we had been back home in March. We definitely needed these issues addressed before we started heading to Alaska.

Our next destination was the San Luis Obispo area and no matter how much we calculated, it was unavoidable, we had to drive through Los Angeles. Neither of us was really interested in the Hollywood/Rodeo Drive/beautiful people scene so we were literally just passing by. I will never complain about traffic on the Don Valley Parkway in Toronto again. It took us almost three hours to cross from one side of L.A. to the other, sitting in stop and go traffic the entire way. This on a freeway that was 7 lanes across, in each direction–14 in total! I don't know how people do it. I have nothing more to say.

The reason for heading to San Luis Obispo was in order to tour Hearst Castle, although technically, it is actually near San Simeon, not far from Big Sur. But there are no campgrounds in the San Simeon area, and we didn't want to take the coach along coastal Highway 1, no matter how scenic it is. We have driven that road before, and given its narrow, winding turns and precipitous drop-offs, it is no place to drive anything over 25 feet. Reserving a campsite was again a challenge and when we found availability at a county park in Pismo, we jumped without reading too much of the fine print. We pulled in late at night, set up in the dark and the next morning found out why the place still had vacancies. We were literally between Highway 1 and a set of railroad tracks. No exaggeration. The highway was about 20 feet off our front bumper and the railroad tracks about 30 feet behind. Thankfully the trains were infrequent, and we were out all day anyway, so it wasn't too bad. We've stayed in worse places. The only thing that ticked me off was that in addition to the camping fee, they charged $3.50/night for Porter. Really?!? If we'd had a smaller rig, we could have dry camped out on Pismo Beach itself for $10.00, only 1 mile away. There was just no making sense of their policies out there.

The drive up to San Simeon was beautiful. John wasn't all that interested in touring Hearst Castle, which was just as well since dogs were not allowed, so he and Porter went to the beach while I paid my $25.00 for access to an example of one man's material excess. I'd heard a fair bit about the "castle" and was really looking forward to it but at the end of the day, came away feeling somewhat disenchanted. It took me a while to figure out why. There is no question the place is grand. Over-the-top grand. Three "cottages", the smallest one being 2,550 square feet, and the Casa Grande at 68,500 square feet (still only half the size of Biltmore in North Carolina) are surrounded by terraces and landscaped gardens. Perched high on a hillside with the Pacific Ocean in the distance, the views in every direction were magnificent. The building façades equally magnificent. And the huge interior rooms, also magnificent. At least in size. But there was something wrong with the overall picture. To me, it seemed like a hodgepodge of stuff that didn't really fit together. I'm no interior designer but what does a 3,000-year-old statue of the Egyptian Goddess Sekhmet have to do with an antique Spanish ceiling? And 16th century Flemish tapestries with a 2nd century sarcophagus? Plus, an entire monastery. And lengths of church choir stalls used as wainscoting. Talk about eclectic! A bit of history and context is in order. Randolph Hearst was a very successful newspaper magnate who inherited much of his wealth from his mother. The family owned 40,000 acres around San Simeon and used it primarily for cattle ranching although Randolph entered the world of journalism where he added to the family's already sizeable fortune. When his mother passed away in 1919, Randolph went on a collecting and building spree that lasted 28 years. WWI had just ended, much of Europe was in ruins and many aristocratic European families found themselves in financial difficulties. They had heritage but no money. Randolph had money, but no heritage. So he travelled around Europe buying whatever antiquities he could get his hands on. And when he brought them back to La Cuesta Encantada (he never called it Hearst Castle), he had his architect build another room, wing, or salon to incorporate his newly acquired treasure. No wonder he never stopped building. But everything is so ornate it can only be described as gaudy. Today, the property is technically a California State Park, although the 67 direct descendants of Randolph can pretty much come and go and use the place as they please. I'm not sure how that works. It was worth seeing, for sure, but nothing I'd need to see again.

After joining back up with John, we drove north a few miles to check out the beach at Piedras Blancas, where Elephant Seals like to hang out. Those beasties were huge. The males weigh between 3,000 and 5,000 pounds (that can be over 2 tons), while the females are more svelte at 900 to 1,800 pounds. The males grow a long proboscis, hence their name "elephant" seal. During the 18th and 19th centuries these odd-looking creatures were hunted, almost to extinction, for their blubber – at one point, numbering only 50. In the early 20th century Mexico and the US placed them on the protected species list and their numbers have since rebounded to about 250,000. Today, their only predators are orcas and white sharks. Given it was spring, just the females and pups were on the beach and it was very entertaining to watch them as they snarled, sparred and bickered with each other, over what, I don't know. They spend most of their lives at sea, so we were very lucky to see them lying around, waiting for the pups to mature. I could have easily spent hours with them, but the weather was not cooperating. It was overcast, very cold and very windy. Time to move on up the coast to Monterey, where more entertainment awaited us. We avoided Hwy. 1 however. As mentioned, that route is simply too windingly steep with too many hairpin turns for a vehicle our size. But even had we been in something considerably smaller, the highway remained closed through Big Sur, following a huge landslide in May 2017 that took out the road for almost half a mile. Crews had been working 24-7 and it was projected to re-open in September. Uh-Huh.

So we drove north along highway 101 and although we were travelling just a few miles inland, everything was agricultural – field after field of meticulously laid out lettuce, parsley, artichokes and other greens. And the closer we got to Salinas, the more Janis Joplin's *Me and Bobby McGee* played in my head... *"One day up near Salinas, Lord, I let him slip away..."* We didn't actually get to Salinas but turned west to reach our campground, about a 30-minute drive from Monterey Bay. And an interesting place it was too. I've never had the pleasure of staying at a raceway before – the Mazda Raceway at Laguna Seca – to be specific. Thank goodness the Ferrari Challenge had ended the weekend before and there were just a few drivers out practicing when we pulled in. It turned out this raceway is quite renowned throughout California. It was built in 1957 in order to keep car racing alive and well in the Monterey area, after the original Pebble Beach Road Race along the iconic 17-Mile-Drive was deemed too dangerous. I don't pretend to have even a passing knowledge of (or interest in) the racing world, so the names of the cars, the racers and the sponsors meant nothing to me. (Although I have heard of Mario Andretti and he won a race there in 1975.) But there was one name that did catch my attention. Paul Newman! Go figure. After getting over the shock of where we were set up, I must say that it was one of the loveliest campgrounds we have ever stayed in. The surroundings reminded me of a cross between Vermont and the pasture-lands of Switzerland. The sites were all set on a high hill, overlooking the green rolling countryside, with only a portion of the track itself barely visible out our front window. Apparently on race days, the sites can't be had for love or money, but we lucked out and it was pretty peaceful and quiet. The only concern...we were advised not to use the water since it had very high levels of arsenic! What?!? Something about the well, but they weren't sure!!! Thank goodness we had filled the coach's fresh-water tank before we arrived.

Monterey was fun, even if the weather was less than perfect. In the mornings it was always foggy, but that usually cleared by noon. One day we decided to bike from Monterey along Hwy 1, and then on 17-Mile-Drive, out to the Lone Cypress – supposedly the most photographed tree in North America. The route was lovely with manicured golf courses on one side (Spyglass and Pebble Beach were particularly appealing), the ocean on the other side, and just enough roll to keep the legs and lungs working. But wouldn't you know it, when we got to Lone Cypress, the road out to the viewpoint was closed! We couldn't see anything for all the high-end real estate and lush landscaping blocking our view. It's just as well. From what I read, the 250-year-old tree is barely hanging onto its granite outcropping and has been braced with steel cables for the past 65 years. Anything to keep those tourists coming.

Monterey itself was originally a fish-canning town when sardines were in great demand between 1900 and 1950. Naturally, with 200,000 tons being processed annually, they quickly ran out of fish and the canning industry collapsed. As one information placard stated, "Boom to bust in 50 years." But the boom lasted long enough for Steinbeck to immortalize the town in his novel *Cannery Row*. (Great book!) There is nothing left of Steinbeck's Monterey, and not to be judgemental, but I suspect a large number of the visitors had no idea who Steinbeck even was. The canneries have been turned into higher-end hotels (which were lovely), there is a huge aquarium (which we didn't get around to touring) and hundreds of harbour seals lounge along the wharf to amuse even the most jaded visitor. We went kayaking in Monterey Bay twice, although it was quite windy and the water rather choppy but staying inside the kelp beds helped. And it was in these kelp beds that the real fun started. Sea otters make their homes there, just hanging out, floating, sleeping and when the mood strikes them, doing summersaults. It was all well and good until one little guy decided to climb up onto John's kayak. Actually, he wasn't all that little, and keeping in mind that a kayak is a very tippy boat, the water was very cold and sea otters weigh anywhere from 30 to 90 pounds (we estimate this one was about 50), it made for a dangerous combination. Of course I was laughing at John's predicament while at the same time trying to take pictures, when the rascal decided to swim over to me and do the same. It was no longer funny. I had my

good camera with me! We were about 100 feet from shore so I started paddling in, with Ollie Otter along for the ride. Thankfully he preferred the safety of the kelp beds and soon slid off, but not before providing some entertainment for the folks sipping coffee on the raised boardwalk. What an experience!

THE GUILTY PARTY...

We continued up the coast planning to spend a few days in San Francisco but ended up spending more time out by Point Reyes National Seashore. We had been to San Francisco in the past, and really enjoyed returning, if even for a short while. A quick stop in the Haight/Ashbury neighbourhood was a must. Epicentre of the hippie counterculture of the 1960's, it still hangs on to its psychedelic roots. Judging by some of the locals, a younger generation is wishing for a return of those hallucinogenic days, while some members of the older generation never quite left, physically or mentally. Still, it's hard to beat that music. We had to make an obligatory stop at the shrine of all things chocolate – Ghiardelli Square – where Domenico Ghiardelli started his factory in 1852, and from there it was a short stroll to Fisherman's Wharf for lunch. We walked around Chinatown, admired the patience of all the people lined up in their cars just to drive down a portion of Lombard Street (the crookedest street in the world – been there, done that), admired the Victorian architecture, and marvelled at the cable cars as they chugged up and down the incredibly steep streets. All very touristy, all very rushed, but fun just the same. The day was mostly sunny but cool and exceptionally windy, and Golden Gate Bridge was shrouded in a bit of a mist. By the time we ended our day, the legendary fog was rolling back in, with just one last ray of sunshine beaming onto the downtown core.

The weather was slightly more agreeable just north of the city at Point Reyes National Seashore, although right at the beach it was still rather windy. We were staying near the town of Olema and it is here that some of the best examples of earthquake activity can be seen. In fact, we were camped smack dab on top of the San Andreas Fault, where the North American and Pacific continental plates meet. You couldn't get any closer to tectonic ground zero. The Point Reyes peninsula sits on the eastern edge of the Pacific Plate, which is slowly drifting northwest at a rate of about one to two inches a year. The North American Plate is moving due west. The fault zone is where the two abut although in reality, several large and small faults running parallel and at odd angles to each other cause the damage. At times, they get caught up on each other causing pressure to build. Eventually, the underlying rock breaks loose and this is what causes the sudden jolts that we know as earthquakes. In 1906, when San Francisco experienced its great quake, the peninsula where we were now situated, jumped 20 feet northwest in less than a minute! The Point Reyes Visitor's Centre had great displays on this seismic activity as well as an interesting walking trail where blue posts demarcate the actual centre line of the San Andreas Fault Trace (which is about 1 mile wide). We joked about falling into the abyss, but it really is no laughing matter. No one seems to be able to predict when the plates will shift, and everyone keeps waiting for the next "big one." In "recent" memory, the October 1989 quake with its epicentre about 60 miles south, killed 68 people, injured 4,000 and caused 6.8 billion in damage (including a partial collapse of the San Francisco Bay Bridge). This at a time when building codes are much more rigorous when it comes to withstanding seismic activity. I did learn, however, that not all tectonic plates move in the same manner. There are places on our planet where the plates move apart (creatively called Divergent Boundaries) and new material is then added to the earth's crust. There are other places where one plate slides underneath another (Convergent Boundaries) producing mountains and volcanoes, and then there is San Andreas where the plates slowly slide past each other (Transform Boundaries). Interesting stuff. The landscape on the peninsula is very steeply pitched rolling pastureland, like foothills on steroids, indicative of the turmoil going on not so far below the ground. Ranching appears to be the primary enterprise and even the cows have learned to walk at an angle. We managed to find some terrain that was bike-able for our (my) fitness level, but there were cyclists tackling hills that truly defied belief. It would be tough walking up never mind biking! How fit do you have to be to do that? I was envious and consoled myself by suggesting we have ice cream after dinner.

Gas and diesel prices in California were quite high – more like Canada than other parts of the U.S. – and that was a concern because we were bouncing around and back-tracking a fair bit when it came to route planning. Leaving San Francisco, we headed south again towards Sequoia National Park. And since the park has no room for big rigs, we stayed at an Army Corps of Engineers campground about 90 minutes west of the park boundary. More driving. But it did give us the opportunity to see how varied the state can be. The campground was in the midst of what was once ranch country (with a few cattle herds still roaming around) and the grass on the surrounding hills had already turned yellow. California is still in a drought. But outnumbering the cattle ranchers by a long shot were citrus growers. Primarily orange and lemon groves, with a few olives thrown in to mix things up. In every direction, small trees planted in neat equidistant rows, meandering up the hillsides with much of the irrigation coming from a dam built across the Tule River. I'm not sure how I feel about creating a citrus oasis in what is really very arid country, but perhaps the rain and snow that falls on the Sierras immediately to the east offsets the water problems. One thing was for sure, though. Prices were very cheap. Five lemons right off the tree; one dollar. Three large red grapefruits; one dollar. Juicy and delicious.

Visiting Sequioa National Park was both great yet a bit frustrating. It is a place of incredible beauty, and it is very difficult to describe the feelings evoked by standing at the base of a huge sequoia tree and gazing skyward. Awe at its grandeur and majesty.

Humbled at the insignificance of my own presence and existence. But Sequoia NP was the sort of place where to do it any justice, you have to stay for at least a week. Without a dog. And start hiking. Most of the park cannot be accessed by vehicle. We did what we could as car tourists and the drive up into the Sierra Nevada was truly spectacular along a steep, winding road. We managed to get in a few sights, not the least of which was General Sherman – the biggest living tree in the world. The "biggest" designation comes not from its height (Redwoods are taller) but rather, its girth. Sherman is 110 feet/33 meters around at its base; 37 feet/11 meters in diameter. No tree has more volume (i.e. wood) in its trunk. However, Sherman is not the oldest tree. Estimated to be about 2,200 years old, it was the right location and growing conditions that allowed it to surpass other sequoias a thousand years older. Viewing access is gained by a twenty-minute walk downhill along a paved trail from the parking lot, so we left Porter in the car (he was rather put out) and headed into a large sequoia grove. No problem going down but coming back up, at 7,000 feet elevation, entailed a bit of huffing and puffing. But it was certainly worth it. The thing was massive! We drove to some other sequoia groves where these huge giants have been standing for over 2,500 years and could only marvel at their size and longevity. We even drove through one that in the 1950s had fallen across the roadway so park staff just chain-sawed a tunnel into it. And we managed to walk/hike/huff our way up to the top of Moro Rock, Sequoia's answer to Yosemite's Half Dome. A huge monolith at 6,725 feet, it provided an all-encompassing view out over the surrounding landscape. Not that we hiked 6,725 feet. We drove most of the way and only had to negotiate the last quarter mile. No sense exerting ourselves. We were saving that for Half Dome. But the day was soon drawing to a close and we still had to drive 90 minutes back to our campsite. Needless to say, it was maddening with so many trails left un-trod. Plus, the long drive back and forth dampened my enthusiasm. We didn't stay in the area too long because ten days were up and the RV had a service appointment just outside of Sacramento in the suburb of Rocklin.

We made it to the appointment in plenty of time, the problem was identified in short order (a leaky hydraulic valve just as John suspected) and the replacement part ordered. Five business days to deliver. Okay. It was Wednesday afternoon. Now what? Turn around and head back south. Yosemite was a go after all. A bit more scrambling and we managed to find space at a RV "resort" just outside the park boundary with doggie daycare an hour's plus drive away. Or we could stay in the town of Mariposa at their Fairgrounds, with the daycare only 15 minutes away. Neither were what could be termed ideal choices as both involved a lot of driving, but that was all we could find. We opted to split the difference and stayed in Mariposa for a few nights, dropped Porter at daycare and then drove to the park with the plan to get in some serious hiking, and then moved to the "resort" about 2 miles from the park gate (but still a 30-minute drive from the valley), where we could engage in dog-friendly activities. (Read: stay on paved trails and roadways.)

Yosemite requires more superlatives than I have in my vocabulary. Majestic. Moving. Impressive. Imposing. Spectacular. Stunning. I don't want to get into rating parks since they are all so very different and therefore difficult to compare, but I'm going to have to say that Yosemite is my favourite. Zion and Grand Canyon rank up there too, but Yosemite has the most scenic vistas I have ever seen with waterfalls around every corner, fantastic, challenging hikes and beautiful meadows for relaxing strolls. To describe all we did would take too many lines, so I'll stick to some highlights (and inevitable annoyances). On day one, we dropped Porter at daycare, (which was really just an eccentric older man who loved dogs and cared for them in his home) and headed for the park in high spirits. Yes! It was sunny! It was warm! We were finally going hiking! "Sure you are," said God. Road construction and traffic volume turned the one-way drive into 2 prolonged hours of frustration. It was noon before we arrived at the park and realizing we no longer had time to tackle the longer routes, opted for two shorter hikes (Sentinel Dome and Taft Point) with trailheads part way along the winding road to Glacier Point. Half-way to the point, we found that parks staff had closed the road and diverted all vehicles to a staging area, saying that parking at Glacier Point was full. "But we aren't going that far! We want the Sentinel Dome trailhead! It's just a few more miles up the road!" No. We were told to either turn back or get in line. The wait time was anywhere between 30 and 90 minutes. Decision time. We had come this far, 30 minutes was okay, but what if its 90? There was no way to predict. So we opted to wait. And wait. And wait. After 90 minutes we were waved forward. And to add insult to injury, it started to cloud over. I was thinking very uncharitable thoughts about the staff and all the other people who were out and about, crowding my wilderness. It was over 4-1/2 hours from the time we dropped Porter off to the time we finally reached the trailhead. So we made another adjustment. We decided to drive all the way to Glacier Point, take a quick look and then backtrack to start the hike. I am so glad we did.

The view from the point was indescribable. It could quite possibly rank as the best overlook ever. The entire valley was visible, with Half Dome (Yosemite's signature peak) directly in front, and Vernal and Nevada Falls off to one side. Hiking was put on the back burner while we sat and soaked it all in, watching the clouds as they moved in and at times obscured the very top of Half Dome – and talked about the feasibility of hiking past Vernal Fall, to the top of Nevada Fall and then on to at least the base of Half Dome.

An ambitious plan. But (and isn't there always a "but") gazing out over this incredible panorama, I realized I didn't have the same level of satisfaction I felt from other beautiful overlooks. Why? After some contemplation, it came to me. I had not "earned" this view. No exertion. No shaking legs. No pounding heart. No gasping for air. It had been handed to me, if not exactly on a silver platter, then on smooth asphalt. We just drove there. Where was the price to be paid? It didn't seem right. Well, I paid it the next day because I got my wish.

We undertook something considerably more challenging – hoofing it to the top of Nevada Fall, a 5-mile round trip with a 2,000 feet (610m) elevation gain – the route taking us along Vernal Fall, where spray from the waterfall makes the footing slippery and treacherous. People have died there. I had actually hoped to reach the base of Half Dome (the chains were up but we didn't have a summiting permit and if I am honest, I don't think I had it in me to risk life and limb for that T-shirt) but once again, we were stymied in our efforts for an early start. This time by lack of parking near the trailhead. We circled for ages until another driver simply moved a "no parking" sign over by eight feet, thus creating two new spaces. The lesson here? If you want to go on a longer hike anywhere in Yosemite, accommodations within the park are a must. Driving to the boundary, getting in the gate, driving to a trailhead, and then finding a parking spot, all conspire to make it virtually impossible to start on time. However, securing acceptable accommodations within the park means planning six months ahead. And not all accommodations are created equal. If not bringing my own gear, my choice would be the old Ahwahnee Hotel, (now re-named The Majestic Yosemite), built in 1927 and where Queen Elizabeth stayed in 1983. Very old-school posh. I would never stay in the canvass tents they have set up in Curry Village (now re-named Half Dome Village). Reminiscent of the tents at Sidrabene, although darker on the inside and much closer together than complete strangers should be situated. Not to put too fine a point on it, but let's just say that if someone in the neighbouring tent was suffering from a bout of gastrointestinal distress, it would be a shared auditory and olfactory experience. The parks people were aware of this issue so installed "upgraded" tents with canvass draped over plywood frames in an effort to alleviate the complaints. It was a health hazard in the making. The space between the frames and the canvass created unanticipated homes for the numerous deer mice, chipmunks and squirrels that have practically taken over the grounds. And guess who carries Hantavirus? Five years ago, three visitors came down with Hantavirus Pulmonary Syndrome, contracted after staying in these tents. Two died. Today, there are signs in several locations warning of both Hantavirus and the Plague being carried by these little rodents. Yet the tourists visiting from Europe and the far East, naïvely "camping" in the great "outdoors" take an inordinate sense of pleasure from feeding and photographing the little critters (and keeping food inside their tents), despite the warnings. Apparently it's still an issue.

But I digress. The portion of the hike along Mist Trail to Vernal Fall was the most challenging part of the day, not just because the terrain was steep, wet and uneven (600 irregular and jagged granite steps at one point), but because there were a large number of day-trippers moseying along with no concept of trail etiquette. For example: Hikers going up have right away over hikers coming down. Clueless. Stopping to rest is fine. Stopping to rest in the middle of a narrow trail with precipitous drop-offs on either side, is not. Hiking in a group is fine. Blocking the trail as a group, is not. Taking pictures is fine. Taking pictures from the centre of the trail and again, impeding other hikers, is not. These minor inconveniences can be overlooked if things are not too busy but if a trail is crowded (and the hike is hours long), it becomes very annoying. Does fantasizing about pushing someone over a cliff make me a bad person? Given our late start, we never did make it to the base of Half Dome, another 4 miles past Nevada. Foiled again.

Yosemite Falls (Upper, Middle and Lower) combine to form the tallest waterfall in North America and the fifth tallest in the world at 2,425 ft/740 m. Sounds very impressive. But because the water comes tumbling down in three separate sections, it doesn't really seem all that high (relatively speaking). From the bottom looking up, it is impossible to see the entire length in one unbroken section. But since it is one of the more easily accessed falls in the park, along a flat paved trail where both bikes and dogs are allowed, it too was very popular. The water that flows over the lip comes from Yosemite Creek, water that is fed entirely by melting snow, draining an area of almost 50 square miles. Peak volume hits in early spring (9,000 litres per second) but by late summer, when the drainage area has completely melted, the falls usually run dry. No wonder there were so many people there in May!

On a lazier day, we set up the camp chairs in a meadow near the base of El Capitan to watch the rock climbers as they slowly inched their way upwards. What a sport! El Capitan is a massive granite monolith, the world's largest exposed rock, rising 4,500 feet (1,370m) almost straight up from the valley floor. Climbers from all around the world make a pilgrimage to test their skills and endurance on the sheer rock face. It takes several days of hanging out on the wall to reach the summit, with fit climbers taking 4 to 5 days to reach their goal. El "Cap" is so huge that it is almost impossible to spot the climbers without that aid of binoculars and a fair bit of patience. On our day, we counted fifteen of these fanatics on and in numerous ledges, fissures and cracks. Needless to say, the spectators outnumbered the climbers by at least 50:1. There is something for every fitness level in this park. But El Cap also has its tragic side. During the 1980s, BASE jumping became popular (see "Is This Where We Shoot Out the Tires") and the National Park Service actually began issuing permits to the hopeful dare devils in an effort to regulate the congestion. Regrettably, the jumpers were more concerned with the jump than the environment and after ten weeks of mayhem, the programme was shut down. If only it had ended there. In 1999, an illegal jump was performed wherein the adventurer landed safely, but subsequently drowned in the fast-flowing Merced River while fleeing apprehension by park rangers. An indignant compatriot decided to perform a protest jump in response, and only compounded the tragedy when her parachute failed to open, and she didn't "stick the landing." Well, she did "stick" but not as intended. Sad, but also ironic in a twisted dark humour kind of way. There have been no recorded BASE jumps since.

Because Yosemite is located at such a high elevation, parts of it (namely Tioga Pass/ Hwy 120) are only open during the summer months when all the deep snow has melted. Lucky for us, they opened the road on our second last day, so we were able to do some exploring away from the more heavily visited valley floor. But it was decidedly chilly and there was still a fair bit of snow along some stretches of highway We stopped for lunch at one drifted in little valley and Porter was in heaven. Running up and down, jumping, rolling around, chasing snowballs. The way he carried on you would think we kept him locked in a crate 24 hours a day and this was his first taste of freedom. None of the campgrounds were open yet, understandable because the forest floor was still very wet, and we drove as far as Olmsted Point, which provided fantastic views of the valley and Half Dome from a completely different angle. However, the change in temperature was significant. On the valley floor we registered 75F/24C, yet at Olmsted we only reached 52F/11C. Maybe that adds to why they don't open the campgrounds until later.

We also walked down about a mile along an old narrow road (the original 1840s tourist route into Yosemite Valley) to Yosemite's Tuolumne Sequoia Grove, but having seen the giants in Sequoia NP, this was somewhat of a disappointment. Not the walk, that was lovely, with Pacific Dogwoods in full bloom the entire way. But these sequoias, despite their size were no match for what we had seen just over a week ago. Still, it was interesting to learn a bit more about them including that the oldest ones have bark up to two feet thick. We also got in a few days of biking the valley floor too, a respectable little pedal of about 20 miles/32k, nothing too strenuous with only a few ups and downs. It was a great way to see quite a few of the popular waterfalls – Bridal Veil and Yosemite, but also some that I never learned the names of, and which despite their power in May, will have pretty much disappeared by August.

We ended up staying in the Yosemite area longer than anticipated because the "five business days" for the hydraulic pressure switch turned into seven. On one hand, that was okay with me because I wasn't ready to leave. There was still so much to see and do. On the other hand, it meant we would not be able to get to Redwoods National Park or drive anywhere else along the coast. Time was running out and we had to be in Canada June 1st for a regular service appointment on the engine. That, and we were reaching the 180-day limit for being in the US. No sense upsetting the border crossing people considering we were going to be in Alaska soon enough. We returned to Sacramento and found we had not won the lucky RV repair lottery. In fact, we had won the booby prize. The ordered part had arrived all right, but it was the wrong one! You have got to be kidding me! Clenching our teeth and curbing our tongues, we had to fall back and regroup. John ended up ordering the necessary part, plus a flush nozzle for the black tank, and a blower wheel for the a/c, from Tiffin in Alabama and arranged to have them shipped to Whitehorse in the Yukon, where he had managed to get at service appointment June 18. One thing that became very apparent to us was that when it comes to service, the RV industry is sorely lacking. Great on sales. Abysmal on service. Yeah, yeah, when life gives you lemons... I figured by the time this trip is over we would have perfected lemonade.

Making our way north, we considered stopping for a few days at Lassen Volcanic National Park, but they had just had a fresh dump of snow and all the roads were closed. No big surprise really. It sits, after all, in the Cascade Range. And driving along I-5, it was beautiful to be surrounded by high green rolling hills and then periodically seeing a white-capped mountain in the distance – Lassen, Shasta, Hood, Rainier. Like a string of pearls. Given that we had an extra day, we made a short detour to the coast and drove along Highway 101 for a stretch, between Reedsport and Newport. The Oregon coast is breathtaking, and in my estimation, more appealing than California's. The terrain is more rugged, the weather less predictable, the trees bigger. We camped for a couple of nights at a great beachfront campsite where Porter was able to get in one last frolic in the ocean waves before we made our way to the border and thankfully, crossed without incident. Home at last!

26.

INTO THE GREAT
WHITE NORTH

MOST PEOPLE NEVER GET AROUND TO VISITING THE FAR NORTH. The Yukon, the Northwest Territories, Alaska. It is a long way away. It takes a long time to get there. It is expensive. It has a short tourist season (unless you like darkness and sub-zero temperatures). It is sparsely populated. It is, for the most part, wilderness. No lions, no tigers, but bears? Oh, my! So it had been on my bucket list for quite some time. It is also the sort of place that requires continuous planning. Gas stations are not on every corner. Tow trucks or emergency assistance can be hours away. Some communities don't even have 911 service. Forget about reliable wifi. The roads can be quite bad and carrying more than one spare tire is recommended. We dutifully purchased *The Milepost*, the northern visitor's travel bible, along with other tour books and plotted our route. We gave ourselves until mid-September to pack in as much as possible.

The expedition started on a sunny day as we left Vancouver, driving along beautiful highway 99, the Sea to Sky Highway, with expansive views out across Howe Sound, and then continued on towards Whistler. Blue skies soon turned to the drizzle that B.C. is known for. There were still patches of snow on Whistler's lower elevation runs and I was half-tempted to suggest we turn in to see what was going on up top, but there was no sense teasing ourselves. We planned to spend winter on Vancouver Island so hoped to pop up for a ski week then. Past Pemberton, towards Lilooet, the drive was very scenic with high mountains and steep winding roads, although the low-lying dark clouds obscured the tops of the snow-capped peaks and prevented us from experiencing the full wow factor. It's amazing how gray days can have such an impact on your psyche. In some places, the driving was a bit tricky. Along one downhill stretch, the first road sign said

13% grade for 1 km. Okay. Did that no problem. Further along, 13% grade for 2 kms, plus some curves thrown in. Then even further, 13% grade for 3 kms. Come on!!! By the time we reached our campground near Seto Lake we could smell the brakes despite John having used the lowest gear. The campground was lovely, and free of charge. Located at the confluence of Callaghan Creek and Cheakamus River, it had some short hiking trails and a small suspension bridge, and is maintained by BC Hydro who supposedly just want to give something back to the community. If they are anything like Ontario Hydro, they are probably giving back to the community because of a court order, but regardless, thank-you. Past Lillooet, the scenery continued as we followed the Fraser River Valley with CN railroad tracks to one side and a steep drop to the Fraser River on the other. Lots of sparkling blue lakes and soaring mountains although they gradually decreased in size until by the time we reached highway 97, the terrain could be characterized as steeply rolling (of course from an Ontario perspective, we would probably still call it mountainous). After 100 Mile House, the landscape was reminiscent of northern Ontario (maybe a bit more undulating) and by Prince George there was farm country around town that quickly gave way to Ontario-type forest. No sky-high redwoods or cypress here. Maybe those were all on the logging trucks that passed us every 3 minutes. (I timed them.) We then had the misfortune of setting up camp in a secluded provincial park (Prophet River – we were the only ones there) where we had our first experience with northern BC's mosquitos. They didn't seem all that bad when we went for a short walk, but unbeknownst to us, they had burrowed into Porter's fur and hitchhiked back into the yacht. We spent the better part of the evening swatting away and killed at least 50. No exaggeration. This was a concern. What were they going to be like in Alaska where some people are lobbying to have them declared the state bird?

We had planned the route so that driving time between overnights was 3 to 4 hours in case there were sights or trails to explore along the way. Nope. Not much. At Chetwynd we made a quick stop to check out some of the over 100 chainsaw carvings that are located throughout town, and while they were pretty impressive considering they were done with a chainsaw, and competitors come from all around the world for the yearly competition, it didn't take long before we were back on the road, heading for Dawson Creek. Not to be confused with Dawson City in the Yukon, Dawson Creek is the childhood home of opera tenor Ben Heppner (they named City Hall after him – go Ben!) and more importantly to most people, Mile "0" of the Alaska Highway. Running 1,520 miles (2,432 kms) to Fairbanks, Alaska this highway has an interesting history. Originally called the Alaska Military Highway, then Alaska-Canada Highway, then Alcan and finally the Alaska Highway. Those who built it simply called it The Road.

There was U.S. interest in building a land link between the lower 48 states and their northernmost territory as far back as 1930, but things never got rolling until the Japanese bombed Pearl Harbour in 1941. Almost overnight, it became an urgent issue. A supply road north was needed in order to defend North America against Japan. Building started in Dawson Creek in March of 1942 and finished 8 months later. Imagine something like that happening today! Ha! They did have a lot of cooperation and help, however, not the least of which was good will and amicable relations between the U.S. and Canada. (My, how things have changed.) The U.S. paid for the actual construction while Canada paid for materials along the route. It was agreed that once the war ended, the Canadian leg of the highway would be turned over to the Canadian government. Bring on the army. Over 11,000 U.S. troops and 16,000 civilians from both countries worked 7 days a week (sometimes 20 hours a day under the midnight sun) averaging 8 miles a day through a wilderness of mountains, muskeg and mosquitos. It cost $140 million dollars. Of course the road they built is not the road we travelled along. Back then, there were sections with 25% grades and 90-degree turns. Surveying was done by sight, with workers often climbing trees or standing on bulldozers to pick a distant point to work towards. Today, it has been re-routed with most of the curves straightened out, bridges re-built, and residential areas by-passed. Even the pavement is fairly smooth (for the most part). At some turn-offs, it is still possible to see/visit the original roadway and in many places, it really was just a one-lane dirt track. So to call what they built back then a highway is a bit of a stretch.

After Fort Nelson the road veered west and that was where things got really pretty (and the pavement pretty bad). The snow-covered Rockies were in the distance (we finally had a sunny day) and the area's moniker as Serengeti of the North was well deserved. At first, we started counting: 10 black bears (one was light brown in colour, although technically that is still a black bear), a young moose, a small fox, 14 Stone Sheep and a small herd of Wood Bison, all along the shoulder of the roadway. By Liard River, a distance of about 300 kms, we gave up the count. There were too many bison and too many sheep. The campground at Liard River Hot Springs Provincial Park was a real treat. Apparently it is a very popular stop for those travelling the Alaska Highway, but we had not heard too much about it. We were stopping because it just happened to fit with our driving schedule. Turns out the mineral hot springs there are the largest natural mineral springs in Canada with temperatures ranging between 42 and 52C (depending on where you situate yourself in the water) and were used by many a trooper during the building of The Road (although once a week the men cleared out so the women of the camp could have a turn). The spring is in a completely natural setting with the water coming from one very hot source (it was actually boiling, bubbles and all) and several cold sources, combining into a small stream/river where the BC Parks people had built a tiered wooden deck making it easy to get in and out. The water had a faint sulphur smell that was strong enough to be noticeable but not so strong as to be off-putting. Twelve varieties of orchids and other warmth loving plants grow around the area. And despite being in a lovely Shangri-La setting, within a provincial park, and just a short walk from our campsite, it never really got crowded. During our forays, there were never more than 10 or so people around. Of course, with the water so hot, no one really lasted more than 30 minutes anyway. And while these hot springs are classed as the "largest" in Canada, they didn't feel that way. To the contrary, they felt rather intimate. Perhaps because everything was so natural and not having a concrete pool in sight is what made all the difference. And best of all, very few mosquitos. That was such a pleasant surprise after our experience a few days before. But we were lucky. Apparently the little pests get quite bad during the summer months. Just one thing was lacking. There weren't any hiking trails around to create the type of sore muscles that only a hot soak can ease. We soaked anyway. A much-needed stress reliever. John had been cleaning the day's bugs and driving dust off the yacht's front end and noticed a stone chip in the windshield. Low down and small, but something that would need attention. We hoped for a repair in Whitehorse because to replace the whole thing would be in the 4 to 5-thousand-dollar range. Ouch!

LIARD RIVER HOT SPRINGS – NATURAL AND RELAXING.

Just outside the park entrance, we came across two more small herds of wood bison, including calves, wandering back and forth across and on the highway, and further along more stone sheep, a porcupine and another black bear. But as much as it was beautiful to observe these animals in their natural habitat, it was also sad to see nature in action. While watching the bison herds grazing their way along the highway verge, we saw in the distance (about ½ km back) two more bison hurrying to catch up with the rest. They were both limping quite badly and as they passed, we could clearly see that neither could put much weight on a front leg. They kept trying to catch up, but the herd kept moving forward at a pace these two could not maintain. And the herd's pace was not fast. The poor stragglers would lie down, panting to catch their breath, and the distance would widen again. They were definitely weaker and leaner, and there is no doubt that sooner or later they will be dinner for some hungry wolves. I couldn't help but feel sorry for them. Wait a minute. I love wolves! Somebody ring the dinner bell! We stayed at the park three days and one morning, I noticed a park ranger staring into the thick brush while talking on his radio. I used to be a trained investigator. Something was going on. I stopped to chat and found a huge bison had situated himself between two wooded campsites. Staff were using bear bangers to scare it off and the tactic was certainly effective. The big guy came crashing out of the undergrowth, crossed the road, went through two other campsites and last we saw him he was back foraging his way along the side of the highway. Sadly, that very afternoon we passed by another large male lying at the side of the road, surrounded by four official looking people. Two parks vehicles (emergency lights flashing) and a front-end loader were parked nearby. It didn't look good. How fast do you have to be going to hit a bison? You can see them a mile away! I inquired with the parks people and was advised that the unfortunate bison was "Fred." He had been hit last year, injured, but managed to survive the winter. Ministry staff had been monitoring him and decided to put him down. He was in great pain, had lost considerable weight and there was no sense prolonging his suffering. The guilty culprit? One of the huge transport trucks that race up and down the highway. Probably the same idiot that gave us our stone chip. And the difference between woods bison and plains bison? The experts can't agree. Some say they are one and the same species while others argue woods bison are larger and travel in smaller herds. For protection purposes, woods bison are considered an endangered species (which is good in a way, I suppose) while plains bison are not. To my inexperienced eye, the northern BC/Yukon guys definitely looked different than the ones that stood between me and the safety of our car in Grasslands National Park, Saskatchewan. But who am I to say? We also managed to get the kayaks into the water at Muncho Lake, a very scenic lake just south of Liard River. The water was that beautiful turquoise colour often found in the mountains, not quite as vivid as Peyto Lake in Alberta, but still lovely. There was very little breeze, so the paddling was easy, and Porter was happy to be in the water once again. The Muncho Lake/Liard River Hot Spring areas were amongst the most wonderfully natural places we experienced in this area. The only negative? Filling the car up with gas at a nearby lodge. $1.95 per litre! Most we had ever paid.

On to Watson Lake. Not much there except the one-and-only Sign Post Forest. Started in 1942 by a homesick soldier working on The Road, he made a wood sign with the name of his hometown (Danville, Illinois) on it, and added it to an army mileage post. Since then, people from all over the world have been adding their names and hometowns in signs of varying creativity. The current count is around 78,000! We too decided to leave our offering, although our little marker was rather improvised and lacked the finesse of other pre-planned placards. But who knows? Maybe someday a traveller will see our little sign and say, "Hey! I know those guys!"

About 175 kms south of Whitehorse, we stopped in at the Teslin Tlingit Heritage Centre, an average sized building showcasing the history of the inland Tlingit people, as well as some incredible mask carvings created by contemporary artists. The Centre is relatively new and functions to both preserve the Tlingit culture by passing it on to the next generation, and to display that heritage to the wider world. Classes in the Tlingit language, traditional carving and beading, cuisine, healing and heritage are presented on a regular basis. It reminded me a little bit of how the Latvian community worked together to preserve and pass on its culture at a time when things looked rather bleak. It seems we are all the same in wanting to keep alive the customs and traditions of our ancestors. And this tribe is doing it quite well. In fact, most of the Yukon first nations people are doing remarkably well compared to other parts of the country. Here goes the history lesson: In the early 1700s, the Teslin Tlingit journeyed from the southeast coast of Alaska to the Yukon interior, in order to enhance their fur trading capacity with the newly arrived Russians, Europeans and English. Living a semi-nomadic subsistence life, they integrated with their Athapaskan neighbours yet kept many of their own traditions. In 1876 The Indian Act became law and amongst other things defined who was an Indian, and how band money and resources were to be managed. Two years later the Klondike Goldrush (more on that later) brought thousands of prospectors with gold fever into the Yukon, negatively impacting the Yukon First Nations way of life. Within a few years, they were petitioning Ottawa for compensation due to loss of land and hunting grounds. We all know how that went over. Building the Alaska Highway in 1942 opened their world to even more contact from "outside", yet at the same time, served to dilute their already pressured lifestyle. They went from a hunter-gatherer society to living in permanent communities along the highway. I can't say if that was good or bad. It took until 1973 before the Yukon leaders presented a formal document to then Prime Minister Pierre Trudeau and created the Council for Yukon Indians to negotiate land claim settlements on behalf of all the Yukon First Nations people. It took another twenty years before there was any movement on these claims but when the ball started rolling, it rolled very effectively. Just under 9% of Yukon's land mass has been identified to become Settlement Land and will be owned by individual Yukon First Nations. Of the 14 tribes, 11 have already signed treaties making them self-governing. In effect, having the same powers over land, governance, management of resources, heritage etc. as our provinces and territories. Very impressive, considering how little has been resolved in the rest of the country.

And speaking of country, being constantly on the move, I lost track of how far north we had travelled and only realized our latitude when looking at a map of traditional Tinglit lands. We were 200 kms north of Juneau! No wonder I was having difficulty sleeping. At midnight it was so light outside I could have easily read a book. Not that I went outside. The mosquitos were horrific. The Liard River hiatus was just dumb luck. We subsequently spent several sleepless nights fighting off the little vampires that kept coming inside with Porter, and by the time we reached Whitehorse, my first stop was Canadian Tire to purchase a mosquito net canopy for over the bed, and a mosquito trap for the rest of the coach. And we hadn't even reached the North West Territories! I was starting to question the wisdom of this choice of destination. By the time you reach a certain age, you know what you like and what you don't. What you can tolerate and what you cannot. I cannot tolerate biting insects. Mosquitos, black flies, deer flies, horse flies. I learned that when I was 10. Was it too late to turn around and head back south?

The Yukon is an interesting place. Almost complete wilderness. Total population around 36,000 with 75% living in Whitehorse. That's like all the people of the territory living in Georgetown, Ontario with room left over for 5,000 more. We stayed in the thriving metropolis of Whitehorse for several days, primarily taking care of maintenance and safety issues. The yacht's windshield chip was repaired with an epoxy resin injection (for less than $100 thank goodness), four new heavier tires were purchased for the Jeep (the old ones already had 74,000 kms and we wanted two spares for driving the Dempster Highway and up to Tuktoyaktuk), an extra gas can was rigged up next to the kayaks (there are no gas stations for 370 kms after Dawson City and the Jeep sucked gas like no tomorrow), the yacht went in for our pre-booked repairs on the blower wheel and black tank nozzle, and John attempted to wash the calcium chloride off both vehicles. Calcium chloride is something they spray onto the gravel roads in the north country to keep the dust down but when wet, it sticks like glue (along with airborne pieces of gravel) to just about everything. No wonder every other person around Whitehorse drives a beater. There is just no way to keep a vehicle clean and shiny with that on the roads. We set up in the Walmart parking lot, along with 40 other motor homes and trailers (we counted), that varied in size, vintage and condition. And some of these folks were permanent residents. I can't imagine what they do in the winter. There was one unit in particular that caught my attention. It was a 25-foot white panel truck with a residential door fitted into the back. No windows. No licence plates. Soft tires. An exterior generator ran almost constantly. At one point, a man came out with a little girl around 8 years of age, and they both walked hand-in-hand over to the Walmart store. This was obviously their home. It would have been interesting to find out their story, because there is more than enough work to be found in the area. We chatted with two people (one the young mechanic who worked on our coach, and the other along a hiking trail) who had moved to Whitehorse specifically because the cost of housing was so affordable, and there was so much work to be had.

And Whitehorse itself? It started out as a tent city where Klondike strike-it-rich hopefuls heading for Dawson City had to dry off and re-group after navigating the White Horse Rapids and Miles Canyon, treacherous going back in the day, and it eventually became a transportation and transhipment centre used by both the railroad, and stern-wheelers on the Yukon River. And of course, it played a role in the building of the Alaska Highway. But despite this history, the place can't be described as charming. Sprawling unimaginative two story buildings (John called the architectural style "northern utilitarian"), wide streets that still had much of last winter's gravel on them, garbage, plastic bags, coffee cups etc. blown into the surrounding brush, no landscaping to speak of, vacant lots, huge parking lots, box stores. A few independent cafes and restaurants trying to make a go of it but nothing that would draw me back. John said he thought the place had a "nice feel" to it but we must have disparate definitions of "nice".

And what is there to do in Whitehorse when the chores are done? Not much. At least not anything that requires 4 full days! We visited the Beringia Interpretive Centre where we read up on the Bering Land Bridge, and the flora and fauna that lived upon it during the last ice age. While most of the North American continent was covered by glaciers, this area remained ice free allowing for various species to thrive and flourish. It was the time of the woolly mammoth. Scientists estimate these giants went largely extinct about 11,000 years ago yet somehow a few managed to survive on Wrangel Island just north of Siberia until about 3,700 years ago. Wow! They were building pyramids in Egypt at that time! Interesting stuff. Using DNA, scientists also estimate that the first Americans split from their Asian ancestors about 25,000 years ago, living on the land bridge for thousands of years before moving into present day Alaska and Yukon about 14,000 years ago. So have the first nations people been here "since time immemorial?" Nope. We are all immigrants. Some along the oceanfront just got here considerably sooner.

We also checked out some more recent history by visiting the National Historic Site of the restored S.S. Klondike, the largest sternwheeler to carry passengers and cargo up and down the Yukon River between 1937 and 1955. Sternwheelers were first used on the lower Yukon River in the late 1860s to supply mining camps and trading posts but when the gold rush started in earnest after 1897, their numbers and distances travelled greatly increased. I must confess, I found all this only mildly interesting. But there wasn't much else to do while our own vessel was in dry dock. We hiked a short way along Miles Canyon, that section of the Yukon River that used to have the nasty White Horse Rapids (prior to a dam being built in 1957) and this was more interesting both from a natural perspective (it was a lovely walk with beautiful wild blue lupines in full bloom) and a historical perspective. Whitehorse would not exist in its present location if not for these rapids. Of course it wouldn't exist at all if not for the 1896 Klondike Gold rush but more on that later.

Leaving Whitehorse, we turned north towards Dawson City, driving along the Klondike Highway, another misleading term if there ever was one. It wasn't so much a highway, as more a country road with constant potholes, rough pavement and the occasional frost heaves thrown in to make the ride even more enjoyable. Of course this was supposed to be nothing compared to the Dempster Highway. A mere warm up if you will, so there were some concerns about what lay ahead. We reached Dawson relatively unscathed. "Relatively" being the operative word. We picked up another stone chip in the windshield. Exploring Dawson right away was not in the immediate plans since the focus was mostly on getting to Tuktoyaktuk in the North West Territories, as far north as it is possible to go by road in Canada. We arranged for the yacht to stay in a RV park while we packed up the Jeep for the journey into the wild yonder. Although some people do take their campers and smaller recreation vehicles up that way, it would have been sheer insanity to try it with a coach.

The first day's drive along the infamous Dempster saw us cover a distance of 400 kms from Dawson to Eagle Plains – population 9. Yes, nine. And they are all owners or employees at the only gas station/garage/motel/restaurant compound. We had set out at 10am and got to Eagle Plains around 4pm., not stopping too many times simply because of the weather. It was raining at the outset, eased up a bit, stopped for a stretch

allowing for some pictures, and then came on in a deluge. Trees and mountains gave way to rolling tundra around the half-way mark. But it was beautiful. Such a wide, open expanse where, similar to the Grand Canyon, the mind has difficulty comprehending the scale. Photographs don't do it justice. It cannot be described. Only experienced.

STARTING OUT ALONG THE DEMPSTER – SO FAR, SO GOOD.

Near Tombstone Territorial Park, we stopped for a break, and while I was inside the Visitor's Centre, John took Porter for a short walk. Beside the Centre was a gravel path leading to the camping area, where he stopped to read a small information placard. Within a few seconds, some movement by a spruce tree about 15 feet in front of him caught his attention and looking up, he saw a little cinnamon coloured bear cub come out of the brush. John jumped. The cub jumped. And then they both just looked at each other for a few seconds. John quickly realized bear cub equals bear mama, so cautiously and quietly beat a hasty retreat. Porter, ever the city dog, was oblivious to the whole thing. John didn't have a camera with him, so there is no documented proof of this interaction, but I do believe he was telling me the truth about his encounter with little *ursi catulum*.

The building of the Dempster itself was started in the late 1950s as a way to access the resources of the north and was optimistically called the Road to Resources, but after 124 kms of construction, the project was cancelled, and it became known as the Road to Nowhere. When oil was discovered in the Beaufort Sea in 1971, it took off again, was completed in 1979, and formally named after Inspector Jack Dempster of the Fort McPherson RCMP detachment (more on him later). The road surface was not as bad as threatened. We had certainly driven on much worse. It was all gravel and quite well graded although we did pass numerous areas where the remains of shredded tires were scattered about and at least 3 times, overtook people out changing tires, including one older couple (i.e. older than us!) with a flat on their trailer. I remembered them specifically because they had been in the NWT Visitor Centre in Dawson where the attendant advised them the drive to Eagle Plains would be okay but not to go beyond there. Apparently crushed shale is used in some sections of the road and this is particularly hazardous to tires. That, and the constant presence of the dreaded dust supressing calcium chloride. In some respects, we were lucky because the rain kept the dust to a minimum but what was kicked up stuck to the car like glue. And twice (once going north and once going south) we passed big transport trucks (semis) that had obviously left the road and ended up in the tundra. It almost looked as if the drivers had pulled off and parked, but these were definitely not rest areas. We heard the tow charge alone for the northbound mishap was $30,000.00! Everything was expensive in the north. Staying at Eagle Plains motel was like stepping back in time. Built in 1979, it has not changed nor been upgraded since, and the only really positive thing I can say is that it was very pet-friendly. Porter was allowed into the lounge, where we had dinner while he slept under the table. The owner sat at the bar holding court, chatting with regulars and new guests alike. We thanked him for his relaxed dog-welcoming atmosphere, and he laughed saying, "Fuck, this is the Yukon. If the health inspector comes in again and wants to write me up, I say, whatever, go ahead, I'll pay it. If someone comes in and doesn't like the dog, I'll kick them out." Great attitude. Of course his own dog wandered all around the facility so what was he going to say. But the place needs a lot work, including in the area of customer service. At "the kitchen", when I asked the fellow behind the self-serve coffee/tea area where I could find milk, he responded with a surly, "Not my problem." Okay then. I used Coffee Mate. But this is literally the only place to stop for 360 kms so they don't have to try too hard.

North of Eagle Plains, the road was considerably worse and the weather not much better. While there were periods of respite (notably at the Arctic Circle and after crossing into the North West Territories) for the most part we had precipitation varying from drizzle to mist to rain. This of course limited visibility and turned the road to mud although thankfully we passed through the dreaded crushed shale section without issue. Not everyone was as lucky. At the Arctic Circle stop, one traveller advised he had set out with three spare tires but was now down to his last one! We took the obligatory pictures right at 66 degrees latitude, where the distance around the Earth at that point is less than half the distance around the Earth at the Equator. It was still quite windy and chilly but for that, I was grateful. Even at 10C, stepping out of the wind was inviting a mosquito onslaught They were just awful. It's hard to imagine what they must be like during July and August. Perhaps that is why so many people like to visit in the autumn. They don't get the midnight sun experience, but they probably don't risk losing a pint of blood either.

It was an odd feeling driving along such a remote stretch, picturing our location on a map of North America. We were so far from everything!!! In a few places, the road actually widened into a landing strip for small aircraft should an aeronautic emergency be encountered, but that was it. And while there were considerable miles upon miles of empty tundra, there were equally as many, if not more, miles upon miles of stunted birch, spruce and tamarack trees, none taller than five feet, and many listing precariously to one side or another. This because of the permafrost that prevents their roots from anchoring and growing down into the ground. And of course, permafrost doesn't just affect the trees. The Dempster was built on it, and in several sections, we were simply driving along a raised four-foot gravel embankment. By definition, permafrost is ground that remains at or below freezing for at least two years, and consists of gravel, soil and sand bound together by ice. During the summer, the first 3 meters thaw, and this causes the surface area to sink (and later heave) causing all kinds of structural damage to roads and buildings, and leading to some creative construction techniques. Interesting fact?

About 20% of the Earth (including ½ of Canada) is underlain by permafrost. Still, I somehow had not imagined seeing trees above the Arctic Circle, but apparently the Mackenzie Delta creates an environment suitable for their growth. Another interesting fact? The Delta is the muskrat capital of the world and trapping for pelts is big business. Who knew. There were two ferry crossings along the way, the first at the Peel River, which took about 2 minutes, and on the north side we stopped at the only other community between Eagle River and Inuvik – Fort McPherson. There wasn't much there. It is a Gwich 'In community and looked incredibly unkempt and run down but we stopped in to see the cemetery where the officers of the Lost Patrol are buried. It is a very sad story. During the late 1800s, the RCMP had established outposts in remote locations of the north in order to secure Canada's sovereignty over the area. In December of 1910, four officers set out from Fort McPherson on a patrol en route to Dawson City, a distance of 765 kms. They never arrived. A search party under the direction of Inspector Dempster, together with an aboriginal guide, set out in March 1911 to locate them. They were found only 25 miles from Fort McPherson. Not being familiar with the terrain, losing recognizable landmarks, hampered by bad weather and sparse game, they had starved to death. Two of them were in their forties, two just in their twenties. They lie buried in the neglected cemetery by the church. I certainly hope that the current RCMP detachment officers pay them a visit from time to time. We continued on, sobered by how unforgiving the wilderness can be.

The ferry crossing at Mackenzie River took about 5 minutes, and I must confess to having skipped the odd geography class in school because I did not know the Mackenzie is Canada's longest river, at 1,738 kms. Just goes to show, you are never too old to learn. And finally, we were in Inuvik. Depending on whose translation you accept, "Inuvik" means "Place of the People" or "The Real People" or "Place of Man" in the Inuvialuit language. And the pronunciation is not IN-u-vik but rather i-NU-vik, with the emphasis on the second syllable. It is an artificial government created community, to which many Inuvialuit people moved when it became clear their traditional lands around Aklavik (place of bear) were disappearing due to erosion and flooding. The new settlement is nothing to write home about. Also sitting on permafrost, the mechanicals are all above ground using a system called utilidors. Water pipes, sewer pipes, heating pipes all running underneath and alongside the buildings (which are on pilings, some sunk as deep as 30 feet) in plain view. So basically, an above ground sewer system. Very unsightly, but this is the great white north. And no sewage treatment plant either. Everything just gets dumped into the ocean. Lovely. The only aesthetically pleasing building in the whole place was the church, shaped like an igloo and built in 1960 without the use of blueprints.

Historically, the two main cultural groups living in the Yukon and NWT were the Inuvialuit and the Gwich 'In. How do they differ? In the past, the Inuvialuit were called Eskimos and the Gwich 'In called Indians. Completely different peoples. And despite the whole peace and harmony with nature and each other myth, they didn't always get along when it came to hunting territory. The Inuvialuit live primarily in the Western Arctic including the Mackenzie Delta while the Gwich 'In are in northeast Alaska, over to the northern Yukon, parts of the NWT, and around Fort McPherson. It all gets so confusing. Then add some more recent immigrants to the mix. At our hotel, staff were from India, Sri Lanka and Ghana. In order to get their Permanent Resident status, they need secure full-time employment so many head north to take those positions the long-time residents deemed undesirable. Another story as old as time.

And then there was the Arctic Ocean and the Inuvialuit hamlet of Tuktoyaktuk. When I was in my teens, a disc jockey on Toronto's CHUM am radio station (whose name I can't recall) ended his show by providing the current air temperature in Tuktoyaktuk. I had been curious about the place ever since. I wish I could say nice things about Tuk but it's going to be a stretch. Charming. Scenic. Picturesque. Natural beauty. Quaint. None of the above. There is very little to recommend. Not that I expected much but given how it is promoted in NWT tourism literature, there should have been something! As recently as the spring of 2017, "Looks like Caribou" or "Place of Caribou" (depending on whose translation you use) could only be accessed by ice road during the winter months (basically eight months of the year) but come the summer melt, nothing but muskeg, mud and mosquitos. It was an expensive plane ride in or out. However, over the past four years, a year-round road had been in the making. The prevailing sentiment was, "Build it and they will come" but after the official opening in November 2017, it changed to, "There are so many coming!" The community was just not prepared for what was in their estimation, an onslaught of outsiders. Really it was just an additional 30 people a day, but for a village of 900, it was overwhelming. And this is not a prosperous place full of entrepreneurs. It is, as the landlord of our B&B said, "a government town." Euphemism for 70% being on welfare or some other form of government assistance. And it looks it. The road in leads past the garbage dump with much of the refuse resting in the water. It then passes by boarded up buildings, machinery and drums from the earlier oil exploration years. One of the NWS (North Warning System) radar stations was on the horizon (replacing the old DEW line – Distant Warning System), adding yet another layer to the already industrialized look. Heaven help us if the Russians decide to cross there. It's hard to tell when the town proper begins because things don't improve. Run down houses with all kinds of junk strewn about, cannibalized snowmobiles, sleds, four by fours and dirt bikes parked out front in a haphazard manner. I couldn't tell if I was looking at a parking lot or someone's front yard. Mangy looking dogs on 5-foot lengths of chain, attached to dilapidated doghouses are situated right beside the road. These are outside sled dogs, left over from a time when they actually had a purpose hauling sleds across the ice. Long since replaced by snowmobiles, some people insist on keeping them as a "cultural" thing yet in reality, the poor creatures are clearly neglected. They are chained because if they run loose, they will be shot. In the city office there was a job posting for a Dog Officer Position where the lucky applicant would be tasked with capturing or shooting stray or unwanted dogs within the town's boundary. Our landlord told us that when a dog does get shot, there is no delicate disposition of the carcass either. It is attached to the back of a pick-up truck and dragged along the road through the mud and dirt to the dump. How barbaric is that! There was a large industrial trailer near our B&B that functioned as a restaurant of sorts (the only one in town) and by "The Point" three local guys were smoking fresh caught whitefish that they sold to visitors. The pungent smell of pot surrounded them as well so I'm not sure how much of the fish was smoked with traditional driftwood and how much was laced with THC. No wonder it was popular fare!

Other than providing an opportunity to dip your toes into the Arctic Ocean (which we did – it was really cold!) and viewing some pingos, there was really very little to see. I had never heard of pingos before but have since learned they are a unique geological feature found only in permafrost landscape. They were rather underwhelming. Explanation. A pingo is a dome or volcano-shaped mound of earth that has a core of solid ice. Yawn. The Tuktoyaktuk area has the highest concentration of them (around 1,400) with the largest one in Canada, the Ibuyuk, rising around 50 meters from the tundra floor. Yawn. It is estimated to be around 1,000 years old and still growing as its internal core of ice continues to be forced upward by the freezing of an old lake bed beneath it. Yawn. I suppose that isn't fair. In a land that is primarily flat, any raised area, no matter how small, is cause

ALONG THE ARCTIC OCEAN IN TUKTOYAKTUK WITH PINGOS ON THE HORIZON.

for celebration, and they are quite proud of their pingos. The Government of Canada had built a boardwalk out to one of these marvels, but the access point could only be reached by water. So we launched the kayaks and set out. Unfortunately, Tuk had been having a late spring and ice sheets up to a foot thick soon blocked our way. I can't say I was too heartbroken. Although 24 hours later, when we were leaving, most of the ice had melted under the midnight sun. And there is midnight sun here. And 1am sun. And 2am sun. It was easy to lose track of time. We found ourselves puzzling over why we were so tired, and then realized it was well after midnight.

We wanted to find out as much as we could about this community and located an advertisement for someone offering one-hour "cultural" tours. It turned out to be more talk than tour. We went to our host's home on "The Rez" which was relatively clean if somewhat cluttered, were warmly greeted by a mother and son duo who treated us to smoked whitefish (not too good) and caribou roast (very lean but very flavourful) and bannock with wild cranberries. And then we just chatted about living in the area. There was no structure and topics were all over the map. It was clear they had not done this very often (if ever) but they did try. The mom, who works for the housing authority, showed me a traditional parka hood made from wolf pelts, as well as a quilted parka she was making by hand, having harvested the down for the filling herself from the Arctic Geese her son had shot, and trimming it with a wolverine pelt, complete with claws dangling as decorations in the front. Much of the family's time is spent going to their hunt camp about three hours out of town, where they have found old whalebone fishhooks and other artefacts that an archaeologist would kill for. But a few things they said really troubled me, especially given this era where most people are concerned with climate change and its impact on large mammals. They maintain that given their heritage (and recently settled land claims of which they are very proud), they engage in subsistence hunting. "Subsistence" by definition means "for survival". They hunt everything from caribou to wolves and grizzly to polar bears. But other than the caribou, they only take the bear and wolf hides, and leave the carcasses to the elements. Well that isn't entirely correct. Having shot a polar bear, they occasionally take the paws too because some people eat the paws (that are similar to pork hocks) and then make mittens out of the fur. The dad makes his living by guiding hunters out on trophy shoots. No matter how you twist it, that is not subsistence hunting! "Oh, but it's part of their heritage," goes the argument. Maybe at a time when hunting was with spears and sled dogs, but nobody uses that mode of transportation anymore other than to give tourists a thrill. How challenging is it to chase something down on a snowmobile using a high-powered rifle with a scope? I ground my teeth but said nothing. John was thankful. And what about the carvings and beadwork the Inuvialuit are known for?

In town at the city "hall", a few small crafts and carvings of average quality were on display for purchase, but staff advised that at 1pm Tuesdays an art market takes place at the community centre where local artisans have all kinds of items for offer. We were due to leave that morning but hung around to attend the market. I really wanted to buy something to commemorate our visit. Big mistake. Just before 1pm, eight of us tourists were dutifully arrayed outside the centre, but the doors were locked. Shortly, a young lady came up and unlocked the doors, but when we went inside, the hall was empty. Five tables had been arranged in a semi-circle but not a craft nor artist in sight. "I'm sure they will be here soon," she said. Right. By 1:15 we left, with no craftsmen on the horizon. They really need to step up their game. Enough said.

The drive back to Inuvik and on through Eagle Plains was pretty dismal. It rained almost the entire way and the mud on the road was so thick and deep in places that many motorcyclists chose to remain at the Eagle Plains motel and wait for things to dry up. The "car wash" (as at other locations in the north), was just a simple pressure hose. It was in great demand as drivers tried to rinse 50 pounds of mud off their vehicles. No pretty coloured suds, no swinging cloths, no tire wax, no blow dry. Just the hose. Everyone was grateful. And almost all conversations revolved around the road. "How was the road?" "Did you come from the north or the south?" And said road? After five days of on-again, off-again rain, it was completely different from what we had travelled on heading north – rutted, wash-boarded and full of potholes. Reaching Dawson, we were so thankful to have made it without getting a flat, although we did pick up yet another stone chip during the last 40 kms. Road etiquette on the Dempster is such that when vehicles approach each other, both should slow down and move as far over to their respective shoulders as possible. Some do, some don't. On this particular occasion, it was a fifth wheel being pulled by a pick-up truck that made no effort to either slow or move. We wondered if the windshield repair guy in Dawson would give us a two-for-one special.

Back in Dawson, we immersed ourselves in the history of the Klondike Gold Rush and while there wasn't a ton of detailed information readily available in the Visitor's Centre, I was reading Pierre Berton's book *Klondike: The Last Great Gold Rush* and was completely enthralled. I never really knew anything about this period of Canadiana so it was all news to me. As gold rushes go, the Klondike was neither the longest, nor the richest, nor drew the most prospectors. But it was the most intense and most frantic, insane really, and although it lasted a mere 3 years (at least the traditional hand panning phase) there had never been anything like it before, or since, for that matter. They say over 1 million people from all parts of the world made plans to go to the Klondike once gold fever hit, but only 100,000 got around to setting out, and of them, only about 30,000 actually made it. And considering word only reached the outside world a full year after the first strike (in July 1896), odds were not good that anyone arriving late to the game was going to get rich. Not good at all. Yet they came by the thousands. A virtual stampede that more often than not exposed man's insatiable greed and brutal cruelty when overcome by the disease. It also exposed man's stupidity and gullibility. Some came by water, some on foot. Most turned back before ever reaching the gold fields, but not before killing thou-

sands of horses, mules and dogs, and at times, each other and themselves. Those who did succeed were often tricked or robbed of their treasure and returned home poorer than when they arrived. I won't get into the details here. Read the book. It is excellent.

PORTER HELPING JOHN PAN FOR GOLD — WITH NO SUCCESS.

Dawson City today is really a mere shell of its former self and seems to exist only for the benefit of tourists who wish to somehow experience the more romanticized part of the gold rush. Diamond-Tooth Gertie's advertises itself as Canada's oldest gambling establishment, complete with can-can dancing girls and honky-tonk piano but it really only opened in 1971. There are opportunities to go panning for gold at Claim No. 6 on Bonanza Creek, just half a mile upstream from where the first big strike that started the madness occurred. It is owned by the Klondike Visitor's Association, so we rented some pans for $2.00 and spent the day playing in the dirt. It was kind of fun although the odds of finding anything are incredibly remote. The area has been picked over for more than 120 years. At the end of our day we had nothing to show for it but aching backs and mosquito bites. But digging for gold still continues in the area, only today's process is industrialized with huge dredging machines and bulldozers that are basically ploughing through the landscape leaving behind massive piles of tailings and deep ponds full of stagnant brown water along each and every road. It was ugly. There is no other word for it. Shops sell all manner of jewellery made from locally found gold, as well as woolly mammoth ivory, and it is quite pleasant to walk around on the raised wooden sidewalks and poke about. Sadly, many of the original buildings have collapsed over the years, leaving behind vacant lots, and others are in the process of soon following. Quite a few were boarded up and looked abandoned. But literature has a place there too. A small museum about Jack London (remember *White Fang* and *Call of the Wild*?) is nearby, since apparently he too succumbed to the lure of gold and made his way to the Klondike during the rush. He didn't get rich and didn't stay long, but certainly collected enough material to write those classic books. They are next on my re-read list. And the cabin of poet Robert Service (of whom I am ashamed to admit I knew virtually nothing) who authored such classics as *The Spell of the Yukon* and *The Cremation of Sam McGee*. And of course, Pierre Berton's childhood home. It was hard to image these literary giants roaming about this little town with its never-paved dirt streets, wood plank sidewalks and corrugated metal buildings. Reading Berton's depictions of life and times in this place and then walking the very same streets made the descriptions so much more poignant.

And so June drew to a close. At the risk of sounding un-patriotic, for July 1st we opted to skip the Canada Day celebrations and started our journey towards Alaska. Timing is everything. We heard that the Prime Minister was scheduled to arrive in Dawson that day, and we couldn't get out of town fast enough.

27.

AIN'T NO SUNSHINE

AFTER ABOUT A MONTH, I CAME TO THE CONCLUSION THAT I WAS NOT CUT OUT FOR THE FAR, FAR NORTH. At least not for any lengthy periods of time. I was tired of dressing like a bum. I'd forgotten how to put on make-up. I missed my hairdresser. "Manicure" became a foreign word. Spa? What's a spa? And I decided I preferred pavement and concrete to dirt and gravel hands down. At least pavement when it was not full of frost heaves, lateral cracks and ruts. I don't know what happened. I used to love the great outdoors – getting away from the city and getting back to nature. But perhaps that saying about too much of a good thing is correct. We had been on the road for two full years by this time and it was starting to show. From time to time, I found myself daydreaming about how I would redecorate the house when we moved back, and I looked forward to reading the Saturday paper at our local coffee shop. But a deal was a deal. There was another year and a bit to go, at least until fall of 2019, and we were going to enjoy it, damn it! On to Alaska!

We left Dawson City July 1st following the Top of the World Highway and crossed into Alaska at its most northerly land border post, Poker Creek. Population: 3. The border crossing actually closes between September and May due to inclement weather and its remote location. The road was not too bad on the Canadian side with ruts, gravel and potholes as expected, but do-able. The American side (where it is called the Taylor Highway) was the worst we had experienced anywhere to date. Why do they insist on calling these goat paths "highways?" We didn't go much faster than 20 km/h, often less. Driving into the most remote northern Ontario cottage after a heavy rain is better. Coupled with tight hair pin turns, no shoulders and steep drop offs, it took us 3 hours to cover about 60 kms before finally reaching the tiny community of Chicken, population 23 during the summer and 7 in the winter. Chicken started out as a gold mining town and that is still its primary industry (along with tourism in the summer). Although calling it a town is being rather generous. They have three "businesses". A bakery/café, a small pub and a mercantile shop, all side by side just off the "highway". No telephones. No flush toilets. And mail comes by plane every Tuesday and Friday, weather permitting. And where did the name Chicken come from? Legend has it that in the late 1800s the local miners decided to name their town after a common chicken-type bird, the Ptarmigan, widespread throughout the area. Sadly, being neither scholars nor ornithologists and not having a dictionary amongst them, they could not agree on how to spell "ptarmigan" so settled on "chicken." A large chicken sculpture constructed of flattened school lockers graces the landscape of Gold Camp RV Park should anyone need reminding of where they are. The grounds are situated near an active gold mining claim and many people actually come for a week or two simply to try their luck in the creek. The owner advised she has two guests from Germany and Sweden who return every year just to go panning. It was a fun little place and in the morning I too, took some time to hone the craft, actually finding a few miniscule specks. And by miniscule, I mean smaller than a grain of sand. You practically needed a magnifying glass to see them. I would have stayed longer to keep looking for the mother lode but could see John was itching to get going. Searching for gold is somewhat addictive. Almost like gambling. You always think the next pan will yield something really big. One man I chatted with had nicknamed his wife, "One More Pan Anne." And just to set the record straight, John did not drag me away screaming, "My Precious! My Precious" like Gollum from *Lord of the Rings*. (Although I did buy a pan just in case we camped by a promising creek.)

Our destination was Anchorage but the plan was to mosey along the Tok Cutoff Highway (there they go again) for a few days, and then pick up the Glenn Highway for the final leg. Driving those roads was like grabbing a handful of Bits 'N Bites. You never knew what you were going to get. At times it was smooth sailing and then back to the usual bump and grind. I am not going to comment further on the road conditions other than to say they made it virtually impossible to accurately predict driving times. Very frustrating. But the scenery was breathtaking with the mountains of Wrangell – St. Elias National Park quickly coming into view. This park is actually the largest in all of North America but can only be partially accessed by two short roads that I suspect you'd need a tank to negotiate, so we left that to more intrepid travellers. We saw several moose along the way, including a cow and calf that crossed the road directly in front of us. Just like in the travel brochures.

We were blessed with great weather along the Glenn, with wildflowers in shades of purple, blue, yellow, cream and white along the highway verge. Even wild irises. And the views can be best described by the eloquence of our conversations during the day – variations on the theme of "Wow!" "OMG!" "Holy shit!" "Do you see that?" "Look over there! Look over there!" Fantastic mountains and mountain ranges that were huge, yet so far away. And one human interest observation. There were lots of neglected shacks of varying sizes along the way, as well as boarded up buildings collapsing in on themselves. I'm not sure if this is because the winters are so severe or because the owners have neither the means nor the motivation for their upkeep. I suspect the latter because there were occasional nice log cabins as well. Such is life in the middle of nowhere. We overnighted at the Matanuska Glacier parking lot and could not have asked for a nicer place to stay, especially towards evening after the day trippers moved on. Gold panning in Caribou Creek was a bust so we set up the chairs and just enjoyed the view, all by ourselves. The Matanuska Glacier is what is referred to as a "stable" glacier, in that it has not advanced nor retreated in over 400 years. Because of that stability, the tree line (with 200-year old trees) goes right up to the toe, unlike the Athabaska Glacier along the Columbia Icefield in Alberta where, as the ice retreats, it leaves a long unsightly path of gravel and stones in its wake. Much prettier here.

Just past Palmer we stopped in to tour a Musk Ox Farm, the only "domestic" herd of Musk Ox in the entire world, and it was fascinating! I must admit I had thought they would be bigger, more along the lines of bison, but even though they weigh between 600 and 900 pounds, they were not that tall. Males only stand about 4 to 5 feet at the shoulder. So really, huge blubbery bodies with thick coats on short stumpy legs. But all that blubber means they are able to swim! They have survived more than one ice age when other animals like mammoths and saber-toothed cats died out, and they even expanded as far south as Florida. But being cold weather animals, when the ice sheets retreated 10,000 years ago, the Musk Ox retreated with them and wild herds are now found primarily in Greenland and northern Canada. Alaska is another story. With the arrival of "modern" human beings, all of the indigenous Musk Ox were extinct by the late 1800s. Quelle surprise. But in 1930, U.S. Congress provided funding for a project that saw 34 musk oxen re-located from Greenland to Nunivak Island (off the coast of western Alaska) where they had no predators (the four or two-legged kind). The animals thrived and by 1964 the herd had reached such a size that some were "transplanted" to the rest of Alaska. Today they number around 8,000. Finally, an animal success story. In 1954 a fellow by the name of John Teal decided to experiment with domesticating these ancient beasts. He managed to set up a small farm in Vermont (although it has since been moved to Alaska) and began harvesting Qiviut (pronounced *ki*-vee-ute), a fine under wool that protects these beasties from the harsh Arctic temperatures. It is a remarkable product. Eight times warmer than wool, it never shrinks no matter what the water temperature because it is really a hair fibre. And being one of the rarest fibres on earth, it costs $95.00 per ounce! No knitting bulky sweaters with this stuff. Although I did buy a few ounces for some projects for loved ones. But it takes about 250 years to domesticate an animal so the musk oxen we visited on this farm were not quite there. Yet even at this semi-domestic point, they exhibit remarkable personalities and show an intelligence level comparable to that of dogs. Our guide told us that they constantly try to escape from their enclosures, often by just leaning their massive weights, cooperatively en masse, onto the wire fences. While the guide was talking, I had bent forward to take a picture of one beautiful female about 80 feet away, when she suddenly charged at me full speed. All I could think was, "Oh, God. I hope that fence holds!" But she stopped short right at the fence, leaned in towards me and then snorted all over my camera. The guide laughed and said that she was just being playful. Oh sure. Tell that to my cardiologist. Being a one-of-a-kind place, the farm has a celebrity supporter too. Alex Trebek of Jeopardy fame has taken a liking to these guys and has donated funds to help keep the farm (really a non-profit organization) going. Apparently they are his favourite animal. Remember that next time you play Jeopardy.

And finally, Anchorage. Ahhhhh. Concrete. Cars. Coffee shops. Civilization. Okay, maybe civilization is going a bit too far. We were set up in a small municipal campground in what can best be described as the less-than-tony suburbs of town (lots of struggling businesses, lots of traffic) yet a large black bear persisted on nonchalantly walking through the grounds. A section of the park had already been cordoned off to campers because of him but apparently he didn't care. John had taken Porter out for a walk one morning and there was Yogi, ambling along like he owned the place. Campers and staff alike used bear horns to scare him away, but the bear's departure never seemed to last for long. Such excitement! It wasn't the best of parks, however. We were fortunate to have a site near the office so didn't have any issues, but other campers complained of local druggies coming in late at night and hanging around in the far corner. I don't believe they caused any harm, but it can be unsettling to people not used to the negative side of urban life. And while downtown Anchorage was not huge, I really liked it. Perhaps I just needed an asphalt fix, (or perhaps my opinion was influenced by the sunny warm weather) but even Porter had a spring in his step, not being set upon by mosquitos nor being on the look-out for bears. I can't say I had any expectations about the place, but I was very pleasantly surprised by it all. Every Thursday evening during summer a band plays in the small town square, and the surrounding landscaping was amazing. Flowers, with their 20 odd hours of daylight grew in deep, rich shades of orange, yellow, red and blue. And interspersed amongst them, almost as colour co-ordinated accent plants, were huge cabbages and Swiss chard. However, being edibles, some people had obviously helped themselves to the decorations because the odd cabbage plant was missing its head. And these were big cabbages! Apparently this part of Alaska (and in particular Palmer, just outside of Anchorage) is known for its huge vegetables, holding records for largest cabbage (105.6 lbs), radish (9.5 lbs) and rutabaga (53 lbs). It's that continuous sunlight that does it. But back to Anchorage. The place had a lot of tourist shops selling the usual tourist kitsch (eg. T-shirts: "Keep Calm and Play Dead" below the image of a running bear) but there were several stores that had genuine art for offer. In one shop in particular we were able to observe and chat with the native carvers as they worked on walrus ivory, scrimshaw (the fine carving or engraving of ivory or bone), whalebone and even pieces of baleen over 8 feet long. It was captivating, although the smell as they cut through bone wasn't very pleasant. There were also several fur shops to explore and while I have long since outgrown my whole fur coat phase, there was one parka that I fell in love with. If only I'd had the money to buy it and a place to wear it. It was a work of art! Besides fur garments (coats, vests, hats, gloves etc.) the shops also sold fur pelts and, to my indignation, wolf pelt rugs, complete with snarling stuffed wolf heads. I fully realize that hunting and trapping is a part of life up there, but it is so ironic that in some parts of North America people are working diligently to re-introduce wolves to their previous range, and in other parts, this magnificent keystone species is hunted and stuffed. Save the wolves!!!

One day we hiked two thirds of the way up Flattop Mountain, a very popular local hiking trail whose proximity to town belies its intensity. As hikes go, it wasn't long, but what it lacked in length it made up for in pitch. The going was pretty steep with several poorly maintained sections and an elevation gain of 1,350 feet in 1.7 miles. We had not hiked for quite some time and our regular fitness regime had long since been abandoned, so my legs really felt it. Even Porter, who was starting to show his almost 8 years, began to drag. (Although if we had been headed towards water there is no doubt he would have picked up the pace.) But it was all pretty much open tundra so the views down towards Anchorage and out over Cook Inlet were great, despite it being a rather hazy day. And far in the distance, almost like a faint mirage, loomed Mt. Denali. It was 250 miles away! I couldn't wait to get there. But we still had a few more outings near town, including a short drive to Hatcher Pass, a road that leads to Independence Mine State Historical Park. The drive was lovely with the road paralleling the Little Susitna River, steadily climbing higher and higher into Alpine like meadows complete with mountain heather and a babbling brook. Other than the breathtaking views, the park

314 — DISPATCHES FROM THE DOGHOUSE

itself was meh! It used to be a hard-rock gold mining community (for 10 years the most productive one in Alaska second only to the Treadmill Mine in Juneau) but closed down in 1955. Work is underway to restore some of buildings but much of it is beyond repair. We had a nice walk around, but I found myself considerably more awed by the surrounding scenery than by some collapsed shacks and rusting engine parts. And besides, I prefer to pan for my gold instead of crushing rocks! Porter found himself a huge patch of snow to roll around in so I suppose the outing was not a complete loss.

And on the topic of loss, there are not too many places you can go in Alaska without coming across information panels describing the great Good Friday earthquake of 1964, the largest ever recorded in the Northern Hemisphere (and the second largest ever recorded in the world) measuring 8.6 on the Richter Scale (or 9.2 according to other sources). The initial tremor lasted an incredible 4-1/2 minutes. The epicentre was not quite halfway between Valdez and Anchorage but its effects were catastrophic up and down the entire west coast. The seabed floor (an area 60 miles by 240 miles in size) actually slipped, displacing land and water by as much as 50 feet. There were 11 aftershocks measuring above 6.0 within 24 hours and the resulting tsunami (230 feet high) swept up Valdez Arm carrying boats over 1 mile inland, and swept back carrying people, buildings and cars out to sea. The town of Valdez was destroyed and within 5 minutes, so too were the coastal towns of Seward and Cordova, both moving 46 feet south within minutes. It is hard to comprehend that kind of destruction. And the threat remains very current and very real. In 2002 the Denali Fault decided to take a turn, measuring 7.9 and offsetting land by 29 feet. We always hear about "the big one" hitting San Francisco and given its population the human toll could be tragically sizable, yet Alaska certainly seems to have problems of its own. We took a drive out to Earthquake Park where an entire community ended up in the sea. It was nice to get a bit of a visual on what we had read about, but in reality, all that remains today is a high bluff overlooking the mud flats of Cook Inlet. Not all that interesting. However, our next destination was a waterfront RV park in Seward so we were hoping things remained quiet.

Fortunately, while in Anchorage, and along most of the highway towards Seward we had pretty good wifi so I was able to check in and follow along with how things were going at the XXVI Latvian Song and Dance Festival in Riga. The Latvians need no synopsis but may themselves not even realize the festival has been included on UNESCO's list of Masterpieces of the Oral and Intangible Heritage of Humanity. Happening every 5 years and lasting about one week, it brings together Latvians from all parts of the world (although primarily from all regions of Latvia) to celebrate their culture, heritage and history through song and dance. Given this was the 100th year, the participants

(18,000+ dancers and 16,000+ singers) and spectators were out in record numbers. I knew that when I was really old and gray I would look back at that time and wish I had been there. Never mind "when I was old and gray." I wish that now. But to everyone who went and to everyone who sang and danced, "*Es dzīvoju jums līdzi ar visu sirdi.*" It was surreal to be sitting by the ocean in Seward, Alaska watching the final choral concert with those thousands and thousands of voices being broadcast live from Riga. With a lump in my throat and tears in my eyes, I had such a sense of pride knowing that in some small way, I too was a part of that amazing culture. I kept returning to all the Youtube posts, trying to recapture the moments. They are indescribable!

And Seward? Seward is described as "one of Alaska's most scenic locations." Well it's a good thing it is described that way, because I sure didn't see much of it. The drive along the Seward Highway (listed as one of America's most beautiful drives) was rainy with low-lying cloud the entire way so not much to ooh and aah about there. And our campsite directly on the water? Also a bust. We couldn't see across the bay (a fjord really), never mind see any mountains. We knew they were there because we had seen pictures, but all we had was rain and clouds. Not exactly Biblical forty days and forty nights type rain but pretty close, I'm sure. Non-stop heavy for the first two days and nights. And it wasn't just the precipitation that was depressing. Even rocks contributed to the overall sense of doom and gloom. Rocks, stones, gravel, sand, even the soil were an unappealing dark slate gray in colour, and when wet, turned an even darker charcoal hue. Together with the dark green of the trees and the oppressing clouds, it was enough to make you want to just pull the covers over your head and stay in bed. I'd had such great plans for kayaking past calving glaciers. Insert a big sigh here. We whiled away the hours by reading, watching other campers try to set up in the downpour, and at one point when things eased to a mere Irish mist, let Porter out to play in the ocean. Then, as if by some miracle, a short break on the third day. We scrambled to get the boats in the water and managed a brief 2 hours kayaking. It drizzled on and off but at least we could see the other shore. Staff at the campground (Miller's Landing) had a pat line about living in a rainforest but somehow, I just hadn't thought of Alaska in rainforest terms.

Seward itself (pronounced like "sewer" with a "d" added) is named after William Seward who was secretary of state in 1867 during Lincoln's presidency, and who negotiated the deal whereby the United States purchased Alaska from Russia at a cost of $7.2 million. Or about 2 cents per acre. Not a bad deal, although the Russians might disagree. Seward is also technically the starting point for the Iditarod, that extreme dogsled race that covers a distance of 1,049 miles in the dead of winter (okay early March), challenging both man and beast, all the way from Anchorage to Nome. But the race as we know it today only started in 1973. In reality, the Iditarod was just a system of trails (pack, sled, wagon and railroad) that had been blazed by the early gold miners, leading from Seward into the gold fields of central and western Alaska, enabling dog sleds to bring in mail and bring out gold to the ice free port in Resurrection Bay. It's always about the gold.

In retrospect, the dismal weather was a harbinger of things to come. My sister called to say that my Dad was in the hospital and things were not looking good. His health had been declining the past several years and that was no surprise given his age. But following Mom's death in March, it seems to me he lost his will to live. He said he would hang in there. He said he still had much to do. And he did. He was in the process of transcribing the handwritten journals he had kept as a young man fleeing war torn Europe, as well as the letters that he had exchanged with his parents as a young refugee in Canada, while they were still in displaced persons camps in Germany. And he was typing out over 100 love-letters that Mom had sent him when they were courting. He had kept them all. Whenever I called, I would ask him how things were progressing and he would say slowly, but that he was keeping busy. Yet during those conversations, I could hear that the old tenacious bulldog was gone. There were only flashes of his usual stubbornness and grit. Without Mom, he was lost. I booked the first flight home from Anchorage while John stayed behind to once again, pack up the yacht. I didn't make it in time to say good-bye. While waiting to board my flight, my sister called again to say that the man who had loomed so large in our lives was gone. Peacefully and on his own terms. Everything was always on his terms. For John, to drive home for the funeral from Seward, a distance of almost 6,800 kms, was too far and would take too long, but he managed to find a nice off-leash boarding facility for Porter in town and flew home as soon as he was able. And there we were again, four short months after Mom left us, going through another roller coaster of emotions and making the same arrangements. It was unreal. Following the funeral, John returned to Anchorage within a few days, and I stayed a bit longer to take care of a few practical matters and spent a lovely therapeutic cottage weekend with friends. There was still much adjusting to do.

I had hoped that upon my return to Seward the weather would have improved but if anything, it was worse. Adding to the alternating bouts of rain and drizzle, we now had fog and the dulcet tones of a foghorn. It was just dismal. The campground host (who was 83 years old) said he had not seen so rainy and cold a summer in 50 years. Just our luck. One afternoon things eased enough so that we were able drive over to Kenai National Park to check out Exit Glacier, one of the few glaciers in Alaska that are relatively easy to access via a short hiking trail. We took turns since Porter was with us and if we had not known before, we would certainly have known by the time we got to the trailhead, no dogs on trails in national parks! The constant reminders got very tedious. From where we parked the car to the Visitor Centre (a distance of about 50 yards), we were told by three separate park rangers, no dogs! Followed up with the usual b.s. about how his presence would disturb the wildlife – but we were welcome to walk him along the state park trails. I guess we were supposed to believe that wild animals know the difference between national and state park boundaries. I ultimately didn't get to see much of Seward although John assured me that it really was very beautiful on the one day of sunshine he had the privilege of experiencing.

Back at the yacht, I scrambled to re-schedule our remaining Alaska itinerary, opting to shorten our time in Denali and cancel the swing north to Fairbanks in an effort to keep the reservations we had for Juneau. Alaska is a popular place in the summer so spots for big rigs were hard to come by. But we managed to squeeze in a few days in Homer, and that was a good thing because Homer was a considerable improvement over Seward and partially restored my faith in Alaska. While I can't say it was total sunshine, we at least had periods of blue sky and could actually see some of the mountain tops. The temperature ranged from a balmy 55 to 59F (13 to 15 C), although it was considerably cooler out on the water.

Alaska really does have an interesting history, what with the Russians being the first white settlers to come ashore. They were incredibly brutal in their treatment of the indigenous population (what else in new?) but remnants of their early settlements can still be found, particularly in the little villages inhabited by the "Old Believers", settlers who split from the Russian Orthodox Church after it aligned itself more closely with Greek Orthodox in the 1650s. We drove to two such places, Nikolaevsk and Ninilchik, but could have probably saved the gas. Nikolaevsk, in particular, supposedly had the Samovar Café, serving a really good borscht. Well, one drive by was enough to convince us that this was one place we were not going to be having lunch. Actually, we drove by twice just to make sure it was the place recommended by the Lonely Planet travel guide, which is generally pretty reliable. Boy were they ever off the mark on that one. Located along a stretch of run-down homes that were spread out along a rural gravel road, it looked pretty much abandoned except for the neon "open" sign lit up in one grimy window. There were no cars in the parking area and no signs of life. It was hardly inviting. Ninilchik at least had a history. Settled in the 1820s by members of the Russian-American Company, it is amongst one of the oldest communities on the Kenai Peninsula. After Russia sold Alaska to the United States, many of the inhabitants stayed on and their descendants supposedly form the heart of this little community. I can't vouch for the size of that community since we didn't see any people, but there was a charming little Orthodox church at the top of a hill, looking out over Cook Inlet. The "village" itself was just a rambling collection of unpainted wood frame buildings, many of which looked uninhabited. There was a little gift shop we hesitantly went into, but it was run by an elderly woman who knew very little about the old Russians except to say that they just used the place during summer. Okay then. Back to Homer, the Halibut Fishing Capital of the World.

PORTER ENJOYING THE SPIT IN HOMER, ALASKA

If truth be told, I quite liked Homer. We were staying at a campground on The Spit and although it was really just a gravel parking lot, we were facing directly onto the water with beautiful mountains and glaciers across Kachemak Bay, so it was quite lovely. The Spit itself is about 4.5 miles long and geologists theorize it is the moraine of a long-retreated glacier. During the quake of '64, it dropped in elevation by 4 to 6 feet and since then, engineers and construction crews have been reinforcing some of the shoreline in an effort to prevent it from being completely washed away by ocean storms. It is rather touristy but in a cute instead of tacky sort of way, with numerous gift shops, small restaurants, and fishing and bear-watching charters all competing for tourist dollars during their relatively short tourist season. But while the season may lack longevity, the operators make up for it with their pricing. Everything was expensive. We wanted to kayak in the waters across the bay in and around Kachemak Bay State Park but that required a water taxi at a cost of $75.00 per person. Kind of steep for a few hours paddling. But the water was calm, and we saw numerous sea otters and bald eagles along the way. We also managed to secure a spot on a halibut fishing charter and while it was fun, it was not something I am likely to repeat. The boat held 22 of us anglers and took us 1-1/2 hours out to sea before we dropped our lines. Fishing for halibut is not difficult. They are a bottom feeding fish so all that is required is to sink your hook and wait. Nor are they a fighting fish, but they are dead-weight heavy. At least in my estimation. Hauling a 10-pound fish (in addition to the 2-pound lead sinker) up from a depth of 200 feet was exhausting. I can't imagine how the folks who bring in the 300-pound record holders do it! Apparently, when halibut first hatch, they swim in a vertical position, like fish normally do, but at some point become horizontal. The bottom side becomes white in colour while the top turns a mottled brown to act as camouflage. And their eyes move to the top of the camo side. Needless to say, they are not a pretty fish. We each caught our limit of two, the deck hands filleted them during the return voyage, arranged for flash freezing and voilà, halibut for dinner. However, once we factored in the cost of the trip, the cost of the fishing licence, and the cost of the freeze, we could just as easily have

bought some off the guys at the dock. But this was something that we did "for the experience" so no complaints, other than really sore muscles the next day. I'm not much of a sailor and had taken some Dramamine to be on the safe side and had no issues while on the boat, but later that night getting ready for bed, felt as if I was still out at sea, pitching and rolling. Not very pleasant.

CATCH OF THE DAY! IT WAS HARD WORK!

I didn't sleep well either and was quite tired when the alarm went off at 5:00am the next morning. We were going on a bear watching excursion that required us to check in at the airplane hangar at 6:00am. At least that is what we thought. We showed up at the appointed time only to be advised that the weather report indicated heavy fog at our destination so to come back at 9:30. This was troublesome since we had arranged (with some difficulty) for a dog walker to go to the coach and take Porter out for a walk twice during the day. But it worked out okay and the dog walker texted a picture showing all was good with the brown menace. We flew off in a six-seater Cessna 206, taking off and landing on several beaches in Lake Clark National Park, about a one-hour flight time from Homer. Considering my discomfort with flying, I think I did admirably well. And the take offs and landings were much smoother than anticipated. From a photography perspective, the weather could not have been much worse. Heavy cloud cover, flat light and a fine mist to coat the lens every time I lifted the camera. But the bears! Oh my! These were the Alaskan Brown Bears, called Grizzlies in Canada and the lower 48. Huge creatures to be respected and feared, although not as huge as the sub-species Kodiak bears on Kodiak Island. Lake

Clark and Katmai are the only two places in the word where humans can get close to these magnificent creatures without being in any real danger. The bears in these parks have been protected from hunting for so long, they do not view us as a threat. Nor do they associate us with food or as a food source. The area is so isolated nobody lives there (although there are some wilderness lodges) and there are no garbage bins, dumps etc. to divert them from their natural diet. This diet consists primarily of clams that they dig out of the huge shallow, muddy bays, and sedge grasses from the meadows. Prior to our initial departure we had been instructed not to bring any food stuffs that might crumble or in some way be left behind and definitely no bear spray. (Funny story about tourists and bear spray to follow.) Upon landing and disembarking, we moved slowly in our group of six (keeping together in a pack so as to appear "large") to within 50 feet of them and then just crouched and watched. We had been kitted out with heavy-duty hip waders so other than possibly getting stuck in the mud, the danger level was pretty low. We watched as one sow with her cub dug for clams, another with two yearling cubs dined in a meadow and a third with two older cubs lazed around on a beach. There were many other bears off in the distance, but these three families were the highlights. At one point, a sow walked past another tourist group at a distance of not much more than ten feet, totally ignoring the clicking of the cameras. It was amazing! Yet despite their relative acceptance of our presence, safety cannot be taken for granted. In 1990 a young man by the name of Timothy Treadwell decided that these bears needed protecting and spent 13 summers camped out amongst them and basically living with them. All was good until 2003 when his girlfriend joined him for the summer and in October a large 23–year-old male decided he'd had enough and attacked them. Treadwell's video camera had been turned on at the time and although there is no video, 6 minutes of audio captured their screams as they were mauled to death. And partially eaten. There is no definite explanation as to why after so many years the bear turned but some naturalists suggest that October is a dangerous time of year when the bears are trying to fatten up for winter hibernation and become more aggressive in seeking out food sources. A movie, "*Grizzly Man*", was made of Treadwell's life and experiences but I'm not sure I want to see it.

A RELAXING DAY AT THE BEACH — LAKE CLARK NATIONAL PARK.

And then there is the sheer stupidity of some tourists. It never ceases to amaze. People have been scared silly about entering bear country, so they equip themselves with all manner of defensive items including "bear bells", supposedly so as to make noise and thus not startle any bears. In reality these are just golf ball size jingle bells that neither man nor beast can hear over a rushing stream. Completely useless but some entrepreneur somewhere is making lots of money. The running joke is that these bells are constantly being found in bear scat. And then there is bear spray. A capsicum-based agent that comes in aerosol containers, it is used as a diversion tactic to temporarily blind and distract an aggressive bear, thus facilitating a head start on hopefully a quick and successful getaway. To be of any use, you'd have to be in fairly close proximity to said aggressive bear, so easy access is obviously an issue, yet naïve hiking enthusiasts tuck the bottles neatly away into their backpacks. But the anecdote that takes the cake is that some tourists were actually spraying themselves with the bear spray, à la mosquito repellent style, prior to setting out on their hikes. The mind boggles. I cannot think of anything else to say.

By month's end we had not finished with Alaska and planned on exploring Denali and Juneau next, hoping the weather gods would be kinder during August.

28.

LOVE-HATE RELATIONSHIPS

WE WERE HEARTLESSLY DENIED ENTRY TO THE 30% CLUB. That marginal figure represents the number of people who, at great time, effort and expense, made their way to Denali National Park and Preserve and were fortunate enough to gaze in awe at The Great One. Also known as Mt. Denali. Formerly known as Mt. McKinley. The highest peak in all of North America. The rest of us? Too bad, so sad. Yet when planning the Alaska leg of our adventure, I never thought we would be shut out. Flipping through numerous travelogues, happily drinking the kool-aid, and imagining all the wonderful things we were going to do, it never occurred to me our main goal would not be realized. In my mind we would ride our bikes along the only access road with bears and wolves nipping at our heels, hike in the tundra while admiring the soaring peaks all around, take numerous pictures of caribou and mountain flowers under a sparkling blue sky, all with Mt. Denali visible at every turn. Maybe even take in a flight seeing tour and land on the mountain itself. Talk about crash and burn. The reality was practically heartbreaking, and for this I blame Alaska tourism. I have come to believe that every picture ever taken in that blasted state was taken on the one and only day of sunshine they had in an entire year. Maybe even two years.

In all fairness, weather is something no one can control, but come on! We had scheduled an entire week in Denali, hedging our bets that on at least one of those days, the mountain would be out. Nope. Not even close. It rained every single day, and when it wasn't pouring, it was drizzling, and when it wasn't drizzling, it was misting with low clouds obscuring any scenic views. That is why the rest of the continent was aflame. All the precipitation was following us around Alaska! We did our best to make lemonade. Denali National Park itself is over 6 million acres in size with a negligible 92-mile gravel road leading part way into the interior. Only the first 15 miles are accessible by private vehicle. After that, a shuttle bus must be booked. That in and of itself is not unique. Many national parks, in an effort to limit traffic congestion, and preserve some sense of pristine wilderness, have similar regulations. Zion and Grand Canyon come to mind. But the difference in Denali is that here they charge you big bucks for the privilege of riding on what is essentially a school bus. And there are no other choices. You either pay or you don't go. There are several bus options to choose from, ranging from $200.00 per person for the entire 92-mile route in and out, to $60.00 per if going as far as Eielson Visitor Centre, where supposedly the views of Mt. Denali are amongst the best. We chose the Eielson Route which took 8 hours return and other than seeing some of the local wildlife (4 moose, 1 wolf, 1 grizzly sow with 2 cubs off in the distance and 3 caribou) it was not really worth it. Blame the weather. Not a mountain peak in sight. And the Eielson Visitor Centre was so sparse both in exhibits and information there was little to do other than wait for the announcement to re-board for the return journey. We also had the misfortune of having 26 members of a Polish tour group on our bus and not understanding English (and accompanied by a tour guide who did not translate for them), they constantly ignored the rules that are in place to protect wildlife (eg. no hands or arms out the bus windows). They annoyed our driver to such a point that he simply drove away from one great photo op – a beautiful caribou walking towards us in the centre of the road. To be fair, he did warn these passengers to get their arms back inside the bus, but to no avail. Needless to say, I didn't get any good shots.

Considering the size of the park, there are very few marked hiking trails (only a handful along those first 15 miles) and visitors are encouraged to hop off the money bus at any point and forge their own path into the tundra or along one of the numerous braided creek beds. Quite a departure from the usual "stay on the marked trail" mantra of all other national parks. Given Denali is known for its high concentration of grizzlies and wolves, we didn't see too many people choosing this option. Then again, maybe nobody wanted to pay ridiculous amounts of money (in addition to the park entrance fee) just to go for a walk in the rain. One day, we drove the Jeep to the end of the 15-mile private vehicle limit and optimistically started hiking out along the marked Alpine Ridge trail, a fairly strenuous climb, hoping the weather would hold. But after 45 minutes, drizzle turned to downpour, so we retraced our soggy steps, walked a two-mile loop along the Savage River and then packed it in. It just wasn't worth it. And the most frustrating thing? The RV park where we were staying had on-site dog daycare so we had time do all the hiking we wanted! Sometimes you just can't win. Another day, we visited the park's sled dog kennels and watched a short demonstration on how these dogs run. They were beautiful animals, quite friendly and somewhat larger than those used for the

Iditarod. The ranger explained that the Denali dogs were working dogs, used for patrolling the park and for hauling supplies to different outposts during the winter, while the Iditarod dogs were strictly for racing. Somewhat like the difference between Clydesdales and thoroughbreds, although these guys were a combination of Malamutes, Samoyeds and Siberian Huskies. They have 31 dogs in the kennels with over 80 volunteers who come to walk them during the summer months when there is little sled-pulling work to be done, and it was heartening to see how well cared for they were. When they reach retirement age (generally around 8), or just aren't cut out for sled pulling, they are usually adopted by one of the volunteers.

And Mt. Denali itself? At 20,320 feet (that is almost 4 miles) it is taller than Mt. Everest, keeping in mind there is a difference between the "tallest" mountain and the "highest" mountain. "Tallest" is measured from base to summit while "highest" is measured to the highest point above sea level. So Denali, with its base sitting 2,000 feet above sea level, rises another 18,000 feet, while Everest sitting 17,000 above sea level, rises another 12,000 feet. Apparently size matters. But tallest or not, we didn't get to see it. Rangers advised that the mountain is usually visible one out of three days, but not in any predictable way. Sometimes it is out for a week straight and then remains obscured for an entire month. They don't advertise that in any Alaska tourism brochures! We did our best to stay optimistic but after five days were forced to accept reality. Seven more days of rain were forecast, so we threw in the towel and have classified Denali as a "do-over." Not sure when. Not sure how. But we are going to see that mountain! Sadly, as we were getting ready to leave, we heard that a small sightseeing plane had crashed on one of Denali's slopes killing the pilot and his four Polish tourists. What are the odds that they were the same people as on our bus tour? And what was that plane doing up there anyway? Visibility was zero! Search and rescue had to wait several days for a short weather window in order to assess the situation and came away with the recommendation that the bodies and plane remain where they lay. They were sitting on too precarious an angle on a narrow ridge, just above a crevasse (and slowly sliding towards it) and any attempts at retrieval would have been too dangerous for rescue crews. The investigation into what happened was still ongoing. I'm definitely re-evaluating the whole "land on the mountain" scenario for when we return.

We finished packing up the coach and made our way towards Haines. Not that the weather got any better along the way. It poured all day and all night and then all the following day too, only stopping momentarily near Tok. The entire drive from Denali to Fairbanks and then towards Delta Junction and on to Haines Junction and eventually Haines itself was neither exciting nor picturesque, although maybe it was. We had no way of knowing. Occasional glimpses of distant mountains were all we got. In many places there were miles and miles of black spruce, one of the few things that can grow on permafrost, and after a while, even their scrawny silhouettes started to look pretty. We cut alongside Kluane National Park in the Yukon and while it is supposed to have some lovely hikes we pressed on to Haines, spending a few soggy days there, before boarding the Alaska Marine Highway ferry to Juneau.

I was really starting hate Alaska. Nothing but rain, rain, rain, day and night. And not the sprinkle of a passing cloud type rain, nor the deluge of a passing summer thunder-storm type rain. This was unrelenting, never-ending, heavy rain without mercy. And when it paused, it was only to allow the oppressive dark clouds to sink even lower and envelop everything in a misty fog. And it was cold. Around 54F/12C. I wanted to go home. If not home, then at least back to Death Valley where warmth and sun were guaranteed. John said I was imagining things, but I swear it was even starting to feel damp inside the coach. Although having an electric fireplace that kicked off a fair bit of heat helped prevent total depression and despair from setting in.

Just outside of Haines, we camped in a beautiful state recreation area (Chilkoot Lake) that is known for its abundance of bears (both Grizzly and black) that fish for salmon along the banks of the Chilkoot River where it flows into the Lynn Canal (really a fjord). Each day scores of fishermen in hip-waders would be thigh deep in the rushing river, competing with bald eagles and supposedly the occasional bear, hoping to snag one of the spawning salmon as they made their way upstream. Going for walks along the road that followed the river, I didn't see any bears but there was certainly lots of bear scat. Fresh bear scat. Every morning, a few new piles. So we knew they were around. And on our last day, while driving out, we finally saw one. A 3-year-old Grizzly making himself at home on the fishing weir, jumping in and out of the water in his efforts to catch some lunch. And he succeeded, carrying a plump salmon off into the forest to dine in privacy away from the prying eyes and clicking cameras of us tourists. Normally, there were parks staff sitting out on the weir counting and measuring the number and types of salmon coming up-river but I guess the bear waited until they had gone on break so he'd have the place to himself. It's an interesting project they have set up there. The Chilkoot River Weir Project has been running since 1976 when someone finally caught on to the fact that there was something wrong with the salmon stocks on the west coast. Could it possibly be the countless fish canneries that had been operating unchecked in virtually every inlet since the 1800s had finally exhausted a seemingly inexhaustible supply? More on the salmon fishery later.

One afternoon, we took the kayaks out onto Chilkoot Lake and although the water was calm, it was very drizzly with low misty clouds obscuring the glacier at the far end so that outing was rather short lived. There were lots of bald eagles around, with the Haines' resident population being about 350. However, come November, when many of the other Alaskan rivers have frozen, 3,500 of them gather along the still flowing Chilkoot watching for fish. Residents say there are so many, they sit like vultures in the trees. Now that would be a sight to see.

Haines itself is a very small town with a modest historical/cultural museum and a few shops but nothing to really write home about. Supposedly the surrounding mountains are the spectacular drawing card but... okay, no need to belabour the point. We didn't see them. The town also has a Hammer Museum, yes really, dedicated to man's first tool. Supposedly it contains 1,800 artefacts but we just weren't quite that desperate to entertain ourselves. Then again, it might have been interesting to ask the proprietor for a demonstration on how the implements work. One day we finally had a break in the clouds and while strolling around town, John came across a fellow in his woodworking shop/gallery, carving an eagle. They got to talking and the next thing I knew, John was signed up for a three-hour wood carving lesson. So I went kayaking by myself back at Chilkoot Lake. There were patches of blue sky and the water was fairly calm when I set out, and following some local advice for bear watching, headed around Bear Point to a quiet, sheltered bay. And sure enough, I briefly saw three black bears as they thrashed their way through the brush along the shoreline. They were moving fairly quickly so no time for pictures, but they looked pretty big. Being out by myself, I stayed fairly close to shore, but half-way down the lake had the bright idea to cross over to the other side and check out a very tall, narrow waterfall. I was about a third of the way across when the skies darkened, the wind picked up, and fair-sized waves started coming at me broadside. This was not good. Forget the waterfall. I angled the kayak and paddled as hard as I could. My arms were aching by the time I reached the other side and then still had to make my way into a headwind, back to the boat launch area. I will admit to being a bit scared. That water is glacier fed and very cold. Tipping would have been very bad.

It may have been nice to stay in Haines a few days longer but when planning this leg of the journey, we had reserved a spot on the Alaska Marine Highway ferry Fairweather quite some time earlier. Haines to Juneau, and two weeks later, Juneau to Skagway. Our original plan had been to leapfrog our way down the entire Alaska coast by ferry all the way to Prince Rupert, getting off to explore the numerous communities along the way, but that entailed several 8+ hour crossings where Porter would have had to remain in the coach by himself. No dogs allowed off the car deck and no people allowed on the car deck. That was not going to work for us. So we opted for these few shorter sailings with the thought that we may return to do the entire stretch some day on our own. Perhaps even as far as Unalaska/Dutch Harbour. Reservations were not necessarily required but given the length of the coach we wanted to make sure they could accommodate us. Boarding room is measured by linear feet. The Alaska Marine Highway system is really quite outstanding. And a lifeline for many communities that can only be accessed by air or by water. No connecting roads up in this neck of the woods. Alaska Marine is the road.

The Fairweather was true to its name. It was a great sailing day with the best weather we'd had to date and while the skies were not exactly cloud free, there was a fair bit of sunshine and gorgeous views of huge glaciers, soaring snow-capped peaks and green forests throughout the 2-1/2 hour ride. (The Fairweather is a high-speed ferry. Normally the trip takes about 4 hours.) And while I wouldn't say I fell in love with Alaska, I was willing to give it another chance. In many ways the coastline was similar to British Columbia's except everything seemed higher and the glaciers bigger. Upon arrival, the ferry docked in Auke Bay, a short distance from downtown Juneau, where all the huge cruise ships come in. And thank goodness for that. On some days there were four behemoths moored up and dwarfing the town's modest sized buildings. Juneau itself has a population of just over 32,000, and when all the ships arrive, they can add another 10,000 people! The cruise ship business up there is insane. Some residents say it is trying, and to some degree succeeding, in turning Alaska into a Disneyland of the north, albeit with a gold rush theme. This is how one Haines local explained it:

Only the odd ship goes into Haines, but the industry practically owns Skagway, as well as half of the waterfront in Juneau and parts of Wrangell and Petersburg. And with much of Skagway owned by these companies (except for the National Parks Service areas), they naturally advertise and encourage their passengers to frequent certain establishments and buy "local" souvenirs. The town is promoted as a great destination to re-live America's gold rush past, complete with saloons and good-time girls. The cruise companies have little invested in Haines, so when ships do stop there, passengers are urged to take a day trip on the high-speed ferry to Skagway for a "genuine" Alaska experience. There may be some truth to this. Strolling along the waterfront in Juneau, the first two blocks were side-by-side jewellery shops with sparkling window displays selling diamond, tanzanite, ammolite, and other semi-precious stone rings, pendants and charms. With accompanying specials of "free gift" to cruise ship passengers just to go in and look. Do people really go on these cruises simply to get off, walk fifty feet and buy sub-standard gemstones? It was only after a couple of blocks that we started seeing "locally owned and operated" signs in the shop windows, where there were some incredible Tlingit (pronounced klink-it), Haida and Tsimshian artworks for sale, as well as Inuvialuit and Yupik from the far north. Sculptures, carvings, weavings and the like.

Coastal Northwest art is very distinctive with its black and red colours depicting various creatures – eagle, raven, bear, wolf – using what is referred to as formline style, where carved or painted lines are fluidly curved and interconnected. I tried to understand the difference between a Haida eagle vs. a Tlingit eagle, but the variation is so nuanced that apparently sometimes you just have to know the artist's background in order to tell. And if there is a modern or stylized twist to it, forget it. Although it is the Tsimshian who incorporate blue paint into some of their work. Or maybe it was the Tlingit. I forget. There was so much I wanted to buy. Just that small matter of price acted as a deterrent. Okay, I did succumb and purchased one fantastic Tlingit panel carving by a local Juneau artist, but exercised admirable restraint the rest of the time. The entire coastal northwest was the traditional homeland of these three tribes whose art, music, traditions, ceremonies and stories are similar, but interestingly, not their language. Because they interacted, traded and fought with each other, there are some words in common, but not enough to carry on a conversation. I suppose similar to the Latvian *labdien* and the Lithuanian *labas dienas*, but there the dialogue ends. I did learn a few fitting Tlingit phrases though. *Séew daak wusitán* – It is raining. And *Séew daak satánx* – It rains regularly. Official estimates are that Juneau gets rain 230 days per year, although the locals maintain the number is closer to 300. I believe the locals. We were in the Juneau area for 14 days and only had 4 without some type of precipitation. Had the weather been good, 14 days would have been too long, but as it was, it was just enough for us to engage in some of the outdoor activities we had planned. Plus, being cold and rainy does have a positive side. We were spared the dreaded Alaska mosquitoes. Even they couldn't tolerate the weather and we didn't see even one. I'm really trying to be a "glass-half-full" type here.

Like most places in Alaska, Juneau owes its existence to gold. The location was originally a Tlingit fishing village but when gold was discovered in 1880, the rush was on. Across the Gastineau Channel on Douglas Island, the Treadwell Mine was once the largest gold mine in the world and only its 1917 massive slide/cave-in ended its reign. Today, Juneau's primary industry is government, followed closely by tourism, with some fishing and one mine still in operation. And while the population, as mentioned, is over 32,000, that number fluctuates by season. A full third of the inhabitants leave at the end of September when the tourists stop coming, and don't return again until May. A migration of sorts, if you will. That seems to be the norm for much of Alaska.

And this chapter's Trivial Pursuit question, "What U. S. state capital city is named after a Canadian?" That's right. Joseph Juneau, born in Quebec, Canada in 1833. Actually, Sitka used to be the capital, but lost it to Juneau in 1906. And Juneau almost lost it to Willow in the 1970s. Plans were underway for the big move but once the actual cost was figured out, the decision was reversed in 1982. Why they didn't consider Anchorage or Fairbanks is beyond me.

Our home for our two weeks in the Juneau area was a campground at Mendenhall Lake in Tongass National Forest. The setting was wonderful but surprisingly, there were hardly any other campers. Of the 70 sites, only 6 were occupied. This was very odd (almost creepy) especially since it was relatively inexpensive yet had full hook-ups with 50-amp service. The stumbling block seemed to be the price of accessibility. Getting to Juneau with any kind of vehicle requires a ferry ride and depending on the size of that vehicle and the point of departure, it can be quite costly. Our short Haines-Juneau-Skagway jaunt was over $1,000, so coming from further afield is decidedly pro-hibitive, especially for the average one-week family camping vacation. Add on glacial flight-seeing trips or boating excursions and things can get quite pricey. That said, the campground was right on Mendenhall Lake, so Mendenhall Glacier was easily visible. We could put our kayaks in the water and paddle across the lake or drive a short distance to the Visitor's Centre and launch from there, cutting down on the paddling distance by about a mile. Being Alaska's most accessible glacier, the Mendenhall is Juneau's big draw. People say if you go to Juneau and don't see the Mendenhall, it is like going to Rome and not seeing the Coliseum. That may have been true 30 years ago, but the picture has changed dramatically, and no one is publicizing that too much. Given the warming period the earth is currently experiencing, the glacier has retreated considerably over the past 30 years and scientists estimate that within the next 25, it will have retreated to the point where it will no longer be visible from the Visitor's Centre. I asked what they plan on doing when that happens and was advised they hope to build a bridge across the Mendenhall River and transport people by boat across the lake. In my humble opinion, that has disaster written all over it. There were already so many tour buses disgorging cruise ship passengers it would be nothing short of a never-ending ferry service, disrupt-ing a beautifully quiet and serene wilderness and traumatizing the numerous bears that fish for spawning salmon in the surrounding streams. But maybe the cruise ship industry has already added the glacier and lake to its list of Alaskan purchases and its full steam ahead. I'm glad we had the chance to see it when we did.

The Mendenhall is around 13 miles long and is considered a "valley" glacier, in that it calves off into Mendenhall Lake (as opposed to "tidewater" that calves into the ocean or "hanging" that literally hangs over a cliff), so we set out in the kayaks to see how close we could get. In fact, we went out on three separate days under three different weather systems. Cloud and drizzle one day, sunny the next, and overcast on the third. The water in the lake was incredibly silty, but it was relatively calm every day with the odd smallish iceberg floating by. Actually, I should use proper iceberg terminology. There were growlers and bergy-bits. "Growlers" are small pieces of floating ice, less than 6.6 feet long, while "bergy-bits" are bigger but less than 15 feet, and icebergs are the ones that ruined the party on the Titanic. I broke off a few pieces of one growler and could only marvel at the crystal clarity of the ice. And the glacier itself? Fantastic! I cannot find words to describe the colour. Bright blue? Turquoise blue? Azure blue? Ice blue? Robin's egg blue? Sky blue? Aquamarine blue? All of the above. It redefined the colour "blue". Neither pictures nor words can capture it. And when we were there on the cloudy day, the blue was an even deeper shade. And where does this incredible blue colour come from? It's a combination of air, water and light. When snow originally falls, the snowflakes, in their beautiful and varied shapes are 80% air, and that air reflects white light back to our eyes. As the snow settles, the air is compressed and the snowflakes start losing their star-like crystals, becoming more like rounded grains of rice. And as more snow falls, the grains are further compressed, reducing further the amount of air between them. Over time, these compacted grains form a solid mass of ice and when light hits them, it is refracted inside the ice with only the blue spectrum transmitted back to our eyes. That's the mechanics of it. Why the shade of blue is of such an unworldly hue, I have no idea.

PADDLING PAST BIG BLUE...

One day we kayaked along the face of the glacier, keeping in mind that we were pushing the envelope a bit since some unexpected calving could ruin the day. But no issues. We took out at a rocky beach off to one side – a popular spot for small tour groups to start their glacier walks – and felt quite safe. Mind you, the tour folks were kitted out with crampons, harnesses, helmets, ropes and poles but I think that was a bit of overkill considering they didn't go further than fifty feet out onto the surface. It may

PADDLING TOWARDS MENDENHALL GLACIER.

look expedition-like in their photos, but I wonder if they felt a bit foolish when we walked by in just our hiking boots. Although in retrospect, crampons might have been helpful. Scrambling along the moraines was a bit tricky with fairly precarious footing, and in some places, we realized we were actually walking on gravel covered sections of the glacier itself, but we managed to make our way along one side to some ice caves without incident. If the face of the glacier was fantastic, the caves were even more so. We crawled part way into one, although most of the bottom was covered by a shallow lake from the melting ice as it dripped from the ceiling, and with the sun moving in and out of the clouds, the light inside the cave constantly changed. I've never seen anything like it. A second cave, a bit further along, was not quite as inviting. It sloped steeply down into some unknown depth and in places the ice was so dark as to be almost black. We just peeked into that one. I never thought I'd take so many pictures of what is really just ice. The most mesmerizing ice I have ever seen.

Seeking more glaciers and bergs, we booked a full-day tour on the Captain Cook, a 65-foot, 50-passenger vessel that took us out into Tracy Arm Fjord, a waterway that ends at the Sawyer tidewater glacier, with one branch reaching the South Sawyer. Some say that Tracy Arm is like Glacier Bay National Park without the big cruise ships and without the big price tag. I can't agree or disagree on that assessment but what we saw more than exceeded our expectations. The day started out with low cloud and fog, so some of the larger icebergs at the mouth of the fjord just appeared out of the mist. They were captivating. And again, that indescribable blue. The cruise up the fjord could have been better if the soaring cliffs would have revealed themselves, but the low wispy clouds did add a primeval air. Judging by the growlers, bergy-bits and bergs floating in the water, there had been some calving before our arrival, but we didn't get to see that phenomenon. The glaciers were impressive none-the-less. Certainly higher, bluer and more jagged than the Mendenhall. And on the ice floes closer to the glacier itself, numerous seals lazed about, having found themselves a safe haven from the predatory orcas. And once again, I took way too many pictures. I couldn't help myself. By the time we made our way back out of the fjord, the clouds had lifted, and on the ride back to Juneau we saw a couple of humpback whales diving (with their classic tail in the air moves) and a few orcas in the distance. An almost perfect day. My only complaint? It was freezing! The air temperature alone registered 43F/6C. I have no idea what it was with the wind chill on a moving boat. All I know is I spent most of August wearing gloves, a headband covering my ears and long underwear beneath my hiking pants. This year will be remembered as the summer that never was.

There was still more glacier viewing to be had. The Juneau Icefield covers approximately 1,500 square miles reaching well into Canada and feeds 40 large glaciers and about 100 smaller ones. There was no way to see them all, but we were going to try for a few more. This time, we booked a flight out to Taku Lodge on one of their DeHavilland Otter floatplanes. Perhaps I was gradually getting over my fear of flying. No. Not really. I just wanted to see more glaciers. Built in 1923 as a hunting and fishing camp, the lodge is on the Taku River, opposite Hole-in-the-Wall glacier. It has changed hands numerous times over the years and has been used for raising sled dogs, as a private retreat, and as a tourist resort. Today it functions strictly as a daytime "look and lunch" outfit. And I can't say which I enjoyed more. The looking or the lunching. We flew out of Juneau harbour on a 40-minute sight-seeing jaunt over the mountains and over several glaciers that looked exactly as they are often described – wide rivers of ice. The Taku was the most impressive, being the world's deepest and thickest. At one point, the pilot flew a bit closer to where it had calved within the past hour and from the air it looked as if pieces of bright blue glass had shattered into the water. Once at the lodge, lunch consisted of freshly caught Taku River salmon grilled over a smoky alder wood fire. Delicious. Apparently the resident bear thought so as well. We had lingered in the dining room after most of the other guests had gone on a short hike, when looking out the window I saw a large black bear casually stroll over to the BBQ area, get up on his haunches and lick clean the grill. The staff were neither surprised nor concerned, saying he did this quite often. I am of two minds on this. On the one hand, it was very entertaining, and I managed to get some great pictures. On the other hand, the 11th commandment is, "Thou shalt not feed wildlife." Everywhere we had been, the mantra, "A fed bear is a dead bear" had been drilled into our heads. Once bears associate food with humans, it is a short descent into decreased fear and increased familiarity. Sooner or later, there is bear/human conflict and the bear always loses. I suppose given that the lodge is quite isolated and 40 minutes by air from Juneau, the risk is rather low, but still...

The weather gradually improved until one day we had completely blue skies. And just like in a cyclical domestic violence relationship, all was, if not forgotten, at least forgiven. Alaska was back in my good books. On that one perfectly sunny day, we hiked up Mount Roberts, a fairly steep climb that started just north of town, increased 1,800 feet in 2 miles, and offered great views up, down and across the Gastineau Channel making all my huffing and puffing worthwhile. The less ambitious can take a tram that runs from the centre of town and terminates at the same location, but we figured a walk in the woods might be nice. At the top, there was a small wilderness centre, cafe, and naturally, a gift shop showcasing local native crafts. The tram is owned by Goldbelt, a Tlingit corporation that was founded as a result of the Alaska Native Claims Settlement. They opened for business in 1996 and have been running a successful operation ever since. In large part, that success is due to the tram's easy access point, a short 100-foot stroll from the cruise ship dock. And there was no mistaking the cruise ship passengers as they trundled off the tram at the top of the mountain in their bright white running shoes, plastic enclosed identification tags dangling from lanyards around their necks, heading straight for the gift shop. Okay, a few stopped to admire the view and a few actually hiked several hundred feet further along the trail, but most were content to stay within the relative safety of the viewing platform. The round-trip tram ride was $32, but if you hiked up and purchased something in the gift shop, the ride down was free. Since Porter was with us, we hiked back down as well, only learning later that he would have been allowed on the downhill ride. This reasoning made no sense to me whatsoever. Why not uphill too? We also learned later that given Juneau's gold mining history, the inside of Mt. Roberts is laced with over 100 miles of tunnels on 13 levels. I started wondering about the stability of the whole thing and had a vision of one of those glass enclosed criss-crossed ant farms that junior naturalists like to get for their birthdays. Just waiting for a collapse. Earlier in the week, we had driven across the Gastineau Channel onto Douglas Island to check out what was left of the Treadwell Mine, but there was little to see except rotting pilings of what used to be a huge wharf, and a gritty "sand" beach from all the pulverized tailings. Porter had a blast, happy to be running around in the water once again.

Being in Alaska, we had to of course indulge in some King Crab. Tracy's Crab Shack, a very casual eatery on the wharf, offered 3-pound buckets of the gigantic legs so what the heck. How filling can they be? Despite our best efforts, we didn't manage to finish even one bucket between the two of us. We are weak sauce. But it was interesting to learn a little bit about the crabbing industry, apparently one of the more dangerous occupations in North America, with fatalities being quite frequent. At least that is what the tv show *Deadliest Catch*, that showcases the inherent dangers, says. I've never watched it but being a reality show, it must be true. At Tracy's we learned that the crab pots they use weigh between 700 and 800 pounds, and some crab boats carry up to 250 pots. The pots are baited with herring or cod and lowered with huge hydraulic systems to the ocean floor. One or two days later, they are pulled back up and the catch is sorted, measured and held in seawater tanks until the boat gets back to shore where it unloads its prized cargo for our dining pleasure. That was certainly one very positive aspect of coastal Alaska – access to fresh, local seafood. Although this is where a bit of controversy comes in.

We saw many shop signs along the theme of wild salmon good, farmed salmon bad, and restaurants seemed to serve only the wild stuff. Locals with their fishing poles were at or in virtually every stream, and for those who don't fish, wild salmon was even available for purchase at the local Costco. I'm all for walking on the wild side, but that is not very easy to do when most of us live so far away from the source. I have certainly never seen fresh, wild coho at any Toronto Costco! That said, salmon stocks on the west coast are in not much better shape than cod stocks on the east coast. We briefly toured a salmon hatchery where each year millions of fry are raised and released in an effort to reverse the plummeting numbers and thus enhance future opportunities for commercial and sport fishers alike. But that involves a bit of "farming" as well, since smolt (baby salmon) are kept in saltwater pens for one to three months until they have imprinted on a specific location. They have to be fed something. The theory is that by returning to spawn at the hatchery, pressure on true wild salmon spawning in streams will be limited. Yet despite these efforts, most will still fall prey to other larger fish, wading birds, raptors, bears and humans, and never return to continue the life cycle. We actually had a close-up view of that interrupted cycle back at Mendenhall Lake where a viewing platform has been built alongside the Mendenhall River. Numerous Sockeye salmon had returned to spawn and it was interesting to watch them, as well as the black bears that knew exactly where and when to show up. From a distance of about 20 feet (on the raised boardwalk), I watched as one mama polished off her catch, refusing to share it with her cub. Apparently he had to learn how to fish for himself.

We left Juneau on yet another soggy day and boarded the Fairweather again for the 2-hour ride to Skagway. Fortunately, Skagway was not quite as dire as Haines residents had predicted although it too had the gem-stone hawkers, male and female alike. They stood in the doorways of their shops hoping to engage customers with their free samples and, "Come on in and take a look" invitations. I couldn't help but think that there was a similarity between them, and the historic photos of the prostitutes who tried to entice customers into their cribs in virtually the same buildings, 120 years earlier. Only the merchandise differed. Skagway certainly had more to see than Haines, what with its

Klondike Goldrush National Historic Park status, but it was not as diverse as Juneau. And I don't mean diverse in the politically correct way. Rather, Juneau just had more variety by way of museums, restaurants and shops. No one can deny the role Skagway played during the gold rush, and many of the buildings have been saved, restored and/or reconstructed to reflect that period in history when people went completely insane in their efforts to reach the goldfields of the Yukon. The town was a major jumping off point, and it was from there that so many started their arduous and at times deadly treks along the infamous Chilkoot Trail en route to Dawson City. Some opted for White Pass that was slightly shorter but not any better. In fact, one stampeder who had traversed both said, "One was hell and the other damnation. Regardless of which one you choose you will wish you had taken the other." Yet off they went. And it was here that Jeff "Soapy" Smith, the leading bunco man of his time, plied his trade and deprived so many of their life savings going out to and/or coming back from the Yukon. He really was a very nasty piece of work but in keeping with America's fascination with crime figures, has been made into a somewhat if not romantic figure, at least a fascinating one. While his grave at the local Skagway cemetery is rather neglected, his gambling/bunco parlor has been restored by the parks service to look exactly as it did when he lived there. The daily non-stop tours are always booked up. And the honest fellow who shot him? He has a large granite monument at his place of eternal rest, erected by the grateful townspeople of 1898, but today no one has a clue as to where he lived or what happened to his stuff. Most would be hard pressed to even know his name. Soapy's story goes like this. At the time of the gold rush, Alaska had no laws. Despite having purchased it in 1867, the U.S. government had not seen fit to enact any legislation that would ensure any sort of legal system. No police, no courts, no judges. This was a bonanza for early organized crime. When all the thousands and thousands of fortune seekers descended on Skagway, they were easy targets for people like Smith. He had over 200 confederates and during the winter of 1897, he ran the town. But after robbing one stampeder too many, some of the townspeople formed a vigilante group and decided to take action. A shoot-out between Soapy and local engineer Frank Reid, resulted with Soapy being killed outright and Reid dying of his injuries 12 days later. But other than the National Park Service run historical buildings (of which there are only a dozen or so), and the White Pass/Yukon Route railway (more on that later) the town truly is one big outdoor tourist mall catering to the cruise ship crowd who wander aimlessly in and out of the various shops along the main street, purchasing Alaska T-shirts and other soon-to-be-forgotten trinkets. With so much natural beauty around, you would think they'd want to get out and see some of it. Nope.

On one of our two sunny days, we decided to tackle a segment of the Chilkoot Trail. We met 6 people doing the 3 – 5 day through-hike (all 33 miles, across the border into Canada and on to Bennett Lake) and only a handful of day trippers like ourselves, going as far as Finnegan's Point and back. Other than a steep and rocky climb at the beginning, the trail was quite flat, paralleling the Taiya River most of the way. Lots of fresh bear scat here and there, but no bears. At least none that we saw. Apparently the hike gets nasty after the first day, especially crossing the actual Chilkoot Pass, but that wasn't on our agenda. However, it was sobering to sit for a while on the banks of the river contemplating what life must have been like for those desperate souls as they set up camp at the very location where we ate lunch and Porter played in the water. There are no reminders of their passing save but a few photographs of moustachioed men with grim expressions standing by their white canvass tents. Then again, I have little sympathy for them after reading about how they treated their animals. Thousands upon thousands of horses, mules, oxen and dogs were starved, beaten and overworked, literally to death, all for the sake of getting to the gold. And when the animals died, the would-be miners just went out and bought more to repeat the horrid dance all over again. It was sickening. I wish I had never seen those photographs. There are just some things you can't unsee.

But it wasn't all doom and gloom. One other draw that gave Skagway an edge over Haines was the narrow gage White Pass/Yukon Route Railroad. Built in 1898 to carry supplies during the Goldrush, it ran from Skagway to Whitehorse, in some areas literally paralleling the White Pass Trail of old. Only 3 feet wide, it travels through some incredibly beautiful scenery and visitors can take a short 3-hour round trip to White Pass (at the Canadian border) and back. So we did. And the scenery did not disappoint. We finally had a great weather day and were able to see the expansive mountain tops (some with glaciers), wide valleys and deep gorges. Although chugging over the wooden trestles towards the tunnels was a bit unnerving. It was a long way down. Along one stretch, a small black bear was running along the tracks and the conductor had to slow to a crawl, waiting for it to veer either right or left. It took a good blast of the train's whistle before the little guy made up his mind which way to go. But this iconic and historical railroad has also fallen victim to cruise ship hegemony. That industry purchased it a few years ago and they are currently in the process of restructuring and rerouting. The work has already begun. Sections of the track are being widened and the thrice-daily trips are soon going to be every hour on the hour. Just like a lengthy ride at an amusement park. Prior to boarding for our excursion, John and I noticed that the first car was elegantly appointed with tub chairs and a bar area serving croissants, coffee etc., while the rest of the cars were strictly bench seating. We enquired as to why the more up-scale option had not been available to us (we bought our tickets at the railroad office in town) and were advised that car was only for select cruise ship passengers. And so it begins...

We closed our Alaska leg of the journey with one last hike out to Sturgill's Point, about 4 hours round trip, paralleling the south side of the Lynn Canal inlet. There is such beauty and peace to be found walking in a rain forest on a sunny day, with mosses and mushrooms of every variety beside almost every fallen log or exposed tree root. The footing got a bit tricky near the shore but the view down the canal was worth every step.

And finally, there were two terms that, while not much in use today, still popped up from time to time in tourist areas. Sourdough and cheechako. Sourdough refers to a person who has lived in Alaska for some time (at least one full winter) and knows through experience how to endure in such a harsh environment. The expression comes from the very early years when the first trappers and miners carried sourdough starter close to their bodies while travelling during the winter months, thus ensuring the culture would survive until the next bread-baking day. Cheechako, on the other hand, is someone who is new to the state (and/or the north in general) and has yet to learn about its customs and winter survival. And so ended my love-hate relationship with Alaska. There is no doubt it is beautiful and one day I hope to return and see those places we missed this time around.

But I don't want to, and will never be, a sourdough.

29.

SAIL ADJUSTMENT

A POPULAR QUOTE ON MOTIVATIONAL GREETING CARDS AND OTHER ENCOURAGEMENT-BASED MESSAGES IS, "WE CANNOT DIRECT THE WIND, BUT WE CAN ADJUST OUR SAILS," OR SOMETHING TO THAT EFFECT. I am not a sailor, and our yacht had no sails, but the beginning of September had us doing a fair bit of adjusting. The original plan was to drive down highway 37, the Cassiar Highway (more like a paved country road), where it starts at the Yukon/BC border, go as far as Prince George and then head west towards Bella Coola along the one and only road in. There is a portion of this Bella Coola Road known as "The Hill", a narrow 20-km unpaved stretch with hairpin turns, 18% grades, precipitous drop offs and no guardrails. So treacherous that some tourists who drove in, refused to drive back out, electing to leave their vehicles behind and return home by ferry or float plane. I suspect that story may be somewhat embellished, but the warnings (and Youtube videos) were enough to convince us not to try it in the yacht. So we arranged to register at an RV resort on the east side of the hill, drive to Bella Coola with the Toad, stay a few days in a dog-friendly motel, and then return, pick up the coach and continue back into southern B.C. Reservations were made and all was good. Except for those pesky forest fires. The worst in the province's history, scorching 945,000 hectares (that would be over 2.3 million acres or an area around the size of Yellowstone National Park!) This wished-for plan would have had us driving through some of the worst zones, including ones already evacuated or under evacuation orders. Fall back, regroup, cancel the reservations and make new ones. Sail adjustment number one. We then decided to drive part way down the Cassiar and turn east at 37A towards Prince Rupert, catch a BC ferry through the inside passage to Port Hardy, and land on Vancouver Island where we planned to spend most of the winter anyway. (We had pretty much used up our 6-month allotted allowance for the US and hoped to return there again in the spring.) Excellent plan except the earliest sailing we could get was almost two weeks away, on September 14ᵗʰ, a very important date for the two of us. Okay then, we'll take our time driving down the Cassiar, really explore the area, and spend some extra time in Prince Rupert. A nice way of saying we would just be spinning our wheels. Adjustment number two. Cast off!

The summer ends quickly in the far north. September 1ˢᵗ at the Yukon/BC border had many of the trees dropping their already yellow leaves, there was fresh snow at higher elevations, the air was crisp and at night the temperature was hitting low single digits. Like 2C low. Yet the drive was pretty in a decidedly autumn kind of way. There aren't many communities along the Cassiar and we quickly found out, no internet or phone signal either. For 600 kms! It is amazing how important instant contact and communication has become, and how unnerved we get without it. How did we ever manage before? Incommunicado. Adjustment number three. Our first stop was at Jade City, which is not really a city but just a stop along the highway where all 20-odd residents work for the one family-run jade business. It was an interesting and informative stop none-the-less. There are two types of jade in the world. Jadeite (which can come in different colours and is virtually impossible to get today) and Nephrite (that rich green everyone is familiar with.) Around 92% of Canada's Nephrite Jade comes from the Cassiar Mountains, with half of it being exported to countries like China, Indonesia and Myanmar for detailed carving. The finished products are then shipped back to Canada for sale at various markets, complete with bright red maple leaf stickers saying, "Canadian Jade." I found that a bit misleading. If I hadn't asked, I would have thought the lovely $25,000.00 jade polar bear I was admiring had been carved locally. Nope. Like most everything else, it is cheaper to produce overseas. Not that there was ever any question of buying that little number. Way above our pay grade. However, the store did have an extensive selection of raw jade creations that had been sliced, diced, formed, polished and then sealed with wax. What? Wax? In its natural state, even after cutting and polishing, jade is a dull gray. It only takes on that beautiful green hue when wet or when coated with paraffin. Hmmm. Really? I need to do more research. Then again, who knows how many pieces of jade I have kicked off a trail or left laying on a beach, because they weren't coated in wax.

Given there was no hurry to reach Prince Rupert, the next plan was to leave the coach at an RV park in the community of Dease Lake and drive along the scenic albeit steep and winding 70-mile Telegraph Creek Road to Telegraph Creek, a village with many turn-of-the-century buildings left over from the gold rush days. When we got out of the coach at Dease Lake, there was a very noticeable smell of stale smoke in the air.

Not the pleasant outdoorsy smell of a campfire, but more along the lines of an old arson scene. When we went to register at the RV park, the owner asked what we planned on doing in the area. Why drive to Telegraph Creek, of course. Don't think so. Not this time. He advised that some of the worst forest fires had been in the Dease Lake area, and residents of Telegraph Creek had been evacuated more than a month ago. They were still waiting to get back home. Not sure how we missed that little important news item.

Okay then. Adjustment number four. Let's continue south and take a 65-km side trip along Glacier Highway into Stewart-Hyder, located at the head of the Portland Canal. Now that was a detour worth taking. The drive was very scenic with soaring peaks and glaciers along the way, although the international boundary at the end was rather curious. Stewart is in British Columbia and Hyder in Alaska. But the border crossing is only staffed on the Canadian side, with entry to the US completely unregulated. In other words, you can freely drive into the United States, but you need your passport to get back into Canada. Huh? Hyder is pretty much a ghost town ("the friendliest ghost town in America"), with only a few derelict trailers, run-down buildings and abandoned shacks. It had its heyday in the early 1900s when mining was lucrative on the Canadian side, and although a handful of people are still hanging on, there was really nothing of interest. Mind you, Stewart was only marginally better. But like many of these small northern communities, they go through cycles of boom and bust, depending on which natural resource is being exploited. Today, the only reason to drive through Hyder is to get to Salmon Glacier, which is on Canadian soil. There is only one narrow, gravelly, pothole filled road to follow and part way along, a posted sign "welcome to British Columbia" was the only indication we had crossed the border yet again.

All very loosey-goosey, but considering the road only goes 50 kms before ending in complete wilderness, there is very little concern about illegal aliens sneaking into either country. Which makes me wonder why the Canadian Border Services Agency has a post there in the first place. Our tax dollars at work.

OVERLOOKING SALMON GLACIER, B.C.

Salmon Glacier was spectacular, rivalling and in many ways surpassing anything we had seen in Alaska. It is the world's largest car-accessible glacier and Canada's fifth largest overall. Although by car-accessible, that means access to the viewpoint. The road does not reach the actual ice itself. The drive was incredibly bumpy with high cliffs on one side and precipitous drop offs into a deep gully on the other (and no guardrails!) In some places large boulders had rolled down onto the road, and in other places, the gully side edge was washed out and unstable. Passing oncoming vehicles was done with considerable care. After 37 kms, we reached the glacier overlook, parked in the small visitor area, set up our chairs on an outcropping, and had our picnic lunch while enjoying the view. Outstanding. Given it was not the easiest place to get to, there were not many people around and those who had put in the effort, were just as content as us to gaze about in quiet contemplation. However, the road didn't end there, but continued another 10 kms to the abandoned Granduc Mine, so we went to check that out as well. The mine had been in operation for 20 years (closing in 1984 due to low copper prices and operational issues) and all that is left now is a huge concrete bunker-type building and lots of twisted and rusted metal scraps strewn about. Very ugly. But the surrounding scenery, including the Berendon Glacier, was magnificent. I could only imagine having that as my office view every morning. Then again, most people worked down in the mine so saw very little by way of vistas. What was I thinking? Apparently there are quite a few grizzlies in the area too but we didn't see any, which is just as well because we didn't have Porter on a leash. My bad.

It was in Stewart that we developed an issue with the coach's gas/carbon monoxide detector. The coach heating system was electric, but we also had the option of switching to propane if there was no shore power and we didn't want to run the generator. And the three-burner cooktop used propane. We were plugged into shore power at a RV park, and I was cooking with all three burners lit, the microwave/convection oven on, the clothes dryer running and the electric fireplace glowing. That is when the CO alarm started with its ear-piercing beeping. Despite shutting everything off, opening all the vents and running all the fans, the alarm kept going off, every 15 minutes or so. Without any rhyme or reason. It was making poor Porter crazy. He sat by the front door with the most distressed look I have ever seen. And when he got outside, he would not come back in. John eventually cut the wires to the CO monitor and shut off the propane just so we could get some sleep that night. The following morning, he purchased a battery-operated detector, but prior to turning it on, decided to re-connect the built-in, just in case. All worked as it should. The best we could figure is that there might have been a problem with the campground's power. Perhaps electrical surges were being interpreted by the monitor as a fault? I don't know.

Continuing south, we stopped in at Gitanyow, a native community of about 450 souls, designated a National Historic Site in 1972 because at one point it had "the largest number of original totem poles of any Coastal First Nations village, many dating from the mid 19th century. Magnificent poles, carving sheds... contribute to the magical feeling of the site." Uh-huh. Don't think so. No magical feelings being evoked during our visit. Whoever wrote that descriptor hasn't been there in quite some time. While the poles were truly remarkable, there were no carving sheds in evidence and there was no-one around to talk to. When we first pulled into the village it had the stereotypical "Rez" look. Dilapidated houses, unkempt lawns, junk strewn yards, cannibalized cars. But the totem poles, over 20 of them, were primarily along the main street with what looked like a Visitor Centre, built in the traditional west coast long house style behind them, and a shabby gas station/grocery store complete with foil covered windows, beside them. I walked around admiring the poles for a bit, trying not to get distracted by the surrounding trash, and then headed over to the centre. But it was locked. A sign clearly reading "welcome to the interpretive centre" lay on the ground, off to one side. Around the back, in what can best be described as a covered alcove, another 20 or so additional shorter poles leaned up against the walls, and judging by their condition and carving detail, were considerably older than the ones out front. But they were not really protected from the elements and in the crack of one, some bees had made a hive and were busy flying in and out. The entire place had a neglected, abandoned air to it. A local resident was selling a few beaded crafts in a near-by outbuilding, so tourists obviously frequent the place, but on that particular day we were the only ones around. We talked with him for a bit, but he was not able to provide much information other than to say that the chief had taken over the interpretive centre for his own use some time ago. He didn't know anything about the poles other than helpfully advising the oldest one may have been from the 1940s. What? Emily Carr was supposed to have painted these poles in 1928! Some independent research showed that one particular pole (Hole-in-Ice/Hole-in-Sky) had been standing there for 120 years. Turns out, some of the poles were originals from the mid 19th century, while others were replicas, with the originals having been sent to the Royal British Columbia Museum in Victoria around 1960. Lord only knows what was up with the seemingly abandoned ones in the back shed. So much for knowing about your local history. Nobody was around and nobody seemed to care. Arghhhhh! I will get to my politically incorrect rant in a moment.

We headed off towards Prince Rupert, driving along the Yellowhead Highway where it parallels the Skeena River (one of the longest undammed rivers in world) for 240 kms. And while the weather was technically sunny, smoke from the forest fires had created a haze so thick that most of the mountains were completely obscured, with only faint outlines visible. Shades of the previous summer in Banff/Jasper. Although on the plus side, we were spared the views of damage from clear-cut logging (more on logging later). Starting out, the river seemed more like a fjord with high cliffs on either side but as we got closer to Prince Rupert, it grew wider and wider until it looked more like a large lake. Apparently it is crucial to spawning salmon in the area. By the time we reached Prince Rupert, the rain came again and that was no surprise as locals proudly proclaim that Prince Rupert is the rainiest city in the country, receiving four times more rain that Vancouver. Some studies don't necessarily support that claim but be that as it may, it certainly lived up to its rainy reputation the first several days. We sure could pick 'em. However, being trapped indoors gave me time to re-organize and tidy up a bit. Despite all the innovative and ingenious places motor coach builders have incorporated for storage, with all the rocking and rolling along these many miles, a lot of things had shifted. So I took the time to take stock of what we had inside and see what could be moved to "the basement". Not much. And wouldn't you know it, once that was taken care of, we discovered that many of the fires inland had been brought under control and theoretically, we could have returned to plan "A" but by then it was too late.

Other than fair weather dependant outdoor activities (hiking, kayaking) there is not much to do in Prince Rupert. We did check out the Museum of Northern British Columbia, which was very nice and like many visitor buildings in B. C., constructed in a modernized northwest long house style. Walking inside, the aroma of cedar from the massive cedar beams was fantastic. The interior was neither huge nor overwhelming but there were many beautiful exhibits of northern BC's history from the early native peoples to early settlers to current artists. However, I was getting very tired of the over-used phrase "since time immemorial" when describing native presence on this continent. If you've got a specific date or timeline, then use it! While learning about native art and culture, it was difficult to get away from political correctness, and what was expressed privately was tempered and sometimes completely different from what was said publicly. I spoke with individuals who awkwardly acknowledged that several hundred years ago life was not always comfortable, nor harmonious. Being a hunter-gatherer society dependent on nature, starvation was often a real problem. And while various tribes did trade with each other, they also beat the tar out of each other, warred, raided, defended property, hunting and fishing territory, took slaves, and killed slaves. And the great respect they had for the earth and all its creatures came from the fact that they depended on that earth, whose changing seasons could bring intense misery and whose many creatures could easily kill them. Definitely not a utopian world that only disappeared because of white contact. And without diminishing or denying some of the atrocities that took place in the residential schools, some individuals told me that residential school was the best thing that ever happened to them. Which brings me to my rant on the preservation of aboriginal culture.

Gitanyow with its totem poles was not the first time we ran into a certain apathy and disinterest displayed by native people when it came to preserving their own heritage. In our travels, we visited many places of seemingly historic and cultural importance. Yet other than placards saying they have "been here since time immemorial" (I thought if I read one more pamphlet with that expression I would scream), there seemed to be limited interest in maintaining or displaying this heritage. Yes, there were federally and provincially funded museums, a few cultural centres and a few dedicated artists here or there, but little by way of a truly encompassing community commitment to the issue. Demands have been made for the repatriation of totem poles, ceremonial masks and other artefacts from museums around the world, including the Museum of Civilization in Ottawa, yet when items are returned, they are not necessarily displayed in any easily accessible way, if at all. Or like in Gitanyow, left with no explanation as their history, creation or meaning, for either visitors or locals alike. The U'mista Cultural Centre in Alert Bay is an exception and more on that later. And don't get me started on "cultural appropriation." Oops. Too late. There has recently been a big hue and cry over non-native artists incorporating what has been traditional native design into various art forms, be it painting, weaving or sculpting. Yet so few native people seem interested in learning to do it themselves. We ran into that in Tuktoyaktuk, NWT, in Homer Alaska, in Prince Rupert BC. In Haines, (where John had his carving tutorial), the session was with a local white guy, who advised he takes a fair bit of ribbing from his native friends because he carves totem poles, and while they joke about cultural appropriation, there is an unmistakable undercurrent. Yet they are not interested in learning to carve themselves. In Prince Rupert, we attempted to gain access to the "carving shed" which was promoted as a place where visitors could watch local Haida masters at work. Constructed again in the traditional western long house style, we only found it based on a picture we saw on-line, but there was no sign outside to indicate what it was or what the hours of operation were. We figured the Visitor Centre would know. Nope. The girl there said, "I think the guy just shows up when he feels like it." She said it was run under the auspices of the Museum of Northern B.C. and attempted to call over but could not get anyone on the phone. So off to the museum. The girl at the front desk there didn't know either. Maybe someone in the gift shop might? Okay. They had the answer. The carving shed project was defunct, there was no interest and the place only gets rented out from time to time as studio space if anyone wants it. This in a city with a population of almost 12,000, of whom over 25% are native. Come on! Nobody? But heaven forbid anyone non-native produce anything in that style. And that is just carving. What about weaving or basketry? I certainly don't know the answer and don't profess to have any in depth knowledge of the machinations of the Truth and Reconciliation Committee, but it seems to me that one should wear pretty high rubber boots when reading some of that material (or at least listening to the media's spin on it). Okay. I'm getting off my soap box now. In true Canadian style, I feel I should apologize for any offense I may have caused but won't. I'm calling it like I'm seeing it. Back to Prince Rupert.

The town itself was rather tired looking, except for the area around Cow Bay down by the Atlin ferry terminal, where the odd cruise ship docks. A handful of average shops and restaurants catering to tourists didn't take long to explore, although Cowpuccino's coffee shop on the corner was a nice place to sit and people watch on a sunny day. But along the main retail strip frequented by locals, many of the shops were either for sale, for rent, boarded up or simply abandoned, broken windows and all. And driving through the residential streets, many of the houses were in dire need of what a real estate agent might term "TLC", although I suspect a bulldozer might be more effective. Rotting, sagging wood decks and window frames, moss covered roofs, paint peeled siding, zero landscaping. And that was just the outside. There is supposedly a huge deer population too, with many of the ungulates wandering along these residential streets eating whatever flowers may have survived the winter. They are supposedly so numerous, residents say that the way to hunt deer in Prince Rupert is with an apple and a ball peen hammer. We only saw one deer, and that was in our campsite.

There were a few good weather days, so we seized the opportunity to drive a short distance out of town and walk along the Butze Rapids Trail, a 5-km loop that took us through a beautiful rainforest, made even more beautiful by the fact that it was sunny! There were signs posted that wolves and bears frequent the area, but we passed at least 10 people, some with dogs (off leash) so figured things were pretty safe. The rapids were ho-hum, but we bumped into an aboriginal couple collecting leaves for Labrador Tea, and Salal berries from which they will make jam. They couldn't offer a description of what the tea tastes like, but that is just as well. A google search revealed it acts as a diuretic and cathartic, so forget that. But jam? I'm in. They advised where some of the bigger berries were and we returned the following day with plastic bags and scissors to start foraging. Salal bushes grow everywhere along the coast and the berries look almost like very large dark blueberries, only in a cluster, are very sticky, and stain the fingers (and tongue) something awful. They don't have a distinctive flavour, like strawberries or raspberries, but you could possibly say they are like a very very mild blueberry with an earthy undertone. While it was a labour-intensive process (made even more so because the skins have to be strained and my RV kitchen was lacking a few canning essentials), we ended up with about 8 cups of delicious jelly. Bon appetite! Only problem? That darn CO detector started going off again so John disconnected it a second time. What was with that thing? We decided to depend on the portable one until such time as we could order a new unit.

Taking advantage of the sunshine, we took a quick drive out to the North Pacific Cannery, a national historic site that promotes itself as "the oldest intact salmon cannery on the west coast." One of the last canneries remaining of what was once a huge industry up there. It is an open-air museum today, operated by the Port Edward Historical Society, but they would not even allow Porter on the grounds, much less into a building, so that was one tour we didn't take. Then again, I can't say I was really all that interested in seeing the remnants of a business that helped decimate salmon stocks. But it sure was in a lovely setting. Almost everything in B.C. is lovely. Especially when the sun shines.

The idea of having to spend an entire week in Prince Rupert frustrated me at first, but in retrospect, it was very much what we needed. With limited exploring options, we could have easily hopped on the ferry for a 7-hour ride to Haida Gwaii (Queen Charlotte Islands). But we didn't. Why not? We had been there before and quite liked it. Actually, we were there September 11, 2001 on a kayaking trip (who doesn't remember where they were that day?) and found ourselves in a remote little outpost called Rose Harbour, away from civilization and reliable communication. It was like something out of a Gilligan's Island episode, only with serious consequences. All 10 of us paddlers huddled around a transistor radio that kept cutting in and out, trying to understand what was happening. It was 4 days before we returned to the main town of Sandspit and actually saw the visuals. And between grounded flights and fog banks, we were stranded on the island for a few extra days. But I digress. The reason we didn't go was that being in the third year of this journey, we were becoming road weary. My parents' passing had taken a fair bit of wind out of my sails and worry about John's elderly friends was also taking its toll. There is no such thing as footloose and fancy-free. People who are still in the employment phase of their lives sometimes fantasize about retirement, when they will sell everything and just go travel around the world. I had an acquaintance at work who did just that. But I suspect it takes a certain kind of person to successfully pull it off. Perhaps someone without close family ties, without close friends, without children? Because despite having the luxury of going home several times a year and catching up with people, it was not the same, and it was not enough. I was still glad we were on the journey, and would still do it all over again, but it came at a price. I missed "home."

We were scheduled to leave Prince Rupert at 11am on September 14th, our 22nd wedding anniversary, and planned to spend an idyllic day enjoying the scenery of the inside passage. Nope. Not this time. The ferry was having trouble with its starboard engine, so departure was delayed until 10pm. Oh no! Another day in Prince Rupert! We decided to tire Porter out by hiking the Tall Trees Trail up to the top of Mt. Hays for a bird's eye view of the harbour. The trailhead was across the road from the Butze Rapids trail and as we pulled into the parking area, two RCMP officers advised us to be careful because that very morning several wolves on the Butze had attacked a small dog, carrying it off into the water. The dog managed to escape but needless to say required some veterinary attention. They cautioned us to keep Porter on his leash. Okay, this was one time I would follow orders, but I still think it was pretty cool. Wild wolves! Maybe they had been watching us while we blithely picked Salal berries. On second thought, Yikes! The Tall Trees hike was pretty steep through another lovely rainforest with all kinds of wild mushrooms along the way, and while I am familiar with some of the edible ones, I am not confident enough to add them to any dinner menu. Someone more schooled in the art of identification would have had a field day. The view from the top was so-so and we returned to the car without seeing any of my spirit animals. Save the wolves!

Boarding the ferry went smoothly (fantastic bright fuschia sunset from the parking lot) and Porter stayed in the coach while we took a berth for the night. Nothing fancy, but at least there were beds to lie down on. Quite a few travellers simply rolled out sleeping bags between the rows of seats in the lounges, but that might be taking economizing a bit far. I didn't sleep well because in the back of my mind, I was very cognizant of the fact that in 2006, the ferry Queen of the North had sunk on this very journey after her distracted captain missed a turn and ran into an island. She went down with the loss of two passenger lives, in water that is 1,400 feet deep, so there will be no attempt to raise her. The officer at the helm has since been convicted of negligence, although he maintains he followed all the rules. At least he didn't claim to have fallen into a lifeboat, à la the Concordia captain. The scary thing was that we had been on that very vessel just 6 months earlier! This new boat, the Northern Adventurer, had a pet area but it was really just a small 10 x 5-foot room with stacked dog crates and a three-seater bench. Not comfortable for man nor beast. Thankfully, there were two stops before we reached Port Hardy on this 20-hour sailing, one in Klemtu at 7am, and one in Bell Bella at 11am, so we were able to disembark with Porter for a 30-minute walk each time, as well as go down and walk him around the car deck a few times later in the day. There were several other dogs on board so there was a fair bit of tail wagging and meet and greet sniffing. The unpleasant thing was that the dogs were expected to do their business on the car deck. Pee on the tires, so to speak. Poop had to be scooped up, naturally, but urine just left there. Yuck. And very confusing for the dogs. They are trained not to "go" anywhere indoors, yet here they were encouraged to do so. Surely BC Ferries could have designated a specific area with some artificial turf. Sailing along the inside passage was lovely and very relaxing. Overcast with a few sunny stretches, calm seas and only some minor swells when crossing the open water towards the northern tip of Vancouver Island. Periodically there were "point of interest" announcements, describing historic lighthouses along the route or which side of the vessel to look for whale sightings. I kept waiting for them to say, "Ladies and gentleman, we are now passing directly over the Queen of the North where we sank her in 2006, and if you look closely you can see the top of the smoke stack..." but they were mum on that topic. No sense panicking the passengers. We saw a few humpback whales and dolphins but none that were overly close. I must admit that despite the majestic beauty of the Alaskan coastline with its high mountains and impressive glaciers, I prefer British Columbia. While the scenery is not as dramatic, and there is mist, clouds and rain a-plenty, the feeling is one of serenity. Ahhhh. Vancouver Island. I belong there.

We used Port Hardy and then Telegraph Cove as home base to explore a bit of the northern end of the island and sad to say, it is really just one enormous logging operation with the odd ecological enclave still hanging on. While big trees are visible in every direction (some still actually old growth) most is second growth (in places even third), with trees that have been planted following the clear-cut of an area, a process known as reforestation. Most of the roads are active logging roads and even along highway 19 (which runs the length of the island), the "forests" on either side are only about 50 feet deep. A green gauntlet to delude the casual observer into thinking they are still in a pristine paradise. But looking sideways instead of straight ahead, it was easy to see where the clear cut began. And driving along some of the logging roads themselves, it could get downright ugly, with only stumps remaining on the completely denuded hillsides and no attempt to hide the carnage. The terrain is so steep in most places, you would think many of these trees would be inaccessible, yet somehow the companies manage. There is no end to man's ingenuity when profit is at stake. It brought to mind the original illustrations in Dr. Suess's book *The Lorax*. Given that we are rapidly moving towards a paperless society, you have to wonder where the rapacious appetite for more, more, more comes from. But it is not all doom and gloom. With the days of activists chaining themselves to trees seemingly in the past, there appears to be a détente of sorts between loggers and conservationists, with the former possibly engaging in the odd environmentally responsible activity. While the Sierra Club maintains that too much old growth is still being logged (and they could be right on that one), the logging companies have their own PR firms working hard to mitigate the bad press. If Sierra reports are to be believed, the harvested logs are shipped to Asia as is, for milling there, thus providing jobs overseas as opposed to here. We saw quite a few log sorting facilities along our drives, yet no mills. However, going for my morning walks along the roadway leading into Telegraph Cove, three separate logging facilities were situated by the shoreline and the "aroma" in the air could easily be mistaken for the lumber section of Rona or Home Depot. Information placards at the viewpoint advised that loggers work in concert with a fish processing plant across the bay. While logs are sorted, graded and shipped to mills down island, any debris generated during this process is turned into wood chips. Fine debris left over from chipping is composted together with fish waste from the fish processing plant and used to make garden soil products. Just one big eco-friendly family. But I am getting ahead of myself.

We drove along one logging road to get to Cape Scott Provincial Park on the northwest tip of the island and a short 45-minute hike through a beautiful (protected) rainforest led us to San Josef Bay where at low tide a vast expansive beach awaited us. Porter was so happy he didn't know what to do. Racing back and forth, running in circles, at one time even bucking like a horse. There were sea stacks to

THROUGH THE RAINFOREST TO SAN JOSEF BEACH.

explore but little by way of beachcombing and we didn't see any wildlife, be it wolves, bears or cougars (although warnings were posted at the trailhead). Vancouver Island has about 3,500 cougars and apparently the rule of thumb is if you see one, it has already been watching you for 10 minutes, so I suppose we should consider ourselves lucky. We chatted with a couple who were camping in the area and they advised that their neighbour in the adjoining site had fallen asleep on the beach and awoke when a black bear standing at her head licked her hair. Both frightened of each other, they scrambled away in opposite directions. Now that would have been something to write home about! Some people have all the luck.

And while Port Hardy doesn't have much to recommend it, we ended up spending well over a week at Telegraph Cove, about a 1-hour drive south. At first glance, it appeared to be a small charming boardwalk community and that is what it originally was. Built in

1911 as a telegraph station for northern Vancouver Island, by 1922 it was an active sawmill, and was then expropriated by National Defence at the outbreak of World War II. At its peak it had 60 residents. Following the war, it was returned to the original mill owners who produced custom lumber for most of the boats, buildings and docks built on the north end of the island. After the mill shut down, it became a seasonally operating community that caters to tourists from all around the world who come for a chance to see the whales that call the Johnstone Strait home. Our visit revealed it is really a resort, with the original humble cottages converted into rental units. There are only about 10 people who live there year-round. But the overall air is more original than engineered, more rustic than chi-chi, yet with all the modern comforts anyone could ask for. Cozy café, a couple of restaurants, passably stocked general store, comfy patios and best of all, easy access to kayaking in the crystal-clear waters of the straight. We spent a fair bit of time on the water as the weather was often sunny and the water for the most part calm. Except for those occasions when the current was going in one direction, the tide in the other, and the breeze blowing in from the third. Then, the water was literally roiling and churning as if in a boiling cauldron, with white caps amongst the swells and an accompanying sound like rushing rapids. Definitely intimidating. It was easier to paddle inside the bull kelp beds that floated about 20 feet offshore and thankfully acted as a great break water. Paddling south from Telegraph Cove was by far prettier than heading north (where the 3 logging outfits were), but we did make our way over to the fish processing plant where we found the remains of an old cannery. Just the rotting pilings were left but it was interesting to paddle in and around the area. The water was incredibly clear, and I was particularly taken with the bull kelp as it floated gracefully in the current. Further along near the logging operations, it was a bit unsettling as we made our way past the huge log booms. What if those wire bands holding several tons of logs together gave way? We had no issues. But then again, we didn't see any whales, humpbacks or orcas, either.

JOHNSTONE STRAIGHT…STILL VAINLY LOOKING FOR ORCAS.

One day we took a small ferry that runs 25 minutes from Port McNeill to Alert Bay on Cormorant Island, and this was where my faith in aboriginal viability was partially restored. (Only partially – the entire subject is just too complex.) We primarily went to see the U'mista Cultural Centre which had been built in 1980, specifically to house returning potlatch artefacts that had been seized by government authorities in 1921. Short synopsis. Potlach is a ceremony practiced by aboriginal peoples of the Northwest Coast to mark important life passages such as marriage, mourning the dead or transferring rights and privileges. As I understand it, almost a way of legitimizing or validating these events. Guests at a potlatch are in effect witnesses and are given gifts by the hosting Chief. The more gifts that are distributed, the higher the status allotted the host. The celebration itself involves the showing of masks, dances, songs, speeches and lots of food. In 1884, Canada's government, pressured by missionaries and Indian Agents who were concerned this ritual was frustrating their attempts to have aboriginal peoples adopt a more western lifestyle, passed a law outlawing potlatch ceremonies. In defiance of this law, a large potlatch was held at Village Island in 1921, whereupon the authorities arrested and charged 45 people, of whom 22 received suspended sentences based on an agreement that they would surrender their potlatch regalia. (Those who refused received sentences of 2 or 3 months.) The seized artefacts were sent to Ottawa and subsequently divided up amongst several museums and collectors. After that, potlatch celebrations went underground. Thirty years later, the Indian Act was revised and the section pertaining to the potlatch ban deleted. In the late 1960s the Kwakwaka'wakw people (no matter how much I tried, I could not get that pronunciation right) lobbied the government and museums to have their collection repatriated. This was acquiesced to on the condition that a proper museum be constructed to house it. So just over 50 years later, most of the property has been returned. A few pieces are still outstanding and searched for. The display was impressive. The masks and accompanying rattles, coppers and related regalia were beautiful (although not necessarily in a conventional sort of way) and it was wonderful to have a wealth of information available to help understand the concept and importance these items had and continue to have for the community. I would have taken pictures, but photography was forbidden. The only downside? Getting to view the collection is not easy. It is a 5-hour drive from Victoria to Port McNeil, then a half-hour ferry ride, and then about 2 kms to the centre. This is where the paradox comes in. On the one hand, accusations are levelled that the larger Canadian community does not know enough about aboriginal culture, yet informative displays such as this are located in areas that most people will never get to. There is supposedly an even larger cultural centre on Quadra Island opposite the town of Campbell River, but we hadn't made our way that far south and by the time we did, it was closed for the season. I obviously don't have the answer and still have much to learn.

But there was more to Alert Bay than just the U'mista Centre although that day, it was the main drawing card. Since we took turns touring that facility, Porter was able to spend time splashing around in the ocean, which pleased him to no end, and we then strolled along the raised boardwalk about 3 kms to the other end of town. There were numerous impressive carvings and totem poles still standing, many in the local cemetery, and the Visitor's Centre provided a pamphlet detailing who built them, when and why. Some were carved and painted as recently as 2015, so obviously traditional carving was alive and well in this community. In some locations the poles had toppled over but in accordance with tradition, family members elected to leave them there in the belief that they had served their purpose and now return to mother earth. Other families replaced the fallen ones with new ones. There are no hard and fast rules. But other than marvelling at totem poles and enjoying the simplicity of real life in a remote community, we were pretty much done in a day. Alert Bay was at its peak between 1950 and 1970, thanks to fishing and logging but as usual, once the resource exploitation was complete, most people moved on. The population today is around 900, equally divided between aboriginal and non, and we returned to the yacht, happy to have had the opportunity to go on this little excursion.

We ended up spending more time in Telegraph Cove than anticipated because the sun kept shining, it was relaxing, and we couldn't pull ourselves away from just one more day of kayaking. I was seriously starting to think about the feasibility of purchasing a building lot right on the water, overlooking the strait. More than 25 years ago, an entrepreneur from the U.S. had fallen in love with the place, invested millions upon millions of dollars (80?) in blasting, grading and putting in numerous serviced lots, few of which sold. I can only surmise it is because of the area's remote location (a five-hour drive from Victoria can seem a bit far) and generally rainy weather. But sun, rain, cloud or fog, I loved it. The possibility was not off the table. *Dream a little dream for me...*

30.

SURF'S UP DUDE!

THE CITY OF CAMPBELL RIVER, ON THE CENTRAL-EAST SHORE OF VANCOUVER ISLAND, IS KNOWN AS THE SALMON FISHING CAPITAL OF THE WORLD. In fact, it was there that in 1924, the Tyee Club of British Columbia was formed (a Tyee being a Chinook salmon that weighs over 30 pounds). To get into the club, you have to reel in one of these behemoths. Since neither John nor I know much about fishing, there was never any question of trying to join the club, but it was early October and the Coho were running so in keeping with the spirit of the place, we too decided to try our hand at this revered sport. If only it were that simple. Going out with a professional outfitter cost a ridiculous amount of money, anywhere from $600 to $800 dollars per person per day. We wanted to go fishing for heaven's sake, not dig for diamonds. But on the Quinsam River in Elk Falls Provincial Park, as well as along the banks of the Campbell River itself, lone anglers were standing both in the water as well as on the shore, so obviously this was something that could be accomplished without the high price tag. We just needed the gear. Hmmm. The girl at the Visitor's Centre advised that many people fished from the long pier right on the Strait of Georgia and had been pulling in some fairly respectably sized fish. The hut at the entry to the pier rented poles for $5.00 per hour. Now that was more in keeping with my budget and skill level. However, there were quite a few rules to be aware of first, not the least being the requirement for a fishing licence, so off we went to the tackle shop to take care of the necessary paperwork. It turned out that if keeping any caught salmon, the licence also needed a salmon stamp. Right. Stamp away. I was feeling optimistic. But wait. There were more rules. For example, salmon from a hatchery could be kept but wild ones had to be released. How do we tell the difference? Hatchery salmon have had their adipose fin clipped. That's the fin that is located on their back, just forward of their tail fin.

Doesn't everybody know that? If keeping a Chinook, it had to be longer than 24 inches, but a Coho only had to be 11 inches. There was also something about black tongue, black mouth and bigger teeth vs. possibly black tongue, white mouth and smaller teeth, but by this time, my eyes were rolling back in my head.

Off we went to the infamous pier and collected our rental rods. I had watched a local guy cast, "jig" and reel for a while and engaged him in conversation, hoping to pick up a few pointers. He was more than happy to oblige but unfortunately, spoke a completely foreign language. Tossing around terms like spinners, spoons, green buzz bombs, jacks, tri-hooks and drop-nets, he might as well have been talking about flying purple people eaters. About the only thing I understood was that it's best to fish at slack tide because during ebb and flow, the fish are too tired to bite. It just so happened it was slack tide, so cast away. There are now two hours of my life that I will never get back. The entire undertaking was quite boring with neither of us getting even a nibble, (nor did anyone else on the pier, for that matter) and about the only positive thing I can say is that it was sunny. The local fellow consoled us on our lack of success by saying we were probably using the wrong lures anyway. Ours were bright pink and only Pinks (yet another type of salmon) go for those. Then again, he said Coho will pretty much bite on anything so you never can tell. I think it's all just dumb luck. Between what we spent on licences and rentals it would have made more sense to just go buy a nice big fillet, ready for the BBQ. Come to think of it, I don't know what we would have done had we caught anything. Who would have cleaned it? Certainly not me! I'd need professional assistance. Maybe we should have sprung for the high-priced experience after all.

Elk Falls Provincial Park, our home base in the Campbell River area, was one of the loveliest provincial park campgrounds we have stayed at. Huge, private sites with many right on the Quinsam River. We had originally set up for a few nights at a remote Hydro BC camping area by the Strathcona Dam (the tallest one on Vancouver Island), where it was also very nice and scenic, but it was also a 30-minute drive from town and we had quite a few errands to take care of prior to setting out for Tofino. And the camping area itself was a bit troubling, situated directly below the earth-filled dam, not above it. Who came up with that genius idea? Reading the posted notice at the entrance didn't ease my concerns either. The campground is being relocated in 2020 to an area above the dam because engineers have determined that should a major earthquake occur, there is a good likelihood the dam (having been constructed in 1958) might give, ("at risk of failure", as they put it) and there would be no time to evacuate those people in close proximity. And we all know how easy it is to predict earthquakes. So after a few days we relocated to Elk Falls. No hook-ups but very peaceful. From our front window we were able to watch bald eagles flying low along the river, the odd spawning salmon and a lone fly-fishing angler. John had an opportunity to catch up with a work colleague who had moved to Vancouver Island after retirement, and one sunny day we went on a beautiful hike to Elk Falls, crossing a suspension bridge and strolling through some great stands of old growth Douglas Fir. All was good. Except for Thanksgiving Day celebrations. Those were a bit meagre. Being en route to Tofino, we couldn't make it to my uncle and aunt's place in Vancouver to join up with family, and it was pretty hard to muster up any enthusiasm to make Thanksgiving dinner for two. So I bought a pumpkin pie. Woo-hoo. A far cry from turkey with all the trimmings that I used to enjoy preparing. We vowed to make up for it the following year.

A quick overnight in Port Alberni (there was really no reason to linger, despite its claim to fame as being the birthplace of Kim Campbell, Canada's first female prime minister, whose exalted status was achieved not by vote but rather by default) and we were off to what is my favourite vacation place in all of Canada, Tofino! If my count was correct, I had been there five times before and loved it every time. John and I spent part of our honeymoon there and back then, toyed with the idea of purchasing some vacation beach front property, but at that juncture, our heads were in the wrong space and we have been kicking ourselves ever since. Certainly land values are well beyond our pay grade now, so that is another dream not to be realized. Unless of course we win LottoMax. Then my first call will be to a real estate agent. Fingers crossed. I don't know what it is about the place. The air. The ocean. The trees. The sky. It just feels right. As if I belong. If there is such a thing as reincarnation, perhaps I lived there in a previous life. It is definitely my happy place. Rain or shine. And it rains a lot.

We had arranged to stay at Crystal Cove Resort on MacKenzie Beach until December 1st and were delighted to find that they were extremely dog-friendly. Dogs were welcome everywhere! Porter quickly made friends with the office staff and determined the exact location of the treat jar in no time. The facility has RV sites, glamping sites (RV rentals for people who don't have their own rigs but would like to try that type of accommodation) and individual log cabins complete with wood burning fireplaces and hot tubs. Our site was a bit tight but very private, next to a massive cedar. We settled in for what we hoped would be a wonderfully relaxing stay but did end up moving after several days. The original site received not one ray of sunshine and despite not having a single drop of rain during the first two weeks, the mat and steps outside were constantly damp. So we switched over to where we could get a bit of dappled sun and that helped considerably. The rest of the month just flew by. We managed to establish a bit of a routine, although nothing too rigid, with most mornings dedicated to some sort of physical activity and most afternoons enjoying the sunshine on the beach by the cove. We made friends with two women from Vancouver (one a very talented artist) who also enjoyed sitting by the water and John dubbed us the Afternoon Club. When the sun was not shining, the plan was to check out the various shops and galleries in town, but we didn't quite get around to that. Bad weather days found us occupied with the usual mundane chores of daily living – grocery shopping, laundry etc. There was a yoga studio a ten-minute walk from the resort (Coastal Bliss Yoga) so we signed up in the hopes of recovering some of what we had lost over the past year. The first "foundations" class left my legs wobbly, but it was a great place with the faint aroma of cedar from the construction beams permeating the air, and friendly instructors for every lesson. We went twice a week. We also frequently biked along the Pacific Rim Highway as far as Long Beach and back, exploring the occasional side road, and while some drivers had difficulty with the whole "share the road" concept, most were fairly considerate, giving us a wide berth. The only negative thing I can say is that there was a fair bit of trash in the ditches. Primarily empty cans (Red Bull, beer, Coke) and the odd piece of clothing (underwear, bandanas, socks). That was quite surprising given that the area prides itself on being very environmentally conscientious. One time we actually stopped to pick up a very nice, new hiking pole that someone had obviously lost so not everything was deliberately tossed out a window. And if the weather was not conducive to biking, we went on "power walks" along Chesterman Beach, although John throwing sticks for Porter and me stopping to examine seashells kept the pace from getting too brisk. We kayaked out oceanside once, but the water was pretty choppy and there really wasn't any place to go other than parallel the shoreline, and we talked about putting in on the Clayoquot Sound side but never got around to it. One of the locals advised that the current through the narrows is quite strong and with changing tides, can create whirlpools that have sucked both boats and people underwater. It's all about timing.

And then we discovered surfing. Perhaps we were coming to this sport a bit late in the game, but one positive aspect was that falling in water didn't hurt quite as much as falling on a ski hill. Getting copious amounts of saltwater up your nose, while unpleasant, doesn't count as pain. And as luck would have it, I never had my board hit me in the head. How did we get to this point? A bit of context. Tofino used to be a town dominated by loggers and fishermen, with weather that is often less than ideal. It's in the middle of a temperate rainforest after all. Average yearly rainfall is about 130 inches. And it is situated literally at the end of the road. In fact, the western terminus of the Trans-Canada Highway is near Main Street and First Avenue. And it was not until 1972 that the road across the island was actually paved! The environmentalists and loggers went at it back in the early 1990s (more about tree hugging later), but things have quieted down considerably on that front. And while the more intrepid vacationers did make Tofino (specifically Long Beach) their destination of choice in the 1960s, it was also the destination of choice for urban drop-outs, American draft dodgers and other people who wanted to disappear. Pacific Rim National Park Reserve was created in 1970 but it wasn't until many years later that the place really showed up on mainstream society's radar. Today, the permanent population is about 2,000, with that number swelling to around 35-40,000 in the summer months! Numerous campgrounds, cabins and resorts line the many miles of beautiful sandy beaches (except Long Beach, which at 16 kms lies within the National Park boundary) and many of the privately-owned places are rented out through AirBnB and the like. The original humble cottages along Chesterman Beach have been replaced primarily with mega manses where price tags start in the 2-million dollar range (just under 2 mill. will get you a vacant lot) and climb rapidly, and older locals decry how much the place has changed. And while there are some average residential homes and low-rise condos in town, there are also many enclaves seemingly hacked out of the forest where dilapidated trailers that have seen better days are tucked out of sight. So it's a very wide ranging socio-economic demographic. And what struck me most was the large number of young people, primarily of the surfer-dude variety. Some very obviously transient, working at service type jobs, making just enough money to pay for a roof over their heads (or a van to sleep in) while waiting for an opportunity to get out in the water, and then moving on to the next surfing destination when the mood strikes them. Others, a bit more established, arrive specifically for surfing vacations, and there are 9 separate surf shops offering rental gear and/or lessons. Tofino today is a surfing mecca. *Outside Magazine* went so far as to name it "North America's Best Surf Town" (and here I always thought that was some place in California). I don't know enough about the sport to offer any opinions on wave size or quality, but I do know that every other car we saw had surfboards strapped to the roof, and every day at every

beach, neoprene clad surfers bobbed about in the water on their boards, like flotsam after a storm.

So when in Rome... Based on the recommendation of a young couple staying at our resort, we signed up for a 3-hour group lesson with Surf Sisters. Ten of us newbies met with two instructors at the parking lot

SURF'S UP DUDE! GETTING READY FOR MY FIRST-EVER SURF LESSON.

of Cox Beach and were advised our lesson would cover ocean safety, surf etiquette, surf gear maintenance and technique. One hour would be spent in the water. One hour in the water? Is that all? We were going to spend two hours on safety and etiquette? Really? I was a bit miffed. It didn't take long to figure out the realistic rationale behind this schedule. It wasn't the safety or etiquette that took up the bulk of our land time. It was getting into and out of the 5mm wetsuits! OMG! Talk about squeezing 10 pounds of shit into a 5-pound bag. All the while standing on one foot in a gravel parking lot, trying not to get any grit on the inside of the suit! And keeping in mind that a wetsuit has to fit very snugly in order to be effective. Thank goodness no-one had a camera out at that point! And I now know that the only thing worse than putting on a wet bathing suit, is putting on a wet wetsuit. After everyone had struggled through their contortionist routines, standing or hanging on to car doors and bumpers, tugging and jumping, muttering and cursing, we reconvened (many still gasping for air) for a brief lecture on surf gear maintenance. Rule number one – don't pee in the wet suit. What?!? We have to be lectured on this? Someone might have peed in my suit?!? Yuck! And you couldn't tell me this before I squeezed into it? Never mind. It's too late now. We picked up the boards and marched down to the beach where the more practical aspects of the lesson commenced. We drew surf boards in the sand and practiced paddling, keeping our chests up and eyes looking ahead, and then "popping up" on the board. Another OMG. I was out of breath and we were still on dry land! And then the water fun began. It was fantastic! An incredible work out for arms, legs, abs and cardio (with the added benefit of sinus cleansing saltwater nettipots). Once I got the hang of timing the incoming waves, I actually managed to pop up (i.e. stand up) five times for the short ride in to shore. We were learning in the "white waves" (i.e. belly deep water where the waves break), leaving the "green waves" (i.e. deeper water where the bigger waves are just cresting), for the more experienced participants. And my scepticism about only having 1 hour in the water? I was done before the instructor called "time." My mind was saying, "Pop up! Pop up!" and my legs were saying, "No. Don't think so." As best I can describe it, imagine holding a yoga forearm plank or cobra pose for a period of time and then hopping straight into a crouch position (from which you will quickly stand up), all the while atop a tippy board gliding along the water with loud and frothy surf pushing you along. And once you fall off and clear the saltwater from your nose yet again, struggle against the incoming waves to get out there and do it all again. Yeah! It was great! Seriously! Within two days of our lesson (and popping several Advil), we went out and purchased some used wetsuits and surfboards. The suits required a few minor repairs that we effected with dental floss and neoprene glue, but that was considerably cheaper than renting the stuff for 6 weeks, so we officially became "surfers." We had the gear. We had the music. Cue The Surfaris' 1963 hit *Wipe Out*. Sadly, our first solo foray was not very successful. I'd like to say the song was very apropos, but then you have to get up before you can wipe out. We went on a day when there was a very high tide (12 feet) with waves that were much too big for our ability. It was like having taken a ski lesson on the bunny hill in the morning and heading over to a black diamond in the afternoon. Not pretty. I didn't get up even once. Although I did clear out my sinuses quite nicely several times, thank-you very much. At one point, John managed to get the board between himself and an incoming large wave, resulting in some pretty sore ribs, so we called it a day, promising to return when the waves were more our speed. After all, I wanted to start using my new-found surfer vocabulary. Everything will be "sweet" and "awesome" once I learn to "hang ten" on the "face" of a "bomb." Right now, I am still a "kook."

About 40 kms south of Tofino, along the Pacific Rim Highway, is the small community of Ucluelet. Situated on rocky headlands, it lacks Tofino's close proximity to beaches, but does have dramatic views out over the Pacific Ocean. And real estate is marginally more reasonable. Over the years, I have monitored sales in both communities, dreaming of that perpetually elusive vacation property. In Ucluelet, a relatively newish condo-hotel resort (Black Rock) had some units for sale that warranted further investigation. We drove out and found that as per conventional wisdom, if it's too good to be true... Despite the lovely pictures and write-ups, the entire complex left me cold. A large, cavernous concrete structure decorated in shades of dark gray loomed like a bunker from the cold war. To one side of the main building were 2 and 3 storey complexes containing 1 and 2-bedroom units, advertised as being deluxe, but the whole air was one of faux-luxury without real depth. We decided to have a coffee at the outdoor restaurant/patio overlooking the ocean to get an objective feel for the place (I really wanted to like it) but after sitting there for some time (and being ignored by the server who looked over at us several times), John went inside and was informed that service had ended 15 minutes prior to our arrival. I suppose it was too much effort for that server to let us know. We were done. And the town of Ucluelet (or Ukee as the locals call it) just didn't cut it. I have tried to like it before and I truly tried to like it this time, but nothin' doin'. John said Ucluelet is like Tofino's Cousin Eddie. Ouch. But there is some truth to that. I'm back to buying lottery tickets and pinning my hopes on Tofino's beaches. We all need a dream.

The entire stretch of coast between Tofino and Ucluelet is dotted with fantastic beaches, but one of my favourites was Florencia, in part because it is not as easily accessed as the others, and thus less visited. Up until 1930, it was officially called Wreck Bay because in 1861 the brigantine Florencia, en route to Peru with lumber, got into difficulty and shattered on an islet in the bay. Situated about 30 kms south of Tofino, we drove there on John's birthday and spent a glorious afternoon wandering along the beach, collecting sea-shells (my sand dollar collection was growing on a daily basis) and trying to exhaust Porter by throwing sticks into the surf. We didn't see any bears but did pass two huge piles of scat on the trail in, and two more huge piles on the beach itself. Given all the people-activity in the general area, it is easy to forget that this place is still mostly wilderness, home to bears, cougars and wolves. Even on populated Chesterman Beach, a news item from September 1ˢᵗ warned people to exercise caution with respect to their dogs. Apparently, a local family had let their medium-sized dog out of the house unsupervised early one morning, and doing what dogs do, it wandered down to the beach proper. Two wolves, assuming it was an interloper, attacked and killed it. Most dogs we saw on the beaches were off leash (as was Porter) but their owners were all within close proximity. Except for one chocolate lab (without even a collar) that made friends with Porter at north Chesterman and followed us all the way to Frank Island (well over a kilometer) before turning back. No owners in sight. A tragic news item in the making. And wolves will get the blame.

ANOTHER GREAT DAY AT FLORENCIA BAY

Closer to town, a different news-making story has almost been forgotten, although this one involves a tree. Along the road into Tofino on the east side of the highway, stands a huge western red cedar, seemingly held in place by massive cables attached to metal bands that encircle the tree's trunk. Called the Eik Cedar, it is not situated in the most picturesque of settings and the 64 tonne metal support braces only make it look worse, but be that as it may, it was the source of much angst at the turn of this century. The tree is estimated to be over 800 years old, and in 2001, not even 10 years after the more contentious logger/ environmentalist conflicts (environmentalists were protesting clear cutting in Clayoquot Sound – one of the last old growth areas of B.C.), an arborist deemed this particular tree unsafe (rotted inside), on the verge of toppling over and possibly causing extensive damage to nearby buildings. With typical liability concern, City Council voted to cut it down, but that elicited a big hue and cry from the tree huggers. What kind of message would that send? Two men truly devoted to the cause actually climbed up the 94-metre thing and refused to come down for over a month. What to do? What to do? The solution? Raise $60,000.00 to pay for said bracing. The town, concerned citizens, environmentalists and artists all got into the act. Even Robert Bateman donated some art for auction. And they pulled it off. Raising enough funds to keep Herbie (as the locals called it) from chainsaw carnage. Sadly, most people drive past the tree today without even noticing it. I say sadly because although it is not as spectacular as other trees we have seen, when considering the timeline, it truly is something to marvel about. When it was just a sapling, around 1200 AD, the Tower of Pisa was under construction in Italy. When it was 25 years old, King John of England signed the Magna Carta. When it was 400 years old, Quebec City was founded. Really helps put things into perspective.

The completely sunny days of our first two weeks did not last of course, and when it rained, it really rained. Night-time was the worst because when all is said and done, we really were living in a tin can, and heavy rain on the roof made for sleepless nights. Other times it drizzled. Or misted. Or dripped. Or was foggy. And the perpetual dampness did get to be a bit of a pain. Whenever Porter went out to do his business and came back in, we had to towel him off. Whenever he went to the beach (which was almost every day), we had to towel him off. And this made for a lot of wet towels. Unfortunately, the RV sites at the resort only had 30-amp service, and the clothes dryer in the coach required 50-amp. So we tried hanging the towels in front of the fireplace to dry but that was only marginally effective. It was electric after all. We ultimately stocked up on loonies and used the dryers in the resort's laundromat. A small inconvenience, all things considered. But what was not a small inconvenience was the condensation that kept building up on the windows, especially the big front windshield. So heavy it ran in rivulets down onto the dash. And the interior of the entrance door was constantly beaded with water. Then, after more than a week of unsuccessfully trying to resolve this, John went to get a sweater from the storage cupboard above the bed and found condensation in there as well. Not good. We had always opened vents and run fans when showering or cooking, but with the outside humidity sometimes hitting 95%, that was a rather futile gesture. So we did some research and bought a dehumidifier tout de suite. An unanticipated expense but it saved the day and our clothes.

We looked forward to another full month in this beautiful place and while I suspected the sunny days were behind us, I refused to complain. After all, surfing was possible rain or shine.

31.

PARADISE FOUND

ANGEL WINGS IN PARADISE TO ME. A TYPE OF RAZOR CLAM TO OTHERS.

TOFINO. What is there to write about everyday life in paradise, keeping in mind that what is paradise to one person (me!) is not necessarily paradise to someone else. Which is probably a good thing. When too many people discover paradise, there is a tendency to start paving. Thankfully, that has not happened much in Tuff City. It is still pretty wild. And it is not a conventional sort of paradise. There are no palm trees, no white sand beaches, no warm turquoise waters, no perpetual sunshine. The frequent rain of the Pacific west coast can put a damper on land activities, and a wet suit is required for comfortable water activities. But it is still paradise to me. And because of that, I haven't given up on the idea of one day possibly purchasing a little vacation place. The travel distance from home may be a bit far, but this is how I rationalize it. Many greater Toronto area people have summer cottages in Muskoka, Haliburton, Kawarthas etc., and spend every Friday evening from May/June through to September/October, sitting in traffic for at least 2 hours, often more, just to get to their little corner of heaven. And then every Sunday evening, turn around to do it all again in reverse. By my rough calculation, that is at least 64 hours of commuting time per season. And not that many days of actually being at the cottage. If the place is winterized, add some additional challenges. In comparison, if we had a place in Tofino, we could go out for several months at a time (retirement has its benefits), flying 5 hours Toronto to Victoria, and then driving 4 hours to Tofino. Overall, considerably less time spent in transit with more time kayaking, snorkelling, surfing and strolling to our heart's content along endless miles of beaches. And even if we went in January, the temperature rarely drops below 8C. And people surf year-round! I realize this logic has huge holes in it, but what are a few holes when you are dreaming the impossible dream. So with that mind set, I contacted a local real estate agent who showed us two properties that had potential. The first one we ruled out fairly quickly. It was a smallish condo/hotel complex where we could put our unit into a rental pool whenever we were not using it, if we chose. And we could use it as often or as little as we liked. At first blush, that sounded quite efficient. But "hotel" is the operative word here. Although the individual condos themselves were architecturally acceptable (only 3 stories high), many in a loft style with okay living rooms, kitchens etc., the furnishings and entire feel of the place was very, well... hotel-like. No individuality. Minimal charm. Very impersonal. The second place, however, was lovely – part of a condo/strata community with two and three-story units. The model we looked at was priced a bit high for us and sold before we finished our journey, but we hoped another one, more in keeping with our pay grade, would come up. I may need to start a GoFundMe campaign, but I'm not ready to give up on the dream just yet. Telegraph Cove is out. Tofino is in. ♪*You may say I'm a dreamer...but I'm not the only one.*♪

The entire month of November just flew by and weather permitting, we managed to get in a walk along one of the many beaches almost every single day. November is generally very rainy, but we lucked out and although it wasn't constantly sunny, it wasn't always raining either. The locals said that was quite unusual. Except the last week. It poured. A lot. I now know what the phrase "bucketing down" really means. Some of our beach walks were only an hour or two, with MacKenzie virtually right out our front door, but for others, we'd pack a lunch, drive to Beach "X" and start strolling. I can no longer say which beach is my favourite. Possibly Schooner Cove since that had the most shells and driftwood. And where John saw wolf tracks in the sand. If we missed a beach day, I truly felt like something was off. As if I hadn't had my morning cup of tea or forgotten to brush my teeth. And Porter? There has never been a happier dog. Into the water. Out of the water. Back into the water. Crunching on shells, crabs or whatever else he thought might be tasty. One of his favourite activities was tearing up the bull kelp that often washed up with the tide (or wading in and dragging it ashore), and then having us use the pieces as a fetch toy. And whenever he'd come out of the ocean, he'd roll in the damp sand, coating his fur with a kind of wet, granular paste. Thank goodness the resort had a dog wash station, although even that did not prevent sand from making it back into the yacht. The entire Tofino community was very dog-friendly and there were always several dogs on any given beach that he could run around with. I kept adding to my seashell collection though things may have started to get out of hand there. But I couldn't resist picking up just one more. And it was interesting to see how with each tide, the type of shells that washed up changed. The first few days, sand dollars were quite abundant, and I was somewhat selective about which ones to keep, but they soon disappeared, replaced with olives, and then the olives disappeared to be replaced with clams, then scallops and so on. Always something new. It never got old. John asked what I planned on doing with all these marine mollusks and while I didn't have an answer at that point, I'm sure something creatively artistic will come to mind sooner or later.

We continued surfing, although our skill level progressed rather slowly, and we didn't get out as much as anticipated. Fitness levels aside, there is a lot more to the sport than just squeezing into a wet suit and wading out. The size of the waves, their spacing, their speed and their direction can all make the difference between looking fairly accomplished or looking like a kitted-out poser. Some days, the waves were good but the weather itself a bit dodgy – other days, nice sunshine yet minimal waves. But we persevered and managed to shakily get up on our own a few times without too much damage. Other than injured pride. For every successful rise, there were at least ten tumbles. John took a bit of a dive during one foray and somehow managed to pull/strain the muscle the runs down the entire length of his inner forearm, resulting in a rather large, greenish bruise. Painful, but not enough to call it quits. We traded boards a few times and agreed that John's board, being about a foot longer and considerably heavier, was much more stable and therefore easier to balance on. But mine was prettier. We took Porter with us one day, but he kept swimming out into the water after us, and when not actually trying to climb up onto the board, kept getting in the way of incoming surfers. His retriever gene tends to kick into

overdrive if he sees anything floating in water. So we had to leave him in the yacht after that. But it was fun. And if it was that much fun in November, with air temperature 8 to 10 C, it must be fantastic in the summer (although I'm certain considerably more crowded). I'm willing to give it a try.

I'M UP! I'M UP! CUE THE MUSIC!

And on the theme of physical activity, the local yoga studio that we attended about twice a week in October, ran a 30-day challenge in November, so in a burst of questionable enthusiasm, we signed up. There were many class times to choose from and we figured it would be a great way to ensure we got in some daily exercise while working on our strength, balance and flexibility. Things went quite smoothly at first because several of the classes were geared specifically towards deconstructing the foundations for many of the postures, and the tempo was rather moderate, allowing us to actually think about what we were doing. But about mid-month, the pace picked up and the next thing we knew, we were being instructed on how to do handstands! Not even headstands! Full on handstands! It wasn't going to happen. I may have been a bit of a gymnast in my younger day, but that was a long time ago. And while I don't really consider myself old, I am wise enough to know that there are just some things best left to younger, more limber bodies. Thankfully, the instructors always provided less-challenging options to work on, and I was rather proud of managing to get into a reasonable facsimile of Wild Thing. The age demographic of many students was in the late 20s to 30s range, but there was one couple closer to our own vintage. We started chatting with them (okay, they were a bit older than us) and it turned out she was Latvian! Māra! With family in London, Ontario! What were the odds? She and her husband Robert had moved to Tofino years ago and now lived there full time, right across the road from Chesterman Beach. It must have been fate that we met. Because this particular year, on November 18th Latvia was celebrating its Centennial Year! I had been following along both on Facebook, and in Latvian news feeds, all the activities that were scheduled to take place throughout the various Latvian communities in Canada, the United States and of course Latvia itself, and was quietly lamenting the fact that I would not be participating in any of them. No Latvians around to share in this momentous anniversary. Enter Māra! So on November 18th, John and I baked a traditional *klingeris* (carefully following the instructions we had painstakingly written out from Ausma Mikelsons' workshop at Sidrabene back in June 2017), and went to celebrate with Māra and Robert at their home. It was lovely. Well, visiting with them was lovely. Baking the *kilngeris*... not so much. It was actually a frustrating and humbling labour of love.

I had taken copious notes during Ausma's tutorial and was confident that we could turn out a fairly respectable product. Alas, our efforts were only marginally successful. Finding the correct ingredients started the challenge. Tofino is a small town, after all. I had cardamom in my spice drawer, but no saffron. I located that at the local co-op grocery store, but the price? It was $18.00 for 0.5 grams. Wow. Then the candied citrus peel. Not so lucky. I did find a glacé mixture full of maraschino cherries and other unidentifiable, questionable pieces so bought that and then painstakingly picked out the orange and lemon bits. We carefully measured out the required ingredients and optimistically started stirring. It wasn't long before we realized something was not quite right. The entire mixture was way too runny. Okay. Add more flour. Oh. Oh. We used up all the flour, so John made an emergency run to the grocery store. Something still wasn't right. Now it was too sticky and not coming away from my hands or the sides of the bowl. We double checked our measurements and realized that we had misread ¼ cup for ¼ pound of butter/lard. I won't say who was responsible for that gaffe, but his initials are J.L. Okay. Add more butter and lard. We threw in some extra yeast too, to compensate for all the extra flour. Still too sticky. It was obvious that this was a science experiment going from bad to worse. And time was running out because we had planned to mix everything up and leave it to proof while we went to our yoga class. We placed the bowl in the microwave to keep it away from any draft, rushed off to yoga and hoped for the best. Upon our return, nothing had changed. It was still just a heavy clump of dough. I searched the internet for advice on getting dough to rise and was reminded it should be placed in a fairly warm space. Since we didn't have an oven proper, I wrapped the dough bowl in tea towels and then placed a heating pad around it. Things were getting ridiculous. To make a painful story short, the dough never really did rise, we shaped it the best we could, left it to proof a second time (still no rise), baked it anyway and while the flavour was nice, the texture was nowhere near what it should have been. But given the occasion, it was worth the effort. Happy 100th Birthday, Latvia! Next time, we'll do better.

Latvia's Centenary was not the only community event we commemorated. November 11th we joined the locals for the Remembrance Day Ceremony. On the one hand, being used to the parades and marching bands of larger cities, this one was almost sad in its scale. The "participants" (maybe 30 in total) milled about outside the volunteer fire-hall waiting for someone to tell them what to do, while the "spectators" lined up along the other side of the street. Judging by their age and medals, there appeared to be only three army veterans in the entire "participant" group. And one of them did not wait for the "parade" to start but rather, walked down the street by himself and went into the church, about 2 blocks away. I have no idea why. About 20 minutes later, the rest of the assembly (4 uniformed RCMP officers, a few Coast Guard and Parks Canada employees, ambulance personnel and firefighters – so pretty much anyone who wears some kind of uniform) fell into several rag tag lines and walked (there is no way it could be called "marching") down the same street and into the same church. There was no band of any kind. Not even a high school one. And not even one drummer to beat out a step. The rest of the crowd fell in, followed along behind, and then waited around outside until the short church service was over. Then everyone shuffled over to the legion, just around the corner, where a simple cenotaph stands outside. Actually, not everyone went. Part way over, the firefighters split off, apparently called out to some emergency somewhere. Yet despite the lack of military precision, it was heartening to see so many regular people in attendance, listening to the usual speeches and standing quietly as wreaths presented by numerous local businesses (including our own Crystal Cove Resort) were laid at the base of the modest monument. They had managed to rustle up a trumpeter who played a shaky Last Post and all ended as it should. We estimated there were about 600 to 700 people at the ceremony. Pretty respectable numbers for a town with a full-time population of less than 2000. Of course the weather helped too. It was a clear and sunny day so there really was no excuse to stay away. Lest we forget...

With so much of our time spent walking along the beaches, I must confess that we neglected many (most) of the numerous hiking trails in the area. However, one day we did check out the Rainforest Trail in Pacific Rim Park Preserve. It wasn't too lengthy (about 2 kms in total) along a raised boardwalk with a few sets of stairs that led through dense foliage and some old growth trees. Spectacular, as usual. Especially one old cedar that is estimated to be close to 800 years old. A sapling when Marco Polo travelled to the Far East. I still find it hard to get my head around that kind of timeline. We also hiked along the Tonquin Trail that led from our site at Crystal Cove, along MacKenzie Beach, through to and along Middle Beach, then Tonquin Beach and on towards town, a distance of about 3 kms. It was very similar to Rainforest except interspersed with beaches. We had set out at high tide, so some sections were a bit dicey, and John managed to get a pretty good soaker, but overall it was a very nice walk combining sand and soil, ocean and forest, and more huge trees. However, we were a bit more vigilant with respect to our surroundings this time. Despite the trail leading towards a more populated area, there was a fair bit of chatter and warnings about a recent cougar sighting. Fairly reliable chatter too. Staff at the Cove advised, and even posted a notice, that people in the neighbouring property reported seeing a female cougar outside their trailer around 1am one night, along with a few kittens up in a tree. How exciting! I'm sorry we missed it. Then again, there is that saying that if you see a cougar...

There were also several reports of wolves in the area, although that was nothing unusual since they are known to spend much of their time on the inlet (Clayoquot Sound) side, closer to the mud flats. But they do venture further afield as well. One young lady told me that she had been chatting with her father (face time) while standing in the parking lot at the town's "outskirts" coffee shop (where there is also a surf shop, hair salon, grocery store, and 2 eateries, about 3 kms from town proper), when her father asked, "What is that behind you?" She turned and saw a wolf several meters away, just watching her. No threatening behaviour or anything. Just watching. And then he (she?) turned and went off into the bush. This is also the place where our yoga studio was situated, so less than a 10-minute walk from our RV site! Yes! My spirit animals were all around! Another evening, we attended a presentation at the community theatre about wolves, hoping to gain more insight into these magnificent creatures but unfortunately that was a bit of a bust, despite the good turnout. The presenter was an "award winning" author who was promoting her recently published book and the event was advertised as being accompanied by "remarkable images." So we anticipated some current information either on wolves in the area, or wolves in general, but there was very little of that. Perhaps the author didn't want to provide too much information for fear no-one would buy her book afterwards, but I hoped her writing was more compelling than her speaking. The presentation was simplistic, and there was nothing "remarkable" about the projected images either, other than they were of wolves. Perhaps I am being too judgemental. Not everyone is a good public speaker. I purchased the book and hoped for the best. Save the wolves!

We ultimately couldn't muster up the enthusiasm to browse the various "touristy" shops in town either (except House of Himwitsa, which was great), but did check out Roy Henry Vickers Gallery (which we have done on previous visits) and still found it as impressive as ever. Built in 1986 and resembling a traditional northwest coast longhouse, it contains many of Vickers' works (mostly limited-edition prints) along with a few carvings, and has the requisite gift shop in the back. It was a bit like going to a small museum, except with the option of purchasing the pieces on display. I was happy just to admire them. It's funny how when we were "on the road" and only staying a week or two at a given destination (and knowing we would probably never return), I often wanted to buy something as a memento. Yet in Tofino, I didn't feel like I was visiting, and thus had no desire to purchase anything. Except real estate. (Insert a wistful sigh here.) Perhaps if we hung around long enough we would be considered honorary locals.

Despite our arrangements to ride out winter on Vancouver Island (with a few excursions home, south and skiing) we also started to turn our minds towards the upcoming spring and summer destinations – roughly Washington, Oregon, Colorado, Montana, Wyoming and South Dakota. One of the main issues to address was when to actually resume traveling. Many of these places are at higher elevations and there was no sense looking for snowy weather. December, January and February would definitely see us situated in Victoria, but what to do about March and April? It's such an unpredictable time of year weather wise. Well, it didn't take much discussion. We booked ourselves back into Crystal Cove until May 1st. And not a moment too soon. It is such a popular place, a considerable number of the RV sites had already been reserved, and the cabins were almost all fully spoken for. The beauty of the surroundings speak for themselves, but the staff were also incredibly friendly and helpful. They were more than understanding when we had an issue with the RV's levelling jacks. Long story short, we had requested a change of site after our initial arrival (one with a bit more space and light) and since this was in effect a change to our reservation, part way through the month we were supposed to switch back to our original site for a few days. But on the slated day of change up, we could not get the jacks to retract. We had brought in the slides and were ready to go, but for some reason, turning the ignition key to the left (necessary prior to hitting the "jacks button") activated the hydraulic pump. That is not supposed to happen. And we could not get them to retract manually either. When I tried the key a third time, the front driver's side slide started going back out, totally on its own. Which should definitely not happen! John called Tiffin and the mechanic walked him through a few checks before finally advising that it sounded like one of the solenoids had malfunctioned. Now there is a word I had never heard before, never mind used in a sentence. I now know that a solenoid is an electrical part in a hydraulic system. I didn't need to know any more. Just as long as it got fixed. Tiffin shipped out the replacement part and it arrived 10 days later. John got to work. Problem solved? Nope. Turning the ignition key in either direction still activated the pump. Back on to Tiffin again. This time, the suggestion was to replace the entire forward electronic breaker panel. Considerably more expensive and as per the law pertaining to warranties, this one had expired several months ago. Ouch. John ordered the panel to be delivered to Victoria and decided to change it up there. We hoped that would get us back on track. Until then, Tiffin talked John through the jack/slide bypass process which although somewhat cumbersome had to do until the part arrived. Thankfully, we were not actually in transit, so it was just a bit of a hassle one or two times.

And another RV maintenance issue came up. One evening, as we returned from yoga, our neighbours in the adjoining site advised that something was very wrong with the RV's heating system. While we had been away, there had been a very loud banging and clattering noise coming from one of the heating units on the roof. John immediately suspected that it was the front blower wheel, since we had experienced this once before, about 6 months earlier, albeit on the rear unit. Given that we were due to depart for Victoria a week later, John held off ordering the replacement part until we were re-situated. It too came from Alabama. There was no urgency since we had the option of switching to propane if need be. But what was most distressing about this inconvenience was that Porter had been inside the coach while the blower wheel was shredding itself up on the roof. The racket would have been unbearably loud until the whole thing quit, and he must have been very frightened. There were times when we wondered if we were overly protective and overly indulgent when it came to the brown menace. But then something like this happens and we were reminded there was a reason for why we didn't like to leave him alone in the yacht, despite the "Rescue Our Pet" sign and contact phone numbers that we usually placed in the window. Worse things than this could and have happened to other people, and we didn't want to go there. Porter went off to his bed very early that evening, which was most unlike him, but by morning was his usual self, excitedly leading the way down to the beach just in case we had forgotten how to get there. If he could talk, I'm sure he would be urging us along, "Hurry up! Hurry up! The water is going away! Come on! Come on! I know how to get there!" He lives in the moment, and most of his moments were great. As were ours.

32.

SILVER LININGS

OUR THIRD DECEMBER AND OUR THIRD CHRISTMAS IN THE LAND YACHT. If all went according to plan, it was going be our last "on the road". The first year saw us in Florida where it was nice and warm, the second in south Texas where it was sort-of warm, and the final year in Victoria, B.C. where it was not warm at all (although still warmer than Ontario). Given the time spent in Alaska during the summer, we had used up our 180-day per annum stateside allotment and were forced to remain north of the 49th parallel for a few more months. This was not a surprise and we had made a 3-month reservation at Salish Seaside RV Resort early on, calculating that it would be about the warmest place in Canada to wait out the winter. We rather reluctantly pulled out of Tofino December 1st, a beautifully clear and sunny day, made one quick stop at Chocolate Tofino to pick up a pint (or more) of the best gelato outside Italy and we were off. The drive was uneventful, the scenery lovely and we made it to Salish Seaside in good time. Our site was great. Right on the water of West Bay in Esquimalt, facing Victoria's Inner Harbour where if the wind was from the east, we could watch the seaplanes take off out our front window. A bit noisy but interesting none the less. At night we could see the beautiful city lights. The resort itself was small (only 36 sites) but had recently undergone a complete overhaul, and everything was so new that the lofty yet cozy clubhouse still had that off-gassing new smell to it. Hardly anyone ever used the place, so it made for a great private yoga studio for us, and a nice space to hang out and read the paper from time to time. There were numerous floating homes on the same little inlet, and a boat launch ramp less than 50 feet from our site. It was odd seeing people kayaking, canoeing and sailing past our coach in mid-December. Cormorants were a regular fixture on the pilings out front, harbour seals and river otters (six at one point) swam back and forth, with occasional forays up onto the dock and deck of a neighbouring boat. A boardwalk/paved walkway along the shoreline lead directly past Victoria International Marina and into downtown and could be comfortably walked in just over an hour. Weather permitting, we'd stroll along it with Porter, admiring the Olympic Mountains in the distance, and the beautiful water birds (Hooded Mergansers, Harlequin Ducks and Common Goldeneyes) in the water close by. The first few days were relatively sunny (although only 5 degrees) so we took care of some maintenance and cleaning issues that had been long neglected. Clear out the car, dry out the kayaks, re-organize the basement. John replaced the blower wheel on the roof so we finally had both heating units in full operation, and we picked up an inexpensive area rug at Costco in an effort to insulate the cold tile floor a little bit. That was only marginally effective and if I were doing this all over again, I would definitely opt for a RV model with heated floors. John decided to wait until January to tackle the hydraulic jack issue, concerned it could prove to be tricky, but everything else went rather smoothly. Except for a few concerns regarding Porter.

Given that we were flying home for Christmas and could not take Porter with us, it was necessary to locate a good off leash daycare / boarding facility for the brown menace. One that would actually be open during the requisite time period. A Google search showed a promising place only a few kilometers away. Perfect? Not so fast. There is much wisdom in the old adage that you can't judge a book by its cover. Or by its website either. Positively or negatively. When we checked Porter in for a trial visit, it was with considerable consternation. By this point we had used doggie daycares all across North America and the reputable ones all have pretty standard requirements. They want to actually <u>see</u> vaccination records, require veterinarian, owner and emergency contact information, request an authorized financial amount should emergency vet care be required, discuss any health and habit issues the dog may have, and of course, conduct an assessment to see if the dog fits in with the pack. This particular place did none of the above. There was a form I signed releasing them from liability in case of injury and three areas to check off indicating his vaccinations were up to date, but that was it. The facility itself was very small and cluttered with all manner of water buckets, bedding and boxes scattered about. There were way too many dogs for the cramped space, and the more excited ones were spritzed in the face with water to break them out of their barking/ humping/excited behaviour cycles. Water spray is a common and very effective distractor with dogs, but the minder was using it with such frequency and enthusiasm that the concrete and tile floor was soaking wet. Any exercise the dogs would get required a walker to take them out and around the block in groups of six. The place was clearly way over capacity and we returned after leaving Porter there for less than 3 hours. I just couldn't imagine leaving him there for 10 days! We found a second place about a 15-minute drive away and they were very thorough in asking for all the necessary info. The daycare facility itself was fairly spacious, with an option for dogs to be driven out of town to a fenced acreage where they could run around outside. Lobo Land, they called it. Any overnights would be spent at this acreage and in the owner's home. It was prefect. Except they were full up for Christmas. I half-jokingly (but hopefully) tried to bribe them with offers of chocolate and wine, to accept just one more pup, but they wouldn't budge. I suppose that is a good thing. What to do? What to do? Then, as if I wasn't worrying enough, I noticed a rather large lump on Porter's belly, which was definitely not there a month earlier. It was in all likelihood a benign lipoma – quite common in labs – but we were off to the vet just in case. During the examination, the vet found that Porter had a badly chipped rear molar with the dentin partially exposed. The tooth would have to be pulled under general anaesthetic. The lipoma would be removed and sent to pathology at the same time. Ka-ching! Ka-ching! We scheduled the surgery for January 15 when the good doctor was back from holidays. He probably upgraded to a first-class ticket to someplace extravagant in anticipation.

With the Porter issue only partially addressed, we caught the ferry to Vancouver and did some semi-housesitting for my favourite uncle and aunt, while they wrapped up some sun time in Mexico. It was such a treat to live in a space where the ceiling was higher than 7 feet. When the weather was sunny, we went for a leisurely drive and stroll along the walkway around Stanley Park, and Porter thoroughly enjoyed himself wading in the water of English Bay and running around on Third Beach. That is, until I noticed the sign indicating a $2,000.00 fine for dogs on the beach. Ooops. Retreat! Retreat! There had been a fairly heavy foggy frost the previous night, and the rime patterns on the leaves, plants and logs were just fascinating. And great for artsy photographs. Downtown, we checked out the Bill Reid Gallery but disappointingly, found that to be rather underwhelming and quite light on content. One guest quote in their brochure described it as, "the best gallery of Indigenous Art I've ever had the pleasure of visiting." All I could think in response was, "Wow. Whoever wrote that needs to get out more." Bill Reid was an acclaimed Haida artist (goldsmith, sculptor, carver) with seminal works such as *The Spirit of Haida Gwaii*, and *Raven and the First Men*. *The Spirit of Haida Gwaii - Black Canoe* is in the Canadian Embassy in Washington, while the *Jade Canoe* version is in Vancouver International Airport. Magnificent pieces both. Reid is also credited with reviving interest in Indigenous art, and inspiring and teaching future artists and carvers. Sadly, none of this came across in the gallery bearing his name. And while there were a few pieces to admire, I think we should have gone to the Museum of Anthropology at UBC instead.

Next up, we hit the Vancouver Art Gallery to see the extravagant *Guo Pei: Couture Beyond* exhibit. Given all the news with respect to China over that past little while, I felt a bit guilty praising this exposition, but it was definitely worth the price of admission. Guo Pei is a Chinese designer and the only Chinese national invited to present her collections at the Paris Haute Couture Fashion Week. Of course her creations are not really meant to be worn in any practical way. They are more works of art where the human body is just the frame upon which they are draped. Colourful, whimsical, theatrical, with unbelievably intricate embroidery and detailing. And some weighing as much as the average suit of armour. One masterpiece on display was the canary yellow number Rihanna wore to the Met Gala in 2015. Sometimes caustically referred to as "the omelette dress", it weighs 55 pounds and poor Rihanna needed three attendants to help carry the train. Such is the price of uber-stardom. I could have spent the entire day wandering back and forth admiring the ensembles, but compassionately took pity on John, who despite being more than a good sport, couldn't quite match my level of enthusiasm. I forget what other exhibits were on at the museum, but in comparison to this, they must have been merely meh! The weather was definitely cold the first few days and we were not equipped for any lengthy walks outdoors. That is just as well. We were forced to cross Grouse Mountain off the list since dogs had been banned from the hiking trail up (in an effort to "enhance the visitor experience and minimize ecological impact." Oh, please!) and they were certainly not allowed in the tram. So no picturesque views out over the city this time.

One evening, we caught up with friends from back east who moved to Vancouver over 30 years ago, and now live in a floating home community on the Fraser River. I originally called them houseboats, but that is not the correct term. These truly are homes, in every sense of the word, that simply float. Some on wooden barges, some on cement bases, some on metal pontoons. They are just not motorized. Never having been on one, or in one, I suppose I had imagined something a bit more boat-like, but these places were two and three stories high with every modern convenience imaginable. And with beautiful, unencumbered views out towards the mountains to boot. What a novel way to live! As luck would have it, we were able to see and compare several of these abodes because our friends' floating community was having a bit of a neighbourhood open house, celebrating the sail past of the carol ships. What?!? I had no idea what a "carol ship" was but apparently, it's a Vancouver phenomenon. On given December evenings, any and all manner of participating boats (including a kayak one year) are decorated with Christmas lights and cruise along the shoreline as a festive flotilla. Carols are sung, music is played and wishes of "Merry Christmas" are exchanged between the mariners and the landlubbers. It was a lovely way to start celebrating the Christmas season. And in the spirit of Christmas (which I hoped they wouldn't regret), our friends offered to look after Porter while we were away. They were temporarily "dog-less", were staying put over the holidays and were in need of a fur fix. This required a minor adjustment to our flight plans, but it certainly took a load off our minds knowing Porter would be well cared for and fussed over. We couldn't say thank-you enough.

Returning to Victoria, we had less than a week before departing for Toronto but did manage to get in a visit to the Royal BC Museum. What a fantastic place. The featured exhibit was *Egypt - Time of the Pharaohs* and while it did have some interesting pieces (and a basic IMAX movie), much of the information was somewhat rudimentary. Is there really anyone who does not know that the Ancient Egyptians mummified their dead? But that is not really fair. Five years earlier, when our son was working for the UN in Cairo, we took the opportunity to visit him and experience Egypt first-hand. This was just after the Arab Spring when tourists were staying away in droves (I don't believe they have returned in any great numbers) and we were able to sail along the Nile and tour the ruins from Aswan to Luxor to Cairo in almost complete privacy. Except for the discretely armed security escort but that is another story. Still, the museum was a nice way to "re-visit" the pyramids albeit through IMAX. Another section, the Natural History Gallery was excellent, with numerous dioramas depicting the vast variety of flora and fauna found throughout British Columbia, and many of the scenes were so life-like it truly felt as if some of the animals were about to move. There was also a section on the history of B.C. from first contact, sailings, forestry, fishing, mining and the like (as is to be expected) but the area that we enjoyed most was the First Peoples Gallery, a fantastic collection of Aboriginal totem poles, ceremonial masks and other carvings. There is just something about that formline art style that appeals to me. However, given the repatriation of artefacts issue, almost every item had a small placard indicating not only its location of origin but also its lawful purchase or legitimate donation by a specific chief or tribe. No sense upsetting the Truth and Reconciliation applecart at this point in the game. We spent a fair bit of time in that gallery. And the last area I found most informative (and to a certain extent, sad) dealt with First Nations languages and the efforts underway to preserve them. A sizable 60% of Canada's Aboriginal languages are spoken in British Columbia (34 languages with 61 dialects) and an interactive map showed which languages originated where, how many fluent speakers still remain, how many merely understand and how many are actually learning. The Nisga'a (northwestern BC) have the highest numbers with 16% fluent, 35% understanding and 9% learning, but most regions are in the 0.5 to 2% range and many at 0%. That is very discouraging considering the preservation of culture is so closely tied to the preservation of language. And while one information panel romantically indicated that the "0% spoken/understood" languages have not died but are rather "sleeping", there is no waking them up from that slumber. "Our languages will never die... they are born on the land... our voices will not be silenced." Another heart-warming sentiment, but the reality is that many of those voices have already been permanently silenced. The argument is presented that Canada's education policy should support First Nations language fluency through investment, that money and additional resources would help these floundering languages thrive. Really? Not only has that ship sailed, it sank quite some time ago and no wishful thinking and no government infusion of resources will see it float again. Sad. Realistic. A story as old as time.

And speaking of time, with Christmas fast approaching, we decided to visit Butchart_Gardens to see the festive lights and decorations that are put up at this time of year. I was actually surprised that the gardens were located so far from the city proper. They are always referred to as Victoria's Butchart Gardens so I somehow imagined they were, if not actually within town, at least in close proximity. Not so. It was about a 30-minute drive towards Brentwood Bay and I am glad we went in the late afternoon, which gave us the opportunity to walk around and see things in daylight, and then stay for the light display when it got dark. (Fortune favours the foolish. As we were departing – around 6pm – the line-up of cars to get in, had to have been 5 kilometers long. I have no idea how long people waited before getting to the sizeable parking lots.) And while the gardens have been declared a National Historic Site, their ownership still remains with the descendants of Robert and Jennie Butchart who got the ball rolling in the early 1900s when they operated a limestone quarry on the vast acreage. In fact, the beautiful Sunken Garden is set on the actual quarry after the limestone had been exhausted. Spring and summer are supposedly the best times to visit but even in December, it was beautiful. With the Christmas lights, it was magical. The acreage is very walkable and at various points along the decoratively lit pathways, tableaus were set up depicting the Twelve Days of Christmas. Children (and more than a few adults) had corresponding sheets where they ticked off the various scenes. Some of them were very clever, as in three hens sitting and having tea by the Eiffel Tower and four birds holding cell phones (Three French Hens, Four Calling Birds – get it?) Apparently they start putting up the decorations in October in order to be ready by December 1st. There was a small skating rink, the usual gift shop (very dog-friendly where Porter was invited inside and fawned over), an old-fashioned carousel, carol singers, a brass band and had we planned for it, places for afternoon tea or dinner. It truly was an enjoyable feast for the eyes.

And on the topic of feasts, we discovered something else in Victoria that was enjoyable, although not necessarily good for us. The Saltchuck Pie Company. OMG! Located around the industrial area of Esquimalt, dangerously close to our RV resort (we had to drive by it to get home), it is a café/take out place serving up savory and sweet pies with crusts so flakey you would be hard pressed to find a Michelin-starred pastry chef who could match them! The salted caramel apple pie was melt-in-your-mouth delicious. The savory pies could probably use a bit more filling but with crusts like that, who wants to quibble? You can even purchase the crust dough to make your own pies at home if you wish. Be still my heart! And hide the bathroom scales! It really was rather unfair, considering how much over-indulging takes place during the holidays. We just added to the new year recovery woes by getting a head start.

Returning home for Christmas was a double-edged sword. I missed Matejs a great deal and we had all reached the point where we wanted our lives to be more intermingled, with more chats over coffee, more family dinners. Skype just didn't cut it anymore. So seeing him, family and friends was something to look forward to with great anticipation. But at the same time, I was dreading Christmas Eve without my parents. How could it not be so? Sixty years of celebrating *Svētvakars* with them in the same place, in the same manner. It was going to be difficult. But before heading home, we had to get Porter settled. Anticipating he would be staying in Victoria, we had jumped the gun and booked our flights – Victoria to Toronto with a plane change in Vancouver, before the doggie daycare debacle. And our friends lived on the mainland. So John flew as scheduled from Victoria, and I took the ferry from Swartz Bay to Tsawwassen, spent the night at their place to help Porter get acclimatized to his new floating digs and then told a little fib at Vancouver International that I had missed my flight out of Victoria. I had originally called the airline (Westjet) to advise I wanted to legitimately make the departure locale change but was told that would cost an additional $430!! Seriously!?! I wasn't adding a leg, I was dropping one! The call taker was very helpful and said that while they don't recommend this strategy, to just show up at Vancouver and say I didn't make the Victoria flight. So that is what I did without any issues. Thank goodness. I really hate flying. And thankfully I left when I did, because B.C. was hit with some pretty serious windstorms 24 hours later and numerous ferry crossings were delayed or cancelled. Even the ferry that runs from Victoria to Port Angeles in Washington was cancelled for the first time in 22 years.

Being home for only a short time was exhausting, especially since we wanted to see as many family and friends as possible, but we were not complaining. Matejs surprised me with a delightful (and thoughtful) early Christmas present, by taking me to a performance of Handel's Messiah at Roy Thomson Hall with the Toronto Symphony and the Mendelssohn Choir, and it was the perfect way to get into the Christmas spirit. We used to attend almost every year but being on the road had interrupted that tradition, so it was wonderful to get back to something beautiful and familiar. We both agreed that the conductor had the tempo up at a pace that was a bit quick for our liking (laughing that perhaps he had a hot date after work) but the soloists and choir were excellent as usual, and the entire evening uplifting.

And then Matejs made the Christmas season all that more memorable by proposing to Erica, and she completed the joy by saying "yes." We knew what he was planning (she did not) and were delighted to see pictures of him down on one knee amidst the flowers and greenery of Allan Gardens. Such happiness and excitement! However, I suspect Matejs was also quite happy when we returned to the road so I couldn't meddle too much in their wedding plans.

Christmas Eve was tough but not as much as I had expected. We went to the cemetery and lit candles as is customary, made it to church on time, and returned to "my parents" house for a traditional Latvian meal that my sister had worked hard to put together, preparing all the dishes Mom would have made. There is no denying that Mom and Dad's absence was difficult, but it was more surreal than sorrowful, and the shift in the family dynamic was profound. On the positive side, however, we had four additions joining us. My sister's three boys all had their significant others with them, and Erica was with Matejs so it was heartening to see the future unfolding in front of us. And while it was sad to reflect back on all the losses we experienced during the year, we had much to look forward to in the future.

And then the holidays were over. John returned to Vancouver to pick up Porter while I remained a few more days to take care of some practical matters and spend one more full day hanging out with Matejs. We would see both him and Erica again soon, but as I have touched on previously, the allure of travel was losing its lustre, in large part because we missed our family and friends. John met with our tenants and advised that our return date was set for October 1st, but I suspected it would be sooner. They had a little boy who was starting school in the fall, and wanted him settled in their new digs, wherever those may be, by the start of September. It all seemed to be falling into place. We just had to start turning our minds toward selling the land yacht.

SHE SAID, "YES!"

33.

LIVING THE PURA VIDA?

I HATE COMPUTERS. I hate everything about computers. I hate how they intimidate me. I hate how they have a language all their own – one which I do not understand. I hate how when they stop working, a simple re-boot sometimes, but only sometimes, fixes the problem. How does that even make sense? I hate how they won't work for me but will for John. I hate how staff at the Apple store look at me with a mixture of pity, incredulity and frustration as I inarticulately attempt to explain my problems. But most of all, I hate those people who create the programs we use, and then feel compelled, for no apparently good reason, to generate unnecessary "updates", deliberately triggering my Tourettes, throwing my tenuous grasp on all things digital into disarray and expediting my rapid descent into technology hell. Given that I was able to develop and create my own blog-site, complete with dedicated url, and had been fairly proficient at posting monthly blogs, you would be forgiven for thinking that I was fairly competent in computer use. That is not true. John maintains that the massive blackout experienced on the Eastern Seaboard in 2003 was entirely my doing, and that when I walk into an Apple store, the lights momentarily dim due to the massive amount of negative electrical energy that follows me around. He calls me the anti-Midas. There may be some truth to his assertions. Programs that work smoothly for most people do not work at all for me. Even simple e-mails can be a challenge. I still do not have an explanation for why my November 2018 blog group e-mail was not delivered for 3 days. And why the December 2018 was not delivered for 2 days. I had been following the same steps religiously for 2-1/2 years without issue. But what set me off on this particular rant was that Wordpress, the platform that hosted my site, (as opposed to Hostgator that held my domain name), (sounds like I know what I'm talking about, right?) decided to "update" to something called the Gutenberg Block Editor. When I went to upload both my written text as well as my photos for the December blog, it was as if I had been working in Spanish for over 2 years and they decided to switch to Swedish. WTF!!!! And it had taken me a long time to learn Spanish. So what had previously taken a couple of hours, now took an entire day, and this was after contacting the help desk and being talked off the ledge and through the new process. Future posts became frustratingly more labour-intensive and less labour-of-love. I was too stubborn to quit, and I'd be damned if some computer geek was going to force me to throw in the towel so late in the adventure. Game on! My apologies to anyone who works in IT.

Our final year in the yacht started rather quietly. I flew back to Victoria on December 31st and with the 3-hour time difference, it was all I could do to keep my eyes open long enough to exchange a happy new year kiss with my darling husband. And then it was lights out. No party animals in this RV. The first few days saw us engaged in the usual year-end clean up, trying to purge, consolidate and organize. It was amazing how even in as small a space as an RV, useless papers and pamphlets had piled up. John finally managed to get an appointment for some minor body-work required at the back of the coach (cracks in the fibreglass resulting from when we had it in for service at Tiffin in December 2017 and they failed to properly reattach the tailpipe) and the repair was scheduled to be completed while we were in Costa Rica (more on that little detour later). He also put on his mechanic's overalls, having patiently waited for a completely sunny day to replace the main electronic panel that governed most of the hydraulic-dependent moving parts on the yacht. You may recall that while in Tofino, we found our levelling jacks were not working properly, and some wire somewhere was responsible. I wish I could say that all went smoothly but Murphy's Law came into play. Switching up the crucial panel went without a hitch, but it was the mounting brackets that caused the headache. Apparently, the new panels were just marginally different from those that had been installed in 2016 models, with framing now required to be horizontal as opposed to vertical. You would think they'd have a supply of 2016 parts for 2016 vehicles but that would have been too easy. And of course there did not appear to be any logical reason for the change up. Probably some guy who used to work with computers had transferred over to auto-mechanics and thought everything needed an update. As it was, John had to take off the brackets, reposition them, drill new screw holes and re-attach. Thankfully he was able to borrow a drill from the on-site property manager, but it was a long and frustrating day. All I can say is it's a good thing we were staying put in one place while all this was going on. I couldn't imagine what we would have done had we been actively travelling and boondocking in some remote locale. Which brings me to another point that contributed to an overarching air of discontent at this point in our travels. At least for me, anyway.

Staying put in one place was definitely beneficial from a domestic perspective (i.e. I knew where the grocery store was and could navigate the aisles quite effectively.) But it also had a downside. There was a tendency for a certain lethargy to set in, and the less you do, the less you want to do, so the less you do, so the less you want to do… it's a downward spiral. We had to force ourselves to get out even if the weather was less than ideal. Sunny days are few and far between during the winter months in Victoria and while an air temperature of 8C may seem great for January, that positive is negated by the clouds and/or rain that usually accompany it. Adding to my feeling of ennui was the fact that we had been to Victoria before, more than once, and the excitement that comes with exploring uncharted territory was absent. To use a military analogy, I felt like we were marching on the spot. I left my comfortable home in Port Credit for the experience of travelling about and seeing North America, not for the experience of living in a motor home, no matter how well appointed. And while it was nice not to have to contend with snowdrifts and sub-zero temperatures, even the rare sunny days did not exactly lend themselves to sitting outside or going for long, leisurely walks. The thermometer usually hovered between 5 and 8, but it felt considerably cooler. However when the sun came out, there was much rejoicing in the land, and the walkways and parks were full of activity, both human and canine. And most parks, at least the ones we came across, all had unfenced, off-leash dog areas. Those folks who didn't favour dogs, just stayed away from the off-leash areas. Very civilized.

And a further positive, if we had to stay put in Victoria, Salish Seaside RV Resort was certainly the best one around, and I have nothing but good things to say about it. However, it is situated in a part of town that is decidedly downmarket, and while there were signs of gentrification with new condos being proposed and popping up around every corner, it is not an area that will see a return to the grand mansions of yester-year. Or more accurately, yester-century. The odd one is still standing but most were long since replaced by nondescript apartment buildings and more "modest" single-family homes, many built by the Department of National Defence, so not exactly contenders for Architectural Digest. The Victoria area can roughly be divided into 7 regions. The Inner Harbour & James Bay (think Empress Hotel & B.C. Legislature Building – businesses, government and tourism), Oak Bay (beautiful views and high-end real estate), Uplands (towards University of Victoria), Fairfield & Cook St. Villages (cozy arts & crafts homes with great community feel), Fernwood (central town but away from the water), Vic West (other side of the Inner Harbour – struggling to gentrify) and Esquimalt (lots of DND presence with accompanying poorly maintained buildings and Canada's western naval base.) An eclectic mix to be sure. Victoria was founded as a trading post in 1843 by the Hudson's Bay Company (is there anywhere HBC didn't set up?) and on the condition of colonization, HBC received title to Vancouver Island itself. Build it and they will come. Victoria currently has a population of about 86,000 (368,000 if you include the surrounding area) so it is really a very comfortable size and it doesn't take long to get from point a to b.

But there were no endless beaches to explore, so how did we fill our time? Well, one afternoon we went to the Robert Bateman Centre located in the old Steamliner Building by Victoria's Inner Harbour. To those unfamiliar with Bateman's work, think wildlife paintings that look like photographs. I can't say that his realism style is such that I would necessarily hang any on my wall at home, but his ability to paint nature in a manner where each blade of grass, each snowflake, each feather, each hair combines in such detail to look so real, is incredible. Bateman himself does not consider the praise he receives for this detail to be complimentary. I'm not sure I quite understand that, but what can I say. He's an artist. And to think he grew up and spent much of his early life in the GTA. The centre itself is not large and didn't contain as many pieces as I expected (and some of the works were just numbered limited edition prints) so it didn't take long to see everything, but it was a nice way to spend an hour on a rainy day.

On the few occasions that weather allowed, we walked Porter along a stretch of Dallas Road, overlooking the Juan du Fuca Strait with the majestic Olympic Mountains across the way. A long, paved pathway bordered by off-leash green space runs from Beacon Hill Park to Clover Point Park, so Porter was able to do a bit of doggie socializing plus get into the water to splash around a bit. But then I saw a posted sign indicating that the pebbly beach (such as it was) was closed for swimming due to high bacteria levels in the water. And judging by their condition, the signs had been there for quite some time, so this was not a new problem. Okay, what was up with that? This is the Juan de Fuca Strait, a massive body of rapidly flowing tidal ocean water. How can it be contaminated to such a degree that it poses a health hazard? Well, we may have been in environmentally conscientious British Columbia but apparently Victoria didn't get the memo about not dumping the city's untreated raw sewage into the ocean. Actually, most of B.C. didn't get the memo (or simply chose to ignore it) because the province of B.C. has the third highest percentage of untreated waste being released into waterways, eclipsed only by Nova Scotia and New Brunswick. And the discarding of this waste in this manner is a very contentious issue for provinces with coastal communities, since despite the "yuck" factor, it is a very inexpensive way to deal with what goes down the toilet. In Victoria, proponents maintain that the sewage is "filtered" for plastic type products and the outfall pipes vent not only an entire kilometer away from shore, but 50 meters below the surface, into the fast-flowing ocean waters where rapid dilution renders the waste products "almost" harmless. But they don't recommend any snorkelling within the vicinity. You think? The opponents, meanwhile, claim that polluted scallops and sick kelp near the discharge pipes speak for themselves, and in 2014 the governor of Washington State issued a "formal reprimand" over the supposed contamination of their shared waterway. In 2012 the federal Conservative government brought in new standards for sewage treatment across the country, and made funds available for new infrastructure, but incredibly, many municipalities chose to use the money for road improvement. Victoria, the last major city in North America to simply dump its raw sewage, voted to build a treatment plant, work was underway, and things should be operational by 2020 despite the usual government sanctioned cost overruns. In the meantime, I tried to keep Porter out of the water but that was fairly futile. He is a water dog after all, and despite the signs, there were no overt indicators of contamination. Read: we only saw logs of the wooden kind floating in the Strait. I know that whales and other marine creatures both large and small use the ocean as their personal privy, but do we humans really have to contribute to it, en mass? It was really quite awful to contemplate.

We then decided to check out Chinatown, with its claim to fame as being Canada's oldest and North America's second oldest, San Francisco being awarded the longevity honour. Its inception dates to about 1858 when the first Chinese immigrants arrived on their way to the gold rush (is there any part of the world that gold seekers did not come from?) Back then, the

DRAGON ALLEY IN CHINATOWN. THE OPIUM DENS ARE LONG GONE... I THINK.

settlement covered 8 city blocks, and was comprised of crude wooden shacks joined by a seemingly confusing maze of narrow back alleys and secret passageways that led to opium dens, gambling parlours and brothels. Two of these laneways still exist, with Fan Tan Alley considered to be one of the narrowest "streets" in the country. As pedestrians, we could easily touch the walls of the brick buildings on either side. Back in 1858, the Chinese community made up about 1/3 of Victoria's inhabitants, but considering the entire populace was only about 500 souls, that isn't really saying much. Within a few short years the population exploded and by the early 1900s it was the largest Chinese settlement in Canada. Then from 1920 to 1970 it saw a massive exodus as people moved on in search of a better life. Things were rather neglected until the 1980s when revitalization turned it into the tourist attraction it is today, albeit with a still functioning core of Chinese shops and gathering spaces. The area now is only 2 city blocks in size, and it made for a very enjoyable stroll, certainly not as overwhelming or exhausting as Toronto or San Fran. And while many of the turn-of-the-century buildings have been restored and repurposed into all manner of chic boutiques and salons, there were just as many great Chinese restaurants and retailers.

Mid-month Porter went in for his tooth extraction (note my use of the singular word tooth) and lumpectomy. We had actually discovered a second lipoma under his left armpit just after our first consultation in mid-December, and then a third one literally popped up on his muzzle two days before the surgery date, January 16th. What was going on? Lipomas are generally benign fatty tissue tumours that form under the skin, appearing in twos and threes, sometimes more, and while unsightly, do not cause any discomfort unless they are in a joint or interfere with gait. Some dogs, like labs, are more prone to them than others. Being that I wanted to ensure the veterinarian knew what he was talking about, I thought it best to check this all out on Google. Big mistake. I came away convinced these were liposarcomas, malignant growths that lead to more surgery, radiation and chemotherapy. There was considerable anxiety until the pathology reports came back a week later signalling all was clear. And while that was good news, the tooth extraction did not exactly go smoothly. We had dropped Porter off at 8:30am and were told he'd probably be ready for pick-up around 3:30pm, but the office called around 1pm, advising they had found a second tooth that was broken and needed extraction as well. We gave the go-ahead. Then the vet called a third time to say that a third tooth was loose and needed removing. By this time, I was starting to wonder what kind of a money-making operation they had going on there. Certainly this fellow seemed sincere enough but I longed for the advice of our trusted vet back home. When all was said and done, Porter had been under anaesthetic for 3 hours, the vet advised that the extractions were the most difficult he has ever had to perform, and the final bill was $1,900.00, about $600.00 more than the estimate. But we shut up and paid up. The brown menace was back home with us and at the end of the day that was what really mattered. The first 24 hours were quite difficult for him, being disoriented from the anaesthesia, in pain from the incisions and bleeding from the teeth extractions. We gave him the prescribed pain meds and took off the lampshade he came home with (John made a pool-noodle ring the next day – which apparently allows for better peripheral vision and hearing), but it was a long night for all of us. We had also noticed Porter had lost a bit of weight since December, which was a concern since his appetite was as voracious as ever and his activity level average, but elected to take a wait and see approach. If things didn't improve once he had fully recuperated from this barrage of treatments, we'd take him back to the vet again. To complicate things a little further, we were booked to depart on a week-long trip to Costa Rica together with our friends Andrew and Ilze, routing for a few days through Toronto, eight short days after the surgery, so that meant Porter was going to off-leash boarding despite not being fully recovered. The timing could not have been much worse but all we could do was hold our breath and pray that the people who profess to "just love him" would follow the recuperation instructions and take good care of him in our absence.

Around the same time that Porter was going through his ordeal, I managed to throw my back out. Doing yoga! How humiliating. I guess I'm neither as young nor limber as I thought and shouldn't have worked on Wild Thing without supervision. My bad. Recovery took quite a few days of muscle relaxants, together with lying on the floor (much to Porter's confusion) and by the time we left for Costa Rica I was only at about 75%. Because we flew through Toronto, we were able to have a quick breakfast with Matejs and see how the wedding plans were progressing, but he didn't disclose much, with his own upcoming trip to Bali being forefront in his mind. Not to worry. I planned on getting more out of him the following month.

Costa Rica was a lovely break from the ordinary every-day. It could be argued that our "every-day" was not exactly "ordinary", but regardless of how we were living, there comes a time when even the novel can become routine. And truth be told, we were longing for some hot sunny weather where we could bake our bones, and soak up some natural Vitamin D. In Costa Rica we got it in spades. It was sunny, sunny, sunny and hot, hot, hot. Based on a friend's recommendation, we had chosen a boutique hotel at Portrero Beach on the Pacific Ocean side in the arid province of Guanacaste. I must confess to having very little knowledge about Costa Rica and in retrospect, wish I had researched further and stayed longer. I felt like one of those ill-informed visitors to Canada who expect to see moose, wolves and grizzlies around every corner, except I was expecting to see toucans (the Fruit Loops birds), tree frogs and sloths. And if not sloths, at least the infamous howler monkeys. It was not to be. Costa Rica is divided into seven provinces that are as disparate from each other as British Columbia is from Saskatchewan. Given where we were situated, to see the incredible biodiversity of Costa Rica would have meant going to the rainforests, and those were located primarily on the Gulf side or up in the mountains. That would have meant six-hour plus round trips and none of us were up for that. We added yet another return destination to our ever-expanding list. And one week was definitely not enough.

Portrero Beach was a gem. While most visitors head for the tourist town of Tamarindo (which we did check out and found to be fun for a day trip), Portrero was a diamond in the ruff. Our small resort had all the usual amenities, but its location was what made all the difference. To one side was an open-air shop renting the requisite beach toys (sluggish plastic kayaks, small sailboats, paddle boards etc.) and to the other side was what appeared to be a wire-fenced, humble homestead complete with crowing rooster. Further along were some higher-end vacation homes and then considerably more simple abodes. The odd herd of cows occasionally wandering along the beach, much to the consternation of some of the sun-bathers, only added to the rural charm. It was eclectic to say the least. Quiet, unassuming and entertaining. I loved it. The only sad thing was the malnourished stray dogs, ribs showing, that roamed up and down the beach, seemingly looking for food. They were quite friendly but despite their hunger, refused the Cheetos that Andrew offered them. Apparently even they have standards. Fortunately, there are efforts under way to curtail the whole stray dog matter although I can't speak to how successful it is. While out for dinner at a small local restaurant one evening, we found the waitress run off her feet and the service rather slow. It turned out they were short two staff members who were away at a "castration clinic." I didn't ask for details.

The sand on our beach was not of the white Caribbean variety but rather brown volcanic, and boy did it get hot! Heading from the resort towards the water, everyone would start walking at a leisurely pace that gradually increased as feet started burning, with the last few meters a veritable dash for the relief of the surf. And the water itself was incredibly warm. So much so that I was able to snorkel without a shortie. We went on an afternoon catamaran sail to a rocky promontory and while the water visibility was not the best, we did add some new species to our "never seen that before list" including a King Angelfish. It was a wonderful day capped off with a beautiful sunset. The daytime sun was incredibly hot, be it 8am or 5pm, with temperatures hovering around 35C, and even lounging in the shade of palm and Matapalo trees would have been brutal if not for the constant gentle breeze. Not to rub salt into the wound, but we were well aware that Toronto was suffering through a major snowstorm and double-digit sub-zero temperatures, and although we weren't exactly gloating, we were quite happy to have escaped the brutality. The beaches were also quite "clean" in that there were few seashells to collect, no seaweed and thankfully almost no garbage. I did, however, find a washed-up spiny puffer fish that I thought would make an excellent addition to my beach debris collection, but John would not even entertain the notion of somehow getting it home. However, there was other fauna and flora to experience. Iguanas were quite common, with one particular large specimen (about two feet in length) often sunning himself on the peaked roof of one of the resort's cottages. Except for the afternoon when he situated himself at the top of a large Matapalo tree, directly above some chaise lounges. And bombs away! A poor fellow vacationer, innocently dozing underneath, lulled into complacency by the sound of the surf, didn't know what hit him until it was too late. Splattered not just with dark green/black liquid guano but with some fairly large chunks too. About the size of what a small dog would produce. Eeeeww. I really felt for the guy but at the same time, was quite relieved because John's lounger was just a few feet away. There but for the grace of the guano gods... Another afternoon, Andrew and I decided to sample some unique Costa Rican fruit called Caimito (or star apple), which Andrew had purchased from a street fruit vendor in Tamarindo. While she was able to pantomime how to cut and eat this thing that looked somewhat like an apple but was the colour of purple eggplant, the language barrier prevented her from explaining its more nuanced subtleties. Namely that it is sticky. So sticky that it was almost like scraping dried LePages Glue from your lips and fingers afterwards. Other than being mild and

sweet, it didn't really have much flavour and the consistency was rather slimy. We stuck to mangos and papayas after that. The handful of restaurants in the area were truly "local", requiring a short stroll along a fairly busy yet poorly lit roadway (only recently paved) and it was refreshing to find that big chain eateries had not yet secured a toehold.

OUR COAST RICA BEACH WAS PRETTY CASUAL.

With a population of about 5 million, the countryside of Costa Rica is what one would imagine of a typical Central American country, albeit impoverished by North American standards, with homes running the gamut of corrugated tin to humble cinder block to lavish hacienda. There were quite a few places with cactus growing from rocky outcroppings but supposedly come the rainy season, the dusty brown disappears, and everything becomes a lovely shade of green. As Central American countries go, Costa Rica has the most stable democratic government, a very high literacy rate and is very environmentally progressive – with almost 30% of all land set aside as nature preserves or national parks. Tourism has overtaken the export of coffee, bananas and pineapples combined, and all one can hope for is a balanced approach to expansion, so the monkeys still have a canopy in which to howl. Tamarindo, while good for picking up souvenirs, is typical of the busy tourist towns that can develop when demand outpaces urban planning. Lots of t-shirt and trinket type stores, surf shops with their requisite apparel, numerous places for casual dining and unfortunately, street hawkers selling everything from beads to ceramic pots to clay bird whistles that they irritatingly blew as they walked up and down the street and beach. And while these wandering vendors were not as bad or persistent as their counterparts who sell "silver" on Mexico's beaches, they did become annoying. Over lunch at an outdoor beachfront restaurant, at least 18 came by during the course of our meal. Come on! But the week flew by and we reluctantly departed for Toronto, fortunately arriving after the worst of the deep freeze was over, and grateful for friends with whom it was a joy to travel with. It was a great vaycay and we looked forward to our next adventure.

34.

CHERRY BLOSSOMS
AND SNOW BUNNIES

WHEN IT COMES TO WINTER IN CANADA, EVEN IF YOU ARE ABLE
TO RUN, YOU CANNOT HIDE. Sooner or later, the freeze will find you. Even in
Victoria, where cherry trees are supposed to bloom in February. Not for us. For us,
temperatures were well below seasonal, and that translated into several nights of -8C.
And nary a cherry blossom to be seen. It was even snowing and blowing for several
days with serious accumulations, resulting in a lot of confused and miserable people
wandering around. Including us. We ran the coach on propane heat because using the
electrical system only blew cold air through the roof ducts. There were also a couple of
days with pretty high winds, gusts up to 90 km/h, causing the usual cancelled ferries,
downed trees and widespread power outages. Our neighbour's outdoor dining tent was
completely shredded, although he never used it so I suppose it was no great loss. We
were forced to bring the front slides in simply because we learned the hard way (back in
January) that high winds can wreak havoc with the toppers, those heavy canvass sheets
on rollers that are designed to keep rain and debris off the tops of the slides themselves.
That one particularly blustery evening, as we listened to what sounded like a full-on gale
howling outside, and not knowing what kind of wind tunnel these coaches have been
tested in, we commented to each other that maybe we should bring the slides in, just
in case. Coulda, woulda, shoulda. The following morning, we found that the retention
springs (which help support the rollers upon which these toppers sit) were broken. On
both sides! The replacement parts did not arrive until the end of the month, so that was
another repair to be done somewhere down the road. The slides still worked fine but we
were not going to take any chances. Those springs are there for a reason. Almost 3 years

on the road and we were still learning the hard way.

Overall, February got off to a shaky start. We left Costa Rica on the 2nd, spent a couple of nights in Toronto and flew back to Victoria, landing just before 5pm. The flight was a bit bumpy, we were delayed getting into Calgary and our luggage didn't make it onto the connecting flight. No problem there. WestJet, true to their promise, delivered it the same evening. We easily picked up the Jeep from long-term parking and drove over to the conveniently close big bus garage/shop, where we had left the RV for its much-delayed body work around the tailpipe. At least things went smoothly there. Well no, not exactly. The body work was fine, but the mechanics had neglected to turn off the house batteries while the coach was in the bay, so without shore power they were completely drained. Everything inside was dead. Refrigerator, microwave, heating system, hot water heater, generator. Even the steps would not retract. Thankfully the engine batteries were fine, and the owner was still around, so he drove the beast back into the garage to replace the house ones. All six of them. Ka-ching. Somebody some-where was going to miss out on his "employee of the month" award.

Porter didn't seem too much worse for wear after his daycare stay, although his belly incision was a bit inflamed, so we took him back to the vet for a follow up. I wasn't impressed. The vet gave the belly a cursory look but didn't even enquire about the other areas. It was as if he had either no recollection of the other procedures or he simply didn't care. And as we left with yet again more antibiotics, I'm sure I saw the good doctor leafing through another travel brochure. I really missed our vet back in Oakville.

But things were not all doom and gloom. Chinese New Year fell on February 5th – starting the Year of the Pig – so we bundled up and on the 10th attended the Lion Dance parade taking place along the streets of Chinatown. Colourful. Loud. And a real learning experience, although accurate information was not easy to come by. I'm still not sure I've got it straight. Accompanied by percussion instruments (drums, cymbals and gongs) as well as some smiling Buddhas, the "lions" danced their way to the door-ways of participating businesses where offerings of lettuce, together with either a red envelope containing money (or straight out bills without the envelope), had been tied to the lintel beam. After some enthusiastic stooping, springing, twisting and swaying, the lions ripped down the lettuce, shredded it and scattered it about (the envelopes were pocketed) before firecrackers had them moving on to the next establishment. It took 3 lions (2 large and 1 small) about 3 hours to cover the route, and it must have been exhausting since from time to time, the dancers would switch up. Okay then. What did this all mean? I asked several people, including shop owners hanging the offerings, as well as participants of the dance, but the best I got was, "It's a tradition." No kidding.

How very insightful. I finally lucked upon one fellow who was able to elaborate a bit although I still had to do some additional research. The lion dancers were all members of local Kung Fu clubs and the Lion Dance, dating back to the Tang Dynasty of the 7th Century, is performed at important cultural events to ward off evil spirits, and bring forth good fortune and prosperity. Interestingly, despite playing a very important role in Chinese folklore as peaceful and noble creatures, and symbolizing wisdom, courage and strength, there have never been real lions in China. The dancers require not just stamina, balance and flexibility as they incorporate various Kung Fu stances into their steps, but strong arms to raise and lower the lion's head as well. Very impressive. But what's with the lettuce? Apparently, the Cantonese language is full of all kinds of homonyms, not the least of which is the word *"choy"*. It describes a leafy vegetable – as in *"bok choy"* but *"gong hei fat choy"* means to wish someone great happiness and prosperity. Hence the suspended greens. When the lions ripped the lettuce apart and threw it around, they were distributing this good fortune to the surrounding crowd. It is a routine called *"cai qing"* or "plucking of the greens." And the firecrackers? Since the lions are chasing away evil spirits, the loud noises just help them with their task. To me, the lions looked very much like dragons, but while symbolically their activity and function is the same, they are very different when compared side by side, with the biggest distinction being that lions employ two dancers while dragons with their long coiling bodies can use nine or even twelve. So there you go. The Lion Dance in a nutshell. I hope I've understood it correctly.

And whatever good fortune these lions were bestowing upon others, it certainly bounced back to them as well, because the weather during the parade was the best it was going to be all week. The day prior to the festivities was incredibly cold and windy with those 90 km/h gusts, and the day after the parade was snowmaggedon. At least from a Victoria perspective. We received a dump of 25 cms! It was the snowiest February in Victoria's history. Schools were closed for 3 days, (naturally) but so were most of the retail businesses downtown. That may have been a bit unwarranted. We drove in because I needed to exchange some knitting needles at the yarn shop and found the major roads to be in fairly decent shape, but the shop itself had a sign posted in the window that it was closed "due to inclement weather". Weak sauce. I took Porter for a long walk along the seawall and through some parks and he was in heaven, rolling and running around in the chest deep stuff. As were all the other dogs we met. And then there were the kids. Having snowball fights, building snowmen (I think some adults helped there), making snow angels, sledding down hills. It is hard to say who was having more fun. The dogs or the kids. I even saw one older couple cross-country skiing. It was probably the lady who should have been at work in the yarn shop. John borrowed a shovel from the resort manager to clear a path around the coach (as did everyone else in the place) and then to make things completely incongruous, a guy on a paddle board made his way across the inlet. Only in Victoria.

Yet despite this meteorological aberration, Victoria remains in my estimation one of the most civilized cities in North America. Why? They know how to serve up a perfect cup of tea, something that is sorely lacking in most cities on this continent. I will go off on a bit of a tangent here although I suspect only tea drinkers will be able to sympathize. Have you ever noticed that when eating out, especially breakfast but it happens at dinner too, coffee drinkers get numerous offers for refills from the wait staff who arrive with pot in hand. Yet the tea drinkers? Nada. It's as if we aren't even sitting there. They don't even make eye contact. We have to make a specific request to get more hot water for our already expended tea bag. And that begs another grievance. Why do we have to re-use that already used tea bag? Why don't we get a fresh one? Are the coffee drinkers getting their second cup of coffee made from previously used grounds? I think not! So on behalf of all tea drinkers, thank-you Victoria for upholding that fine tradition of tea drinking, as well supporting the many tea-rooms that serve the more elaborate "afternoon tea." I should point out here that "afternoon tea" is different from "high tea" although there is a tendency to interchange the two terms. Afternoon tea (or low tea as it is sometimes called because it is often served at a low table) contains the conventional scones, clotted cream with preserves, crust-less cucumber sandwiches, cakes et. al. while high tea is more substantial with meat and fish dishes added. A bit like a light dinner, only with tea. Most places serve "afternoon tea", including the Empress Hotel where people pay exorbitant prices more for the location than for the actual culinary experience. Full disclosure, we succumbed years ago and quite enjoyed it but this year, to celebrate Valentine's Day we opted for another establishment, just around the corner. It was relatively just okay by comparison, but regardless of the scone quality, there is something about drinking tea out of a fine bone china cup that makes everything perfect.

And then as if by magic, another birthday rolled around except this time, instead of boondocking in the desert of Quartzite Arizona, I was at the opera – a performance of La Traviata by Pacific Opera Victoria. Obviously not The Met, but very well done none-the-less, providing a much-appreciated musical boost. It was also refreshing to see the audience stay and actually applaud the cast until the final curtain, unlike in Toronto where there is a stampede for the door with patrons wanting to be first out of the parking lot. Did I mention Victoria was civilized?

With all the chilly temperatures and snow, we tried to maintain a positive attitude and while not exactly adopting an "if you can't lick'em, join'em" approach, embraced the white stuff by going skiing. Matejs and Erica flew out for a week and we all headed up to Whistler, and had a blast despite being a mixed bag of schussers. Matejs snowboarded, Erica was a first-timer, and John and I had not been on skis for at least nine years. So we were all content to stick mostly to the easier runs. No black diamonds for us! We rented our equipment (except for Matejs who brought his own board) and I have to admit that although not being anywhere close to expert level, not having my own gear made a big difference when it came to confidence and to a certain extent, ability. Perhaps not so much the skis themselves but good boots are crucial. Something you just don't get when renting. But I am not complaining, even though reawakening muscles that had long been neglected was a tad painful. I really had thought my skiing days were behind me, but perhaps not. It was such a great feeling to be out again that I immediately started planning for the following winter. However, things in the sport have changed a fair bit. Boards are considerably wider now and almost everybody wears a helmet. On the one hand, that is very commendable. Supposedly safer with fewer head injuries. But on the other hand, there is a tendency for some helmeted people to now feel invincible and recklessly barrel down the mountain at speeds well beyond prudent. In many places there were banners warning the more enthusiastic participants to ease up and in other places there were actually staff on the slope signalling people to slow down. All that was lacking were radar guns. And lift prices? OMG! Obviously being at Whistler/Blackcomb factored into it, but a single-day lift ticket purchased at the wicket was $182.00! One day!!! A half day was $142.00. Hardly a savings. Purchasing multi-day tickets on-line a week ahead of time offset that ridiculous rate somewhat, but not enough to make this a sport accessible to everyone. Where is it going to end? At some point the law of diminishing returns must kick in.

Our first few days were wonderful with bright blue skies and good snow despite being a touch on the chilly side. And the expansive views in every direction were almost enough to make you forget why you were up there in the first place. But things can change rapidly in the mountains, and one day, while John, Erica and I were on the Seventh Heaven chairlift, we had such blowing wind and driving snow, coupled with -16 air temperature, it can only be described as miserable. And of course the lift stopped just short of the top and we were left huddled together exposed to the elements for what seemed like an eternity but was probably less than 5 minutes. They closed the lift shortly after we got off. The ski down was no picnic either, with whiteouts and near-zero visibility at times. We made sure to keep Erica positioned between us so that she did not inadvertently ski off the wrong side of the mountain, but she was a real trooper. Another day we had several inches of new snow and that made everything magical. There is nothing quite like gliding through calf deep snow – floating actually – in the quiet stillness of a forest. Regrettably for Matejs, a last-minute work commitment popped up so he was forced to hang back at the chalet writing reports for some of the time, while the rest of us crammed in as much as our tired legs could handle. But he did get out every single day so by the end of the week we were all exhausted. Thank goodness for hot tubs! The time flew by much too quickly, and we all emerged relatively unscathed, if battered egos and wounded pride are not taken into consideration. I say "relatively" because Erica

did end up with a nice bruise on her backside, Matejs took a spill resulting in a rather hard landing on his tailbone (nausea-causing hard), and John caught an edge and managed to throw in a few summersaults before coming to a inelegant stop. A "yard sale" you might say. He somehow managed to chip a tooth as well although we are still not sure how that happened.

PICTURE PERFECT DAY AT THE TOP OF SEVENTH HEAVEN… PRIOR TO THE YARD SALE..

And Whistler/Blackcomb itself? It is supposedly North America's No.1 ski resort with its two mountains linked by a peak-to-peak gondola but then again, other places claim the same ranking fame, including Jackson Hole in Wyoming and Vail in Colorado. But it all depends on what criteria are factored into the analysis. Total vertical, number of runs, number of lifts, longest run, longest season, best après-ski, easiest access etc., etc. Blackcomb has 1,609 meters of vertical, in other words 1 mile from top to bottom while Whistler is slightly lower at 1,530 m and both have their longest runs at 11 kms (6.8 miles.) The peak-to-peak gondola is very convenient, although either summit can be accessed via numerous high-speed chairs and other gondolas, several that start at the village. Combined, there are over 8,000 acres of skiable terrain. Only Matejs and Erica made it over to the Whistler side to put in a run. I was happy where I was and despite skiing every day, didn't get around to crossing the entire mountain. I've not skied Jackson Hole or Vail so can't comment on them, but of all the places we've been in North America (Ontario, Quebec, Alberta, Colorado) Whistler/Blackcomb is still my personal favourite. Europe doesn't count because there is no sense comparing what we have here to the sheer perfection of what they have over there. I really do wish my legs were younger. Actually, I wish a lot of me were younger.

The only hiccup during the entire week (and isn't there always one?) concerned Porter. We had left him for a couple of nights at a dog "hotel" in Pemberton, an off-leash boarding facility on several acres that was rated quite highly. (Strange at it sounds, Whistler has absolutely no dog care facilities of any kind.) When we went to pick him up, I noticed what looked like a raised, burnt welt on the top of his muzzle, along with a blistered area on top of his actual nose. It was a great mystery to everyone what caused it. Reluctant to contribute yet again to the vet's vacation fund, we took a wait-and-see approach and while Porter did not appear to be in any pain, his muzzle took a long time to heal. Even a week later, the area was still raised and heavily scabbed over. I did some searching on the internet and the physical appearance of his injury was similar to that of dogs that have been exposed to Giant Hogweed, a toxic plant that looks similar to Queen Anne's Lace only much, much larger and considered a relatively new invasive species in B.C. The images of other dogs similarly afflicted seemed to support my amateurish diagnosis except for the fact most of the ground was snow covered. There was nothing we could do other than monitor his progress, and eventually everything just healed over.

We reluctantly left Whistler behind (I could have easily stayed) and returned to Vancouver where daffodils were already starting to bloom. Such a contrast to the deep snow just an hour's drive to the north. And then like leaves scattered to the four winds, it was over. Matejs was on a flight back to Ontario, Erica stayed an extra day to catch up with a friend, and John and I were on the 5pm ferry heading back to Victoria. It was a clear evening and as the sun slowly started its set, I watched Vancouver recede in the distance, wondering when I would return. Probably not soon enough.

35.

OH, IT'S YOU AGAIN

HOW MUCH TRUTH IS THERE TO THE OLD ADAGE, "YOU CAN NEVER GO BACK?" I suppose in certain circumstances quite a bit, with some things best left cocooned in memories. Particularly if they are good memories. Because what if you go back and things are not as you recall? What if the sun doesn't shine as brightly? If the people are not as friendly? If the scenery is not as breathtaking? If the feelings are not as intense? What then? Happily, such was definitely not the case in returning to Tofino. We went back and loved it just as much as every other time. It is our happy place.

We pulled out of Victoria just as the beautiful spring flowers the city is known for were emerging from their winter hibernation and those darn cherry trees were finally starting to bloom. I was sure there would still be much to admire when we passed through again in May, but any regrets we felt about leaving were off-set by the anticipation of returning to our own corner of paradise. The drive across the island went smoothly although it was odd seeing snow along the shoulder of the highway, quite substantial at the higher elevations and over Summit Pass. We were fortunate that it was a precipitation free day with clear views of the mountains in all directions. Settling into Crystal Cove Resort's RV site #24 was a bit of a tight squeeze and came with a bit of a hiccup. When we had made our two-month reservation back in November, the resort took full payment for the first month and all was good. Yet for some inexplicable reason, the assistant manager had then cancelled the reservation but not advised us nor refunded the money, and subsequently over the course of the winter, booked three other parties into our site at various times during our scheduled stay. He was very apologetic, had no recollection of having done so and could not explain what happened. He quickly contacted these three groups, two of who were willing to accept another site so that we would not have to shuffle around, but the third party was completely uncooperative. He wanted site 24 and site 24 only. And he was only coming for two nights! In the interest of not being assholes, we accepted the manager's offer of a complimentary two-night stay in one of their cozy cabins overlooking the beach, complete with fireplace and king size bed, for that particular weekend. Despite the hassle of moving the yacht, it was a very enjoyable break. (More on the cabin later.)

We learned that the winter in Tofino had been rather dry (by their standards) and much colder than usual with several severe windstorms, including one that uprooted trees, ripped off cabin skylights, toppled a chimney and left the entire community without power for three days. So lots of repair and pruning work going on. We didn't care. The weather was quite sunny and there was much beach walking to catch up on. Interestingly (and I suspect much to John's relief), there were not all that many seashells washed up for me to collect and I still don't know if that is because the ocean was very calm or if seasonal temperatures had any impact. Still research to be done there. But despite the shortage of shells, something else unidentified was on the beach and Porter managed to chow down on it. He was as sick as we have ever seen him. Frighteningly so. It was our own fault.

When walking off leash, Porter never really strays too far from us. Even on forest hikes, he may get 30 feet ahead but will always look back to ensure we are following. On beaches he generally stays close by, always hoping we will toss a stick or toy into the surf. One particular morning, as per our usual routine, we were strolling along Mackenzie Beach talking about wolves (of all things) and commenting that it was a good thing Porter never ventured too far on his own. And where was this epitome of obedience while we were chatting? About 100 feet back, running to catch up with us, but still licking his chops. Oh. Oh. We didn't know what he got into because the evidence was now in his belly. He didn't seem to be any worse for wear the rest of the day, so we skated on that little misadventure. Or so we thought. The following day, we were at Wickanninish Beach, where I walked with Porter while John situated himself amongst the driftwood to start work on a carving project. All was good except yet again, Porter managed snap something up out of the surf. I'm still not sure if it was part of a washed-up dead crab or mussel but either way, not good. The following morning, he started vomiting, and it went on all day, eventually turning to dry heaves. He had zero interest in food or snacks (actually turning his head away, which for him was unheard of) and could not even keep water down. By evening he was completely lethargic and at times given to episodes of shaking/tremors. What to do? Why take him to a vet of course. That was easier said than done. Neither Tofino nor Ucluelet have veterinary services of any kind, and the one in Port Alberni (2 hours away) was closed. This was a Saturday

OH, IT'S YOU AGAIN — 399

evening. The 24-hour emergency clinic was 3 hours away in Nanaimo. So off we went, driving along narrow, winding highway 4 in the pitch dark. It was not fun. That's how worried we were. Bear with me on this next segue.

Historically, as well as currently, members of the legal profession (i.e. lawyers) are both lauded and denigrated, as evidenced by a proud parent's announcement, "My son/daughter got into law school" and Shakespeare's line from Henry VI, "The first thing we do, is kill all the lawyers." Much of the negative sentiment comes from the fact that people generally do not understand the law very well and generally believe lawyers make too much money. No argument from me on that one. Well, I am about to add veterinarians to this love 'em / hate 'em group because they have us pet owners over a barrel and they know it. They can tell us just about anything and we will believe them because the average person has very little insight into animal anatomy and illness. And they know we will do almost anything and pay almost anything to alleviate our furry family member's suffering. We located Nanaimo's animal hospital very easily and found the staff there very friendly, very willing to suggest all manner of tests, yet very reluctant to commit to any diagnosis. Let the games begin. It was either acute pancreatitis, a partial blockage in the digestive tract somewhere, a complete blockage in the digestive tract somewhere or severe gastroenteritis. Blood work. X-rays. IV fluids. Anti-nausea medication. Clinic admission and overnight monitoring. More X-rays. Digital consultation. Ka-ching. Ka-ching. Ka-ching. Pancreatitis and blockage were eventually ruled out, so we were left with gastroenteritis brought on by "an unspecified dietary indiscretion." ?Que? A veterinarian's high-priced way of saying he ate something that didn't agree with him. And for this we paid over $1,400.00, plus drove 6 hours to and from Nanaimo. Twice. Were we complaining? Maybe a little bit but it was our own fault for not keeping a closer eye on him. Were we relieved? Yes. Although keep in mind that "relieved" has two meanings: as in "relieved" that he would be okay, and "relieved" of another considerable chunk of change. One day, I am going to tally up how much money we have spent on Porter's day cares, boarding fees and vet visits. It might just about equal the cost of a degree in veterinary medicine.

When we returned to Tofino and ran into other dog owners, questions were naturally raised about Porter's health because he now had a shaved front leg from his IV site. It turned out two other labs got sick at exactly the same time, although not as severely as our brown menace. Someone advised that a rumour was going around of dogs being poisoned on Chesterman Beach, but no-one wanted to believe that. It is such a dog-friendly community, the friendliest we have ever been in. Someone else opined that given the amount of pot left lying around these days (it is so prevalent no-one worries about saving their roaches or crumbs) that might be the culprit, because marijuana is very toxic to dogs. But it was all just speculation. However, on the topic of mood-altering substances, it does seem that the legalization of pot somehow opened the floodgates for the smokers to feel they must indulge at every opportunity. Either covertly or overtly. And whether they realized it or not, the smell of that joint they just finished puffing on followed them into the grocery store, the coffee shop and the bookstore. Even on one of our morning beach walks past Mackenzie Beach Campground, the tantalizing aroma of bacon sizzling over a cedar wood fire was overpowered by the pungent stench of weed. Bongs for breakfast. Pathetic.

It took Porter several days to return to his usual self but once recovered, he was back in the water again, joining the die-hard surfers who despite the air temperature (anywhere from 4 to 8C the first two weeks) were still out there riding the waves. They surf year-round in Tofino, regardless of the weather but that was too hard-core for me. I was waiting for at least 15 degrees. Maybe 20. And walking along the beaches it was interesting to see how things had changed over the winter. Huge logs that had once teetered precariously on rocky outcroppings were gone and new ones were in their place. I could only wonder about the size of the waves that would have been necessary to effect these changes. Beaches that had once been littered with all manner of large and small driftwood pieces were now covered with miniscule shell fragments. Porter's favourite pastime remained nosing around in the tidal pools, disturbing the anemones and starfish that waited to be rescued by the next high tide, and I continued to add to my shell collection albeit at a slower rate. John just kept asking where I planned on storing them all.

The complimentary log cabin we settled into after the booking mix-up (cabin #2) was directly at one end of Mackenzie Beach, which is itself about a kilometer long, configured in a shallow arc. It was wonderful to see that the two bald eagles that had been around in the fall were still in residence, occasionally perched at the top of tall cedar trees, each at either end of the beach, like bookends. From the cabin's large picture window, I could watch one of them as he (she?) sat on his lofty perch, waiting to swoop down on unsuspecting crabs or fish. The cabin itself was very cozy with a wood-burning fireplace, spacious gated deck and steps leading directly down to the sand. But it was the view that made up for the inconvenience of having to pack up and relocate. It was easy to lose track of time watching beachcombers stroll along, children dig in the sand and dogs race back and forth into and out of the surf. We became thoroughly spoiled and started wondering if perhaps we could stay there for the remainder of our Tofino hiatus. Alas, that would have required a sizable lottery win, so back to the coach we went.

With respect to beaches, I decided that South Beach, Schooner Cove and Florencia Bay were my favourites, in part because they were more remote and required a marginal level of effort to reach them. There were no parking lots providing direct access (as at Long Beach), so there were no large families with picnic coolers and beach toys disturbing the peace of the natural wilderness. South Beach and Florencia Bay both necessitated a short walk through the forest (500 meters?), and to reach the extreme end of Schooner Bay meant waiting for low tide, parking at Incinerator Rock by Long Beach and walking about 3 kilometers along the surf. There used to be a 1-kilometer walk along a trail as well, but that had been closed for quite a while. At the same time, any sojourns to these locales did require a certain level of vigilance because wolves like the solitude as well, and do not always take kindly to anyone encroaching on their territory. Sadly (I suppose) we didn't see any signs of my spirit animals. South Beach is not very large and is covered with small, smooth pebbles, like jellybeans in various shades of gray, and has lots of rocky outcrop-

pings and lots of tidal pools. The fog rolled in while we were there so despite being iconic west coast majestic, it was quite cool and we didn't linger very long, planning to return on a sunnier day. And because Schooner Cove sees so few visitors, it was a mecca for shell collectors such as me. I'm sure I saw John biting his tongue as I rejoiced over yet another find.

SCHOONER COVE — DIFFICULT TO DESCRIBE THE VASTNESS.

Notwithstanding the chilly weather at the outset, the temperatures were in the occasional double digits by mid-month, with one day even hitting 24C (but that was a fluke). Sunny much of the time, but not always. What more could we ask for? Most days were spent walking along the various beaches or basking in the sun, although any sitting by the water for extended periods of time required a bit of bundling up. It was easy to become lazy. However, we did manage rouse ourselves and undertake one hike to a destination that is in theory, a local secret. Secret in the sense that no-one is supposed to recommend it, but once brought up in conversation, directions to the trailhead were readily volunteered. There was certainly nothing about it in Parks Canada literature. I refer here to the Canso Bomber Crash Site.

Given that British Columbia is noted for its natural beauty (not to mention being an outdoor enthusiast's paradise) it is easy to forget that during the Second World War, especially following the attack on Pearl Harbour, the entire west coast was on alert, fearing a Japanese invasion. Numerous radar stations were built, strung out along the shoreline from Alaska to California, watching and waiting, waiting and watching. One such place was Radar Hill, now located in Pacific Rim National Park Reserve, 12 kilometers south of Tofino. It is a nice drive and short hike to the top with views out over the Pacific Ocean, and information about it is readily available in Park literature. But the hike they don't mention is to the above noted Canso Site. Late one 1945 February night, a Royal Canadian Air Force Canso Bomber carrying 12 crew members, 3,400 litres of fuel and 4 100-kilogram depth charges took off from the Tofino airfield intending to return to Coal Harbour at the north end of Vancouver Island. Within minutes, the plane lost power to its port engine, began falling at 300 meters per minute and crashed into a steep hillside in the rainforest. The pilot is credited with saving the lives of everyone on board by stalling the plane and thus slowing its descent and ultimate impact. Not having studied aerodynamics, I cannot independently corroborate the efficacy of this manoeuvre, but that is apparently what the subsequent investigation showed. By some miracle (not withstanding no lives lost), the depth charges did not explode on impact. But because the crash site was in a remote and difficultly accessed area, it was decided to detonate the charges there, since hauling them out would have proved too problematic. The explosion created a large 6-meter deep crater that is now full of water and still visible today. Together with what is left of the plane.

The hike out was interesting to say the least and instructions for locating the unmarked trailhead very easy. Park at the bottom parking lot of Radar Hill, walk back out to Highway 4, turn south and count out 15 telephone poles. On the fifteenth pole, a rudimentary black marker drawing of an airplane, about 3 inches large, indicates where to head off into the forest. Okay then. Found it. Off we went. The first bit was very easy, flat and wide enough to walk abreast with only the occasional blow down to step over. Then we came to an abandoned graffiti-covered building that judging by its rusty equipment had served some industrial purpose a long, long time ago. After walking through that, the fun began. We had been warned ahead of time that the route can get quite muddy and in some places was just a thigh deep bog. And that the trail was not well marked. Just the occasional coloured ribbon tied to a tree branch here and there. And that there would be many side trails leading off into dead ends, where previous hikers had tried to skirt the more difficult sections. Being warned and living the experience are two different things. This was not a hike that challenged strength and endurance with high elevation gains or extreme length. This was a hike that challenged balance and agility. Numerous exposed, gnarly roots made the footing quite tricky, but we were grateful for those because they often acted as stepping-stones over the muddier sections. And we used the fallen logs like balance beams to ferry us across the really deep stuff. At the outset, we both were diligent in trying to find the driest spots in an effort to stay out of the muck. Muck that was so thick and deep that if you hadn't laced up tightly, chances were pretty good you'd be leaving a shoe or boot behind. But our efforts were in vain. Despite our best two-steps and side-shuffles, we had both sank into stuff that came well over the shoe tops and up to our ankles. By the time we were hiking out, we acknowledged we had lost the battle and were no longer concerned with trying to keep our feet dry, but rather, with keeping our boots on.

The plane itself was much larger than I expected, although over the years, souvenir hunters have walked away with just about anything they could pry off and carry. And it still amazes me how even in remote areas such as this, people bring spray paint cans with them, indulging their delusional desire to enhance the scenery and commemorate their attendance with crude drawings and simplistic slogans. The plane was covered in graffiti. But it was still pretty remarkable to walk around this aircraft, seemingly sticking out of the side of a heavily forested steep hill, knowing that everyone survived. There is some talk that Parks Canada may actually create an official and maintained trail out to the sight but I'm not sure that is a good idea, despite the fact that every year, people get lost along the way and have to be rescued. I think having to navigate the boggy terrain was half the fun and walking out along a smooth boardwalk would not just detract from the experience, but would remove any sense of how unforgiving and treacherous the topography really is. Some destinations should remain a challenge.

ANYONE MISSING A WWII CANSO BOMBER?

By the end of the month, many spring flowers were in full bloom. First came the snowbells (which achingly reminded me so much of my mom, who used to rejoice at this sure sign that winter was over), then the crocuses, daffodils, hyacinths and finally tulips. Even the forsythia bushes with their yellow blooms were out. But despite the sun and its relative warmth, the breeze was still quite cool, so summer wear had to wait. Children, of course, are immune to the cold. It was March break in B.C. (which, OMG, lasted 2 weeks!!!) and families with their energetic (and noisy) children were out in full force. Many of these kids ran around in shorts and t-shirts although they did put on wet suits to brave the water. And every evening, like moths to a flame, everyone gathered on the beach to watch the sunsets. Some of them were spectacular in fuschia, pink, salmon and orange colours. If only I could have captured those hues on camera. We really looked forward to the coming month when the children would have returned to school (and a great peace returned to the valley), the weather would be warmer, and we could finally get back to the surfboards and kayaks. It would be our last hurrah by the ocean before we started heading inland.

36.

SOME GOOD-BYES ARE
HARDER THAN OTHERS

APRIL WAS A RATHER QUIET MONTH. That is not a complaint, but more of an observation. And it's not that we didn't enjoy it. I've already stated on several occasions – we loved Tofino. But we did settle into a routine more akin to everyday living than enthusiastic exploring. I re-read some of my earlier blog posts and was reminded that we had so much fun hiking and biking and kayaking the first few years. What happened? Well, the weather was partly to blame. It was unseasonably chilly, rarely above 10C with the breeze making it feel much cooler, and quite rainy. I know, I know. It's a rainforest. But it was very frustrating. Too cold for water sports (at least for us sane people) and too rainy for hiking or hanging out on the beach. No bicycling either. At one point, just to rub salt into the wound, we were suffering through 8C and heavy downpour while back home it was 18C and sunny (although it didn't last). Azaleas and rhododendrons were starting to bloom by mid-month, but it was hard to appreciate their beauty through the rain.

We signed up for another 30-day yoga challenge at Coastal Bliss Yoga and I was amazed at how much I had backslid over the winter, despite my best efforts (and intentions). It was great to be back at the cozy studio with its very welcoming instructors but that said, several of the classes we attended seemed geared towards a considerably younger age dynamic. There was no way I was ever going to master Pincha Mayurasana (Feathered Peacock Pose) like some of the twenty-somethings. While to a certain extent I agree that aging is largely in your head, there are occasions when the more mature body just says, "F this. Not going to happen." To borrow a phrase from the Ontario Lottery Corporation, "Know your limit. Play within it." I was being forced to play within my limit. And to add insult to injury, I came down with a very bad cold two weeks in, missed 12 days straight and had to admit defeat in the challenge. But on the positive side, was motivated to get back to practicing on a regular basis. Perhaps I will be able to perfect Bakasana (Crow Pose).

On the weather-permitting days, we managed to get in a few hikes, first along parts of the Wild Pacific Trail near Ucluelet. The entire trail is just under 9 kms long, broken into several manageable sections – Ancient Cedars, Artist's Loop, Big Beach and Lighthouse Loop. While the walking path itself is fairly easy with beautiful and dramatic vistas out towards Barkley Sound and the Broken Group Islands, the terrain off-piste is very rugged in an inhospitable sort of way, and evokes a sort of uneasy respect for the sea, with huge waves crashing onto the rocky headlands and rushing into the surge channels. In 1988, a shellfish farmer ("Oyster Jim" Martin) proposed a trail along the cliff edge that would run from the Amphitrite Lighthouse all the way to Pacific Rim National Park. A major undertaking because the wished-for route passed through federal, provincial, municipal and private land. It took 10 years of negotiating, compromising, cajoling and conceding to get the first section opened up and plans are still underway to keep expanding north, although it seems Oyster Jim has passed the torch and that battle is now being waged by the Wild Pacific Trail Society. The lighthouse itself was not exactly romantically picturesque like some in Prince Edward Island, (it looked more like a bunker) but given the massive storms that batter this coastline, that is out of necessity. Built in 1915, it is not the original one either. The first one was constructed of wood in 1906, after the steel sailing barque Pass of Melfort was tragically wrecked on the rocks nearby in 1905, with the loss of all 35 lives. But given the building materials, this first lighthouse was destroyed by storm waves in 1914. We checked out the replacement on a fairly windy day and it was easy to see the power these waters can generate. There are countless shipwrecks along this coast, with some estimates saying that for every nautical mile along the western shores of Vancouver Island there lies a wrecked ship (or what's left of it) on the ocean floor. When not awed by the power of the ocean, we were quite taken by the trees in the old growth forest, many twisted and bent into all manner of odd shapes. Sometimes it was hard to discern whether I was looking at roots, branches or trunks. And being early spring, Skunk Cabbage flowers were blooming in the wet boggy sections along the way.

Skunk Cabbage is an interesting plant. Its leaves are huge and can sometimes grow to 5 feet high and 1-1/2 feet wide. But it's the flowers that caught my attention. In some ways reminiscent of calla lilies (but much larger), they emerge well before the leaves and are a bright yellow colour, almost neon. The smell of these flowers (and leaves if they are bruised or crushed) is supposedly similar to the odour of a skunk, but while I must admit that their aroma would never be mistaken for a bouquet of roses, describing it as skunk-like seems a bit harsh. I didn't find it all that bad. Then again, they can also change their scent during warmer parts of the day to attract different pollinators so perhaps we were just lucky. But what makes this plant unique is its supposed correlation with bears. Apparently, the strong smell emitted by the flowers causes bears to wake from their hibernation. They then forage for the roots which in turn, act as an early nutrition source as well as a laxative. Nothing like a good poop after a long sleep. The relationship between flora and fauna really is fascinating.

All along the trail at various viewpoints high above the crashing surf, there were solid, heavy park-like benches, most dedicated to the memory of departed family or friends, where we could sit and just soak in the view. And watch whales spouting in the distance. At one spot, a short path down an embankment made it possible to access the shoreline of a little bay, and we found so much foam floating around it looked as if someone had dumped a few gallons of Mr. Bubble into the water. In the strong breeze, bits of this foam were even blowing across the beach. At first glance, it seemed rather unsightly, but from an information placard I learned that sea foam is really an indicator of a healthy body of water. It is in fact nothing but saltwater and air, mixed with tiny single-celled plants (phytoplankton). The foam is created when either strong winds or strong waves mix air into the ocean water. Organic matter in the water (mostly from dead plankton) contains protein, and that protein gives the water enough surface tension to form lasting bubbles. These bubbles then get piled up into suds along the surface of the water or onto the beach. Directly or indirectly, every living thing in the ocean feeds off plankton, so the presence of sea foam is then really an indicator that the ocean off this specific coast is producing literally tons of food for bigger creatures up the marine food chain. Here endeth the oceanography lesson. Despite the damage being caused by plastics and oil spills elsewhere, this particular corner of the ocean at this particular time, was doing quite well. Hallelujah!

We also checked out the aquarium in Ucluelet and although very modest in size when compared to the likes of Ripley's in Atlanta or Toronto (truthfully, there is no comparison), it was perfect for the location. It highlights only marine life from the immediate area and operates on a "catch and release" format. That is, all the creatures (fish, urchins, anemones, crustaceans, even an octopus) are captured in the local waters, moved into the aquarium's viewing tanks and hands-on tanks (which are constantly flushed with fresh seawater) and after about 9 months, returned to the ocean and a new crop rotated in. Because the tanks are not large, the focus is on the smaller creatures that don't get the same press as large predators. I read up on nudibranchs and sea cucumbers (and promptly forgot what I read), poked at some sea urchins and sand dollars, but what was most intriguing (and in a way unsettling) was the Plankton Tank. In this particular tank (about 30 gallons in size), back in 2012, staff had placed a simple bare slab of concrete. Water from the ocean was continuously circulated directly into and out of the tank. That was it. Nothing but constantly flowing saltwater. Saltwater that was full of microscopic sea life – plankton. Over the span of 7 years, numerous sea creatures in their miniscule form made this concrete slab their home, latching on and creating a miniature sea world in every colour of the rainbow. It was amazing. And disconcerting at the same time. Is that what I ingested when I fell off my surfboard and accidentally swallowed a mouthful of ocean water? Yuck!

We also visited the Tofino Museum and Heritage Centre but found that to be a bit of a misnomer. Located in the musty lower level of a building that also houses the Vancouver Island Regional Library (we never did get around to investigating that) with the Royal Canadian Legion upstairs, there were only a handful of display cases containing a handful of artifacts, and a couple of photographs of days gone by on two otherwise bare walls. Overall very little information on the original aboriginal population groups, who the early explorers were, or even how the town was settled. I did, however, find one placard that offered a bit of an explanation on where the name "Tofino" came from. The area was named after a rear admiral in the Spanish Navy, Captain Vincent Tofiño de San Miguel. In 1792, two commanders of the Spanish Navy were surveying the area and decided to name this nearby inlet after their buddy. Most original. People didn't really start settling there until the late 1890s, well after the Spanish were gone, and they dropped the tilde over the "n", taking until 1932 to incorporate the town. That was about all I learned at the "museum." I suspect to get further information, a visit to the local bookshop would be more informative.

And on the subject of history, the bee in my bonnet continued to buzz with respect to the aboriginal community. I just can't figure it out. There is no question that Tofino has difficulties regarding employment. The population swells from less than 2,000 full timers in the winter to 30,000 vacationers in the summer and those in the hospitality industry, be it hotels, restaurants or outfitters are in desperate need of employees. We heard quite often that places were forced to close or operated at half service simply because there was no-one to cook food, wait on tables or engage in housekeeping. We personally saw a sign in one restaurant window "closed due to staffing shortage." Young people migrate there in droves during the "tourist season" and easily walk into those jobs, but then staff housing becomes the issue. There is literally no-where for them to stay and they often end up sharing tight quarters in less than ideal conditions or living in their beat-up vans or run-down campers. Many are from Australia, Europe and Indonesia, and they come primarily to surf.

So where does the aboriginal community fit into this picture? There are several villages in the Tofino area, one across the bay on Meares Island (Opitsaht), and a couple on the island proper, south of town closer to Long Beach (Esowista and Ty-Histanis). Is there some reason members of these underemployed communities are not filling the jobs? They live here year-round. They have accommodation. They have transportation. Why are they not the ones to be hired? Supposedly there is an explanation. And it was only talked about in hushed tones because it is just not politically correct to say anything disparaging about aboriginal people. Especially as a generalization. We heard over and over again that as employees, they were simply not "reliable." They would show up for work one week but not the next, would work until their first paycheck and then disappear. You can't run a successful business that way, be it a hotel or a restaurant. Yet at the Co-op Grocery store, as well as at the gas station, and the Himwitsa Native Art Gallery we saw the same aboriginal faces day in and day out, so obviously this generalization does not hold true. Or does it? At the south end of Wickaninnish Beach is a large aboriginal owned Visitor/Information Centre – Kwisitis – but during our 4 months there, we never saw it open, despite the fact that it is technically located in Pacific Rim National Park Reserve and its hours of operation are actually posted on the Parks Canada web page. Locals advised there used to be a nice restaurant there, but once ownership transferred to the tribe, you never knew if it would be open when you showed up for dinner, so they stopped going.

The Esowista community near Long Beach exemplifies the stereotypical derelict "Rez." The community obviously came into some money at one point because the road leading in was newly paved with nice curbs and a large log signpost with their name "Esowista" is letters 3 feet high. But there it ended. The houses were completely rundown, many with busted out windows, neglected front yards, and rear yards literally used as garbage dumps. Hundreds of plastic bags filled with household refuse and other junk in large piles that only became obscured when the spring underbrush started to green up. The smell must be just awful, not to mention the health hazard. I have never seen anything like it. But what is most frustrating is that there is no reason for it! This reservation is situated on one of the most beautiful beaches in the country, between two towns that are constantly in need of employees, and has no issues such as those that plague other aboriginal communities in Canada. No toxic water, no extreme weather, no geographic or social isolation, yet they live in absolute squalor. There is no other word for it. Those community members who do hold down jobs and take care of their homes, and those who work on their behalf must just despair. I don't have a solution. But so far, it seems that the billions of tax dollars spent have achieved very little. And you can't blame everything on the residential schools. Stepping off my soap box now.

Despite its rather placid pace, April was not entirely without excitement. On one of the rare sunny days, we returned to South Beach (actually we returned several times) enjoying the 1-kilometer stroll along the boardwalk through the dense forest and marvelling at how quickly the skunk cabbage grew. It was surprising how few people hung out at this beach (we never saw more than six) given that it really wasn't hard to get to, and was such an oasis of tranquility and solitude. On this particular day, there was only one other couple sitting near the northern end, so we walked across a short promontory at the southern end to a second beach where John situated himself amongst the driftwood to work on his carving project. The beach here is a combination of coarse sand, stones and pebbles of various sizes, rocky outcroppings and is covered in all manner of sun- bleached shells. It was also a bonanza for sea glass. At low tide, the beach itself ranges anywhere from 50 to 150 feet wide and has lots of tide pools. This particular day, the swells were huge and put on quite a display as they crashed onto the rocks, with spray flying well over a hundred feet into the air. Porter and I wandered over to the complete southern end (about 300 feet away from John), where I looked for sea glass and Porter alternated between nosing around in the washed-up kelp and wading in the tide pools. All was well with the world. At one point, I had crouched down to pick up several small pieces of glass, confident that Porter was wading around in the surf. I don't know what caused me to raise my head. Certainly there was no barking or snarling or snorting or anything else to cause alarm. But I went from serene to scared in a nanosecond. There was Porter, about fifty feet away from me, running aggressively towards the tree line. And fifty feet in front of him, at the tree line but still on the beach, a large black bear jumping up the embankment back into the forest. I ran after Porter yelling his commands, "Leave it!" and "Come!" but although that slowed him down somewhat, he wasn't entirely convinced he should give up on this interesting creature. He was channelling his inner Karelian Bear Dog. Thankfully the bear disappeared into the brush and I managed to grab Porter and walk him back towards the surf. But then I became concerned that the bear might return. Or worse yet, be heading towards John. Were there cubs around? I shouted "Bear!" for John but given the distance and the sound of the crashing waves he could not hear me. All ended well but we certainly kept a closer eye on Porter in case he decided chasing after bears was a fun pastime. And I guess the information about the skunk cabbage and bears was accurate. Hibernation was definitely over.

And Easter? We had been invited to my uncle and aunt's place in Vancouver for the holiday so in preparation decided to bake *pīrāgi* and colour eggs using the traditional Latvian method of onion skins as dye. This dyeing technique requires a considerable amount of skins and I should have started saving them months ago but had not. Thankfully, our Tofino Latvian friend Māra had some to spare, and I had scrounged a few extra handfuls from the local grocery store, so there was enough for 10 eggs. I experimented with Salal berry jelly as additional colour and cedar sprigs for design, and the eggs turned out quite nicely, if I do say so myself. And baking the *pīrāgi* went smoothly too, although it was a bit time consuming since the coach's micro/convection oven only allowed us to bake 10 at a time. We left early on Saturday morning and not a moment too soon. The RV resort was full to capacity with families and their high-octane offspring hopped up on chocolate, with the added anticipation of more to come during the annual Easter egg hunt. We learned later from staff that it had been bedlam. Thankfully, we were enjoying a sunny, leisurely drive across the island to catch the ferry from Nanaimo to Horseshoe Bay. The leaves on the trees were just starting to unfurl and were a bright light green that contrasted beautifully with the dark green of the conifers. All manner of fruit trees in bloom, including pears and apples, and the Rhododendrons were indescribable. (Actually, some of the blossom clusters in Tofino were the size of volleyballs!) And Vancouver? On a sunny spring day, it must be the most beautiful city ever. Although the cherry trees were just past peak bloom, they were still impressive, and flowers were all around. When not over-eating, we got in a few walks, one through the forests of the University Endowment Lands/Pacific Spirit Regional Park – 874 hectares of paths amongst spectacular old growth, and another day, out along the Spanish Banks which offered a vantage point of downtown Vancouver that I had never seen before. It was wonderful to spend Easter with family, even though we were so far from our Ontario home. But typical of B.C. weather, although we arrived on a beautiful sunny day with 15C temperature, our departure two days later was a rainy 9C. Returning to Tofino, we learned that our selfie-loving Prime Minister had spent the weekend in town and had been spotted surfing at Cox Bay. Terrific. A snake had arrived in my paradise.

So perhaps it was fitting that we started making plans for our departure. Not knowing how long it would take to sell the yacht, we decided to list it for sale in several Canadian and U.S. publications at the beginning of May, with a negotiable availability date of July 31st. We researched current listings (not many out there) to determine a fair market price for our type of unit and took numerous photographs of the interior so as to present it in its most appealing light. This necessitated moving all our personal things out of view, and that was a bit of a pain, but the same way that houses are "staged" for the market, so too are motor coaches. And we were a bit annoyed with ourselves over all this as well. Back in September, while set up at Telegraph Cove, a couple in a neighbouring site approached us and advised they were in the market for a Tiffin motor coach. They gave us their contact information and said to call when we were ready to list. So naturally, we put that contact information "in a safe place." And everyone knows what happens when you put something in a safe place. We tore the coach apart. Nothing! We also decided to sell our surf boards. Alas, my surfing career was a non-starter. Despite our initial enthusiasm in the fall, the weather in March and April was just too cold and miserable to continue. Although the water temperature does not vary by too many degrees over the course of the year, it's the air temperature and cool (read cold) breeze that prevented my budding interest from taking off. We listed them in the local on-line buy-and-sell late one afternoon and by 9am the following morning, both were sold. Did I mention surfing is popular in Tofino? We had also hoped to unload the area rug we used to insulate the floor during the winter, as well as the dehumidifier that was such a necessity, but there were no takers.

As the days counted down to our departure, we both got into a bit of a funk, wondering when we would be able to return, if ever. And almost as if to spite us, or perhaps remind us of what we were going to miss, or maybe to give us a great send-off, the weather during the last week was great. Sunny and warm-ish, so we packed in as much as we could. First, we scrambled up to the top of Cox Peak (officially called Vargas Peak) which at a height of about 400 meters gave us a fantastic panorama of the entire area. The going was a bit tricky in that there was no marked or maintained trail to the top, but rather, a confusing array of paths going off in various directions, sometimes just looping back down. There were lots of roots to scramble over and in one place, some sympathetic soul had rigged a nylon rope to provide a hold while navigating the steeper, rockier section. But what a view! Definitely worth the price of exertion. Another rather windy day (BC ferries across the Strait of Georgia were cancelled again) we hiked out along a 1-km trail to Half Moon Bay and then along adjacent 2-km Willowbrae Trail to south Florencia Bay beach. Again, fantastic old growth trees along the way. The walk was quite easy, most of it along a boardwalk but to get down to the beaches required navigating some steep stairs – 123 at Half Moon Bay and 173 at South Forencia. The going down was not bad and just required watching your footing but coming back up? Oh my. I really needed to get in some cardio! Despite the wind (gusts around 50k) it was very beautiful, and the water was that turquoise colour more reminiscent of the Caribbean than the northern Pacific. It must be extraordinary on a calm day. Too bad we discovered it so late in our stay. We only got the kayaks into the water once over the

two months and that was on our last day, but for that I am blaming the uncooperative weather, although inertia and laziness on our part contributed. We had planned to
paddle in Clayoquot Sound, but the water was so calm we launched on the ocean side
and paddled along the coast, almost into town. It was, as expected, lovely.

We said good-bye to Māra and Robert (who gifted us with two delightful books
about the Tofino area written by local authors), attended one last yoga class, had one last
fish taco at Tacofino (fantastic fish tacos!), purchased one last tub of homemade strac-
ciatella gelato, took one last walk along South Chesterman beach to gaze longingly at
my desired vacation home, took in one last sunset, collected one last handful of seashells
and said farewell to the wonderful staff at Crystal Cove. It was time to move on.

OUR HAPPY PLACE.

37.

ONE MORE TIME, WITH FEELING

ON THE ROAD AGAIN... OR SO THE SONG GOES. We left Tofino on a warmish, sunny day and the drive across the island was uneventful, except for a little stretch near Kennedy Lake where work crews were busy shoring up the highway and blasting out what seemed to be half a mountainside in order to move the roadway inland by a few feet. Having driven back and forth with the car a number of times, I had forgotten how winding and constricted this area was, and sitting high up in the coach made the sheer drop down into the lake seem even steeper. But John navigated the route with no issues and we soon found ourselves back in Victoria taking care of a few practical matters. The coach went in to have the slide toppers repaired after the damage caused by December's windstorm, Porter needed more flea and heartworm medication, and I was determined to return to Butchart Gardens to see it in the springtime. Oh my goodness! I wish I could have posted every picture I took on the blog because words cannot describe the beauty of all the early flowers. Narcissus and Daffodils set amongst blue, white and purple Forget-Me-Nots (I always thought Forget-Me-Nots were just blue), huge multi-coloured Rhododendrons, light and dark purple Magnolias, Violets, flowering trees, and most dazzling of all, the countless varieties of Tulips. I have never seen anything like it! Some looked more like large roses, some had feathered petals, and still others looked like and were as big as peonies! Some striped, some solid. I never realized Tulips came in such a variety of shapes, sizes, details and colours. After wandering the grounds at our leisure, we savoured Afternoon Tea (at least I did) on the patio of the old historic Butchart home and simply sat admiring the beauty around us. Porter was allowed on the porch although not directly by our table, but it worked out okay despite the cool temperature. If I lived in Victoria, I would purchase an annual pass and go back every week to see what was new. Definitely worth the visit.

We had a bit of a hiccup on our last night on the island but that worked out okay as well. Given that we had a reservation for the Black Ball ferry from Victoria to Port Angeles in Washington state at 10:30am, and were required to check in 90 minutes prior to departure, I called the office and asked if it would be permissible to boondock in their parking lot the night before. It would save us from having to get up at the crack of dawn, with the added bonus of saving us almost $100 in site fees at the campground. "Sure" the friendly voice replied but advised we should show up after 7:30 pm when the last scheduled ferry for the day had departed. Excellent. We checked out of the RV resort and spent the afternoon hanging out at Beacon Hill by the Juan de Fuca Strait. Porter splashed around in the water and we enjoyed the lovely sunny afternoon. Promptly at 7:35pm, we drove over to the ferry terminal and found everything locked up tight as a drum, including the access gate to the parking lot. There was no way there had been a 7:30 sailing! People might leave work in a hurry but for everyone to be gone in 5 minutes? Don't think so. There was no answer at either their Canadian or US numbers, so we hurried back to the RV resort and snagged one of the last 3 spots that were still available. Not sure where we would have gone had they been full up. So much for sleeping in and saving a hundred bucks.

The crossing on The Coho the following morning took about 90 minutes and although the water was very calm, the boat must not be outfitted with very effective (if any) stabilizers because I could really feel the swells. On the civilized side, dogs were permitted everywhere except the dining area, so we were all happy sailors. Upon arrival in Port Angeles, US Customs decided to give the yacht a cursory search and seized our basmati rice (about 3 cups of it) because it was in a glass jar and not in its original packaging. Rice?!?! Really?!?! The officer very gravely informed me that without the packaging, he could not determine its country of origin. Wow. It must have been a slow day at the border crossing. He also took a good look at my spice drawer. Was that oregano? Good thing he didn't check the freezer and spot Porter's marrow bones, or the basement with John's cedar wood carving. I guess if they had to seize something, it might as well be rice.

We spent the next 3 days boondocking at a casino near Sequim (although they provided 30-amp service free of charge so technically that isn't really boondocking) and explored the general area, with Olympic National Park topping the agenda. However, a fair bit of time was also devoted to taking care of some minor RV repairs, things that had been ignored for far too long. The undermount kitchen sink support needed bracing, a few screws here and there needed tightening. We wanted the yacht to be in tip-top shape prior to listing it for sale, just in case a serious purchaser materialized sooner rather than later. Then again, it could take 6 months to sell too, so I wasn't sure how long we could maintain living in a spotless abode. But winding down this practical aspect of our journey had been forefront in our minds. Where to list. How to word. Which pictures to post. What paperwork to complete. What price to ask. It sure was easier when we were in the buying phase! The first listing was on RVT.com (a U.S. site but accessible to anyone) followed by a Facebook Buy & Sell page dedicated to diesel coach owners, and the old stand-by AutoTrader. Within a few days we had three interested buyers, one in Florida, one in P.E.I. and one near Ottawa. It turned out the first two were just Looky-Loos and the Ottawa fellow thought the US listing price was in Canadian dollars. Sticker shock was too much for him when he factored in the exchange rate. The entire process at this point in the game was such a double-edged sword. On the one hand, I was eager to sell and get home but on the other, could not believe that 3 years were already up! What would we do with ourselves once we returned? And while the travel bug may have gone into a mild state of hibernation during our 6-month hiatus on Vancouver Island, it re-emerged just fine as soon as we crossed into the U.S. There was still so much to see!

But when not worrying about sales strategies, we took the time to enjoy the warmth and sunshine of the Olympic Peninsula's north-east corner. Situated in the rain shadow of the Olympic Mountains, the town of Sequim receives very little rainfall, and combined with relatively warm temperatures, is perfect for growing lavender. It is in fact the lavender capital of North America, but it was too early in the growing season for full-on blooms and farm visits, so we had to be content with strolling around town and making a few purchases at the very aptly named Purple Haze lavender shop, complete with Jimmy Hendrix poster on the wall. Actually, I made the purchases. John isn't really into lavender. We had also hoped to stroll part way along the Dungeness Spit that juts out into the Juan de Fuca Strait (and at 6+ miles is the longest natural sand spit in North America) but given the last several months of relaxed freedom in Canada, had forgotten that any place in the United States containing the word "National" really means "no dogs allowed." In all fairness, this spit is also the Dungeness National Wildlife Refuge, protecting critical habitat for all manner of waterfowl and shorebirds, so I can't fault them for wanting to keep the likes of a duck hunting dog as far away as possible. Instead, we drove to Port Angeles and walked out along the spit there, but it wasn't all that exciting.

The following day we drove about 17 miles up to the Visitor's Centre at Hurricane Ridge in Olympic National Park (there is that "N" word again) resigning ourselves to a limited alpine experience with dogs only being allowed on the roadway and in the parking lot. The weather was sunny, clear and fortunately quite calm (they don't call it Hurricane Ridge for nothing) and the views of the Olympic Mountains to the west were spectacular, as was the view northeast across the Juan de Fuca Strait towards Mount Baker. There was still a lot of snow on the ground at this elevation (5,750 feet) and we took advantage of a road closure at the top (due to a winter wash out) to walk along a paved stretch for a short distance. The scent of the cedar, fir and spruce trees, the dried needles and pinecones on the ground, all combined to remind me once again why I love camping. Even though there is much to be said for the comforts of coach travel (not the least of which is easy access to the bathroom at night and not having to fumble for a flashlight) I sometimes missed the smell of the earth while sleeping on the ground in a tent, listening to the sounds of little night creatures as they scurry about. But that was in another life. I suspect we won't be returning to it any time soon. At least not for more than a few nights in a row. Given the great weather, however, I initially regretted having scheduled so little time in Olympic N.P., but with our hiking options so limited (I use the term hiking very loosely here), it is just as well that our next destination was Fort Worden State Park in Port Townsend. But not before an amusing incident involving some tourists from Shanghai. Although it was still early in the season, two large tour buses pulled up to the Visitor's Centre where the views out to the Olympic Mountains are amongst the best. We were having lunch on the patio, enjoying the scenery and Porter was lying in a snowbank cooling off. (If he can't be in water, his second favourite place is snow.) Most of the sightseers wandered along the patio wall, got a chuckle upon seeing him, some venturing to ask what breed of dog he was, but by and large spent most of their time taking pictures of themselves with the snow-capped mountains as a backdrop. Except one couple. They could not get enough of him and took picture after picture. Porter in the snow. Porter in the snow with me at the picnic table beside him. Then Mrs. crouched down beside him. Then Mr. crouched down beside him. With constant oohing, ahhing and giggling. It went on and on. A regular photo-shoot. I didn't see them take one picture of the mountains. Are there no dogs in Shanghai?!

The camping area at Fort Worden State Park in Port Townsend was great. I was always a bit anxious pulling into a new campground simply because it can be a real gamble making reservations for RV spots sight unseen, and there are so many factors to keep in mind when travelling in a coach our size. While most parks indicate site dimensions (i.e. they provide length and width), they don't necessarily address other crucial considerations such as low-hanging tree branches, rocky terrain, slope or even maneuverability. Paper maps just can't convey the reality. In this case the campground was basically an open field, so not the most private of places, but the sites were at least 60 feet apart. Wide open, easy to get into and easy to get out of. And less than 200 yards from the sandy (and in some places pebbly) beach of Puget Sound. Set on 360 acres, Worden itself is one of three defensive forts that were built between 1898 and 1917 to safeguard the north entrance to Puget Sound. It still has all the old wooden buildings (officer's row, mess hall, parade square etc.) that have been renovated and repurposed into museums, dining rooms, gift shops, meetings rooms and dormitories, and if the military style and layout of these buildings didn't do the trick, the 12 concrete batteries strategically situated throughout the grounds would definitely remind you that this used to be an active military base. It was closed in the 1950s and they have since done a great job of making it a place for rest and relaxation. Porter was of course very happy to be back in the water and I spent most of my time sifting through the beach pebbles looking for sea glass. This was both therapeutic and addictive at the same time. Just like panning for gold. The next handful was sure to yield the desired reward. Most of the polished glass on this beach was either brown or white, although the blue and green pieces were hard not to miss despite being quite small. None larger than a dime and some as tiny as the grains of sand they were lying in. The phrase "separating fly shit from pepper" comes to mind. I even got John into it, although he was not quite as dedicated to the whole painstaking procedure as myself. The weather was sunny and so clear that we could see Mt. Baker (at 10,775 feet) 65 miles to the north and Mt. Rainier (Washington's highest peak at 14,410 feet) 110 miles to the south (as the crow flies). Both these peaks are not quite dormant volcanos in the Cascade Mountain Range, and they are so high they generate their own weather systems. So we were fortunate to see them both and looked forward to exploring Rainier closer up later in the month. But first we were off to check out the Victorian town of Port Townsend.

Named by none other than Captain George Vancouver himself, after his good friend the Marquis of Townshend (they dropped the "h" somewhere along the way – either that or there is a spelling error on the commemorative plaque) he landed there on May 7, 1792. Officially founded in 1851 with native peoples displaced or absorbed by the larger population, development was moderately paced until the California Gold Rush, and that changed everything. Lumber and sawmills brought boomtimes, and the strategic location at the head of Puget Sound made it the headquarter for U.S. Customs. Every foreign ship entering the Sound stopped to pay taxes and all the business associated with maritime enterprises (legal and illegal) brought big bucks into the community. But the good times only lasted until the mid-1890s when the population dropped almost overnight from 8,000 to 2,000. Why? The anticipated link to the transcontinental railroad failed to materialize, and steamships started replacing sailing craft. Many of the beautiful Victorian era homes were left empty, some not even finished. But thankfully the town hung on and now it's an attractive tourist destination with a charmingly restored historic downtown and many opulent mansions operating as B&Bs, sitting on a bluff high above the commercial district. That was one thing I had not anticipated. I can't say I had ever given much more than a passing thought to what the coastline along Puget Sound looks like, but certainly high sandstone bluffs never figured into it. And they were high. Not exactly White Cliffs of Dover high, but still high. And some of the houses seemed precariously close to the edge. Nothing like a shrinking front yard to bring down property values. Still, we spent an enjoyable day strolling around the ornate buildings downtown which now house all manner of interesting shops and galleries, and then drove around ogling the mansions on the bluff. Wandering into some of the shops, it struck me that no matter where we had been on this journey, the creativity of people can only be described as amazing. Regardless of the medium – be it paints, pebbles or pieces of glass – the imagination conjures up such wonderous things. If only there had been room in the coach to make a few more purchases. I had to make do with my own lovingly collected pieces of glass and my own limited talent.

Next up, Mount Rainier. Or so we thought. It turned out we were too early in the season to easily see this snow-covered volcano up close. The campgrounds did not open until the May long weekend but fortunately, we found a boondocking spot in the Baker-Snoqualmie National Forest at Ranger Creek Airstrip, located to the north-eastern side of the mountain. The north-east side is more arid than the south-west side and the forest fire rating was already at moderate. That was surprising because highway 140 into the park at the northern White River Entrance was still closed while they were still blasting for avalanches and plowing the road around Cayuse and Chinook passes further on inside the park itself. Plus, there were countless little water falls along the highway's embankments from the snow runoff. But first the airstrip. What's up with that? There is some disagreement on how it came to be. One story is that the area was specifically built and used as an army camp during WW II (called Ranger Creek) and following the war, between 1950 and 1990, was utilized by rangers, army, special forces and the like. But from the mid 90s on, less and less until around 1998 the army demolished the remaining buildings, leaving the airstrip intact. The other theory holds that in the 1950s, the airstrip was specifically built by the state of Washington as an emergency landing area for planes flying across the Cascades. Having seen the airstrip, this second explanation doesn't seem that reasonable. It is less than a mile long so you really wouldn't be able to land anything too big on it. I really know next to nothing about aeronautics, but it makes for an interesting story. Currently used for small Piper-type pleasure craft to fly in and out, it is apparently "not for the faint of heart." Pilots note that the windsock, set at the top of a 10-foot pole, is surrounded by 80-foot trees, and therefore difficult to locate. And the strip itself is at a 2,650-foot elevation in a 1.5-mile-wide valley dwarfed by 5,000-foot ridges all around. Of course, I think any kind of flying is not for the faint of heart, so these concerns just confirmed my misgivings. Carved out of the forest, set amongst mountains, beside an active volcano. What could go wrong? The surrounding area is maintained by the forestry service for relatively free camping (i.e. you just need a parks pass of some kind, but no fees are charged) and it was great. Some tent camping sites were nicely secluded in the forest while others, for the likes of us, were set pretty much near one end of the runway. Over the weekend, 13 small planes flew in one day and out the next. Literally past our front door. Is there such a thing as fly-in camping? Actually, they were there for "clean-up day" as this was the first weekend that the airstrip was open for the season. There were only a handful of campers (RV and tent), mostly families, set up during that weekend but by Monday there was only us and 2 other parties, who were so far off we could neither see nor hear them. From one perspective, the total privacy was great but from another, a little bit creepy. Sometimes it's nice to have people around. And there was a downside to this locale. No cell or internet service

of any kind. We had to drive 40 minutes to the town of Enumclaw to check mail and make phone calls. There were quite a few elk roaming the area and we saw several of them along the highway but none at the campground or airstrip itself, although every morning abundant evidence of their prior night's presence was quite noticeable. We had to watch our step.

BOONDOCKING AT RANGER CREEK AIRSTRIP — FAR FROM THE MADDENING CROWD.

We were determined to see Mt. Rainier up close and the only entrance to the park that is open year-round is Nisqually, at the southern end. That involved a 2-1/2-hour drive by car one way around the base of the mountain along smaller roads, pretty much through hill and dale. Very picturesque, heavily forested in some places, with occasional glimpses of snow-covered Rainier getting closer and closer. The downside? (And isn't there always one?) It also provided way too many views of the huge swaths of clear-cut logging that goes on. Massive forests denuded to the top of the highest ridge. In every direction. Thank goodness Rainier is in a National Park because I'm sure they would figure out a way to log that too if they could. Once in the park, the drive up to Paradise Park (basically a valley 1 mile up the mountain) along the steadily climbing and constantly winding road with huge trees on either side was beautiful, and we naturally stopped for photo ops along the way. And then we reached the Paradise parking lot. Oh my goodness! It was not at all what we expected. Or remembered for that matter. (We had done some summer hiking up there 11 years ago.) The snow was incredibly deep – easily 8 feet in places – and people were everywhere. Having snowball fights, sliding down the hillsides, mugging for photographs and even skiing! I spoke with one fellow who advised that they put skins on the bottom of their skis, walk up and then ski down. It takes all day to put in one run. I could only envy the fitness level that must require. We walked around a "road closed" sign to escape the crowds a bit and found ourselves looking out towards the Skyline Trail that we had hiked all those may years ago. It was just a snow-covered bowl and in the distance we could clearly see where they had stopped plowing the road. And then I understood why it is closed during winter. There is no way plows would be able to keep up with this amount of white stuff. Rainier receives on average, 56 feet of snow each year. I'd say each "winter" but it can snow there in May with serious accumulations. The most they ever received was 108 feet! This year was a paltry 43.

One of nicest views of the peak is supposed to be from the Sunrise Visitor's Centre (elevation 6,400 feet), and that would have been a leisurely 20-minute drive from our camping area, if only the road were open. Being too smart for our own good, we decided that while barriers may keep cars out, bicycles could easily navigate around them. So we kitted up and set off. OMG! It was tough going and I could only lament the fact that my fitness level was nowhere near what it had been at the beginning of the journey, when we peddled sections of the Cabot Trail on Cape Breton Island. I specifically recalled that back then, I did not have to get off my bike even once for any of the climbs, but at Rainier? I had to dismount several times to gulp my lungs back into my heaving chest and gasp in some oxygen for my burning legs. And it wasn't that the incline was really all that steep, but it just never, never, ever stopped. Never. Ever. There were no downhills, no flats, just a relentless upward grind. At times I was only going 7km/h. Can't most people walk faster than that? It took me close to an hour to cover 8kms. The only positive thing (aside from the scenery) was that since the road was technically still closed, there was no motorized traffic (except for two parks vehicles) so we could ride along the centre line without fear of being hit. And that is just as well because I was so tired, I was criss-crossing from left to right shoulder, as if going at an angle would somehow ease the gradient. We stopped to rest with only 26 more kilometers to the top. It wasn't going to happen. Thankfully, my demoralized ego was saved by some parks department employees who drove up in their truck and advised that we should not go further because they were still clearing snow from the road further along. I did my best to look disappointed. Really? I have to turn back? Gosh darn. Well that sure is upsetting but rules are rules. The ride down did not involve much peddling but rather, considerable use of the brakes. I got up to 45km/h but considering there was nothing between me and the asphalt, tried to keep it around 30. Wheeeee! Look Mom! No hands! And one last comment on Mt. Rainier. It was named by again, none other than Capt. George Vancouver, after fellow naval officer, Peter Regnier. What was it with this guy and spelling?

Making our way further south, we set up camp at a state park about half-way between Tacoma and Portland. This was by design since there were some things we wanted to see and do in both cities, although the park itself didn't have much to recommend it other than having full hook-ups. The big draws were Powell's Book Store in Portland and the Museum of Glass in Tacoma. And in between was Mt. St. Helens. The two weeks of sunshine enjoyed at the beginning of the month didn't last and it was soon drizzly gray, more in keeping with the reputation of the northwest. Everything was a very lush green and lots of moss! We tried to time our indoor activities with the more inclement weather but that didn't really work out all that well. Predicting the weather was next to impossible. Sunshine when it should have been rain and rain when it should have been sunshine. It was sun/cloud mix while hanging out at Powell's, more sun than cloud while learning about glass, and drizzle, cloud and fog at Mt. St. Helens. So needless to say, we didn't see much there. But all three places were more than worth the visit.

Full disclosure – we had been to this part of the U.S. before, so we knew what we were in for upon returning to Powell's City of Books, the world's largest independent bookstore. It takes up three floors on an entire city block and at the entrance, visitors can pick up a floor map to help navigate their way through the nine colour-coded rooms, each with their own subject matter: blue room – literature & poetry, orange room – cooking & music, purple room – religion & health, and so on. They stock both new and used publications, all shelved side by side, so it was a great place to browse, find out-of-print books and get a good deal on prices. Because it was so easy to lose track of time, we had to phone each other in order to stay in touch. "I'm in the green room. I'll meet you in the red room." I could have stayed there all day, but we limited ourselves to two shopping bags. There was only so much weight the yacht could carry.

We then headed over to the International Rose Test Garden which is considered to be the oldest continuously operated garden of its kind in the United States with more than 10,000 roses (over 600 varieties) spread across 5 acres. The gardens were established in 1917 to test new varieties of roses and of course give awards for the best ones. Peak bloom time is between May and July but it must have been a late spring because despite visiting in mid-May, most of the roses were still tightly closed buds. Another week or so and they'd be fantastic. However, the Rhododendrons were full out. Maybe even a few days past their prime but magnificent none-the-less. And huge! While at home we refer to them as "bushes", in Portland they could easily be called "trees" because some were at least 25 feet high. And they weren't limited to just this garden. All over the north-west, they were blooming in a variety of vibrant colours in front of a variety of homes, from those with lavish gardens to those with humble yards. Even in the woods and along the interstate. It was just lovely!

And then there was the Museum of Glass in Tacoma. I found my artistic medium. It started with beach glass but now that I have seen true artists at work, I am inspired to take on a new hobby. Seashells are out. Glass is in. Honestly, I knew virtually nothing about glass beyond the fact that I could see through it (sometimes) and break it (if I tried hard enough) but that was all about to change. Pulling up to the museum, the architecture (mostly the Hot Shop Cone that contains the kilns) seemed strangely familiar. I was sure I had seen a similar design somewhere before. Once inside, it turned out that the architect was none other than Arthur Erickson. Of Toronto's Roy Thomson Hall fame. My father was the Electrical Consulting Engineer on Roy Thomson and the one summer I worked for him, I saw a lot, and I mean a lot, of those drawings. So entering the MOG, I felt right at home. However, information plaques stated that Erickson got his inspiration for the Cone from the historical sawdust burners that were quite common throughout this region, but I find that a bit suspect. The MOG opened in 2002, considerably after Roy Thomson Hall's 1982 inauguration. Hmmm. Was he recycling his ideas? It is not a huge museum but one of its biggest draws is the Hot Shop. A soaring 90 feet high, visitors sit in a semi-circular elevated theatre to watch the artists at work (both resident and guest), learn from the on-going real-time narrative and can have any of their questions answered. It was mesmerizing. And on the second weekend of every month, wanna-be artists can participate in fusing workshops and have their creations fired in these kilns where the glass reaches 2,300 degrees Fahrenheit! If only we had the time! The inspiration for the museum itself came from glass maestro Dale Chihuly who studied glass blowing techniques in Murano, Italy during the late '60s, and was motivated to bring one major approach back to North America. Instead of working as solo artists, collaborators operate as a team with one individual conducting the creation. This enables them to construct huge magnificent works that would have been impossible to produce alone, while at the same time, pushing the boundaries of glass as a medium. Within a short time of Chihuly returning to his native Tacoma, the Pacific NorthWest became one of the most innovative glassblowing centres in the world. Who knew? The MOG displays some of Chihuly's work inside, but most of it can be viewed along the 500-foot long Chihuly Bridge of Glass outside – really a pedestrian overpass above Interstate 705 – connecting the museum to the rest of the city. It was odd viewing these fantastic works of art with cars zipping by underneath. And they were fantastic works of art. Bold colours. Creative, way-out-there shapes. Vases, flowers, tubes, plates. The "ceiling" in particular looked somewhat familiar, and then I read that the lobby ceiling of the Bellagio hotel in Las Vegas was also a Chihuly creation. People are more likely to visit Las Vegas than Tacoma, so if ever in Vegas, head over to the Bellagio to admire this over-the-top art! Definitely worth it!

But one thing we didn't really get to "admire" was Mt. St. Helen's and that was most frustrating because it was exactly 39 years ago, on May 18th, that one of the most beautiful of the Cascade peaks blew her top. Many can recall the images of volcanic ash spewing into the initially clear blue sky and then blanketing cities like Portland many miles away but despite the drama at the time, for most of us, it all faded from memory. Not so for the people who still monitor this active volcano that has erupted, albeit on a smaller scale, numerous times since, with the last serious activity being between 2004 and 2008. Quick recap. Along the Cascade Mountains through Washington and Oregon lie a row of not-so-dormant volcanoes: Baker, Rainier, Adams, Hood, Jefferson and others. All beautiful snow-capped peaks that rise majestically above the surrounding green forests. After 123 years of quiet Mt. St. Helens decided to put on a show, first by releasing a bit of steam and ash, and producing some minor earthquakes. A belch, if you will. That was in March of 1980. Geologists and volcanologists were soon crawling all over the place, measuring and monitoring, and in April, found that the north flank of the mountain was "growing" between five and seven feet per day! In early May, a 5.0 magnitude quake was recorded. Local people as well as visitors were still hoping to hike and enjoy their leisure activities around their favourite mountain but several volcanologists, including one fellow, David Johnston, pushed to have the area closed to recreation. It was too dangerous. They were waiting for the big one. On May 18th, Johnston was set up on a ridge about 5 miles from the mountain, a safe distance it was assumed, filling in for a colleague whose turn it had been to monitor the activity. At 8:32am, the entire bulging north face collapsed causing the largest ever recorded landslide in history. This unleashed a hurricane-force blast that travelled laterally at a speed of over 300 miles per hour, reaching Johnson's location in 40 seconds. His last transmission was an excited, "Vancouver! Vancouver! This is it!" Then nothing. (His body was never found and road crews building a new by-pass unearthed his camper in 1993.) Massive trees were snapped like matchsticks, leaving only mangled stumps behind. Within 3 minutes, 57 people were dead (although if not for Johnson and his colleagues it could have been many more) and almost 230 sq/miles of forest was devasted. Then 9 hours of ash plumes (over 12 miles high into the air) and pyroclastic flows. It is hard to comprehend that level of destruction. Yet the recovery has also been astounding. An observatory built on the ridge where Johnston had been set up (fittingly named the Johnston Ridge Observatory) and numerous hiking trails in the area stand testament to both the devastation as well as the regrowth that has taken place.

John and I had done a bit of hiking around Mt. St. Helens 11 years prior and at that time, the surroundings were still quite barren with lots of cinder, rock and ash but now there was quite a bit of green scrub, fair-sized trees and numerous wildflowers (including Trilliums!) Animals as large as elk and as small as tiny toads have all returned. Yet the volcano continues to smolder. The Observatory was quite informative showcasing all kinds of volcano and earthquake measuring devices, and presented a fifteen-minute movie covering the St. Helens blast itself, put together from actual footage and some recreations. The ending of the film would have been very powerful, if only the weather had not conspired to make it almost anticlimactic. On the day of our visit, it was very foggy with lots of low cloud. There wasn't even a glimmer of the mountain itself. Denali all over again. The movie was shown on a huge floor to ceiling screen, behind which was a huge floor to ceiling curtain, behind which was a huge floor to ceiling glass wall. After the credits had rolled, the screen went up, the curtains opened and theoretically we should all have been dramatically gazing straight out at the magnificent crater and what is left of the mountain. Instead, all we saw was a wall of fog. Lunch bag letdown. So we walked around outside on a few of the shorter trails hoping the fog would lift but nothin' doin'. Snapped off tree trunks was about as impressive as it got. We had left Porter in the car (three guesses as to why) and with the limited visibility, there really wasn't much reason to linger. Yet I wish we could have stayed to soak it in a bit more. I can still hear the sound of Johnston's voice, yelling into the radio, "Vancouver! Vancouver! This is it!" He was only 30 years old.

Ideally, we could have remained in the area longer and returned when the weather improved, but that was not expected to happen any time soon, so we packed up and headed south towards the Columbia River Gorge and Hood River in Oregon. We ended up staying there longer than planned and enjoyed almost every minute. When viewing a map of North America, the distances between Portland, Hood River, Mt. Hood itself and The Dalles seem insignificant, but there really are quite a few miles between them and in exploring the area, we put quite a few extra miles on the Jeep. It all started with the drive along the Gorge which can be done quickly along Interstate 84, or at a leisurely scenic pace following Historic Road 30.

By the early 1900s America was a nation already in love with its cars, and subsequently came to love the roads upon which they were driven. Scenic rides in the countryside were fashionable and when it came to Highway 30 (then called the Columbia River Highway), engineers designed it to complement the beautiful and winding landscape through which it passed, endeavouring to make country cruising as enjoyable as possible. That was accomplished in spades! If a road can be described as gorgeous, this is the one. We set up the coach in Memaloose State Park, about 6 miles east of the town of Hood River and opted to explore in both directions in the Toad, on our bikes and on foot (including those sections where motorized traffic is now prohibited). The scenery was stunning with high cliffs on both the Washington side and the Oregon side, and the wide Columbia River acting as a boundary between the two states. At over 80 miles long, the Gorge was formed by the com-bined forces of volcanoes, glaciers, massive floods, earthquakes, erosion and landslides, evidence of which can easily be seen in the exposed cliffs and eroding rocks (we came across more than our share of recent rockslides). It also contains the greatest concentration of "high" waterfalls in North America (some claim 75 of them while others cite a mere 45), so there was considerable sightseeing to do. Of course there was no definition of what constituted a "high" waterfall, but the ones we visited were very beautiful. Especially Multnomah, the most popular of all, with a combined height of 620 feet (the 4th tallest in the U.S).

MULTNOMAH FALLS.

There were numerous trails both around and connecting the waterfalls but sadly, most of them were still closed following a catastrophic fire in September of 2017. There is always some idiot somewhere doing something stupid and in this particular case that idiot happened to be a 15-year old boy in Eagle Creek Campground who decided to throw firecrackers into a canyon despite a burn ban being in effect. This started a massive forest fire that lasted for 3 months and burned nearly 50,000 acres. While it raged, it actually jumped the Columbia River (which is about 1 mile wide at this point), brought all train and marine traffic to a stop, caused the evacuation of numerous towns and shut down Interstate 85. The closure of the hiking trails remains in effect mainly because the vegetation that kept the Gorge's steep walls in place had burned away, thus destabilizing the ground surface and resulting in numerous and unpredictable rockslides. We hiked along a few of the shorter trails that had re-opened and were grateful for at least a taste of this dramatic landscape. And the convicted arsonist? He was put on 5 years probation and fined a reasonable 36 million dollars. As if that will ever be collected.

We also found a couple of great biking routes along Historic 30, my favourite being the section that lead from the town of Mosier to the Rowena Overlook, a distance of about 13 miles return, with some challenging yet do-able inclines heading east, and great downhill cruising heading back west. Along this stretch, the road winds along near the top of the Gorge so the views out across the Columbia River and into Washington were spectacular. Maybe it's just me, but whenever I hear the word "gorge" I envision something deep, dark and narrow but this gorge, while deep, is wide open and bright. One sunny day we could see the top of Mt. Adams to the north and Mt. Hood to the south! Some rolling sections passed through vineyards while others through cherry orchards. And so many wildflowers in bloom. Blue, purple, yellow, cream, pale lilac! My favourite were the cornflowers. Fields of them! And not just blue ones. They were also purple and pink and two-toned as well. Just lovely. I'm glad we were able to bike it several times.

Another route was along a 6-mile section of hwy. 30 that was only open to pedestrians and bicycles, from Mosier, through some old tunnels, towards Hood River. It also involved a fair bit of huffing and puffing but the dramatic and scenic overlooks were well worth it. We also walked it one afternoon with Porter but I'm sad to say that halfway into his 9th year, Porter was really lagging by the 3-hour mark. John said that if there had been a beach in front of him his energy level would have dramatically improved, but I was not so sure. He was really struggling by the time we got back to the yacht. I started thinking 2-hour walks might be his new max. Hood River itself was a cute little town with a charming downtown core (really just a two-block strip) with all kinds of small shops and cafes. And its claim to fame is being the windsurfing capital of North America. During the day, as the air warms and travels east up the Columbia River, the

Gorge acts as a big wind tunnel creating ideal conditions for this sport (as well as kite-sailing). We only saw a few people out on the water, but it was still a bit early in the season. I can't say it's an activity I'm too keen to learn. I tried many years ago in the Caribbean but could never quite master raising the sail and spent too much time falling off the board. There is only so much saltwater you can get up your nose before you give up and return to your chaise lounge.

Naturally, Mt. Hood was a big draw so one sunny day, we drove there as well, stopping for a 2-hour hike to Mirror Lake which supposedly offers up a wonderful view of the mountain reflected in the calm waters. Sure. If its sunny and there is no wind. The hike itself was on the steep side and by the time we reached said lake, clouds had moved in to obscure most of the mountain and the wind ripples on the lake foiled any mirror effect. All in all, an okay walk in the woods that required too much effort for minimal reward, so we weren't about to tackle that again no matter how nice the weather forecast. Instead, we drove higher to Timberline Lodge, about as far up Mt. Hood as it is possible to get by vehicle (6,000 feet). It's really a ski resort at that point and while the lifts had been shut down for the season, the snow was still so deep it was impossible to walk anywhere without snowshoes. A few intrepid skiers had slogged their way uphill on foot in order to cruise down unimpeded, but it didn't look like much fun to me. The lodge itself was quite large and antiquated in a "ski chalet" kind of way with huge wooden beams and a massive fireplace in the lobby, but its mainstream claim to fame came from Hollywood. The exterior was used in the film *The Shining* with Jack Nicholson, based on Stephen King's novel. Ho hum. And one other comment about Mt. Hood. It was named by... yes, you guessed it, Capt. George Vancouver, after yet another buddy, British Naval Admiral Lord Samuel Hood. At least he got the spelling right this time.

This general area was also the near terminus for the infamous Oregon Trail, that wagon train pioneers followed for 2,000 miles from Independence, Missouri to Oregon City, Oregon, a crossing that took over 5 months to complete. I hoped to see additional sections of it as we made our way east, but one particular segment here really showed how arduous that trek must have been. Naturally there were several branches of the route but in this area, some settlers opted to cross along the southwest flank of Mt. Hood instead of floating down the treacherous rapids of the Columbia River. Here, it was called the Barlow Toll Road (parts of which were paved over in the 1920s) but one section remained as it was back then. Laurel Hill Chute, a rough steep drop with a 60% grade on the "road" and then a sheer cliff thrown in just to make things really exciting. Settlers were forced to lower their wagons by ropes down the cliff, after they had already cut down huge trees (three-foot diameter) which in an effort to navigate the road, they tied to their wagons with the branches facing downhill to act as brakes! Ingenious. Who comes up with these ideas? On a more sobering note, there was also the grave of a pioneer woman (descriptively called Pioneer Woman Grave) along this roadway as well. In 1924, when engineers were constructing the first Mt. Hood Highway, they came upon this grave, marked with an old wooden wagon tongue, containing the remains of a pioneer woman. Her body was reinterred, but there was no information as to identity. How sad to have almost reached the end of such a long and grueling journey, and then to die virtually within sight of your destination. And be forgotten. Buried alone in a vast wilderness. I found myself thinking about her a lot. What was her name? How old was she? Where was she from? What did

she die of? Did she have family? Did they wonder what happened to her? I think in today's political climate where our leaders are hastily apologizing for all manner of decisions made by yesteryear's governments, we sometimes forget these nameless souls whose struggles were in vain and whose lives ended well before their dreams could be realized...

PIONEER WOMAN GRAVE — ALONE AND FORGOTTEN.

Finally, the reason I say we enjoyed "almost" every minute of our time in the Gorge was that one afternoon I just happened to glance over at the right rear tire of the coach and noticed a 4-inch gash in the sidewall. We had no idea how or when it got there but John said it was a blowout waiting to happen. Naturally, this was over the Memorial Day weekend, so all businesses were closed but first thing Tuesday morning John contacted the big tire place (Les Schwab Tires), sent over some pictures and we had an appointment for Thursday morning. Being that the yacht rode on commercial truck-sized tires we had to wait an extra day to have one shipped in, but once it had been replaced (Kaaaching – Ouch!!!) we were off, making our way towards Klamath Falls. Time to visit with family.

38.

IT AIN'T OVER UNTIL THE FAT LADY SINGS

IT IS ESTIMATED THAT APPROXIMATELY 60% OF AMERICANS DO NOT HAVE PASSPORTS, THUS MAKING IT IMPOSSIBLE FOR THEM TO TRAVEL OUTSIDE OF THEIR OWN COUNTRY. And it's not as if they are not <u>allowed</u> to have passports. They have simply not bothered to obtain them. At first, I thought that was just ridiculous. How can anyone not want a passport? There is so much to see and do in the world! But our travels through Oregon and Wyoming had me re-evaluating my opinion. There is so much to see and do in those two states alone it would take years of exploring to do them any justice. Why go further afield? As it was, we barely scratched the surface.

The month started with a visit to Klamath Falls in southern Oregon where we were able to spend some quality time with John's sister, brother-in-law and niece. Their hospitality and assistance (providing a boondocking spot, getting our bikes tuned up, taking us for great dinners, spoiling Porter) was very much appreciated, and catching up with family at a relaxed pace is always preferable to the rushed exchanges that tend to take place at weddings and funerals. One of our first group outings was to Lava Beds National Monument, just south of the Oregon/California border. Much of the area (including around Klamath Falls) used to be covered by shallow lakes, crucial to migrating birds and water fowl, but over the last one and a half centuries, the water has been diverted, dyked and otherwise re-routed enabling huge swaths of land to be transformed into farm and pastureland. Needless to say, the avian population has plummeted, and moves are underway to try to restore some of the grassland back to wetland. Resistance from farmers and ranchers is a no-brainer. But at Lava Beds, the land rises to an elevation of 5,700 feet, with rocky out-croppings, several scrubby overgrown cinder cones, sagebrush savannahs and miles and miles of lava created tunnels and caves. The entire landscape was formed by a massive volcano (Medicine Lake Volcano) which has been gently erupting (bubbling, really) on and off for the past half million years. (The last bigger bubble was about 900 years ago.) And although Lava Beds N.M. covers an area of 73 square miles, that is only 1/10th of the volcano's actual size. During the 30-odd separate lava flows that have occurred over the past tens of thousands of years, more than 700 lava tube tunnels and caves were created, many of which can be entered and explored. They are all very "natural" in that there is no artificial lighting or artfully illuminated displays of stalactites (like Luray Caverns in Virginia) so carrying our own lanterns and headlights, we descended into the depths. Some of the caves were a bit like walking through a dark subway tunnel, except there were random places to smack your head if you didn't crouch down low enough (yep, did that), and the floor underfoot was very gnarly and uneven. Perfect for twisting an ankle or scraping a knee. In one cave, we went down so far, ice had formed on the floor, a product of moist cold winter air that does not rise back out. In another cave John suggested we all turn off our lights, and despite waiting for my eyes to adjust, they never did. That kind of inky darkness is not something I want to relive. Claustrophobic. Suffocating. Thankfully, we all emerged relatively unscathed and I must admit that although it was pretty cool (literally and figuratively) I'm not too keen on being that far underground without clearly marked exit signs. Plus having the information pamphlets warn you to mark your route so as not to get lost didn't ease my jitters any either. And we didn't even go into the more challenging ones where we would have had to crawl on hands and knees. Spelunking is not going to be a future activity for me.

Originally, this general area of northern California, including Lake Tule, was home to the Modoc Indians (less than 400 strong) but by the 1850s, conflicts with arriving settlers reached a point where the Modoc were persuaded to relocate to the Klamath Reservation in southern Oregon. The Modoc and Klamath tribes did not get along and when officials running the Reservation did not satisfactorily address Modoc complaints, a young Chief by the name of Captain Jack (Kintpuash) along with half of the tribe (169 individuals) packed up and headed back to their original homeland. Naturally, the settlers did not appreciate their return and we all know who wins in that situation. Violence ensued, Modocs, soldiers and settlers were killed, and Captain Jack fled with what was left of his followers to the rocky outcroppings of the lava beds, setting off the Modoc War. Outnumbered (60 to 600), the lava beds formed a natural fortress for them, and they were able to last 5 months before finally surrendering. Their holdout became known as Capt. Jack's stronghold and two hiking trails led in and around the rocky terrain. A National Parks pamphlet described various stations along the way and explained pretty much who did what, where, and walking along I tried to imagine the thoughts of both the aggressors and the defenders. I found myself almost philosophically reflecting on the rise and demise of cultures throughout humanity's history. How desperately we all want to preserve our heritage. No matter how small or insignificant others may consider us to be. Unfortunately, the pamphlet ends with the following quote: "The cultural identity of an entire people was lost here... just so settlers could graze a few cows." I find that a rather flippant summary to a very complicated time in history, and certainly expected better from an official publication. But the bias of political correctness has a way of seeping into everything. How unfortunate. Leave it to the government to continue its alienating diatribe. As if they hadn't done enough damage 150 years ago. We also checked out some petroglyphs that had been etched into a cliff face on an "island" in Lake Tule, which with the lake's drainage, could now be accessed by car. The Indians used to paddle out to the island and chisel their creations while sitting in boats, and their placement on the cliff reflects the fluctuation in water levels over the centuries. Sadly, a high barbed-wire fence has been erected around the petroglyphs to prevent treasure-hunters from cutting these artefacts out of the rock, and to prevent modern-day morons from adding their own artwork. Some people are such idiots.

Our second group outing was to Crater Lake, although John and I also returned on our own when everyone else went back to work and school. Less than an hour's drive north of Klamath Falls, it is one of those places where I would have been content to just sit and stare at the mesmerizing blue colour of the water. It is hard to describe. Almost sapphire. Yet deeper. Apparently, when Kodak first processed colour photographs of the lake, they apologized to their customers believing that the resulting brilliant blue shade was caused by an error in their lab. During our visit, the lake was still ringed by snow in many places and that only seemed to intensify the colour. The lake was formed 7,700 years ago, when 12,000-foot high Mount Mazama, one of the many volcanoes along the Cascade Range, erupted in a massive explosion. Scientists estimate the blast was 50 to 100 times bigger than Mt. St. Helens. As the magma chamber emptied, the mountain could no longer support its own weight and collapsed inward, forming a deep caldera. Over the centuries, rain and snow filled its entire depth. Since there are no streams or other lakes feeding into it, there is very little sediment, so the water is incredibly clear. Statistically, it is the deepest lake in the United States, seventh deepest in the world. Six miles across and 1,943 feet deep. And what makes it so remarkable is that you don't so much gaze out at it, as you gaze down into it, basically standing on the edge of the caldera. In places the crater walls are 2,000 feet high and numerous signs warned people to stay away from the edge. This was particularly germane in the spring because given the combination of still-deep snow and the onset of tourist season, one misstep could result in a tragic slide down a slippery slope from which there is no crawling back up. In fact, about a week after our visit, one hapless holidaymaker did exactly that. Got too close to the edge and whoops, slid 800 feet down into the freezing waters of the caldera. Rescue crews were not able to reach him despite climbing down 600 feet, so a helicopter was brought in. He survived despite the odds. Thankfully, we did not experience any drama of that kind. While in the summer it is possible to drive (or bike) a 33-mile loop around the lake (the rim road), most of that was still closed because of snow, with sections not expected to open up until July. But a few miles were clear and accessible to pedestrian (and bicycle) traffic so we went for a lovely stroll, enjoying not just the lake but also views of other peaks in the distance. Porter of course had a blast rolling in the snow and playing with his cousin Jubel, another chocolate lab who is only 2 years old and needless to say, wore the brown menace out. I wasn't sure if his age was catching up to him, if he was not well, or if he was just depressed but it seemed that ever since we left Tofino, he just didn't have that same spring in his step. Almost as if someone had flipped a switch. He'd rally for a time when faced with a new situation, but generally was much more lethargic and prone to napping. We decided that when we got home a visit to our vet would be a top priority.

Leaving Klamath Falls, the terrain change through south-eastern Oregon towards Wyoming was completely unexpected. We had become accustomed to dark green forests with huge pines and snow-capped peaks but within a short time we had mile after never ending mile of sagebrush covered flats, as far as the eye could see. No sign of human habitation or presence save for the pavement upon which we were driving. Gradually, a few rolling hills with the odd western juniper but still mostly sage. Yet despite the seemingly inhospitable landscape, quite a few herds of cattle. I recalled from our swing through Texas that cattle rarely move more than one mile from a water source, so there must have been water somewhere, but we certainly didn't see it. Eventually we got into some river valleys and stopped for the night at Massacre Rocks State Park, on the shores of the Snake River. Not exactly a welcoming park name but given what happened near there in 1862, it was a place of some apprehension along the Oregon Trail. At least for those settlers who were passing through.

Going off on a tangent here... Imagine you've had a job transfer 2,000 miles (well over 3,500 kilometers) away, to a remote location nobody really knows much about.

And your company isn't going to provide a moving van. And you won't have a map because there are no roads on how to get there anyway. And you and your family will have to walk the entire way. And there will be no conveniently situated motels or grocery stores. And you've heard rumours of violent attacks by residents whose territory you will have to pass through. So you pack up whatever belongings, supplies and foodstuffs that can fit into a cart, buy a couple of oxen, and start walking. Kids and all. What would possibly motivate you to undertake such a journey? Couldn't you just get another job?

Over a 30-year period, (roughly between 1840 and 1869) more than 500,000 people had the requisite motivation, most starting in Independence, Missouri (just outside of present-day Kansas City, MS) heading west. Why? Economy, politics and religious persecution. In 1837 and 1841, there were two considerable economic depressions so for some, the promise of a better life out west was the lure. An opportunity for farmers and businessmen alike. Others bought into the political objective of Manifest Destiny – that it was God's intent the United States stretch from coast to coast. In reality, the government of the day just wanted a stronger American presence in the Pacific Northwest in order to wrest the area from British control. And the third group, The Mormons, wanted to practice their faith free from harassment and persecution. They all started out from pretty much the same jumping off point and followed the same route, with several spurs, but then diverged with one group heading to Oregon (hence the Oregon Trail), one to California (hence the California Trail) and one down to Utah and Salt Lake City (hence the Mormon Trail). But along the way they faced the same challenges and hardships. Rough terrain, inclement weather, debilitating accidents, disease, violence and death. From one 1852 journal, "... a man must learn to endure heat like a salamander... dust like toad... learn to eat with his unwashed fingers, drink out of the same vessel as his mules, sleep on the ground when it rains, share his blanket with vermin and have patience with musketoes [sic]... to be sick without a home, to die and be buried like a dog."

These are the things not depicted in movies or on television. In fact, almost everything we see in the Hollywood portrayal of this great migration is wrong, not the least of which is the interaction between the emigrants and the local Indian tribes. There was very little circling of wagons and running bow & arrow/gun fights. Very few wagon trains were ever attacked, and the majority of contacts were peaceful and at times even lifesaving. A considerable number of emigrants completed their entire journey without even having seen an Indian. This is not to say conflicts did not arise. And when they did, they were very ugly. On both sides. Complete with scalpings, eviscerations and worse. By both sides. Sadly, it was often the hapless settlers paying for the atrocities committed by U.S. soldiers at some earlier time in some different locale. Reading about the accounts of what happened at the Sand Creek Massacre under Colonel John Chivington (they are too gruesome to describe here – google the Commission's findings at your own peril), it is no wonder that at times the Indians wanted to extract some measure of revenge or retaliation. But the migrants struggled on. And not in large Conestoga covered wagons either. Most made the journey in carts that were 10 feet long, 4 feet wide and only 2 feet deep, walking because it was too jarring to ride along the uneven terrain. A large number of Mormons actually pushed and pulled their belongings in hand carts. For 5 or more months! It gives "motivation" a whole new meaning.

Massacre State Park is located close to where, in August of 1862, one of the traveller/native skirmishes took place. It is unclear why the Indians attacked this one particular wagon train, but robbery may have been a motive since after killing a few emigrants, they stole as much property as they could manage. They were pursued by men from a second train and after all was said and done, 10 settlers were dead along with an unknown number of Indians, possibly as many as 40. This all took place along a very well established and busy part of the Oregon/California Trail. In fact, so many had already passed this way, deep swales left by the thousands of wagons can still be seen in the surrounding hillsides. We went for a short walk along a designated path where we could stand in the hollow of these swales and I tried to imagine what it must have been like to be in a wagon train, slowly crawling along, covering anywhere from 4 to 20 miles per day. And you really do have to stand there and feel it. Neither the artist's sketches from that time period, nor the journals so painstakingly recorded by the travellers can convey the vastness of the land they crossed. It is almost unfathomable. Unfortunately, large parts of the trail have been paved over by I-86 and the roar of passing semis and speeding cars kept interrupting my reverie, making it difficult to channel the emigrant experience. And the difference between a swale and a rut? Swales are almost like deep, relatively wide eroded ditches where the earth has been worn down by the passing of thousands of wagons and feet. Ruts, on the other hand, are narrower grooves left in dirt or rock, made primarily by wheels alone. Back in the coach, we continued the journey across this vast expanse of almost arid wasteland at 60 miles an hour in air-conditioned comfort. It boggled my mind to consider doing it on foot. More on the Oregon Trail later. There were other fish to fry. Fish in the form of fossils.

I cannot recall when I first heard about the Green River Formation. Certainly, a long long time ago. And while fossils have never really been my thing, I am fascinated by the idea that the remains of creatures that had lived millions and millions of years ago can be seen, touched, even held. At one point (also long long ago) I had considered purchasing some pieces from a fossil company, but their prices were beyond my meager income and I'm just not that kind of collector. I want to get my own hands dirty and find my own treasures. I had heard there were quarries that provided the hands-on experience I was seeking, but while I had always wanted to go, I somehow never seemed to arrive. Green River Wyoming, and more specifically Kemmerer, is a long way from anywhere. And all the area has going for it are fossils. Fish fossils mostly, but also avian, mammal, insect, reptilian and plant. So off we went to Kemmerer, driving through sparsely inhabited terrain that was punctuated by an increasing number of natural gas wells. They did somewhat mar the scenery.

About 52 million years ago, during the Eocene Epoch, the areas of present-day Wyoming, Utah and Colorado were covered by three large lakes, the smallest being Fossil Lake (where we were headed.) And as the climate changed and the lakes dried up, the sediments left behind formed limestone, mudstone and volcanic ash layers in the Green River Formation. For some reason, the limestone sediment of Fossil Lake contains the richest Eocene fossil deposits in the world. Mostly fish but also animals and plants. Scientists are not certain why there are such large concentrations of fish fossils found at the same sedimentary level, but some believe it to be an indicator of a mass die-off attributed to a catastrophic event. In this case, a sudden change in water temperature or water chemistry. A volcano perhaps? They don't know. But they do know it is "the world's best Paleogene record of a freshwater lake ecosystem."

There were three quarries in the area that offered a paleontology experience but after chatting with our neighbour at the RV park (who had been to all of them), we settled on American Fossil about 10 miles north of Kemmerer. Their website provided very specific directions to the quarry and while not difficult to follow, we had to drive along a winding dirt road, over rolling terrain for quite some time. Only us and a few wandering cows. On the road, no less. Once at the quarry we had the option to sign up for 1 hour, 4 hours or the entire day. I could have stayed the entire week. Such fun! Even John conceded that it was pretty interesting. At least more interesting than digging for dinosaurs. We were each issued a narrow chisel and rock hammer, shown how to split rocks and advised what to look for. On his first slab, John found part of a rather large fish, and we were off to the races. I'd like to say that we uncovered numerous exotic species previously unknown in the paleo world but sadly such was not the case. Exoticism does not come easy. We managed to unearth numerous pieces of fish, mostly quite small and although we turned up a few entire specimens, they were only about 3 inches long and of a very common genus. The staff were incredibly helpful in identifying them, "Oh yes, that is a *Diplomystus dentatus*. Or possibly a *Knightis eocaena*." Sure it is. They could have said it was a *Fishius Fossilus* and I would have nodded wisely in agreement. The entire process was all more a matter of luck than skill. I did however split open one rock to reveal what appeared to my untrained eye to be a small bird's wing. No more than two inches long. It very obviously wasn't a fish, so I put it to one side and didn't think much of it. After a few more fish finds, I decided to show it to the staff, and this generated some excitement. They took pictures of it, consulted with each other, called over someone supposedly more knowledgeable, asked to take a picture of me with it (sure, why not?) and spent a fair bit of time trying to pinpoint the specific location where I had found it. Apparently, this was a rare find! One of them said he had never even seen a bird fossil in his three years at the quarry. Stupid me. I should have paid more attention because apparently if the other wing and head were located, it would have been worth anywhere from 10 to 20 thousand dollars! And at this quarry, guests can keep anything they find. I spent a bit of time trying to retrace my steps, but it was a bit like searching for a needle in a haystack. I can't really say it was all that upsetting. I did not go there with any financial reward in mind but rather for the sheer joy and incredulity of being the first person, ever, to look at and hold something that had not seen the light of day for 50 million years. Get your head around that! I may just add Kemmerer to our "return to" list.

We also made our way over to Fossil Butte National Monument, still within the Green River Formation, where there was a small museum. Interesting if for no other reason than to pride ourselves on having found some fish fossils that were comparable to what they had on display there. Not all of them, of course. They also had some pretty large and rare specimens alongside turtles, snakes, stingrays, leaves and palms, reflective of the area's earlier tropical climate. As I said, I wish we could have stayed longer and done some more quarrying. It was, curiously, almost like panning for gold. The next rock was sure to yield up that new species.

An interesting observation. Throughout our journey, we found that almost every little town, regardless of size, strives for some type of recognition. Something that will set it apart from all the other faceless forgettable little towns that dot the landscape. In Kemmerer, aside from its proximity to Fossil Lake, it was J.C. Penney. Hard to believe that in 1902, in this little community with a population of about 1,000 (it is only 2,700 today), the J.C. Penney chain was founded. Kemmerer is primarily a coal mining town and at one point had the largest open pit coal mine in the world. Not exactly something to brag about. But there it was on the corner – J.C. Penney Company Mother Store. And still open for business. Not that I went shopping. John said had it been Neiman

Marcus or Nordstrom, that would have been a different story. Further along, another otherwise forgettable town, Montpelier, had billboards proclaiming that Butch Cassidy had robbed one of their banks in 1891. No explanation as to what the Sundance Kid was doing at the time. We drove on.

Our next stop was Independence Rock, an important landmark and waystation along the Oregon/California/Mormon Trail. When emigrants got to this unique rock formation, they knew they had reached their approximate halfway point, having travelled over 900 miles, with anywhere from 1,100 to 1,300 more to go. They also knew that if they did not reach it by early July, the weather (i.e. snow) could get problematic down the "road." We boondocked in the parking lot/ rest area and after all the daytime traffic was gone, it was easy to imagine what it must have been like for those early pioneers. The geography has not changed, and other than the rest area, the landscape is almost exactly as it was 180 years ago. This large, isolated granite formation, some say resembling a whale, is more than a mile in circumference (700 feet wide, 1,900 feet long) and about as tall as a twelve-story building. We scrambled up to the top of it, dog and all, and in the evening sun, the views in every direction were spectacular. We could even make out the shallow swales demarcating the old route. This had also been a resting area of sorts for the early travellers because the Sweetwater River, a clean uncontaminated stream, flowed nearby. And after having contended with alkaline water during much of the earlier journey it was a huge blessing to both man and beast. One of the main causes of death along the trail was cholera contracted from stagnant contaminated water. So while chillin' for a few days, the emigrants also explored their surroundings and much like ourselves, clambered up and around the monolith. And much like today's graffiti artists, they painted their names with tar or axle grease, or chiselled them into the hard granite to mark their passing. Except for those in sheltered alcoves, or of a deeper nature, most have been worn away by the ravages of time. The earliest signature found was of "M. K. Hugh 1824" (no longer legible) and the oldest one we could make out was from May 29, 1850. Of course the usual idiots have also been out adding their John Henrys but fortunately, the area is now monitored with video surveillance and most people seem to realize its significance. However, it was interesting to note that at one end of the rock, several plaques had been mounted lauding the efforts of those who had worked to have the site declared a nation landmark, and that section was cordoned off with barb-wire fencing. Yet the names of the early emigrants have been left to the elements to slowly fade away. I guess their contributions were not significant enough.

Our next planned destination was Grand Teton National Park, but not without a quick stop in Casper where we had to purchase a new tire for the Jeep. The low-pressure warning light had come on and thinking we might have a slow leak, we stopped in to have it checked. If only. Turned out we had two large nails in the tread, with one of them protruding from the sidewall. Yikes. We suspect we must have picked those up somewhere in or en route to the fossil quarry because most of the other roads had not been too bad. And given how remote those roads had been, we were grateful that although we could have done without this little problem, it came up while we were relatively close to a larger centre. Or at least one with a tire place. We would have been toast as early pioneers.

Heading west again along highway 20/26 we passed by what had once been a state-maintained rest area with scenic overlooks, viewing platforms and picnic shelters, but was now a seemingly abandoned and fenced off parking lot. There were no facilities, the viewing platforms had long since rotted away and the picnic shelters were inaccessible. Hell's Half Acre. There really is such a place! It was in some ways reminiscent of Bryce Canyon only on a much, much smaller scale and without the magnificent colours but we weren't sure why the fencing. Possibly because the entire edge is eroding, and it had become too dangerous? There was no explanation. A few quick pics and we were off.

As we continued the drive along #26 towards Jackson Hole and the Teton Mountain Range (which is really the smallest of several mountain ranges in the area but has the most striking silhouette) the landscape became increasingly picturesque. Green rolling pastureland interspersed with acres of sagebrush and rocky outcroppings, grazing horses and cows, the odd pronghorn sheep, and snow-capped peaks drawing ever nearer. The fact that it was a sunny day helped of course. The closer we got, the rockier the terrain, in places similar to the red rocks of Utah. And then finally, more and more trees, deeper valleys, more dramatic landscape. By 9,000 feet elevation, many of the trees were dead (not sure why – possibly pine beetle?) and there was snow. Lots and lots of snow. Then once over the Continental Divide and dropping back down into the valley, beautiful yellow flowers and the full Teton effect. One of the most photographed and easily recognized mountain ranges in North America, due in no small part to the work of Ansel Adams and other black & white photographers.

What makes this range so spectacularly different from all others is that it rises up so dramatically from a wide flat valley (which is technically called Jackson Hole) and where there are no foothills to block the view. But only on the eastern, Wyoming side. The western side of the range is in Idaho and nowhere near as breathtaking. Most of the peaks and valley are situated within the boundaries of Grand Teton National Park, first established in 1929 with only 96,000 acres set aside. Shortly thereafter, John D. Rockefeller visited the area and was dismayed by what he considered to be rampant haphazard development of the valley floor (despite said valley being 48 miles long and 8 to 15 miles wide). So he quietly bought up over 32,000 acres and in 1950, donated it to

the federal government with the understanding that it would remain protected for all to enjoy. I wish I had that kind of philanthropic capability. Today the park is just over 310,000 acres so needless to say, we only explored a mere fraction of it. By foot, by bike and by car. I can't say which I enjoyed most. The hiking or the biking.

IT IS SO BEAUTIFUL IT HURTS.

One popular activity in the park is watching for wildlife, and with the right timing, bison, elk and pronghorn can be seen grazing in the valley and sightings of grizzlies, black bears and moose are quite regular. We saw lots of moose (one directly in front of our RV about 50 feet from our campsite, on five separate occasions) lots of bison (one walked about 3 feet in front of our car where we had pulled over at the side of the road), numerous pronghorn (one stopped in the centre of the road staring us down), one coyote trotting across the road, some elk in the distance, but sadly no bears of either kind until our very last day and that was just as we were leaving. A lone grizzly about 200 yards away. Barely visible but enough to cause a traffic jam, or as they called them out here, a bear jam. But most of our sightings were simply as we drove to or from our camp-site at Gros Ventre Campground. I did feel a bit sorry for some tourists however, who had gone to considerable expense in order to view this same wildlife. Perhaps they were just gullible. Or maybe really keen. Several times we saw Jeeps kitted out like African safari vehicles complete with canvass roof and rolled-up sides, "Wildlife Viewing Safari" painted on the hood, looking as if they were heading off into the wilds of the Serengeti, but in reality, slowly cruising along the same asphalt where we were bicycling. Someone should have told these folks their faux-safari vehicles were not permitted to leave the pavement, and the bison and pronghorns were easily visible along highway 191, the main north-south artery in the park anyway. A fool and his money are soon parted.

But then we weren't impervious from ridiculous expenditures either. Our campground was quite expensive considering what was offered by way of amenities, yet we paid it. The location itself was quite nice along the Gros Ventre River, somewhat removed from the hustle and bustle of the park's inner campgrounds, and there was lots of space between sites, but they charged $50 per night just for electric hook-up! No water or sewer. And no hot running water in the washrooms either, never mind showers. So we were fully dependent on the RV tanks and used our water sparingly. That is generally no biggie when camped for a few days, but when staying put for more than a week, it means that at some point, sooner or later, we were packing up and heading off to dump the gray and black tanks and take on fresh water. At this point in the journey, I was tired of all that. I wanted full hook-ups. John wanted them even more than me. But we considered ourselves lucky. At least with the coach we did have hot running water. I have no idea how the people in tents managed. The maximum stay at this campground was 14 days, but who is going to go 14 days without a hot shower? And to make things completely ridiculous, the inner park reservable full hook-up RV campgrounds charged $83.00! In a national park! Crazy! I don't think that is quite what the founding fathers of the national park system envisioned back in the day, but the demand is such today that they can get away with it.

A FOOL WITH A DEATH WISH, GIVING TOURISTS A BAD NAME.

We spent almost two weeks in Grand Teton N.P. We hiked. We biked. We moseyed. We meandered. And from every new vantage point the view of the Tetons seemed more spectacular than the one before, whether it was from across the valley floor, in the centre of the valley or at the foot of the mountains. Truly magnificent. The only challenging thing was that the valley floor sits 6,237 feet above sea level, so I found myself out of breath quite often. Age had nothing to do with it this time. The weather upon our arrival was very warm and sunny but towards the end of our stay, had turned cold and cloudy with one night dropping to below freezing. Not fair! I had hoped to kayak in Jackson Lake on our last weekend but by the time we got our act together it was simply too windy and miserable. Foiled again.

Our good friends from Atlanta have a place in Teton Village at the foot of Jackson Hole ski resort, just outside the park boundary, and as luck would have it, were in town with their family for one of those weeks. This gave us ample opportunity to catch up, create some new memories and rekindle some old ones. We all took in the local rodeo in Jackson one evening and although it was somewhat small-town with third-tier riders (hardly anyone could stay in the saddle), it was fun just the same. Although I'm still very conflicted about the whole rodeo concept. These animals run and buck because they are scared, stressed or uncomfortable. For us to make that the foundation for a "sport" just isn't right. But it is certainly a way of life out there. We saw lots of cowboy hats and lots of cowboy boots that evening. Another day (cold and cloudy – again) we all checked out historic Jackson Lodge at the north end of the park and walking into the beautiful lobby with its cozy fireside chairs, and high floor to ceiling windows framing the mountains across Jackson Lake, I was struck by how much I still wanted to savour these magnificent national parks. But only from the comfort of a luxury lodge. I was done with "roughing it." Even if the Tiffin motto is "Roughing it Smoothly."

The town of Jackson, at the southern end of the park boundary, was quite nice with numerous galleries and shops that were very heavy on the Western theme – lots of wildlife, and "Cowboys & Indians" motifs, and many cater specifically to the well-heeled tourist set, with price tags to match. One particular gallery, Images of Nature (which has locations across the United States), showcased the work of Tom Mangelsen, a world-renowned wildlife photographer and environmentalist, and his photographs truly are amazing. He was the first to capture that iconic shot of the spawning salmon flying directly into the jaws of a waiting Grizzly at Brooks Falls in Alaska. And that was definitely in the days before photoshop. However, I think spending $15,000 on a photograph is a bit much, regardless of its limited-edition status or National Geographic endorsement. Even if I had that kind of spare change. And on the topic of famous, what do Herb Alpert (of Herb Alpert & the Tijuana Brass) and the National Museum of Wildlife Art just outside of Jackson have in common? Not much if you ask me, but I'm not the curator. The museum houses a wonderful collection of paintings and sculptures depicting wildlife as it has been perceived by artists through the centuries (including Robert Bateman's famous "Bison") and was a joy to visit. Many of the sculptures outside were larger than life, some very realistic and some more avant-garde, but ol' Herb may have taken modern to a level that I obviously fail to appreciate. He designed twelve abstract bronze sculptures, collectively entitled Spirit Totems, which were prominently displayed on the walkway from the parking lot. But I couldn't see how they related to anything, much less wildlife. John said, "I don't know much about art, but I know what

I like. And I don't like that." Personally, I think Herb should have stuck to his trumpet.

And then there was the curious matter of food. While we don't eat out a lot, we do know a little bit about the culinary world. For example, Eggs Benedict, while having a few modern twists, has as its main ingredients poached eggs and Hollandaise Sauce. I hadn't had eggs benny for quite some time so when we went out for breakfast on Father's Day, I was quite looking forward to savouring this low-cal treat. The eggs arrived fried. Cooked medium, as requested, but fried. I asked the waitress if perhaps there had been some mistake? "No. That's how we serve 'em." Hmmm. And dinner? I know that if Steak et Frites is on the menu, John will order it. At two separate restaurants, he placed his order and was asked if he wanted mashed potatoes or fries. In fact, at the first restaurant, they actually brought him mashed. No fries. What part of "frites" don't they understand? Very curious. And another thing. Since we prepared most of our own meals, we went to the grocery store a fair bit. And since leaving British Columbia (where people seem to work quite diligently at reduce, reuse, recycle) we received more plastic bags in one month than we did in the entire five months we were in Tofino. Check-out clerks dispensed them as if they got a prize at the end of each week for the most distributed. It was really very dispiriting. Save the whales!

Our time in GTNP passed in a flash and we didn't even come close to hiking all the trails we wanted, never mind getting out on the water or exploring further afield. Perhaps that is because we had so much fun with our friends. Or perhaps it is because we subconsciously wanted to leave something for a return visit. Or perhaps it is a combination of the two. We plan to go back.

No trip through North America would be complete without a stop in that incredible place that is Yellowstone National Park, situated primarily in Wyoming but with a small stretch in Montana at the north west, and an even smaller stretch in Idaho at the southwest. Of course word has been out for a long time about the amazing sights to be seen there, so everybody and his brother has included it in their vacation itinerary. Needless to say, it was pretty crowded. Although it is still possible to find a bit of solitude if you got far enough away from the more touristy, developed areas. We were forced to check into a KOA in West Yellowstone, about 12 miles outside the park's western boundary because we had not made any reservations a year in advance for spots inside the park, and their only full RV campground was closed for renovations anyway. The KOA wasn't the most scenic of spots compared to what can be found inside the park, but we had full hook-ups so John was doing his full hook-up happy dance. Our plan had been to stop in at the Old Faithful area for a few hours on our first day (and leave Porter in the yacht while we walked the basin) since we were driving right past it en route to the KOA, but that did not work out as hoped. Despite two huge parking lots, there is no provision whatsoever made for coaches or even trailers. Cars were parked haphazardly, a few early birds had managed to snag some double spaces but all in all, it was a mess. After circling a few times, we gave up. We've never seen such disorganized parking.

For a national park, especially one touted as America's first national park (and the first national park in the world) the roads were in surprisingly bad shape. A bit of a national embarrassment if you ask me, considering how many international tourists come to view its geothermal features. And make no mistake. A car is a definite must if there is any hope of seeing the sights. The park is huge (2.2 million acres – about the size of Rhode Island), the points of interest far apart, and there are no safe cycling routes even if you could cover the distance on your bike. Theoretically, it would be possible peddle along the roadway but there really aren't any shoulders to speak of and car accidents are quite common, with drivers forgetting to keep their eyes on the road and instead, looking at wildlife in the clearing. We saw two horrific accidents (one a head-on) which caused incredibly long back-ups and there were no alternate routes to take when the road was shut down. I'm not sure why people get so excited about seeing animals in the wild (I include myself in this grouping), throwing caution to the wind, parking only half off the roadway and walking well within the recommended safe distance (75 feet for bison and 300 feet for bears). All for a photograph? (I should talk.) The animals don't look any different from the specimens that can be viewed at the zoo. And it's not like we work for National Geographic and need to get the money shot. Perhaps because they are totally wild, fending for themselves and at the same time, capable of inflicting serious harm. No fences between you and them out there. But I doubt that fascination will ever change. We sat in a 2-mile long line for about 40 minutes because one Yogi happened to be wandering in the meadow 200 feet off.

So about the animals... Bison were everywhere. If it was exciting to see them in Grand Teton, that was nothing compared to the herds that roam at will throughout Yellowstone. It's a bit unfair, but comparing the bison of Grand Teton to those of Yellowstone is like comparing your local Mini-Putt to The Masters in Augusta. Not that there is anything wrong with Mini-Putt. They were in the distant valleys. They were in the near valleys. In the parking lots. On the road, beside the road, off the road. Along the trail. Everywhere! I didn't bother counting. They went wherever they wanted, whenever they wanted. And no-one was going to stop them. It was only after one medium sized herd, complete with calves decided to wander back and forth across the road a couple of times, causing a considerable traffic backup, that a park ranger showed up and cleared them off with a few soft buzzes of her siren. Interestingly, the Yellowstone herds are the largest ones on U.S. public land that have not been hybridized through interbreeding with cattle. Who knew? The males tend to be solitary roamers or hang out with just a few buddies while the calves, yearlings and females all stick together in herds. The calves were so cute! A light reddish-brown colour, referred to as "red dogs" and only a little bit taller than Porter. Several times throughout our stay, people commented that Porter looked like a bison calf. I don't know what bison calves they had been looking at because there really was no resemblance. The Lamar Valley (in the northeast of the park) was the best place to see them, along with other wildlife. We saw numerous moose, including a cow leading her two calves across a clearing and into some trees (moose will often birth twins), lots of elk (we watched three of them fording a river), a few pronghorn, several

black bears but sadly, no grizzlies. Then again, we have no right to complain. Nothing will ever top our experience in Alaska's Lake Clark. One afternoon while we were out in the Lamar Valley, there was a sudden and heavy thunder shower, and after the clouds moved on, the sweet aroma of sagebrush perfumed the air. It was heavenly. We were truly blessed.

PORTER WASN'T GOING TO TAKE ANY CHANCES.

More often than not, when the name Yellowstone comes up, people think of hydrothermals. And there were a lot of them. Ten thousand hot springs, geysers, fumaroles, mudpots and travertine terraces. The largest concentration in the world. The park actually has a lot of "in the world" claims to fame. So how did this come to be? A large part of Yellowstone lies atop a supervolcano. A supervolcano that created it, fuels its present-day wonders and will continue to shape its future. In the very distant past, the area experienced three huge volcanic eruptions, and the last one, 630,000 years ago, collapsed inward forming a 30 by 45-mile caldera. The heat that generated that eruption still feeds all the geothermal activity that goes on in the park today. In numerous places the earth's crust is so thin that caution signs were posted warning tourists to stay on the boardwalks lest they break through and fall into some boiling pit to be poached alive. It happens to the odd wandering bison from time to time although there were also lots of buffalo chips lying about, quite close to some of the hot springs, so obviously there are places that can hold a fair bit of weight. However, walking along the boardwalks it was a bit unnerving to hear all the boiling and hissing going on practically beneath my feet. And of course, stories of tourists who just can't follow the rules and have their vacations cut short in the most unpleasant of ways.

The most popular geyser is Old Faithful, and I am still wondering why. It is not the highest, certainly not the prettiest, and definitely not the most unique. The area surrounding it is very developed with the charming (and historic) Old Faithful Inn and somewhat dreary Old Faithful Lodge within rather close proximity. The eruptions can actually be viewed from the Lodge's windows. There are massive parking lots, a huge Visitor Centre, a large grocery store and well stocked gift shop. And hundreds and hundreds of people. I had to keep reminding myself I was in a national park and not an amusement park. That was challenging given the numbers of small children whining for ice cream and displaying other fits of pique. But Old Faithful's eruptions are fairly predictable (about every 90 minutes) so it draws huge crowds. In reality, the whole thing is more hype than substance. Yet you want to see it because who goes to Yellowstone and doesn't see Old faithful? So we joined the teeming throngs, waited dutifully on the viewing platform for the show to begin and after the 3-minute spectacle was over, came away wondering what all the fuss was about. All these people just sitting there awaiting to see what is in effect a water fountain. And some of them were not the brightest of folks either. Just before the eruption, I couldn't help but overhear the conversation going on between a couple in their 70s. This is not a direct quote, but the conversation went something like this. "I wonder what kind of remote mechanism they use to get this thing to go off on time. Is there a switch or something?" That was Mr. The Mrs. then tried to explain that it had to do with water and pressure, but he didn't seem convinced. I kid you not. And this was a serious conversation. I thoroughly admit that I am no rocket scientist (and never will be) but come on.

Leaving Old Faithful, we then took turns walking along the boardwalks of the Upper Geyser Basin. Porter + National Park = Same Old Story. Despite not being able to share the experience together in real time, I did find many of the geysers and pools fascinating. It was a 3-mile loop so over that distance the crowds thinned out considerably. My favourites were the Grotto Geyser and the Morning Glory pool. Geologists speculate that the Grotto is hundreds or even thousands of years old and actually emerged amongst a stand of dead or dying trees. Over the years, the eruptions deposited layers and layers of silica on top of the stumps and branches, resulting in its odd shape. And when it erupts, it can spurt anywhere from 1 hour to 24 hours! Morning Glory is a deep, beautiful, serene hot spring in a lovely shade of almost robin's egg blue although sadly, the colour is not as brilliant as it used to be. This because stupid people throw coins, rocks and other garbage into it, clogging its vent and thus lowering the water temperature. Bacteria in shades of brown, orange and yellow prefer the cooler water and are gradually turning the vivid blue to a murky green. Almost like a swimming pool where you forgot to add enough chlorine before you went away for the weekend. And every year park staff use a huge suction tube to try to vacuum out the detritus. My lack of faith in humanity continues to be reinforced.

But the most impressive of all the hydrothermals was Grand Prismatic, the largest of Yellowstone's hot springs at about 200 feet across. Its water temperature is around 160F (70C) so there is usually steam rising from the surface and that often obscures the view of the vibrant colours. But when the breeze blows the steam aside, it is spectacular. We first hiked a short distance to an overlook to get a bird's eye view (and jostled for elbow room with everyone else on the platform) but in my opinion, its beauty was best appreciated from the boardwalk, right at the water's edge. The colours were so intense I can only describe it as being up close to a rainbow! The rich azure blue at the centre is a result of sunlight hitting fine particles that are suspended in the water. The green, yellow, orange and brown in the rings around the edge are from thermophiles – heat loving micro-organisms that can survive in the high-heat environment. And occasionally, a small hint of purple at the very, very core. It was glorious. Of course the usual crowds were there too so I harnessed my inner Zen as best I could, gritted my teeth and restrained myself from pushing anyone onto the thin hot surface crust. After all, I was just like them, trying to view this beautiful work of nature. Actually, no. I was not like them. I waited patiently to get a clear shot instead of pushing my way to the front. While John's enthusiasm for these waterworks waned rather quickly, for me, they continued to hold a certain fascination: the colours they projected, the sounds they emitted, the heat they radiated, the water and steam they propelled.

And the difference between all these water-based features? Hot springs are pools of hot water where the temperature is anywhere from to tepid to boiling. Their "plumbing" can be narrow or wide and the water is in constant circulation, with the cooler surface water sinking and the hotter deeper water rising. They are the most common hydrothermal feature in the park. Geysers are really hot springs where the plumbing narrows near the surface and prevents constant water circulation, forcing the hot water to stay deep below ground where it continues to heat, often reaching a point where it is twice as hot as the surface boiling point. Eventually steam forms, and near the top of the constricted area, forces out the water above, causing the geyser to erupt. That was getting too technical for me. Fumaroles, also known as steam vents, are simply hot springs that do not have enough water to erupt. Because there is so little water, it quickly boils away leaving only steam or gases to escape. They are often the noisy ones and are the hottest of all the features. And mud pots occur when gases interact with surface water and organic matter, creating acid. This acid breaks down the mineral filled rocks, turning them into clay which given the heat becomes very viscous. Simply put, they are pools of scalding, bubbling mud that lie on top of steam vents. So there you have it. The technical explanation. Although I prefer painter Ann Coe's more romantic description. They are, "the place where the centre of the earth finds an exit and gives us a glimpse of its soul." It certainly makes our little corner of the world in southern Ontario seem so tame.

We also checked out the Norris Geyser Basin, about 25 miles north of the Old Faithful area, which contains rare acidic geysers and is located in a very active earthquake area. Sadly, we did not feel the earth move. But we did spend a bit of time hanging out by Steamboat Geyser, the tallest active geyser in the world. When it blows, it hits heights of over 300 feet and goes for anywhere from 3 to 40 minutes. However, unlike Old Faithful, its eruptions are completely unpredictable. Days, months, even years have passed between major eruptions. It had actually erupted two days prior to our visit, expelling a fist sized rock from its bowels that flew about 75 feet to smash the warning sign on the visitor's platform. Thankfully no-one was hurt. All I saw were some occasional spurts of steam. I might have lingered a bit longer except I couldn't stand listening to one windbag who had set up his lounge chair, sun umbrella and various photography accoutrements right on the viewing platform and was holding court, spouting off to anyone who would listen his theories on when it would go next, and how the parks people should pay more attention to his sage advice. Perhaps he is still there, sitting, waiting, and by now, talking to himself.

YNP is basically in the shape of a square and if divided into four equal quadrants, I would say the top right is the most scenic with the most animal sightings, and the bottom left has the most hydrothermal activity. But overall, the National Park Service needs to step up its game. Yellowstone is tired. Its signs were old, its trails poorly marked, its roads in bad shape, and they don't seem to be able to handle the huge numbers of visitors who make their pilgrimage to this national park mecca. There are not enough picnic areas and definitely not enough campgrounds. But it seems they are sinking money into a new hotel/lodge by Canyon Village near the Lower Falls, complete with yet another gift shop instead. So much for minimizing the human footprint. They should also consider implementing a shuttle bus service between all the major attractions to help ease traffic congestion and if not, build more parking lots to accommodate the steady never-ending stream of cars, vans and motor homes that circle round and round looking for a place to pull over. Despite its massive size, Yellowstone is a victim of its own popularity and we are loving it to death.

39.

THE END OF THE ROAD

THE LAST FULL BLOG POST IN THE JOURNEY WAS A DIFFICULT DIS-
PATCH TO WRITE. Not because there weren't interesting things to describe, but
because it was the last report from the road. After that installment it would all be over
except for the crying. I must admit that once we decided it was time to return home
and actually proposed a target date out loud, our enthusiasm for continued exploring
did somewhat wane. Whereas in the first or second year, if there was a biking, hiking or
kayaking opportunity, we couldn't take it fast enough. During the last full month? Not
so much. In fact, hardly at all. Although by the time we had reached our last national
park, I was starting to wonder if perhaps we had been a bit hasty. Couldn't we stay out
a little bit longer? Things were ending too fast. Did I want to be home? Yes! Did I want
the journey to be over? No! Such inconsistency. So to begin...

We started in Montana and our first impression was very positive. It is a beautiful state. More so on the western side. Lots of ranches with lots of horses and cows.
Huge rolling green hills dotted with Ponderosa Pines, expansive valleys, meandering
rivers, the occasional deep gorge and wide, wide open spaces. They don't call it Big Sky
Country for nothing. I'm sure more people would make it their fulltime home if not for
the bone-chillingly cold winters. Yet those who do live there don't seem to mind. "If you
are lucky enough to live in Montana, you are lucky enough" the saying goes.

Our first outing was to try our luck at sapphire mining, something that I didn't
even know was a thing. Turns out it is a very popular tourist activity. There are two
ways to mine gem-quality sapphires in Montana, pretty much the only place in the U.S.
where they can be found. The first, for the real professionals, is hard rock mining, using
drills and heavy machinery. We would have never been allowed near anything like that,
even if we had wanted to go. The more common is alluvial. Gravel along riverbeds and

other areas of deposit is scooped up with front-end loaders, sifted, washed and then combed through. For tourist purposes, the gravel is transported to specific areas where "miners" like us place it in smaller 12 by 12 inch sieves, "wash" it in a water trough to rinse away the mud and sand, invert the "clean" gravel onto a table and then pick out any small rough gems using fine pointed tweezers. Since sapphires are heavier than their surrounding stones and grit, they will generally be sitting at the top if the "washing" is done correctly. The entire process was very addicting. Again, just like panning for gold. The next wash was sure to yield up that 5-carat. A bit about sapphires. True sapphires are pure gem-quality aluminum oxide crystals that come in a variety of colours. Mostly green and blue shades, but some yellowish, pink and mauve. No red. If they are red, they are considered rubies. There are four main areas in Montana where significant sapphire deposits have been found and we were mining the Rock Creek deposit near Philipsburg, a lovely little town with a very charming main street and several historic buildings, one home to a very well stocked candy shop.

We drove out to the Gem Sapphire Mine, located along a gorgeous stretch of roadway that typified the wide open rolling Montana countryside, joined about 30 like-minded people (some local rock-hounds and others tourists just like us), purchased two 5-gallon buckets (at $27/bucket) and set to work. Well wouldn't you know it, we collected a small handful of stones. A very small handful. Of very small stones. So we purchased another bucket. Got a few more. I wanted to buy yet another one but by this time, 6 hours had passed (in a flash, I might add) and it was getting close to quittin' time. Darn! We took the stones into the small office/gift shop to be sorted and appraised, and this was where the increased cost came in. The majority in our collection were either too flawed or too small to do much with. The best suggestion was to place them in a jar with white vinegar for about two weeks, shaking it frequently. The vinegar would remove any hard water stains and then the stones could be rough set. Sounded good to me. But about 10 of our beauties were suitable for heat treating (a common practice to enhance colour) and faceting. This particular company heats the stones on site and then ships them to Sri Lanka to be cut. The more we left for treating, the lower the cost per stone. Oy vey. Such a deal. So we selected three of our more promising ones (having been advised that close to 75% of the stone will be lost in the faceting process) and we would see the finished product in six to nine months! I wanted to return and do some more mining the following morning, but this particular site was closed for the next three days. Fortunately, the company had a facility right in Philipsburg that was open 7 days a week. Perfect. We tried a bucket there too. More stones. But we were curious. Gem Sapphire wasn't the only game in town. We also checked out the Sapphire Gallery, a somewhat more "genteel" setting where the gravel is purchased in a heavy plastic bag and already contains a tiny faceted sapphire – about .14 of a carat. An enticement if you will. As if I needed any more enticing. And .14 of a carat is so small, the head of a pin almost looks larger. At this place, the washing was done by an employee, so John didn't have to splash muddy water on himself and within 30 minutes we were finished, having found several more rough nuggets. These folks also appraised and sorted our find, and we left three stones for treating and faceting with them as well. However, they keep the work in-house, so we received their finished product sooner. (In comparison, the final products from both companies were great and I'm still working on a design setting for my beauties.) We could have also purchased bags of gravel to take home and "mine" at our leisure, and quite a few people did this, but after checking with Matejs regarding the rules on importing soil products to Canada, that was a no-go for us. I'll have to be content with our little meager treasure trove. But despite the fact that these were genuine gemstones, and we had a lot of fun finding them, I have no illusions that the "virgin gravel" we were playing with hadn't already been put through some larger sifter or some other such screening device, that would have removed everything of a larger carat quality. There is just no way any mine owner would risk losing the big stones to the likes of posers like us. Still, if I'm ever in Montana again, I know where I'm heading.

ALONG GOING-TO-THE-SUN ROAD.

Our next stop was Glacier National Park, and if I thought Yellowstone was crowded, this place took it to a whole new level. It is not a huge park, and actually abuts Waterton National Park in Alberta, together forming the Waterton-Glacier International Peace Park, created in 1932. Of course it is all wilderness so no-one is going to do any illegal border hopping without first fording raging rivers, climbing mountain peaks and eluding roaming bears (black and grizzly), but it's a nice neighbourly concept just the same. Most of the campgrounds are along the western boundary and did not accommodate large motorhomes (even if we had bothered to make the absolutely necessary reservations) so we stayed in a privately-run RV park near the southern edge, about a 30-mile drive from the west gate. That was a bit of a pain, but we managed. And for our troubles, got to see several mountain goats (with their little kids) foraging just off the roadway. So sweet. And so sure footed! We didn't seriously plan on doing any major hiking simply because of the no-dogs rule and prior to getting there, I was mildly put out by that. But once I saw the parking chaos at the trailheads and the countless clueless wanderers setting out with their overloaded packs and not-yet-broken-in boots, I didn't feel too bad. I would have hated to share the trail with them. I think fall would be the perfect time to return. We did, however, drive along the Going-to-the-Sun Road. Arguably one of the most scenic, if not the most scenic road we have ever driven. It is a 50-mile stretch that transects the park east-west, and we drove it in both directions. Completed in 1933 it only opens up in late June given the deep winter snows, and then closes again usually sometime in October. Naturally, given the brief weather dependent window of opportunity, everyone wants to enjoy the drive, so it was a steady stream of cars and motorcycles (no motorhomes, trailers or anything over 21 feet allowed) travelling in both directions. In places it was like sitting in rush hour traffic but generally, we moved along at about 25 mph. And I didn't want to go any faster anyway. The winding road was so narrow there often wasn't much space between the cliff face, the oncoming traffic and the straight plunge into the deep glacier formed valley below. But the views were jaw dropping with numerous scenic pullouts along the way. In one place we got out of the car and walked into a meadow full of Bear Grass, Indian Paint Brushes and other mountain wild flowers, and if not for the numerous people (including one bride and groom posing for pictures – that is a long way to drive for the perfect backdrop!) I would have set up the chairs and just stayed there. Low clouds rolled in and out, so visibility was not always the best, but I'm not complaining. It was lovely. I can only imagine what the solitary hikes into the backcountry must be like. Add another destination to the return-to list. Huckleberries were also a popular thing (similar to blueberries only smaller) so there was a lot of huckleberry pie to eat, and it was a good thing we moved on while my pants still fit. There hadn't been much in the way of regular fitness during the preceding few months.

THREE BILLY GOATS GRUFF.

As soon as we left the eastern boundary of the park, the landscape changed as dramatically as if someone had drawn the proverbial line in the sand. All of a sudden it was pretty much flat prairie. And we were on the Blackfeet Indian Reservation. We stopped in the small town of Browning to check out the Museum of the Plains Indian and although not large, it had excellent exhibits describing and displaying life of the Plains Indians. Clothing and tools, both decorative and functional with intricate bead work. Just exquisite. We chatted with the man at the admissions desk (about our age) who advised he was a member of the Blackfeet tribe (one of the ten largest tribes in America) and married to a Navajo. He related the same discouraging story we had heard elsewhere throughout North America. Given this was a Saturday, he would not normally have been in to work, but the scheduled guy had just not bothered to show up. As was typical. He advised his own father had moved their family off the reservation in an effort to instill a work ethic in the children and break the cycle of dependence that is so prevalent amongst so many Indian people. He worked in Silicon Valley most of his life and had now returned to his roots. But nothing had changed. As he put it, he knows that he can provide all the training necessary for the museum jobs but after receiving their first paycheck, half of his employees will not show up the next day. He has tried to explain to the young people that these jobs are not there for their convenience but are a necessity, that they need to be responsible, but it is a psychological barrier he has not been able to breach. Would doing away with the entire reservation system help the problem? We parted, not having reached any answer. Outside, a stereotypical intoxicated Indian tried to hit us up for money. And so it goes.

Our next stop was another Indian story with another less than happy ending. Bear Paw Battlefield, site of the last battle of the 4-month long Nez Perce War of 1877. I'm not sure why I am drawn to these places, but I suspect it has something to do with a book I read as part of my university studies in minority group relations. Yes, that was a long time ago, but it had a definite and lasting impact on me. And all these years later, I am glad I can go to some of the locations and actually see some of what I had only read about. *Bury My Heart at Wounded Knee* by Dee Brown. History written not from the perspective of the victors, but from that of the vanquished.

In a nutshell, the Nez Perce were comprised of several tribes that lived in the Pacific Northwest. By 1877 the usual lack of agreement about accepting reservation status on the part of the tribes (some for, some against), and broken treaties on the part of the government (this is your land, no, just kidding, it isn't), had led to a situation whereby the government ordered all "non-treaty" Indians (those who had refused reservation life) to be forcibly removed to Idaho. Armed conflict ensued and the Nez Perce fled north hoping their Crow neighbours would help them. The Crow refused. So much for a united front. They then continued towards Canada, hoping to enlist the aid of Sitting Bull of the Lakota Sioux. (Sitting Bull had himself just fled to Canada a year earlier in order to avoid the repercussions that were sure to come following his involvement at the Battle of the Little Bighorn aka Custer's Last Stand.) Keep in mind that this Nez Perce migration was a mass transposing of not just warriors but of women, children, the elderly and the ill. The U.S. army pursued them for over 1,200 miles (2,000 kilometers), with battles and skirmishes along the way. By the time the Nez Perce reached the Bear Paw Mountains (less than 40 miles/65 kilometers from the safety of Canada's border) the army had caught up and the final stage was set. Following a five-day battle, a large majority of Nez Perce survivors under the leadership of Chief Joseph surrendered (a smaller contingent under Chief White Bird managed to escape to Canada) and it was here that Chief Joseph is said to have uttered the famous words, "*Hear me, my chiefs! I am tired. My heart is sick and sad. From where the sun now stands I will fight no more forever.*" Of course this was said through a translator and recorded by a U.S. aid-de-campe who also fancied himself a bit of an author and poet, so there is considerable dispute over whether Chief Joseph really said that. But regardless, it was pretty much the end of Nez Perce independence and ultimately resulted in the Nez Perce nation being scattered throughout the United States and Canada. While all that is left of the battlefield are undulating fields of grass, there are also markers indicating where certain tepees had been set up when the army attacked, and where certain Nez Perce Chiefs and U.S. soldiers had fallen during the battle. It was quiet. It was sad. And as the available pamphlet read, "This is a place of mourning not just for memorializing the past, but as a place for letting go of what might have been."

Since we were on the war path (no pun intended – ok maybe a little bit) we also made our way to the battlefield that most Americans and many Canadians have heard of – the site of Custer's Last Stand. Its official name used to be Custer Battlefield National Monument but in 1991 was renamed Little Bighorn Battlefield National Monument, to acknowledge the Indian perspective in the conflict. It truly was, as the literature describes, "a clash of cultures." The Monument commemorates one of the last armed efforts made by the Northern Plains Indians to preserve their independent nomadic way of life, and simultaneously, the worst rout the United States Army suffered in their efforts to impose reservation life. I wasn't sure what to expect but given all the renown attached to the name of "Custer", I somehow thought the battleground would have been physically more remarkable. A high hill with a steep incline, perhaps. A gully, possibly. Maybe even a ravine or two. No, it was just another grassy rolling hillside. Nothing remarkable about it at all. And conceivably that is what contributed to my sense of emotional ennui. It was all so average-countryside looking. Not to bog down in the minutia of military maneuvers, but basically, the U.S. army, comprised of 3 separate expeditions (Custer 's 7th Cavalry being only a part of one of them) took on between 1,500 and 2,000 Lakota, Cheyenne and Arapaho warriors under the leadership of Sitting Bull, Crazy Horse and other Chiefs. The army was outnumbered from the start, setting into motion the eventual slaughter of Custer and his men. There were casualties from other companies as well, bringing the U.S. losses to 263, and it is estimated the Indians lost no more than 100. All over the battleground, markers have been placed to indicate where both soldiers and Indians fell – white and red respectively. The highest concentration of white markers (as well as a tall monument inscribed with the dead soldier's names) are found on the rise where the "final stand" took place. It was both very moving and disturbing. Especially after having read that over 42% of the men who served under Custer were foreign-born immigrants, looking to learn about their new country, learn English and experience a bit of excitement. While the mandatory age for enlistment in the army was 21, many lied about their age. The youngest to die on that hill was only 17 years old. Not that the Indians were much older. Their average age was approximately 22. Such a cruel waste of life. In 2003, after much political negotiating, an Indian Memorial was unveiled just west of the army monument, and in 2013, its circular granite walls were engraved with the names of the Indians who had died, together with commemorative words from the various tribes that participated in the battle. Some were a little stark ("We had killed soldiers who came to kill us."), others more conciliatory ("I have been in many hard fights, but I never saw such brave men."), but the overall theme of the memorial is "Peace Through Unity", acknowledging the need for cooperation not just between the various Indian tribes, but between the tribal and federal governments as well. I suspect this is a much-needed outlook considering two of the tribes (Crow and Arikara) were actually sided with the U.S. army during the conflict. While I found it to be a beautiful memorial and hope things continue to move forward in the right direction, there is still a ways to go. It was interesting to note that U.S. Park Rangers were delivering presentations about the battle more from a Custer perspective, while Indian guides had their own tours going, presumably delivering a differently weighted version of events. And so it goes.

Leaving the war trail behind, we continued along I-90 towards Devils Tower National Monument, a place my parents had taken us three girls as children, and a place where in turn, John and I had taken our own kids. The drive was again beautiful, but most striking was the profusion of yellow flowers that covered the rolling hills in an almost bright lime green colour. I've never seen anything like it. A bit of research revealed it was a plant called "sweet yellow clover", and its fragrant aroma permeated the air. Just stepping outside of the coach and inhaling was like burying your face in a bouquet of freshly picked white or purple clover back home. The reason for the blanket coverage was that the Montana/Wyoming/South Dakota areas had received an unusual amount of rainfall that season. As one park ranger explained, by late June/early July most everything is a dried-out brown, but this was a banner year for precipitation. Well lucky for us, I thought. Until we hit a thunderstorm, but more on that later. We were heading for The Tower.

D-E-C-C-G OR RE-ME-DO-DO-SO.

Devils Tower is America's first national monument and is located in the northeast corner of Wyoming. Movie fans would recognize it from the 1977 Steven Spielberg film *Close Encounters of the Third Kind*. It is a geological anomaly and geologists are still not in full agreement on how it was formed. I won't try to summarize their theories because I really didn't care to learn. It's enough to say it is a massive 867-foot tall column of rare igneous rock that was formed through some kind of volcanic activity, sometime... they didn't say when. The top is slightly rounded and just over an acre in size. Huge hexagonal columns appear as lines or grooves rising from bottom to top and are the result of "columnar jointing" that occurred during the formation, and are not, as may appear, the result of weathering (although large sections have fallen off, as evidenced by the rock piles near the bottom, but not in anyone's memory). Yawn. I prefer the Indian version. The columns are the result of a bear's claws as he tried to scramble up to the top in pursuit of some young girls. But geological or ursine, between four and five thousand climbers use them to test their skills each year, taking anywhere from 18 minutes to 16 hours to reach the summit. The average time is 5 hours. We were walking the 2-kilometer trail around the base of the tower when we saw two such brave souls. I'd still like to try this sport but suspect I should begin with something a bit more modest. The surrounding area is very picturesque and peaceful with wide valleys, pine trees and red cliffs all around, and I almost wished we had planned to stay longer than one day. But we had made reservations at Badlands National Park in South Dakota, and wanted to stop in at Deadwood, Mt. Rushmore and the Crazy Horse Memorial along the way. Ambitious as always.

Pulling away from the Tower, we made a quick stop in the town of Sundance, another one of those small forgettable towns that try to attract a few tourists during the summer season. Their claim to fame? Harry Longbaugh, aka The Sundance Kid (Butch Cassidy's sidekick), spent 18 months in their jail after being convicted of stealing a horse, gun and saddle. Serious time if you consider what today's bandits get for considerably more serious offences. It was during his time in Sundance that Longbaugh adopted his Sundance Kid moniker. There was a statue of him beside the courthouse so naturally we had to stop for a quick pic. Walking back towards the yacht, we passed two women and a man (about our age), chatting on the sidewalk, the man sporting a stars 'n stripes cowboy hat, and wearing a white sleeveless T-shirt and blue jeans with suspenders. Nothing to write home about. Except for the open-carry semi-automatic pistol holstered on his right hip. Only in America.

And on the topic of guns and shoot-outs, our next destination was Deadwood, the town made famous in the HBO Series by the same name. Another wild west frontier town, it sprang up in the Black Hills after gold was discovered there in 1876. Settlers flooded in, breaking yet another Government/Indian Treaty. In its day, this town, full of the usual gambling halls, saloons and brothels, had the dubious of honour of being the place where James Butler Hickock aka Wild Bill was murdered – shot in the back during a poker game. He was buried in Mt. Moriah Cemetery, so we decided to stop in and pay a visit. Buried next to him was Martha Jane Canary aka Calamity Jane (although she died 27 years later.) There is considerable speculation as to the relationship between these two with most theories leaning towards that of unrequited love. Hers for him. Her supposed last words were, "Bury me next to Wild Bill." So they did. He may not have agreed, but what could he do? Despite being promoted as a tourist attraction, the cemetery is still consecrated ground with many burials not all that old, and is divided as per the day, into Jewish, Chinese, Masonic, Civil War Vet etc. sections. And this is where I got ticked off.

Upon entry (and after paying a $2 entry fee), visitors are advised that despite some of the notorious wild west personalities buried there, it is still first and foremost a cemetery and should be afforded the respect any final resting place deserves. Fair enough. Yet while standing by the Hickock/Calamity graves, a local tour bus pulled up and the commentary from the guide to his charges can only be described as appalling – cracking tasteless jokes, making lewd innuendos and behaving in a manner better suited for a haunted house at an amusement park. At least the majority of his passengers had the grace to look rather embarrassed. I hope they complained because I certainly did. At the end of our walk, I marched right back to the front gate and advised the sexton (who thankfully happened to be standing there) what I had overheard. I'm not one to make formal complaints and I don't offend easily, but I can only imagine what someone visiting their loved ones might feel when overhearing that inexcusable drivel. With a microphone, no less. But I'm off on a tangent… back to the burials.

Seth Bullock, the town's first sheriff is buried about ¼ kilometer up a steep hill away from all the other graves, ostensibly at his request, so that he would be able to "see" the friendship tower he had built on Mt. Roosevelt (several miles away) for his good friend Theodore. We huffed and puffed our way up the hill, and although Roosevelt's monument is no longer visible given the trees that have grown in, it was a lovely spot providing a nice view of the town down below. Unfortunately, a summer thundercloud decided to let loose (with little bits of hail, too) and we were forced to take cover at the base of a pine tree. I know, I know. Thunder. Lightening. Hilltop. Tree. Bad idea. But we were spared and quickly returned to the car, a bit damper than when we set out, passing half a dozen mountain sheep dining their way through the flowers on some of the graves. Such an odd place. But the cemetery was about the only thing worth seeing in the entire area. Having the wisdom of hindsight, I have no idea why anyone would go there. Historic Main Street still has remnants of its old architecture and that would have been charming except all the interiors have been repurposed into T-shirt shops, arcades and cheap gambling halls complete with flashing lights on the slot machines. Old Deadwood had a reputation as being a lawless wild west town full of bars and brothels but if you are going to promote history, keep it real instead of turning it into a half-fast, tawdry imitation of mini-Vegas. This was one detour we could have skipped. And not just because it simply wasn't worth it. It also put us well behind schedule, so we were not able to stop in to see what progress had been made on the Crazy Horse Memorial, located not too far from Mount Rushmore (which we weren't all that excited about anyway). I suppose we could have made more of an effort, but we were driving through a very severe thunderstorm, complete with high winds and warnings of golf-ball sized hail and wanted to get that behind us. The rain was very heavy and the sky very dark but on the positive side, we had a beautiful rainbow stretching all the way across I-90 in front of us.

And then we reached our last national park of the journey. Badlands NP in South Dakota. Another one of those places where my parents had taken me as a child, and John and I in turn, took our children. (Not that our son remembers much. All he can recall is being tired of having bagels for lunch!) The first thing most summer visitors comment on in the Badlands is the heat. Average high temperatures in July are 92F (33C) but it felt much hotter. Summer was finally upon us, arriving as Matejs would have said, "Like a punch in the face." It was unbearable and any plans we had for hiking were quickly revised. Actually, the first day was not so bad since those serious thunderstorms from the day before had cooled things down considerably. And the strong breeze kept any biting bugs at bay. But the heavy rains had also flooded several of the campsites, making it impossible for some visitors to even set up their tents. And they were still being charged a camping fee! Bad form. There had actually been so much rain that this desert-like locale had a lot of green vegetation around, mostly sweet yellow clover. Something that is quite rare. The following day, the breeze died down and things really heated up. Wandering out onto the baked, vegetation-less buttes that have eroded over time into all manner of canyons and spires was not to be done without a bit of planning. The terrain is so inhospitable, the few hiking trails that there are, are very short, and carrying water is an absolute necessity. We went out fairly early in the morning (having left Porter in the yacht with the a/c going full blast), and came back after about an hour, thinking we'd go out again in the late afternoon when the setting sun would make for some great pictures. Never made it. It was just too darn hot. And at dusk the darn mosquitoes and no-see-ums came out. That was all the incentive I needed to move inside.

The next day, we decided to drive over to Wall Drug. After all, it was too hot to engage in any outdoor activities. A bit of an explanation for this excursion is required here. Anyone who has ever driven along I-90 will remember seeing sign after sign after sign extolling the virtues of stopping in at Wall Drug. "Kids love Wall Drug!", "Free Ice Water! Wall Drug!", "Western Wear. Wall Drug!", "201 Miles. Wall Drug!". Sign after sign from Minnesota to Montana. Well we are certainly proof that advertising works. Because curiosity got the better of us and off we went to see what all the fuss was about. And lived to regret it. Wall Drug, in the town of Wall, is basically a bunch of older buildings that have been cobbled together to form a shopping mall of sorts, complete with western-themed shops (cowboy boots, cowboy hats, ropes, spurs etc.), Indian crafts and artwork, a faux petting zoo with numerous stuffed wild animals that kids could paw at, tourist trinkets, an arcade, a food court, a Western art museum, a chapel (!) and yes, an actual pharmacy. Some of the hallways were lined with historic photographs so that was at least somewhat interesting. But overall it was one of those tasteless places that attract a certain class of people about whom your mother would have said to you, "It's not polite to stare." Yes, I'm being judgmental, but wow. Some of them made "Walmart shoppers" look elegant. We are living during the decline of Western civilization and sometimes I truly do despair for the future of humanity. Yet there we were.

Once we left Badlands NP, the push was on to just get home. The weather was very hot and muggy. The drive along I-90 seemed interminable. The Missouri River was like a dividing line with everything to the west of it ranching and to the east, farming. Corn field after corn field. At one point, I noticed that the geographic centre of North America was a mere 300 miles (500kms) to the north of us. Near Rugby, North Dakota. Nope. Neither of us was up for the detour just so that we could say we had been there. And we elected to skip the Corn Palace as well. There is only so much tawdry kitsch I can handle, and I wanted this journey to end on a positive note. Having spent so much time in the national parks and the wide-open spaces of Montana and Wyoming, and even though the return to more populated areas was gradual, it was still a bit of a shock. It is hard to explain because it's not as if we'd been in the back country for the entire past three years. But as soon as we crossed the Missouri, the evidence of human habitation was increasingly more prevalent. Wind farms, grain silos, cultivated fields. And no issues getting a signal for the internet. And something else changed east of the Missouri as well. The Interstate. It became progressively worse so that by the time we were approaching Chicago, we elected to veer off and take secondary roads lest we sustain spinal cord compression fractures from all the jarring. It was unreal. At one rest stop we found that the entire spring mounted double blind unit (solar and night shade) had fallen from one of bedroom windows. It was worse than anything we had experienced by Detroit and we still had to pass through there! Yet despite the discomfort, I started to feel a bit envious of all the people who were just heading out on their adventures. Some for a few weeks vacation and others more long term. That was us, such a short time ago. It is truly unfair how quickly time passes.

As much as I had anticipated our journey would end on a high note, we did manage to hit one more bump in the road. A very unpleasant one. Our tenants had run into a bit of a problem with respect to their new home and were not moving out until the second week of August. No biggie. We could stay at my parent's house with my sister, which still contained some of our earlier stored property. Timing was the key. Mississauga does not allow overnight parking on city streets without a permit so the plan was to arrive mid-morning, unload the coach and still have ample time to drive it out to Sidrabene where we could give it a thorough cleaning later in the week, prior to sale. So that meant spending one more night "on the road." We drove as far as London and decided to boondock in the Walmart parking lot, for old time's sake. It would certainly be the last time I'd be doing anything like that. We obtained the store's permission and set up as usual. It was a very hot night, so we kept the windows open, but that meant street noise prevented a sound sleep. Or so we thought. We both must have slept very well because the following morning when John took Porter out for a walk, he found that some @*#&%$^ dirtbags had stolen both our bicycles from the back of the Jeep. They had been secured to the bike rack with both a lock and cable, bungeed, and covered with a bike cover. The reprobates obviously had bolt cutters. We couldn't believe it. After all the places we had stayed over the past three years (some a touch on the dicey side), to be victimized not only on our last night, so close to home, but in the town where John was born, where I went to school and where we both felt so at ease! Come on! I'm not sure what lesson we were supposed to learn from that.

Unpacking the coach took considerably longer than anticipated (the entire day), and the humid heat wave (34C without the humidex) didn't help matters any either. My hair hadn't been that frizzy in three years! And the cleaning took much longer than anticipated as well. But we were giving it a thorough detailing, complete with Q-Tips and toothbrushes, hoping our efforts would have the desired effect on any prospective buyers. John engaged in a rather prolonged text message/phone conversation exchange with a potential private buyer in California (back and forth well over two weeks) but at the end of the day, this guy wanted a brand-new high-end coach with a used low-end coach price. It wasn't going to happen. The whole private sale thing was a bust, which in retrospect isn't surprising. I don't think I would shell out the kind of money we were asking without some company name behind it either. We ultimately took the yacht to an RV dealer near the town of Grimsby where we contracted them to take care of the sale for us and retain 15% of the selling price. They advised it would go within a month, but I wasn't holding my breath. It was an odd feeling as we drove out of the parking lot, leaving our home of the past three years behind. A bit sad. Reflective. Appreciative. Hopeful. A lot of emotions to process.

Given that we weren't moving back into our own home for some time yet, I can't say that we comfortably settled back into a bricks and mortar life. But I can say that I missed the freedom of the road in no time. Obviously we were happy to be reunited with family and friends, and looked forward to seeing more of them, but there is much to be said for exploring and experiencing new things. We just had to find the right balance.

40.

THE LAST POST –
AKA EPILOGUE

VERY FEW PEOPLE ARE EVER GIVEN THE OPPORTUNITY TO LIVE A DREAM. And of those who are given that opportunity, very few ever seize it. To do so takes a certain combination of faith, support, determination and gumption, and for this type of dream, planning, patience and flexibility. In all honesty, I cannot say that RV'ing through North America was ever a real dream of mine. It was more a variation on an overall travel theme that morphed, as dreams do, into this incredible journey. A journey that took 3 years, 1 month and 16 days. A journey that covered almost 42,000 miles/67,000 kms by coach and 53,000 miles/85,000 kms with the Jeep. A journey that saw us spend 418 nights in private RV parks and resorts, 136 at my childhood summer home of Sidrabene, 117 in provincial and state parks, 112 in national parks, preserves, monuments and recreation areas, 81 in city, county & regional parks, 75 in friends' and family driveways and homes, 39 in Walmart parking lots, 29 on BLM land, rest areas and wherever we could safely pull over, 23 in dealer/repair facility lots, 11 with Boondockers Welcome, 9 at casinos and 1 on a ferry. Not included are the motels and b&bs heading up to the Arctic nor the driving days/nights to get home for Christmas and funerals, nor the sun or ski holidays. With the coach we stayed everywhere from high end resorts at $$$ per night, to free roadside stops where we wondered if perhaps we weren't pushing the safety envelope a bit too close to the edge. We met wonderful people with whom we hope to stay in touch, and weird people we were happy to leave behind.

And the people we were very appreciative of were those who travelled along with us on this incredible ride. Comments sent to the blog, e-mails, messages, facebook "likes" and remarks, phone calls and even face-to-face chats reminded us that while we may have been out of sight, we were not completely out of mind. It was like receiving letters from home and in many ways kept us grounded. Sincerely, thank-you.

Did we get to see everything on our list? No. In particular, the Eastern Seaboard eluded us. Maine, Cape Cod, The Outer Banks. Even New Hampshire and Vermont for that matter. And of course, Mt. Denali. And some parts of the Rockies around the Alberta/B.C. border. Sometimes weather (rain/fog), sometimes natural disasters (hurricanes) sometimes nature (fire) conspired against us but towards the end of the journey, when we could take that extra detour, we were too tired. I never thought I would say it, but I was tired of travelling. At least full-time travelling. For the time being. But what of those places we did see? Some of our favourites, in no particular order – Yosemite, Zion and Grand Teton National Parks, southern Utah in general, Key West, New Orleans, and of course, Tofino. Some of my favourite experiences, again in no particular order – walking with wolves in B.C. (and having one come up and lick my hand as he passed by), snorkelling in the St. Lawrence River along the Gaspe Peninsula and having a little harbour seal climb up on top of me, watching a sea otter try to haul himself onto John's kayak in Monterey, mining for sapphires in Montana, splitting rocks while looking for 50-million-year-old fossils in Wyoming, watching Grizzly Bears walk within 10 feet of us at Lake Clark in Alaska, kayaking up to and crawling into the ice caves of Mendenhall Glacier in Alaska, and all the hiking and biking! Of course there were also places that could be put into the "been there, done that" category. This is not to say we didn't enjoy them. We were very glad for the experience, but they didn't have the kind of appeal that would draw us back. Tuktoyuktuk in the NWT, Big Bend National Park in Texas, the drive along the Gaspe Peninsula, even Saskatchewan. Definitely worth a visit but not a return. And then there were the places that we wished we had never bothered, but thankfully those were very few. The tourist traps of Wall Drug and Deadwood come to mind. Others might disagree.

Of course not everyone likes to travel. It is just not their cup of tea, although I find that hard to understand. My thinking aligns more closely with that of St. Augustine of Hippo – "The world is a book and those who do not travel read only one page." I want to read the entire book. The entire weighty tome. I want to turn the next page and see what is around the next bend. For me, travelling is like reading that fantastic novel that you don't want to put down, that keeps you awake well into the night, enthralled, giving you something to ponder and think about, and in the end, is finished too soon. And just like reading a well written book, this journey had twists and turns and unexpected outcomes from which I learned and was changed. And in many ways, it was also over too soon. So what exactly did I learn? Other than the obvious natural and historical matters. What did I learn about RV'ing, about travelling full-time, about myself?

With respect to RV'ing, it was more expensive than originally thought. Especially in the United States where the exchange on the dollar generally added about 30% to any expenditures: food, lodging, sightseeing, gifts, clothing, souvenirs, veterinary and dog daycare, even fuel (although without the exchange that was almost half the price of what we pay in Canada). And adding 30% to the budget for 6 months of the year was at times painful. Things were more challenging from a domestic perspective as well: not knowing where the better-stocked grocery stores were and once located, not knowing what products were in which aisle. And unfamiliar product names. Yes, I want a jar of pickles, but where are the Bicks? And where is Porter's Purina dog chow? Finding a hair salon that actually knows how to style hair. One time I found myself in an all-black salon with all-black clientele and all-black stylists. It was interesting chatting and comparing notes, but they knew next to nothing about treating straight hair. And travelling in a large motor coach (as opposed to a smaller B-class) definitely ruled out impromptu stops, whether at roadside fruit stands or small-town farmer's markets. There was just no place to pull over, given that with the Jeep in tow, our total length was about 57 feet. You can't stop, turn or park that thing on a dime. Although we were certainly happy not to have succumbed to the lure of a tag-axle, 45-foot coach back when we were still in the purchasing phase. While they look pretty snazzy in the showroom, they are more for travelling from "Point A" Resort in the north to "Point B" Resort in the south. The national, provincial or state parks can rarely accommodate anything over 40 feet, and if they did have anything for that size, it was only a couple of sites. Our coach alone was 38 feet, bumper to bumper, and if reservations were made early enough, we could just fit. If not, we were checking in at private resorts where fees were higher and privacy was limited, at times non-existent. However on the plus side, we'd be guaranteed a wifi signal, something that was scarce in the parks.

From John's perspective (given that he was stereotypically responsible for the mechanics of the coach) it was a near constant learning curve. An RV really is both a vehicle and a house on wheels, where in addition to the usual vehicular maintenance, everything from plumbing to electronics is vulnerable to all the bumps in the road. We had screws backing out of the shower stall, a DVD player that decided to transmit its signal intermittently, a fuse panel that needed replacing, a leak in the hydraulic leveling system and a carbon monoxide detector that would randomly go off. And lots of other minor stuff. John had to repair almost everything himself. Thankfully the Tiffin company provided excellent phone support and their mechanics would literally walk him step by step through any required process. The biggest challenge was being able to understand their verbal instructions which were delivered in a very heavy southern drawl. But if repairs requiring specialized tools were necessary, finding a willing facility was very challenging. The RV industry has incredibly poor to almost non-existent service, definitely not what is available to car owners. Yes, all RV manufacturers have some variation on the "RV Care" package, which covers the financial end of all warranty issues, but locating a facility to do the work within a reasonable period of time? Nope. For these bigger issues, most places wanted to know if we had purchased our coach from them, and if not, offered 4 to 6-week wait times. Ridiculous. It is no surprise that so many owner-generated help forums are available on the internet. Thank goodness.

Having a Toad was an absolute must. Prior to setting out we had read that some people simply rent a car upon reaching their destination but that would have been impossible given the places we explored. Maybe if we had travelled from Point A to B and back again, but our route was too vast, too varied and too far from any car rental agencies. Climate was also a consideration, especially in Canada when the weather turned chilly. I was very thankful for the electric fireplace which surprisingly kicked out a fair bit of heat but if we were to do this again, I would also opt for heated floors. However, one thing our coach did have was a heating system that could be run off both propane and electricity. Many newer models are strictly electric. Propane gave us much more flexibility when boondocking, off the grid or where generator use was restricted. And propane heat warmed things up considerably faster. But I have defaulted to the more negative lessons. On the positive side, it was great being able to experience the wonders of our national parks without having to worry about inclement weather. If it rained, we were nice and cozy with a solid roof over our heads and comfy furniture to lounge around on. With a three-burner cooktop there was no fussing to light a Coleman stove, and having a residential sized refrigerator meant no worries about leaky coolers or having enough ice. At nighttime, there was no fumbling for flashlights and reluctant resentful treks to locate an outhouse. All the comforts of home literally at your fingertips, albeit somewhat scaled down. And overnights could reasonably be wherever we could safely find a parking spot, something that is impossible with a tent. "Home is where we park it", was a common catchphrase for many an RV'er.

RV travelling, however, is different than fulltime RV living. We met quite a few people (Americans) who had sold their bricks and mortar homes, purchased their coaches and now simply travelled around, following the sun. Many had adult children who lived in different parts of the country, so they bounced around from the first offspring to the second to the third, with some vacation time built in. No permanent roots anywhere, but it appeared to suit them. Occasionally we met people who were living fulltime because they had sold their homes but were not yet sure where they wanted to plant new roots. They were travelling the country searching for the perfect town in the perfect state. These folks tended to be without any family ties – no children, no parents – so had no issues about returning home for Christmas or for a grandchild's birthday. But most of the RV'ers we met were people who still had their homes or condos or apartments (and jobs) and were using their coach as their moveable cottage. Summertime was vacation time. There were very few fulltime RVers like us, who were temporarily displaced and who planned on returning home after a set period of time. I think we only met one other couple. And an interesting observation with respect to mode of travel. Canadians prefer trailers and fifth wheels over coaches, hands down. The reverse is true for the United States. I am not sure why. Perhaps those who live north of the 49th parallel like being behind the wheel of a pick-up truck as opposed to a bus.

Another thing I learned from this journey is that everyone needs to have a sense of belonging, and being on the road for an extended period of time, away from family, friends, neighbors, community and all that is familiar, takes that away, resulting in a certain psychological isolation. I suppose that is why so many RV'ers create or join affiliations of one type or another. For example, the Tiffin Allegro Club, the Tiffin Motorhome Owners Group, the Airstream Club etc. Now many of these forums are a place to exchange travel tips and address maintenance issues, but they do provide a sense of community in what can at times seem like a lonely existence. For myself, I had no interest in joining these groups yet at the same time, came to dislike the transient nature of our lifestyle. At least from a community perspective. Even when we stayed put for a few months, (3 in Victoria and 4 in Tofino) there was no sense of permanency. No little garden to plant. No decorating to do. No point in doing anything remotely long-term since we would just be moving on. While there are so many beautiful places in North America, from natural wonders to cute villages and historic places, nothing can replace family, friends and community. And while we met some wonderful people and did make friends in Tofino, our RV home was a constant reminder that we weren't even semi-permanent residents.

Living in a motor coach also hammered home to me what an incredibly materialistic world we live in. Most of us are mildly aware of our consumer-driven existence, our susceptibility to advertising, our penchant for purchasing unnecessary stuff simply because it was on sale or "a good deal", keeping up with the latest fashion, decorating or technology trends, and in the process, generating tons and tons of garbage. Living in a small RV space meant not buying much simply because there was just no place to put it. We started out with a policy of "one new T-shirt purchased, means one old T-shirt discarded" and that was marginally successful, although John maintains that his T-shirt supply dwindled while my shoe collection grew. But once you get your head around the fact that only necessary items will be purchased, there is no need to go window-shopping. And once you stop thinking about buying stuff, you realize how many tourist areas are geared towards just that – buying stuff. Everything from that never-to-be-displayed pottery piece to that never-to-be-used keychain. Stuffed animals, "local" jewelry, regional themed clothing to be worn when preparing recipes from that regional themed but rarely-to-be-used cookbook, seashell picture frames, "cute" beachwear, replica this and reproduction that. This is not to say we did not purchase a few items over the course of the journey as mementos, but we did try to keep it to a minimum and only supported local artists. I was truly amazed by the creativity of people, in all parts of the continent and from all walks of life. Whether using paints, pebbles, clay or wood, there are so many incredibly talented artists whose many works I would have happily purchased. If only there had been room in the yacht! We both came away inspired to explore our own creative sides, with John, grateful for the teachers he encountered along the way, looking forward to mastering the art of Aboriginal wood carving and I plan on working with glass in its many shapes and forms.

Did the journey change me? Of course. How could it not? I can't say I returned home a full-on environmentalist, and I'm not about to start voting for the Green Party but I definitely have a greater respect and increased concern for our environment. I'm trying to make a difference in my own small way with little things like not using plastic bags or water bottles, and biking to the grocery store instead of driving, but it does seem like the proverbial drop in the bucket when I look and see the madness around me. I still want to travel and explore new places, but I know that I need to have a home base to return to. Not necessarily a *Cheers* type neighbourhood bar, "*Where everybody knows your name*," but at least a place where I don't need a map to find my way around. Overall, it was a fantastic trip although I must admit my attitude was occasionally quite fickle. There were days when I thought I could live that way forever, awakening in new places with new landscapes, wondering what new experiences the day would bring. Then there were days when all I wanted to do was go home and spend time with family and friends in a community where my ties run so deep. And towards the tail end, there were days when I just wanted to return to Tofino to walk along the endless beaches and breath in the ocean air. It's like something out of a *Seinfeld* episode. I wanted "This, That and The Other." And losing both my parents two years into the journey really took the wind out of my sails. I never realized how even at my age, I still wanted to say, "Hey Mom! Guess what I just did!" A variation on the theme of, "Look Mom! No hands!" I suppose. And

I did so many new things I would have loved to tell her about. Things I had never even considered (learned to surf), and things I had never even heard of (mined for sapphires). Got up close with Grizzly Bears and fished for Halibut. Snorkelled with barracudas and crawled into ice caves. And re-visited places my parents took me to as a child.

The journey was over so fast. A large part of me didn't want it to end because that meant acknowledging three years had passed. And that we were three years older. We slowly settled back into "normal" life, there was much unpacking to do and while we were in familiar territory geographically, it took quite some time before we felt like we belonged. As if we have left a parallel universe out there somewhere. A universe where each day brought something new. I missed that. I saw a motor coach on the highway one day and immediately perked up. Was that a Tiffin? What are they towing? Where are they going?

By mid-August, the coach had not yet sold so I started wondering if perhaps that was a sign. Yet when it did sell (a week later), the feeling was bitter-sweet. It was what we wanted. It was what we planned for. But it left us feeling a bit lost. The dream was definitely over. And the sale was so impersonal. We handed over the keys and the ownership, the dealer said he'd cut us a cheque in a few of weeks and that was that. A couple around our age were the buyers, upgrading from their older model Tiffin. They looked like nice people so I hoped they would enjoy it. And then we easily started slipping back into behaviours and thought patterns that I had assumed were behind me. Apparently not. Instead of researching our next destination, I was fretting about what colour to paint the living room and how to re-do the kitchen. Regrettably, our tenants had left the house in considerably worse condition than expected and it took a bit of work to get it back into shape. Whatever they were paying their cleaning lady, it was way too much. So were we glad to be back? Yes. In a way. Would we leave to do it all again? In a heartbeat.

And Porter? We hustled him off to the vet for a thorough check-up within days of our return. Overall, he was in great shape for a dog his age, save for one troubling diagnosis. Laryngeal paralysis. It is quite common in older larger breed dogs, with Labrador Retrievers being the poster pups for the condition. In a nutshell, the larynx ceases to function normally and in hot humid weather, or during periods of prolonged exercise or exertion, the folds within it become swollen and inflamed, causing a partial obstruction of the airway. Hence, laboured breathing and decreased energy. It is not necessarily fatal, but it does mean that Porter will no longer be running with the hounds. A more sedate lifestyle is in his future although that may be easier said than done, since he is still a puppy in the head. We have decided to let him set the pace and call the shots. As if that was anything new.

At the end of it all, my most overarching feeling was one of gratitude. Gratitude that we had this opportunity. Gratitude that we took it. Gratitude for what we experienced. Gratitude that we returned home, safe and sound. And John added, gratitude that we are still together. Yes, there were bumps along the way, and places where we were forced to adjust course. There were some sights we didn't get around to visiting and some we wish we had not bothered. And there were huge family adjustments as well. Negative and positive. Life unfolding as it should. But my mind is a kaleidoscope of colourful images that I will carry with me always. And I hope that this journey is only one chapter in my travel book. I wonder what kind of RV's they have in Europe?

YOU CANNOT DO ALL THE GOOD THE WORLD NEEDS… BUT THE WORLD NEEDS ALL THE GOOD YOU CAN DO.

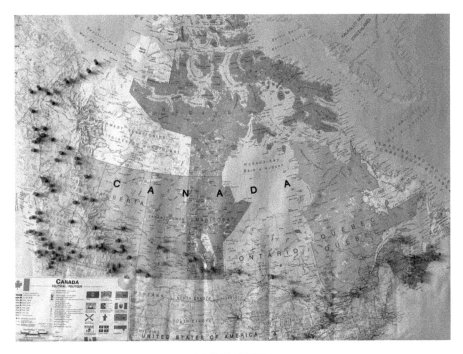

OUR CANADA STOPS.

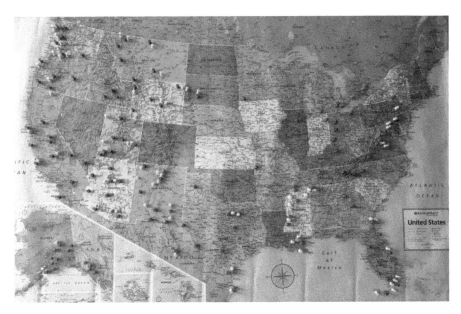

OUR U.S. STOPS.

CPSIA information can be obtained
at www.ICGtesting.com
Printed in the USA
BVHW091201301120
594238BV00002B/11